Africans and
Native Americans

Africans and Native Americans

The Language of Race and the Evolution of Red-Black Peoples

SECOND EDITION

Jack D. Forbes

University of Illinois Press

Urbana and Chicago

Illini Books edition, 1993
© 1993 by the Board of Trustees of the University of Illinois
Manufactured in the United States of America
P 5 4 3

This book is printed on acid-free paper.

Library of Congress Cataloging-in-Publication Data

Forbes, Jack D.
    Africans and Native Americans : the language of race and the
evolution of Red-Black peoples / Jack D. Forbes. — 2nd ed.
        p.   cm.
    Rev. ed. of: Black Africans and Native Americans. Oxford and
New York: Basil Blackwell, 1988.
    Includes bibliographical references (p.   ) and index.
    ISBN 0-252-06321-X (pb)
    1. Indians—Mixed descent. 2. Miscegenation—America. 3. Afro-
Americans—Relations with Indians. I. Forbes, Jack D. Black
Africans and Native Americans. II. Title.
[E59.M66F67   1993]
305.8'00973—dc20   92-29849
                                                          CIP

Contents

Acknowledgements

I wish to thank the faculty and staff of the Erasmus Universiteit Rotterdam for honoring me with the Tinbergen Chair for 1983–4 and for graciously assisting me in my work. Similarly, I wish to thank the faculty and staff of the Institute of Social Anthropology, Oxford University, for welcoming me as a Visiting Scholar during 1986–7 and for helping in many significant ways. Some of the early chapters were also prepared while I was a Fulbright Visiting Professor in Comparative American Studies at the University of Warwick or in the United States (at the University of California, Davis).

I wish to thank individually Dr P. G. Rivière of the Institute of Social Anthropology for his scholarly assistance and Sally Sutton for her typing. At Erasmus University I wish to thank the staff in the Juridische Faculteit who have assisted me with typing – Joke Martins, Marion Ammerlaan and Ada Verschoor, and Dean Professor Dr D. J. Rijnov and Wim de Jong of the Faculteit for providing research assistance. Paula Heady and Carole Hinkle of Applied Behavioral Science and Nancy McLaughlin and Janet Kendrick of Anthropology, University of California, Davis, also should be mentioned for typing part of the manuscript. Finally I wish to thank A. S. C. A. Muijen for her research assistance and Dr Donald C. Cutter for his valuable help.

I wish to acknowledge that portions of this work have appeared previously in the *Journal of Ethnic Studies*, vol. 10 (1982), pp. 46–66 ('The Evolution of the Mulatto Concept'); in the same journal, vol. 12 (1984), pp. 17–61 ('Mulattos and People of Color'); in the *American Indian Quarterly*, vol. 7 (1983), pp. 57–83 ('Mustees, Half Breeds and Zambos . . .'); and in *Explorations in Ethnic Studies*, vol. 7 (1984), pp. 11–23 ('The Use of the Terms "Negro" and "Black" . . .').

It is my desire to dedicate this study to Professor L. H. C. Hulsman of the Erasmus Universiteit Rotterdam.

Jack D. Forbes

Introduction

Thousands of volumes have been written about the historical and social relations existing between Europeans and the Native Peoples of the Americas and between Europeans and Africans, but relations between Native Americans and Africans have been sadly neglected. The entire Afro–Native American cultural exchange and contact experience is a fascinating and significant subject, but one largely obscured by a focus upon European activity and European colonial relations with 'peripheral' subject peoples.

Africans and Americans must now be studied together without their relations always having to be obscured by the separations established through the work of scholars focusing essentially upon some aspect of European expansion and colonialism.

It is especially important to note here, at the very beginning of this study, that those relations do not begin only in the Americas. On the contrary, they also take place in Europe and in Africa and perhaps also in the Pacific.

Contacts in Europe can be seen as significant because both the African and Native American ancestry there has tended to be absorbed into the general European society, and whatever earlier cultural developments have occurred have now become part of modern European culture. The impact of non-European peoples upon European societies directly *within Europe* has not, as of yet, been fully explored; and, of course, there is now a large new group of Native Americans and people of African background in Europe.

Contacts in the Americas have been studied to some extent but much work remains to be done. Contacts in Africa have been studied very little.

The fact of a relatively small but steady American presence in Africa from at least the early 1500s onward may well prove to be a vital area for future research, since one would expect to find Native American cultural influences in regions such as Angola–Zaire and Ghana–Guinea–Cape Verde especially.

It is, of course, interesting to note that some Africans were already exposed to American cultural influences before leaving Africa. The cultures brought by

Africans to the Americas may already have been influenced, especially by Brazilian Native Americans. The extent of such cultural exchange will obviously have to be worked out in careful field research in Angola, Ghana, Guinea, Cabo Verde, and other places, as well as in archival records.

This study has a modest objective, in that it seeks to introduce the subject and to primarily deal with a series of basic issues or questions which have to be resolved before proceeding to a detailed analysis of the precise nature of African–American relations. Raymond Williams, in *Keywords* (1976), has shown the importance of confronting the issue of meaning as a fundamental aspect of scholarship. I propose to apply his example to the basic terms which inform our understanding of African–American contact and mixture, terms which are part of a nomenclature developed under colonialism and racism.

Long ago, when first working with my own Powhatan-Renápe people of Virginia, Maryland, Delaware, and surrounding areas, I discovered that the meaning of racial terms was a controversial issue.

I learned that terms such as 'mulatto' and 'colored' were used, or had been used, in Virginia in a quite different way from their usage in most books including modern dictionaries. I also discovered that many questions were not answerable within the context of the latter, such as: 'what do you call a person of mixed American, European and African ancestry?' No one provided any answer, because, it seems, the American mixture with the African was generally subordinated to a focus upon (or a fascination with) only the black–white nexus.

The modern dictionaries all stated that a mulatto was the child of a black and a white or someone of mixed black and white ancestry. But where did that leave those who were also part-Indian?

In any case, I discovered that Native American descendants had been legally defined as mulattoes in Virginia in 1705, without having any African ancestry. Thus I knew that the dictionaries were wrong and that there was a lot that was hidden from view by the way most authors had written about the southern United States, about slavery, and about colored people. I later discovered also that the same thing was true as regards the Caribbean, Brazil, and much of the rest of the Americas.

The unraveling of *mis*-conceptions is almost as important as the creation of new conceptions, it would seem, and this is nowhere more true than in the realm of race relations. So before one can seriously reconstruct Black African–Native American contacts one must clear away a lot of mistakes, mistakes arising out of the very nature of discourse in a racist-colonial setting as well as mistakes arising from the assumption that the current meanings assigned to racial terms have an equal validity for the past.

As the reader will see, there is hardly a racial term which has a clear and consistent meaning over time (and space). For example, the term 'Indian' (or *indio*) has been applied to many peoples including the Indians of South Asia as well as all groups found in the 'West' Indies (the Americas) and the 'East' Indies (Filipinos, Chinese, Japanese, etc.). The term 'negro' has been applied to Black Africans, the Indians of India, Native Americans, Japanese, and slaves of whatever ancestry. 'Black' has been used for all of the above and for non-whites in general.

By way of illustration, in attempting to grapple with the problem of Black African–Native American mixture and especially with the question of to what extent African-Americans throughout the Americas are part American Indian, it is first necessary to focus upon a clarification of such racial or ethnic terms as were used in the colonial and early national periods. Key terms include: mulatto, *pardo*, colored, free colored, negro, zambo, or sambo, mustee and mestizo.

As noted, many modern writers, whether popular or scholarly, have simply assumed that they could transfer sixteenth-, seventeenth-, or eighteenth-century racial terms to contemporary usage without any critical examination of meaning. For example, it has been assumed generally that a mulatto of, let us say, 1600, would be of the same racial background as a mulatto of 1865 or of 1900; or that a 'colored person' of 1830 would be the same as a 'colored person' of 1930.

Moreover, it has also been assumed that terms such as 'free negro' and 'free colored' can be used interchangeably and that one could, in more recent usage, substitute 'free Black' for either of these.

Many prominent writers have, it seems, been very lax in their failure to consider that the 'meaning' of a word is never a timeless, eternal constant but rather is a constantly evolving changing pointer. Thus the word 'coach' as used in the ninteenth-century (stage coach or other horse-drawn vehicle, then later a railway coach) has today become something different (for example, motor coach). And while we can trace the obvious connection between stage coach, railway coach, and motor coach it is still quite clear that we would be badly mistaken to interpret 'get on the coach' of 1840, for example as meaning 'get on the bus' of 1960! And, of course, the term 'coach' has other meanings today, aside from motor coach.

We may think we know what the word 'negro' means today but do we know what it meant in 1800 in Virginia? And did it mean the same as 'colored'? The answer to these questions is not and cannot be an exercise in deductive logic or *a priori* reasoning. It is, rather, an empirical problem which can only be solved by discovering through documentary and other evidence exactly how such terms were used. This is not an easy task, for reasons which will become clearer later.

In short, we cannot move, historiographically, from word to word or concept to concept across the centuries. We must instead actually engage the primary data in order to 'touch reality'. When we discover that one of Sir Francis Drake's pilots (not an airline pilot, incidentally) in 1595 was 'ysleño de nación mulato' and sailed from Plymouth, England (although being an 'islander' in origin), we should not picture him as if he were a *mulato* of 1981 or of 1900. *His precise racial background is not established by the use of the term 'mulato'*, as we shall see. We must ascertain from other evidence, if we can, what the Spanish author meant by his usage of this category.

During the summer of 1981 newspapers in the United States carried stories about 'blacks' rioting in British cities. What they failed to tell their readers was that in Britain today the term 'black' is applied not only to Africans or West Indians (of whatever shade or mixture) but also to people from India, Pakistan, Bangladesh, Sri Lanka, and even to Latin Americans. (For example, a very light-skinned Chilean lady refugee living in Oxford was surprised to be referred to as a 'black'. Her dark hair, Spanish accent, and immigrant status had caused her to become 'black', at least to some English contacts.)

I have before me an appeal to 'Drop All Charges against Black Youth' which refers to the arrest of some 'young Asians' in Bradford during the summer of 1981.[1]

This modern British usage (which usage extends well back into earlier years) reflects very vividly the problem of assuming that English terms such as 'black', 'negro', 'mulatto', or 'colored', can be interpreted easily when found in documents of earlier eras.

When the Europeans first established intensive contacts with Africans and part-Africans, they met people with a great variety of physical characteristics. This was especially true in the Iberian peninsula and Mediterranean area, but undoubtedly many of the 'Moors' and 'Blackamoors' who came to England in Shakespeare's day were of north African as well as sub-Saharan background and from many distinct nations. Later in the sixteenth and seventeenth centuries, diversity was also encountered, as when most English vessels sailing to the Caribbean dropped anchor at the Cabo Verde Islands. One writer in 1647 commented on the extreme variability of physical types met there and the great beauty of the mixed Cabo Verde women.[2]

We must realize, therefore, that at the very beginning of the modern period racial terms as used by Iberians and as acquired by the English were going to refer to part-African peoples who might not only have the features of the Gulf of Guinea (variable as they are) but also every conceivable combination of central African, Ibero–African, Afro–Arabic and American–African mixtures.

And for our purposes it is important to stress that many Africans from the Sahel or 'savannah' belt (Hausa etc.), as well as from parts of East Africa, sometimes resemble American–African hybrids (with various combinations of high cheekbones, prominent aquiline noses, semi-wavy or 'bushy' hair, 'oriental' eye shapes, etc.). Why is this important? Simply because many part-American, part-African persons (with no European ancestry) could easily be subsumed under a racial term applicable to 'pure-blood' Africans, and would not, in any case, be especially recognizable to most observers as being part-American. The predominant physical type of the slaves brought in from Africa may have been that of coastal West Africa, but enough variability existed so that terms such as 'Blackamoor', *negro*, and 'black' cannot *a priori* be assumed to be useful for determining precise genetic identity.

Many color terms, such as 'dark', 'swarthy' and 'brown' are also quite ambiguous, as should be obvious. In a 1756 list of militia-men in King and Queen County, Virginia, for example, one finds, in addition to fair-complexioned persons, Thomas Delany as 'dark', Benjamin Wilson as 'dark', James Willimore as 'Brown', John Major as 'Brown', John Kemp as 'swarthy' (but with light hair and freckles), John Evans as 'dark', and Richard Riddle as 'dark'. All or most of these men were born in Virginia and several were 'planters'. Were they part-American or part-African? Certainly we cannot judge their 'race' from such color-referents alone.

Similarly, in 1768, an advertisement appeared in New Jersey for 'an apprentice lad named John Foster, born in the Jersies, about 5 feet 8 inches high, of a dark complexion, and pitted with the small-pox, wears his hair with a false que to it.'[3]

In any case, the colonial and state courts in the United States frequently had difficulty in determining exact racial status. In 1859 a North Carolina court called in a planter as an expert who could distinguish between 'the descendants of a negro and a white person, and the descendants of a negro and an Indian.' He could also, allegedly, differentiate between a pure African and a 'white cross' or an 'Indian cross'.[4] Unfortunately, most of us today lack that kind of certain expertise, whatever phenotypical features are seized upon as evidence providing 'proof'.

In our efforts to reconstruct the story of Black African–Native American relations it is necessary, then, to begin with an analysis of the evolution of the meaning of racial terms, for only in this way can we hope to identify people of American and African ancestry in the past. But the study of words alone does not, in fact, reveal the subtleties of actual usage. And thus I have had to delve into many aspects of Native American–Black African history in order to reconstruct the environments in which racial and color terms have evolved and been given a new or different content.

The reader will find a great deal of the social and cultural history of Afroamericans and Native Americans in this work, woven together with broad social history as it relates to colonialism, slavery and racism. *But the primary purpose of this study is not to write a comprehensive account of Native American–African relations but rather to establish a sound empirical and conceptual basis for further study in this area and, more importantly, to demonstrate beyond any doubt that old assumptions must be set aside.* This latter is especially true as regards the extent of Native American–African mixture and the significant genetic contribution of Americans to present-day 'black' or 'Afroamerican' populations in the Caribbean, Brazil, the United States, and elsewhere.

This work will, I hope, make a major contribution to the field of the history of race relations and, more specifically, to the study of the formation of plantation, creole, and colonial cultures in the Americas and elsewhere. Because of the data presented herein, a great deal of revision will have to be made in these areas, as well as in the fields studying the evolution of modern African, Afroamerican, and Native American cultures.

Finally, I hope that this study of interethnic contact and racial classifying will lead to progress in the field of human rights by highlighting and clarifying a major area of abuse: the arbitrary and often racist practice of defining the identities of other human beings by powerful outsiders, as well as by governments and institutions.

1

Africans and Americans: Inter-Continental Contacts Across the Atlantic, to 1500

AMERICANS CROSSING THE ATLANTIC BEFORE COLUMBUS

The meeting of Native Americans and Africans, of people from two great continents of the earth, can be described in many ways. A fitting mode in which to begin is to cite a Native American story from Guyana, presented by Jan Carew, in which Nyan, an African sky-spirit, along with the African earth-mother, the African river-mother, and Anancy the Spider-trickster met the Great Spirit, the Father Sun, and other spirit-powers of the Americans.[1]

The next day, all the peoples of the earth complained to Father Sun and for the first time, the ebony people, who were neighbors of Tihona, made themselves heard. . . . The Great Spirit invited Nyan, the anthracite-coloured Sky-God . . . to share his domains. . . . They [the African spirits] agreed on condition that the Great Spirit, in turn, shared the distant kingdoms of earth and sky that Nyan ruled.[2]

Pia, an American child of the Sun and of Tihona, the Mist-woman, became a brother to Anancy the Spiderman, and both agreed to live among human beings.

Thus the spirit-powers of the Black Africans are said to have established a close cooperative relationship with the spirit-powers of the Americans. This same cooperation and reciprocal relationship can also be seen in Brazil, where Tupinamba and Guaraní *candomblés* exist side by side with those of Congo–Angola and Nago orientation and where Native American and African spiritual powers are called upon for assistance in various contexts.[3]

The dimensions of African–American contact can also be seen in a painting by the Dutch artist Jan Steen (1645) in which the making of a marriage contract in the Netherlands area is depicted. The future bridegroom is of African ancestry while a man of American race is an active onlooker on the right-hand side of the scene. The bride is of European Dutch background.[4]

Thus in spiritual as well as secular contexts, the American and African peoples have interacted with each other in a variety of settings and situations. These interactions may well have begun in very ancient times.

J. A. Rogers, Leo Wiener, Ivan Van Sertima, and others have cited evidence, including the "Olmec" stone heads of Mexico, pointing towards early contacts between American and African cultures.[5] I do not propose here to explore the early archaeological evidence which, in essence, requires a separate study, but instead, I will cite briefly some tantalizing data which suggests contacts in *both* directions.

It is now well known that the Atlantic Ocean contains a series of powerful 'rivers' or currents which can facilitate the movement of floating objects from the Americas to Europe and Africa as well as from the latter to the Americas. In the North Atlantic the most prominent current is that of the 'Gulfstream' which swings through the Caribbean and then moves in a northeasterly direction from Florida to the Grand Banks off Terra Nova (Newfoundland), turning then eastwards towards the British Isles and the Bay of Biscay. This current has carried debris from Jamaica and the Caribbean to the Hebrides and Orkneys of Scotland. Moreover, Jean Merrien tells us that valuable hardwood was commonly washed ashore along the coasts of Ireland and Wales: 'This timber from the ocean, borne by the Gulf Stream, really came from the rivers of Mexico.' Merrien, a student of trans-Atlantic navigation by small vessels, also states that

the first attempt – the first success – [of crossing the Atlantic by one man] could only come from the American side, . . . because the crossing is much less difficult in that direction. A French writer has said (justly, in all probability) that if America had been the Old World its inhabitants would have discovered Europe long before we did, in fact, discover America.

This is because of the prevailing winds from the west as well as the currents. One can, says Merrien, sail in a 'straight line' from Boston via Newfoundland to Ireland or Cornwall 'with almost the certainty of fair winds'. The other direction requires 'twice the distance, thrice the time, and four times the sweat'.

In the 1860s a 48-foot-long sloop, *Alice*, was navigated from North America to the Isle of Wight in less than 20 days with very favorable winds; and in recent times a wooden raft was propelled from Canada to northern Europe by means of this ocean river. Moreover, Stephen C. Jett cites the 68-day passage of one William Verity from Florida to Ireland in a 12-foot sloop as well as the crossing by two men from New York to the Scilly Islands in 55 days in a 17-foot dory powered only by oars. Thus the Gulfstream demonstrably can propel small craft successfully from the Americas to Europe.

Perhaps this is the explanation behind the local Dutch tradition that holds that in AD 849 one Zierik arrived by boat to found the coastal city of Zierikzee and why the local people believed that he had arrived in an Inuit (Greenland) kayak which was on display there for several centuries. The kayak may, indeed, not have been Zierik's original craft but it very possibly points toward a genuine folk tradition of a crossing of the Atlantic from the west.[6]

In this context it is also worth noting a report that Columbus had information about strange people from the west who had reached Ireland prior to 1492, doubtless via the Gulfstream. Merrien tells us that Bartholomew or Christopher Columbus had made marginal notes in their copy of Pius II's *Historia* (1477) to the effect that 'some men have come from Cathay by heading east. We have seen more than one remarkable thing, especially in Galway, in Ireland, two people tied to two wrecks, a man and a woman, a superb creature.' Merrien also believes that the first documented case of a single navigator crossing the Atlantic consists in the record of a Native American who reached the Iberian peninsula long before Columbus' day.

In the Middle Ages there arrived one day on the coast of Spain a man "red and strange" in a craft described as a hollowed tree. From the recorded description, which specifically states that he was not a Negro, he might well have been a native of America in a *piragua* – a dug-out canoe . . . the unfortunate man, ill and enfeebled, died before he had been taught to make himself understood.

To return to our own discussion of the Gulfstream, it should be noted that this eastward-flowing current has a southern extension which swings southwards along the west coast of Europe to the Iberian peninsula and on to the Canary Islands. From the latter region it turns southwestwards and then westwards, returning to the Americas in the vicinity of Trinidad and rejoining the Caribbean segment of the Gulfstream. Thus it would be theoretically possible to float in a great circle from the Caribbean to Europe and northwestern Africa and then back again to the Caribbean.

A North American archaeologist, E. F. Greenman, has argued that the crossing of the North Atlantic was 'feasible' before the end of the Pleistocene period (about 11,000 years ago) 'for a people with kayaks and the Beothuk type of canoe [from Newfoundland], if at that time the ocean was filled with floating ice from the Scandinavian and Labrador glaciers, and from freezing of the sea itself.' The same author attempts to show many parallels between Pleistocene European and American cultures, but sadly neglects African comparisons. In any case, his argument is based solely upon hypothetical European movements towards the Americas, movements which would have had to fight *against* the currents (and winds) rather than flowing *with* them.[7]

Bartolomé de las Casas, in his monumental *Historia de las Indias*, cites examples of rafts or canoes (*almadías*), dead Americans, and debris reaching the Azores Islands before 1492. This evidence will be discussed below. Here it is only necessary to note that the Azores lay in an area of weak currents but that, even so, with the help of winds from the west and northwest some boats could reach the islands from the Americas.[8]

In the South Atlantic, as noted, a strong current runs from the west coast of North Africa towards Trinidad. Below that a counter-current is sometimes shown, running eastwards from South America to the Gulf of Guinea. Then a strong current runs westwards from the mouth of the River Zaire (Congo), to the north of the Amazon, where it divides, part joining the northwesterly current which becomes the Gulfstream and part swinging southwards along the coast of Brazil until it veers eastwards across the Atlantic to Africa again, reaching southwestern Africa, from whence it curves northwards to rejoin the Zaire–Amazon current. Thus, as farther north, a great circle is formed.

Fundamentally, what we see are two great circular rivers in the ocean, the northern circle running in a clockwise direction and the southern circle in a counter-clockwise direction, with a smaller counter-current in between, running eastwards. In the South Atlantic Americans might have reached Africa via the counter-current or, more likely, via the Brazil to southwest Africa current. Africans could have used either the southern (westwards) swing of the North Atlantic circle or the northern (also westwards) swing of the South Atlantic circle, coming from the Sierra Leone–Senegal region or the Congo–Angola region respectively.

Of course, one of the problems with the argument for early trans-Atlantic crossings is that in the modern period such islands as Iceland, Bermuda, the Azores, the Madeiras, the Cabo Verdes, Tristan da Cunha, Ascension, and even São Tomé (off Nigeria and Cameroun) were uninhabited prior to documented Irish, Norse, and Portuguese occupations. On the other hand, some of these islands are small or far from major currents. Bartolomé de las Casas states that the Azores were the *islas Cassitérides* mentioned by Strabo in his *Geography* and which islands were repeatedly visited by the Carthaginians. Allegedly, there lived in the Azores a people who were of *loro* or *baço* color, that is to say, people of the color of Native Americans or intermediate between white and black.[9] The Canary Islands were inhabited in the fifteenth century by a people who were isolated from nearby Africa and whose cultures somewhat resembled those of some Americans. Moreover, the personal names of the many *canarios* enslaved by the Spanish have a decidedly American 'ring' about them (although such resemblances do not always mean a great deal).[10] The *canarios* are sometimes described as a *loro* or brownish-colored people in the slave registers.

The fact that the islands of Cabo Verde and Madeira were uninhabited in the fifteenth century does indeed pose a problem for African navigation to the Americas; however, that will be discussed later. Now it is necessary to consider briefly evidence relating to the maritime capabilities of Americans in the late fifteenth century, to see whether voyages across the Atlantic might have been feasible.

The Americans of the Caribbean region were outstanding navigators and seamen, as noted by the Spaniards and other Europeans. Christopher Columbus was impressed everywhere by their skill. He noted, for example, that their boats (*barcos y barquillos*) 'which they call *canoas*', were excellently made from a single tree, were very large and long, carrying sometimes 40 or 45 men, two or more *codos* (perhaps a man's breadth) in width. The American boats were unsinkable, and if in a storm they happened to capsize, the sailors simply turned them back over while swimming in the sea, bailing them out with goards carried for that purpose.[11] Andrés Bernaldez recorded (from Columbus) that the

Americans navigated in their *canoas* with exceptional agility and speed, with 60
to 80 men in them, each with an oar, and they went by sea 150 leagues or more.
They were 'masters of the sea'. (A canoe was later discovered in Jamaica which
was 96 feet long, 8 feet broad, made from a single tree.)[12]

Columbus found that the Lucayo people of the Bahamas were not only very
well acquainted with Cuba (one and a half days away via canoe) but also knew
that from Cuba it was a 'ten days' journey' to the mainland (doubtless Mexico
or South America since Florida would have been closer than that). He also saw
a boat which was 95 palms long in which 150 persons could be contained and
navigate. Others were seen which were of great workmanship and beauty, being
expertly carved. A canoe was also seen being navigated successfully by one man
in high winds and rough sea.

At Haiti, Columbus learned that that island, or Jamaica, was ten days' journey
distant from the mainland and that the people there were clothed (thus
referring to Mexico or Yucatan most likely). In another place he learned of a
land, 100 leagues away, where gold was mined.[13]

The Arawak and Carib-speaking peoples of the Caribbean were well
informed geographically. Columbus captured Caribs in the Antilles (such as
Guadeloupe) from whom he learned of the South American mainland, but he
also learned of the mainland from Americans living on St Croix and Borinquen
(Puerto Rico). Americans who were taken into Europe drew maps there which
showed Haiti, Cuba and the Bahamas, as well as 'many other islands and
countries' which were named in the native language.[14]

It seems quite clear that the geography of the Caribbean basin and the
Bahamas, including that of the adjacent mainland, was accurately known to the
Americans. Moreover, it seems clear that voyages of 60 to 150 leagues were
undertaken (about 180 to 450 miles, figured conservatively at three miles per
league although the Spanish nautical league often exceeded that distance).

When Spaniards reached the area of Yucatan in 1517 and again in 1518 they
found that the Maya people were already aware of what had transpired on the
islands invaded earlier by the Europeans. The Maya were uniformly hostile
and, at Campeche, 'they then made signs with their hands to find out whether
we came from the direction of the sunrise, repeating the word "Castilan"
"Castilan" and we did not understand what they meant by Castilan.' In the
latter year the Spaniards met an American woman from Jamaica on the island of
Cozumel. She told them

that two years earlier she had started from Jamaica with ten Indians in a large canoe
intending to go and fish near some small islands, and that the currents had carried them
over to this island where they had been driven ashore, and that her husband and all the
Jamaica Indians had been killed and sacrificed.

It seems more likely that the Jamaicans had fled from their home to avoid
Spanish slave-raiders and that they did not want to fall under European control;
hence her story. In any case, all of the Maya towns along the coast in 1517 were
well aware of the threat posed by the Spaniards. This news could have been

conveyed by two Spaniards living among them, but whatever the source the 'news' had spread very widely.

Even more significant, for our purposes, is the fact that when the Spaniards reached Yucatan in 1517 they

saw ten large canoes, called piraguas, full of Indians from the town, approaching us with oars and sails. The canoes were large ones made like hollow troughs cleverly cut out from huge single logs, and many of them would hold forty Indians.

The fact that these boats were equipped with sails is indeed interesting, because it means that wind-power could be used to run against currents or to navigate rapidly even where currents were lacking. Clinton R. Edwards also cites other evidence documenting the use of sails by Carib and other American peoples in the Caribbean and by Ecuadorian–north Peruvian sailors in the Pacific, both at the time of initial Spanish contact.

As an example of the navigational capabilities of the Caribbean natives, we can cite the case in 1516 when 70 or 80 Spaniards in a caravel and a *bergantíne* (brig) sailed from Santiago de Cuba to the Guanaxa Islands off Honduras (now Roatan). There they enslaved many Guanaxa people and carried them in the caravel to Havana, Cuba. The Americans were subsequently able to overcome their Spanish guards, seizing the sailing ship 'y haciéndose a la vela, cual si fueran expertos navegantes, volvieron a su patria que distaba más de doscientas leguas.' In short, the Americans were such 'expert navigators' that they were able to sail from Havana to Honduras, a distance of more than 200 leagues, in a European vessel with no assistance from any non-Americans; and this after having been kept below decks during their journey to Havana.

The navigational capabilities of the Americans of the Caribbean–Mexican coastal area extend back well into pre-Columbian times, as attested to by pictures of boats found in various codices, murals, and sculptured walls in the Mexico–Yucatan region. In about the tenth century AD also the Mexican leader Quetzalcoatl is recorded as having sailed with a raft to the east (rising sun) from the Gulf coast of central Mexico.[15]

Along the Atlantic coast of North America, Americans also went out to sea. On the South Carolina coast, for example, the Sewee outfitted boats with sails and on one occasion a group of natives decided to visit England. They outfitted a canoe with sails and went out into the Atlantic but were picked up by a British vessel and sold as slaves.[16]

In 1524 Verrazano saw dugout boats outside Chesapeake Bay which were 20 feet long, while canoes were seen in Narraganset Bay, going out to sea, with 14 or 15 men in them.[17] One report of a later date states that Americans navigated between New Jersey and Chesapeake Bay, using canoes specially fitted out with sails and decks.

But when they want [to go] a distance over the sea, as for instance to Virginia or New Holland, then they fasten two punts [canoes, dugouts] together broadwise with timbers over them, right strongly put together, the deck made completely tight and side board of planks; sails of rugs and freze [cloth] joined together; ropes and tackle made of bast and slender spruce roots; [and they] also mason for themselves a little fireplace on deck.[18]

To the south, along the Brazilian coast, the Portuguese and other Europeans also witnessed American navigation at sea. An Italian traveling with Magellan in 1519 noted that the Brazilians' boats were made from the trunk of a tree, and were so large that each boat held 30 to 40 men. In the 1550s Hans Staden noted that the dugout boats of the Santos–Rio de Janeiro area could hold up to 30 men, were four feet in width, with some being larger and some smaller.

In these they move rapidly with oars, navigating with them as far as they wish. When the sea is rough they take the canoes ashore until good weather comes again. They do not go more than two leagues straight out to sea but along the coast they navigate far.[19]

In 1565 the Jesuit José de Anchieta stated that the Americans of the same region had dozens or more *canoas* made from a single tree, with other pieces of the same cutting used as 'boards' well attached with vines. They were large enough to carry 20 to 25 persons with their arms and supplies, and some held up to 30 persons. With these boats they were able to cross 'such fierce [*bravas*] seas that it is a frightful thing and not to be imagined or believed without seeing'. Anchieta also noted that if the canoes turned over, the navigators simply bailed out the boat, turned it right side up, and carried on.

Thus the Brazilian boats were also very well made, were very fast and manoeuvrable and could be righted at sea if necessary. They were used to carry warriors and supplies over considerable distances along the coast, as, for example, from Santos (São Vicente) to Rio de Janeiro.[20]

In general, it would appear that the Americans of the Caribbean built the biggest boats and were most accustomed to going far out to sea, while the Atlantic coastal groups were more oriented to staying within a certain distance of land (six miles or so). On the other hand, all were capable of being carried out to sea by strong winds and currents and yet surviving rough water.

It should also be noted that several groups along the Pacific coast manufactured seaworthy craft and were capable of reaching Polynesia by means of favorable currents. It is beyond the scope of this study to discuss such voyages but one must note that many Pacific island peoples may very well be of American ancestry mixed with varying proportions of 'Oceanic Negroid' (African?) and Malayo–Indonesian stocks.[21]

Returning to the Atlantic, it is interesting to note that there is some additional evidence to support the notion that Americans crossed in an easterly direction. For example, Pliny, in his *Natural History*, reported that

Nepos de septentrionali circuitu tradit Quinto Metello Celeri, Afrani in consulatu collegae sed tum Galliae proconsuli, Indos a rege Sueborum dono datos, que ex India commerci causa navigantes tempestatibus essent in Germaniam abrepti.

Thus we learn that Cornelius Nepos, an author of several works in the last century BC, and virtually a contemporary observer, recorded that as to the northern circuit of the seas (from France northwards)

that Quintus Metellus Celer, colleague of Afranius in the consulship [of Rome] but at the time pro-consul of Gaul [south of the Alps] received from the [Suevi] king . . . a present of Indians, who on a trade voyage had been carried off their course by storms to Germany.

In order to interpret this event, which occurred about 60 BC, we must keep in mind that for Pliny Germany commenced far to the south of Denmark (that is in the Belgium–Netherlands region most likely). Pliny states that in the time of Augustus 'Germaniam classe circumvecta ad Cimbrorum promunturium' (a fleet 'sailed round Germany' to the promontory of the Cimbri, in Denmark).[22]

Also Pliny believed that the *Indos* had reached a Germanic-speaking zone by way of a fictitious sea which was thought by him to have connected India with the Baltic. We know, however, that the only way that people looking like 'Indians' could have been driven by a storm to northern Europe would have been across the Atlantic from America. It should also be noted that the *Suevi* group of Germanic-speaking tribes is thought by some to have included the Angles, a people living at a later date along the North Sea shore of Germany.

Several later writers, citing the Nepos account, assume that the 'Indians' were driven across the Atlantic. Certainly there is no reason to doubt that the builders of Teotihuacan and the Olmecs were engaged in widespread trade or that they possessed navigational capabilities, to mention only two American groups active in the 60 BC time-period.[23]

Archaeological evidence may also support later eastbound voyages, since Inuit (Eskimo) type harpoon-heads have been found at two locations in Ireland and Scotland. For example, a harpoon-head of very worn condition was found in County Down, Ireland of which it is 'absolutely certain, that it is of Archaic Eskimo origin'.

Specifically, this harpoon-head is of 'Thule type', dated probably between the tenth and thirteenth centuries. It was very unlikely to have been carried to Ireland by a seal or a walrus and most likely was taken there by a living Inuit hunter, perphaps on a Norse vessel. The authors of the report on this find state that 'so far no harpoon-head of the mesolithic period has been recovered from Ireland, and the present specimen has no parallels among prehistoric European finds.'[24] The harpoon-head found in Scotland may be of 'old Thule' type and is perhaps earlier in date than the Irish discovery. It was found before 1876 in Aberdeenshire, in sandy ground.[25]

Inuit navigation will be discussed below, but here it is worth noting that the Angmagssalik people of east Greenland in the eighteenth century used umiaks to journey all the way around the southern tip of Greenland to barter on the west coast. Often they did not beach the umiaks but moored them in the water, having no need to dry them out. Such boats *might* have survived the kind of strong easterly winds which in 1347 drove a small Norse boat all the way from Markland (Labrador) to Iceland.[26]

Las Casas and other writers report that Columbus knew before his 1492 voyage of Americans reaching the Azores, along with 'reeds', pine trees and other debris driven by westerly and northwesterly winds. Certain Azorean settlers had told him that the sea had tossed up on the island of Las Flores the bodies of two dead persons, 'who seemed to have very wide faces and features unlike those of Christians'. Moreover, on another occasion, it was said that in the Cabo de la Verga and its vicinity *almadías* or canoes were seen outfitted with a sort of 'house'. These canoes were driven from place to place or island to island by the force of winds, and the occupants had apparently perished or disappeared while the vessels drifted for a time in the Azores region.

Also it was known that a Portuguese pilot had seen an 'ingeniously carved piece of wood' some 450 leagues to the west of Portugal, which wood was being driven from the west and had not been carved with iron tools.[27]

Columbus was also aware that Africans may well have utilized ocean currents to navigate to the Americas. His 1498 voyage specifically used the southern route from the Cabo Verde Islands to Trinidad, an easy crossing travelled consistently thereafter by Spaniards, Portuguese, Britons and others. Columbus was especially intrigued to see what lands lay in the South American direction, since the king of Portugal had said that there was *tierra firme* in that direction and was greatly inclined to make discoveries to the southwest 'y que se habían hallado canoas que salían de la costa de Guinea, que navegaban al Oeste con mercadurías.' In short, the Portuguese had found boats (*canoas*) which left from West Africa to navigate to the west with merchandise.[28]

In the Gulf of Paría area, near Trinidad, Columbus found that the Americans

trajeron pañezuelos de algodón muy labrados y tejidos, con colores y labores como los llevan de Guinea, de los ríos a la Sierra Leona, sin diferencia, y dice que no deben comunicar con aquéllos, porque hay de aquí donde él agorá esta, mas de 800 leguas; abajo dice que paracen almaizares.

Thus he saw well-made multi-colored scarves or sashes, identical with those of Sierra Leone, but because of the distance he thought that the two peoples 'ought not' to be in communication. Later Columbus stated that each American wore scarves which resembled *almaizares* (Moorish sashes), one for the head and one for the rest of the body.[29]

Nonetheless, one of Columbus' motives in examining the area around Trinidad was to

experimentar lo que decían los indios desta Española, que había venido a ella de la parte del Austro y del Sueste gente negra, y que trae los hierros de las açagayas de un metal a que llaman guanín, de lo cual había enviado a los reyes hecho el ensaye, donde se halló que de trienta y dos pantes, las diez y ocho eran de oro y las seis de plata y las ocho de cobre.

Thus, Columbus wanted to verify the truth of what the Americans of Haiti had stated previously, to the effect that 'black people' had come from the south and southeast and that their *azagaya* (spear) heads were made of *guanín*, a brass or bronze-like mixture of gold, silver and copper.

Las Casas doubted the truth of one of Columbus' stories, about an island with only women,

como lo que aquí dice que entendía haber isla que llamaba Guanín donde había mucho oro, y no era sino que había en alguna parte guanín mucho, y esto era cierto especio de oro bajo que llamaban guanín, que es algo morado, el cual cognoscen por el olor y estímanlo en mucho.

Thus the existence of an island of Guanín where much gold was to be found was also doubted. Probably in some region there was much *guanín*, which was a base type of gold (*oro*), somewhat 'purplish' (*morado*), esteemed much by the Americans and known by its smell. Significantly, the Americans of the Gulf of Paría area possessed pieces of gold but it was 'muy bajo, que parescía sobredorado' (very low-grade, appearing to be alloyed with, or gilded over silver or base metal). No evidence of 'black people' was found in the Trinidad–Paría region, the Americans being either of *indio* color or near-white, many being 'tan blancos como nostros y mejores cabellos y bien cortados' ('as white as us and better hair, well-cut')[30]

Thus it seems likely that *guanin* was a base alloy or gilding of gold which was quite common in the Caribbean region. It may well be that the 'black people' who brought spears tipped with it to Haiti were only Americans painted black (a common practice) and not Africans. (One must also remember that Columbus' knowledge of American language was virtually non-existent.)

In 1464–5 Alviso da Ca'da Mosto wrote a description of his visit of a few years before to the West African coast. He noted that the West Africans of the kingdom of Senegal (to Cape Verde) were using *azagaie* (spears) with worked and barbed iron heads, and that the Wolofs of Senegal obtained from Gambia curved *alfanges* (swords) made of iron 'sem nenhum aco (azzale)', without steel.

He also noted that they did not have ships, nor were any seen, but those Africans living along the river of Senegal and by the sea had some *zoppoli*, called *almadie* (*almadías*) by the Portuguese (dugout boats), the largest of which carried only three or four men and which were used for fishing, as noted:

Non hanno navilii né mai li viddero, salvo dapoi che hanno avuto conoscimento de' Portogallesi. Vero è che coloro che abitano sopra questo fiume, e alcuni di quelli che stanno alle marine, hanno alcuni zoppoli, cioè almadie tutte d'un legno, che portano da tre in quattro uomini al piú nelle maggiori, e con queste vanno alle volte a pescare, e passano il fiume e vanno di loco a loco.[31]

Only very small *almadías* were seen beyond Cabo Verde also and this, coupled with the fact that the Cape Verde Islands were found to be uninhabited, without any trace of occupancy, would seem to argue against much West African marine navigation, at least in the years 1455–63.[32] The use of iron spear-points also tends to argue against the accuracy of Columbus' information relative to 'black people' reaching Haiti with spear-points of a softer metal.

(One should note that the Africans of the Cape Verde mainland were reported as using bows and arrows, rather than spears, in the Ca'da Mosto narrative.)

It is possible that Columbus, who probably never did understand what the Americans of Haiti were saying, was confused and that the *guanín*-using people were different from the black people mentioned. On the other hand, the evidence is perhaps unconvincing by and of itself.

There are, however, bits and pieces of data tending to at least provide some support for West African voyages to the Americas. For example, Pedro Mártir de Anglería obtained information (at second hand), to the effect that in 1513 Vasco Núñez de Balboa met members of a 'tribe of Ethiopians' in Panama. While crossing the peninsula, Balboa reached the native village of Cuarecua on the Caribbean side of the summit of the mountain and

encontraron allí esclavos negros de una región que dista de Cuarecua sólo dos días, en cual no se crían más que negros, y estos feroces y sobremanera crueles. Piensen que en otro tiempo pasaron de la Etiopia negros a robar y que, naufragando, se establecieron en aquellas montañas. Los de Cuarecua tienen odios intestino con esos negros, y se esclavizan mutuamente o se matan.

Thus the Spaniards actually are said to have seen black slaves belonging to the Americans but they learned that these slaves came from a totally black village located two days' journey away, and they conjectured that the blacks had come from Ethiopia (Black Africa) at some earlier date.

López de Gómara also reports that when Núñez de Balboa reached Cuarecua he found *algunos negros* (some blacks) who were slaves of the American ruler. The Spaniards could only learn that there were 'men of that color close to there, with whom they have frequent war'. López goes on to state that 'these were the first *negros* which they saw in Indias, and I think that no more have been seen since'. The *negros* were 'as of Guinea'. López never visited the Americas and his 1552 work is based on reports received in Spain.[33]

Since Panama lies along the current coming westwards from Africa via Trinidad, such a journey is quite possible. On the other hand, it is perhaps more probable that these Africans were runaway slaves from Haiti who conspired with their American hosts to fool the Spaniards about their origins. (It was very common for Americans to concoct stories designed to fool the Europeans, once the latter's avariciousness and imperialistic designs were understood.) Runaway Africans had already joined the Americans on Haiti by 1502 and doubtless some would have tried to leave the island. (Nonetheless, prevailing currents would probably have taken them towards Florida rather than towards Panama, unless they knew how to take advantage of American navigational skills.)

A Jesuit also makes reference (in 1554) to his judgement that some Ethiopians were living beyond the Amazon River region, 'in alia parte maris' (Latin) or 'na outra banda do mar (Portuguese) but this was secondhand information. Moreover, Black Africans are recorded as having escaped to the forest from Bahia with the help of Americans who captured a Portuguese slave ship prior to July 1559.[34] The 1554 account may indicate that Brazilian Americans knew of the existence of Africa, rather than that Africans were in America.

Thus we are left with intriguing possibilities, but with no hard evidence. Thor Heyerdahl has noted that a rubber boat was able to travel from the Canary Islands to the West Indies in recent times, but early sources tell us that the Canary Islanders had 'no means of navigation'.[35] Thus, one sort of evidence tends to balance out the other.

We are, however, still left with a number of significant problems, such as how plants of the banana-plantain family reached the Americas and West Africa, how certain species of cotton spread, whether the yam was present in the pre-Columbian Caribbean, and so on. The spread of banana-plantain-pacoba is of special significance, since it could not remain viable if carried in salt water. The *pacoba*, a banana, was clearly indigenous to South America.

A Brazilian author states that 'if the banana was known in Asia and Africa, what the first chroniclers called the pacoba, i.e., the "golden" banana, was not.'[36] About 1535 a Portuguese pilot described the bananas of São Tomé Island, Africa. He states that 'they have commenced to plant' there and they are called *abellana*: 'vi hanno cominciato a piantar quella erba che diventa in un anno cosi grande che par arbore, e fa quelli raspia modo di fichi che in Alessandria di Egitto, como ho inteso, chiamano *muse*; in detta isola la domandano *abellana*.' In the 1520s Leo Africanus described the *muse* of Egypt, the same plant as above.[37] A report on the Mina area (Ghana) in 1572 stated that bananas were also planted there, 'which in the Indies of Castilla were called *platanos*', and also that near 'Agri' the bananas grew in thickets so that it seemed that no one had to plant them there.[38]

In Brazil bananas and pacobas were quite important in the food supply. *Bananas asadas* (roasted bananas) were eaten by the Jesuits in 1561 when the wheat supply failed at Bahia, while the Jesuits at Espirito Santo in 1562 had many fruits, 'especially that which is called bananas, which last all the year' and is 'a great aid to the sustenance of this house'.[39] When lands were donated for the college of Bahia in 1563 one of the first tasks was to plant *bananas* on them.[40]

In the 1580s Gabriel Soares de Sousa stated of Brazil:

Pacoba é uma fruta natural d'esta terra, a qual se dá em uma arvore muito molle e facil de cortar . . . na India chamam a estas pacobeiras figueiras e as fruto figos . . . e a estas pacobas chama o gentio pacobuçú, que quer dizer pacoba grande.
Ha outra casta, que as indios chamam pacobamirim que quer dizer pacoba pequena.[41]

Thus Brazil had several types of native bananas, called pacobas, some large and some small, the latter being the size of fingers and called *pacobamirim*. The large pacobas were said to be known in India as 'figs' and in Brazil as *pacobuzú*.

Brazil also had, by the 1580s, bananas derived from São Tomé of Africa, which in India were said to be called *figos de horta*. 'Os negros de guiné são mas

affeiçados a estas bananas que ás pacobas, e d'ellas usam mas suas roças . . .'
The *negros* of Guinea preferred the São Tomé bananas to the pacobas. In the
1640s George Marcgrave, the young naturalist, described the Brazilian
varieties botanically.[42]

Varieties of the banana-plantain family were widely dispersed throughout the
Caribbean region and descriptions of them date back to at least the 1530s. An
early English visitor to Barbados (1650s) has drawn pictures of the native
varieties on that island, while an English traveller among the Miskito people of
Nicaragua found in 1681 that one of their main agricultural plants was the
plantain (along with the yam).[43]

The problem of the dispersal of the banana-pacoba by human action
demands more thorough study, but, in any case, it stands as a strong argument
for ancient maritime contact between the Americas and either Indonesia,
southeast Asia, Africa, or all of these. The dispersal of the sweet potato and
other crops from the Americas through the Pacific stands as a related
phenomenon. It should be noted that with the exception of American plants
being dispersed in the Pacific, virtually all writers dealing with the ancient
diffusion of crops and other cultural influences exhibit an extraordinary anti-
American bias. If a trait is, for example, found on both sides of the Atlantic most
diffusionists *a priori* favor an east-to-west dispersal and simply ignore any
possible influences from west to east.[44]

KIDNAPPED AMERICANS IN EUROPE BEFORE 1492

In any case, Americans did not reach Europe and Africa solely by means of
voluntary voyages or storm-driven adventures. European expeditions to the
Americas are known to have taken thousands of Americans to the east, and
some of these involuntary journeys preceded the time of Columbus.

By the ninth century AD, the European frontier was advancing northwards
and westwards with Irish and Scottish hermits or monks reaching Iceland.
Close behind them were Norse-speaking settlers and raiders from Norway and
the various islands north of Scotland. Our knowledge of what happened in this
region is shrouded in mystery because the earliest detailed sources, the
Icelandic sagas, are of a much later date and are oriented towards the
adventures of particular individuals only.

According to the sagas, Greenland was not reached by the Norse until very
late in the tenth century, being named at that time by Eric the Red. On the
other hand, several bits of information might indicate earlier contact.

First, a papal bull attributed to 834–5 reportedly already mentions both
Iceland and Greenland. Secondly, a pale-colored woman with chestnut hair
was reportedly seen among the Americans of Vinland (Newfoundland) in
c. 1006. Thirdly, when the Norse reached Greenland in *c.* 985–6 they found

both towards east and west, traces of human dwellings as well as fragments of small
boats made of skin and such instruments of stone which made it clear that the same kind

of people had lived [or had journeyed] there, who had peopled Vinland and whom the Greenlanders [Norse] call Skraelings.

Archaeology does not, thus far, support Inuit occupation of the south of Greenland in the 900s although Inuits of the Dorset culture were there in earlier times. Nonetheless, the remains seen by the Norse were clearly of recent origin. This suggests that the abandonment of south Greenland by Dorset people could have been due to raiding by Norse or Celtic pirates in the years prior to 985. If so, it is conceivable that captives were carried back to Europe since both the Norse and Irish possessed slaves in that era.[45]

The Norse who settled in Greenland before AD 1000 made several journeys westward to Markland (Labrador) and Vinland (Terranova or Newfoundland). In 1009 they captured two young Americans in Markland and carried them away to Greenland and, in all probability, to Norway. The Norse sagas state: 'Those boys they kept with them, taught them their language and they were baptized. They gave their mother's name as Vaetilldí, that of the father as Uvaegi.'[46] Thorfinn Karlsefni, the owner of the captives, did not stay long in Greenland but sailed with all of his belongings directly to Norway in *c.* 1009, later returning to Iceland. Since the Americans were his property and since the information about their learning to speak Norse and being baptized is recorded in an Icelandic saga, we must assume that they were taken to Norway with Karlsefni and perhaps from there to Iceland.[47] Thus in the year 1010 or thereabouts we have record of the first Americans to reach northern Europe involuntarily in the late pre-Columbian period.

The Norse of Greenland and Iceland thereafter made visits to Markland to obtain timber and other goods, one voyage being as late as 1347 (when their very small vessel was blown from Markland to Iceland). The Greenland Norse also began having military contacts with Inuit people in Greenland in the early 1300s and sporadic hostilities continued for a century or more. Since the Norse had a history of using Irish and Scots as slaves, we can assume that a small number of Inuit or other American captives would also be taken, even as several Norse were captured by the Inuit.[48]

It should be noted here that the 1347 wind-driven voyage of 17 or 18 Norse Greenlanders in a very small boat from the coast of Markland to Iceland, a boat that was not even equipped with an anchor, tends to reinforce the possibility that Americans in similar-sized craft could also be storm-driven to Europe. Prevailing winds in the North Atlantic also sometimes drove Norse vessels eastwards to Ireland.

In this connection, it is worth noting also that in old Shetlandic folk tales 'Finns' (Inuits) often arrived in those islands in the form of seals, and then casting their skins aside, became human beings. It has been suggested that this refers to the arrival of people in skin-covered kayaks. (Some folklorists prefer other symbolic interpretations.) In any case, the presence of Inuits in kayaks around the islands north of Britain will be discussed below.[49]

Very little information exists from the fifteenth century but it appears that Norwegians captured Inuits perhaps on more than one occasion, along with one or more kayaks. Claudius Clavus Swart, a Danish geographer who drew his maps in the 1420s, places in the Greenland area

the little pygmies, no more than one ell tall; I have seen them myself after they had been caught at sea in a skin boat which now hangs in Nidaros Cathedral. In the cathedral there is also a long boat of skin which was taken with the same kind of pygmies in it.[50]

A Norse report of the early 1200s also refers to the Inuit as 'very small people'.[51] For many years an Inuit boat was on display in Trondheim Cathedral in Norway.

Thus, most certainly, we have a record of Inuits being in Europe in the early 1400s.

A century after Clavus Swart, a German Jacob Ziegler met some Danes and Swedes in Rome and learned about the *Pigmei predatores*, or Inuit predators.[52]

Other European nationalities also seem to have come into contact with Americans before 1492. One author mentions a voyage to the Greenland–Labrador area in the early 1000s allegedly made by some mariners of Friesland. They were

cast on the rocks and took refuge on the coast. They saw some miserable looking huts hollowed out in the ground, and around these cabins heaps of iron ore. . . . But as they returned to their vessels, they saw coming out from these covered holes deformed men as hideous as devels [sic], with bows and slings and large dogs following them.[53]

One Frisian was slain while the others escaped.

Between *c.* 1418 and *c.* 1500 there is no official record of a Scandinavian ship reaching Greenland, partly due to the depopulation of Norway and Iceland carried out by the Black Death of 1348–9 (which may well have spread to Greenland). After 1349 English and Scottish pirates began to raid Iceland and Norwegian–Icelandic navigation fell into decline. Soon Basque and Portuguese vessels were joining in the exploitation of Icelandic waters. They alternately raided and traded with the Icelanders.[54] It appears also that some ships (probably Basque or Breton) visited the surviving Norse in Greenland between 1400 and 1500 (since European goods of that period have been found in south Greenland Norse archaeological sites). It is also believed by at least one historian of Greenland that Basque 'pirates' may well have exterminated or carried off the last Norse Greenlanders in *c.*1500. On the other hand, European reports had it simply that a 'pagan and barbarous' fleet from neighboring shores had carried them off, suggesting perhaps a move to Newfoundland or Labrador.[55]

Certain Basque traditions point towards their having made contact with Newfoundland in the 1370s and Iceland by 1400. Maps of 1436 and 1448 definitely show a 'Stocfish Island' (Codfish or Bacalao Island) west of Iceland, which undoubtedly is the same island which later came to be known as Terranova or Newfoundland. Extensive pre-Columbian contact cannot be doubted, even though there are arguments as to whether Basques, Bretons or others first reached the area.[56]

The subject is extremely interestiong for several reasons, one being the possibility that captives from Newfoundland and/or Greenland were carried back to the coasts of France and Spain.

It seems highly likely that vessels from Denmark and England reached Newfoundland in the 1470s and 1480s but as there is no mention of Americans being abducted we shall proceed to evidence relating to captives actually being taken.[57]

In November 1494 a German, Dr Jerónimo Münzer, wrote a letter about his impressions of Lisbon, Portugal. He reported that there were many *nigri* (blacks) in Lisbon and that the king of Portugal had sons of Ethiopian kings with him for educational purposes. He also stated: 'Habet item rex nigros varii coloris: rufos, nigros et aubnigros, de vario idiomate . . . O Rei possuía pretos de varíos côres: acobreados, pretos e anegrados, e de linguas diferentes.'

Thus by late 1494 there were in Lisbon *pretos* or *nigros* (blacks, non-whites) of various colors, including reddish or copper-colored people.[58] These latter were probably Americans, perhaps brought from the West Indies by Columbus, from Brazil by an unknown Portuguese navigator, or, most likely, from Newfoundland.

Interestingly, on January 11, 1503 a sailor from Lisbon presented for sale in Valencia, Spain, five *negros*. One of them was 'Miguel, de 20 años, de Terranova, aspresado cuando era pequeño y llevado a Lisboa, donde lo bautizan.' In 1505 was presented also (as a slave) 'Juan de 16 años de Terranova, no sabe si aun vivirán sus padres; cautivado cuando pequeño, fue llevado a Portugal y luego a Castilla.'[59] Thus Miguel was born in 1483 and was taken from Newfoundland to Lisbon when he was small, so probably before 1493. Juan was born in 1489 and was captured when small, so before 1499. They are among many slaves from Terranova sold in Lisbon, Seville, and Valencia after 1500.

It is well documented that in October 1501 some 50 or 60 Americans from the Newfoundland region were brought as slaves to Lisbon. This was followed by another shipload in 1502. These could be the origin of the Terranova slaves referred to above, except for the dates of their probable capture.[60]

TAKING THE CARIBBEAN TO EUROPE AND AFRICA: COLUMBUS
AND THE SLAVE TRADE

In any case, by the 1490s Americans were appearing once again in European cities. Although Terranova (Newfoundland) and Greenland continued to be a source of captives from 1501 on, it is best at this point to turn away from northern waters to examine the activities of Columbus and the catastrophic slave trade in American flesh which he initiated in the Caribbean region.

Columbus seems not to have been the first bearded white navigator to have reached the Caribbean region, but his immediate predecessor's name is unknown and no record of any return voyage to European or North African waters exists.[61] Moreover, Columbus' impact was singular in that he was, from the first, a dedicated slaver and exploiter with an extremely callous and indifferent attitude towards culturally different human beings.

Columbus on his first voyage kidnapped at least 27 Americans, two of whom escaped, leaving a total of 25 in his hands. His attitude is expressed as follows, when, after abducting seven males, he says: 'when your highnesses so command, they can all be carried off to Castille or held captive in the island itself, since with fifty men they would be all kept in subjection and forced to do whatever may be wished.' Thus, at the very first island reached (Guananí), Columbus already was able to express his willingness to depopulate the entire island in order that the Americans might be sold as slaves in Europe, or held as captives in their own land. This, it should be noted, is long prior to any disappointment about the failure to find gold or other riches in quantity.

A month later, after capturing five boys, Columbus says:

afterwards I sent to a house which is near . . . and they brought seven head of women, small and large, and three boys. I did this, in order that the men might conduct themselves better in Spain, having women of their own land . . . because *already it has many times been my business to bring men from Guinea*, in order that they might learn the language of Portugal, and afterwards when they had returned and they thought that use might be made of them in their own land . . . when they reached their own land this result never appeared . . . So that, having their women, they will be willing to do that which is laid upon them, and also these women will do much to teach our people their language, which is one and the same throughout these islands of India. (Italics added)

After two boys escaped, Columbus stated: 'and I have no great confidence in them, because many times they have attempted to escape.' His philosophy of conquest and colonialism was extremely well developed: 'And they are fitted to be ruled and to be set to work, to cultivate the land and to do all else that may be necessary, and you may build towns and teach them to go clothed and to adopt our customs.' Also: 'They would make good and industrious servants.'[62]

After learning of the existence of so-called 'Cannibal' (Carib) groups in the Indies, Columbus began to emphasize the enslavement of the latter. While still at sea, on his first return voyage, Columbus advocated the capture of Caribs: 'very fierce people and well proportioned and of very good understanding, who, after being removed from their inhumanity, we believe will be better than any other slaves whatsoever.' On January 30, 1494 he addressed to the Spanish monarchs a plan for sending men, women, and children to Spain to learn the Castillian language and to be trained in service, with more care 'than other slaves' receive, saying that this plan would save a great number of souls while at the same time providing the colonizing Spaniards with the profit needed to supply themselves with goods. In other words, Columbus proposed (after his first voyage) that American slavery be used to finance the conquest.[63]

Subsequently, Columbus began to enslave Taino (Arawak) people who were definitely not cannibalistic and it would appear that the idea of punishing Caribs (for being allegedly so) was simply an expedient financial strategy. The logic of his activities was well expressed by Las Casas who noted that

el acabará en muy poco tiempo de consumir toda la gente desta isla [Haiti], porque tenía determinado de cargar los navíos que viniesen de Castilla de esclavos y enviarlos a vender a las islas de Canarias, y de los Azores y a las de Cabo Verde y adonde quiera que bien se vendiesen; y sobre esta mercadería fundaba principalmente los aprovechamientos para suplir los dichos gastos y excusar a los reyes de costa, como en principal granjería.

Thus Columbus, according to las Casas, was determined to 'consume' the entire population of Haiti by filling every ship with slaves to be sold in the Canary, Azores and Cabo Verde islands or wherever, and planned that these slaves would finance the conquest.

As Las Casas points out, for Columbus the lives of Americans were obviously 'nothing' and the continuous wars to obtain slaves were simply necessary to fill the ships.[64] Columbus wrote to the monarchs that from Haiti

it is possible, in the name of the Holy Trinity, to send all the slaves which it is possible to sell . . . of whom, if the information which I have is correct, they tell me that one can sell 4,000. . . . And certainly, the information seems authentic, because in Castille and Portugal and Aragon and Italy and Sicily and the islands of Portugal and Aragon and the Canaries they utilize many slaves, and I believe that those from Guinea are not now enough. . . . In any case there are these slaves and brazilwood, which seem a live thing [profitable], and still gold.

Thus, even as Columbus was loading five ships with slaves, he was proposing to sell 4,000 in various parts of the Mediterranean and along the coast of Africa.

Columbus was also unconcerned that many Americans would die in the slave trade because, as he said, the blacks and the native Canary Islanders when first enslaved also had died in great numbers. For Columbus the Americans were *piezas* (pieces) or *cabezas de cabras* (heads of goats), and it did not matter if only ten per cent lived to reach a market, according to Las Casas (who, incidentally, possessed Columbus' diaries, letters and notes).[65]

The shipment of Americans to Europe and Africa by Columbus (and by other Spaniards) was, then, not an accident, nor was it a result of armed resistance or alleged cannibalism. It was a direct extension of the style of commercial slavery long practiced by the Genoese and Venetians in the Mediterranean and used by the Portuguese along the west coast of Africa. Columbus' voyages, in a very real sense, were mere extensions of the old galley routes from Italy to North Africa and the Black Sea or of Portuguese routes along the African coast.

What was the result? First, many thousands of Americans were shipped to Spain during Columbus' period of dominance in the Caribbean. It is difficult to calculate the exact number because many ships departed from Haiti without leaving any record of their cargo, but we may be sure that they did not leave empty. On the very first voyage, although Columbus only carried 25, it is likely that Martín Alonso Pinzón (who sailed to Galicia and then to Palos separately) may have carried more. It is possible that Pinzón actually landed the first Americans in Spain, a few days before Columbus arrived in Lisbon.

In any case, at least 3,000 Americans are known to have been shipped to Europe between 1493 and 1501, with the likely total being possibly double that. Most were sent to the Seville area, where they seem to show up in the slave markets as *negros* without a place of origin being mentioned. Others were probably sold in the Azores and other islands, partly to avoid the wrath of Queen Isabel (who, on occasion, expressed hostility towards the dividing up of 'her' vassals without her prior permission).[66]

Columbus reached Lisbon in early March 1493. Many people came to see the captive Americans and it is very likely that some of the latter were taken nine leagues into the interior to see the king of Portugal. There it was that two Americans drew maps which showed the Lucayos (Bahamas), Cuba, Haiti, and other islands. It may be also that Columbus left some Americans with the Portuguese, as discussed earlier.[67]

Shortly thereafter some of the Americans were taken to Seville, perhaps seven to ten being still alive and together. Some were left in that area, while about six or seven were taken overland across Spain to Barcelona where they were displayed before the monarchs in mid-April. In the fall of 1493 some Americans were taken on Columbus' second westward voyage, but only two of these reportedly arrived alive. One was able to run away immediately upon landing in Haiti.[68]

The process whereby Columbus began loading ships with slaves need not concern us here, in any detail. The flavor of it is conveyed by a report of Miguel de Cuneo, a member of the second expedition:

When our caravels ... were to leave for Spain, we gathered ... one thousand six hundred male and female persons of those Indians, and of these we embarked in our caravels on Feb. 17, 1495, five hundred and fifty souls among the healthiest. ... For those who remained, we let it be known in the vicinity that anyone who wanted to take some of them could do so, to the amount desired, which was done. And when each man was thus provided with slaves, there still remained about four hundred, to whom permission was granted to go where they wished. Among them were many women with children still at suck. Since they were afraid that we might return to capture them once again, ... they left their children ... and began to flee like desperate creatures.

About two hundred died on the voyage and were cast into the ocean, the rest being disembarked in Spain.

Columbus gave to Cuneo 'a very beautiful Carib woman'. Cuneo says, 'I conceived the desire to take my pleasure' with her. She valiantly resisted Cuneo's efforts at rape but eventually he had his way, after thrashing her mercilessly.[69]

Thus the veil of evil descended upon the Caribbean and many long years of rape and genocide commenced. As Todorov has stated:

the sixteenth century perpetrated the greatest genocide in human history ... in 1500 the world population is approximately 400 million, of whom 80 million inhabit the Americas. By the middle of the sixteenth century, out of these 80 million, there remain ten.

If the word genocide has ever been applied to a situation with some accuracy, this is here the case.[70]

But the tens of millions of Americans who disappeared after 1492 did not all die in the 'holocaust' inflicted within the Americas. Many thousands were sent to Europe and Africa where their descendants still live.

2

The Intensification of Contacts: Trans-Atlantic Slavery and Interaction, after 1500

THE ARRIVAL OF AMERICAN SLAVES IN SPAIN AND PORTUGAL

It will perhaps be surprising to some readers to learn that the greatest degree of intensive contact between Americans and Africans did not occur initially in either the Americas or Africa, but rather in European cities such as Lisbon, Seville, and Valencia. This contact has not heretofore been studied for a variety of reasons, one of the principal ones being the myth that the enslavement of Americans was a temporary phenomenon. Another reason, equally mythical, is the notion that in modern times 'slavery' and 'negro slavery' were virtually synonymous concepts.

Slavery was quite common in the Mediterranean world in the thirteenth and fourteenth centuries. In Iberia Islamic laws recognized slavery and Muslims were even allowed to hold other Muslims as slaves if the latter were black or *loro* (of intermediate color).[1] In Christian Barcelona one finds numerous slaves between 1275 and 1288 classified as *moro lorum* (Muslim of intermediate color), *sarraceno blanco* (white Saracen), *sarracenum nigrium* (black Saracen), *sarracenam lauram* (Saracen of intermediate color) and *sarracenam albam* (white Saracen). In the thirteenth century, Barcelona had many *tártaros* (Tartars), Greeks, Bulgarians, Bosnians, Albanians, and so on, as slaves, including an *esclava blanca tártara* (white tartar slave). In the fourteenth century, Muslim slaves became more common again, and one finds many white, *loro* (intermediate), and black slaves. In 1439, Simon, an Ethiopian slave, killed a Russian (*ruso*) slave. Turkish and Tartar slaves were also present, along with many Russians, Bulgarians, *sarts* (probably *Sardos* or Sardinians), and others called *Abguas*, *Xarqueses* (Circassians), and so on, probably from the Caucasus mountains. In 1429 two runaway black slaves were recaptured in Redome, France, but others escaped to Tolosa (Toulouse) where slavery was not recognized. Between 1243 and 1296, of 50 slaves listed in Barcelona, 18 per cent were *laurus*, 10 per cent were black, 20 per cent were Saracen only, and about 52 per cent were *blanche* (white).

In Provence a 'Sarrazin noir, un esclave blanc, une fille circassienne', and 'un garçon turc' were all sold as slaves in the fifteenth century.[2] This characterizes slavery in the period, with white, black and brown, European, African and Asian slaves being treated basically the same, and with a tremendous ethnic variety – although most were from the Balkans, the Black Sea region, or northern Africa.

In 1266–71 several *olivastre* (olive-colored) slaves were sold in Gênes (Genoa), while of 48 slaves named between 1401 and 1499 in that city, 25 were *albi* (white), 15 *neri* (black), six *olivegnii* (intermediate or olive), one *endeco* (*indaco* or Indian), and one *lauro* (intermediate or brown). There were many Tartar and other eastern slaves in Italy during that period, along with a substantial number of blacks and others from North Africa and the Iberian peninsula.[3]

In Portugal slaves of Muslim background were present in the thirteenth century along with some who were *Moçarabes* (Christians who lived in an Arab fashion). During the fourteenth century Porutuguese vessels began to raid the Canary Islands and many *canarios* were introduced as captives, along with additional Muslims. In the fifteenth century Berber and black Senegalese (Wolof) slaves became common, especially after 1440–50.[4] During certain periods the term *sarraceni* was synonymous with *servi* or *captivi* (slave or captive). *Maurus* (moor) corresponded to a free or slave Muslim, while later slaves were known as 'negro e guineu, preto e sobretudo escravo'.[5] Thus, slaves as a class might be called – depending on the time period – *sarraceni* or *negro* or *preto*, or slave (*slav*).

Quite early, in both Portugal and Spain, the status of a child was determined by the status of the mother. If the mother was a slave, the child was also a slave.[6]

In the western Mediterranean the slave trade was dominated by the Genoese and Castillians by means of slave factors in Fez, Morocco, but slaves from the east were also introduced. In 1455, for example, a Tartar slave was mentioned in Seville. At about that time, however, the Portuguese began to dominate the black African trade by successfully reaching Agadir and then Senegal in the mid-fifteenth century. In 1452, Pope Nicholas V permitted the Portuguese to enslave infidels, pagans, and 'enemies of Christ'. By 1479 the Portuguese were dominant insofar as black slaves were concerned, but *canario* and Muslim slaves continued to be obtained by the Spanish directly.[7]

For a long period of time Muslim slaves continued to arrive in Seville and other Spanish cities, some from Granada and others from Algiers, Oran and other places which were raided in North Africa. Canary Islanders were also shipped in by the Spaniards who had replaced the Portuguese as the oppressors of the *canarios*. Thus, all during the fifteenth, sixteenth and seventeenth centuries, the slaves of the Iberian peninsula were of all colors and of many nationalities including Greeks, Slavs, Turks, Egyptians, Asians, Indians,

Americans, and so on.[8] A Portuguese expedition to the Gambia in 1457 took with it an Indian interpreter, Jacob.[9]

The Christian Castillians possessed slaves of many kinds in the thirteenth and fourteenth centurties, most of whom were *maures* (moros) or *morezno* (children of *moros*, perhaps *moreno*). Some were classified by color (white, black, *loro*) as in Cataluña, while a few in 1266 were called *mamelouks* (slave in Arabic, especially soldier-slaves). In 1475 a royal order established for Seville the position of

Mayoral e Juez de todos los Negros e Loros, libres e captivos que estan e son captivos e horros en la . . . Sevilla, e en todo su Arzobispado; y que non pueden facer ni fagan los dichos Negros y Negras, y Loros y Loras, ningunas fiestas nin juzgados de entre ellos, salvo ante vos, el dicho Juan de Valladolid, Negro, nuestro Juez y Mayoral de los dichos Negros, Loros y Loras; y mandamos que vos conozcais de los debates y pleytos y casamientos . . . e non otro alguno, por quanto sois persona suficiento para ello . . . ; e Nos somos informados, que sois de linage noble entre los dichos Negros.[10]

Thus in 1475, Juan de Valladolid, a black of noble ancestry, was appointed as the judge and mayor of the blacks and *loros* (browns) of the Seville area, with authority over their communal life, whether they were free or slave.

This policy of self-government for blacks and browns conformed to the established Castillian and Aragonese policies towards free Muslims and Jews, each community of which had its own laws and courts separate from those of the Christian community. This attitude of tolerance and autonomy was later abolished but it set a direct precedent for later policies favoring American autonomous pueblos in the Americas after the 1520s. In any case, American slaves were probably integrated into the non-white community structure in Seville.

Thus, the arrival of American captives after 1493 did not, in any sense, present a new spectacle. Both Spaniards and Portuguese had become accustomed to financing their wars and expeditions by seizing men, women and children wherever possible. This is not to say that it was at all clear that all such captives were *legal* slaves, especially if they were not taken in 'just war' but, in practice, laws were often ignored. One finds, for example, Christians capturerd by Muslims being treated as slaves in Spain if purchased from Muslim slave-dealers. In the records which have been published from Seville and Valencia, 'possession' seems initially to have always been accepted as proof of the rights to sell a slave and for the authorities to impose a tax on the sale.[11]

Columbus was the major supplier of American slaves prior to 1500. As noted earlier, he caused some 3,000 to perhaps 6,000 slaves to be sent to Europe and also, if we are to be believe that his plans were implemented, to the Azores, Canary, Madeira, and Cabo Verde Islands. By the year 1500, however, a great escalation began in the shipment of Americans across the Atlantic since other Spaniards and the Portuguese became directly active.

In the year 1500, Americans were directly transported to Europe from the Caribbean islands, from the coasts of South America, and from the Terranova

(Newfoundland) region. Three major new sources of slaves were thus opened up and it is necessary to examine this subject before proceeding to an analysis of what happened to the Amerians when they arrived in eastern lands.

As mentioned above, Gaspar Corte Real and João Fernandes were among Portuguese navigators from the Azores who reached the Newfoundland–Greenland area in 1500 or perhaps earlier. Fernandes may have taken captives to the Azores but if so no record exists. In October 1501, however, Corte Real sent some 57 captives to Lisbon. Their description is worth noting:

Les habitants son un peu plus grands que nous. . . . Ils son très semblables à des tziganes; leur visage est peint à manière des Indiens, quelques-uns avec six signes, d'autres avec huit au moins. Les cheveux des males sont longs et flottants en boucles. Leurs yeux de couleur presque verte . . . les femmes . . . leur couleur est plutôt blanche, le mâle, au contraire est beaucoup plus foncé.

Thus, the Americans were slightly taller than the European observers. They resembled Gypsies with their faces marked in signs like those of the 'Indians'. The hair of the males, who were darker than the females, was long and curly, and their eyes were greenish in color. (Thus it is quite possible that these Americans were part Norse Greenlander or part Breton or Basque.)

We do not know exactly where these green-eyed Americans came from; whether from Newfoundland or Labrador, however, they were in possession of what appeared to be part of a sword and jewelry manufactured in Italy. This tends to confirm early contact with Europe, as discussed above.[12]

In 1501, Miguel Corte Real sailed back to the *Terranova* region, where he disappeared. One of his ships returned to Portugal, with 'certain men and women whom he found'. In 1503 the Portuguese sent out two ships and thereafter the Newfoundland area was visited regularly, so much so that in 1506 a royal tax was imposed on the fishing catch.[13] The Bretons, English and perhaps Basques were also active in the area, but that will be discussed below.

Slaves from *Terranova* show up in the slave-markets of Seville and Valencia very soon after 1500. In Valencia during the period to 1516, we find in 1503 Miguel (age 20) and Manne (age 10); in 1505 Juan (16) and Pedro (16); in 1507 Antonio (8) and Juan Amarco (18); in 1515 Ali, now Melchor (20); in 1516 Catalina (28). These eight slaves were, with one exception, all obtained from Portuguese sources. They were all classified as *negros* with the exception of Juan and Pedro, called simply slaves.[14]

In Seville, between 1510 and 1515, some 13 *Terranova* slaves were registered and sold, including: in 1510 Isabel (age 20), Cristóbal (age 20), Virgida (17); in 1511 Pedro (20), Antón (25), Felipa (14); in 1512 Pedro (25), Catalina (18), Antón (25); in 1513 Fernando (20) and María (25); in 1514 Francisca (14), and in 1515 María (20). Two of these slaves were categorized as *negro*, one as *loro*, and ten as slaves only.[15]

In 1525 a Spaniard, Esteban Gómez, made a voyage up the Atlantic coast of North America, bringing back 'many Indians' as slaves. Allegedly, they were set at liberty but perhaps some *Terranova* slaves after 1525 were derived from Gómez' voyage.[16]

Interestingly, between 1548 and 1560, some 20 slaves from *Terranova* appeared in Peru (out of 256 who can be identified geographically in the records). Between 1560 and 1650 about 143 slaves from *Terranova* showed up in Peru, coming by way of Iberia probably. An additional 11 were classified as *bozales* (not familiar with the Spanish language or culture at all).[17]

The location of *Terranova* has heretofore been a matter of debate, with writers generally placing it somewhere on the west coast of Africa. On the other hand, there is very strong evidence that *Terranova* was, at least in the first half of the sixteenth century, Newfoundland.[18]

First, António Brasio in his collection of Portuguese missionary documents and royal communications relating to Africa (1471–mid-1500s) does not mention any place called *Terranova*.[19] On the other hand, in a contract written in the Canary Islands in 1543 a reference is indeed made to a black slave as being a 'native of Terranova de Guinea'.[20] I will argue, however, that whenever *Terranova* is mentioned without *de Guinea* it refers to Newfoundland.

First, although the Portuguese referred to Brazil as *la Terra nuova* (the new land) in 1500, thereafter they virtually always used *Terranova* for Newfoundland. Documents relating to *Terra Nova* were found in the Torre do Tombo in Portugal and *Terra Nova* is used repeatedly by Portuguese sources of the sixteenth century for Newfoundland or Cape Breton. The Ruysch map of *c.*1508 has *Terra Nova* on it and reflects Portuguese nomenclature. Many other maps, including that of Verrazano (1524–9) also use *Terra Nova* for Newfoundland. This usage persisted so that in the 1630–46 period Brazilian Portuguese were referring to 'o comericio com a Terra Nova' in codfish. There was regular trade in fish between *Terra Nova* and Recife in Brazil.[21]

For the Spanish *Terranova* was used consistently for Newfoundland. Early maps used by the Spanish, such as the Oliveriana (1503), the Pesaro chart (1503–8) and the Ruysch map (*c.*1508) located *Terra Nova* (*Terra Noba*) at Newfoundland. The Ribero map of 1529 places *Tiera Nova: de Cortereal* near Cape Breton. In 1511 Spanish royal correspondence relates to a voyage to *Tierra Nueva*, using Breton pilots. This usage continued, as Martín Navarette (1829) entitled a section of his work 'Sobre las navegaciones de los vascongados á los mares de Terranova'. He cites documents from 1561 referring to Newfoundland as *Tierranueva* and *Terranova*. Finally, La Farga Lozano in his work on the Basques uses *Terranova* for Newfoundland without qualification, including references from the 1690s.[22]

The French, it may be added, also used *Terre-Neuve* or *Terre Neuvfe* consistently for Newfoundland.[23] Thus, we must, it seems, acknowledge the fact that for the Spanish, Portuguese, and French, *Terranova* was the proper name for Newfoundland (or for the Newfoundland–Cape Breton area) and that slaves from *Terranova* would have to have been from that area unless specified as being from the very obscure *Terranova de Guinea* (especially before *c.*1540).

It should also be noted that *Terranova* fell outside of the realm of Spain (in practice) and for a time was thought to be within the Portuguese sphere. In fact, Portuguese under João Álvarez Fagundes attempted to colonize the area in the 1520s, but the attempt failed.[24]

The *Tabios* people from *Terranova* (being often described as 'sooty' or dark-colored) might well be regarded sometimes as *negros* rather than as *indios* (this will be discussed in a later chapter).[25] Americans were usually regarded as *pardos* (Portuguese) or *loros* (Spanish) in terms of color in the early period (1492–early 1600s), but *negro* was also used for them.[26]

The *Terranova* slave trade helps to explain the early depopulation of Newfoundland and the ease of the subsequent extinction of the American native inhabitants by the English.

The second source of slaves after 1500 was the Caribbean region which, very soon, included the adjacent coasts of South America, Florida–Carolina, and Meso-America. Many Americans were taken as slaves to the east, to Spain and to the Canary Islands, often as a result of the direct authorization of the Crown. In 1499, for example, Vicente Yáñez Pinzón was authorized to discover islands and mainland in 'the Indies' and permission was given to take 'all manner of slaves, *negros*, *loros* or others, who in Spain are held as slaves': 'vos fasemos merced de toda manera desclavos negros o loros o otros de los que en españa son tenidos por esclavos e que por razon lo deven ser.' Moreover, the authorization given by Ferdinand and Isabella to Rodrigo de Bastidas, June 1500, allowed for the importation of slaves to Spain who were '*negros* and *loros* who in the kingdoms of Castilla were held and reputed for slaves' of whom the Crown was to receive a quarter share. A similar clause was inserted in another authorization of the same year.

Speaking of the late 1499–1503 expeditions to northern South America, José Antonio Saco states 'that one of the objects of these expeditions was that of robbing human beings in order to sell them as slaves'. The expeditions were to obtain slaves from among the *negros* and/or *loros* who lived in the discovered lands. As we shall see in a later chapter, *loro* was regularly applied as a color term for Americans while *negro* was also used (but in this case the usage meant simply that *any* brown or black people found could be enslaved if people of similar status were already held as slaves in Spain).

A series of voyages then ensued, including that of Alonzo de Ojeda who, in 1500, disembarked more than 200 American slaves at Cádiz. Américo Vespucci also reports having sold more than 200 Americans in Spain but some authorities feel he was simply reporting on the Ojeda expedition. In 1500 Yáñez Pinzón captured 36 Americans in northern Brazil as well as some from other places. These were landed at Palos, Spain, where a legal dispute ensued.

It seems that Pinzón had promised one slave from his expedition to a Diego Prieto. When he did not receive a slave, Prieto seized one of the American slaves of Pinzón in Palos. In order to settle the dispute Pinzón offered to pay Prieto the value of another common slave and the king commanded that this be done. This royal decree of June 20, 1501, shows that the Crown was ready to accept the enslavement of Americans in Spain, in spite of several exceptions noted elsewhere.

In 1499 Diego de Lepe also departed from Palos and proceeded to enslave Americans in the Amazon region and the gulf of Pariá. The slaves were turned over to Bishop Juan Rodriguez de Fonseca in Spain. Interestingly, an American from Marañón (Maranhão or the Amazon) showed up in Seville in 1500. He was named Pastor, age 13 or 14, color *loro*, and sold for 10,000 *maravedis*.

In 1501 Cristóbal Guerra and his brother Luis brought a large number of slaves from Pariá, the Isla Margarita and other areas to Spain. These slaves benefited, however, from an order to enslave only Americans taken in 'just war' and Guerra was ordered to return them at his own cost. On the other hand, in 1503 Juan de la Costa sailed to the Cartagena region, seized 600 Americans, the majority of whom were sent to Spain with Luis Guerra, brother (or other relation) to Cristóbal Guerra. Costa went on to seize other Americans in the Gulf of Urabá.

It would appear that if the Americans resisted (as many did) then 'just war' could be alleged and enslavement became legal. Moreover, as a result of the above incidents, in which several Spaniards were killed, the Crown was persuaded in 1503 to authorize the enslavement of the alleged *caribes* of Cartagena. In 1504 a royal decree stated that 'rebel Indians' were to be enslaved, a portion going to the Government. With the death of Isabel that same year no restraint existed. (In 1512, for example, Ferdinand authorized the enslavement of Borinquen natives, with an 'F' being branded on their 'fronts' and with a fifth part going to the crown.)[27]

After 1510 Spanish slave-raiding reached out increasingly towards the outer islands of the Caribbean and the adjacent mainlands. Much of the raiding was designed to meet the labor needs of Haiti (where the native population was being greatly reduced), but numerous Spanish expeditions such as those of Magellan (1519), Sebastián Cabot (1529, to Brazil), and Gómez (1525) captured Americans who were taken to Spain or who died en route. Cabot also purchased 50 to 60 slaves from the Portuguese in Brazil, for later sale in Seville. By the 1520s slave-raiding in Florida and the Carolina coast area was common also.[28]

It is not necessary here to review all the data relative to the enslavement of Americans in Panama, Venezuela, Nicaragua, Mexico, Peru, and other countries, but there is sufficient evidence to indicate that, at least through the 1550s, large numbers of slaves were procured and shipped to various locations.[29]

Saco notes that King Ferdinand had been considering the large-scale introduction of American slaves into Spain. In a dispatch of July 3, 1510 he asked several royal officials what profits might be derived from shipping slaves for sale in Spain. But the rapid decline in the native population of Haiti forced Ferdinand to change his opinion. By decree of July 21, 1511, Ferdinand ordered Columbus that no American slaves could be sent to Castille; this was to prevent the depopulation of the islands. Because the Spaniards did not abide by the order (as was customary, according to Saco) the king strengthened his opposition in 1512, imposing a fine and the loss of the slaves sent. This order was also not completely obeyed and other orders had to be issued in 1528, 1543, and 1556.

But the Crown also vacillated in its policies. An order of 1526 prohibited the capture of natives and their shipment to Spain without license. They were to be returned unless the license had been obtained. In 1530 further American enslavement was prohibited; however, violations were common and the ban was lifted in 1534. Two years later a decree again prohibited the shipment of American slaves to Spain unless accompanied by a document issued by the provincial governor giving his approval. A decree of 1543 prohibited the taking of free or slave Americans from one province to another in the Indies.

Efforts were also made to enforce some of the above provisions. In 1529 the officials of Seville were ordered to facilitate the verification of the legal status of Americans introduced there. In 1531 arriving ships were to be examined for clandestine slaves. Decrees of 1536 and 1538 ordered the examination of the proof of slave status. Finally in May 1549 the officials of Seville were commissioned to liberate the Americans in Spain (in a manner similar to what was then being attempted in the Americas).[30]

Especially in the years around 1500 some Americans were actually freed and returned to the Caribbean from Spain, but the numbers seem few in comparison with those actually shipped.

In 1541 the bishop of Santa Marta (now Colombia) wrote to Emperor Charles V that in that region

se habían vendido públicamente muchos indios exportados del Perú, y que los castellanos que allí tenían repartimientos vendían sus indios sacando otros muchos para Castilla con el objeto de servirse de ellos lo cual se hacía con facultad de los que gobernaban.

Thus, Spaniards were exporting American slaves from Peru to Colombia and many were being sent to Spain, with the help of officials (and in spite of laws to the contrary).

The New Laws of 1542 which supposedly ended several forms of American slavery did not immediately result in the suspension of the slave trade or in the shipment of Americans to Spain. On December 18, 1547 a royal official wrote from Santo Domingo that

contra el mandado de Vuestra Magestad se sacan indios, especialmente mujeres, y se venden públicamente en Sevilla, y de dó llevan muchos de Tierra Firme dó se venden en almoneda. De consentirlo en Sevilla nace el atrevimiento de aquí.

Thus in 1547 American slaves, especially females, were still being sold in Seville and the acceptance of such sales in the latter city gave birth to the impudence of Spaniards in the Indies (who continued to ship American slaves in defiance of the laws). During this period the northern coast of South America seems to have served as a major source of slaves, with slave ships arriving at Haiti from Paría and Cumaná as late as 1544.[31]

Clearly, the legislation enacted by the Spanish Crown at various times to control or prevent certain types of American enslavement was only partially effective. One of the major objectives of the early legislation was to prevent the diminishing of the labor pool in the Indies by shipments to Europe rather than to end slavery as such. Much has been made by writers of the significance of this legislation but even the famous laws of 1542 did not bring an end to enslavement. First, it must be noted that the Spaniards developed several categories of 'partial slaves', categories which continued to allow for effective enslavement. Thus, there were *naborías* (slaves who could not be resold), 'useless' Americans (natives who could be moved from an island without gold to a place of labor shortage), 'apportioned' Americans (natives who were apportioned to Spaniards as laborers or, later, as tribute-paying retainers), *chichimecos* (natives of dispersed living settlements who could be forcibly reduced to missionary control and mandatory labor), and *rebeldes* (such as all alleged 'caribs', the Mapuches of Chile, and others who could be legally enslaved at various times even after 1542), all of which allowed for quasi-slavery or actual slavery to continue to exist.[32]

An Italian, Girolamo Benzoni, was in the Indies from 1541 to 1556. He later wrote that:

All the slaves that the Spaniards catch in these provinces are sent to Cubagua. . . . The slaves are all marked in the face and on the arms by a hot iron with the mark of C [for *caribe?*] . . . when ships arrive from Spain, they barter these Indians for wine, flour, biscuit, and other requisite things. And even when some of the Indian women are pregnant by these same Spaniards, they sell them without any conscience. Then the merchants carry them elsewhere and sell them again. Others are sent to the Island of Spagnuola [Haiti], filling with them some large vessels built like caravels.

Benzoni also noted that: 'although an almost infinite number of the inhabitants of the mainland have been brought to these islands as slaves, they have nearly all since died.'[33]

As we shall see, some Americans were still being shipped to Europe by Spaniards in this period, even though labor shortages (more than royal decrees) operated to favor their being retained in the Americas. It was primarily Cuba, Haiti, and Borinquen which absorbed Mayas from Yucatan, Huastecas from Mexico, Miskitos from Nicaragua, and various other nations during this era, rather than Spain itself.

Note should also be made of the many Americans sent to Spain in capacities other than that of slave. Many were sent to become interpreters or to be instructed and baptized. Others went as curiosities or as entertainers. In 1528, for example, Hernan Cortés took a group of Aztec and Tlaxcalteco chiefs, including a son of Montezuma II, to Spain along with a troop of jugglers, acrobats, and dancers. These also were taken to the court of Pope Clement VII in Rome. A different kind of figure was Juan Santos Atahualpa of Peru, taken to Spain and Angola by the Jesuits. Later Atahualpa led a major rebellion in Peru, one feature of which was the use of black African allies. Part of eastern Peru (the Campa region) remained liberated for many years as a result of Atahualpa's efforts.[34]

THE PORTUGUESE ENSLAVEMENT OF AMERICANS IN BRAZIL AND ELSEWHERE

A third region which served as a major source of slaves for Europe and Africa was the coast of Brazil.

In 1500 Pedro Álvares Cabral, sailing to India, touched along the Brazilian coast. It appears that at least one American was sent back to Portugal with Gaspar de Lemos.[35] This initially friendly contact was not to last, however, since the king of Portugal seems to have envisioned the coast of Brazil as a second slave-coast, to be harvested in the manner of West Africa. In 1502 he let a contract to Fernão de Noronha and a company of merchants 'to trade in brazilwood and slaves'. They were to send to Brazil six ships each year. Four ships were sent in 1503 and they returned to Portugal full of wood and slaves. It is known that the trade was fairly regular after 1504. From the very beginning, then, Americans were acquired as a commodity and shipped to Europe, as well as perhaps to Africa.

Portuguese slavers may have also ventured into regions claimed by Spain. In July 1503 a letter reached the Spanish court with the news that Portuguese ships had gone to the area discovered by Rodrigo Bastidas (part of Colombia and Panama) 'y traido esclavos indios y palo del Brasil' (and carried off American slaves and brazilwood).

In 1511 the Portuguese ship *Bertoa*, with two *negros* and one non-negro slave on board, carried some 35 American slaves from Brazil to Portugal. Another ship in the following year was described as having the deck loaded with young men and women. From then on there are frequent reports of Americans being taken to Portugal, some for showing to the king and some for more ordinary servitude. As Capistrano de Abreu noted, 'o Brasil exportou escravos ante de importa-los' (Brazil exported slaves before it imported them).[36]

As noted above, Cabot was able to purchase 50 or 60 slaves from the Portuguese of San Vicente (Santos) in 1529, for resale in Spain. The Portuguese of this area, intermarried with prominent Tupiniquin leaders, were already actively exploiting inter-American rivalries, especially with the Tamóio of Rio de Janeiro (allied with French traders) and the Carijó (Guaraní) to the south.

The Portuguese Crown in the 1530s authorized the creation of about 12 feudal domains in Brazil. Each of the grantees (*donatarios*) was entitled to enslave as many Americans as were needed for local labor, but only 24 per year (48 for one *donatorio*) could be sent to Portugal by each for sale. This authorization continued until 1549 and allowed about 216 slaves to be sent each year for some 15 years, for a potential total of 3,240 or more. Of course, Portuguese laws were frequently not enforced in the colonial areas and many more slaves may have actually been transported, especially since American slaves could legally be used *without limit* to man the ships for the passage to Portugal.

The Portuguese began quite early to try to find markets for Brazilians outside of the Portuguese Empire. In 1538 three Portuguese ships reached Borinquen with 45 Portuguese and 140 American slaves and a few free Americans. A Portuguese captain later proposed to ship Brazilian slaves to Haiti, and initially six or seven were sent. In 1550, however, Charles V resolved not to allow the introduction of Brazilians as slaves. Some years later, a Portuguese ship reached the island of Margarita with 300 American male and female slaves. They were sold but in 1556 the Spanish Crown ordered the guilty to be punished for violating the law. On the other hand, in 1570 consideration was given to authorizing the importation into the Spanish colonies of Brazilian slaves enslaved by other Americans. This category of slave (as well as *caribes*, that is, alleged cannibals) could be imported.

In any case, one can see that between the 1530s and 1570s, the Portuguese were actively attempting to market American slaves far and wide.[37]

Within Brazil, the enslavement of Americans proceeded very rapidly, primarily for use in the sugar cane and cotton industries. Letters of the *donatarios* between 1535 and 1550 document this process, as in 1545 when Pero de Góis wrote to the king that in the fields and sugar refineries of São Tomé there were enough slaves. The population of San Vicente in 1548 included 600 free persons and more than 3,000 American slaves, according to a letter of Luiz de Góis.[38]

In 1549 the Jesuits began preaching to the Americans, free and slave, as well as to the *mamalucos* (mixed-bloods) and Portuguese. Their letters, from 1549 on, contain frequent references to the '*escravos da terra*' (American slaves) who were very numerous.[39]

A few black Africans (*escravos da Guiné*) began to be introduced in the Pernambuco area where, from the beginning, they worked together with American slaves. In 1548, for example, Hans Staden found 'Moren und Prasilianische Schlaven' ('Moores' and Brazilian slaves) used together against an enemy group. (These 'Moores' could have been Tapuya slaves, however.) Two years later, in San Vicente, Staden frequently mentioned American slaves (usually Carijós) and said that the Portuguese had 'many'.[40] Ulrich Schmidl, who passed through the same region in 1553, carried 20 Carijós to Lisbon with him, where two of them died. He very likely took some of the remainder on with him to Antwerp.[41]

The development of the sugar industry created increasing labor demands and Africans began to be taken to Brazil regularly after 1550–70. For the next 50 years, however, Americans continued to be a source of labor even in the sugar industry, being only gradually outnumbered by Africans and American–African mixed-bloods. In 1584, for example, the Pernambuco area had 60 or more sugar refineries 'com muita gente branca, Negros da Guine e Indios da terra'. Bahia had some 40 refineries, with 'Portugueses, Indios da terra e

Negros de Guiné'. To the south of Bahia only American slaves were mentioned as forming the labor force in 1584.[42]

Especially in the southern and northern parts of Brazil (São Paulo–San Vicente and Pará–Maranhão) and in the interior, the enslavement of Americans continued to be the major source of labor for centuries. Between 1630 and 1650, for example, from 100,000 to 200,000 Americans from the Paraguay region were enslaved and sold in São Paulo, Rio de Janeiro and elsewhere.[43]

In 1570 the Portuguese Crown attempted to limit the enslavement of Americans to those captured in armed combat or those from certain specified nations such as the Aimores. In 1587 enslaved *Brasis* (Americans) were to be seen as free workers, serving for a term whether fixed or otherwise. In 1595, Philip II, ruler of both Spain and Portugal, prohibited enslavement except in a war which he declared. None of these measures eliminated native slavery, however, and it increased greatly again during the 1630s.[44]

Under the conditions of labor shortage in Brazil after *c.*1580 it would appear that the shipping of Americans to Portugal would have declined in significance. But we must keep in mind that the Portuguese had to have a way to pay for African slaves and also, perhaps, sometimes wanted to be rid of potentially rebellious Americans. C. R. Boxer noted that as late as *c.*1719 the Portuguese of the Piaui region were trading 'three or four redskins . . . for one Negro from Angola'. In that area the Americans were 'disliked and despised'. It is possible, therefore, that 'cheap' American slaves (captured in slave raids) were sent to Africa and Portugal, in exchange for Africans.[45]

In 1578 an Italian living in the Portuguese Empire wrote that Brazilian natives were not then being imported into Portugal because they 'sono gente cattiva e ostinata e como é si veggono schiavi, si deliberano di morirsi, en viene loro fatto'. We must, however, view this assertion of obstinacy and self-destruction within the context of the continuing enslavement of hundreds of thousands of Americans in Brazil itself as well as in relation to the possibility that the women and children might have been more easily transformed into slaves than were adult males. In any case, Chief Martín of the Carijó nation complained to the Spanish in 1576 that the Portuguese of southern Brazil were carrying their children off to 'other parts of Brazil and then to Portugal to be sold as slaves'. A Jesuit witnessed, in 1635, a slave-raid using 15 sea-going ships and many large canoes, designed reportedly to secure 12,000 slaves from the Carijó nation. One must suppose that many were to be secured for sale outside Brazil.[46]

We can, I think, be confident that Americans soon appeared in the Portuguese colonies in Africa and in the Cabo Verde Islands. The high death-rates on Portuguese sailing vessels of the period would make necessary the replenishing of crews in Brazil and, at a somewhat later date, the use of the Brazilian natives and mixed-bloods in the African trade in various capacities.

It may well be that Americans were introduced into the Portuguese African outposts soon after 1500. As noted above, Fernão de Noronha was given a contract to ship slaves and brazilwood from Brazil, beginning in 1502. John Vogt states of Noronha (called Loronha): 'during 1502/3 this merchant's involvement with San Jorge da Mina [Ghana] included supplying all slaves and wine to the port. Simultaneously, Loronha held leases for Brazil and the Guinea pepper monopoly.' Most of the slaves taken to Mina were gathered together on São Tomé island but it seems highly likely that Noronha would have utilized some of the Brazilian slaves he acquired in his African activities, at the very least as mariners and laborers.

A Brazilian scholar, José Honório Rodrigues, has written that: 'from the seventeenth to the nineteenth century Brazil had more contact with and greater bonds to Angola, Dahomey, and parts of the coasts of Mina and Guinea than did Portugal itself. . . . Many Brazilians went to Angola as soldiers, peddlers, businessmen, prostitutes, and exiles.'[47]

It will be very interesting to trace the first Brazilian American impact directly upon Africa but doubtless it is more or less simultaneous with the first African impact upon Brazil. By the 1550s native Brazilians were in Portugal in some numbers and at about the same time the regular shipment of Africans to Brazil commenced. The Brazil–Africa trade at first went largely via Portugal but gradually became direct.[48]

Portuguese vessels were noted for having crews of diverse national and racial origins. From Madagascar to Japan, crews were often of African or Indian (South Asian) origin but in the Atlantic we can assume that a high proportion were of American background. Just what percentage is not certain.

Black Africans reached Macao and Japan in the sixteenth century in Portuguese ships but it is also possible that a few Americans or part-Americans reached the east coast of Africa and then went to the Far East. Japanese drawings of the Portuguese at Nagasaki show many Africans but also a few brown men of possible Indian (Asian or American) appearance.[49]

An early instance of a person of American ancestry being in the western Pacific is seen in the case of the son of Juan Carvajo (Carvalhos), who was left behind on the island of Borneo near Burné in July 1521. The father, a Portuguese accompanying Magellan, had lived for four years in Brazil and there his son had been born, of an American mother certainly. Carvalhos had taken the son with him to Europe, where both later joined the Magellan expedition. Young Carvalhos remained in Borneo after becoming lost, while his father remained in the Moluccas.

An interesting example of a person of American ancestry going with the Portuguese to Africa, India and the Far East can be seen in the career of Antonio de Albuquerque de Coelho (1682–1746) a Brazilian-born man who served as governor of Macao, Goa, and in East Africa between 1700 and 1746. Albuquerque's mother, Angela de Bairros, was from Pernambuco and had 'white, negro and Amerindian blood . . . in about equal proportions'. The fact that he was of mixed race and born out of wedlock did not prevent Albuquerque's rise to fame and fortune, and his case is certainly not unique. Because of the rarity of Portuguese women in Brazil, we must assume that a high percentage of Brazilians who later served in Africa and Asia were of at least part-American racial background.[50]

Some Americans were utilized as military auxiliaries to Portuguese soldiers as well. In 1641 auxiliaries were to be sent from Bahia and Rio de Janeiro to reinforce the troops in Angola, and in 1644 the king approved a project to send Henrique Dias with non-white auxiliaries from Bahia to Angola. Dias was needed instead in Brazil to fight the Dutch but in 1645 an expedition left Rio de Janeiro for Angola. Again in 1648–9 some 2,000 men were sent from Rio de Janeiro to Angola. The Portuguese troops in Angola were accompanied in their campaigns by 'auxiliary native troops' and thus we can be confident that the Brazilian contingents included persons of American origins.[51]

After 1650 Angola was virtually a colony of Brazil and we can be sure that many persons of American ancestry went there. In addition to the normal kinds of contact, Angola was used as a place for sending Americans and other persons who proved troublesome in Brazil. In Ceará, for example, mixed-blood and American 'undesireables were periodically rounded up and shipped off to Angola' (1720s onward). After about 1740 the island of Fernão de Noronha was also used 'as a dumping ground for such people'. In the south of Brazil Americans and other non-whites were deported to Angola for gold-smuggling or for using a route passing through a region exposed to attack by free American forces (1720s).[52]

Quite early, Americans were used in the settlement of Fernão de Noronha island. In 1602 a Portuguese man was residing on the island with 13 or 14 *negros*. In 1612 a French vessel found only 'a Portuguese, with a few Tapuyas of both sexes'. The French removed the Americans to Maranhão.[53] (The Portuguese generally referred to Tupí-speaking Americans of coastal Brazil as *Brasis* or Brazilians, while the non-Tupí nations were often referred to collectively as Tapuyas.)

AMERICAN SLAVES IN EUROPE AND AFRICA

Now we shall examine data relating to the Americans who arrived in Europe and along the coast of West Africa, beginning with Portugal. The impact of Americans upon Portuguese life has not been studied although Camoens in his epic poem *Lusiadas* refers to the *tristes brasis* (sad Brazilians) arriving in Lisbon. Moreover, there exists a painting from the early 1500s wherein a Portuguese artist substituted a Brazilian (in native dress) for 'the black king' in his *Adoração dos Reis Magos* (Adoration of the Holy Kings).[54]

In 1552 or thereabouts Lisbon had some 10,000 slaves out of a population of 100,000, including Asians, south Asians, Muslims, black Africans, Americans, and others. A Flemish priest wrote in 1535 that 'todo o servico é feito por negros e mouros cativos' (all service is done by captive negros and Muslims). In 1552 a Brazilian slave was chained together with another slave trying to escape.[55]

In 1562 one Maria de Vilhena liberated by her testament 'two Indians, a white, a brown, a black, a mulato, two Moors – a man and a woman, a "chino Azamel" and two other captives where the race was apparently unknown.'[56] About the year 1550 the king of Portugal declared that, in order to avoid disputes as to who could get water from the river at certain places, for the purpose of selling water in Lisbon,

que a primeira bica indo da Ribeira, fôsse destinada exclusivamente aos homens pretos fôrros e cativos, como a mulatos, indios e mais cativos que fôssem homens; na segunda poderiam encher os mouros das galés . . . ; na quinta encheriam as pretas, mulatas, indias, fôrras e cativas.[57]

Thus, sections along the river were set aside for various groups, Americans being included in the group with black and mulatto males, or black and mulatto females, slave and free, rather than with Muslims. We can, then, picture the interaction of these various kinds of persons, trying to earn money by peddling water through the streets of Lisbon.

Towards the end of the sixteenth century there existed in the church of São Tomé in Lisbon a *confraria* (confraternity) limited to '*Indians*'. In a letter of 1591 the king responded to a petition from the judge, overseers, and members of the group by granting for three years the right to ask for alms along the river, in the Alfama and the Barrio dos Escolares, provided that the right was limited to those who were very old or ill and could not support themselves. Some Americans, especially after intermarriage with Africans, probably also belonged to the confraternity of 'Rosario para pretos', a *confraria* founded by 1496 to provide mutual assistance and communal life for *pretos* (blacks). This group petitioned in the interests of the community as, for example, in efforts to keep officials seeking runaway slaves from breaking into the homes of *negras* and *pretas* who were honest women, married to *linguas* (interpreters) and *mareantes* (seamen) (1521, 1529, 1646).[58]

Many American slaves were resold from Portugal to other countries, and this trade continued for at least a century. In 1592, for example, a widower of Lisbon sold Beatriz, aged 12, originally from Pernambuco, Brazil, to the Canary Islands.[59]

Many Americans were sold as slaves in Spain, as revealed by the notarial records of Seville and Valencia. It is not possible to be certain as to the numbers involved since not all of the slaves seem to have been properly registered, and also baptismal records are relatively scant. Moreover, many slaves are classified only as to their color (and for some even that is lacking). The color terms used, such as *loro* (intermediate), *negro* (black or very dark), *blanco* (light), *loro casi negro* (brown, almost black), and so on are not diagnostic as to 'race' because they refer to color as perceived by the authorities and not to ancestry. It is especially helpful when the place of birth is given but otherwise it is not possible to tell whether a given *loro* (for example) is from the Americas, from the Canary Islands, from northern Africa, from India, or from Spain itself. The major exception is when an Arab or Islamic proper name accompanies the color designation.

About 102 *loros* were registered in Seville between 1472 and 1513. Of these, some 30 can be identified further as follows: 17 were born in Spain, of whom at least one was of Islamic background, six were from North Africa, three were from the Americas (two identified as *India* (female) and *Indias* (the Indies), and one as from Marañón), one was from 'Meni' in Guinea, one was from Portugal, one from the Azores, and one was the daughter of a *negra*. Thus 72 remain from unknown backgrounds and ten per cent of those identified were from the Americas.[60]

It is significant that during this same period of time Americans in the Caribbean were being referred to as *loros*, as for example, when Fernández de Oviedo states that 'la gente desta isla es lora' referring to Borinquen (Puerto Rico).[61]

In one case (above) a female slave from Guinea in 1504 was classified as *de color lora*, possibly a result of Portuguese–African mixture (but perhaps she was from a lighter-skinned group). Later, in 1524, another slave from Guinea was categorized as *negro como loro*.[62] Persons from Calicut (India) were also registered as slaves in 1508 and 1513 but no color designations were given.[63]

The term *negro* is, of course, very commonly used for Seville slaves. Often the individuals so categorized can be linked with a particular region or kingdom in Africa. Others, however, are not so identified and could be, in some cases, Americans of darker color. Sometimes non-Christian personal names suggest such an origin, as with 'Pitijuan', a *negro* sold in 1500.

Those Americans recorded as specifically being from the Americas are as follows:

1500 Pastor, age 13–14, *marañón*
1501 Francisca, 11–12, *India*
    Alfonso Pérez, 25, *Antilla* (*enfermo*)
    Zumbay, *India* (*enferma*)
    Pedro, 12, *Indio*
    Francisca, *India* ('vendida en su mitad')
    Cosme, 12, *Indio*
1503 Gonzalo, 10, *Indio*
    Leonor, 25, *la Española* [Haiti]
1504 Rodrigo, 13, *Indio* (*fallecio*)
1508 Beatriz, 25, *Luque* [*Lucayo?*]
    Francisco, 18, *La Española*
1509 Constanza, 20, *La Española*
    Juan, 20, *Indio* [with 3 *negros*, liberated by a Florentine merchant]
1511 Gonzalo, 18, *Indias, Loro*
1512 María, 8, *India Lora.*

In addition, four other Americans were registered in 1500, 1503, and 1506.

Between 1513 and 1525 another twenty-one Americans were registered in Seville, of whom ten were males and eleven were females. From 1500 through 1512 males numbered eleven and females numbered eight or nine. The sex ratio was much more balanced for Americans than was true for black Africans. The greatest numbers appeared in 1501 (six) and 1525 (six also). In the latter year two females with two children *a los pechos* passed before the officials of the Casa de Contratación without interference. After 1534 the numbers may have increased still further as Charles V lifted the prohibitions on American enslavement.

In actual fact, there were many slaves from the Americas in Seville who never appeared in the notarized registers. Franco Silva has stated that there were about 40 Americans in Seville in 1500–1 but that there could have been more.[64] Other evidence for their presence includes the following: 1500: two appear in the *padrón* (census) of San Vicente; 1502: two females baptized in Santa Ana de Triana church; 1503: another female baptized; 1511: a male named Baltasar *hijo de India* was baptized in El Salvador church and in the same year the only *loro* was baptized at Santa Ana (slaves constitued ten to fifteen per cent of the total baptisms in Seville to 1525 but race is often not mentioned); 1516: Catalina, age 25, *india* from Brazil mentioned; 1517: Antón, *indio* sold for 10,000 *miravedis*; 1518: a Portuguese sold an *india* from Brazil, Juana; and 1525, Juan, an Indian from Española, fled. He had been captured in the first war of Higuey province, when he was a boy. He had a finger cut off from the right hand, and had a 'sign of iron' (that is, he had been branded). Most American slaves were from Haiti, Borinquen, and Brazil.

Between the 1490s and 1525 some 1,153 slaves were freed in Seville, of whom 319 were *negros*, 234 Muslims of all colors, 11 American males (no females), 16 *canario* males and 11 women, 44 male *loros* and 45 female *loros*. The balanced sex ratio of the Americans registered would suggest that some of the *loros* must have also been from the Americas.

Other American baptisms, after 1525, include: 1530: a male and a female baptized at San Vicente and Diego, *indio*, baptized at San Ildefonso; 1533: *una india* baptized at San Ildefonso; 1534: another male baptized in el Sagrario and also one at San Vicente; 1539: a female baptized in el Sagrario; and 1540: a female baptized in el Sagrario.

In 1533 *una esclava india*, age 20, accompanied by a girl was given as part of a marriage dowry. In 1542 Isidro, age 25 years, wounded in both *carrillos* of the face, was freed along with Pedro, *indio*. Both were *mejicanos*, natives of New Spain.[65]

In 1549 Benjamin, *un esclavo indio*, was in jail after having fled from his owner, a *tintorero* (dyer) of Seville, Juan Núñez. In the middle of the next century (*c.*1650) three *esclavas indias* were donated by a rich Spaniard from the Americas to a nun of the monastery of La Encarnación de Mula. Interestingly also, in the annals of Seville for 1607 occurs the following: 'Empezó a verse el tabaco; tomábanlo en humo algunos negros bozales.' That is to say that some new slaves (called *negros* but certainly Americans) introduced the smoking of tobacco to Sevillanos.[66]

By 1565 there were more than 6,000 slaves in Seville, including Muslims from Granada, Turks, Berbers, black Africans, Americans, and so on.

Reportedly, the inhabitants of the city were not really white or black, while another source states that there were as many *prietos* (dark people) as whites.[67] These were joined by other slaves later, including 2,000 Turks, Greeks, and Slavs sold in Cádiz as a result of a victory of the Austrians over the Turks in the late seventeenth century.[68]

There are a few references to persons in the interior parts of Spain who may well have been of American ancestry. For example, a suspected fugitive was apprehended in the Valencia area in 1579. He claimed to be free although his mother was a 'negra, de les indies de Portugal' while his father was white and was from Algofrin near Toledo. The suspect was called a *negre* and was age 23. Because his mother was probably from Brazil he doubtless was half-American.[69] In 1599 a traveler coming from Portugal noted that in Ayamonte and also in Gibraleón:

Hay aquí muchos esclavos y principalmente hembras negras y morenas, que vienen de las Indias y Isla de Santo Thomás, muy hermosas y amorosas, de manera que los vecinos de esta villa se casan muchas veces con ellas.[70]

In that area, then, there were many black and darkish brown women from the Americas and from São Tomé Island who were so beautiful and amorous that the local males often married them.

Valencia, as a major port on the Mediterranean, was an important center for the trans-shipment of slaves to Italy and to other parts of Spain. The situation was quite similar to that of Seville in that there were many *loros* (called *lors* or *llors*), large numbers of Muslim slaves (*loros*, *negros* and *blancos*), even larger numbers of black Africans, and quite a few Canary Islanders, Asian Indians and Americans.

Some differences show up, in that many more Americans, *canarios*, and Muslims are classified as *loros*, while some Americans, many Muslims and almost all Asian Indians are classified as *negros*. A high percentage of *loros* seem to be of Muslim extraction (from North Africa) or are said to have been born in Spain. Nonetheless, there are a number of *loros* who are not identifiable by place of origin.

The Asian Indians are usually not called Indians but are identified as *negros* from Calicut, Bombay or 'Malacca, India'. One or two are identified as of *loro* color or *lor casi negro*. South Asia is usually called *la India* or, as in the case of Gonzalo in 1515, *de Chochiti, India*. As we shall see, however, there is a possibility that *Indias* was sometimes used for southeast Asia or Indonesia (even as some writers used *India* for Brazil or America).[71]

Although the large majority of unidentified *negros* probably came from Africa, many could also have been from Asia or America. Here are some examples of shipments with no place of origin given: 1510: 228 very unassimilated, from Lisbon; 1510: 227 from Portugal, also *bozales*; 1511: 112 from Portugal, very unassimilated; 1511: 88 from Portugal; 1512: 101 from Portugal; 1514: 95 from Portugal; 1514: 27 from Portugal, six of whom were sick; 1516: 130 *negros*, of whom 15 died; and 1516: 66 *negros*, of whom three died. These figures leave room for wide speculation since also in 1516, of a load of 88 *negros*, 85 were from Brazil (and were Americans). Similarly, in 1516 a *lor*, Pedro from Calicut, was registered who had been part of a group of 50 Indians captured by the Portuguese and brought to Lisbon in 1514.[72]

The following is a list of known Americans arriving in Valencia to be registered, through 1516:

May 27, 1495: two merchants presented 'una cautiva "des les illes noves"' [the new isles], age 7, de 'les Indies e illes novament trobades'; [from the Indies and islands newly discovered]. 'She did not confess because no one could understand her.'

June 6, 1509: Martín, 10 years, of Brazil *terra de negres* [land of *negros*], along with a group of Berbers.

September 6, 1509: a Venetian merchant presented a *lora*, 15, who was native 'de les Indies de la terra ahon porten lo Brasil, lo nom de la qual n'os sab com no sapia parlar.' [Name unknown because no translator.]

August 17, 1514: Axa, now Beatriz, 16, *de Indias*; Sana, now Felipa, 13, same place, alli por un moro que lo vendio a cristianos qe lo llevaron a Portugal.' [From the Indies, seized there by a Muslim who sold him to Christians who carried him to Portugal.] [May refer to the East Indies.]

August 17, 1514: Axa, now Beatriz, 16, *de Indias;*' Sana, now Felipa, 13, same place, to Valencia from Portugal. [Axa is a name common to Muslim women, probably pronounced 'Asha', but could be from many lands.]

January 9, 1515: 'presenta seis negros [including] dos loros oscuras': Joha, *lora*, now Isabel, 16, *de Brasil*, Camane, now Catalina, 10, from same place. [Thus the dark *loras* from Brazil were also categorized as *negros*.]

February 6, 1515: two *negros*: Allo, now Jorge, 15, *de Hireo*; Arago, now Alvaro, same place. [These were the only slaves in Valencia from Hireo, which was probably Iere or Trinidad.]

1516: four *blancos indianos* presented: Olmiren, now Antonio, 14, *de Paranonpol*; Boy, now Isabel, 16, same place; Yaya, 14, same; Parahimpo, 15, same. They were purchased in Portugal. [Paranonpol was probably Pernambuco, Brazil.]

December 9, 1516: 88 slaves presented, 85 from the 'island' of Brazil, formerly pagans but now Christians, and three *negros*. A Spaniard testified that of these he had seen '23 *negros*' die and taken them to be buried. [Thus the Brazilians were called *negros*.]

December 12, 1516: *una blanca*, Francisca, 14, of the island of Brazil, brought from Lisbon.[73]

Thus the Americans were variously categorized as whites, *loros* or *negros*, depending upon their perceived color.

I have not seen any detailed data for Valencia between 1517 and 1569; however, statistical summaries relating to new and runaway slaves are available from 1569 to 1686. During this period new color terms appear, largely replacing *loro* and representing various shades of brown. Some 2,999 slaves and captives were categorized as follows:

negros	1,401	
blancos	363	
membrillo cocido	365	[stewed quince color]

morenos	53
mulatos	22
claros	1
llors	3
oscuros	2
no classification	789
	————
Total	2,999

Thus 'blacks' made up less than half of the total, but some of the other shades of brown could have referred to interior West Africans (such as *Fulos*) thought to have a brownish color.

Of the above, 435 were runaways (421 males and 14 females) while 2,564 were new slaves (1,253 males, 836 females and 475 not stated). Most were quite young (usually age 15 to 25).

The numbers coming from the *Indias* (Indies) of Portugal were as follows:

1569–1570	1571–1578	1579–1585	1594–1603	1609–1666	1607–1620	1666–1686	
new	new	new	new or fugitive	new or fugitive	new or fugitive	new or fugitive	total
7	4	7	0	1	3	0	22

In the same period, 12 came from Cabo Verde, 23 from São Tomé and 23 from Angola, thus illustrating that Brazil (probably) was contributing about as many slaves as were each of the Portuguese islands and Angola. On the other hand, 84 came from 'other countries,' 576 from Guinea, 481 from Granada, 81 from Turkey, and so on. 'Las Indias de Portugal' doubtless refers to Brazil rather than to India.

Insofar as color terms are concerned, the Brazilians were apparently categorized variously as *membrillo cocido, moreno, llors, mulato,* or perhaps occasionally as *negro* or *blanco*.[74]

One of the problems in tracing the history of Americans in Spain is that with so many slaves (100,000 to 300,000 in all) of so many shades of color, the Spaniards tended to record those characteristics lending to individual identification (that is, appearance) and not ancestry. Likewise, the term *negro* was probably used broadly for many types of slaves. In 1560, for example, the *moriscos* (Christianized *moros*) were forbidden to purchase 'esclavos negros, ni los tengan, ni de Berberia'. It would make no sense to forbid *moriscos* from having Berber or black slaves, if they could purchase American, mixed, or brownish slaves.[75]

As mentioned previously, the officials of Seville were commissioned in 1549 to liberate Americans in Spain. A few months later it was ordered that Americans who asked for their liberty would be heard and that justice would be done. In 1555 two additional officials of the Casa de Contratación of Seville were assigned to aid in the above process.[76] Nonetheless, it is clear that some remained in slavery (and doubtless all part-Americans whose mothers were of African or other non-American ancestry and whose status was that of a slave were *not* affected by any of the emancipation provisions whatsoever. The greater proportion of the children of Americans would have fallen in this category, in all probability.)

The American and African slaves in Spain (as in Portugal) merged into the general population. Doubtless many contributed to the growth of the *Gitano* ('Gypsy') group in cities such as Valencia and Seville. A Spanish historian has noted that after the 1490s, the *Gitanos* grew in numbers:

This was partly because the genuine thoroughbred Gypsy was being joined by others from the oppressed classes of society – fugitive slaves, *Moriscos*, even Christians wanted by the law, criminals, adventurers and vagabonds.[77]

On several occasions, as in 1637, the Crown ordered all slaves and *gitanos*, including 'negros, mulatos y berberiscos' to forcibly serve in the military galleys regardless of their owners' wishes. This should act as an indication that although the slaves were assimilated fairly rapidly into Spanish society, the assimilation was not always easy or just. As early as 1496 some 50 Americans were sold to serve in the galleys of Spain, provided that they were not later found to be legally free (and by that time many would doubtless be dead).[78] Thus we can be sure that both Americans and Africans who entered as slaves tended to be absorbed into the proletarian level of society. Their cultural impact upon Spain (and Portugal) needs to be explored more thoroughly in a separate study.

Many Americans were also sent to the Spanish and Portuguese islands off the African coast. Data is available for part of the Canary Islands during the sixteenth century which shows that Americans were present throughout the period. At Tenerife, to 1525, about ten per cent of the slaves sold were native *canarios*. In 1506 *una india* was sold in the Tenerife slave market by a Genoan. At Las Palmas, no native *canarios* were sold after 1510. There were about 1,956 slaves registered for the market, of whom *negros* constituted 1,371 (70 per cent). *Moriscos* constituted 12 per cent and the balance tended to be Muslims from North Africa. The sex ratio of the *negros* was heavily male (60 per cent), but the *moriscos* were more evenly balanced.

Many *loros* and *mulatos* were sold at Las Palmas, with the category *loro* being gradually replaced by *mulato*. Nonetheless, *loro* is used as late as 1599. Some of the *loros* and *mulatos* could have been Americans. In 1580, for example, Melchor, age 30, was referred to as *mulato-indio*.[79]

The Americans sold in the Las Palmas market after 1510 and who can be identified are as follows:

1537 Gaspar, 25, *indio blanco*
1546 Luis, 26, from *india de Portugal*
    Antón, 6, Brazil, *bozal*
    Catalina, 15, Brazil
1555 Francisco, 20, *Indio*

1557 Antonio, 25, from *India de Portugal*
1558 Bastián, 40, *India*
1559 Leonor, 20, *Indio*
      Gabriel, 28, *Indio*
1567 Pablo, –, *Indio*
1575 Pedro, –, *Indio*
1576 Roque, 48, *Indio*
1579 Pablos, 30, *Indio*
1580 Melchor, 30, *mulato-indio*
1582 Luis, 22, *Indio*
1592 Beatriz, 12, Pernambuco [from Lisbon]
1600 Antón, 30, *Indio*

As one can see, the vast majority of Americans were males (14 of 17) suggesting that some females were called *loras*, *mulatas* or *morenas*, or had no color mentioned.

The compiler of the above data believes that the number of Americans probably exceeded the number actually registered (as was the case with slaves in general). Other Americans were mentioned in various sources, such as in baptismal records or in lawsuits. Also in 1563 an American was accused of a robbery for which he was condemned to eight years in the galleys, while another *indio* (Agustín Inglés) was condemned for a sexual perversion. The records of the Inquisition also mention a *caribeño*. The baptismal records of el Sagrario mention a *cacique* (chief) from Mexico and 'el indio Luis, natural de la India de Portugal' who had been in Seville before reaching Las Palmas.[80]

From the above evidence it is clear that the enslavement of Americans and their shipment to Europe and Africa was not a short-term experience. We cannot be certain of the numbers involved (because so many slaves were not identified ethnically in the records) but we can be sure that their presence was not limited to the areas cited. Doubtless Americans were resold to many countries just as African slaves were resold. Italy was perhaps a major market but the Spanish-controlled Netherlands were probably also a place of trans-shipment (along with, of course, the various Portuguese islands off Africa).

DUTCH EXPANSION AND THE AMERICAN DIASPORA

There were early connections between the Flemish–Dutch region and both the Azores and Canaries. In 1495 a ship from 'Flanders' brought Ubay Chimayo, a *canario* slave, from Tenerife to Valencia. Similarly, in 1502 some *naves alemanas*, Germanic vessels, delivered a *mora lora* captive from Valencia to Oran, North Africa, after ransom had been paid.[81] Thus we can suggest that in the 1490s and early 1500s slaves from the Canary Islands, Africa and the Americas probably began to appear in the low countries and other northern areas, carried there by Dutch and Germanic vessels (as well as by Venetian, Genoese, Portuguese and other ships which frequented northern waters).

After the Portuguese occupation of coastal Brazil, a close connection developed between the San Vicente (Santos) area and Antwerp. Peter Rösel, the factor of an Antwerp banking and commercial house, was in charge of a sugar refinery (using American slaves) close to San Vicente in the 1550s. In 1554 he was also operating a ship along the Brazilian coast.[82]

Antwerp was known as a city with many slaves, including blacks, Muslims, and Jews. We know that Americans were among them since, in the early 1500s, one Baltasar the Moor (who was freed) was said to have been 'born in the Indies of Portugal of Christian parents'. We know that he was from Brazil because he alleged that the 'whole land' from which he came was inhabited by Christians, which could only be applicable to the areas where the Jesuits had been Christianizing Americans since 1549. Earlier, in 1516, two non-Christian *mooren* (non-whites) who belonged to one George de Sulco Lobo from Portugal fled from slavery.

It is evident that there were many Portuguese merchants in Antwerp. Albrecht Dürer, in his journey to the low countries, met a Portuguese factor with a female (*Moorin*) slave whom he painted. In 1532 a slave fled from the house of the Portuguese factor, and in 1540 a Portuguese merchant sold to a Genoan a *zwarten* (black) slave named Duarte.[83] The close Portugal–Antwerp–Brazil connections virtually guarantee that many Brazilian slaves, along with many Africans, arrived there in the 1500s.

In the latter part of the period the Dutch living to the north of Antwerp began to wage a successful struggle against their Spanish rulers. Part of their strategy was to send out ships which raided Spanish and (later) Portuguese shipping and colonies in the Americas. As early as 1580 some Dutchmen established Nieuw Zeeland in Guyana and thereafter they frequented the coasts of South America. As early as 1601 and 1609 they made contact with Brazilian natives and it is possible that some were conducted to the Netherlands even as some were taken there from the Bahia da Traição.

Não se sabe com segurança o número de indios então embarcados, mas é de presumir que alguns sejam os interrogados por Kilean de Renselaer em 1628 a aos quais Hessel Gerritsz se refere pelos nomes – Gaspar Paraupaba, então de 50 años, Andre Francisco, de 32 ãnos, ambos de Ceará, Pieter Poty, Antonio Guiravassauay, Antonio Luis Gaspar, todos da Baía de Traição.

Thus, the Dutch took the above-named Brazilians, among others, to the Netherlands where they were interviewed and provided important data to those who planned the attempted capture of Brazil from the Portuguese.

Jan de Laet, the Antwerp man who played a major role in the above, referred to the Brazilians whom 'he saw many times in Holland':

nous avons veu souvent [os índios] en les Provincies Unies, apris en nostre langue, sçavoir escrire e entre instruicts aux principes de la Religión Chrestienne; nous avons reçue en quelque façon d'eux la cognoissance de ces regions.

The Brazilians in the Netherlands had learned the Dutch language, been taught to write, and been instructed in the Christian religion. In turn, they informed the Dutch about the Brazilian region. As will be noted, Pieter Poty especially became a major leader against the Portuguese.

While in the Netherlands: 'êles andavam nos meios universitários e no mundo dos negócios – locais da activadade de Laet'. The Americans went about in the world of the university and that of business, areas where de Laet was active.[84]

Dutch expansion in the early seventeenth century also served to accelerate American–African contacts elsewhere. From the 1590s onward Dutch warships frequently captured Spanish and Portuguese vessels, many of which were loaded with slaves or possessed crew members of non-white race. Some of these slaves were taken to Europe while others were sold to the English in Virginia or were sent to Dutch ports in the Americas (New Amsterdam and Curaçao, for example). We know that some of the captives were persons with Spanish (Christian) names and were not new slaves from Africa. In fact, some of those who arrived in Virginia were Carib people.[85] The Dutch also sent Esopus captives from the Hudson River area to the Netherlands, Bermuda and Curaçao in 1644. In 1660 some 15 or 20 Esopus (Lenápe) captives were sent to Curaçao and Bonaire by Governor Peter Stuyvesant, to work for the West Indias Company. Before 1664 slaves arriving in the Netherlands 'from the Indies' were set free.[86]

Along the South American coast the Dutch attempted to establish posts at various places, such as at the mouth of the Essequibo River where one Jan de Moor [John the Black] was in 1616. In 1624–5 an effort was made to capture Bahia but, as with certain of the posts to the north, this was a failure. In general, a long-term struggle ensued in which the various American nations were pawns in a power struggle between the Portuguese and other Europeans.[87] The Dutch were able to capture Recife-Pernambuco and thereafter gradually dominated a significant part of Brazil and Maranhão (the lower Amazon region).

As soon as they seized Pernambuco the Dutch began to make use of some of the Brazilians educated in Holland. In 1631 three were sent to Brazil to be employed as interpreters and go-betweens, while others returned later. At the same time many Americans remained in Holland and in 1635 it was reported that they were speaking Dutch as their 'own' language in place of their native tongues. The Brazilians were numerous enough in Amsterdam in 1636 to have their own 'synagogue' (probably a reformed church), according to an Irish visitor who had been in Brazil previously. The Americans gave him messages to take back to their relatives in Brazil.[88]

During the period from 1631 to 1654 many Brazilian natives, both Tupí-speaking (called Brazilians) and Tapuya (called *Tapoeijers* and *Daboyers*) were sent to the Netherlands, for education, to provide entertainment, and for diplomatic alliance purposes. A Brazilian *mamaluco* (mixed-blood) also went to Leiden, where he is known to have married and had children. Moreover, many Dutch in Brazil married Portuguese-speaking and native women, producing a new type of *mamaluco* (often blonde-haired). Many of these mixed families stayed in Brazil but others, after 1654, fled to the French West Indies, Curaçao, and Holland. Black Africans were also taken to Holland during the period.[89] The Americans were absolutely essential to Dutch plans in Brazil. Some 4,000 Tupí-speaking Brazilians lived under Dutch supervision in separate communities and furnished essential labor and military service. Thousands of Tapuya served as allies against the Portuguese. On the other hand, the Portuguese also had Americans on their side and both European groups utilized black, *mulato*, and *mamaluco* troops against each other. In 1538, for example, the Dutch governor had 3,600 European and 1,000 American troops at his disposal. One Antonio Mendes commanded a company of 'tupís, mulatos e negros' for the Dutch.

In addition to 'free' Americans living in communities, there were also many slaves of native origin as well as those of mixed African and American ancestry. The Dutch allowed some Americans to remain in slavery; others (newly captured by Dutch allies) were to serve for seven years. In the Maranhão region and Ceará, however, the enslavement of Americans continued as it had under the Portuguese until the policy began to create problems with the Tapuya allies. Theoretically, in 1642–3, the Americans of the Maranhão were to be considered free, 'as are the Brazilians'. Nonetheless, some Brazilian Americans were sold by the Dutch in the West Indies (to the colony of St Christopher) prior to 1654.[90]

After 1630 the Dutch West Indias Company became fully involved in the slave trade from West Africa, made necessary in part because large numbers of African and American slaves in Brazil fled to the interior during the years of Dutch–Portuguese fighting. The slavery business prompted the Dutch to attack Portuguese trading stations in Africa, beginning in 1637.

Dutch military expeditions to Africa included significant numbers of Brazilian (Tupí and Tapuya) auxiliary soldiers. The expedition which conquered the Portuguese forts along the Gold Coast (1637–8) included many Tapuyas, while the expedition which conquered the Angola forts, São Tomé and Ano Bom included 240 Americans of the Tupí group (1641). In 1642 they also conquered Axim in Guinea. Some 300 Brazilian natives were used on São Tomé, of whom only 60 were later alive.

Given the Dutch use of Brazilian natives as allies and auxiliaries in Brazil itself and in West Africa, it seems also plausible to suggest that Americans were used in connection with Dutch activities elsewhere. In 1641 and 1642 complaints were being made that Tupí numbers were diminishing because they were being taken to fight in foreign lands.[91]

The influence of the Tapuya auxiliaries taken by the Dutch to West Africa needs especially to be traced, since there is evidence of long-standing Tapuya influence in Elmina (Ghana). Albert van Dantzig, a Dutch scholar working in Ghana, has written to me that 'down to the 19th century (when the Dutch sold Elmina Castle to the British) the Dutch continued to refer to mulattoes as Tapoeijers.' William Bosman, a Dutch slave-merchant who fathered a mixed-blood son on the Gold Coast of Africa (where he resided from 1687 to 1701) had some nasty remarks to make about the *Tapoeijers of mulatten* (Tapuyas or mulattoes). He notes that the *Tapoeijers* were serving as soldiers for the Dutch but otherwise they and their women are described as bad characters, idolators (although nominal Christians), prostitutes, and 'knaves'. He states also that they were born from the mixture of a European with a *neger* woman, a statement which betrays his lack of knowledge of their actual history but which also reveals that they had become Africanized (or that by *neger* he meant any non-white). Doubtless the Tapuya men of the 1640s had married African or African–Portuguese–Brazilian mixed women already living on the Gold Coast. It should be noted, however, that an earlier Dutch writer refers to the *Daboyer* as *Moren* (blacks, non-whites) even in Brazil.[92]

That Tapuyas remained on the Gold Coast is not surprising since after 1654 they would have probably been killed by their Portuguese enemies if they had returned to Brazil.[93]

It should also be noted that the Dutch, like the Portuguese, sent civilians from Brazil to Africa. In 1644 *mulatos e negros* who were stonemasons were taken from Pernambuco to Luanda, Angola, to help build a fort. The *mulatos* were doubtless part-American.

In this connection, it is interesting to note that J. A. Rogers refers to the tradition of American ancestry in West Africa at a much later date:

Today the West African mulatto has castes of his own. The oldest group are the Portuguese–Brazilians. . . . They live chiefly in the larger towns as Porto Novo, Cotonou, Whydah, Grand Popo. . . . Some even have an American-Indian strain brought by their earliest mulatto ancestors from Brazil. These Portuguese–Brazilians are the aristocrats of the mulatto group.[94]

After being expelled from Brazil in 1654, the Dutch (or many of them) and the Portuguese Jews who had joined them, retreated with slaves, servants and a plantation ideology to other places. For example, 900 such persons, free and slave, left Brazil and migrated to Guadaloupe and Martinique. In addition, the Dutch had been actively selling slaves in the French islands, as noted. We know that many of the slaves on the islands were 'Brazilians' (Americans from Brazil) and *Aroüaques* (Arawaks, perhaps from the Guiana coast). In 1656 some 20 Brazilian slaves helped suppress an Angolan rebellion on Guadaloupe. As late as 1767 the Brazilian term *mamaluco* was still being used on Martinique.[95]

The Dutch, along with the French and English, were active along the Guiana coast during this same period. The Dutch, in particular, developed for a time a route from the Essequibo River, via the Rio Negro, to the Amazon, bringing back canoe-loads of slaves to the coast. They made peace with the Lokono (Arawak) people of Surinam and, by the late 1680s, with the adjacent Carib groups. The friendly tribes, especially the Caribs, continued to supply the Dutch with American slaves from the interior until the mid-nineteenth century.

The island of Curaçao was also used by the Dutch as a center for the resale of slaves and it would appear that Americans were still being obtained along the 'wild coast' of South America well into the ninteenth century. The ultimate disposition of the American slaves from the Surinam–Orinoco–Amazon watersheds and the Curaçao region is not known to me. Some Surinam area natives were sent to Barbados from 1627 to help develop the sugar industry there. Perhaps others were sold (with black Africans) to all available markets or were taken to Dutch colonies in Africa and elsewhere.[96]

Regulations issued in the Netherlands in 1764 for the Dutch slave trade at Curaçao mention two kinds of slaves: *neger* slaves and *macquerons* slaves. These *macquerons* slaves were obviously not African and they were of less monetary value than *neger* slaves. The term *makarons* can be interpreted as meaning 'mixed' (as applied to language), as being of light brown color or as referring to long hair hanging down in front of the ears (a 'macaroni' hairstyle, as it was called). My suspicion is that these were, in fact, American or part-American slaves since African-white slaves would not have had a price differential in all probability. It should also be noted that an American group in the Maranhão area was known as the *Macamacrans*.

In 1774 one Frank, a slave of a 'yellowish or mustee complexion', ran away in South Carolina. he 'would feign dress, the wool of his head in the macaroni taste, the which being that of a mustee, he has teazed into side locks, and a queue, but when too lazy to comb, ties his head with a handkerchief.' Thus we have evidence that a 'mustee' (of American and African mixture) of the period wore his hair in a 'macaroni' style. American–African mixed-bloods often were described as having 'bushy' hair, longer and 'wilder' than West Africans.[97]

In modern times, the term *macaron* has come to refer to a person lacking in some type of physical capability. It has been interpreted as referring also to slaves whom the Spaniards would not purchase from the Dutch and who had to be sold in North America, that is, slaves who were old or unable to work hard. A more first-hand source refers, however, to the sweetness of a *hallif-blanks makronsje*, that is, to a young half-white *macaron*, thus invalidating the above thesis. American slaves, in general, were difficult to sell to the Spaniards because their enslavement was technically illegal. Moreover, they were usually used for the less arduous tasks such as hunting, fishing, boating or craft work.[98]

Americans continued to be transported to the Netherlands long after the loss of Brazil. In the 1770s, for example, an American boy named Weekee from the Berbice River (Surinam–Guyana) was living in Bergen-op-Zoom where he learned to be a cook and 'something of a tailor'. He later returned home and 'no sooner touched American ground, than stripping himself of his lumber [clothes], he launched naked into his native woods.'[99]

AMERICANS IN FRANCE AND THE FRENCH COLONIES

The French also are responsible for taking many Americans to Europe, but the earliest of such visits probably are lost in the mystery of early Breton and Basque voyages to Newfoundland and Greenland. In general, the French were active initially in two regions, in the North Atlantic and along the coast of Brazil. In 1503 Captain de Gonneville of Honfleur sailed to Brazil and brought back an

American who was the son of a chief of the Carijó nation. This 15-year-old boy was educated in France, married a Frenchwoman and was still living there in 1583. Thereafter, the French were active rivals of the Portuguese along the coast of Brazil, making friends with the Americans who were enemies of the Portuguese, in particular, with the Carijós of the south, the Tamóios of Rio de Janeiro, and the various groups north of Pernambuco. French individuals intermarried with the Americans, leaving in Brazil many *mamalucos* of French ancestry, especially among the Tupinamba (many of whom were blondish and white-looking).

Numerous Brazilians journeyed to France after 1509, including Paraguazu, the wife of the famous Portuguese founder of the Bahia, Caramuru or Diego Álvares. Paraguazu and Caramuru were legally married in France in 1510 with the king and queen as sponsors. Later they returned to Bahia.

Many other Brazilians lived in Rouen, France. In 1550 a large number put on a spectacle there for Henry II and Catherine de Medici, while Montaigne interviewed three Americans in Rouen in 1563. The Portuguese Jesuits were extremely concerned that Protestant heretics were taking Brazilians to Europe for training in heresy. In 1561 it was reported that 'many young people are being sent to Calvin and to other places for training in their errors.'

As early as the 1590s Americans from the Maranhão were taken to France and in 1612 some six Tupinambas from that area made the same journey, stopping also in Falmouth, England. Three lived to be baptized in Paris with the king and queen as sponsors.[100] It is quite clear that the Franco-American alliance in the Brazil region resulted in large numbers of Brazilians going to France as free visitors, a situation leading directly to contacts with Newfoundland and Canadian Americans as well as with Africans also in France.

If Americans reached France as slaves in the sixteenth century they were probably set free. In 1571, for example, the parliament of Bordeaux set free 'Ethiopian and other slaves' whom a merchant wished to sell in the port, on the grounds that slavery was not legal in France.[101]

The first Americans reaching France across the North Atlantic would seem to have been brought to Rouen from Terranova (the Newfoundland area) in 1508 with another group following in 1509. The first group consisted in seven men, of *suie* (soot) color, tattooed from ears to chin.[102]

In 1524 Juan Verrazano, sailing for France, visited the North American coast, kidnapping a young boy. Ten years later, Jacques Carier took back two youths from Canada and in 1535 he kidnapped nine Americans from the same area. The chief Donacona and his fellows were baptized at St Malo but are said to have died within a year or two. In 1541 Carier returned a young Huron girl to Canada. Later, in the 1680s Iroquois captives were sent to France to serve in the royal galleys.[103]

As the years went by, the French became involved in American slavery in Canada, the Mississippi Valley, Louisiana and the Caribbean. In North America itself American slaves, called *paducas* (1720s) and *panis*, became quite common. It is possible that some of these, along with mixed-blood Acadians, reached France. In 1747 a *panis* slave was sent from Canada to Martinique while in 1732 a Carib slave was taken to Canada.[104]

In the French West Indies a plantation economy began to develop and there, as noted, one finds Brazilian and Arawak slaves by the 1650s. In Louisiana the enslavement of Americans was quite common from the very beginning of the colony, with the Chitimacha people being a special target but also with slaves being brought in from the Mississippi Valley. In the early 1700s the French there are known to have been interested in exchanging American slaves for Africans from Haiti and other colonies. Some were actually traded for supplies. In the late 1720s many Natchez people were sent as slaves to Haiti.[105] In the 1750s the Spanish apprehended three Americans on a French vessel. They were liberated from slavery by the Audiencia de Santo Domingo in 1756 on the grounds that all Americans 'who shall not be *caribes*' were free, whether found inside or outside Spanish territories.[106]

BRITISH EXPANSION AND THE RELOCATION OF AMERICANS

The English may have met Americans at Newfoundland in the pre-1492 period but the first record relating to Americans on British soil is somewhat later. In about 1501–2 a joint Bristol–Portuguese venture seems to have been responsible for bringing three Americans from Newfoundland to England. A source states that: 'three men were brought out of an island founde by merchants of Bristow forre beyond Irelonde, the which were clothed in Beestes skynnes and ete raw flesh, and rude in their demeanure as Beestes.' These newcomers were presented to Henry VII. Two of them were still about Westminster Palace in 1504 when, because of a change of dress, and for other reasons they 'appeared English'. A biographer of Thomas More feels that More 'had probably seen them' prior to his brother-in-law's expedition to Newfoundland in 1516 and the publication of *Utopia*. Several voyages reached that same area in 1504 and 1505 also, but no further references to Americans appear until 1531 when William Hawkins brought back a Brazilian leader who met Henry VIII at Whitehall.[107]

In 1576–7 Americans (probably Inuits) were kidnapped by Martin Frobisher, one of them being sketched by Lucas de Heere, the Flemish artist. Like many Inuits kidnapped in subsequent years, the majority seem to have died away from their home environment.[108]

Contacts with the Atlantic seaboard of North America and with the Orinoco–Guiana region produced a number of visitors in the 1580s, including the famous Manteo of North Carolina and several Guiana natives who served Sir Walter Raleigh in the Tower of London. The English also began to capture Spanish shipping during this period, in the Caribbean and elsewhere, and we know that non-whites began to be present in Plymouth and other ports in some numbers.

Beginning in 1603 the English began to abduct or otherwise convey

Americans from the New England and Virginia coasts to England. The Powhatans brought from the Chesapeake Bay area gave a demonstration of canoe handling on the Thames. Boatsmen 'waited on the Virginians when they rowed with their canoes'. When John Smith was a prisoner among the Powhatans in 1607 he was exhibited to see if he had been on board an earlier ship which had 'taken away some Indians from them by force'.[109]

In any case, abductions began to play a key role in English plans for colonization. Interpreters were needed as well as precise geographical information. In 1605 five Americans were kidnapped from the St George River, the first (apparently) of a large number seized from the New England area. 'By 1610 taking captured Indians to England had become routine. Would-be-colonizers such as Sir Fernando Gorges hoped to impress the captives . . . , to learn as much as they could about the lay of the land, and to acquire mediators with the local Indians.'

Not all of the Americans were treated in such a manner, however. Thomas Hunt in 1614 kidnapped 27 Americans from Massachusetts and took them to Málaga, Spain, for sale as slaves. A few were sold as such while the rest were taken by Spanish 'friars' to be instructed in Christianity. Most of them doubtless remained in Spain but one Tasquantum (Squanto) was able to get away to Newfoundland and England and in 1619 returned to Massachusetts, only to find his region decimated by European-introduced disease.[110]

In 1616 Pocahontas and at least ten other Powhatans were taken to England from Virginia. One of the men, Uttamakomak (Tomocomo) and several girls remained in Britain for some time, the girls being eventually (1621) sent to the Bermudas where they married settlers.

Other Americans did not fare as well. Records in England indicate that Queen Elizabeth in 1596 and 1601 issued orders to be rid of all of the non-white foreigners in her realm (Blackmoores and 'negars and blackamoores') and many were gathered up for resale to other countries. Some Americans or part-Americans could have been among those sold, since in 1621 there is a reference to 'thirteen Negroes or Indian people, six women, seven men and boyes' who were being sold, perhaps to Bermuda.[111]

After the Pequot–English War in New England many American prisoners were enslaved and sold. In 1638 Pequots were sold in the West Indies, many reaching Providence Island off Central America. Between 1676 and 1683 many other New England Native Americans were 'condemned to be sold into foreign slavery' after the so-called 'King Philip's War'.

Thus during the war and for some time afterward, Indians believed to be hostile or dangerous were shipped away to the slave markets of the West Indies, Spain, and the Mediterranean coasts. . . . Both Jamaica and Barbados legislated against their admittance. John Eliot knew of a case in which a vessel filled with Indian prisoners tried in vain to unload its human cargo at one market after another. She finally managed to get rid of them at Tangiers in North Africa, where they were still living in 1683. Probably many a black man today in North Africa and the islands of the West Indies carries some traces of the blood which once surged through the veins of Philip's [Metacomet's] defeated warriors.

Another source indicates that some Americans were returned to Massachusetts from Algiers in 1683. In any case, a policy was developed early in New England of exchanging Americans overseas for Africans. After 1637–8 that policy was effectively implemented by means of wars which provided captives.[112]

Some years after the English took New York from the Dutch one Sarah Robinson, a Native American of that province, was seized in Southampton and sent as a slave to the Madeira Islands. She was fortunate, however, and was later returned to New York.[113]

As the English became more involved in the African slave trade they also became more ruthless in terms of seizing Americans. In 1663 William Hilton kidnapped several Americans from South Carolina and carried them to Barbados where two of them, Shadoo and Wommony, were seen in 1666. From 1670 onwards the English of South Carolina engaged regularly in the American slave trade, sending natives in the tens of thousands to the West Indies and other markets. In 1674 a group was sent to Jamaica. In 1693 a Cherokee delegation at Charleston requested the return of their relatives who had been taken to Jamaica, without apparent success. Most of the slaves were from Florida or the Mississippi area (Choctaws for example) and they were a major source of income to the English.

American slaves from Virginia, North Carolina, and other areas were also sold to the West Indies and Bermuda. Virginia laws of 1660, 1711 and 1723 specifically referred to enslavement and transportation to 'a foreign country' or to the West Indies as a punishment for Americans.[114]

Native American slaves show up in many areas as a result of English activity. In 1688 the *London Gazette* had an advertisement for 'A black boy, an Indian, about thirteen years old, run away the 8th inst. from Putney, with a collar about his neck with this inscription: "The Lady Bromfield's black".' In 1694 the same paper advertised for 'A Tanny Moor, with short bushy hair' who had run away. (This could refer to an American–African mixed-blood.) In 1709 *The Tatler* had an advertisement for a 'Black Indian Boy, 12 years of age'.

It would appear that both Americans and Africans began to appear in exotic pageants and entertainments staged in London during the seventeenth century. It is not always possible to clearly ascertain the ethnicity of the performers, since Africans were sometimes dressed up as Americans, or perhaps vice versa. In 1629 the librette for a pageant refers to: 'an Indian boy, holding in one hand a long *Tobacco* pipe, in the other a dart'. But he is riding an ostrich. A 1672 pageant showed in 'West India' some 'Tawny Moors' working and playing music. Also the audience heard a 'Masculine' Tawny woman declare: 'That I the better may Attention draw, be pleas'd to know I am *America*.'

In 1695 a London pageant featured a plantation scene showing 'Negroes, Tawneys, Virginia-Planters', and so on.

The American presence in Britain was augmented by the activities of the

Hudson Bay Company after the seventeenth century. An interesting article of 1915 notes that:

Many of the most prominent men and the most respected families in the North of Scotland edging in from the Orkney Islands are of Indian descent. Most of these persons are of Cree blood. For many years the Scotch have been active as traders . . . and scores of them have brought back with them their Cree wives. Even the Cree men intermarried with Scotch lassies and so today up in the north of the British isles, Cree words mingle with Gaelic and bronzed cheeks are often seen. . . . the British army and navy even number their descendants as soldiers, marines and officers.[115]

Meanwhile, Newfoundland, Labrador and Greenland continued to be visited by vessels of many nations and by 1566 Inuit people could be seen in the The Hague, ten years prior to Frobisher's kidnappings. The massive growth of the whaling industry as well as the activities of the Danish government led to many Inuits along with their kayaks being taken to Europe, principally to Denmark, the Netherlands, and whaling centers (such as, probably, Hamburg). Between 1605 and 1725 quite a number of Inuit were taken specifically to Denmark, Holland and Friesland. From these places a number managed to escape in their kayaks. Doubtless these Inuits were the same who appeared frequently in the Orkney and Shetland Islands, in the Netherlands and even in Scotland during the period, paddling kayaks apparently in a desperate effort to return to their families in Greenland.[116]

It is worth noting also the existence of many seamen and whalers of native origin, especially since many were active in the Caribbean and Atlantic generally. During the seventeenth century New England Indians were recruited to serve as sailors on English vessels sailing from Boston and other ports. Many served on whaling vessels from 1670 while others were present on vessels trading with Africa and the Caribbean. Herman Melville's novel *Moby Dick* features an American whaling-man.[117] by 1681 Miskito men from Central America were common on board English vessels also.

They have extraordinary good Eye, and will discern a sail at sea farther, and see any thing better than we. [They are also good fishermen.] For this they are esteemed and coveted by all Privateers; for one or two of them in a ship, will maintain 100 men . . . and it is very rare to find Privateers destitute of one or more of them, when the commander, or most of the men are *English*; but they do not love the *French*, and the *Spaniards* they hate morally. When they come among Privateers, they get the use of Guns, and prove very good Marks-Men: they behave themselves very bold in fight. . . . The *Moskito's* are in general very civil and kind to the *English*, both when they are aboard their ships, and also ashore, either in Jamaica or elsewhere, whither they often come with the Seamen. . . . When they are among the *English* they wear good cloaks, and take delight to go neat and tight.[118]

An ordinance adopted by South Carolina in 1823 and by Georgia in 1829 seems to suggest that sailors visiting that area included many non-whites. Any such 'colored' seamen were to be imprisoned while in port but that rule was not to apply to 'free American Indians, free Moors, or Lascars, or other colored subjects of countries beyond the Cape of Good Hope'.[119]

Doubtless as a direct result of American experiences as sailors, Paul Cuffe, an American–African mixed-blood, and his Native American in-laws went into the shipping business in the early 1800s. Most significantly Cuffe acquired his own vessel and actually sailed to West Africa (with other Americans from the Wampanoag Nation). Cuffe was interested in the idea of colonizing free people of color in Africa. Subsequently, the colonization of persons of part-African or African descent occurred in Sierre Leone and Liberia. Some of these persons could, of course, have been part-American in ancestry (since the white racism of the period did not always distinguish between a Red-Black mixed-blood and a 'pure' African).[120]

BRAZILIAN–AFRICAN CONTACTS AND THE CONTINUED ENSLAVEMENT OF AMERICANS

The most important source of continuous contact would appear, however, to be between Brazil and West Africa and especially with Angola. As noted earlier, from the 1630s onward there was continuous contact between Brazil and West Africa and Brazil's population included many Americans and part-Americans. Many 'white' Brazilians were actually half-American and the free non-slave population (as well as the slaves) included large increments of American ancestry. We can be sure that the bulk of the crews sent to Africa were drawn from the lower and therefore 'brown' levels of Brazilian society.[121]

A Brazilian author has stated that: 'Angola was more closely linked to Brazil than to Portugal, it having been Brazil that freed Angola from Dutch rule'. Moreover, there were many other continuous links with Africa including the education of free Africans in Bahia and the return of ex-slaves to Africa, 'taking Brazilian customs, traditions, and language to Dahomey and the whole of the Gulf of Guinea.'[122] From 1807 to 1821 the Portuguese Crown ruled Brazil and after 1825 Brazil was an independent state dominating the Angola slave trade. Thus during the nineteenth century we can be sure that Brazilian–American contacts with Africa were quite extensive.

During all of this period Americans were held as slaves or were being enslaved in Brazil. This was true in the Amazonian region where Native American labor was in constant demand for the Pará–Ceará area. One Jesuit estimated that 'three million Indians were descended (as slaves) from the Río Negro alone in the century up to 1750'. While this figure may be exaggerated, there is no question but that some Portuguese possessed more than 1,000 American slaves each.

As noted, a law of 1755 prohibited the enslavement of persons of American ancestry, but only in the female line. In any case, ways were found to create a new class of *tapuios, seus servos* (Tapuyas, their servants) legally distinct from *pretos escravos* (black slaves) but in actuality also slaves. In 1789 a *cafuza*

(American–African mixed-blood), daughter of '*india* Ana Maria' was sold and held as a slave in spite of being of American ancestry in the female line. In 1854 a Pará newspaper advertised regarding a slave of *côr tapuia* (Tapuya color) while in 1854 an advertisement mentioned a slave who was *mulato atapuiado* (a Tapuya-ish *mulato*). Large numbers of *cafuzo* slaves were present during those years.

During the nineteenth century debates took place in regard to resuming the full use of American labor as a means for excluding further imports of Africans. The bishop of Bahia in 1827 noted that 20,000 Americans in his province were 'suited to all kinds of work and industry'. Another speaker mentioned '200,000 who can immediately settle Brazil'. In the middle of the nineteenth century a British visitor to the Guiana–Surinam region noted 'how prevalent the Indian slave-trade has been, and how recently carried on, even within our boundaries. It still prevails on the southern borders of our colony and the northern tributaries of the Amazon.' He noted further that Macusi of the interior were especially victimized. 'The Brazilians, as well as the Caribs, Acawoios, etc. have long been in the habit of enslaving them.'[123]

Slavery also continued in other sections of Brazil. In 1741 some 8,000 Kaíapo people of Goías were enslaved. Large numgers of *carijós* (servants) were present in the south, sometimes classified as 'administered Indians' but in practice used in a servile status.[124]

In the Spanish Empire and the independent republics established therefrom, slavery or semi-slavery also continued from the late seventeenth through the nineteenth century in spite of laws prohibiting such. Along the northern frontier of Mexico slavery continued during the 1690s and persisted until the 1860s, primarily involving Apaches, Navajos, Paiutes, Yavapais, and other border nations whose resistance made them subject to being captured. Some natives from this region were shipped to the West Indies while others (such as the Yaqui in the 1880s) were sold to Yucatan.

After the abortive Tupak Amaru rebellion in Peru in 1781–3, however, the Inca nobility suspected of disloyalty to Spain were 'executed, imprisoned, or shipped to exile in Spanish Sahara'. Thus some Americans reached still another part of Africa.[125]

It should also be noted that when the Spaniards first began bringing slaves and workers from Spain to the West Indies a number of those transported were *ladino* (Spanish speaking) or of mixed brown appearance. In 1501, for example, Andrés García *de color loro*, formerly a servant and Cristóbal de Palacios, *de color loro* and a resident of Trigueros, went to Haiti under four-year contracts. *Cautivos* of *loro* color were also sent, as in 1521 when Isabel *de color loro* was sold to the Indies. Slaves of Islamic background were also sent (although prohibited by law) as in 1523 when Almanzor (*esclavo blanco*) and María and Catalina (*esclavas blancas*) were transported. All three were natives of Allende in Berbería (North Africa). Of course numerous Africans of non-Islamic background were sent, as in 1501 when Pedro *de color negro* contracted to serve as a soldier with Juan de Saravia for two years in Haiti.[126]

In 1502 a large number of *negros* were sent from Seville to Haiti as slaves but the following year the Crown temporarily prohibited the sending of more because of the difficulties which had been produced by their uniting with rebel Americans.[127]

THE NATURE AND SIGNIFICANCE OF AMERICAN–AFRICAN CONTACTS

Thus in many parts of Europe, along the coasts of Africa, and throughout the Americas the slave trade and European imperialism in general produced a vast number of contacts between black Africans and Native Americans. As a result a great deal of intermixture took place, as in Brazil where one scholar has stated that:

from the beginning Brazil was more a Negro and Tupí product than a Western, Portuguese one. . . . Brazil is therefore a Mestizo Republic, neither European nor Latin American, the synthesis of Tupí, African, Occidental, and Oriental antitheses, a unique and original creation.[128]

In Europe, the Canary Islands, the Azores, and other places, it would appear that both Americans and Africans generally became absorbed into the melting pot of the working classes, disappearing gradually into the general population or into groups such as the *Gitanos* of Spain and Portugal. The story of this process remains still to be written, even as the current intermixture of Native Americans and part-Americans with Africans, Asians, Afro-Americans, and Europeans in the modern cities of Europe has yet to be studied.

In Africa itself, the impact of Americans and part-Americans, whether from Brazil or elsewhere, remains also to be studied. Certain it is that American crops and specific cultural items or habits (such as the hammock and tobacco smoking) have had an impact. Rodrigues has noted that to Africa went tobacco, maize (corn), manioc (cassava), the *anana* (pineapple), and *batata* (sweet potato). Native American words for many of these plants were incorporated into African languages.

Bahian coconut palms were taken to Cape Verde . . . and our cashew has sweetened African palates. . . . So the commodities on which the African native diet is based, like corn, sweet potato, and manioc, are Brazilian in origin. . . . Plants of American and Brazilian origin also went to the Congo. Corn, manioc, coconut, guava, and peanut, . . . were transplanted from Brazil. . . . Rubber was also taken to Angola.

Often Brazilian–American methods of preparation for foodstuffs were directly incorporated into African cultures, as with the use of manioc-cassava.[129] (Needless to state, African crops were brought in the reverse direction with great impact in certain regions.)

In the direct Brazil–West Africa trade, enduring from the 1600s (or earlier) until the latter part of the nineteenth century, there must have been many opportunities for other American influences upon African cultures, especially in the Angola region but also in Ghana and other areas. Writers who have concentrated solely upon the Black African influence on Brazil and other parts of the Americas have perhaps overlooked the fact that communication was, of necessity, in both directions.

This issue is especially important in relation to the assumption fostered by some scholars that Black Africans did not experience American acculturative influences until arriving on American soil, but it is also significant in relation to the assumption that one can (or could) examine West African cultures through twentieth-century fieldwork and assume that what one finds is (or has been) largely unaffected by external influences.

Needless to state, one must also acknowledge considerable African impact upon Native Americans in the Americas. Up to four or five centuries of contact cannot be without cultural interchange.

In America itself Black Africans and, to a lesser extent, North Africans were thrown into intensive contact with Americans soon after 1500 in the Caribbean and shortly thereafter in Brazil, Mexico, Central America, and Peru.

The nature of these contacts varies, of course, according to the region and the time period. We can be sure that Americans and Africans did not automatically see each other as friends or as allies against a common Spanish or Portuguese foe. In essence, each Black African and each American national probably saw most outsiders as aliens just as the Spanish, Portuguese, Dutch, French, and English saw each other as enemies or rivals.

There is much evidence to show that Americans and Africans often collaborated against European exploitation, as, for example, in Mexico. On the other hand, there is also considerable evidence suggesting that in locales such as Peru, Africans sometimes became exploiters of the native people, modeling themselves on the Spaniards. Needless to state, the imperial powers often attempted to keep black and red people apart, the better to divide and conquer.[130]

We can also expect that many free mixed-bloods identified with colonialism's rewards and did not, *a priori*, possess any feelings of loyalty towards unmixed Americans or Africans.

Nonetheless, slavery and general labor oppression soon began to create conditions favorable for the establishment of especially intimate relations between Africans and Americans. The nature of the European empires determined that the overwhelming majority of non-whites were to be severely exploited and that only a handful, in comparison, could expect to escape from the lowest rungs of colonial society.

Virtually everywhere, from Brazil to Mexico and Peru, the initial *peón* or slave populations consisted in Americans. Black Africans only began to be imported in significant numbers after 1510 (Caribbean) and 1550 (Brazil), and the subjugation of Americans also continued during that epoch.

The Europeans sought out labor wherever they could find it and many thousands of Americans were absorbed into the slave cauldron during the same period that Africans were being brought in. (It is true, as noted, that efforts were made by the Spanish Crown and by the Jesuits in Brazil to prevent American enslavement, but such efforts were seldom very successful.)

In any case, *the initial slave population was American.* In the second stage *it became African and American.* In the third stage *it became increasingly Africanized* in certain regions (such as plantation areas of Brazil, the British and French Caribbean, the Atlantic seaboard of North America), but other areas saw the continued enslavement of Americans (such as northern and southern Brazil) or the replacement of slavery by peonage or low-wage labor using people largely of American ancestry.

As time went by, the initial African *and* American nature of the slave population became obscured by Africanization, on the one hand, or Americanization, on the other. But the fact remains that there are large areas of the Americas where the modern-day 'Indians' or *mestizos* are part-African, and conversely there are few areas where the modern-day Afroamericans are not part-American.

Of course, this process of African–American mixture also involved the 'free people of color', the *pardos, mestizos, ladinos,* and *cholos* of the Americas. I discuss the evolution of this population elsewhere but it should be noted that almost everywhere it originated from free American mothers who produced free children from fathers of various races (African, European, or American). Needless to state, white mothers occasionally produced free mixed children but outside of North America there were very few white women available. Also European fathers sometimes freed their own mixed children (if from a slave mother) but, in fact, most mothers must have been American women in the early period (because African women were greatly outnumbered by African males; indeed, the sexual imbalance among African slaves runs as a continuous theme throughout the era of importations).[131]

Mention must also be made of Africans who fled to Native American nations or who were initially enslaved by Americans but later often became absorbed by marriage and adoption. This is a complex subject which cannot be explored here but it seems to have been a common phenomenon from southern Brazil (at least) to the northern United States.

As early as 1559 Americans in the Bahia region captured a Portuguese slave vessel from São Tomé and, as a result, 'os negros de Guiné fugirão e esconderão-se pelos matos'. Exactly where in the *mato* the Africans fled to is not clear, but this incident may have led to the founding of an early mixed African–American free community.[132]

Africans often escaped from slavery to form independent *quilombos* or *cimarrón* (maroon) communities. In many instances, as in Jamaica, Surinam, Mexico and Brazil, there is evidence of initial collaboration with American *cimarrones* or, at the very least, the abduction of American women. Such communities were, of course, not always on friendly terms with neighboring American groups but warfare has never served to prevent inter-group marriage (when females or children are captured).

One of the most famous *quilombos* was that of Palmares in Brazil. In 1644 the

Dutch with American allies attacked and burned part of Palmares, capturing in the process 31 prisoners of whom seven were Tupís (Brazilians) and some of whom were young mixed-bloods (*mulaetjens*). Thus, the freedom-seekers at Palmares included Americans among the Africans, as well as Red-Black children. Similarly, in Surinam when a young boy and his mother were captured in 1775 on a raid against the rebel leader Bonny there is evidence of an American presence. The young boy could not bear to be touched by any white person and he constantly referred to the latter as 'Yorica, which in his language signifies the devil'. Reportedly *Yorokan* is a Carib word for 'evil spirits' probably being related to *Uracan* (hurricane).[133]

Individual Africans running away also excercised a great impact upon Americans, especially in Brazil but throughout the Americas as well. In some cases their influence lay in a so-called 'Europeanizing' direction but there was also considerable Africanizing influence. Rodrigues states: 'I don't know to what degree that action was more Europeanizing than Africanizing. Both whites and Indians underwent a definite Africanization – in food, dress, language, music, religion, and folklore.'[134]

Finally, mention must be made of the impact of modern urban developments which have seen the migration of people of American and African ancestry to the great cities of the Americas from Buenos Aires to Toronto and Montreal. In such settings, especially from New Orleans southwards, a vast melting pot seems to have ensued in which American and African strains, mixed often with European, become lost in a complex although uneven process of fusion. In North America the ghettoization of ethnic groups has tended to slow down this process but the autobiographies of musicians from New Orleans reveal that, at least in that area, much American–African mixture has gone on in recent times. Moreover, there is occasional intermixture of Afroamericans (already often part-American) with Puerto Ricans, Mexicans and other persons of American of part-American ancestry, including people of reservation 'Indian' background.

It is clear, then, that Africans and Americans have been interacting in a variety of settings for at least five hundred years. What is, of course, especially intriguing is that this interaction is not confined to the Americas but extends also to Africa and to Europe (where, incidentally, people of African and American ancestry from Surinam, Aruba, Curaçao, French Guiana, Trinidad, Dominica, Guyana, and other areas are living today in considerable numbers in Amsterdam, Rotterdam, Paris, London and other cities).

We can be sure that this process has been, and is, extremely significant in cultural terms and yet almost nothing has been done to explore the significance of the subject. Histories of black music in North America, for example, very seldom mention 'Indians' in the text or index. It would be tedious, however, to list all of the examples where writers exploring some aspect of cultural evolution have ignored American–African interactions, but elsewhere I will explore some of the reasons for this omission.

The genetic significance of African–American interaction is also extremely significant. In fact, *two* great mixed races have developed in the Americas. The one in which African ancestry is strongest we can call 'Eastern Neo-American' because it is most characteristic of the eastern half of the Americas. The other one, in which American ancestry is strongest, we can call 'Western Neo-American' because it is most characteristic of the area from Chile and parts of Argentina to western North America.

'Eastern Neo-American' people are part-African, American, European and sometimes Asian, with the African ancestry being very clearly evident although not always dominant. 'Western Neo-American' people are part-American, European, African and sometimes Asian, with the American ancestry being clearly evident although not always dominant.

Thus the two Neo-American races are essentially the same, in terms of components, but differ only in the relative proportions of African, American or European input. In many areas around the Caribbean and in the interior from Colombia to Rio de Janeiro the two groups blend and overlap. Needless to state they also meet each other in almost every great city in the United States.

Thus the modern period of interaction which commenced in the 1490s in the Caribbean and the Iberian peninsula has had unforeseen and extremely significant results. It remains now to shed light upon the extent and nature of American–African intermixture by carefully analyzing the various racial terms employed for mixed persons during the colonial era.

3
Negro, Black and Moor: The Evolution of These Terms as Applied to Native Americans and Others

DIFFERENT TENDENCIES IN THE USE OF 'NEGRO' AND 'BLACK'

In 1854 the California State Supreme Court sought to bar all non-Caucasians from equal citizenship and civil rights. The court stated:

The word 'Black' may include all Negroes, but the term 'Negro' does not include all Black persons. . . . We are of the opinion that the words 'White', 'Negro', 'Mulatto' and 'Black person', whenever they occur in our constitution . . . must be taken in their generic sense . . . that the words 'Black person', in the 14th section must taken as contra distinguished from White, and necessarily includes all races other than the Caucasian.[1]

As convoluted as the quote may be, it expresses a strong tendency in the history of the United States, a tendency to identify two broad classes of people: white and non-white, citizen and non-citizen (or semi-citizen).

The tendency to create a two-caste society often clashed with the reality of a territory which included many different types of people, of all colors and different degrees of intermixture of European, American, African and Asian. American Indian people, whether of unmixed ancestry or mixed with other stocks, were at times affected by the tendency to create a purely white–black social system, especially when living away from a reservation or the tribal homeland.[2]

In the British slave colonies of North American, along the Atlantic coast, many persons of American ancestry were at times classified as blacks, negroes, mulattoes, or people of color, and these terms were, of course, used for people of African ancestry. The manner in which Americans and part-Americans were sometimes classified as 'mulattoes' and 'people of color' from New England to

South Carolina and in the colonial empires is explored elsewhere.[3] The purpose here is to illustrate how the term 'negro' has also been applied to people of American descent.

The concept of *negro* needs first to be analyzed in terms of its historical development. As noted elsewhere, the late medieval period in Italy and the Iberian peninsula saw people being variously classified as *albo, alvi, blanco, branco* (white), *nero, nigri, negri, negro, negre, preto* (black), and as of intermediate colors: *lauro, loro, llor, berretini, rufo, pardo, olivastre,* etc.[4]

It is apparent from the evidence that the term *negro* or its equivalent was not used for a race or for a single stock of people or to point to ancestry or ethnicity. It was usually a simple description for perceived color or appearance.

We find many instances where *de color negro* is used when describing persons, or *negro algo loro* or *loro casi negro*, etc. That is, it is quite clear that a perception of color is being described, and not ancestry, ethnicity or race. Muslims or Saracens are often described, as noted earlier, in terms of being *negro, blanco,* or *loro*, for example.

In 1543 the Spanish Crown ordered that *mulatos* could not be taken as slaves to the Americas under the general license for *esclavos negros*:

En virtud de nuestras licencias generales para passar esclavos Negros á las Indias, se llevan, y pasan algunos Mulatos, y otros, que no son Negros, lo que se siguen inconvenientes . . . no dexen passar á ningun esclavo, que no sea Negro, aunque sea Mulato, sin especial licencia nuestra.[5]

In brief, *mulato* and other slaves 'who are not Negroes' were forbidden to go to the Americas without a special royal license.

Thus in the late medieval and early modern period there is no equivalent to the recent North American tendency to utilize the terms 'negro' or 'black' for persons of alleged 'negro' or 'black' *ancestry*. People were usually described as black, olive, brown, red, copper, or whatever, according to their skin (or hair) color only, not according to a racial scheme.

On the other hand there was a tendency to also utilize the term *negro* or its functional equivalent *mohr, moor, more* (German, Dutch, French) in a very broad sense. Albrecht Dürer, for example, although certainly aware of the existence of Americans, is recorded as stating that there were only two types of human beings, white and black (*mohr*). The Portuguese, as we shall see, also tended to use the term *negro* to encompass many non-Africans, people whose skin color was a shade of brown. It would appear that, in this sense, black can be conceived of as the opposite of white and in a dualistic mode of thinking all humans must logically fall into one of the two categories. In this usage, *negro* or *moor* almost becomes equivalent to 'non-white' or 'Third World' in recent usage.

We must, however, briefly explore the use and meaning of *moor, mauri, moro, negro, negre,* etc., before arriving at any premature conclusions. Nevertheless, to summarize we can say that by *negro* and equivalents is meant a range of color-shades – for humans generally dark browns – always less extreme than true black but approaching the 'darkness' of black; and also including very often people of medium shades of brown whose color seems to contrast sharply with white or 'clear' shades.[6]

The issues involved in the perception of brown and other shades of color intermediate between black and white will be discussed early in the next chapter. Here we will proceed to illustrate how terms meaning 'black' have been utilized for peoples whose skin colors are often of various lighter shades.

Latin *niger, negri* would seem to be the predecessor of Spanish and Portuguese *negro*, Catalán *negre*, Italian *nero*, French *noir* (black) and *nègre* (black or dark person). These terms correspond to Dutch *swert, swart*, German *schwartz*, English 'black' ('swarthy' has come to be equivalent to 'dark' rather than black).[7] As applied to humans these terms do not necessarily imply a true black color but merely a range of dark shades approaching black or reminding one of black. Thus there is a considerable range for interpretation. An early Spanish–French dictionary (1607) translated Spanish *negro* as being equivalent to French 'noir, sombre, obscur, offusqué, brun'. 'Negro de la Guinea' is equivalent to 'un nègre, un More'.[8] As will be noted in the case of Dutch, the above allows for dark (*obscur*) and *brun* to be subsumed under *negro* and uses French *more* (moor) as equivalent to a *negro* from Guinea.

THE TERM 'MOOR'

The term *more* and its equivalents were widely used in late-medieval and early modern Europe. According to Simonet in his study of the language spoken by the Mozárabes (Christian Spaniards under Muslim rule before 1492), *maúro* meant *negro* and corresponded to Castillian usage in which *moro* was applied to horses whose color was *negro*. The corresponding *more* (French), *maurus* (Hispanic Latin), and *moro* (Valencian) were derived from Latin *morus* (*negro*) and ultimately from a Greek word meaning *oscuro*. Similarly, Mozarabic *maúro* was related to *moro* (Spanish and Italian), *mouro* (Portuguese and Gallego), *mor* (Provençal), *maure* and *more* (French), meaning 'Moro; negro; hombre de color'. These forms stemmed from Latin *maurus* (also from Greek), 'for the dark (*oscuro*) color of the *Mauritanos o' Moros* (peoples of northwest Africa)'.

The Mozarabic *maurel* and *moreno*, corresponding to Castillian, Catalan, and Portuguese *moreno* (*subniger, fuscus*, that is, less than black, darkish, *pardo*), French *moreau*, Italian *morello*, etc., were derived from Latin *morulus, morellus*, diminutives of *maurus* and *morus*.[9]

Finally Mozarabic *maurixco*, corresponding to Castillian *maurisco* and, later, *morisco*, stemmed from Hispanic Latin *mauriscus* for *mauricus* (*mauritano*), derived as above.

In 1591 an Italian went to Cabo Verde 'a comprar Mori per l'India Occidentali', that is, to buy African slaves (*Mori*) for the Americas.[10] To summarize, the people of northwestern Africa (Algeria, Morocco) were anciently known as Mauri or Mauritanians and this name in both Greek and

Latin came to mean 'negro' or black but also various shades of so-called 'obscure' color, i.e., darkish shades for which terms such as *fuscus*, *pardo* and *loro* were often used in later times. Moreover, derivatives such as *moreno* acquired meanings distinct from, but related to, *negro*. A 1607 dictionary states for *moreno*: 'brun, noir, obscur, couleur d'olives', quite a range.[11]

In any case, one can see that *mauri–more* group of terms (in various languages) did not refer to absolute black or to 'blackish' alone, but could indeed refer to a range of darker skin colors. This is also true as regards *nigri* and its forms. For example a 1494 source states that the king of Portugal possessed 'pretos de vários côres: acobreados, pretos e anegrados. . . . Habet item rex nigros varii coloris; rufos, nigros et aubnigros.'[12] Clearly the term *aubnigros* next to *nigros* indicates a variation, while *preto* (black) encompasses all of the stated colors: copperish or reddish, and so on.

An Irish Gaelic saga of the 900s (copied in 1643) states that Danish–Irish raiders attacked Spain and Mauritania in the 800s. From the latter place they 'carried off a great host of them as captives to Erin, and these are the blue men [of Erin], for Mauri is the same as black man, and Mauritania is the same as blackness. . . . Long indeed were these blue men in Erin.' The Gaelic text uses *Mauri* and *negri* and *mauritania* and *nigritudo*, obviously borrowed from Latin (the concept of 'blue men' is described in original Gaelic words).[13]

From this text we can see how the term *mauri* for *negro* spread to northern Europe and at the same time how both words could be used for shades of brown, since from our modern perspective the Mauritanians (Berbers, Moors, and others) are not regarded as being 'black' (or 'blue') in skin color. (It may be, of course, that they have become much lightened due to mixture with Romans, Spaniards, Arabs, Vandals, and so on, but some of that change in color could have preceded the 800s. Saco describers the *berberiscos* as being *fusci* (dark), *moreno*, and *aceitunado* (olive-colored) in his study of ancient slavery.)

The use of *moor* in the Dutch language will be discussed below, but here it is useful to note that the medieval Dutch understood by that term a very dark color, so that the color of coal was compared with that of a *moor*. Also it was said: 'scijnt swaert ghelike den more', he is as black as a moor.[14]

The spread of *maurus* to the north can also be seen in Scotland where, in 1504–5, several references to 'More lasses' (Moor lasses) are found. At that time a child was born, referred to as 'Moris barne' (a *maurus* born). Late in 1512–13, one finds 'Elen More' and 'Blak Elene' used (one assumes) interchangeably. By 1527 'Helenor, the black moir' is referred to, while in 1567–9 there are references to 'Nageir the More.'[15]

THE PORTUGUESE USE OF *NEGRO* FOR AMERICANS

In so far as the use of *negro* or its equivalents for Americans is concerned, it is well to begin our analysis with a brief review of usage in the Portuguese language. First, it must be noted that Europeans generally regarded the

Americans as being of an intermediate color, *pardo*, *loro*, *berretino*, or *olivastre*. For example, in 1519 it was said of the Brazilians : 'non sono né neri né blanchi, ma di colore di ulivo' (that is, they are not black or white but of olive color), but the same writer also remarked that the Brazilian canoe-men he saw were 'so black' that they could have been taken for sailors on the sea of Styx (in Hell). Another Italian in *c*.1533 described them as 'di color olivastro, e piú presto negri' (that is, olive-colored and almost black). In 1492–3 the Caribbean islanders were said to be 'of *loro* color, white more than black'. But in 1524 the Carolina coast people were said to be 'of dark color not much unlike the Ethiopians' with lighter-colored people farther north. Thus a range of color was perceived, with some being 'almost white' and some of darker shades.[16]

From 1549 through 1565 the letters of Jesuit missionaries in Brazil, usually addressed to colleagues in Portugal or Spain, frequently refer to the Americans as *negros* as well as using terms such as *gentios* (pagans), *brasis* and other forms of Brazilian, and *indios*. In April 1549 Manuel da Nóbrega, the leader of the Jesuits, addressed a letter from Bahia to Simão Rodrigues in Lisbon in which he refers to the Portuguese in Brazil as living in sin because of their having 'many *negras*' and lots of children by the said 'black' women. The editor, Serafim Leite, notes in a footnote: ' "Negras" isto é, mulheres índias. Negras nem negros da África ainda os não havia na Baía.' A few lines later Nóbrega refers to the *Indios desta terra*.[17]

Thus, the Jesuit father called the American women living with Portuguese men *negras*, a term which, according to Leite, could not have denoted people from Africa because in 1549 there were few or no African women in Bahia. Nonetheless, Nóbrega also uses the word *indio*.

This pattern is repeated time and time again, as we shall see. What does it signify? It would seem that the *indios* or *brasis* of Brazil were, in fact, both *negros* and *indios* because *indios* were simply a special (regional) kind of *negros*. We must bear in mind that Brazil was part of *las Indias* or *India*, and that the geographical designation for people native to that would be Indian. But in addition to a purely geographical designation, they might also be considered to be *negros* even as the people of India proper were often called *negros* (as we shall see below). In addition to being *indios*, the coastal Brazilians were also called *brasis* because they resided in that part of *Indias* called *Brasil*.

When Africans are referred to in the Jesuit letters they are always called *negros da Guiné* (blacks of Guinea) to distinguish them from *negros da terra* (blacks of the land or Americans).

In August 1549 Nóbrega wrote to Rodrigues in Portugal about the Portuguese men and 'their *negras* [used] for mistresses'. He also referred to *os negros* who were being enslaved, and to the Carijós as *negros*. Of course, most Portuguese possessed mistresses or wives who were American.[18]

In June 1551 Brother Diego Jácome wrote from São Vicente to the Jesuits of Coimbra (Portugal), referring to Americans as *os negros*. In August 1551 from Pernambuco Father António Pires wrote to Coimbra that 'the *negros* are now very calm'. Also from Pernambuco in August 1551 Nóbrega requested from

King John II 'alguns escravos de Giné' as servants for the Jesuit Colegio da Bahia. In June 1552 António Pires, writing from Pernambuco to the Jesuits of Coimbra, stated: 'Ha nesta capitania grande escravaria asi de Guiné como da terra. Tem huma Confraria do Rosario.' That is, Pernambuco possessed a great number of slaves, both African and American and they had a confraternity of (Our Lady of) the Rosary (the common confraternity for slaves in Portugal, as noted earlier). The editor, Serafim Leite, notes that the Confraria do Rosario in Pernambuco seems to have been for all slaves, American as well as African.[19]

In July 1552 and again on several occasions through 1558 Nóbrega asked for three or four slaves from Guinea for the Jesuit college.

A very interesting letter is one prepared by 'dos meninos do Colégio de Jesus da Baía', that is, by the young Americans studying in the school: Diogo Topinamba, Peribira, Mongeta, and Quantía. Although probably edited by a Jesuit, this may represent the first letter written by Americans in a European language from Brazil. In it they refer to an American leader, 'el Grillo', as a *negro* and to other natives as *negros*. We find, for example, 'el Grillo, who is a *negro* very well-known and feared among them' and that el Grillo 'es negro muy grave'. 'El Grillo' was at the same time an *Indi pagan* and a friend of the Portuguese.[20]

In August 1552 Nóbrega wrote from Bahia to Lisbon, referring to the native people as *negros*. In May 1554 António Blázquez from Porto Seguro wrote to the Jesuits of Coimbra that: 'Yo estoy en este Puerto Seguro, y la vida que hago y en lo que me ocupo es esto: enseño la doctrina a los negros y negras.' That is, he was preaching to the Americans, called *negros*. He also referred to the *negros* and 'los mamalucos desta tierra' as pupils. The editor notes that by *negros y negras* he meant *Indios e índias*.[21]

In 1556 or 1557, Nóbrega prepared one of the first works of literature written by a European in the Americas, a fictional dialogue on the question of the enslavement and conversion of the *gentios* (pagans) of Brazil. In it Nóbrega frequently used *negro* for *indio*, as when he refers to the people of el Gato, an American leader, as *negros*. Leite, in a footnote, states that Nóbrega used

Negros por oposição a Brancos, mas trata-se de Índios. Na mesma acepção escreve Nóbrega a D. João III, de Olinda, 14 de Septembro de 1551. . . . "negras forras do gentio . . .", falando de indias livres. . . . Com a palavra Negros, Nóbrega emprega tambem a de Índios, como se le varias vezes neste mesmo Diálogo, en particular na fala do Nogueira sobre os índios convertidos da capitania de São Vicente.

In other words, Nóbrega used both *negro* and *indio* for Americans, *negro* being used in the sense of the opposite of white, and Leite gives several examples.[22]

In May 1557 Pires wrote to Nóbrega that: 'batizé el hijo del Gato y lo casé con su negra. . . . Fué hecho este oficio con poca solenidad por quanto el yndio estava doliente e quasi pudo venir a la yglesia.' Thus Pires refers to el Gato's son's wife as *negra* while a sentence later he says *yndio*. A month later António Blazquez wrote from Bahia to Father Ingatius Loyola in Rome to the effect that an American with his *negra* wished to be baptized. In April 1558 Blazquez in another letter to Rome noted that most conversions were being made among the slaves (American) whom the Portuguese treated like horses and beasts, burying them in *los muladares* (mule yards or dung heaps) and that the Portuguese 'todos tienen negras con que estén em peccado, y los más tienen esclavos que no lo pueden ser'. That is, the Portuguese were all living in sin with American women and most possessed slaves.

In February 1559 António de Sa of Espirito Santo, writing to the Jesuits of Bahia, used *negro* for American and noted that el Gato, alias Vasco Fernandes, had come with French goods 'de maneira que quasi todos os negros vinhão vestidos'. Thus el Gato's native people, called *negros*, were wearing French clothes. In June of 1559 Sá referred to 'Vasco Fernandez, Principal de los Indios' and to his son Manemoaçu as *el pobre negro*. Similarly one of *estos gentiles* (these pagans) was called *el negro*, etc.[23]

In July 1559 Nóbrega wrote to Portugal that the Christians (Portuguese) were, for the most part, 'living in the interior areas with their *negras* as mistresses' and that their slaves were also living together without proper marriage. Nóbrega also wrote, in a letter to the governor, that 'eight *negros* of Guiné' were killed by a party of 'sixty valiant *negros*'. By using '*negros* of Guiné' for Africans and *negros* for native Americans, Nóbrega is able to refer to both in the same sentence.

In September 1561 Father Leonard Do Vale wrote to Rome that another Jesuit was *muy suave* to 'whites as to *negros*' in his work in Brazil. The next year, June 1562, Do Vale also wrote to Rome using *os negros* for Americans while in June 1565 he wrote to the Jesuits of Portugal about *hum negro bautizado* and he also uses *o negro* for a Tamóio. In a footnote the editor states:

"Negro" por "Indio" (não negro de África); o que é evidente na sequência deste mesmo parágrafo, aplicado ao Indio Tamóio. . . . Donde se segue que a intromissão aqui de negro por indio parece da responsabilidade de quem no momento superintendia na Europa as trabalho destas cópias.

Thus *Negro* is used for 'Indian', not for someone from Africa. The editor suggests that a European copyist might have been responsible for this usage, but as we have seen it is too consistent over the years to require such an explanation. In any case, it is clear that many Iberians and Italians, whether in Europe or America, were comfortable in using *negro*, *negri*, etc., for Americans.[24]

Father Joseph de Anchieta, another prominent Jesuit in Brazil, between 1570 and 1584 carefully refers to Africans as *negros de Guiné* while calling Americans *Indios da terra*, *escravos da terra*, or *brasis*. Other Jesuits sometimes use the form *yndia brasílica*, *concubina brasílica* or *lengua brasílica*.[25]

In 1587 a secular author, Gabriel Soares de Sousa, mentions Africans as *negros de Guiné* and *pretos de Guiné* while Americans are usually called *indios da terra*. On the other hand, Soares refers to an American (Tupinamba) woman as being *muito preta* (very black) as contrasted with her son who was *tão alvo* (very white, an *albino*). The father was not very *preto*.[26]

The occasional use of *negro* for Americans seems to continue into the eighteenth century. In 1602, for example, a Portuguese reportedly was living on Fernão de Noronha Island with 13 or 14 *negros*. In 1612, however, the French found a Portuguese there 'with a few Tapuyas of both sexes'. In 1648 the Jesuit Antonio Vieira wrote 'sem negros não há Pernambuco' meaning 'without *negros*, no sugar, and no Pernambuco'. Since American slaves served in the sugar industry of Pernambuco from the very beginning through the 1580s and later, the term *negro* in this case is very probably equivalent to 'slave'. This meaning will be explored further below.[27]

In a letter of Antonio Vieira from the Rio das Almazonas (sic) to Portugal, March 24, 1661, he writes:

e que bastava levar un moço secular branco ou indio. . . . e agora no Pará fez grandes instâncias por levar consigo para a Aldeia um moço secular, propondo dous, um branco outro negro, para os ter das portas a dentro.

In this case, it would seem that Vieira uses *negro* for *indio* in the second sentence quoted.[28]

In 1712 Raphael Bluteau's dictionary of Portuguese and Latin was published, a significant development in that he was one of the earliest dictionary-makers to incorporate Brazilian terms. Of special interest is his definition for: 'Mameluco. No livro 8. de sua historia cap. 4 *De incolis Brasiliae*, diz Jorge Marggravo, que no Brasil chamâo Mameluco ao filho de pay Europeo, e mãy negra.' Bluteau thus states that in Marcgrave's natural history of Brazil (1640s) the term *Mameluco* was used for the child of a European father and a *negra* mother.

Georg Marcgrave had gone to Brazil during the Dutch occupation. His notes on the natural history of the area were edited by Jan de Laet and published in 1648 in Latin. What the original Latin edition actually states is 'Qui natus est ex patre Europaeo & matre Brasiliana nominatur *Mameluco*'. That is, that the child of a Brazilian mother and a European father is called a *mameluco*.

Somehow Bluteau (or some predecessor) chose to substitute *negra* for Brazilian. (Marcgrave had used 'Ethiopian' for African rather than *negro*.)[29] *Mameluco* in the period referred to an American–European mixed-blood primarily if not exclusively.

In 1755 a Portuguese law extended personal freedom to the Americans of Grão Pará and the Maranhão in Brazil, with the exception of those whose mothers were slaves of African descent. Clause 10 stated:

Among the many regrettable practices . . . which have resulted in the disparagement of the Indians, one prime abuse is the unjustifiable and scandalous practice of calling them *negroes*. Perhaps by so doing the intent was no other than to induce in them the belief that by their origins they had been destined to be the slaves of whites, as is generally conceded to be the case of blacks from the coast of Africa. . . . The directors will not permit henceforth that anybody may refer to an Indian as a *negro*, nor that they themselves may use this epithet among themselves, as is currently the case.[30]

This Portuguese usage is extremely significant, not only because American or part-American slaves could be referred to as *negros* in early records, but also because it very much affects one's analysis of population statistics in colonial Brazil (where, in fact, the categories of *negro* and *escravo* must have often included enslaved American Indians and mixed-bloods). An analysis of modern Brazilian census data would, I believe, demonstrate that Americans and part-Americans are still being classified as *negros* (*pretos*) for certain purposes.[31]

In India the Portuguese also frequently used the term *negro* for Indians as well as *baço* (darkish). *Alva* or *branco* (white) was sometimes used for light-skinned persons of *mouro* (Muslim, Arab) background. Afonso de Albuquerque in the very early 1500s encouraged his men to marry the 'white' widows of dead Muslims at Goa but he did not want them to marry the 'black' women of Malabar. Nonetheless, in 1524 it was said that the Portuguese of Goa who were married were almost all married to *negras*. This usage continued and, in fact, the term *negro* came to be used in 1640 in such a broad way that it was applied as an abusive epithet even to Indian-born Portuguese.

In 1645 an Italian Franciscan in India referred to the Indians generally, the people 'of the country', as 'blacks'. A Christian bishop of Brahmin ancestry, consecrated at Rome in 1635, was never allowed to officiate in Portuguese territory and was called (by a Jesuit) 'a bare-bottomed nigger' (*negro*).

In the 1750s the Portuguese government made it illegal to refer to Indians as *negros* 'and other insulting and opprobrious terms'. In 1759 the Viceroy at Goa issued an edict denouncing 'the contempt with which the natives of this State [of India] are treated by the Europeans who call them Niggers [negros], curs and other insulting names, for no other reason than the difference of color.' Nonetheless the above decree outlawing the use of *negro* for Indians was not promulgated by the authorities at Goa until 1774.[32]

One can see, then, that with Indians and Americans both being referred to as *negros* in the 1500s and later, one cannot be at all certain of the ethnic identity of *negros* sold in Portugal or of those resold in Spain, Italy, the Netherlands and elsewhere. As we review usage in Spain it will become clear that both Indians and Americans were also on occasion called *negros* in that country. A Portuguese–Latin dictionary of 1592 (written before 1569) states:

Negro cativo = Aethiops
Negra = Aethiopissa
Negra cousa = niger, nigra, nigrum, pullus . . . , ater
Preto = niger, nigra, nigrum.

Thus a 'captive negro' is equivalent to 'Ethiopian' which would seem to refer specifically to Black Africa. On the other hand, *negra cousa* (something black) and *preto* refer only to concepts of black. [7]

A dictionary of 1611 is similar except that *Negro de Guiné* is equivalent to Ethiopian. *Preto* and *negro* are both equivalent to Latin black (*ater* and *niger*).[33]

An English–Portuguese dictionary of 1701 had these equivalents:

Blackness = a negridão

Black = cousa preta, négra, escura ou sombría
A black-moor = móuro, móura, os naturães de Ethiópia
Cáfra, Cáfre = Black-a-moor of Ethiopia
Mouro = a Moor
Pretinho, préto = see négro
Negro ou cáfre = a black.

thus the term *cáfre* (Kaffir) is equivalent to *negro* (*cáfre* was widely used in the Indian Ocean region especially). Interestingly, 'black-moor' was equated with *mouro* (without a color qualification) as well as with 'Ethiopian'. Further, black was equivalent to sombre or obscure color as well to *negro* and *preto*.[34]

Bluteau in 1712 stated the following: '*Negro*. Homem da terra dos negros, ou filho de pays negros. Nigrita, ae . . . chama Plinio aos negros. Nigritae, arum.' The *Terra dos negros* was defined as lying beyond Libya and the Sahara. *Preto* is defined as 'Negro. Ater, atra, um. ou Niger, Nigra, Nigrum' but for *pretinho* we find: 'Negrinho. Algūa cousa preto. Tirante a preto. Nigellus, a, um. Varro. Subniger . . . tambem val o mesmo que pequeno escravo. Preto. Servulus niger.' Bluteau also states for *preto*: 'tambem se chama escravo Preto. Servus niger.'[35]

In short, by 1712 Bluteau was able to identify slave status with the term *preto*. Other evidence indicates that as the years went by *negro* became a harsher term than *preto* and more like North American 'Nigger'.

A 1784 Portuguese–French dictionary has: Nègre, -esse = Negro, preto, Mouro, escravo, que se tira das costas de Africa (Traiter quelqu' un comme un Nègre. Fig. Tratar alguem como hum escravo; i.h. feramente, muito cruelmente.' Thus the connotations of *negro* = slave were well established, a figurative meaning being to treat someone harshly or very cruelly, as a slave. In 1836 another dictionary-maker pointed out that *negro* in addition to referring to obscure darkness 'such as on a night without stars or moonlight' also possessed connotations of a 'moral' nature (sadness, for example) while *preto* referred properly to the color of something burned and was never used in a moral sense.[36]

J. I. Roquette in his Portuguese–French dictionary of 1862 equated *negra* with *négresse, esclave noire* and *negro* with 'négre, négresse: homme, femme dont la peau est naturellement noire; esclave noir'.[37] Thus the meaning of *negro* as 'black slave' is made very specific.

Antonio Brasio, in his study of *pretos* in Portugal, states explicitly: 'negros (nós preferimos prêto, mais simpático, pois negro é sinónimo de escravo, têrmo injurioso').[38] Thus *negro* had become synonymous with 'slave' and *preto* was preferred as a nicer term.

It seems very likely that by the beginning of the eighteenth century (and probably earlier in Brazil and the other colonies) *negro* had already acquired its negative meaning of 'slave' or 'slave-like'.

That the Portuguese later used the term *negro* as an equivalent to 'slave' and as a term of abuse is also well illustrated by many works on Brazil and Portugal which cite poems, songs and sayings which convey a negative image of *negros*. A modern Portuguese dictionary says of *Negra*:

mulher de côr negra; escrava; mulher que trabalha muito [woman of black color; a slave; a woman who works a lot].

Negro is similar:

Que é de côr escura; preta; sombrio; fusco; de negrido . . . vil, odioso; indigno; adverso . . . homem de raça negra; homem que trabalho muito; escravo [one who is of dark color; black; sombre; darkish; blackish; vile, odious; indignant; adverse . . . a man of the negro race; a man who works a lot; a slave].[39]

C. R. Boxer, the noted historian of the Portuguese Empire, translates Portuguese *negro* as English 'nigger' and states the following: 'The Portuguese habit of referring to Indians, Sinhalese, and even to Chinese and Japanese as "Niggers" was fairly wide-spread and lasted longer than is usually realized.' He notes that the Maratha War of 1737–40 in India was partly caused when a Portuguese official called a leading Maratha man a Nigger: 'a word which they interpreted as slave, for they were assured that this was what we called the Kaffirs of Mozambique.'[40] The Portuguese were, of course, selling 'Kaffirs' as slaves in India and used the term *negro* as well as *cáfre* to describe them.

It is also very significant that an Italian, Filippo Sassetti, who lived in Lisbon and various Portuguese colonies in the 1570s and 1580s specifically refers, in a letter of 1585, to the Americans of Brazil as *negri* (writing in Italian). He reserves the word *indiani* for the people of India. We may justifiably suppose that his use of *negri* reflects Portuguese usage. We may note again the many Jesuit letters to Rome using *negro* for Americans.[41]

In so far as the term *negro* in the Portuguese Empire became synonymous with 'slave' or with a servile status it, of course, lost any mandatory color reference and became a general term of abuse. This usage accords with an earlier Portuguese tendency to use the words *Sarraceni* and later *mouro* to refer to enslaved persons in preference to *servi* (slave).[42] Unfortunately, many English-speaking authors tend to translate *negro* as 'black' rather than as 'nigger' or 'slave' and have failed to see the implications for Brazilian history of the above distinctions.

THE USE OF *NEGRO* IN SPANISH

The Spaniards in Spain seem to have also been inclined to utilize the term *negro* in a broad sense, to include darker Americans and Indians at least. First, however, it is necesary to discuss the way in which *negro* was used in Spain. In the early years it seems to have been merely a designation of color, usually contrasted with *blanco* or *loro*. In Valencia, between 1480 and 1510, for example, one finds the following kinds of descriptions for slaves: white moorish female; black and white captives; black moorish female; Jalof (Wolof, from

Senegal, without the term *negro*); Turk; Canary Island female; black female of Jalof; white female; black of . . . Barbary; two captives: one of white called Mubarich, age 45 years and the other black, named Azmet, age 30 years; a Jew (from Barbary); *alarbe* (bedouin); moors of Barbary; a white Canary Islands captive; a black female of Tripoli, Almosora age 17 years, Arab; as well as *loros* and Indians and Americans called *negros* (to be discussed below).

It is clear that there was no noticeable tendency to use the term *negro* either for 'slave' or as a general replacement for other descriptions. The children of a white and a *negro* were called either *loro* or white. A Spanish authority notes that 'also some children of a white man and a black female were whites'. In 1525 in the Canary Islands one notes: 'Juanico, child, of white color, his slave, son of Maria, his black slave'. The boy was classified as being of white color and he and his *negra* mother were slaves of the same owner.

In records of the Canaries one finds repeated references to *de color negro* (1523, 1538, 1560), *de color loro* (1538), *de color algo baça* (of somewhat darkish color, 1557), and *de color blanco* in addition to the innumerable cases where the *de color* is clearly implied.[43]

The lists of *negros* and others sold in Las Palmas after 1514 include descriptors such as: *negra berberisca*; *negro morisco*; *negra bozal*; *moro negro*; *blanca*; *negro ladino*; '*Cabo Verde*'; *prieta* and *prieto* (both rare); *blanco morisco*; *negro mandinga*; *morena* (rare); *negro Gelofe* (Wolof); *negro Guinea*; along with *loros*, *indios*, *moros*, *Maguerabombas*, etc. In 1549 one finds Juliana, a *mulata* of 25 as sister to Gaspar, *negro* of 16.

A change perhaps begins in the 1580s when one finds a *negro loro*. This term is repeated on occasion, as in 1563, 1569, 1586–7 and 1591, and might imply that a *loro* was being classified as a *negro*. In fact, however, it appears to be shorthand for *negra algo lora* (black almost brown) (1567), *negra casi lora* (1580), and 'prieta, más lora que negra' (1584). One also finds a *negra* with a *mulato* son (1576), a *negro amulatado* (1582), that is, a mulato-ish *negro*, and *negra* with a *mulato* son (presumably, 1584).[44]

Thus it appears that, in general, it is color which is being described throughout the sixteenth century, along with occasional references to religion, place of birth, or nationality (*Berberisco*, etc.).

As noted earlier, the late sixteenth and early seventeenth centuries witnessed a proliferation of new color terms including *negro atezado* (very black), *membrillo cocido* (stewed quince), *moreno*, *claro* (clear), *mulato*, *leonado* (lionish), etc. Most of these terms were clearly color-focused. Nonetheless there may also have been a tendency in the seventeenth century to broaden the concept of *negro* to encompass lighter shadings. In 1695 a Spaniard stated that it was necessary to include the *negros* captured along the Mediterranean coasts and taken to Sicily as 'infidel *moros*' because 'all these are negros of a lionish (*leonado*) color which is known as *membrillo cocido*, they are *moros* of the religion of Mohammed and it is possible to capture them just as they capture us . . .'.[45] The significant thing here is that these Muslims of *leonado* (lionish) and stewed quince color were called *negros*. Why *negros* if they were not of *negro* color? (*Fulos* (Fulani) were regarded as being of *fulo* color (similar to *membrillo cocido*) although also, on occasion, as *negro*.)

Our analysis must now review the cases where Indians and Americans were called *negro*, since such usage may well imply that the 1695 statement quoted above reflected earlier attitudes as well.

In Valencia one finds in 1504 'Antonio, formerly Sutme, de Calicut, de 12 años' called *negro*; in 1507 'Antonio, de 10 años, de Calicut' called *negro*; in 1515, 'Christóbal, de 18 años, de India' called *negro*; in 1515, 'Neyne, now Francisco, de 22 años, de Calicut' called *negro*; and also in 1515 'Francisco, de 27, de Bombay' and 'Gonzalo, 25, de Chochiti, India' both *negros*. One also finds a few cases where Indians had no color descriptor given or were called *lor* (as with a slave from 'Malaca, India' in 1514). One individual was classed as *lor casi negro* in 1515.[46]

In any case it is clear that Indians were often designated as *negros* in Spain but that a light color might lead to a different designation in a few cases (especially if they were from Malaya).

In so far as Americans are concerned, the pattern is somewhat similar. As noted earlier, many of the slaves from Terranova (Newfoundland) were called *negros*, although some were not categorized at all, and one was classified as *lora*.[47] Other Americans (in Valencia) were classifed thus: 1495: no color mentioned; 1509: from *terra de negros* (Brazil); 1509: *lora* (Brazil); 1512: *negro* (*de Indias*); 1514: no color; 1515: two as *loras oscuras* (Brazil) but also counted as *negros*; 1515: *negros* (Hireo); 1516: 85 from Brazil, as *negros*; 1516: *blanca* (Brazil); 1516: four *blancos* from Paranonpol.[48]

Thus it seems clear that Americans could be described as *negros* in Spain but that other distinctions, such as *loro* or even *blanco*, might on occasion be used.

One must also note the case where *loras oscuras* could be counted as *negros* (1515) because it resembles the 1695 attitude cited above, that is, to somehow use the term *negro* with a double meaning – on the one hand, to refer to black (dark) color and, on the other hand, to point towards some broader concept (such as non-white). My data does not allow for a further clarification of this issue but it is to be suggested that there was a strong tendency to classify all persons originating in the *Tierra de Negros* (Ethiopia or Africa south of the Sahara) as *negros* regardless of actual skin color (for example, Fulanis). By the same token, the concept of *negro* was extended to other tropical and non-Western peoples (if of brown color) but not to the exclusion of the use of other color terms or ethnic names. Moreover, one has to note the Valencian notion (1509) that Brazil was part of the *Terra de negres*.

In 1611 a Spaniard noted that *negro* was

uno de los dos estremos de las colores, opuesto a blanca, Latine niger. Negro: el Etiope de color negra. Es color infausta y triste, y como tal usamos desta palabra, diziendo: negraventura, negra vida, etc. Proverbio: Aunque negros gente somos. . . . En el baño entran todos sin luz, y asi no se pueden distinguir quales son negros, o blancos, sí ellos no se descubren hablando.[49]

Quite clearly, *negro* had negative connotations and was seen as being at an extreme among the colors, opposed to white at the other extreme. Proverbs already existed such as 'although blacks, we are people' and 'in the bath everyone enters without light and therefore one cannot tell who is black or white, unless they are discovered talking'.

Given these ideas it might prove easy to extend *negro* to include unfortunate persons of brown color, especially if being sold as slaves.

It should be noted that during the sixteenth and seventeenth centuries slaves were constantly running away while others were given their freedom. The free people of color could be arrested as fugitives from slavery and if they did not possess a document proving their right to liberty they could be jailed and sold. In 1589 Melchior Díaz, a man 'de color de membrillo cocido, scuro' (*oscuro* or darkish) was arrested. Díaz stated that his father and mother were both free people and that neither they nor any predecessors had been captives or slaves. But 'for being the color he is, it was presumed or pretended that he was a slave'.

Thus a dark skin color was definitely a disadvantage in Spain, when away from friends or neighbours. Similarly, signs of being a Muslim would arouse suspicion.

If a *membrillo cocido* (brown) skin color was a sign of slavery, then it is easy to see how the term *negro* might be extended, in a manner of speaking, to such persons.[50]

In 1579, as noted earlier, Bartolomé Sánchez was captured as a suspected fugitive. He stated that his father was *blanch* and that his mother was a *negra*, 'de las indies de Portugal'. She had been a slave but Sánchez claimed that he himself was free. In spite of being half-white and probably half-American, he was termed a black man (*un home negre*).[51]

The general use of the term *negro* in Spain can also be seen in the instance in c. 1607 when the annals of Seville record that: 'empezó a verse el tabaco; tomábanlo en humo algunos negros bozales'.[52] The new unassimilated *negros* who introduced smoking tobacco to Seville must have been Americans.

In *Indias* (the Americas) the Spanish Crown's official documents seem ordinarily to carefully distinguish between *indios*, *negros* and, after 1550–80, *mulatos* and *mestizos*. Nonetheless numerous American slaves and servants continued to exist even after 1542 and Caribs, Mapuches, and other 'rebel' tribes were being enslaved legally. Moreover, one must assume that many African–American mixed-bloods were categorized as *negros*.

In the early 1560s a Spanish official wrote to the king that

> in the island of Puerto Rico there are above 15,000 negroes and less than 500 Spaniards, and in all of the island of Hispaniola there may be 2,000 Spaniards and there are over 30,000 negroes. . . . the same is the case in the island of Cuba and in Vera Cruz, Puerto de Cavallos, which is in Honduras, and in Nombre de Dios, Carthagena, Santa María, and the coast of Venezuela, where there are twenty negroes to one white man.

It seems certain that the official was using 'white' and 'black' in the sense of 'us' and 'them', that is, those who could be counted on to support Spanish control and those who, because of their status, might aid an enemy. He states specifically that the French could capture Santo Domingo with 500 soldiers 'and by freeing the negroes, most of whom are *ladinos* and natives of the land, and by liberating them, so that they be no longer slaves, they would kill their own masters.' Now how could Africans have been 'natives of the land' at such an early date unless most of them were half-American? Moreover, it is well known that the 'Spaniards' were mostly *mestizos* by that date and that many of the *negros* were actually of mixed ancestry.

It is quite obvious, then, that *negro* was not being used in either a color or racial sense but in the sense of slaves or dangerous 'others'. This is borne out by an estimate for the population of Santo Domingo (Haiti) made in 1560: 5,000 whites, 13,000 mestizos and mulattoes, and 20,000 negroes.[53]

It seems highly likely that the Spaniards referred to slaves generally as *negros* in the Caribbean, partly because the term became the equivalent of 'slave' but also because such usage allowed them to continue to illegally enslave Americans without revealing that fact to the authorities of Spain. It is clear that many Spaniards were extremely reluctant to abandon the enslavement of Americans after 1542.

DUTCH AND GERMAN USAGE

The Dutch may very well have taken up a similar usage, especially since *negro* and *neger* were not originally Dutch words and had no immediate equivalent except *Moor*. Significantly, a Dutch–French–Spanish dictionary of 1639 has the following entry for Spanish *negro*: 'noir, sombre, obscur, offusque, brun' (French) and 'swart, doncker, bruin' (Dutch).

Thus Spanish *negro* could be translated as 'dark' or 'brown' as well as 'black' in the view of a Spaniard residing in Antwerp in the early seventeenth century (the presumed preparer of the dictionary). This ambiguity undoubtedly facilitated making reference to all slaves as *negro* and *neger* in the Dutch language, regardless of precise color, and could have implications for early usage in Virginia (1619–20) when *negers* were purchased from the Dutch.

A Dutch–Spanish dictionary of 1659 also has *Negro* translated as *swert*, *doncker* (dark) or *bruin*, while *morena* is equivalent to *doncker*, *bruin* and *oliijff coleur* (olive color) and *moreno*, *cosa baca* (brown, something dark) is translated as *swert* and *doncker*. The Dutch term *Bruin-brood* (brown bread) equals 'pan moreno, negro, baço, prieto'. Thus wide room for the interpretation of *negro* is apparent. Moreover, it is clear that Iberian intermediate color terms such as *pardo*, *loro* or *moreno* had no equivalent in Dutch except *swert* or *moor*.

It should be noted that for a very long period the Dutch language used *Moor* and *Moriaan* for Black Africans and not *negro* or *neger*. This usage persists from the Middle-Dutch language until the eighteenth century and it undoubtedly reflects the Latin–Romance use of *mouro* for black or dark, as noted. To the

Dutch, *Moor* denoted a black or non-white person, not a Muslim (for whom the work *Turk* seems to have been used in 1639).

A Dutch–French–Latin dictionary of 1573 states: 'eenen Moor = un more = Aethiops, maurus'. During the period from 1450 through 1560 in Antwerp several individuals were identified as *mooren*, one of whom was sketched by Dürer in 1521 and another of whom, Baltasar the Moor, was an American from Brazil. A *zwarten slaaf* (Black slave) may also have been mentioned in 1540.[54]

In the 1550s two Germanic-speaking persons lived in South American, Hans Staden and Ulrich Schmidl. Staden sailed from Portugal in 1547 in a ship which was going to trade with *Weisse Moren* (white moors) of Barbary. He later visited the Cape Verde area where the *Swarte Mooren* lived. In the Pernambuco area Staden mentions '30 Mooren en Brazilaansche Slaven' (30 Moors and Tupí slaves). His translator into Spanish, Edmundo Wernicke, notes that: 'En alemán *Mohr* indica a la persona de cutis obscuro. Los "morenos blancos" eran los "moros" mientras los "morenos negros" eran los africanos en el lenguaje alemán en el siglo XVII.' In other words, *mohr* indicated a non-white or *moreno* person and it could refer to *moros* of North Africa as well as to Black Africans, with suitable modifiers.

The same translator also notes in regards to the reference to '*moren* and Brazilian slaves' that: 'La voz de *Moren* queda explicada como de "africanos" por la de "esclavos" aunque Staden por lo general, a la par de castellanos y Schmidl, usa esa voz tambien como de "indigena".' In short, both Staden and Schmidl utilized the term *moren* to refer to 'natives', as did the Castillians.

In his translation of Schmidl's diary, Wernicke states: '*Mohr* en alemán indica a toda persona de cutis obscuro', that is, that in German *mohr* meant persons of dark skin. Significantly, Staden's diary was published in Dutch (Flemish) at Antwerp in 1558, at Amsterdam in 1563, and three German reprints appeared in the same period.[55]

Filippo Pigafetta's work on the Congo, published in Dutch in 1596, translated Italian 'black' into *swert* and said: 'Of de kinderen van de Portugesen die in dese ghewesten geboren worden van de Vrouwen van Congo, swert, of wit, of geelswert zijn, en dieman Mulacken moemt.' That is, the mixed-blood children of Portuguese men and Congolese women were either black or white or yellow-black (*olivastre, pardo*) and were called *Mulacken* (a Dutch equivalent to *mulatos*). Although *swert* (*swart*) is used in reference to color, the term *Mooren* is used generally for the people from Nubia to Guinea and the Congo. It is also noted that the women, and some of the men, are not *so swart* but are yellowish (*geele*).[56]

The term *Mohren* continued to be used for non-whites. M. Hemmersam's diaries, 1639–45 (published 1663), utilize *Mohren* for both Africans and the Tapuya (*Daboyer*) of Brazil (who are called *wilden Mohren*). He also states: 'So sind die kinder von Geburt nicht Schwartz, wie ihre eltern, sondern bräunlicht, wie die Brasilianer, die aber von Christen und Möhrin erzeuget werden, sind gelblich, wie wachs, und solche nennen sie Mollaken.' The children of *Mohren* of Guinea were not black (at first) but brownish like Brazilians, and those born of Europeans and Africans were yellowish like wax and were called *Mollaken*.[57]

Schoutens, in his voyage to the East Indies, published 1676, refers repeatedly to the *Swarte Indianen* and to *en swarte moeder*, etc. *Mooren* seems to be reserved for Muslims. The *swarte Boeronesen* are mentioned. Thus, *swart* was used for East Indian–Indonesian natives while *moor* was being restricted in meaning, probably due to Portuguese usage.[58] Similarly, the voyage journal of A. O. Exquemelin, originally published 1678, utilizes *negers* and *negros* for Africans and *blanche* or *witte* for whites. But in a later, modernized edition *swartinnen* is used in such a way as to encompass both Americans and Africans, since after describing mixtures of Africans, Americans, and Europeans the modernizer states 'en de meer ander slagh die daer zijn, want de Spanjaerden zijn zeer genegen tot de Swartinnen, meer als tot hun eygen vrouwen.' That is, the Spaniards were said to be more attracted to *swartinnen* (dark or black women) than to their own wives. But the original text states that the Spaniards were more attracted to *negerinnen* (black women) or *getaande Indiaansche vrouwen* (tanned Indian women) than they were to their own European women.[59]

Wintergerst, in his journals (1688–1710, published in 1712), uses *Mohren* in a general sense (to refer to Srilankans, for example) but also uses *Schwartz* to describe East Indians. The inhabitants, he states, of Batavia, Java, were 'Holländer, Mohren und Sinesen' (Dutch, natives, and Chinese). A lady of Cochin was called a *schwartzen Mutter*.[60] De Graaf's journal, published 1704, also uses *Moren* for Indonesians but he refers to 'De Moren of Mahametanen', thus making it clear that *Moren* meant Muslim. In reference to the Javanese and Indonesian wives of Dutchmen, he uses terms such as *een Swarte moeder*.[61]

In the latter part of the seventeenth century, then, the meaning of *moor* began to shift from black or non-white to Muslim, including Muslims of the East Indies. *Swart* began to be used more generally as a term for non-whites, embracing most of the peoples found from India through Indonesia as well as Africans and, occasionally, Americans. Since *moor* and *moren* had also been used for Americans (Antwerp, 1563, and Brazil, 1550s, 1640s), we can see a pattern where both *moor* and *swart* were flexible enough to embrace a broad range of brown to dark brown peoples.

It is significant to note that Staden (1550s) used the term *moor* to refer both to 'white' *moren* and to 'black' *moren*. As we shall see, this is not reflected in most Dutch dictionaries but there are exceptions which need to be noted. First, however, I will cite a French dictionary of 1571 which for *mores* has: 'Libyens, barbares . . . noirs . . . furieus, cruels, vagabonds, nigrites, affricains, . . . numidiens. . . . Il i a deux especes de Mores, à sçavoir noirs & blancs.' Thus there were many negative connotations associated with *more* (such as are also attached to *negro* later) but, more significantly, the author states that there are both 'white' and 'black' *mores*.

A Latin–German dictionary of 1573 also refers to *die weissen Moren* (white moors) although *Aethiopia* is equated with *Morenland*. Ten years later a dictionary states of Ethiopia: 'quasi nigra vel nigredo, Regio Africa'. A 1620

Dutch dictionary defines *Mooren* as: 'Swerte, Barbarische, gekoocte . . . wilde . . . wonderlijcke . . . Lybische . . . ghekrolde, witte, ghele.' Thus negative connotations continue but 'black', 'white' and 'yellow' are color-referents. But what is especially interesting is that from the 1550s until 1620 (in the above sources) only 'white' and 'black' are distinguished for *moren*, brown and intermediate colors being ignored until 'yellow' appears.

Many dictionaries from the low countries continuously equate 'Moor, Maurus; aethiops . . . niger', *Moorman* with *Aethiops* (1588), 'Moor, Moriaen' with 'Un more ou Ethiopien' (1576); *Moor-man* with *Aethiops*; a *moor* horse with *equus niger*; *Moor* with 'Maurus, aethiops: mauros, niger' (1599); and so on.

This tendency continues into the seventeenth century. A 1602 work as well as a 1651 Dutch–French dictionary has *more = eenen Morisch*. A 1701 *woordenboek* has 'Moor, Moriaan = un more, un Etiopien'. Greater detail appears in De la Porte's 1659 Spanish–Dutch edition, wherein we find:

negro = swert/doncker/bruin
negra de la Guinea = Moorinne/oft swarte van Genea
moro = eenen Moor
moreno = doncker/bruin/olijff coleur
morena, cosa baça = swert/Doncker
mezquita [mosque] = turksche kercke [Turkish church].

Thus again, as in 1639, *negro* can be equated with brown and dark as well as black, *moor* is used for a black person as well as a *moro*, and a mosque is called a 'Turkish' church.[62]

A 1691 English–Dutch dictionary has 'moor = *moor*', 'a black-Moor = *een Zwarte, zwarte Mooriaan*', 'a Tawny-Moor = *een Geele Moor*'. Thus English 'tawny' (applied often to Americans) is equated with Dutch *geel* (yellow). A Dutch *woordenboek* of 1704 preserves earlier usage: 'Moriaan, Aethiops . . . Dus noemt men alle mensen die zwart zijn (Thus are called all persons who are black)'.[63]

A 1718 Portuguese–Dutch dictionary is revealing in terms of color connotations. Portuguese *pardo* (applied to Americans) is equated with Dutch *Donkerverwig* and *swartachtig*, i.e., to both darkish and blackish. 'Négro, of Cáfre' is equivalent to 'Een Swart, Moor, Caffer'. *Cáfre* is 'Een Caffer, uit Moorenland'. Thus *swart*, *moor* and now *caffir* (kaffir) are equivalent and *Moorenland* is still used to refer to the 'land of blacks'. As the eighteenth century unfolded *zwart* tended to be used in place of *moor* in Dutch dictionaries but a change can be seen in a 1771 dictionary where the author also uses *neger*: 'Moor, Moriaan, zo danig noemt men zulke mensen die een zwart huid hebben, zo als de Negers, de Ethiopiers enz. (Thus are called such people who have a black skin, such as the negroes, the Ethiopians, etc.).' This would seem to imply that *negers*, Ethiopians, etc. were only examples of *more*.[64]

In 1783 a French–Dutch dictionary states:

More – habitant de la Mauritanie = Moor, Neger, Zwart, Moriaan. Voyez Maure

Maure = Noir, quie est au service de quelque seigneur = Moriaan
Maures ou Mores = Habitans de la Mauritanie = Mooren, inwoners van
Moorenland, Zwarten, Negers
Noir = Zwart
Noir, sombre, obscur = Donker, digt, schaduwagtig
Nègre = Par ce mot on entend esclaves noirs . . . que l'on transporte d'Afrique
dan les plantations de l'Amérique = Neger, Zwart.

The Dutch–French section has:

Neger Z. M. Nègre, More
Negerland zie Moorenland
Moor Z. M. Moriäan, Zwart = more ou Maure, homme noir
Moorenland, Negerland = Mauritanie

Thus this dictionary, prepared by a Dutch author, offers an example of the clear
implication of slave status for *nègre* and also for *neger* and *zwart*. We can also see
that the transition from *moor* to *neger* and *zwart* is being reflected.[65]

By 1844–5 Dutch dictionaries have shifted the meaning of *Moor* to a North
African. In 1913 it was said of *Moor* that it was not in common use as compared
with *neger* and *zwart*. By the latter year also it was noted that *neger* had replaced
negro in the eighteenth century and that: 'By European peoples the negroes
became especially known as slaves in the colonies; from that the word negro
also in our language is a very common term.' Thus the close association of *neger*
with 'slave' is made clear, for the Dutch language. Several other Dutch–French
and Dutch–English dictionaries also list 'slave' as one of the meanings for *nègre*,
negro, *maure* and *zwart*.

Swart (*zwart*) meaning black, as can be seen, was not used as a proper racial
name in Dutch and its application was not restricted to Africans. There is, for
example, an early reference to *de swarte Indianen* (the black Indians) in Sumatra
by a Dutch traveler in addition to the examples cited above. A dictionary of
1728 also translates (American) 'Indian' from French *Indienne* to Dutch
Zwartin. Thus both *moor* and *zwart* were applied to East Indian-Indonesians
and, on occasion, to Americans, as noted.

More recently Asian contract laborers imported into Dutch colonies have on
at least one occasion been referred to as *negerkoelies* (negro-coolies). It is also
significant that the term *zwart* (black) or *zwartje* is used by some in the
Netherlands today to refer to all non-white or non-European people in much
the same way that people in Britain currently use the word 'black'.[66]

USAGE IN ENGLISH

By the sixteenth century the English and Scots were referring to the people of
Africa as Moors, and then later as Blackamoors, Ethiopians, and negroes. In
1591 Richard Percivale equated Spanish *mora* with 'a woman black-Moore' and

morillo with 'browne, a little black Moore'. Percivale was greatly amplified by Minsheu in 1599 and we find the following:

Moŕe, vide Moŕo, a blacke Moore
Morisca, a woman Moore that is become a Christian
Morisco, a blacke Moore made or become a Christian
Morádo color, murrey or yron colour, darke colour
Morél, browne duskish colour
a Moore, v. Móro
a Blacke moore, vide Aŕabe, Négro
Negrillo, a little blacke Moore, somewhat blacke
Negrito, idem
Négro, blacke Also a black Moore of Ethiopia
Prieto, or negro, blacke, browne.

These translations reveal a great deal of flexibility, in that both *moro* and *negro* are equated with 'blackmoore' while 'blackmoore' is equated with 'Arab' as well as *morisco* and *negro*, and *prieto* and *negro* are equated with 'browne' as well as black. In 1617 Minsheu equated Latin *maurus* with 'Niger, black' and in another place stated: 'Moore or Neger = a Moore, or one of Mauritanie, a black Moore, or Neger . . . vid. a Neger and Black Moore and Ethiopian'. 'Negro' gradually came to be a common term, especially after extensive contact with the Spanish and the Portuguese.[67] What is not clear is the extent to which the term *negro* was consciously translated as 'black'. The automatic association of *negro* with 'black' color cannot be assumed for the reasons discussed thus far and since even many 'Black' Africans are actually of medium or dark brown color.

In any case, another association gradually arose in North America and that was between 'negro' and 'slave'. Early legislation commonly referred to 'negro and other slaves' or to 'negro, mulatto, and Indian slaves'. Over the years 'negro' and 'black' both became synonymous with enslavement.

In 1702 an observer wrote that the wealth of Virginia consisted in 'slaves or negroes'. But 1806 Virginia judges ruled that a person who was of a white appearance was to be presumed free but 'in the case of a person visibly appearing to be of the slave race, it is incumbent upon him to make out his freedom.' In 1819 South Carolina judges stated flatly: 'The word "negroes" has a fixed meaning (slaves).'[68]

What the English meant by the term 'negro' when they first began to use it is not clear. Certainly, it was not then synonymous with 'slave' as a great many persons so classified were free, both in England and in Virginia. Did it mean an African, a 'black' person, or any dark-skinned individual? Today the term is not widely employed in Britain, although the word 'black' is used to refer to people of various skin colors from all of south Asia, the Middle East, the West Indies, and Africa. Most unmixed American Indians, if living in Britain today, would be regarded as being 'black' especially if their ancestry were not known.

Several illustrations can be cited to show that not only Africans but also

Americans and Asians were called 'black' or 'negro' in Britain itself in the seventeenth and eighteenth centuries. In 1621 a William Bragge claimed compensation from the 'Company of East India and Summer Islands' for several expenses, including 'for thirteen Negroes or Indian people, six women, seven men and boys. . . . And so much in the name of God as touching that Businesse, and touching the Negroes or Indians.' [Bragge hadn't wanted to sell the captives and refused to value them.][69] In 1688 the *London Gazette* carried an advertisement for: 'A black boy, an Indian, about thirteen years old, run away the 8th. Inst. from Putney, with a collar about his neck with this inscription: "The Lady Bromfield's black." '[70]

In 1709 *The Tatler* carried an advertisement for 'A Black Indian Boy, 12 years of Age'. Similar usage of language is also found in the play *Mangora*, written by Thomas Moore in 1718. In a scene taking place in Paraguay an American warrior chant to an American woman: 'Black beauty come on, I must love thee or none, You see my Face black.'[71]

A student of the history of black people in Britain has written that:

It should be borne in mind that the word *Negro* in this period [1600s] could mean an Asian as well as an African (or other person of African descent). Sometimes a performer [in pageants] is identified as one or the other, or the costume provides a clue though black performers were often required to personate American "Indians".

It seems highly likely that the term 'negro' was used in a very broad manner, especially since it had no more specific color meaning in English than would the words 'African' or 'Indian'. The term 'black' was also used in a broad manner.

In March 1765 English newspapers carried stories about a Native American preacher discovered and helped by the Rev. George Whitfield. This preacher was the famous Samson Occom, a Mohegan from New England. The newspapers referred to him as 'a Black' who could speak English very well and who had preached to crowded audiences. Occom sailed to England that year.

An American did not have to go to England to be called 'black', however. In Connecticut, in 1711, a family of 'Indian servants' consisting in one Rachel and her seven children, were distributed by will and were called 'blacks'.[72]

The 'British habit of calling yellow, brown, or red people "Black" ' is commented upon by Wylie Sypher in his *Guinea's Captive Kings*.[73]

Some examples will now be cited from the Americas to illustrate the use of 'negro' and 'black' in English as applied to people of American ancestry.

An example from the West Indies is useful. In 1764 William Young was sent to St Vincent as a part of the British occupation of that island. Living on St Vincent were about 3,000 'Black Charaibs, or free negroes', about one hundred 'Red Charaibs or Indians' and some 4,000 French and their slaves, according to Young. The British found it difficult to control the Caribs and wars were fought with them in 1771–2 and again during 1795–6. During the latter crisis Young wrote an extremely anti-Carib tract designed to prove that the Caribs (the Garifuna) should be removed from St Vincent. The latter were eventually defeated and some 5,000 were shipped to an island near the coast of Honduras.

Young was anxious to prove that the so-called 'Black' Caribs were not true aborigines but were in fact 'Negro Colonists', Free Negroes, or 'negro usurpers'. This was important to him because he wanted to show that they had no bona fide land rights or aboriginal title.

For our purposes, the interesting point admitted by Young is that the so-called 'Blacks' or 'Negroes' were occasionally of 'tawney and mixed complexion' because of American ancestry and that their customs, personal names, and language were those of the native Garifuna. Still further, Young admitted that they had repeatedly intermarried with American women. He consistently refers to them as 'Negroes' nonetheless. Young also relayed a great deal of hearsay information about how the 'Black' Caribs had originated which is without foundation for analysis here. The important point is this: that a people thoroughly American in identity, culture, and language were called 'black' and 'negro' solely because of being mixed with African ancestry.[74] This tendency continues, incidentally, among white scholars who, even today, often refuse to accept the Garifunas' avowed feelings of 'Indianness' and continue to call them 'Black'.[75]

In 1619 some twenty 'negroes' were brought to Virginia. At least eleven have names of Spanish or probable Spanish character. Later they were joined by 'negroes' and 'mulattoes' with names such as Antonio (several) and John Pedro. These Spanish-derived servants could well have been of part-American ancestry, however, no evidence is available except that they were largely secured from captured Spanish vessels.[76]

In 1676 one Gowin, 'an Indian servant', acquired his freedom in Virginia. Two decades earlier Mihill Gowen, called 'a negro', also acquired his freedom. It would appear that the 'negro' was probably father to the 'Indian' in this case.[77]

In 1670 the population of the Virginia colony was said to be 40,000 including 2,000 'black slaves'. Evidence indicates that there could not have been that many Africans there and also that there were a great many American slaves or servants. Thus the total of 'blacks' must have included a good many Americans.[78]

In 1698 three fugitive 'negroes' were reported in North Carolina, of whom one was an American.[79] Similarly, a list of 'Negroes' imported into Virginia, 1710–18, by sea includes at least 69 'Indians', mostly from the Carolinas. Likewise, lists of 'negroes' brought into New York from 1715 to 1736 include many slaves of probable (or stated) American ancestry from Campeche, Jamaica, Honduras, the Carolinas, and Virginia.[80]

In the 1715–17 period the Vestry Book of King William parish, Virginia, records one year 'Robin, Indian' and two years later, 'Robin, negro'.[81] In a similar manner a 1691 list of 'negro' slaves in York County, Virginia, includes 'Kate Indian' while a 1728 list of 'Negroes' at the 'home house' of a Virginia planter includes 'Indian Robin'. (Robin, incidentally, is a common name for slaves of American ancestry.) In 1748 there was an advertisement in New York for a 'Negro man servant called Robin, almost of the complexion of an Indian . . .

talks good English can read and write, and plays on the fiddle'.[82] In 1723 Virginia adopted a law depriving free 'negroes, mulattoes, and Indians' of certain basic civil rights. The act was disallowed by British officials but in 1735 Lt-Governor Gooch defended it by asserting that he wanted to make 'a perpetual brand upon free negroes and mulattoes by excluding them from that great privilege of a Freeman'. He wished to make the 'free negroes sensible that a distinction ought to be made between their offspring and the descendents of an Englishman, with whom they never were to be accounted equal.'[83] Since the act applied to Native Americans and half-Americans ('mulattoes'), Gooch's language would seem to include them under the general category of 'free negroes and mulattoes'.

A welcome clarification of terminology was provided in 1719 by the government of South Carolina when it decided: 'and for preventing all doubts and scruples that may arise what ought to be rated [taxed] on mustees, mulattoes, etc . . . all such slaves as are not entirely Indian shall be accounted as negroe.'[84] The significance of this act is, of course, that all later enumerations of 'negro' and 'Indian' slaves in South Carolina have to be analyzed with the thought in mind that any 'negroes' could be one-half or other fractions of American ancestry.

New Jersey was also an area where Americans and Africans intermixed with considerable frequency. In 1734 an advertisement appeared for the recovery of 'Wan [Juan?]. He is a half Indian and half negro; . . . he plays the fiddle and speaks good English and his country Indian.' Wan was not specifically called a 'negro' but in a 1747 advertisement we read:

Runaway on the 20th of September last, from Cohansie a very lusty negro fellow named Sampson, aged about 53 years, and had some Indian blood in him. . . . he had with him a boy about 12 or 13 years of age named Sam, was born of an Indian woman, and looks like an Indian, only his hair. . . . they both talk Indian very well, and it is likely they have dressed themselves in the Indian dress and gone to Carolina.

Similarly in a 1778 advertisement we read:

Was stolen from her mother, a negro girl, about 9 or 10 years of age, named Dianah, her mother's name is Cash, was married to an Indian named Lewis Wollis, near six feet high, about 35 years of age. They have a male child with them, between 3 and 4 years of age. Any person who takes up the said negroes and Indian . . . shall have the above reward.[85]

From these examples we can see that people of mixed American–African ancestry could be called 'negroes' in New Jersey. Cyrus Bustill, a Philadelphia baker ('black') born in 1732 in Burlington, New Jersey, married a Delaware Indian woman. His son became a Quaker and an anti-slavery leader and was known as a 'negro'.[86]

In Canada in 1747 four 'Negroes' and a 'Panis' (American slave) escaped from Montreal. A French writer referred to them simply as 'negroes'.[87]

Quite clearly persons having American ancestry, or the appearance of it, could be called negroes in Virginia. In 1774 one Robert Chavers, a fiddler, ran away from the south branch of the Meherrin River in Mecklenburg County. He was called 'a negro man' but the Chavers name is common among Lumbee and other Native American groups in nearby North Carolina. In 1773 Tom, 'a Negro man' of a 'yellowish complexion, much the appearance of an Indian' ran away. His hair 'is of a different kind from that of a Negro's, rather more of the Indian's.' In 1777 John Twopence 'a Negro man' ran away in Essex County from the Blandfield estate of Robert Beverley. Twopence was 'of a yellowish complexion'. The name Twopence is a common one among Americans in King William County at a later date.[88]

In 1759 one Saunders, a runaway slave, was described in South Carolina as a 'Negro man . . . of the mustee breed'. 'Mustee' meant either European–American or American–African. In 1775 the authorities in South Carolina were ordered to apprehend 'John Swan, a reported free negro or mestizo man'. In South Carolina other runaway slave advertisements show that the child of a mustee woman was called a negro (1738), and that a 'negro man' was said to have had Indian blood (1748), and that mustee men were referred to as negroes or as one of a group of negroes (1756, 1760, twice in 1761).[89]

East Indians could also be termed 'negro' in Virginia. In 1786 an advertisement speaks of 'an East India negro man called Jean, a slave born. He speaks French and English and will call himself free.'[90] In the 1780s certain white Virginians began to agitate for the termination of the Gingaskin Indian Reservation in Northampton County. The reserve was described as an 'asylum for free negroes' and it was alleged that the Americans 'have at length become nearly extinct, there being at this time not more than 3 or 4 genuine Indians at most . . . the place is a harbour and convenient asylum for an idle set of free negroes.' In 1812 it was argued that: 'the place is now inhabited by as many black men as Indians. . . . the Indian women have many of them married black men, and a majority probably, of the inhabitants are blacks or have black-blood in them . . . the real Indians [are few].' The reserve was divided (allotted) in 1813 and by 1832 whites had acquired most of it. In 1828 the Gingaskin descendants were described as respectable 'Negro landowners'.[91]

This episode reminds one of Young's attack upon the Caribs of St Vincent in 1795 and also of more recent attempts to allot and acquire Indian lands. A similar attack took place upon the Pamunkey-Mattaponi in 1843 (which failed) and against the Nottoway from 1830 to 1878 (which succeeded). By the 1840s at least two Nottoways were registered as 'free negroes'. The heirs of one family were described in 1878 as 'all being negroes and very poor'.[92]

Aside from Virginia, where persons descended from female Americans imported after a certain date could obtain their freedom, all slaves of American ancestry remained slaves throughout the entire duration of slavery unless they were emancipated or ran away. At the end of the eighteenth century 'Bob, a carpenter fellow, of a yellowish complexion, mustee, has bushy hair' ran away. He was said to speak 'more proper than Negroes in general'.[93]

Other persons of American ancestry who were free also were called 'black' or 'negro'. Paul Cuffe, the noted half-American, half-African merchant was called, at various times, an Indian, 'a blackman', and 'this free and enlightened African'; he signed petitions with 'Indian men' and 'all free Negroes and mulattoes'.[94] Other examples of a similar nature abound; one author writes that: 'the Sampsons and Gallees, property owners and school teachers, though predominantly of Indian blood were leaders among the free Negroes of Petersburg, Virginia, in 1860.'[95]

Virginia tax-rolls and census records from the 1780s to 1850 have numerous examples of people of Indian tribal identity being classified as 'free people of color' or as 'mulattoes'; in fact, the practice was almost universal. Nonetheless, some were also classified as F.N. (free negro) or as 'B' (black) in various records. In certain counties (such as Southampton) in 1830, and in parts of Delaware virtually all free non-whites were categorized as 'F.N.' although enumerated under the 'free people of color' column. These lists included people of the Nanticoke and other tribal groups.[96]

Under certain conditions persons of African descent could be legally classified as members of an Indian tribe or as Indians. In a treaty with the Creek nation the Commissioner of Indian Affairs noted in 1832:

an Indian, whether of full or half blood, who has a female slave living with him as his wife, is the head of a family and entitled to a reservation (of land) . . . also . . . free blacks who have been admitted as members of the Creek Nation, and are regarded as such by the tribe, if they have families are entitled to reservations of land.

In the 1860s all persons of African ancestry who had been slaves were granted, by treaty, citizenship in the 'five civilized tribes' of Indian Territory. The general trend, however, was to enroll the more visibly part-African persons as 'Freedman' citizens and to restrict their tribal status. When lands were allotted in the 1880s to the early 1900s most such persons were not allowed to assert American ancestry and were, therefore, denied future rights as 'Indians'.[97]

During the Seminole wars a new term seems to have been coined, that of 'Indian–Negroes'. One source, General Wiley Thompson, asserted in 1835 that 'they are descended from the Seminoles, and are connected by consanguinity.' Other writers referred to them as the 'hostile negroes and mulattoes in the seminole nation' or simply, 'Indian–negro'.[98] However, in the Euchee language mixed people of that type were referred to as *Goshpi-tchala* or 'Red-Black People'.[99]

In North Carolina many people of Lumbee Indian identity were categorized, at times, as 'negroes'. In 1837 Charles Oxendine of Robeson County was punished as 'a free negro'. In 1842 one of the Braveboy family was called a 'negro' while in 1857 a Chavers was charged as 'a free person of color' with carrying a shotgun. He was not convicted because the act specified 'free negroes' and he was charged as a 'free colored'. The court stated that 'Free persons of color may be . . . persons colored by Indian blood . . . the indictment cannot be sustained.'[100]

In a similar situation, some white men took away guns from the Pamunkey people in Virginia in 1857. The governor had them returned but stated: 'If any become one fourth mixed with the negro race then they may be treated as free negroes or mulattoes.' (Virginia at this time defined a 'mulatto' as one-fourth or more African.)[101]

In Louisiana in 1856 the 'Black Code' was said to refer to offenses involving 'slaves, Indians, and free persons of color.'[102] Many narratives of ex-slaves recorded in the 1830s reveal Indian ancestry. One such person, called an Indian, was Uncle Moble Hopsan of Virginia. He says: 'et come time tuh marry' and he married a black woman. 'Dat mak me black, ah' 'spose.'[103]

In 1871 a white writer of Maryland observed:

In this (Dorchester) county at Indian Creek, some of the last Indians of the peninsula struck their wigwams towards the close of the last century, and there are now no full-blooded aborigines on the Eastern Shore, although many of the free-born negroes show Indian traces.[104]

Quite commonly, however, some of the 'free-born negroes' of the Eastern Shore continued to identify with and survive as Native People. The whites often tried to deny their Indianness, as in 1856 when a marker was erected to commemorate a woman who had testified that the Nanticoke people of Delaware had African ancestry. The Indians were referred to on the marker as 'arrogant negroes that assumed to be what they were not.'[105]

During the eighteenth century most persons of mixed race, especially if free, were classified as mulattoes, mustees, or persons of color. The term 'negro' was perhaps less likely to be used for such people, except as noted in the examples above. This usage continued in some states – such as the Carolinas and Virginia – well into the nineteenth century. For example, the jurists of South Carolina noted in 1852: 'It is not according to the use of language in this region to speak of one altogether black as a person of color. The phrase is almost exlusively applied to one of mixed blood and color.'[106] Nonetheless, a change took place in such states as Indiana (1817), Kentucky (1852), and elsewhere (1850s – early 1900s) as the term 'negro' came to encompass most persons of part-African descent.[107]

This change may not have affected dark people of solely African and American descent, especially if the African ancestry predominated. Since many (but not all) Native Americans were 'brown' or dark-colored *without* African ancestry, many of their descendants when mixed *only* with African blood would very likely be seen as 'negroes' by most Europeans (especially in North America where special terms for such persons – such as *Zambo*, *Grifo*, *Lobo*, *Cafuso*, *Cabra*, and *Caboré* – never became current, and where 'mustee' ceased to be used and 'mulatto' changed its meaning).[108]

The United States census also tended to expand the use of the terms 'black' and 'negro'. In 1890 'black' was to be used for all persons having three-fourths or more 'black blood'. In 1910 'black' was supposed to be applied only to 'full-blooded negroes' while the matter of who was an Indian was left to the enumerator. The term 'mulatto' was to be used for 'all other persons having some proportion or perceptible trace of negro blood'. It is certain that large numbers of Americans or part-Americans were classified as negro or mulatto under these rules. For example, of the Mattaponi only one person was counted as 'Indian' by the census out of a reservation population of at least forty persons. Similarly, the Poosepatuck of Long Island had only one person counted as 'Indian', doubtless because the rest were enumerated as negroes or mulattoes.

The 1910 census counted '2,255 negroes' who were part-Indian and were enrolled members of tribes. Another group of 1,793 tribal members were of mixed European, African and American ancestry. Thus only slightly more than 3,000 persons who were part-African were counted with the Indian population, as compared with the hundreds of thousands who were doubtless counted as 'negro' or 'mulatto' because of living away from a federally recognized reservation area.

In 1930 a person of mixed Indian and Negro blood 'shall be returned as a Negro unless the Indian blood predominates and the status as an Indian is generally accepted in the community.' By 1940 all African–American hybrids were to be counted as 'negroes' unless the Indian ancestry 'very definitely predominates and he is universally accepted . . . as an Indian.'[109]

Even 'pure-blood' Indians could be counted as 'blacks', as in Nevada in 1880 when the census enumerator categorized ninety members of the Duckwater Shoshone Tribe in that manner. In the state of Delaware more recent decades found that 'if a person said he was an Indian, he was recorded as either black or white depending upon his appearance'.[110]

The instructions for the 1980 census indicated that any person checking both the 'black' and 'Indian' boxes was counted solely as 'black', although in oral interviews the race mentioned first for the mother of the respondent would be the one counted. More significantly a long list of countries was supplied to census-takers, with the appropriate category to be counted instead of the country name. A large number of countries, including Trinidad and virtually all of the West Indies, were arbitrarily assigned to the 'black' category. Thus Americans or part-Americans from Aruba, Trinidad or Dominica would be counted as 'blacks'.

Significantly not a single country was assigned to the 'Indian' category, including Guatemala, Bolivia, Peru and Paraguay. Clearly the census methods in 1980 had the effect of minimizing the count of 'Indians'.[111]

In summary, it seems clear that many persons of Native American ancestry, in whole or part, have been at times classified as 'negroes' or 'blacks', in the several languages reviewed. This is a matter of considerable significance for the scholar seeking to understand the actual ethnic or racial identity of non-white persons in the slave trade, in the American colonies and in the United States over the centuries.

It would appear that the terms *moor*, *negro*, *zwart*, 'black', etc., must be used very carefully in historical, sociological, and anthropological writing. To discover the actual ethnicity of persons so categorized one must know the specific geographical location from which they were derived. Of course it is no doubt true that the majority of such persons were usually derived from Africa but it remains an empirical question as to how many were from India, the East Indies and the Americas, especially during certain time periods.

It is especially important, of course, that census data and other enumerations be utilized very carefully since it is quite clear that the category of *negro* almost always included people who were not of purely African descent. This is especially true in Brazil and the United States area but also may be applicable to Spanish-speaking regions.

Such a conclusion will come as no surprise to many people in the Afroamerican community of the United States who have long been aware of extensive Indian ancestry and who have, at least since the Civil War, self-consciously utilized the terms 'negro' or 'black' (and, of course, 'colored') to encompass people of mixed Native American and African descent. Individuals such as Ann Plato, Paul Cuffe, Crispus Attucks, Hiram Revels, and many others have long been referred to as 'negroes' in spite of having perhaps at least as much Native American as African ancestry – and even when living in Indian communities, as was the case with Attucks and Cuffe.

From a scholarly perspective, the 'logic' of evolving white racism (which has tended to classify people in very arbitrary ways) is neither the logic of genetics nor of bona fide ethnicity. The mixture of African and American does not make a person 'black' or 'negro' any more than it makes one automatically 'Indian'. Modern scholars must aver that it is both pernicious and dangerous to read into the evidence, and to affirm for earlier times, the pronouncements of a dominant social caste. Their myths, their prejudices, and their systems of classification and nomenclature must all be subjected to critical and empirical re-evaluation.

This necessity for radical reinterpretation will become still clearer as we proceed to discuss terms used for brown colored persons.

4

Loros, Pardos and *Mestizos*: Classifying Brown Peoples

ASPECTS OF COLOR PERCEPTION: CULTURAL AND
INDIVIDUAL VARIATION

The classification of human beings according to their skin color and other physical characteristics is a very important subject but one which has yielded a great deal of confusion and controversy.

One of the basic problems involved arises from the concept of color itself and, for humans, from the problem of describing intermediate colors, that is, those falling between the extremes of white and black. This difficulty may well arise from the weaknesses of certain languages in terms of their lacking appropriate words, as well as in the complex philosophical and physical issues surrounding the nature of the perception of color.

It is to be understood that, even as the Inuit (Eskimo) languages have very fine distinctions relating to ice and snow, distinctions totally lacking in many languages, so too we may find languages which fail to make distinctions for a whole range of colors typical of human skin. We may find instead a very unsatisfactory use of a few overworked words – such as yellow, white and black – which are applied to colors which other cultures might perhaps see as not being at all yellow, white or black.

It may well be that most color terms evolved in connection with such practical tasks as one would find in the tattooing and painting of the body or, later, the painting of cave walls, murals, statues, canvases, dyeing of cloth, and so on. In any case, all of these practices would involve the use of dyes or pigments which, by their very nature, are of a different order from the colors of the human skin. Black and white when mixed as pigments may produce gray, but when 'black' and 'white' humans mix the result is usually some type of 'brown'.

In any case, we can argue that most or all color terms developed to describe practical uses, of which the classification of human beings was not one. Moreover, color terms native to a particular language seem to often be relatively few in number and are often used symbolically to stand for a range of shades or objects. For example, the 'Greengrocer' sells 'greens' (*groenten*) which are often not green at all (but which can be purplish, grayish, reddish, multicolored, and so on). Thus 'green' has come to symbolize the world of growing 'vegetable' things (as well as many other things, envy, the 'green light', and so on).

It would appear that people living in the Mediterranean zone developed an early awareness of different human skin colors, as witness the ancient Kemi (Egyptian) mural paintings showing the majority people of Kem (the Blackland) as reddish-brown and other peoples as darker brown or black, light or reddish-white, and so on. Other groups such as the Hellenes (Greeks), Canaanites (Phoenicians–Carthaginians) and Romans must also have been aware of intermediate shades between black and white although perhaps not always being concerned with fine distinctions.

The Arabic language, on the other hand, developed a number of terms for human skin color. In *c.*1500, for example, we find these correspondences between Castillian and the Arabic of Granada, beginning with darker shades and proceeding towards lighter (the Arabic being written in the then current Castillian orthography):

negro [black] = açuéd, cuedĭn (pl.)
negra assi = céude, ceudĭn
negro assi = aqhál, cóhal
negro de Guinea = açuéd min Quinágua
negro assi = azmár, çúmar
negra de Guinea = çamra, çúmar
negro un poco [a little black] = ḳamrĭ, ḳamriĭn
loro entre blanco y negro [loro between white and black] = ḳamrĭ, ḳamriĭn
loro que tira a negro [loro which leans towards black] = borgóĭi, borgóĭin

The above are not the only color terms used for people in Arabic as, for example, there is an expression 'the black and the red' which is said to mean 'all mankind': *al ahmar*, the red and *al-aswad*, the black. *Ahmar* means red, red-colored, ruddy, rosy, and pink. Another color, moving in a darker direction, is *ḳamrĭ*, translated above as *loro* and 'a little black', but rendered elsewhere as 'golden brown, reddish brown, bronze-colored (actually, wine-colored)' from a root meaning to ferment. This term is also said by an Egyptian informant to refer to the common skin color of modern Egyptians, meaning 'light black' and being a favorable skin color.

The next term is *asmar*, meaning 'less than black' or, in modern times, a polite way (a more favorable way) of referring to very dark persons who might otherwise be called 'black'. There are several words for 'black', 'dark', and such terms, but the one often used for Black Africans (aside from *asmar*) is *aswad*. Modern Arabic dictionaries use *ahmar* for the 'red' in 'Red Indian'.

In any case, one can see that Arabic has had terms corresponding to Castillian *negro* and *loro* but in addition, has had *asmar* meaning probably *loro casi negro* and *ahmar* (red) for *rufo*. These are in addition to *abiad* for white and relative color terms (dark, and so on).[1] Thus it would appear that Arabic may be one of the richer of the modern Mediterranean languages in color terminology as applied to human beings.

As will be indicated, the Romance-speaking areas by the 1200s–1400s were using a number of terms to refer to intermediate human colors, such as *olivegno*, *louro*, *pardo*, *berretino*, *rufo*, and others. Farther north, in the Netherlands and elsewhere, there seem to have been few such terms. An interesting feature of this lack is the failure of *bruin*, *bruni*, 'brown' to develop as a common term, resort being had almost always to white or black or more rarely to some relative concept such as *doncker*, 'darker'. On occasion, 'yellow' was also used to describe brownish persons by the Dutch in the seventeenth century.

Ludwig Wittgenstein asks:

Why don't we speak of a "pure" brown? Is the reason merely the position of brown with respect to the other "pure" colours, its relationship to them all? . . . Also: brown contains black – (?) – How would a person have to behave for us to say of him that he knows a *pure*, *primary* brown? . . .

What does, "Brown contains black", mean? There are more and less blackish browns. Is there one which isn't blackish at all? There certainly isn't one that isn't *yellowish* at all(?) . . . dark and "blackish" are not the same concept. . . .

Why is it that a dark yellow doesn't have to be perceived as "blackish", even if we call it dark? . . .

Darkness is not called a colour. In paintings darkness *can* also be depicted as black.

The perception of color is a complex subject, the complexity stemming both from fundamental 'physical' and perceptual issues and from social–cultural training or conditioning. As Josef Albers has said:

In visual perception color is almost never seen as it really is . . . as it physically is. . . . In order to use color effectively it is necessary to recognize that color deceives continually . . . it should be learned that one and the same color evokes innumerable readings. . . . If one says "Red" . . . and there are 50 people listening, it can be expected that there will be 50 reds in their minds. And one can be sure that all these reds will be very different.

Everyday language seems to deal with color in a very imprecise and often symbolical manner. 'White' is, of course, a good example since probably few if any human beings are 'white'. That is, white is a 'blank' color with, one could say, no color at all. It is significant that in recent centuries white people have coined the expression 'colored' people to refer to non-whites, thus stating (indirectly at least) that whites are indeed 'uncolored' or 'blank' people. (English 'blank' simply meant 'white'.)

But the fact remains that people called 'white' are perhaps never white. They may be pinkish, light grayish, creamy, very light brown, ruddy reddish, and so on, but not truly 'white'. Thus 'white' as applied to humans is usually symbolic or non-specific. 'Black' can also be seen as a symbolic or non-specific color since few, if any, humans are actually 'black'.

The contrast between 'white' and 'black' must have been enhanced by the use of parchment (blank) with ink (black) for writing as well as by other contrasts occurring naturally. But the application of the term 'white' to humans must have arisen from contrasts with people who were of darker color and doubtless arose as a very gross, non-specific differentiation. The use of white as a referent for most Europeans must have arisen from a poverty of more precise ('off-white') color terms or a disinterest in fine distinctions.

But the problems of color classification may actually extend to a deeper level of analysis. Ludwig Wittgenstein has commented that:

In everyday life we are virtually surrounded by impure colours. All the more remarkable that we have formed the concept of *pure* colours. . . . We must always bear in mind the question: How do people learn the meaning of colour names? . . . And indeed the pure colours do not even have special commonly used names, that's how unimportant they are to us. . . . The logic of the concept of colour is just much more complicated than it might seem . . . not all colour concepts are logically of the same kind.

The concept of color must be related to problems of perception.

The colour concepts are to be treated like the concepts of sensations. . . . In my room I am surrounded by objects of different colours. . . . The place is whitish (because the light wall makes the brown table lighter here), at any rate it is much lighter than the rest of the table, but, given a number of colour samples, I wouldn't be able to pick out one which had the same coloration as this area of the table. . . . Therefore: From the fact that this table seems brown to everyone, it does not follow that it is brown. But just what does it mean to say, "This table isn't really brown after all?" So *does* it then follow from its appearing brown to us, that it is brown?

There is an indefiniteness about colors.

'The colours' are not things that have definite properties, so that one could straight off look for or imagine colours that we don't yet know, *or* imagine someone who knows different ones than we do.

In fact, it is probably true that the greater number of colors (shades) as seen by the eye (and especially shades of skin) have no names, the meaningless term 'flesh' (meat) colored sometimes being used with obvious inaccuracy.

One problem is that colors as pigments (dyes) separately do not at all resemble skin colors and, when mixed, they only serve to approximate to such colors. More importantly, what are the names for the newly created, mixed, colors?

Let us imagine that someone were to paint nature and in its natural colors. Every bit of the surface of such a painting has a definite color. What color? How do I determine its name?

Anyone who takes the time to carefully look at another human being or at one's own body will immediately be struck by the fact that *there is no single color at all*. This is true even in relatively even-spread light. But what is also noticeable is that the effect of lighting radically changes the perception of color.

In short, most or all human beings are of uneven or mixed color to begin with and their color changes with changes in light, at different times of day, whether inside or outdoors, and in relation to clothing, and surroundings. (Exposure to the sun also, of course, often results in tanning, that is, darkening.)

This problem of perception is compounded by the fact that human colors move from the light cream tones of some Europeans to the near-black tones of some Africans (and others) in an unbroken progression providing no clear marking-points for guiding us as to when to switch from gross 'white' to gross 'brown' and so on.

This unbroken stream of color conforms to no known series of color terms, simply because such would require an infinity of terms which remain uninvented. Moreover, the stream actually seems to this writer to possess several currents depending upon whether, for example, a yellow *seems* to underlay a brown or brown-black, or whether a reddish tone *seems* to come through the brown or brown-black, or whether it is a gray undertone (or overlay), and so on. It is not always possible to compare, for example, the relative lightness or darkness of a particular brown-skinned person because of the indefinably mixed character of the color shades. Imitative pictures may be created but they also have to be arbitrarily arranged and lack names. Whether, in fact, numerical values (on a scale) can be accurately assigned to such colors is a subject I won't go into here, except to note that it has no practical relationship to the naming of such shades by humans, in any case.

How subjective is the perception of color? How culturally determined is the perception of color? Ralph Hattersley describes a phenomenon of 'sleeping eyes' called gray adaptation.

Scientists describe it as the habit of seeing a given gray thing as gray, no matter what color the light source used for viewing it. . . . Gray adaptation also refers to the habit of seeing hues, especially gray ones, as more gray or achromatic than they actually are. That is, our brains 'dechromatize' hues pushing them towards neutral.

It would seem that cultural factors might encourage a similar tendency to fail to recognize shades of brown (off-white to brown-black). In short, a process of 'white adaptation' and 'black adaptation' may be characteristic of cultures which were (or are) 'lazy' in distinguishing browns. (In this connection it is worth noting that *pardo*, used for brownish shades in Portuguese and Spanish, also was used for the gray color of wool.)

Hattersley notes further that the majority of (Western?) people have eyes that are barely awake to color. A modest number are, however, 'halfway' awake.

They see hues even in colors that are assumed to have no hues, that is, in the blacks, grays, and whites. And they readily see that a given dark brown color may actually be a low-value yellow, orange, red, or magenta.

Such variation could also be cultural, that is, influenced by the perceptual-descriptive habits of a particular people.

In this connection also Josef Albers has shown that even some art students cannot successfully distinguish lighter and darker light intensity without practice: 'only a minority can distinguish the lighter from the darker within close intervals when obscured by contrasting hues or by different color intensities.'

'Color' is extremely important to us because it gives visual shape and size to all phenomena. Colorless objects are invisible to us, as anyone can affirm who has ever tried to walk through a spotlessly clean clear-glass door!

To be colored, to have color, is to be visible.

But what, indeed, is color? Is it a 'sensation' similar to hot and cold, sweet and sour, hard and soft, and so on?

Some would say that we do not 'see' colored objects, since we do not 'look out' from our eyes upon objects at a distance. On the contrary, according to one level of analysis, reflected light from the object is presumed to somehow stimulate our eyes and connected nerves to send the brain (or mind) a message *about* the object, not the object itself.

In the mind, in some manner, the message is decoded and transformed into a colored, presumed representation of the object.

It is the representation in the mind which is colored, not the object itself. Since we (our minds) have no *direct* contact with the object we cannot say that color is a characteristic which is inherent in the object. Instead, it is a characteristic of *viewing* the object, an act occurring as a part of a 'physical' transaction with the mind. By means of color, we experience visibility, differentiation, spacing, and forming as a mental function.

Of course, one problem with this type of analysis is that it fails to deal with the question of what is left of an object after color is removed. Or, to put it differently, this type of dualistic analysis separates (artificially I would think) the mind's 'seeing' from the presumed 'objective' world 'outside' the mind. Such a view cannot be sustained, in all probability, since the various 'pieces' of the transaction between 'mind' and 'object' are all equally perceived in the mind and nowhere else known to us. That is, the eye, the optic nerves, the nervous system, the brain, the light waves, and light itself (including heat) are all perceptions in the mind of a perceiver, no matter what instruments are being utilized to 'objectively' measure or examine the phenomena involved (since these measurements are only known when perceived in the mind or in a computer programmed by a mind, and the instruments are, of course, also perceived in the mind).

But however we analyze the perception of color we find that it is an extremely complex interaction which cannot be separated from habits of the mind which may be labeled as 'cultural' (social) or 'individual'. Hattersley argues that the grouping or categorization of visual impressions is vital to our survival and that we tend to frequently lump together things which should be seen as only being loosely related.

So the tendency is to form categories (groups or *gestalts*) and put things into them that don't really belong. There is a strange psychological law that we follow in this respect: Things that are alike in some ways are actually alike in all ways until it is proved otherwise. . . . The law of similarity is strongest with respect to things we ordinarily pay little attention to.[2]

This helps to explain why certain language groups tend to lump all brown–

dark brown peoples into a black category. The process of 'lumping' may also be facilitated by a cultural focus upon non-skin color characteristics (such as dark hair, or woolly hair) which are used to 'trigger' the use of a skin-color category even when it may not be appropriate. In this situation, indeed, 'black' may not refer to skin color primarily but to something more complex.

In any case, are the colors which we 'see' individual then? Do we all 'see' the same colors? These questions cannot be fully answered, although 'color-blindness' indicates that we do not all see the same colors. Probably we learn (within a particular culture or language) to call something 'black' or 'red'. If I call 'X' red and someone else calls 'Y' red, it may not matter if X and Y are functionally related to the same object.

In other words, we would not see the same color but we would communicate because we used the word 'red' in connection with the same object.

A problem arises, however, when North American and British whites want to call Native Americans 'Redskins' or 'Red Indians' or 'Red People', while Latin Americans often see Americans as 'copper'-colored, 'bronze'-colored or even 'indio'-colored. Also, Native Americans are perceived as being 'red' while Mexicans (Chicanos) are not perceived as being 'red' (by white North Americans). The latter are, more often, called 'brown'.

These differentiations can have important political and social implications (as also when brown people in the West Indies are called 'black' by outside writers). But my examples may reflect *culturally determined* subjectivity. I nonetheless use them to illustrate the consequences, at the practical level, of perceptually determined subjectivity since it may be that Native Americans look 'red' to some white North Americans, while looking 'brown' or 'copperish' to others.

It may be that there were people (as from northern Europe) who did not see some browns but only saw a blackish color. They may actually have been unable to differentiate between shadings of brown. Thus all darker brown peoples become 'black' to them. Perhaps this is a genetically induced tendency, or perhaps a culturally determined one, or one where the effect is brought about by a combination of 'defective' color discrimination and cultural disuse.

In any case, we cannot know what colors are actually perceived by individuals nor can we say precisely how biology and culture influence what colors are created in the mind (or which ones are emphasized at the expense of others). The practical problem is that we cannot know what a Spaniard of 1560 meant by 'stewed quince' color or what an Italian of 1530 meant by 'olive-ish' color. Nor can we know if there was any agreement among people about such terms or, more importantly, about the colors in the mind conjured up by such terms.

This issue of subjectivity is very relevant to modern 'racial' terms used in most Latin American countries and especially Brazil. This will be discussed below. At this point, it is best to focus upon earlier periods.

It seems quite likely that most Christian Europeans of the late medieval period paid relatively little attention to human skin color, except as an aid in the identification of a fugitive or as one of several ways to describe an individual. Human beings were still understood to be all descended from Adam and Eve.

Thus all human beings, in the biblical tradition, were of the same 'race' or stock. Some had become tanned or burned by the sun of the equatorial zone, but the variations were not of fundamental significance. Most slaves and serfs were 'white' and of the same color (at birth) as were the ruling classes.

As we shall see (and has been noted earlier), concern was directed towards developing a very few terms to describe people of intermediate color (between black and white). There was apparently no concern or need to identify persons of 'mixed race' since the concept of 'race' (as we know it) did not exist and 'race' mixture among humans was not an existent concept.

THE EVOLUTION OF 'HYBRID' AND THE CONCEPT OF 'RACIAL' MIXTURE

The word *hibrida* is interesting in this connection. The term apparently originated in Roman times to refer to the progeny of a tame sow and a wild boar, also called *semifero* (half wild). This meaning persisted for a long time, being used in English texts in 1601 and 1623 for half-wild hogs. Pliny is quoted as referring to 'mixture with wild' in connection with the concept. The term also came to be applied to 'one born of a Roman father and a foreign mother, or of a freeman and a slave'.[3] Antonio de Nebrija in his dictionary (Spanish–Latin) of 1492 states:

Hibrida . . . por hijo de fiero y manso
Hybris. hijo de peregrino y ciudadano

That is, a progeny of a tame and a wild parent and of a traveler (foreigner) and a citizen (resident).

A new concept was recorded by Hieronymo Cardoso in his Portuguese–Latin dictionary (prepared before 1569) when he stated:

(Port.) Mestizo = (Lat.) Ibria, ae
(Port.) Mulata, ou mulato = (Lat.) Hybrida, ae
(Lat.) Hybrida, ae = o homem mulato.

Thus the concepts of *mestizo* and *mulato* in Portuguese were being equated with Latin *hybrida*. (*Mulato* was also defined as a mule and as the progeny of a male donkey and a mare.) The 1643 edition of Cardoso is the same except that 'mestizo = ibria' has been corrected to 'mestizo = Hybris, . . . Hybrida, ae'.[4]

The Nebrija Latin–Spanish dictionary of 1554–61 notes that *Hybridas* in Pliny was an old term for a *semifero* hog, and also that, by extension, it could be applied to *homines semiferi* (half-wild people), and further: 'possunt apellari contumeliose natie' (A name for troublesome nations).

Agostinho Barbosa's Portuguese–Latin dictionary (1611) equated *mestiço* with *Hybris, hybridis* but not refer to the term *mulato*.

Bento Pereira in his Portuguese–Latin dictionary of 1646 states the following:

(Port.) Mulata = (Lat.) Hybrida, ae
(Port.) Mulato, homen = Hybrida, ae
(Port.) mestiço, = Hybris, idis. Hybrida, ae
(Lat.) Hybris, eos; . . . Hybrida . . . item o filho de adulterio, porco, ou câo
mestiço, etc. o mulato, ou filho de natural, e estrangeiro.

Thus a *mestiço* dog or pig and *mulato* are equated with *Hybrida* and the latter is also defined (among other things) as a child of adultery, as the *mulato* (mule or human?) or as the child of a native and a stranger (foreign).[5] Emanuel Pina Cabral's 1780 Latin–Portuguese lexicon quotes Pliny to the effect that *Ibrida* refers to an animal born of two diverse species, and Horace to the effect that a hybrid is 'o filho de pay, e mãy de payzes, ou condicoës diversas'. That is, a child of parents from different countries or conditions. The 1802 edition maintains the same meanings.

The 1778–90 editions of Nebrija add some new information (Spanish–Latin)

(Lat.) Hybris, idis . . . Hybrida = (Span.) Perro de cos castas, atravesado.
(Lat.) Hybridae sues = Puercos engendrados de bravo y manso.
* Etiam. Los mestizos de Español, e India.
* (Span.) Mulato = (Lat.) Aethiops hybrida.
* (Span.) Mestizo = animal engendrado de diversas especies ·. . . = (Lat.) Hybris, idis . . . ae.

Thus *Hybrida* is still equated with a dog of two *castas* (crossed-breeds), and a pig born of a wild and tame parent. But to this has been added (new items were indicated by an asterisk) the concepts that *mulato* equals only a 'hybrid Ethiopian' while *mestizo* equals an American–Spanish mixed-blood and an animal born of two species.[6]

The significance of these changes for our understanding of the terms *mulato* and *mestizo* will be discussed later. At this point it is my intention to call attention only to the fact that *hybridity* for a long, long period of time was associated with non-racial intermixture, that is, with the mixture of tame and wild, of citizen and foreigner, and so on.

This concept of mixture is, I believe, very significant for our analysis of the terms used for intermediate colored people, for instance, *loro* and *pardo*, because these terms did not imply interracial mixture nor did they, in fact, make any assertion about ancestry. It seems that the mixture of native and foreigner, of tame and wild, was of some significance but the concept that racial differences (in the modern sense) were more important than other differences (nationality, religion, being a stranger) did not apparently exist.

THE CLASSIFICATION OF PEOPLES AND THE RISE OF RACIALISM

Consequently, we must always keep in mind that the terms for brownish peoples (to be discussed below) arose in a climate of non-racialism (indifference to 'races') and a period in which emphasis was placed upon 'appearance' as opposed to 'racial' genealogy. Some modern authors have attempted to equate terms such as *loro* with the later term *mulato* and by both to mean 'mixed racially' but, as we shall see, such interpretations are a reading back into the medieval and early modern periods of much more recent ideas.[7]

This is, in fact, one of the greatest obstacles to understanding inter-group relations in the early modern period: the mistake of interpreting the terminology in terms of modern concepts of 'race' and of the importance of ancestry or descent. Problems arise when people 'of black color' are put in a category labeled 'the negro race' or when people 'of *loro* color' are called 'mulattoes' (with a modern meaning) or when *pardos* are called 'people of African descent' and so on.

Before analyzing in detail the terms *loro* and *pardo* it is necessary to say a few words about how people seem to have been classified and/or categorized in the 1200s–1400s in the Mediterranean region. Slaves seem to have been classified according to their ethnic or national names, for example, Russians, Turks, Greeks, Tartars, Circassians. People might be also categorized according to broader groupings, often with a religious meaning, such as Sarracens, Jews, Christians, *Mixtiárabes* (*Mozárabes*, that is, Christians in Spain with an Arabic style of culture), *tagarís* (Muslims of the Toledo area living under Christian rule) and so on.

Color terms were also used to describe many slaves (but not all), and the terms include 'white', 'black', *loro*, *rufo* and *olivegno*. These terms were applied to individuals, as already discussed. In addition, some populations of uniform(?) color, such as the Berbers of southern Mauritania, might be called *berritini* as a group.

No association of color with servitude existed, since most slaves were European or North African. On the other hand, a predominance of a certain type of slave may have resulted in their ethnic or class name becoming almost synonymous with 'slave', for instance, *sarraceni*, *mouro*, *sclavi/slavi*, depending on the period. *Servi* and *captivi* were the most common non-ethnic terms used for captives and slaves.[8]

Religious barriers seem to have been the most important for intermarriage. Evidence from the sixteenth century provides numerous examples of white Spaniards, for example, marrying or cohabiting with slaves of various colors or freeing their mixed children. No legal barriers existed and non-whites seem to have been rapidly absorbed into the population. (Prejudice did exist but it does not seem to have formed part of an exclusionary, racialist system.)[9]

During the 1500s and later, concern developed in Spain and Portugal about *descent*, but primarily as regards descent from forcibly converted Jews or Muslims. Later this concern about 'religious ancestry' (and the possibility of secret non-Christian practices) seems to have become attached to non-white ancestry but the evolution of ancestry-based discriminatory practices is complex and requires separate analysis. In any case, the latter practices arose primarily in the colonies.

In the sixteenth century new terms for brown people and mixed-bloods developed. The slave population was still ethnically very heterogeneous but Black Africans formed a higher percentage than in previous times. People continued to be described primarily in non-racial terms. For example, in Brazil one finds the Americans being identified sometimes by village names, and more often by national names, such as Tupinamba, Tamóio, or Carijó. In addition, geographical or regional designations were employed such as *brasis* (Brazilians) for the Tupí-speaking nationalities and *tapuyas* for non-Tupí-speaking groups. Still broader geographical names were also employed such as *indio* for people from *Indias* (the Americas). Africans were identified as *negros de Guiné* or *escravos* from Guinea.

In addition, Americans were sometimes called *negros*, as noted previously; a term which seems to have sometimes denoted 'non-whites' in general. The Portuguese were called Christians and *brancos* (whites) while Americans were referred to as *gentios* (pagans) if unconverted.

After about 1552 one also finds the terms *mamaluco* and *mestiço* being used for mixed-bloods although, on occasion, half-European mixed-bloods were also called *brancos* (whites). Occasionally also Americans were identified by color, as being *pardo*, *baço* (darkish), or *preto* (black), but these terms were not yet used in any caste-like sense.

In the Iberian peninsula, and even more in the Americas, color terms multiplied in the sixteenth and seventeenth centuries. Our concern here relates primarily to certain early terms which later proved to be insufficient because, in all probability, of the complex process of miscegenation. These early terms (*loro*, *pardo*) were supplemented by a great variety of terms which so perplexed later writers that they began to devise ways to organize, define, and classify both the terms and the people they referred to.

This process of classification, which became, in fact, genealogical or racial, seems to have resulted from a rationalistic, 'scientific' desire to bring a sense of order and logic into what appears to this author to have been an *ad hoc* disorderly world of subjective descriptions of color and other phenotypical characteristics. To some extent, of course, Spanish and Portuguese authorities desired a degree of terminological order since colonial statutory law sometimes differentiated between persons who were European or white, mixed, and Native American.

On the other hand, most classification systems went beyond the strict needs of Iberian law in order to offer a rational structure for fine gradations of phenotypical descriptors which had no immediate relevance for legal status.

In 1735 Carl Linnaeus published the first edition of his *System of Nature*. Living creatures were thereby logically arranged by genus, species and variety. Human beings were divided into two species, *Homo Sapiens* and *Homo Monstruos*. Within *Homo Sapiens* were placed: (1) wildmen, (2) Americans (copper-colored), (3) Europeans (fair), (4) Asians (sooty), and (5) Africans (black). *Homo Monstruos* included Patagonians and flat-headed Canadians (both American groups) as well as 'Hottentots' and Chinese.[10]

Linnaeus was followed by other writers who attempted to organize human beings in various classification systems. Quite naturally, one aspect of this effort was to logically arrange the various kinds of physical types resulting from miscegenation into equally 'logical' systems. A plethora of lists of racial terms resulted, being especially common in the nineteenth century for the Caribbean colonies (Dutch, English, French) and for the Spanish colonies somewhat earlier.

An example of such an effort is the work of Joseph Gumilla, published in 1745 and relating to the Venezuela region. First, Gumilla noted that some *indios Americanos* were 'almost whites', that others were *trigueños* (wheat-brown), and still others were 'prietos, y morenos' (black and darkish) but that, in general, they were 'de color trigueño, ya más, ya menos pardos', that is, of wheat color, now more, now less *pardo* (darkish).

The mixture of Americans with Europeans produced the following line of *ascent* (because to leave the American race was to improve one's grade):

I   De Europeo, e India, sale Mestiza [equal parts]
II   De Europeo, y Mestiza, sale Quarterone (¼ de India)
III De Europeo, y Quarterona, sale Ochavona (⅛ India)
IV   De Europeo, y Ochavona, sale Puchuela – Enteramente blanca [all white in appearance].

Gumilla also notes that Pope Clement XI declared that both the *quartertones* and *ochavones* were to be classed also as *blancos*. He also states: 'quede por fixo, que por los mismos grados por donde blanquèa la *Mestiza*, blanquèa tambien la *Mulata* a la quarta generación.' Thus it was established that the same four grades also applied to European–African mixtures, as follows:

I   De Europeo, y Negra, sale Mulata
II   De Europeo, y Mulata, sale Quarterona
III De Europeo, y Quarterona, sale Ochavona
IV   De Europeo, y Ochavona, sale Puchuela . . . Blanca totalmente (Totally white).[11]

It seems very questionable whether this so very neat system actually ever had any reality. Aside from its appealing symmetry, one notes that *quarterona*, *ochavona*, and *puchuela* are used for both American–European and African–European mixed-bloods, an unlikely occurrence especially in the face of many other alternative terms. Moreover, a few pages later Gumilla himself has resort to *negro atezado*, *mulata blanca* and *mestiza blanca*, terms not found in his charts.

Many of the elaborate charts and paintings developed in the Spanish Empire to describe and properly 'place' mixed persons derived, no doubt, from a desire to clarify the racial caste systems which had evolved in the colonies, but the influence of Linnean rationalism must also have been a factor. In any case, systems developed some 200 or more years after the commencement of miscegenation must inevitably be extremely flawed, since an individual might well look 'black' but possess American and/or European ancestry, might look 'white' but possess American and/or African ancestry, or might look 'Indian' and yet be part-African or part-European. The classification systems assume that, in let us say 1745, if Juan who is an 'Indian' marries Dorotea who is 'white' then the child subsequently born will be a *mestizo*, that is, white and American. In fact, however, Juan may be 'Indian' only by appearance and Dorotea may have African ancestry. The child, then, may have the appearance of a *mulato* of some type and may be classified in practice according to that appearance (in some circles) or according to the appearance of the parents (among those who know them), and so on.

The idea that the mixture of white and American produces a *mestizo* (a common assertion of Spanish charts) is, in fact, a false assertion since some such persons will be totally American in appearance and will be called (and treated as) an 'Indian' while some others will appear 'fair' or light and will be treated as either a *blanco* or some sort of near-white.

This illustration brings to the fore the fundamental flaw in such rational systems, derived from a cultural-ideological battle between *appearance* (and the description of appearance) and *ancestry* (the genealogy of the parents). Were terms such as *lobo, coyote, mulato* primarily based upon a perception of appearance, or were they based upon an inquiry into, or exact knowledge of, ancestry?

The records that we have which assign a color or 'caste' term to an individual are usually based upon self-description or, perhaps more commonly, the perception of the individual by a public official (such as a census-taker or a police authority or a notary describing a runaway slave). It is to be suspected that the parents were never present to be observed, except sometimes in the case of young children. Moreover, the purpose usually was to *describe and identify* the individual. It would perhaps have been foolish to use a statement about ancestry when, very often, the appearance of the individual would require a different term or set of terms.[12]

In any case, there is considerable evidence that, in Latin-influenced cultures, 'racial' terms are used only for the individual's 'appearance' (including perhaps the perception of 'status' as an attribute of appearance) and not as a statement about 'race' or 'ancestry'. For example, Marvin Harris studied the application of 'racial' terms in modern Brazil. He found that, in addition to 'the plethora of racial terms',

in Brazil racial identity involves a much more complicated set of calculations [than in the United States]. . . . I am now of the opinion that we shall never be able to state the general cognitive formula by which particular Brazilians assign a racial identity to themselves, or by which particular Brazilians are assigned a racial identity by others.

The absence of 'a descent rule' was one of the features noted by observers prior to Harris but the latter, by conducting tests in the Bahia region, confirmed that 'a rule of descent was indeed absent from the . . . calculation of racial identity.'

Harris found that not only were siblings with the same parents assigned different descriptors (according to their appearance) but that there was very little agreement as to what descriptors to apply. Moreover, when respondents were asked to describe the abstract qualities designated by a particular term, they were frequently found to be in substantial disagreement. . . . A final note of confusion resulted when spot checking on some of the tests indicated a high probability that a given informant might reverse his position when approached after an interval of a couple of weeks.

Harris suggests that

racial terms mean different things to different people. . . . The use of racial terms appears to vary from individual to individual, from place to place, time to time, test to test, observer to observer.[13]

In short, individualism characterizes the use of color-'racial' terms in much the same way as individualism surrounds the use of concepts such as sweet and sour, hard and soft. As Wittgenstein noted, we must treat color concepts somewhat like sensations. Perhaps it has always been foolish for writers (or officials) to attempt to falsely objectify (organize) an inherently individual process.

It is interesting in this connection to note that sometimes naive efforts to divide humankind up into two, three, four, five or more 'races' and to transform 'race' from a very loose term meaning 'kind' or 'stock' (or breed) into a precise, genetic-based, 'scientific' term, have been themselves a form of, and indeed an extremely important part of, modern racialism. The same process which led to the concept of a number of bioligically separate 'races' then resulted in a desire to chart out what might happen when persons derived from these so-called biological groupings intermixed with each other.

Unfortunately for any kind of accuracy, such efforts came several hundred years too late, if not (indeed) thousands of years too late.[14]

In any case, let us turn now to look at the way in which such important terms as *mulatto* and *mestizo* came into being, beginning with an analysis of their predecessor terms, *loro, pardo* and so on.

THE USE OF THE TERM *LORO*

The term *loro*, its various forms, is recorded as early as 930 as a color description for certain cattle (*vacca laura*). In 1215 a poem has 'many chestnut oxen, others dusky and *loro*' ('muchos buyes castaños, otros foscos e loros', the latter to rhyme with 'toros'). For many centuries *loro* continued to be used as a color term for animals of various shades, typically ranging from reds through browns but of obscure (dark) or multicolored character. In the Mozarabic *romance* language of Spain it pointed towards 'morena que tira á negro, y tambien amarillo y rubio, aplicado al trigo'. That is, a dark color inclined towards black and also yellow and 'blonde' as applied to wheat. But it is clear, as Corominias points out, that *loro* was usually applied to darker shades but with great shifts of meaning because of the infinite variations in color exhibited by cattle and other animals.

By 1246 *laurus* was being applied to slaves in Barcelona. Between 1243 and 1296 about 18 per cent of the 50 slaves recorded in one source for Barcelona were *laura* or *laurus*. All were called *sarrasin* (Muslim). In 1283 the *Sarrasin* Azmet, categorized as *laurus*, was mentioned in Aragón. In Barcelona some personal names of *laurum* and *laura* slaves reveal Islamic origin: Maimonam, and two people called Fátima. Occasionally, however, converts were made, as in Barcelona when the 'Sarrasine neophyte Barbara of 30 year age' was for sale with her daughter 'Marguerite de 14 mois'. The latter was called a 'laura'.[15]

During the fifteenth century *moro* had replaced *sarrasin* in Barcelona but *llor* (*loro*) slaves continued to be sold, as in 1428 and 1431. All were of the 'nació de moros llor' except for one Jordí, a Christian, who might have been a Russian.[16] In Genoa, Italy, a *lauro* slave was sold during this period but *olivegno* (olive) was a more common designation for such persons.[17] In 1460 a Valencian poet, Jaume Roig, described the people to be seen there:

totes
de qualque stat
color, etat
ley, nació . . .
les cristianes
juhies, mores
negres e lores
roges e blanques
dretes y manques . . .
franques, catives.[18]

Thus *lores* were enumerated along with Christians, Jews, Muslims, blacks, whites, and ruddy people as part of the Valencian population.

The Islamic law in Christian-ruled Spain during the early fifteenth century, apparently reflecting usage in Muslim-controlled Granada, possessed a section which stated that 'quando alguno se tornará muçilim, y ganaren los muçilimes aquella billa donde bibe aquel hombre que se combertió. . . . El muçilim puede tener catibo muçilim de los negros o' loros, pero no de los blancos.'[19] That is, in a Muslim-controlled village, a newly converted Muslim could possess a Muslim slave provided that the latter was black or *loro* and not white.

During the period 1472–1521 in Seville, and 1482–1516 in Valencia, the term *loro* was the almost exclusive designation for slaves not classified as either black or white. (One 'ruddy' *moro bermejo* is listed for 1513.)

In Seville the majority of *loros* mentioned, registered or otherwise, had only a Christian name and no place of birth was stated. Many could have been born in Spain of Muslim parents who had been enslaved as a result of the war with Granada, while others could have been descendants of Muslims from North Africa. Franco Silva, who has published the records, feels that 'a good portion' were children of *negros* 'and some were Muslims'. A few, he notes, were *canarios* and Americans. In any case, the majority of *loros* cannot be identified ethnically since only their name and color is recorded.

A few examples will be given here, to illustrate the use of *loro* in Seville:

1475   Fernando, loro, 17, from Seville [born 1458]
1480   Merien, lora, age 22, from Fez, Morocco
1499   Abraham, 21, Cabo Aguer [Agadir] loro
1500   Pastor, 13 or 14, loro, Marañón [Brazil]
1501   Inés, 30, negra. Isabel, 2, lora, su hija. Haxa, 35, lora, Allende. Marina,
        30, negra. Francisca, 9, Bernaldo, 5, loro
1503   Pedro Guillén, 30, lora, Alhama
1504   Catalina, 18, Meni [West Africa] lora
1505   Juana, 30, negra. Juana, 10, Francisca, 8, loras
1508   Pedro, 23, Malaga, loro. Antonio, Portugal, loro
1509   Guiomar [now] Juan, loro. Antonio, 27, loro, Las Azores
1511   Gonzalo, 18, Indias, loro
1512   María, 8, India lora. Juan de Berberia, 9, loro
1513   Francisca, lora, 40, Cabo Aguer [Agadir]. María, lora, 41, Berbería.
        Yaya, 20, Moro bermejo. Juan de Berbería, 9, loro.

In addition, there are these helpful references:

1511   *una esclava lora*, Juana, with her child Francisca; Blas, *de color loro*, native
        of Jérez de la Frontera, child of Francisco de Sanabria Alhamel and
        Isabel de Morillo.
1515   'una esclava lora de Terranova', María, 20.
1517   *un esclavo berberisco*, 13, 'between *loro* and *negro*' and another age 35, 'as
        negro somewhat *loro*'.
1518   *una negra María*, 25, (with) son of 9 months called Francisco, who is
        loro, almost *blanco*; *una negra guineana* María, 25, with her *loro* son
        Francisco, 9 months.
1520   Gaspar, *loro*, 20, *natural de* Calicut.
1521   *una esclava lora*, Inés, 30, and 3 niños, Antón, 4, Lucia, 2, and Juan, 1;
        'una esclava de color lora', Isabel, sold to the Americas.
1522   *un berberisco loro*.
1523   *un loro berberisco*, 20, Pedro.
1524   Juan, *negro como loro* and 'who was born in Guinea'.
1525   Gaspar, 6, born in Mérida, '*negro* almost *loro*'.

From these examples one can see that the following are true: (1) the children
of female *loras* are sometimes not classified (thus probably being 'white'); (2) the
children of several *negras* are called *loras* (thus implying a *loro* or white father);
(3) many *loros* were of Islamic origin; (4) some *loros* were of Indian (Calicut) and
American ancestry; (5) several were from West Africa or from Portugal and the
Azores.[20]

The fact that Juan de Valladolid, a *negro* of distinguished background, was
named as judge of the *negros* and *loros* of Seville in 1475 (as noted previously)
implies some type of commonality among *negros* and *loros* at that date (prior to
the war of Granada when many Spanish Muslims were enslaved). It may well be

that the commonality derived from their converted Christian status and from their origin as slaves (although some were by then free).[21]

The integration of *loros* into the Seville society is illustrated by these examples:

1501 Andrés Garcia, *de color loro*, to go to Haiti along with Cristóbal Palacios, *de color loro*, *vecino* of Trigueros.

- 1502 *una mujer lora* inherits a house from her son, an *albañil* (mason).

1519 Juana Fernández, *de color lora*, places her natural son Cristóbal, age 14 years, with the shoemaker Pedro Fernández, for 4½ years.[22]

Thus we see the people of *loro* color being *vecino* (resident), going to Haiti, inheriting a house, and learning a trade.

In Valencia there were many *loros* from 1480 onward. Examples which illustrate the use of the term are as follows:

1482 Muza, an *alarps*, 'más negro que lor' ran away.

1488 Abdalla, age 35, of Granada 'más blanco que lor' ran away.

1489 Two 'esclavas loras de Canarias', ages 11 and 12, were sold.

1491 'un cautivo más blanco que lor'; 'un negro o lor de Túnez, 25, Acbucacim' [N. Africa]; 'dos blancas casi loras de Canarias', 8 years old, sold.

1497 *captive lor* de Túnez, 26, called Amet; now Francisco; an 'obscure white' captive of Berbería.

1501 *Un cautivo lor*, Floristany, 18, of Alcazar, orphan; his father was free and his mother a captive.

1502 María, *mora lora*, from Arcila; '*una cautiva lora* with a star burned on each cheek'. Her parents were Christians and free in their country; *un cautivo lor*, Perico, 16, from Fez, his mother a captive in Jérez; 'un moro berbersco lor.'

1503 *una cautiva lora*, Beatricilla, of Seville, 'her mother a *negra* captive and her father free white', born in Carmona; also 'un lor casi negro', Juanico, 17, from Málaga, carried to Seville and baptized.

1505 María, *negra*, 20, of Toledo, orphan of captives, has a child *lor* age 1–1½, called Dieguito.

1506 *une cautivo lor*, Francisco, 13, of the island of Madeira; his father was white and free and his mother *cautiva negra*.

1507 'Una lora casi oscura', María, 12; her father 'blanco y libre y su madre cautiva y negra'.

1509 *un lor*, Ali, age 10, from Cafí, *bozal* (unassimilated); Yusef, *blanco lor*, from Orán, 20.

1511 *lor*, 50, Alí Bumbali, native of Fez.

1514 *Lor*, Antonio, 12, *de Malaca, India.*

1515 *lor casi negro*, Rumera, now Roque, 20, from Calicut; *un canario lor*, Pedro, 20.

1516 *cautivo lor*, Pedro, 20, from Calicut, [23]

Of some 67 *loros* in the registration lists, almost half (30) can be identified with certainty as Muslims from Mauritania, Morocco, Algeria or Tunisia. Another six can definitely be identified as Spanish Muslims, while seven were *canarios* and three were from India. Only four are known to be the mixed children of *negras* and *blancos*, while some 17 are of unknown origin (but in many cases appearing to be baptized ex-Muslims).

Thus it would appear that the majority of *loros* were simply brownish-skinned people from North Africa, the Canary Islands, the Americas or India. A certain percentage were mixed-bloods of recent origin but it cannot be demonstrated that many *loros* were of that type.

One can see also that the term *loro*, by being modified, could embrace many shades of skin color. The lightest shade cited above was probably *blanca obscura* (dark white) and then the next would be 'blanca casi lora' or *lor blanco* or 'más blanco que lor' followed by *loro* and then by various combinations of *loro* and *negro*.

The records for the sale of slaves at Las Palmas in the Canary Islands begin in 1519, about the time the early published records for Seville and Valencia stop. Thus it is useful to view the Canary records as providing some insight into the transition period when other terms began to supplement and replace *loro*. From 1519 through 1530 *loro* is the only intermediate color term used. Of the 12 persons classified as *loros*, six can definitely be identified as either Muslims from North Africa or as Spanish Muslims converted to Christianity (*moriscos*). The others are not identifiable.

Between 1532 and 1599 another 32 *loros* were registered but they were greatly outnumbered after 1552–4 by *mulatos*. The different terms used for *loros* are as follows (with date first used):

loro (1519)
loro, moro, berberisco (1519)
loro morisco (1519)
lora, mulata, ladina (1532)
loro 'yudo' (1535)
loro de Berbería (1535)
mulato loro (1546)
negro loro (1557)
negro algo lora (1567)
negra casi lora (1580)
loro-mulato (1581)
prieta, más lora que negra (1584).[24]

It is not possible to state the ethnic origins of most of the *loros* after 1532 since almost all have Christian names; however, several are identified as being *morisco* or of North African origin (as are several *mulatos*).

It should be noted that one North African woman (1557) is described as 'de color algo baça' (of somewhat darkish color) while another woman is termed *morena* in 1563. In 1523 Fátima, *blanca berberisca*, is recorded with two *loro* children.

The term *loro*, as noted above, is used (after 1532) intermittently in the Canary Islands (as also in Valencia and elsewhere). Its decline will be discussed below, but first let us examine other data showing what kind of people were called *loro* by Spaniards.

First, it is useful to note that *loro* (as well as other terms for non-whites) was not always used for the children of black women by white men. In 1525, Juanico the son of María, *negra*, was said to be *de color blanco*. Other cases are also to be seen where such children were 'white'. Thus, *loro* and *mulato* were not automatically applicable to the mixed-blood, as such.[25]

As we have seen from the records cited above, many kinds of people could be classed as *loro* including a Jew, Muslims from North Africa, Berbers from the Agadir region, Canary Island natives, people from India, Native Americans, and the children of white and negro parents. As noted earlier, Las Casas stated that the ancient people of the Cassitérides islands (the Azores, perhaps) were 'gente lora o baça de color'.

It is especially interesting to note that the early Spaniards in the Caribbean regarded the American natives as being of *loro* color. Columbus noted on several occasions that the Americans were 'of the color of the Canarios, neither black, nor white'. Bernaldez, writing from Columbus' data, stated that the Americans were 'de color loros, blancos más que negros.' In 1495 Jaime Ferrer wrote to Columbus that 'lo mas que pude sentir de muchos Indos y Árabes y Etiopes, es que la major parte de las cosas buenas vienen de region muy caliente, donde los moradores de allá son negros o' loros.' That is, the Indians, Arabs and Ethiopians indicated that the greater part of the good things (gold, etc.) come from hot regions where the people are black or *loro* (brown).

Following up on the above usage, Ferdinand and Isabella of Spain in 1499 and again in 1500 authorized the expeditions of Yáñez Pinzón and Batidas to capture 'esclavos negros o loros o otros' found in the Americas.[26]

The Spanish writer Fernández de Oviedo wrote that 'the people of this island [Puerto Rico] *es lora* and that the people who lived in the Orinoco area *son loros*. He also referred to a servant as being *de color loro*.[27]

This usage continued for some time. Prior to 1638 the poet Francisco de Quevedo, for example, made reference to 'al indio cisco, tapetado y loro'.[28] The use of *tapetado* (dark brown) perhaps indicates that *loro* was already archaic and used for purposes of rhyme.

Most certainly, then, *loro*, did not mean 'mixed' nor can anyone reasonably equate the brown-skinned Berbers of North Africa, the Native Americans or the Canary Islanders with such a concept. Certain Spanish writers have attempted to regard Muslim *loros* as being the product of intermixture between black Africans and 'white' North Africans but the color of the ancient Egyptians, 5,000 years previously, would have doubtless fallen within the *loro* range. One cannot assume that brown-skinned peoples are hybrids, since, in fact, white and 'black' peoples may have diverged from an original brown-intermediate human stock.

Antonio de Nebrija (*c*.1495) defined *loro* as 'between *blanco y negro*' and equivalent to Latin *fuscus* (dark, dusky). 'Loro que tira a negro' (darkish *loro*) was equated with *luridus*. John Minsheu (1599) defined *loro* as 'dun coloured. Also a parret'. (By that date the use of *loro* for a type of parrot had appeared.) By 1617 Minsheu stated for *loro*, '*fuscus* (Latin), dunne (English). Also *Papagayo* [parrot]'. In 1607 Cesar Oudin stated: '*Loro*: between white and black (Spanish), brown between black and white, obscure, blackish, dusky, inclined towards the black . . . (French).' This made *loro* virtually the same as another entry for *Morena cosa baca* (*morena* something dark) since the French equivalent was given as *brune, noire, obscure*. In 1639–40 the Dutch equivalent was added to the above: *bruyn, swertachtigh, gheblaut* (brown, blackish, blueish perhaps).[29]

Julio Cejador, in his work on medieval Castillian, says of *loro*: 'obscure yellowish or of clay' and in Portuguese and Gallego, *louro*, 'obscure chestnut color'. In another work he added:

de aqui dijose loro el color amarillo verdoso, mezcla que tira á obscuro . . . prevalece el valor de color oscuro [in some texts] por serlo el de la hoja del laurel, y en las Cantigas louro está por moreno. [But in other sources] predomina el amarillo verdoso y el de barro o amarillo súcio de la raza cobriza americana.

Thus in some sources *loro* referred to a darkish color, standing for later *moreno*, while in other sources a so-called greenish yellow or 'dirty yellow' similar to that of the 'copperish American race' was indicated.

Cejador, as well as Corominas cited earlier, refers to *loro* as being derived from *laurus* or laurel, a tree whose leaves possess an obscure color. In this respect, laurel perhaps resembles 'olive', an equivalent sometimes used by the Italians and French.

By 1778–90 *loro* had been dropped from later editions of Antonio de Nebrija's dictionary but it did appear in Aniceto de Pagés' work: '(del lat. *laurus*, laurel, por el color obscuro de sus hojas y fruto): adj. De color amulatado o' de un moreno que tira á negro. "Cuando el trigo está loro, es el barbo como un loro" Refrán.' It is interesting that Pagés compares *loro* with the color *amulatodo* (mulato-ish) and with a *moreno* that tends towards black. On the other hand, the refrain would indicate that *loro* referred to a ripe wheat color.[30]

THE DECLINE OF *LORO*

Perhaps the ambiguity of *loro* is one of the factors which led to its replacement in Castillian and Catalan. Between 1569 and 1686 the published records from Valencia reveal that *loro* was only applied on three occasions, all for new slaves registered in the 1570s. What were the other terms used (other than *negro* or *blanco*)? They were:

membrillo cocido (*codony cuyt*) used 365 times, with all kinds of slaves, new and fugitive, in all registration books;
moreno, used 59 times, with all kinds of slaves, except with new slaves 1569–70;
mulato, used 22 times, used with new slaves in 1571–85, with fugitives in

1569–78, and in books mixing both new and runaway slaves through 1666; *claro*, used once; *oscuro*, used twice; no color stated, 783 times or for about one-fourth of the slaves.

Occasionally modifications occurred as with *blanco-membrillo*, *membrillo-moreno*, *membrillo-claro*, *moreno-claro*, *lloro-mulato*, *blanca-llora*, or *poco moreno*.

Thus, in Valencia, *loro* declined and was replaced primarily by *membrillo cocido* (stewed quince color) and secondarily by *moreno*. *Mulato* was used in only 22 cases, indicating that, at least to 1686, it was not a popular term. A great portion (perhaps half) of the slaves were of Islamic origin. Individual descriptions included:

'un hombre moreno'
'hombre de color de membrillo cocido, scuro'
'a slave', *de Ora* [Oran], *morenet*
'sclava de Ora, morena de cara'
'un sclau fugitiu de color codony cuit (membrillo cocido)'
'esclau negre attesat [dark black], de Ora, nomenat Amade'
'Juamet . . . nationis alarbis, color mustellino' (1558).

The color terms *negro, blanco* and *moreno* were especially common for Muslim (*moro*) slaves, with *moreno* also being used for a man born of a slaveowner and a slave. Picked up as a fugitive in 1564, he claimed to be free although his mother was a slave of his father.

The published materials do not identify American slaves separately by color, but a few inferences can be made. In Book 205 (1569–70) seven people from *Indias* were mentioned. In the same book there were nine of *membrillo* color along with 59 *blancos* and 195 *negros*. Thus the Americans were classified by one of these three color terms. In Book 207 (1571–8) there were four from *Indias*, with many people called *negro* or *blanco* but only 22 *membrillos*, two *mulatos*, one *moreno* and three *llors*. In Book 208 (1579–85) there were seven from *Indias* who had to be classified as being among the *membrillos* (24), *mulatos* (3) or *morenos* (2) unless they were termed black or white, or were unclassified by color.[31]

In 1659, as noted previously, a Spaniard stated that the *negros* then being captured in the Mediterranean and taken to Sicily had to be regarded as 'infidel *moros*' because they were of a lionish color called *membrillo cocido* and were Muslims.[32]

According to another author, Fulo (Fulani) people were regarded as being also of 'color mulato membrillo cocho' (mulato membrillo cocido color) in the slavery period.[33]

Membrillo cocido spread to the Americas where in 1552 a female slave born in Spain was described as being of that color. In early colonial Mexico, according to Aguirre Beltrán, the term *amembrillados* was used for persons who had lighter complexions than *negros* and especially than *negros atezados* (extremely black).

He stated that it was a color similar to, or the same as, *amulatado*. In Mexico the so-called 'dark mulatto' (*mulato pardo*), a mixture of African and American, was also called *color cocho* as well as *color pardo*, *color de rapadura* (molasses), *color champurrado* (chocolate), *color amarillito* (yellowish), *color de membrillo*, *color quebrado* (broken color), *color zambaigo* (and Zambo), as well as simply *cambujos*, *chinos*, *jarochos* and *loros* (Chiapas).[34]

This array of terms need not concern us here except that it illustrates the proliferation of color designations in the seventeenth century as well as the survival of *loro* for a time in the Americas.

As noted elsewhere, some *loros* were allowed to go to the Americas from Spain but between 1518 and 1530 the Crown began to attempt to prevent any potentially seditious elements from travelling to the colonies. In 1526 only newly enslaved *negros* were to be allowed to go there as slaves. Wolofs of Senegal, Levantines (Middle-Easterners) of whatever color, persons raised among Muslims, and *negros* who had been in Spain for two years were all prohibited (along with all ex-Muslims, ex-Jews, their children, heretics, and others). In 1530 slaves who were 'Blancos, Negro, Loros, ni Mulatos' were prohibited without express licence of the Crown.

In this instance it would appear that *loro* and *mulato* were used as similar or identical terms, with the implication of being associated with Muslims. Such slaves were to be confiscated and, if 'Berberish, of the caste of Muslims, or Jews, or Mulato', they were to be returned to Spain at the sender's cost. In this second enumeration only the term *mulato* is used but since we know that many Muslims were called *loros* we must assume that *mulato* is used to stand for both the *loros* and *mulatos* of the first enumeration. This usage helps to illustrate the period of transition from *loro* to *mulato* (and other terms) to be discussed elsewhere.

In 1551 and again in 1552 King Carlos I issued a decree from Spain stating that: 'los negros, y loros, free or slave, could not carry any type of public arms' nor could they touch hands to arms against a Spaniard. They were to be severely punished indeed.[35] This is the only other known use of *loro* in American colonial legislation and we can assume, I think, that it refers to all classes of brown-skinned non-whites, including Americans. (Some writers have interpreted it as being equivalent to *mulato* but such a usage would seem to exclude *mestizos* and other non-whites – an unlikely intention.)[36]

As will be discussed later, *mestizo* and *mulato* appear in royal decrees in 1549 and replace *loro* after 1552.

The evolution of the term *louro* was somewhat different in the Portuguese and Gallego languages. In Gallego *louro* occurred in two senses: one leaning in the red direction and one leaning towards the black: 'more *louro* than carbon'. In the medieval *Cantigas del Rey Sabio* (according to Julio Cegeador y Franca) the usage is 'white and *louro* Muslims'. On the other hand, Portuguese usage tended to emphasize the reddish-goldish-yellowish quality of wheat, as in Camoens' *Lusiadas* (1572).[37]

In Brazil, in particular, *louro* was used to refer to the descendants of

Frenchmen (many from Normandy) and Tupinamba women 'dos quaes ha hoje muitos seus descendentes, que são louros, alvos e sardos, e havidos por indios Tupinambas, e são mais barbaros que elles.'[38] Thus the French–Tupinamba mixed-bloods were described as *louro, alvo* (white), or *sardo* (Sardinian-colored) in 1587. A dictionary of 1646 equates *loura cousa* (a *loura* thing) with Latin *flavus* (golden yellow) and *rutilus* (red, golden, auburn).[39] The term seems to have referred to hair color in particular or to light brown persons with blondish hair. Brasio refers to '*louro* hair' and Nascentes in his dictionary states: 'De côr media entre o dourado e o castanho claro (cabelo, pelo). De côr proxima da do cabelo louro: louras espigas . . . pessoa de cabelos louros.' That is, a color between golden and clear or light chestnut, applied to hair. In the same vein, Gonsalves de Mello speaks of the *mestiços* and 'tipos louros ou avermelhados (reddish)' found in northeastern Brazil and due possibly to Dutch–Brazilian intermixture, while Gilberto Freyre refers to 'a minority of *louros*' dominating 'a proletariat of people of color'.[40]

The fact that *louro* in Portuguese came to refer to a lighter shade of color is, in part, explained by the widespread use of *pardo* as the more precise equivalent of Spanish *loro*. In short, *pardo* came to fulfil the *fuscus* (dusky), *subniger* (less than black) function exercised by *loro* in Castillian and Catalan, while *louro* in Portuguese became more equivalent to *rubio* (as applied to hair) in Castillian.

THE USE OF THE TERM *PARDO*

The early evolution of *pardo* in Castillian is distinct from that in Portuguese and Gallego. Fundamentally, *pardo/pardillo* pointed towards a gray shade in Spanish, one used to refer to the drab clothing worn by some common people. In Gallego, on the other hand, *pardo* pointed towards the equivalent of *fuscus*, that is, darkish, dusky, and obscure. As a result, one never finds slaves classified as *pardo* in Seville or Valencia in the sixteenth century, *loro* being used instead. But in the Galicia region in 1521 one finds records of two slaves being sold who are termed *pardillo* and *pardilla*, while a third is termed a *loro*.[41]

It is rather important to trace the use of *pardo* in Portuguese (and its later adoptation in American Spanish) because it is a term often interpreted by contemporary writers in a somewhat misleading manner. Corominas traces *pardo* back to Latin *pardus*, derived from Greek *pardos* (leopard) and relates its meaning to the obscure color of that animal. It appears in Castillian and Gallego–Portuguese from the eleventh century onwards. Nebrija, in his dictionary of *c.*1495 states: '*Pardo* color of cloth'.

The Spanish Royal Academy has defined *pardo* as: 'del color de la tierra, o de la piel del oso comun, intermedio entre blanco y negro con tinte rojo amrillento, y más oscuro que el gris.' That is, as an earth color or like the skin of the common bear, intermediate between black and white with a reddish-yellowish tint, and darker than gray.

On the other hand, this definition reflects modern usage and in earlier times, as in a Toledo document of 1582 and many others, Spanish *pardo* is equated with 'gray'. Examples will be given below. In Portuguese the *colore pardo* is mentioned as early as 1111 and 1258. A charter of 1182 (published 1293) from Alfonso I refers to *suam pardum* although it is not certain who the *pardum* was, or if it was a misspelling.[42]

A Gallego chronicle of the second half of the fourteenth century uses *uis* for *castaño* (chestnut brown), *bruu* for *castaño obscuro* (dark brown) and *escuro* (dark), but does not use *pardo*.[43] By the fifteenth century, however, *pardo* was being used in Portugal primarily for 'dusky non-negroids' such as the Idzāgen (Azenegues) of Mauritania (a people called *loros* by users of Castillian). *Pardo* and *baço* were also being used for mixed-bloods in Portugal (the term *mulato* not having appeared yet).[44]

Pardo clearly pointed towards an intermediate color between black and white and not towards race mixture. For example, *pardo* could be applied to unmixed Americans. When the Portuguese first reached Brazil in 1500 Pero Vaz de Caminha wrote that the native people: 'A feicao deles é serem *pardos*, maneira de avermalhados, de bons rostos e bons narizes, bem feitos. . . . Os cabelos seus são corredios.' [Their aspect is that of *pardos*, somewhat vermillion, with good faces and noses, well made. . . . Their hair is worn long.] Pedro Alvares Cabral, the leader of the expedition, said, 'que eram gentes de côr parda, entre o branco e o preto.' In this Cabral not only stated that the Americans were *pardos* but that the color *pardo* stood between the extremes of white and black, a definition repeated over and over in Portuguese dictionaries up to the present time. The people of India were referred to as *baços* by Vasco da Gama.[45]

An early Italian translation (pubished 1550) utilizes *color berretino* for the *pardo* of Alvares Cabral.[46] This correspondence is significant because of a similar usage found in the diary of Alvise da Ca' da Mosto, an Italian who sailed with the Portuguese along the northwest African coasts in the 1440s–60s and then wrote about his experience in 1464–5. In describing the people of southern Mauritania, Ca' da Mosto stated that the Arabs of Hoden 'are brown (*bruni*) men', and that the 'Azanaghi are *berretini* men, and more *forte bruni* than *berretini*'. Later he noted that the Senegal River was the first river of the 'land of Negroes' and that the said river 'divides the Negroes and the *Berretini* of the Azanaghi'. Thus the Azanaghi (Idzāgen) were *berretini* people, bordering upon black people to the south and brown (*bruni*) Arabs to the north. Moreover, the Azanaghi were 'more dark brown than *berretini*.'[47]

It is interesting to see how a Portuguese scholar, Sebastião Francisco de Mendo Trigoso, translated *berretini* and *bruni* into his language several centuries later. The Arabs who were *bruni* in Italian become *pardo* in Portuguese while the phrase which stated that the Azanaghi were 'more *forte bruni* than *berretini*' becomes 'Estes azenegues são de uma côr amulatada e mais pardos do que mulatos.' Thus *amulatado* and *mulato* are equated with *berretini*, and 'more *pardo*' with *forte bruni*, while a few pages later 'dos pardos chamados azenegues' replaces 'da' Berretini detti Azanaghi'. But somewhat later, *os amulatados* is substituted for *berretini*.[48]

In any case, *pardo* can be seen as a color equivalent to *bruno* but also embracing *berretino*. The Azanaghi Berbers of Mauritania and the Native Brazilians fell within this range (which also embraced *amulatado* in a manner similar to that remarked upon for *loro* and *membrillo cocido*).

Hans Staden, in a description of the Brazilians in 1557, calls them 'brown' in English translation and *pardo* in Spanish translation.[49] The Jesuit letters relating to Brazil between 1549 and 1568 along with reports of the 1570s–80s do not use the term *pardo* (*negro*, as noted, being often used instead). One source does, however, use *preto* and *muito baça* in relation to the native people: 'Os Tupinambas são homens de meâ estatura, de côr muito baça, bem feitos e bem dispostos.'[50] 'Muito baça' (very dark), as we shall see, could be embraced by *pardo*.

In discussing the children of Portuguese fathers and black mothers in the Congo (1579–91), a Portuguese translator (from Italian) states:

that the children of white Portuguese, born in those lands, of Congolese women, are *negros* or white or *pardos*, whom the Spaniards call *mulatos* . . . and, so, the children of the Portuguese, who are born to Congolese women, lean more towards the white color. . . . The [native Congo people] are *negros*, and some less, leaning more towards *baço*; and they have black kinky hair, and some also reddish.

Thus the mixed children could be white, black or *pardo* in color, children whom 'the Spaniards' called *mulatos*. *Pardo* was clearly being used as an intermediate color, as was *baço*.

A French translation of the above utilizes *olivâtres* (olive-ish) for *pardos*.[51]

In his epic poem *Lusiadas* (1571), Luis de Camoens used the term '*gente* . . . *baça*' to refer to the people of Arabia and the Persian Gulf. Manuel de Faria commented upon this (*c*.1639) by saying that Camoens meant

that the people of those parts were of a color that is neither white nor black, which in Portugal we call *pardo* or *amulatado*: because the children of a black and a white are called *mulatos*, they who from this mixture of parents have this *color dudoso, o neutral* between the two; very bad without doubt; because *hasta alli* it is bad to be neutral; a horrible thing.'[52]

In this interesting statement Faria equates *baço* with *pardo* and *amulatado* but essentially what is meant is a 'doubtful color', a 'neutral' one between black and white, and this 'neutral' color is without doubt very bad; it is horrible and negative to be of a 'neutral' color.

Why Faria regarded brownish shades as being 'horrible' for human beings is not clear, but perhaps it reflects the growth of racism and disdain for mixed-bloods. On the other hand, it also seems to relate to the color dualism referred to earlier, wherein colors between black and white are regarded as being 'doubtful'. Again, the mixture of black and white pigments produces gray, one of the meanings of *pardo*, as noted. In this case, the artist's gray is confused with the browns of northern Africans, Brazilians, Indians, and mixed-bloods and all are categorized as 'neutral'.

In any event, during the seventeenth century *pardo* was extended to include mixed-bloods of various kinds. In 1681, for example, a writer notes that there were many mulattoes and *pardos* in Angola, a result of white men having children by black women. In the 1680s also certain *pardos* of Bahia protested that they were being excluded from Jesuit schools. Antonio Vieira responded that they had been excluded because upper-class whites would not attend with them since they were 'of vile and obscure origin'.[53]

In the 1690s an Italian visitor to Bahia stated that the population there was divided into four classes: the *bianchi* (white), the *Negri* from Ethiopia, the *mulati* or *pardi*, and the 'Indij nazionali, overo Brazliani'. The *pardos* were 'huomini di colore Olivastro, quali non sono, nè Bianchi, nè Negri, ma di colore d'Oliva: e questi sono bastardi degli huomini Bianchi, generati colle donne Negre, quali verdano, e prostituiscono . . . e comunemente si chiamano mulati, overo Pardi.' That is to say, the *pardos* were of olive color, the illegitimate children of white men and black women, and were commonly called *mulati* or *pardi*. Supposedly, there were about 8,000 to 10,000 of these *mulati* or *pardi* in Bahia.

The native Brazilians were neither white nor black nor *olivastri*, but more the color of 'dark vermilion' and few of them were living in the city itself. The 'whites' numbered some 20,000, the 'black' slaves some 50,000, the 'intermediate' olive-colored people some 8,000 to 10,000, as noted, for a total of 80,000 and more (leaving perhaps 2,000 or less for the unmixed 'vermilion' Americans).

The situation of Bahia in the late seventeenth century represents quite a contrast with earlier periods. For one thing, earlier Italian writers usually regarded the Americans as being of olive color. Secondly, in 1584 the population of Bahia totalled 12,000, of whom 6,000 were Americans, 4,000 were *pretos de Guiné* and 2,000 were Portuguese.[54]

Who then were the olive-colored *pardos* and *mulatos* of the 1690s? We know that they were not a simple mixture of Portuguese and African, first because the 'whites' were very definitely part-American and their children by black women would have to be also part-American. Secondly, as will be discussed later, the sex ratios among African slaves were heavily out of balance (usually two males to one female), and thirdly, the mixed population must have been heavily African and American.

On the other hand, it is significant that Zuccelli's use of the term *pardi* reflects a growing tendency to focus on the black–white nexus and to ignore the American component. This will be discussed in a subsequent section, but here it is useful to quote from a Brazilian author to the effect that in *c.*1769–70 the governor of Pará 'pôde criar a 'companhia dos Homens Pardos' (talvez indios) e outras Companhias dos Homens Prêtos, que se dizem dos Henriques, com exercício na artilharia.'[55] Thus a military company of *pardos* was authorized and the *pardos* in this case were perhaps Americans. Separate companies were authorized for blacks, to be called 'the Henriques' (after Henrique Dias who, as noted, had led non-white troops against the Dutch).

At this point les us examine Portuguese dictionaries to understand more about the evolution of *pardo* and the related term *baço*. In the 1560s Cardoso equated both *pardo* and *Baça cousa* with Latin *fuscus*. This was repeated in the 1643 edition of this dictionary. Barbosa (1611) stated the same: 'Baça cousa, ou parda. Fuscus . . . Subniger.' Periera (1646) repeats the same for *Parda cousa*. Interestingly, he also has 'carafuz – homo fusca facie', thus utilizing a term which later became popular in Brazil for African–American mixed-bloods (*Cafuz, cafuso, carafuz*), that is, 'dusky-face'.[56] Bluteau (1712–20) has the following:

Pardaço = muyto pardo. Cousa de pardo escuro. vid. pardo.
Pardo = côr entre branco, & preto, . . . Homem pardo, vid. mulato . . . Mayo pardo, Junho claro . . . De noyte todos os gatos são pardos.

Thus *pardo* is defined as being a color between black and white but in addition, for a *pardo* person, one is referred to the definition for *mulato*. Several old sayings are then quoted: 'May dark (gray), June clear'. 'At night all of the cats are *pardos* (dark)', thus indicting that *pardo* still essentially means *fuscus* (dark, obscure). This remains basically the same in a 1789 edition.

Bluteau also defines the term *trigueiro* (wheat-colored) as follows: 'Que he pouco alvo, que tira a pardo, que declina a negro. Fuscus . . . Subniger, gra, grũ. Varro.' *Trigueiro*, then, was similar to *pardo* in embracing *fuscus*, gray, and earth colors, but perhaps it was seen as a slightly lighter shade (but one essentially variable and obscure). For Bluteau, native Brazilians were of 'bronze' color.[57]

A Portuguese–Dutch dictionary of 1718 equated *pardo* with *donkerverwig* and *swartachtig*, that is, with both 'darkish' and 'blackish'. An English–Portuguese dictionary of the late eighteenth century, on the other hand, says *pardo* is gray and for 'pardo human, see mulato'. A *mulato* is described as being of a tawny color, from the mixture of black and white. A Portuguese–French dictionary of the same period has: 'Pardo . . . Fusco, escuro. Gris, brun, noirâtre, qui tire sur le noir.' It also has: 'Cabra. Pardo, mulato. Mulatre, noireau.'[58]

Thus we see that *pardo* still pointed towards a range of shades: dark, obscure, gray, brown, blackish, learning towards black; but also the term *cabra* was equated with both *pardo* and *mulato* and a dark-colored person. In Brazil *cabra* came to be used for persons who were a mixture of African and either American or European. (The Portuguese–English dictionary also has *cabra* but equates it with Indians who chewed betel.)

In 1836 Constancio defined *pardo* as: 'de côr como a do leopardo, escura como a dos mulatos. Homens pardos, baços de pelle.' That is, a leopard-like color, obscure like that of *mulatos*; people of dark skin color. A German–Portuguese dictionary of 1891 equated *pardo* with *braun* and *dunkelgrau* (brown and dark gray) but, significantly, German *mulatte* was equivalent to *pardo* as well as to *mulato*.[59]

It seems quite clear that *pardo* in Portuguese, unlike *loro* in Castillian, proved to be a very adaptive term. Its ambiguity has allowed it to evolve in the direction of becoming a class term, especially in Brazil. That is, from being a general range of darker, brownish shades (between black and white) *pardo* has gradually acquired other connotations which make it not only an equivalent of *mulato*, *cafuzo*, *mestiço* and so on in Brazil (as well as still retaining color properties) but also an equivalent of 'colored' in English and *kleurlingen* in Dutch. This evolution will be discussed further under the topic of 'people of color'.

PARDOS AND *MORENOS* IN THE SPANISH COLONIES

Now let us review briefly the use of *pardo* in the Castillian language in order to discover the gradual adoption in the Americas of Portuguese usage. As noted earlier, *pardo* began as a *fuscus* equivalent, but with 'gray' as the most direct translation. In 1520 Nebrija stated '*pardo* color of cloth, *fuscus*'. In 1534 Castillian *pardillo* was equated with Latin *griseus*, *leucopheus*, Dutch *grau*, French *gris*, and Italian *grixo*. Oudin, in 1607, defined *pardo color* as *gris de minime* and *Pardillo* as 'gris blanc, gris argenté'. Covarrubias (1611 and 1647) stated:

Pardo, color, que es el propio que la oveja o el carnero tiene, y le labran y aderecan, haziendo paños del fin teñerle. . . . El vestido *pardo* es de gente humilde, y el mas basto se llama pardillo. De noche todos los gatos son pardos.

Thus pardo was essentially wool-gray, both as the color of sheep and of woolcloth. It was the color of the clothing of the lower classes. The same proverb about all of the cats at night being *pardos* is given as in other sources.[60]

Minsheu (1617) equates *pardo color* with Latin *glaucus leocopheus* and with English 'gray or russet color' but under 'browne' he includes as an equivalent 'pardo, à colore pardi animalis. Latin Fuscus. . . . Subniger.' *Baço* is equated with 'colour *interim fuscum* and *nigru*; a sad gray, or light black'. In 1599 *pardisco* was equated with 'somewhat grayish or duskie color'.[61]

In general, *pardo* continued to be equated with 'gray' in Spanish usage for some time, until gradually conforming with the definition of the Royal Academy already referred to (an earth color, or the color of the skin of the common bear, a yellowish red more obscure than gray). An additional change is reflected in the notation of a 1901 dictionary that *pardo* in Cuba and Puerto Rico was the equivalent of *mulato* (but not in Spain).

Santamaría, in his dictionary of Americanisms, notes that in Argentina and the Caribbean the term *pardo* was used for

al mulato, o hijo de negra y blanco, o vice versa; en el Brasil, a los hijos de india con mulato, o vice versa; en otros países, al hijo de español o de europeo en general con india o con negra, y más generalmente a toda la gente de color, incluso al negro del país, como en Cuba y Puerto Rico.

Thus Santamaría notes that, in general, *pardo* had come to refer to all people of color, including native-born blacks in Cuba and Puerto Rico and especially mixtures of American and African with European. In Brazil *pardo* referred especially to the mixture of *mulatos* with Americans, while in Argentina and the Caribbean it referred especially to black–white mixtures.[62]

We cannot, in fact, accept Santamaría's definitions in every detail but they do serve to illustrate the widespread use of *pardo* in Spanish-speaking regions of the Americas. This usage commenced in the seventeenth century, probably as a result of the widespread mixture of Africans and Americans which produced many children of dark brown shades. Aguirre Beltrán notes that in Mexico in the seventeenth century the *mulato pardo* was half American and half African, while the *mestizo pardo* was half American, quarter African and quarter European. He goes on to say that:

The "Dark Mulatto" (*mulato pardo*) was the result of the mixture of Negro and Indian. The dark mulattoes were, without a doubt, the most numerous single group in New Spain, and their skin color inspired a curious and varied series of adjectives. They were said to have "*color pardo*" (dark color)

along with other color shades listed earlier, including *membrillo*. The *mestizo pardo* was the result of the marriage of a *mulato pardo* with a *mestizo*.[63]

As will be noted later, the mixed children of Americans and Africans were called *mulatos* in the Spanish Empire for some time. The term *pardo* appears, in essence, as a modifier implying 'dark'; however, its meaning could also (with time) become more general. In 1646 Juan de Solórzano completed a work based upon a decade of experience in Peru in the 1620s. He remarked that 'the children of *Negros* and free *Negras* are called *morenos*, or *pardos*, and these [people] are coming to live regularly and in some places there are militia companies of them.' Solórzano then refers to royal legislation of 1623 and 1625 which mentions *los Morenos libres* but says nothing about *pardos* and *negros*. Solórzano also takes note of a law that 'Los Negros y Negras libres deben pagar tributo . . . y tambien sus hijos habidos en matrimonio con Indios o Indias.'[64] That is to say, free blacks ought to pay tribute along with their children by American fathers and mothers. We are left in doubt as to what Solórzano meant by 'the children' of free blacks (in the earlier paragraph) being called *morenos* or *pardos* but it could mean that they were part-American (or part-European) to some degree.

Today *moreno* serves as a euphemism for *negro* among some Spaniards and several writers have supposed that this usage commenced at an early date, especially as the word *negro* came to be equivalent to 'slave'. Indeed, it may be true that some *negros* who were free could have been so denominated, but after a generation or two it is also likely that large numbers of slaves must have been of mixed American and African origin, to one degree or another, and there may have actually been some slight lightening of skin color (especially among *morenos libres*, who may have been descended from an American female). Aguirre Beltrán provides several examples of persons who were mixed African and American but who looked like *negros*. Such persons could have easily been designated as *morenos*, especially in regions such as Panama, Cuba or Puerto Rico, where much American–African mixture occurred.

As early as 1501 Spaniards seized certain Americans of the Gulf of Urabá (Darién) who were *de color moreno*. Likewise, Gumilla in the 1740s described the Otomacos as *prietos, y morenos*. Thus the term *moreno* could be applied to presumably un-mixed Americans.[65]

Oudin in 1607 defined *moreno* as 'brun, noir, obscur, couleur d' Olives', that is as very similar to *loro* and *pardo* or *olivâtre*. Minsheu (1599) has *moreno* translated as 'murrie colour, browne, darke, duskish', an *hombre moreno* as 'a man of swartish hue', and *pan moreno* as 'browne bread'. Minsheu (1617) has *moreno* equivalent to '*fuscus, subniger*, brown, dark, duskish'.[66] Initially, then, we can suggest that *moreno* would maintain some connection with its usage in Spain, where (as noted) it was a color lighter than *negro* and was used for many Muslims. A Spanish decree of 1623 refers to 'the free *Morenos*' of Cuba as being distinct from *Negros cimarrones*. The 'free *Morenos*' had houses, fields, horses and so on, and were being disturbed by those searching for runaway *negros*. We can conjecture that the free *morenos* could have been generally dark-skinned or even African–American peasants since many kinds of persons could have been hiding runaways. *Negro* in this case does seem to be the equivalent of 'slave'.

A document of 1671, relating to Cuba, notes that 'in those parts' the *mulatos* were called *pardos* and that an order of 1634 had prohibited service as soldiers to 'mulatos, morenos, y mestizos' but because of a shortage of whites this order wa partially waived for 'pardos o mulatos' The term *moreno* is not totally clarified by the above but *pardo* clearly refers to non-blacks.[67]

A modern Brazilian dictionary defines *moreno* as 'Branco menos claro. De côr um pouco escura . . . pessoa morena.' In other words, a rather light brown color, leaning towards white.[68]

It may be that the theory that *moreno* was a polite term for *negro* in the Spanish Empire originated with scholars (especially North Americans) who tend to classify all part-Black Africans as 'negroes'. From this perspective any term other than *negro* (black) becomes a 'euphemism'.

In any case, by the 1640s–50s the word *pardo* began to be used in the Spanish Empire as a term referring to persons of mixed American and African ancestry, that is, *mulatos*, or to persons resembling such a mixture. In 1656, for example, there is a story about a Spaniard who met 'an old, well-dressed and white haired Mulatto. Having brought the coach to a stop he asked the Pardo to approach and asked him: "What is your name?" The Pardo told him.'[69] In 1681 a petition arrived in Spain from Peru

por parte de Juan Pascual, Domingo López Blas, Manuel y Francisco de Estela, pardos naturales de esa cuidád, esclavos de Francisco Franco, vecino de ella, se me ha representado el miserable estado en que se hallen. . . . Suplicandome que en conformidad a lo mandado por cédula general del ano de 1609 en que está prohibido el servicio personal de los indios y se encargó la libertad que deben gozar como vasallos míos, fuese servido de ordenar que todos los esclavos pardos y cuarterones que hay en esas provincias, sean libres.[70]

In short, a group of *pardos naturales* petitioned the Crown for relief in conformity with a law of 1609 prohibiting personal service by *indios*, thus implying clearly that *pardos* (and *cuarterones* or quarter-bloods) were of American ancestry.

Pardo also continued to be used as a color term (meaning 'dark'). Joseph Gumilla, in describing the skin colors of Venezuelan natives, stated that those who lived in the forests were *casi blancos* (almost white), those who went about in open countryside were *trigueños* (wheat brown), while the Otomacos who navigated the rivers were *prietos, y morenos*. In general, however, the Americans 'son de color trigueño, ya más, ya menos pardo, al modo que los Europeos son blancos, ya más, ya menos, sin que falten trigueños, y más en la gente del campo.'[71] Thus, *trigueño* was the average color, with some being more *pardo* and others less *pardo*, just as many Europeans, especially in the countryside, were not white but *trigueño*.

The Americans who were *moreno* and *prieto* seem to have been regarded by Gumilla as being darker than *pardo* or *trigueño pardo* would have implied. In any case, one can again see the inherent difficulty of using color terms to differentiate between the various peoples of the Spanish and Portuguese Empires, since Americans themselves could range over almost the entire spectrum of browns, from near-white to near-black.

In any case, the word *pardo* gradually gained in importance. Its very ambiguity and vagueness undoubtedly facilitated its general spread until, as we shall see later, it comes to be virtually the equivalent of 'colored' in many Spanish-speaking regions. It should be stressed that *pardo*, as a relational term (dark), had a vagueness that could make it more useful than a specific color descriptive (such as *pardo* = gray). Thus a shift in meaning made it possible for *pardo* to eventually fulfill similar functions in Brazil and in Spanish-speaking areas.

COLOR TERMS IN ENGLISH AND OTHER LANGUAGES

There is no doubt but that Spain and Portugal led the way in developing color terms which tended to become group designations. Other cultures tended to use color terms which remained only color descriptors. This is true, apparently, with Italian where early use was made of *berretini, bruni olivegno, color di ulivo*, and *olivastro* for the Berbers of southern Mauritania and for the Americans of Brazil. The latter were also called 'of the color of the olive' (as were many Pacific islanders) by Pigafetta in 1519–21 (with Magellan) and 'olivastro, e piú presto negri' (olivish, and almost black) in *c*.1533. Generally, *berretino* and olive were used as equivalents to *pardo* and *amulatado* and both point towards an obscure color. *Berretino* is described as *grigio-verdognolo* or *grigio* (greenish-gray or gray) but the term may have been influenced by *birrus* (obscure rose) or by Latin *venetus* (used as an equivalent to *pardo* by Nebrija).[72]

In English the term 'tawny' for a time almost became a designation for Americans or for similar 'intermediate' peoples. In 1559 one author stated: 'As the world's Sun . . . makes the Moor black, the European white; th' American tawny.' This usage continued for many years. As noted previously, a London pageant of 1672 depicted 'Tawny Moors' working and playing music in 'West India' and a woman with a 'tawny face' declared: 'That I the better may Attention draw, Be pleas'd to know I am America.' (For many centuries 'America' was depicted as a Native American woman.) A 1695 plantation scene depicted 'Negroes, Tawneys, Virginia–planters' and so on.

In 1686 a letter from New England stated: 'Tho' he was a Tawney-more Indian, yet he was a converted one'. We shall have cause to make occasional reference to the term 'tawny' and 'tawny-moore' as a designation for Americans elsewhere. On the other hand, it is a descriptor which did not endure, being eventually replaced by the concept of 'redskin'.[73]

An Englishman who had lived in Spain for many years visited Mexico and Central America in 1625–37. This man, Thomas Gage, served as a parish priest in Guatemala. He wrote (*c*.1645) of the servant women of Mexico City:

Nay, a blackamoor or tawny young maid and slave will make hard shift, but she will be in fashion. . . . The attire of this baser sort of people of blackamoors and mulattoes (which are of a mixed nature, of Spaniards and blackamoors) is so light, and their carriage so enticing that many Spaniards even of the better sort . . . disdain their wives for them. . . . Their bare, black, and tawny breasts are covered with bobs hanging from their chains of pearls.

The use of 'tawny' in this context is not clear, but it would seem to refer to the color of Americans since there must have been a preponderance of 'tawny' American maids in Mexico City. 'Mulattoes (which are of a mixed nature, of Spaniards and blackamoors)' can be interpreted as referring to the mixture of Europeans and Africans with 'tawny' people, although Gage's construction is ambiguous.[74] It may be that Gage meant 'tawny' to include all intermediate colored people.

'Dun' (dull brown or grayish brown), although treated as an equivalent for *loro* in 1599 by Minsheu, never became a group term in English. Minsheu equated 'browne' with Italian *bruno* (*fusco*), with Castillian-Portuguese 'bruno' (*baço*), a colore lienis . . . subnigri', and with *moreno* and *pardo* as well as with *baeticus* (from the people of the Betica region of Spain who were originally *sunt* [soot] color and *castaneus* [chesnut]).

In actual practice, English 'brown' was originally a very dark (dusky) color corrresponding to Portuguese *baço* and *pardo* and Latin *fuscus* (*subniger*). One source of 1570 has 'browne, black, *ater*; Broune *fuscus*'. In 1449 the color of a storm was brown, while in 1325 the world was described as 'wel broun' after the sun went down. In 1668 one writer stated: 'as brown as evening'. Thus 'dusk' would be a good translation. Samuel Johnson believed that a brown color always possessed black as part of its compound.[75]

In a way it is strange that 'brown' did not become a term widely used for *loros* and *pardos* but it would appear that English 'black' was used (and is used) in such a broad manner as to embrace all darker shades of human brown. Even 'tawny', a lighter shade of brown mixed with yellow or orange, has failed to survive for humans except in the form of 'tan' or 'tanned'. The same circumstances seem to hold true for Dutch *bruin* being dominated by *swart*.

THE SHIFT OF OFFICIAL IBERIAN TERMINOLOGY FROM A COLOR TO A MIXTURE EMPHASIS

One of the significant occurrences in the sixteenth century is that the interest of Spaniards and Portuguese begins to gradually shift from simply describing all intermediate colored people by the same general color reference terms to one wherein people of mixed ancestry are singled out by new descriptors, especially *mestizo* and *mulato*. Of course, the use of color terms persists, but as noted with *pardo*, one tends to see a partial identification of this term with a mixed-blood status.

This shift of emphasis is, I believe, quite significant. In general, it correlates with the rise of overseas colonialism and, in all likelihood, with the appearance of racist caste systems in those areas.

Mestizo, which literally means 'mixed', has already been referred to in connection with the discussion of 'hybrid'. As will be recalled, 'hybrid' referred to almost any kind of mixture, of wild and tame, of citizen and non-citizen, of resident and traveler. It possessed no 'racial' implications.

Mestizo and its equivalents (especially *mestis* or *metif* in French) seem to have appeared primarily as a referent to mixtures of a similar nature to 'hybrid' and particularly of different kinds of animals. We might argue that growing prejudice was responsible for their appliction to human beings as physically close as Americans are to Europeans. On the other hand, it may well be that *mestizo* developed primarily as a way to designate persons whose culture and social status were felt to be distinctive from those of either parent group. Thus, initially at least, its use may have primarily pointed not towards biology but towards culture.

An early use of the Latin root *mixtus* occurs in a statement describing the *mozárabes* (Arabized Christians) of Muslim Spain: 'et en los otros logares dechos mixta árabes que quiere dezir mesclados con los árabes e oy chaman los mosçárabes.'[76] Thus 'mixed' was used in a cultural sense, referring to their physical juxtaposition against Arabs.

THE USE OF *MESTIZO*: A SHIFT TOWARDS RACIALISM AND CASTE

The term *mestizo* does not appear in the Nebrija dictionaries of *c.*1495 or 1520 although *mezcla*, *mesturar* and related words are included. *Mestiço* also is not a word found in Santa Rosa de Viterbo's study of the medieval Portuguese language. Its first known appearance is in Cardoso's Portuguese dictionary (1560s) when it is equated with Latin *Ibria* (corrected to *Hybris, hybrida* in the

1643 edition). *Mestiço* is treated as something of an equivalent of *mulato* by Cardoso, since the latter is also equated with *Hybrida*.[77] But *mestiço* refers to a broader range of mixtures.

Minsheu's Spanish–English dictionary of 1599 defined *mestizo* as: 'that which is come or sprung of a mixture of two kinds, as a blacke-Moore and a Christian, a mungrell dog or beast.' This approach is maintained by Minsheu in 1617 when he states of *mestizo*: 'Latin *Hybris*, English a mongrill', and also where he equates 'Mongrill' with French *chien mestis* (mixed dog), Spanish *mestizo* and Latin *Hybris*, *Hybrida*, as well as with *mulato*. *Adulterium* is implied, when *hybrida* is applied to humans, Minsheu notes.[78]

Oudin, in his 1607 Spanish–French dictionary has the following:

mestizo = mestif ou mestis, qui est de deux races, comme un enfant d'un More
& d'une blanche, & au contraire; il se dit aussi des chiens & autre animaux
[one who is of two races, as the child of a Moor and a white, also applied to
dogs and other animals].
podenco = Chien ou chienne mestis [mixed dog].
mestif = mestizo, podenco.
métis = animal mestizo.

The term *mulato* also refers to *demy Mores* (half-moors), the children of a white and a *moor* and also to a small mule. Thus *mestizo* and *mulato* continue to have the same meaning except that *mestizo* (and even more, *métis*) refers to a broader range of mixtures, that is, not just to mules or humans. (*Podenco* is now translated as 'hound'.)

Oudin's 1625 edition repeats the above except that he adds to the definition of *mestizo*: 'c'est aussi un enfant d'un Christien & d'une infidele'. Thus, a half-Christian, half-non-Christian child would be a *mestizo*. Oudin's 1639–40 edition remained the same as the 1625 except that Dutch equivalents were added: 'die van diverse generatie compt; ghelijck moulack . . . oft van hont en katte . . . kindt van een Christen en een heydens.' That is, a *mestizo* was one derived from different origins or nations, the same as *moulack*; or from a dog and a cat; or the child of a Christian and a heathen. *Mulato* was also equated with *moulack* but again, *mulato* was not applied to animals other than mules.[79]

Covarrubias (1611 and 1647) defines Spanish *mestizo* in terms of mixture only among animals: 'el ǭ es engendrado de diversas especies de animales, del verbo misceo, es, por mezclarse.' Barbosa (1611) preserves a conservative Portuguese perspective, in equating *mestiço* with *Hybris*, *Hybrida*, as does Pereira (1646). Pereira also notes that both *mestiço* and *mulato* imply adultery or the mixture of a native and a stranger.

These tendencies continue in Spanish, with, for example, Sobrino's 1721 dictionary:

mestizo . . . quien a nacido de un padre pagano y de una Christiana; o de una pagana y de
un Christiano . . . [repeated in French]; animal nacido de un padre y de una madre de
diversos géneros; métis, animal né d'un père + d'une mère de diverses espèces.

Thus *mestizo* referred to both Christian–pagan and animal mixtures, while French *métis* referred only to the latter.[80]

Between the 1778 and 1790 editions of Nebrija's dictionary of Spanish, a reference to '*los mestizos* of Spaniard and Indians' is added to the earlier 'hybrid' definition. Santamaría's dictionary of *americanismos* (1942) notes that *mestizo* refers to 'the person born of father and mother of different *raza*, and especially to the child of the white man and Indian, or the Indian man and white woman'.[81] thus, we can see a change, from 'hybrid' (including animals) with its variety of meanings, including inter-religious mixture, to the more modern emphasis upon 'race'. Also, of course, the fact that *mestizo* came to be applied in the Spanish-speaking Americas to primarily European–American mixed-bloods is recognized.

Trends in the Portuguese language are, overall, similar to those in Spanish. An English–Portuguese dictionary of 1701 has for *mestiço*: 'any creature of mixed generation, as dogs or swine, etc.' Bluteau in 1712 goes into much greater detail:

Mestiço. Diz-se dos animaes racionaes, e irracionaes. Animal mestiço. Nascido de pay, e may de differentes especies, como mû, leopardo, etc. Misti generis animans. . . . Hybrida. . . . Nascido de hum porco montez, & de hûa porca domestica. . . . Homen mestiço, nascido de pays de differentes naçoês, v.g. Filho de Portuguez, + de India, ou de pay Indio, + de mãy Portugueza. Ibrida.

Thus the *Hybrida* tradition is preserved for animals, i.e., the union of wild with domestic, and so on. For humans, a child born of parents of two different nations is a *mestiço*, the example being the mixture of Portuguese and Indian. In the 1789 edition of Bluteau the example is 'o filho de Europeau com India, de branco com mulata, etc'. Thus, *mestiço* embraces the union of European with *mulato* as well as European with Indian. (It may be that a child born of black and white parents might not have been considered a *mestiço* by Bluteau.)

De Sousa and DaCosta e Sa (1784) state that French *mulâtre* is equivalent to *mestiço* as well as *mulato* in Portuguese. For French *métif* they give both *mistiço* and *molato* and state: 'o que he nascido de pai Europeo, e de Mai Indiana, ou de pais de diferentes qualidades, paizes, ou Religiões; Mestiço, caó ou qualquer outro animal nascido de dous de diversas especies.' The 1794 Portuguese–French version gives: 'Mestiço, nascido de animaes de diferentes especies, ou de pais de diversa casta. Métif . . . ou metis. . . . Pessoas mestiças. Personnes métives.' Thus *mestiço* continued to apply to animal mixtures as well as to mixtures among humans involving parents of different quality (social position, caste), countries or religions. *Mulato* and *mestiço* are treated as equivalents except that only the latter applies to animals generally.[82]

A Portuguese–English dictionary of 1783 states of *mestiço*: 'mungrel, *mestizo*, born of Indian and Portuguese parents; also mungrel in general.' The tendency to use *mestiço* for many (or all) kinds of mixtures continues. Constancio (1836) says of *mestiço*: 'filho de animaes de especies ou racas diferentes; v.g., o mu, ou mulo, mula; item. filho de Europeo e India ou Americana indigena, de branco e mulata etc.' Reference is made to animals of different species or races and to European or white mixture with Indians, Native Americans or *mulatos*. This type of definition continues until *c.*1900 but thereafter the mention of animals is usually dropped.

Characteristically, virtually all modern dictionaries of Portuguese equate *mestiço* with any mixture involving parents of 'different races' and make reference to *mulatos* as a type of *mestiço*. A *pardo* may also be a *mestiço* and the *caboré* of Brazil is seen as a 'mestiço de negro e índio'.[83] Thus *mestiço* in Portuguese has retained its basic meaning of 'mixed' but the kinds of mixture included have been reduced to human ones only and, more significantly, to 'racial' ones as opposed to cultural, social, inter-ethnic and inter-religious mixtures.

The triumph of the rationalist's modern idea of 'race' can, therefore, be seen in the evolution of the term. That is to say that the early modern world placed greater stress on the religion, class, local origin, and culture while the modern 'western' mind has selected so-called 'race' as an especially pertinent criterion.

Of course, dictionaries are usually from 50 to 100 years behind the actual speech practices of people, it would seem, and European dictionaries often were especially slow in reflecting usage in colonial areas. We must, therefore, look at a few examples of actual practice to understand the meanings of *mestizo*.

The widespread use of *mestizo* begins, so far as my data illustrates, not in the Iberian peninsula but in India, Brazil, and the Caribbean approximately simultaneously. The Portuguese by the first half of the sixteenth century began to produce large numbers of mixed-bloods. *Pardo* seems not to have been used for such persons. Instead they were called *mestiços*, *mamalucos* and *mulatos* depending on the geographical region. In India and the East Indies the Portuguese used the term *mestiço* to refer to mixed-bloods who were half-Asian, as early as 1547. Such persons could be half-Indian, half-Malay, and so on. Much later the word *topaz* came to also be used for such persons, derived from an Indian term mean 'bi-lingual, interpreter'. During the sixteenth century, however *mestiço* (and *mistiço*) was used commonly, as noted by the Italian traveler Carletti who stated in the 1590s that the mixed-bloods in Bengal were called *mestrizze*. In 1585 Sassetti used *mestizi*. In the 1601–11 period the Frenchman Pyrard de Laval utilized the French equivalents *métisses* and *métifs* to refer to the Portuguese mixed-bloods of India.[84]

In Brazil the Portuguese do not seem to have utilized any terms for mixed-bloods in the sixteenth century except for *mamaluco* and *mestiço*. *Mamaluco* appears in Jesuit letters as early as 1551 while *mestiça* appears in 1552. Neither term is defined when first used, suggesting that the readers will understand (the readers being Jesuits in Coimbra, Portugal in the case of *mamaluco* and a Jesuit in Lisbon in the case of *mamaluquo* and *mestiça* in 1552).

Mamaluco is later defined as referring to half-white (or half-Christian) and half-American persons and it remains a common term in Brazil for such a mixture. Its spelling is later changed to *mameluco*, a result, no doubt, of the influence of a similar-sounding word of Arabic origin. *Mamaluco* appears to be a Tupí term.[85]

The word *mestiço* was used in a vague and general sense in the Jesuit letters; however, ordinarily it had the same meaning as *mamaluco* since the Jesuits were concerned primarily with Americans and part-Americans. For example, in 1552 a Jesuit father confessed certain women *mestiças* by means of an interpreter, thus indicating perhaps that they were Tupí-speakers.

The later use of the word *mestiço* in Brazil is quite complicated and will be referred to in connection with my discussion of 'people of color'; however, we can say here that in general the Portuguese preserved its very broad meaning so as to encompass all kinds of mixed-bloods.[86]

In the Spanish colonies the term *mestizo* appears by 1553, in connection with *españoles*, *mestizos*, and *indios* living as vagabonds. In the same year, reference was made to the great quantity of 'hijos de españoles que han habido en indias', that is, half-American mixed-bloods, but no special term was used. In 1548 a law made *mestizas* subject to the same rules as governed Spanish women in cases of adultery. From 1549 onward many decrees refer to *mestizos*, usually in conjunction with *mulatos*, thus establishing a separation between two classes of mixed-bloods.[87]

In the Spanish Empire in the sixteenth century *mulatos* were usually (as we shall see) of African and American ancestry. *Mestizo*, on the other hand, came to refer to those who were half-Spanish and half-American. Thus usage doubtless reflects a developing racial class or caste system since *mestizos* would usually be lighter and also be, culturally as well as biologically, more akin to Spaniards. (Of course, there were exceptions since many *mestizos* were raised as Americans and were 'illegitimate', but, nonetheless, those raised by Spanish fathers were accorded privileges sometimes withheld from darker persons as well as from other *mestizos*.)

Juan de Solórzano, writing between the 1620s and 1640s, noted that the *mulatos* ought to be encompassed within the general term *mestizo*, a term which he related back to *hibrida*. Solórzano, however, by the 1640s felt that the *mulatos* were called such in order to compare their origin with that of the mule since they were 'more ugly and extraordinary'. This latter opinion was expressed in his later Spanish version and was not found in his earlier Latin work. Whatever the validity of his argument, Spanish prejudice obviously had come to favor the lighter American mixed-bloods over darker, part-African peoples.[88]

Aguirre Beltrán has shown that, in fact, *mestizo* could be used in Mexico for part-African persons in the seventeenth century, provided that they also had American and Spanish ancestry.[89] Nonetheless, standard usage has tended to favor restricting *mestizo* to American–European mixed-bloods until the present century when, as will be noted later, the term has come in certain regions to be virtually equivalent to 'people of color' or to a particular cultural (as opposed to racial) type. That is, a *mestizo* is one who speaks Spanish, does not live as a part of a so-called 'Indian' group and has some non-white ancestry (usually American).

Nonetheless, in Spain itself the older, more general meaning of *mestizo* still persisted. For example, a friar who was half-African is called a *mestizo* by the historian Antonio Domínguez Ortiz. Vicenta Cortés, in discussing the problem of classifying *loros*, states: 'Ahora bien, el auténtico problema es el de los mestizos, el de los esclavos *lors*, oscuros. Porque mestizos había de mora y blanco, de negro y blanco, de mora y negro, y de toda mezcla en que los hijos apuntaran un ligero tinte oscuro en la piel.' Thus Cortés uses *mestizo* for obscure-colored *loro* slaves and for the mixture of Black Africans and Muslims, Muslims and Spaniards, Spaniards and Black Africans, and of all types of mixed-bloods having a dark tint to their skin.[90]

In general, I think we can say that the appearance and evolution of the term *mestizo* in both the Spanish and Portuguese Empires reflects the kind of caste-like and racialist social orders which evolved in the colonies. Terms such as *loro* and *pardo* were too general to meet the needs of caste societies.

That ultimately *pardo* survived and came to be widely used is a reflection of the extensive and complex miscegenation in the colonies and the need for a general term which could embrace all of the different kinds of mixed-bloods and 'people of color' whose ancestry could almost never be accurately described. *Loro*, for reasons which are not clear, died out as a color term and did not fulfill this function. *Mestizo* itself, especially in Mexico, *ladino* in parts of Central America, and perhaps *cholo* in Peru, came to be used, eventually, as almost the equivalent of *pardo*.[91]

Thus we have a sequence in which first the Europeans began with very general color terms (*loro*, *pardo*, *baço*, etc.); second, when they coined many more color terms (*membrillo cocido*, *moreno*, etc.); thirdly, when they invented or adopted terms for various mixed-bloods *as* mixed-bloods (*mamaluco*, *mestizo*, *mulato*, *zambo*, etc.); fourth, when they attempted by means of such terms to individually categorize most types of mixed-bloods; and, fifth, when it all became so very complicated that they fell back upon very general terms such as *pardo* or made ones like *mestizo* very nebulous. Finally, all of this occurred within a reality where the great mass of colonial people probably used all these terms in pragmatic ways based upon appearance and culture rather than upon actual ancestry.

There is, of course, a considerable difference between the descriptive use of *loro* and the later prescriptive use of *mestizo*. *Loros* were never subject to specific legal limits on their behavior, as *loros*, in Spain. The same was true for most other color-descriptive terms.

The colonial designation of persons as *mestizos*, *mulatos*, and later, *pardos*, was an entirely different matter. The use of these terms in the Americas was designed to identify and to limit, to control, *and*, by and large, *to exclude*.

5
The *Mulato* Concept: Origin and Initial Use

Few racial terms have been of greater importance in the Americas than that of *mulato*. Great numbers of persons have been so categorized and books have been written about groups of people presumed to be mulattoes, especially in North America.

Surprisingly, such an important term seems never to have been systematically studied historically. This is, as we shall see, a sad example of scholarly oversight since the term *mulato*, like most other racial terms, has not had a static or single meaning. We have already seen that *mulato* in the sixteenth century was treated as being equivalent to 'hybrid' and thus applicable to many kinds of persons. It is necessary to be more precise, however, in terms of the changing meanings of this word.

Because of the widespread use of the term I propose to deal at some length with its origin. This is also made necessary because the common interpretation (which basically boils down to 'mulish' or 'young mule') is a nasty one, rather pejorative and dehumanizing. If indeed *mulato* does have its beginning in *mulo* we should eliminate its use as another example of the kind of 'nigger'-like words coined by dominant social castes to refer to the objects of their oppression.

But the birth of *mulato* is shrouded in mystery. It evolved in a period in which Arabic-speaking and Arabized *Romance*-speaking Iberians were passing from Islamic to Christian rule. It evolved, undoubtedly, at the folk level and probably existed as an oral term for some time before it was first written down. Thus we may never be able to fully document its early use but it seems that we can ascertain enough to at least clarify somewhat the murky picture existing heretofore.

There are two major theories which have been developed as to the origin of *mulato*. These theories will be analyzed prior to examining the evidence of dictionaries and of actual usage.

The Mule Theory

Corominas in his etymological dictionary of the Castillian language notes that *mulato* possibly arose 'by comparison of the hybrid origin of the *mulato* with that of the mule'.[1]

The first actual reference to the theory that *mulato*, as applied to humans, was derived from *mulo*, seems to appear in the Covarrubias dictionary of 1611. Covarrubias states 'mulato = he who is the child of a *negra*, and of a white man, or the reverse = and for being an extraordinary mixture they compare it to the origin of the mule'. He also refers to the *mulo* as 'a known bastard animal' and to *muleto* as a small or young mule.[2]

The first thing to note about Covarrubias' assertions is that they occurred some eighty or ninety years after *mulato* began to be applied to humans and more than a century after the earliest documented use of the word *mulato*. Thus Covarrubias was certainly not an eye-witness to the original application of the term and we may suggest that his assertion was based on assumption rather than upon documentation.

Moreover, as we shall see, the use of the term *mulato* in the Spanish Empire was far different from Covarrubias' definition. We may suspect that his assertion about the 'extraordinary' nature of the mixture which produced persons called *mulatos* was a statement of personal prejudice based upon limited familiarity with the reality of race mixture in Spain and the empire.

The next reference to the *mulo* theory occurs in Juan de Solórzano's *Indianum Iure* (written 1626–36) wherein he notes that mixed-bloods were commonly called mestizos and mulattoes and that the latter term was derived from the concept of mule.[3] In his 1647 Spanish language version Solórzano acknowledged Covarrubias as his authority for the *mulo* theory and also added some very disparaging remarks about *mulatos* being the most ugly and extraordinary mixture.[4]

In 1639 Manuel de Faria y Sousa published Camoens' *Lusiadas* with commentary. After mentioning the term *mulato* he described the origin of the mule and stated that the term *mulo* 'que lo es de vos mulato, respetando a la calidad de la junta de objetos contrarios.'[5] This idea, of the mule representing the union of contrary objects, is repeated by Bluteau in 1712. Bluteau also asserts that 'the name mulatto comes from mule, an animal derived from two others of different species'.[6]

The significance of this is that both *mulo* and *mulato* refer to 'hybrids'. The weakness of the theory rests in the fact that the Spaniards had been exposed to many hundreds of years of experience with various types of racial mixtures (e.g. Spanish–Moorish, Moorish–African, Spanish–African) during a period in which North Africans and Black Africans were often conquerors, not to mention the earlier Roman and Carthaginian periods. É. Lévi-Provencal, in his history of Muslim Spain, writes of slaves of various colors being imported into the Iberian peninsula, including 'Sudanese' (Black African) persons, as well as white slaves from various parts of Europe. Andalucia possessed in its cities 'une population d'aspect si peu uniforme, blonds et bruns, blancs, métis et noirs'. That is, blondes and browns, whites, mixed-bloods and blacks could be seen (in the ninth century and later). He also tells us that black female slaves were used as concubines and in domestic service and that *mulâtres* (mixed bloods) were found in the Muslim aristocracy and middle class, while color prejudice was absent.[7]

It is, therefore, strange that human hybrids would be named after the mule, since the latter's special peculiarity arises from its infertility. Obviously, the Spaniards knew very well about different colors or breeds of horses, cattle, and so on, interbreeding quite successfully, just as different colors of human did also.

The *mulo* theory also involves some assertions, made by dictionary-makers, about what kind of mule was first called *mulato*. Before discussing that, however, it is necessary to note that Corominas suspects a *mozárabe* (Arabized Christian) origin for the latter term because of his analysis of how suffixes such as -*ato* and -*eto* or -*ito* evolved. Corominas cites Nebrija's early dictionary for the application of the term *muleta* to the 'female young of the mule species', a usage pointing towards an early non-human application.

W. Meyer-Lübke, in his study of Romance languages, discusses the -*ittus* suffix and how this evolved into Spanish and Portuguese -*ito*. He notes that '-*attus*' served as an ending for the young of a species of animals as in later Italian (*cerbiatto*), French (*louvat*), Provençal (*leonat*), Spanish (*cervato, lobato, mulato*) and so on. Thus Meyer-Lübke supports the idea that the suffix -*ato* in *mulato* is derived from a common Romance suffix referring to the young of animals. Nebrija supported this thesis by stating (as above) that *muleta* referred to the female young of the mule family. But Nebrija used -*eta* instead of -*ata*. Meyer-Lübke also allows that -*ittus* could become -*ato* in Spanish. Corominas allows for -*ato* having been derived from -*ittus* or -*itus* as well as -*attus*.

In any case, the difference for us is slight, since young animals can easily be referred to with a diminutive form meaning small (as in *mulito*) as well as by an ending referring specifically to young animals. As we shall see, *mulato* and its variants are often used with *both* meanings. It should also be noted that the earliest form reported by any scholarly source is *mulita* which Simonet states was used in Hispanic (mozarabic) rabbinical writings for *mula*.[8]

Now, as applied to mules, what did *muleta–mulato* mean? This exercise is necessary because of a tendancy among some Portuguese writers to equate *mulato* with *only* the progeny of a she-donkey and a male horse (rather than the much more common product of the union of the mare and with the male donkey).

Nebrija (*c*.1495, and 1516) states that *mulos* and *mulas* were derived from the union of male donkeys and mares. But *muleta* and *muleto* are defined as of 'asna y cavallo' and the same as Latin *hinna* or *hinnus*. He also states: 'Muleto este mismo, ginnus . . . hinnulus'. Nebrija's Latin–Castillian dictionary of 1492 has (Latin):

Burdo, -onis = por el burdégano
hinnus, -i = por mulo de cavallo y asna
hinnulus, -i = por aqueste mesmo romo
hinnulus, -i = por enodio hijo de ciervo
ginnus, -i = por mulo o mula enana.

The combination of the above tells us a great deal. *Ginnus* refers to a dwarfish mule, while *hinnulus* refers to the faun of the deer or a *mulo* derived from a stallion and a she-donkey. *Burdégano* and *burdo* (French *bardot*) refer to the same type of mule. Thus *muleto* has reference to *both* a dwarfish mule and a female donkey–stallion mixture. The implication is that *muleto* is seen essentially as a diminutive, since the size of mules seems to be intrinsically related to the size of the mother (a she-donkey, therefore, produces small mules).

Clarke tells us that *ginnus* was derived from Greek *yinios* which, in Roman times, meant the progeny of a mare and a mule, while *hinnus* stemmed from Greek *innos* and meant (in Latin) the progeny of a stallion and a she-donkey.[9]

The 1520 Nebreja *dictionarium* offers nothing new. Later editions of Nebrija (1778, 1790) preserve the dual meaning in that *muleta* is defined as a 'new mule' and *mula annicula* (one-year-old mule) as well as the child of a stallion and a *burra* (equivalent to *burdo* and *hinnus*). *Muleta* is also an aid (crutch) for cripples, a usage not found in 1495.[10]

The dictionary of Cardoso (prepared before 1569) has Portuguese *mulato* for Latin *mulus* and *mula* for *mula*, but also adds:

mulata, ou mulato = hybrida, -ae
mulata, filho dasno e egoa = burdo, burdonis
muleta = scipio, -onis [cane, rod].

Thus *mulato* refers to a hybrid and to the child of an ass and a mare, but this is equated with Latin *burdo*. The 1643 edition remains the same except that '*mula*, or *mulato*' is equated with *hybrida*.[11]

Las Casas' Tuscan–Castillian dictionary (first edition, 1570) has:

(Tuscan) mulo = bastardo
(Tuscan) stampela = muleta [crutch].

Further note will be taken of the Italian tendency to equate *mulo* with *bastardo*. It is interesting that Las Casas has no other meaning for *muleta* than crutch.[12]

Oudin's Castillian–French dictionary of 1607 has:

(Castillian) muleto o muleta = petit mulet or mule petite [small mule]
          muletas = . . . pontences . . . bequilles [crutches].
(French) mulet = azemila, macho, mulo, burdegano [mule, burdégano].

the 1625 edition is the same.[13] The 1639 version includes, for French *mulet*: 'born of the union of a stallion and a she-donkey = mohino'.

Mohino is defined by Nebrija as '*animal hinnus* . . . , *burdo* . . . .' that is, as *burdégano.* It may be possible that *mohino* is related to the Greek *imionos*, meaning 'mule'.[14]

Thus Oudin equates *muleta* with a crutch and with a small *mulet* or *mule* but equates *mulet* with *burdégano* (*mohino*) but not with *muleta*. The 1639 edition specifically equates *mulet* with the product of a stallion and a she-donkey. The implication is that *muleta* (-*to*) referred to smallness.

Covarrubias (1611) mentions the *mulo* as a 'well-known bastard' stemming from either stallion and she-donkey or donkey and mare. He defines *muleto* as referring to mules when they are 'small and new' or as referring to crutches for cripples, which *muletas* were used as if they were mounts or beasts of burden.[15]

Barbosa (also 1611) states from Portuguese:

mulato, child of stallion and she-ass. Burdo, -onis
muleta, he o mesmo, que bordão [crutch].

John Florio, in his Italian–English dictionary of 1611, states:

mulétto = a little or young mule
mulo = a horse-mule. Also a bastard or misbegotten.

Thus again we note the use of 'mule' for 'bastard' in Italian.[16]

John Minsheu, a very capable scholar, states that *muleta* and *muleto* were diminutives of *mula* and *mulo* (1617). He also noted that *burdo* was an old term for mule, perhaps related to Hebrew *pered* or *pirdah*, and that it referred to a mule produced by a stallion and a she-donkey. He gives Spanish *mulo* and *azemila* (mule, beast of burden) as equivalents, as well as Dutch *muyl, muylesel* and Portuguese *mulato*. He also notes that Covarrubias had equated *burdégano* with the progeny of a she-ass or *burra* and a male horse, *hinnus* being a Latin equivalent.

The above would seem to indicate that while Portuguese *mulato* was applicable to a *hinnus* or *burdo*, Spanish *muleto* was not the same.[17]

Pereira (1646) for Portuguese has:

Mulata = hybrida [Latin]
Mulato [beast] = Burdo, -onis
Muleta = see Moleta
Muleta = embarcação [embarcation]
Moleta = scipio, -onis [crutch]
Moleta = embarcação.[18]

Thus *mulato*, although generally being equivalent to 'hybrid', is specifically related to *burdo* while *muleta/moleta* refers to a place of embarcation (Spanish *muelle*) and a cane or rod (crutch).

In 1659 De la Porte translates Spanish *muleto, o muleta* into Dutch *muylken*, indicating that *muleto* signifies only a small mule. But in 1701 Portuguese *mulato* is rendered into English as 'a beast so called between an horse and a she-ass'. On the other hand, a Portuguese–Dutch dictionary of 1718 simply translates 'mulato, beast' as: 'A beast, between a horse and an ass, called a muilezel. . . . Mulo, A muil-ezel, muil.' Thus we might well be unsure as to whether Portuguese *mulato* meant only a small mule or a *burdégano*.[19]

Bluteau in his Portuguese dictionary of 1712 states categorically: 'Mulato, Besta. O macho asneiro, child of stallion and she-ass.'[20] This phrase is then repeated by Viterbo (1798–9) and by other Portuguese dictionary-makers to virtually the present day. The phrase *macho asneiro* is likely to mean 'donkey-ish male mule' in this context but it could also be translated as 'donkey-ish male'. Bluteau's usage of *macho* = *mu* (*mulo*) implies that, in Portuguese, *macho* did not simply mean 'male' in 1712 (whereas it reportedly did in Spanish).

The evolution of the word *macho* need not concern us here except to note that there were early forms of *muacho* and *mulacho*. *Muacho*, according to Corominas, signified firstly '*muleto*, *machuelo*, young *mulo*' but later came to be applied to 'all ages' of mules.[21]

Spanish usage continued in a similar vein, at least in so far as we can rely on the dictionaries. In 1721 *muleto* was translated as equivalent to *pequeño mulo* and *petit mulet*. In 1901 Pagés has *muleto*, *-ta* equivalent to 'small *mulo*, of young age'. *Muleta* was defined as a crutch for those having difficulty in walking, as a baton or stick used by *toreros*, and as anything which aids in part to maintain another. To 'have *muletas*' was to be, because of old age, very wise.

Pagés also asserts that *muleto* was the old form of *mulato*. Zerolo, Toro y Gómez and Isaza repeat the above for their dictionary a decade later.[22]

Later Portuguese dictionaries, as noted, usually repeated Bluteau. An exception is Antenor Nascentes' work, of Brazilian origin. He defines (1943, 1960) a *mulato* as a 'mu de pouca idade' (young mule) and a *muleta* as a crutch. Jorge Amado, in his novel *Tereza Batista*, has one of his characters moving about with 'two *muletas*', namely, crutches.[23]

Italian seems to preserve *muletto* as a diminutive of *mulo*, *parvus mulus*, while *mulo* includes both *mulus* and *hinnus* with the implication of *bastardo* (Pasini, 1823). More recently *muletto* is equated with *hinnulus* (Badellino, 1970). Meyer-Lübke notes that *mulo* and *muleto* mean 'bastard' in different Italian dialects while *mulo* also means 'street child' in one of them.[24] These kinds of meanings will be discussed briefly below.

In Marin's Dutch–French dictionary (1710, 1728 and subsequent editions) *mulet* is defined as: 'animal of the species of the Mule, originated from an Ass and a mare . . . *Muil* or *Muilezel*'. Halma's dictionary defines *mulet* as: '*Muil*, *muilesel*. A beast produced by a horse and a she-donkey, or by an ass and a mare.'[25] Thus French *mulet* would seem to include both types of mules.

Before analyzing the significance of the above it is necessary to note that actual early Portuguese usage does not agree with the above tendency to restrict *mulato* to the *burdégano*.

First, I will cite an article by a British veterinarian on mules which states:

There are two kinds of mule – the *Mule* proper (*Equus Asinus* . . .; *Mulus*; Fr. *Mulet* or *Grand Mulet*; Ger. *Grosser Maulesel*), which is the hybrid produce of a male ass with a mare, and the *Hinny* (*Equus Asinus* . . .; *Hinnus*; Fr. *Bardot* or *petit mulet*; Ger. *kleiner Maulesel*), the offspring of the stallion and female ass. The mule is the more valuable of the two, and to its production the attention of breeders is entirely directed. Indeed, *the hinny is so rarely produced*, owing to the antipathy of the stallion to the female ass, *that many authorities deny its existence*. . . . Mules inherit to an extraordinary degree the shape and peculiarities of the sire; *from the mare they derive size*.[26] (Italics added).

Because of the difficulty of producing the *burdégano, bardot* or *hinnus*, we may well doubt whether at any time they were very numerous. Certainly such a rare creature could easily be confused with small mules, derived from small mares, and the latter must have greatly outnumbered *burdéganos* at any time. In fairness, however, we must note that the Talmud recognizes the existence of the latter and states that if a mule's ears are large the mule stems from a she-ass and a stallion.[27]

The earliest known written references to *mulato* as applied to an animal in Portuguese occur in the 1520s and 1530s. In Gil Vicente's poem 'Auto da Cananeia' he uses a line 'nem convertido em mulato'. This is interpreted by the editor as referring to *mulo, macho* and not to a hinny. Moreover it wouldn't make sense to refer to a rare animal in a context where the poet refers to ducks, cats, and so on.

At about the same time (1526–8) Vicente wrote a poem 'Clérigo de Beira' with the phrase: 'Se beato immaculato –, m'emprestasse o seu mulato'. *Mulato* is interpreted as referring to a mule. During the same period Francisco de Sá de Miranda wrote a poem wherein he refers to sleeping on a *mulato* ('dormindo no mulato'). This would seem clearly to refer to a mule or small mule.[28]

In a similar sense Cristóvão Viera in a letter from China refers to '*mulatos* and *asnos*' in such a manner as to indicate clearly that this is a reference to mules and donkeys, as such.[29] Most conclusive of all, however, is a law of 1538 adopted in Portugal under the terms of which: 'No person between Duoro and Minho [rivers] may raise more than one *mulato* for his service'. Clearly this law refers to small or young mules in general and not to some rare animal. Interestingly, the French government at a later date (1717) attempted to suppress or limit the production of mules in Poitou (by having all male donkeys castrated) because so many mares were being lost to horse production by being bred to produce mules. Doubtless, the need for cavalry mounts was a motivating factor in both Portugal and France.[30]

In any case, there is no reason whatsoever to believe that Portuguese *mulato* referred exclusively to the *hinnus*. It would appear likely that dictionary-makers after Cardoso tended to copy from each other and that probably none were mule-breeders or familiar with the industry.

Note should also be made of the fact that while it would appear from the dictionaries that *muleto* (rather than *mulato*) was always used in Castillian for mules, we cannot be sure that actual usage in Andalucia, Valencia or Galicia corresponded with that of Castilla. Moreover, Tirso de Molina (died 1648) used *mulato* to rhyme with *gato* (which *muleto* would not have) in a poem in which it is obvious that he intended to denote a mule. Moreover, the first example found of the word *mulato* (1498, Valencia) seems clearly to be a reference to an animal rather than a person. (This will be analyzed below.)[31]

In any case, what can we make of the above data? First, it seems likely that Portuguese *mulato*, Castillian *muleto*, Italian *muletto* and French *mulet* all referred to small or yountg mules as well as to rarer *burdéganos*. If this is so, however, why did some dictionary-makers (usually Portuguese) assert a narrower definition? Copying from each other is one possibility, as noted, but we cannot discount the sexual and racial implications of such a definition – especially in Portuguese where the same form (*mulato*) was used for humans and animals. The stallion impregnating the she-ass might be felt to be *a priori* analgous with the Portuguese male impregnating non-white women (to produce *mulatos*). It would be more difficult to identify with a *burro* (donkey) impregnating the mare (since *burro* has negative connotations not apparently associated with horse stallions). This would especially be true in the seventeenth and eighteenth centuries when racial–sexual overtones had apparently come to be associated with producing human *mulatos* and with *negras* and *mulatas* as sex-objects.

The second conclusion is that the evolution of *mulato* and *muleto* as two separate words may be of some significance in terms of developing a theory as to the origin of *mulato*. Clearly, in Spanish, Italian and French *muleto*, *muletto*, and *mulet* are ordinarily used *exclusively* for non-humans, while *mulato*, *mulâtre*, and so on, are reserved (ordinarily) for humans. We would be fully persuaded that this distinction (which appears at least by the 1540s–50s in Castillian) reflects a different historical origin were it not for the fact that *muleto* in Portuguese (from 1611) is confined to inanimate crutches, and so on.

Nonetheless, it is very significant to note that *muleto* is the most widespread form for 'small mule' and that it is a different word from *mulato* meaning a hybrid human being, except in Portuguese.

We can be sure that whatever the ultimate origins of *mulato* and *muleto*, they are so close in sound as to be easily confused and to be used, at times, interchangeably. The probable evolution of Castillian *macho* (male) from Latin *masclo* and Portuguese *macho* (mule) from *muacho* (as posited by Corominas) can be used to illustrate how divergent roots can eventually lead to the development of what seems to be a single word with several meanings. In modern Spanish, *macho* (Portuguese) has virtually replaced *mulo* as applied to a male mule, while at the same time *macho* also refers to any male, as in earlier usage.[32]

Before leaving the subject of animals, it is necessary to refer to the nuances of meaning associated with *burro* and *mulo*. References have already been cited which refer to *mulo* as meaning *bastardo* in Italian, along with a similar nuance mentioned by Covarrubias for Castillian.

Francisco del Rosal, writing about 1601, noted that *mula del diablo* (the devil's she-mule) was what the common people called the *amiga* (mistress) of a priest. Rosal felt that *mula* was derived from *mulas*, Greek for 'whore'. He stated that whores were called *mulas* in Castillian.

To Rosal the *mulo* represented *bastardo* and 'the use without purpose of procreation, only for pleasure' and it signified concubinage and bastardy.[33]

The word *mula* was, then, loaded with connotations of a sexual nature, and *mulo* in general pointed towards irregular origin or bastardy. One might be tempted to see in such connotations the origin of *mulato* since doubtless many mixed-bloods were born out of wedlock. On the other hand, if *mulo* itself denoted bastardy then there would have been no necessity for referring to adult persons as *mulatos*. We should expect to see such persons, born out of wedlock, called simply *mulos* and, moreover, such a designation should have applied to white persons as well as mixed-blood persons. As we shall see, *mulato* as used for mixed persons in wills seems not to be a term carrying such connotations.

Mulo and *mula* also seem to have other connotations in Spanish, such as 'mulishness', stubbornness, and being a hard worker. The verb *amularse* means 'to become stubborn'. Mules were extremely important to their owners and, in general, were reliable, necessary members of a farming family or important in freighting goods. Thus being a *mulo* might not be entirely negative; however, the term does imply a worker or servant (albeit a stubborn one).

It is significant in this context that the term *muleta* came very early to be applied to crutches or to other 'aiding' or 'supporting' devices. We can perhaps imagine someone saying of a cripple on crutches that 'he is riding on his little mules.' Again the connotation is that of serving. We can suppose that this concept might be transferable to slaves or to the children of slaves, but, in fact, slaves as a group were called neither *mulos* nor *muletos* nor *mulatos*. Nor does it seem that slave women were called *mulas* or *muletas* or *mulatas* as a group.

Thus although there are many connotations involved with the concepts of *mulo* and *mula* relating to bastardy, sexual license, work, and servitude, there does not appear to be any evidence that these ideas were actually applied to human slaves or to non-whites as a class.

In this connection it is significant to note that in 1506 in Valencia an *esclava lora* named Catalina from Mauritania was said to have had 'a bastard child'. The terms *mulo* and *mulato* are not used. Moreover, such terms were not used in many cases involving children born out of wedlock during the first quarter of the sixteenth century. We can be fairly certain that prior to the 1530s (at least) *mulato* was not used as a designation for illegitimate children.[34]

On the other hand, viewing the mule as a hybrid, which is common in early Portuguese dictionaries especially, offers a more convincing explanation of how *mulo/mulato* might have become applicble to humans of mixed background. The problems with this thesis are two: first, that *mulo* is itself equivalent to 'hybrid', thus why use only *mulato*? If the hybrid thesis were accepted we would expect to find mixed humans called simply *mulos*. Secondly, hybrid in the sixteenth and seventeenth centuries did *not* point primarily towards racial mixture but towards the mixture of wild and tame, citizen and stranger, and so on. This being the case, we should not expect the child of a black and a white, both born in the same village, to be called a hybrid. We should expect instead to find a child of a 'wild' black from Africa and a black native-born resident to the hybrid. (Clearly this argument might not be valid in the eighteenth century, after racisim led to greater stress being placed upon physical appearance rather than upon language, culture and religion).

In any case, we still must investigate other data to see whether the term *mulato* is, in fact, derived from *mulo*. Before doing this, however, note should be taken of the argument made by R. Dozy to the effect that the Arabic language had developed a term for *mulato* derived from a term for *mulo*. Dozy argued that *nagíl* (*mulato*) was derived from *nagl* (*mulo*).[35] The fact is, however, that *nagil* and *nagl* in Arabic seem to refer to date palm trees and palm trees (*nakhl* and *nakhla*) and not to mules. The term for mule is *baghl* and no Arabic dictionary consulted by this writer has *any* term meaning *mulato*, mixed-blood, hybrid, half-breed, half-caste, or mestizo, which can be in any way whatsoever related to 'mule'.

An Arabic–Spanish dictionary of *c*.1500, based on the Arabic of Granada, has:

mulo de asno y yegua = bágla, baglát (pl.)
mulo de asno y yegua = bágal, ábgál
muleta mula nueva   = bugáyla, bugayalĭt (pl.)
muleto nuevo   = bugáyal, bugayalĭt (pl.)

The terms used in the Arabic dictionaries for mulatto etc. are *muwallad*, plural *muwalladun* (translated as mulatto, half-caste, mestizo, hybrid, half-breed, half-blood, as well as other meanings); *hajin*, plural *hujana* (translated as half-breed, mulatto, hybrid); *khelassi* (probably archaic, from *khalat* or *khalata* (to mix), translated as mulatto); and *mojanis* (from *hajin*), translated as half-breed and half-caste.[36]

Dozy also asserted that another term in Arabic for *mulato* is *hudairi*, derived from *áhdar* (green). *Akhdar* does mean green, but no dictionary has any derivative referring to mixed-bloods or to people of color (i.e., 'olive'-skinned, *loro* color, and so on). One of my Arab-speaking informants thinks that *khudairi* 'could' be used in North Africa for a type of skin-colour but that it is in no way similar to the concept of *mulato*. That is, it might refer to a color between black and white but not to mixture. *Khudarī* means, at present, a greengrocer.[37]

The Muwallad *and* Malado *Theories*

The above discussion is of some interest because Dozy was a major opponent of a theory that the term *mulato* was derived from Arabic *muwallad*, a term which we will now proceed to discuss. Before beginning, however, it is important to state that some authors seem to have confused *muwallad* with another Arabic word, *maula*, and that, in fact, the two terms may have merged together in both Spanish and Portuguese. This issue will be clarified subsequently, but we will begin with a focus upon *muwallad* and its supposed Iberian derivatives, *muladí* and *malado*.

Corominas in his etymological dictionary refers to the Hispano–Arabic word *muladí*, used in Spain for a 'Christian Spaniard who made himself a renegade by becoming a Muslim'. This *muladí* was thought to be derived from *muwallad*, signifying '"Arabized foreigner", and at times "mulato"'. Also according to Corominas the term 'was pronounced *muellad* in the Arabic of Spain'.[38]

Let us begin the analysis of *muwallad* by first looking at what scholars have said about the term in *both* its Spanish and Portuguese forms. *Muladi* is usually given as a Castillianized form while *malado* or *maladi* are given as Portuguese forms.

The Portuguese historian Oliveira Marques states that between 868 and 930 a rich Portuguese landowner named Abd el-Rahman ben Marwan ben Yunus called Ibn el-Jilliki (the Galician) ruled the al-Gharb (Algarve). He was descended from a northern family 'which had passed over to Islam and had become *muwallad* (converted). . . . Later on, . . . many Christians were converted to Islam and became muwalladūn (from which comes the Portuguese word *malados*).' In addition, many *mozárabes* (Christians as well as Jews) lived in al-Gharb where they wrote Latin with the Arabic alphabet.[39]

The *Grande Enciclopédia Portuguesa e Brasileira* has a large section illustrating the use of *muladi* in the tenth century especially. *Muladi* was: 'a term which the Arab historians used to designate the indigenes of the Iberic peninsula, children of indigenes converted to Christianity. Its general significance is the child of an Arab father and a non-Arab mother.'[40]

It seems likely that the above passage should read 'converted to Islam' instead of 'converted to Christianity'; however, the latter part is probably as intended: a child of an Arab parent and a non-Arab parent.

González Palencia, in his study of Islamic Spain, described the various classes of Christians converted to Islam:

Renegados y muladíes. Los renegados ocupaban una situación intermedia. Se distinguian: los *maulas*, cristianos casi todos, procedentes de esclavos y siervos visigodos, que alcanzaban su libertad profesando el mahometismo . . . , los *muladíes*, hijos de padre o madre musulmanes y considerados por la ley como musulmanes; a todos se les conocía por el nombre de *muladíes* (*muwallad*, adoptado).[41]

He defines two types of *muladíes* (from *muwallad*), those of *visigodo* origin (West Goths) who had been enslaved and later converted and who were also called *maulas* and those who were of half-Christian, half-Muslim background and who had not been slaves themselves. It is especially significant to stress that he places *maulas* under the broader category of *muladíes* and that the term *muwallad* is defined as meaning 'adopted'.

Simonet does not list *muladi* or *maula* in his *Glosario* as terms peculiar to Mozarabic Spain but in his introduction he states that: 'Not only the Mozarabs, but also the Muladíes or Islamized Spaniards conserve . . . the proper language of the race to which they belonged . . . [the Romance].' By *muladíes* Simonet meant native Spaniards converted to Islam. (The term was reportedly transcribed in Latin as *mollites*).[42]

An historian of Spain also tells us that: 'these mozarabes ("almost Arabs"), as Christians living in Andalus were called, were soon outnumbered by the *muladíes* or converts' [to Islam]. He also refers to the *muladíes* of Saragossa in Aragón, both references being to the epoch of Islamic power in Spain.

Lévi-Provençal states that 'new Muslims' (*néo-musulmans*) in the period of the Caliphate of Cordoba were known as *muwalladun* (plural) and also as *musalima* and *asalima*. These converts, adopted into the Arab-dominated Muslim society during the eighth and ninth centuries, came to form the most numerous part of the population of Andalucia. They, along with the Mozárabes. continued to speak 'Romance' (as well as Arabic).[43]

Now let us look briefly at the term *malado* in Portugal, recalling that Oliveira Marques (above) states that *malados* took their name from *muwalladun*. Santa Rosa de Viterbo, in his publication of 1798 on the subject of archaic terms used in Portugal in former times, wrote a very significant section on *malado* (a term which I have not seen in any of the Portuguese dictionaries from the 1560s through 1798). He states:

Malado: O que vive em terras de Senhorio. . . . Tambem no Seculo XII. se chamárão *malados*, *mancebos*, ou *criados de servir*, os filhos, que ainda estavão de baixo de Patrio Poder. . . . No Foral de Thomar de 1174 onde diz no Latin:Pro suo malado, o Tradutor verteo: Por seu mancebo. . . . No Foral de Pena – cova de 1192 se diz = *Miles, e sui maladi*.[44]

To review his major points: *malado* (*maladi*) referred to someone (such as youth, servants, children) living on the feudal domain of a lord, but also in the 1100s *malado* was used as an equivalent for 'servants' who were the children who continued under their father's power. He then cites the use of *malado* in Latin to mean 'servant' (1174) and the use of *maladi* as a plural form (1192).

Santa Rosa de Viterbo also cites many pertinent examples. A document of 1075 used *malado* for *criado* (servant) as in *vestros mallados* (your *malados*). Maláda referred to 'a female slave, servant, concubine, young girl, maid or servant-girl, who by condition' or by obligation had to serve 'their Lords or Masters'. A document of 1279 used *malada* in such a way, to refer to servitude under certain conditions or obligations to a lord or owner. (It was a concept far broader than slavery, as such.)

Maladía and *maladya* referred to obligatory service or to a demand for service and thus the term was used in a contract of 1297. As late as 1317 the form *maladiis* was used, according to Santa Rosa de Viterbo.

In any case, the truly significant thing about *malado* is that it referred to servants and 'those who must serve', which concepts could easily embrace not only the children under *Patrio Poder* but also half-brothers or sisters, children of slaves or concubines. One can easily see how a half-black child, for example, raised in such a household, could be called a *malado* (in fact, he would have to be one). This is certainly very close to later *mulato*.

José Antonio Saco, in his history of slavery, illuminates the Spanish equivalent of *malado* by referring to the

contrato de recomendación en que un hombre en su pobreza se acoge á otro, para que lo mantega. . . . A la recomendación llamósele tambien en España *maulatum*, voz derivada de la arábiga *maulat*, que significa clientela, proteccion; por eso al recomendado se le dijo *mallatus*, equivalente á *maulá*, apellido que dieron los árabes al cliente.

In short, Saco describes a contract of 'recommendation' which was called *maulatum* in Spain, derived from (Latinized?) Arabic *maulat* signifying 'clientage, protection'. The individual was known as a *mallatus* in Hispanic Latin, the equivalent of *maulá*, the Arabic for *cliente* (client). (Saco also has for *maula*: 'Arab word which signifies being under the protection of someone'). Saco then cites a document of 958 and another of 1007 as using *maulatum*.

In short, *maulatum* in Spain referred to an agreement (Portuguese *maladía*) wherein a poor person might place himself in a feudal relationship with someone else in order to secure maintenance or protection. The *mallatus* (*malado*) was equivalent to a *maula*, according to Saco.

Later, in a reference to the mixed-ancestry of a Christian and a Muslim, Saco states: 'estos hijos y sus descendientes llamáronse *muzlitas, mozlemitas, mauludines* o' *mulados* de donde viene la palabra *mulato.*' That is, the mixed Christian–Muslims and their descendants were called 'little Muslims' as well as *mauludines,* or *mulados,* from which came the word *mulato* according to Saco.

It is important to emphasize Saco's statement that *mallatus–malado* is derived from Arabic *maula* and not from *muwallad* as was suggested by Oliveira Marques. Saco then goes on to derive *mulato* from '*mauludines* or *mulados*', forms which he related to mixed-ancestry children, that is, *muwalladun* in Arabic. Thus, although *malado* and *mallatus* seem to closely resemble later *mulato,* the derivation of the latter is not from them but from *muwallad – muladi,* according to Saco.

Lévi-Provençal also discusses the concept of Arabic *mawla* (plural *mawali*), applicable in Muslim Spain to individuals in a state of *wala* (derived from a root meaning 'to have power'), that is, in a state of feudal obligation or patronage. Lévi-Provençal discusses the diverse modes of the manumission of slaves in Islamic society and describes the way in which liberated slaves were sometimes obliged to preserve a legal relationship with their former owner or the family of descendants. This relationship of 'protection' and reciprocal service was described by the concept of *wala.* The *mawlas,* persons subject to *wala,* 'formed an extremely numerous social class' in Muslim Spain.

Lévi-Provençal also notes that *mawla* was Latinized as *maullatus* and describes the latter in terms similar to Santa Rosa de Viterbo's use of *malado* in Portuguese and Saco's use of *mallatus.* In later centuries *mawlas* included people who were originally free but who came to be under a service obligation, as well as those descended from former slaves.[45]

In any case, the widespread use of *malado* and its equivalents in Spain and Portugal just prior to the beginning of the modern age is worthy of comment. *Malados* (*maulas* or *mawlas*) were said to have been numerous and they were, at the same time, *muwalladun* (converts to Islam) according to some writers. Although *malado – mallat* is not seen as the origin of *mulato* by any writer cited thus far, the resemblances are too close to totally preclude such a conclusion.

At this point, however, let us take a further look at *muwallad* as a source for *mulato.* In 1861 W. H. Englemann published his study of Arabic derivations in Spanish and Portuguese. He stated: '*Mulato* de . . . *mowallad* which designates "one who is born of an Arab father and a foreign mother".' At the same time Englemann rejected the notion that *mulato* was derived from *mulo*.[46]

Englemann also noted that the term *mollita* had been used for a 'renegade', one who had embraced Islam from Christianity. He regarded *mollita* as a contraction of *Moslemita*. On the other hand, *mollita* is very possibly simply a dialectical or chronoligical variant of *muwallad* and one leading towards *mulato*. Corominas notes that the form *mollites* was used in the peninsula, along with *muelled*, and that these forms have survived as place-names such as Meulledes in Salamanca and Moldes in León and elsewhere.[47]

In 1869 R. Dozy brought out a revised edition of Englemann's work wherein he disagreed with the latter as to the origin of *mulato*. Dozy asserted that *mowallad*: 'signifie proprement *adopté* . . . , et en Espagne on appelait ainsi, sous le regne des Omaiyades, les Espagnols qui avaient embrassé la religion de Mahomet; c'étaient pour les Arabes des adoptés. Mais jamais il n'a désigné un mulâtre, un fils d'un nègre et d'une blanche.' Thus Dozy asserted that *mowallad* properly meant 'adopted' and was used to refer to Spaniards who were converted to Islam. Moreover, he states that it was never used to designate a person who was a child of a black and a white. Dozy then goes on to state that *mulato* is properly a Portuguese term, in which language it signifies a *mulet* (mule) and, figuratively, a *mulârtre* (human *mulato*).[48]

There is reason to believe that Dozy was not as familiar with Arabic as he might have been (see above discussion of *nagl* and *khudairi*). Moreover, he obviously had no access to historical evidence except that provided by Antonio de Moraes (who revised Bluteau's dictionary in the 1780s) whom he cites as his authority.

Several authors took Englemann's side in the debate, including Eguilaz y Yanguas (1886) who stated that *mulato* was derived from '*muguallad* [*muwallad*] "he born of Arab father and foreign mother or a slave father and a free mother", and not from *mulus*, as Dozy wants.'[49] It is significant that Eguilaz adds the information that *muwallad* referred to the progeny of a slave and a free person, as well as of an Arab and a non-Arab.

Some Spanish and Portuguese dictionaries began to include *muladi* and *malado* in the present century. These entries tend to reflect the work of Englemann and Eguilaz and need not be repeated here. It is, however, worth noting that both Pagés and Zerolo, Toro y Gómez and Isaza stated that *muladi* is derived from Arabic *mualadi* 'one who is not pure Arab'. This form *mualadi* is interesting in that it represents an attempt to express *muwallad* in an hispano-latinized version which is intermediate between *muwallad* and *muladi*.[50]

Portuguese dictionaries define *malado* as an inhabitant of a *maladía* and the latter is described in two aspects: 'solar ou terra habitada por vasados solarengos, sujeitos a encargos feudais; doença.' A *maladio* is defined as 'Que ou o que habitava numa maladia e tinha o foro de cavaleiro.'[51] *Maladía*, then, referred to a feudal relationship on a given estate or manor, (as well as to 'malady', a totally different word) while *maladio* referred to one who lived on a *maladía* and had a customary or legal right to be a horseman.

Machado states of *muladi*: 'From Arabic *mūlladin*, plural of *mūallad*, adopted; a slave born in [the master's] house; (or) one born of an Arab father and a non-Arab mother, especially a black woman; a borrowed word from Castillian muladí.'[52] Again we see the intermediate form *muallad* but of greater significance is Machado's statement that the term covered 'a slave born at home' and one born of an Arab and non-Arab parent, 'especially of a black woman'. These concepts lead directly to later *mulato*.

The dictionary of the Real Academia Española is similar to Pagés in defining *muladi* but states that the term is derived from Arabic *muwalladi*, 'mestizo of an Arab and a foreigner'. This concept of *muwallad* being equivalent to 'mestizo' brings us very close, of course, to the meaning of *mulato*.[53]

Now let us examine the Arabic roots of *muwallad* and the pertinent forms of the word. Basic are *walada* and *maulid*: to bear (a child), to give birth, to beget, generate, procreate, to bring forth, produce. From this stems *walad*, descendant, offspring, child, son, boy, young animal, young one, and so on; *maulūd*, produced, born, come into the world, birth (plural *mawālīd*); and *muwallid*, generating, producing, procreative, generative (plural *muwallidūn*), procreator, progenitor.

Muwallad is another form of the same root and means:

born, begotten, produced, generated; brought up, raised; born and raised among Arabs (but not of pure Arab blood), not truly old Arabic, introduced later into the language, post-classical (esp. of words); half-breed, half-caste, half-blood.[54]

As one can see, *muwallad* does not mean 'adopted' nor does it refer to conversion to Islam, as such. Its root is 'birth' but it has the special meaning of being born among Arabs and covers all persons (mixed-bloods included) who are not perceived as being originally of 'old' Arab ancestry. In Sudan this includes, in essence, many foreigners born in the Sudan including Syrians, for example. Sudanese cities sometimes have districts which are known as sections of the *muwalladūn* because such persons reside there (although they have been born in Sudan or have lived there for generations).[55]

A scholar has noted that: 'In Sudan, the lighter-skinned offsping of mixed Egyptian–Sudanese marriages is a *muwallad*, a term often used in a pejorative sense' by the darker Sudanese Muslims.[56]

As noted earlier, modern Arabic dictionaries use *muwallad* for 'mulatto', 'hybrid', 'half-breed', and so on. To be more specific, the *Oxford Arabic Dictionary* uses *muwallad* for half-caste, half-breed, hybrid, and mulatto. The Al-Manar dictionary uses *muwallad* for mulatto, as well as other terms. The Elias (Egyptian) dictionary uses *muwallad* for mulatto, mestizo, hybrid, and half-caste. The Al-Mawrid dictionary uses *muwallad* as well as *Khelassi* (mixed) for mulatto and explains both terms as referring to someone born from white and black parents, who is *asmar* (dark brown or less than black in color).[57]

Significantly, the Elias dictionary gives the female form as *muwallada* (for 'mulattress'), a form very close to Hispano–Portuguese *mulata* (feminine) and proto-modern *mualada* (feminization of the *mualad* form). The masculine plural form *muwalladūn* is undoubtedly the source of the pre-Portuguese and pre-Castillian *muladi*, and it may very well be that the latter was also a plural in the vulgar Latin of the times. The singular should have been *mulad-* and, after further hispanicization, *mulado* and *mulada* or *mualado* and *mulada* (as above).

It should also be noted that accenting in Arabic appears to give *muwállad* but in *mualado* and *mulado* this would doubtless shift to the new penultimate syllable.

Any analysis of the evolution of *muwallad* and *maula* as they pass from Arabic into Latin–Romance and still later into Spanish and Portuguese forms must confront the fact that the two terms converge both in terms of application and pronunciation. If it is correct to say (as several writers do) that the *maulas* (liberated slaves, converted to Islam) and the *muwalladun* (half-Arabs) *both* came to be known as *muwalladun*, in the sense of either 'converts' or 'adopted', then it follows that a confusion might have developed. All *maulas* conceivably could have been *muwalladun* but not all *muwalladun* would have been *maulas* (except in the sense that children were under the protection of their father, in the later Portuguese sense of being a *malado*).

In terms of pronunciation, *maula* (or *mawla*) in correct Arabic would not be confused with *muwallad* but when *maula* became latinized as *maulat* (the state of protection or clientage), *maulatum* (*maladía*, the contract), and *maulatus* or *mallatus* (the individual under obligation to serve, *malado* in later Portuguese) one sees a substantial overlap. *Maulat-* (also *mollit-* according to Simonet) became *malad-* in Portuguese (sometimes spelled *mallad-*) as recorded for 1075–1317.

Such forms as *maulat- malad* are, of course, very close to the *mualad- muallad- muellad-* forms for *muwallad* recorded by Corominas and other Spanish dictionary-makers cited above. One also can cite the *mulad-* of *muladí* and the *maulud-* of Saco's '*mauludines* or *mulados*'.

One of the most interesting things about the later convergence of *muwallad* and *maula* is that most or all of the references to derivatives of *muwallad* (*muladí*, and so on) seem to be from the tenth century or earlier. Saco's examples of *maulat-* are from 958 and 1007, while Santa Rosa de Viterbo's examples of *malad-* are from 1075–1317.

It is especially intriguing that Santa Rosa de Vitebo's 1317 example is *maladiis* (plural, latinized) for a derivation of *maula* (presumably) which is terribly close to the *muladí* form for *muwallad* cited by Spanish dictionary-makers.

In analyzing the above further we must keep in mind that it is very unlikely that Christians converted to Islam in the eighth to tenth centuries would be *perpetually* known as *muwalladun*. Lévi-Provençal makes it quite clear that the new converts (who were a majority in Andalucia) intermarried with both Berbers and Arabs to form an Andalucian ethnic group.[58] Subsequently these and other Muslim Iberians were known to the Christian Spaniards as *moros* and not, to my knowledge, as *muladíes* or any other derivative of *muwallad* or *maula*.

Indeed it would seem very far-fetched to argue that the term *muellad- mulad-*

was ever used by Christians for the masses of Andalucian, Valencian, or Granadan Muslims after, perhaps, the tenth century and especially after the reconquest of Córdoba and Seville (thirteenth century). And, as suggested, it is unlikely that the term was used by Muslims after the first century or two of the Arab conquest (except, of course, for designating new mixed-bloods or converts).

Thus I would suggest that *muladí* was very likely a term used in the tenth century and earlier and that it declined subsequently, being overshadowed by *maulat- malado* forms emphasizing feudal service and patronage relationships.

Of course, *muwallad* as a term would have survived in Muslim communities from Granada through Aragón into the sixteenth century but it is likely to have been modified into a Romance form, such as the *muellad* suggested by Corominas and *mualad* suggested by others. It is interesting that the *ue* combination in Spanish often becomes *u* in Portuguese, thus yielding *mulado* and then, perhaps, *mulato*.

It should be noted here that *maula* is close in sound to *mula* (mule) and it is possible that Spanish–Portuguese *muleto* (implying crutch, support, aid, service) might have come from the enriching of *mulo/mula* by the incorporation of the idea behind *maula*.[59]

Oliveira Marques may be correct in deriving *malado* from *muwallad*, but the path must have been a complex one since it would seem clear that *maula* (servant) became somehow grafted onto *muwallad*. This could have come about, as noted, if most *muwalladun* in Iberia were involved in some type of service relationship to more powerful masters.

In any case, it seems to this writer that a strong case exists for the evolution of *muwallad* (or *maula–muwallad*) into later *mulato*. A gap of documentation exists from about 1317 to the early 1500s, time enough for the change from *mulado/mulad* to *mulato*. It also seems likely that *muleto* and *mulato* had a different history and that the former term may have come from *mulo/mulito* (and *maula*) rather than from *muwallad*. It is very likely, however, that these terms were confused to some degree at the oral level and that the hybrid nature of the mule facilitated a gradual overlapping of meaning. In Portuguese the line of demarcation between *mulato* and *muleto* consequently developed at a different point than in Castillian.

in 1509 a group of 17 Muslim captives from Oran (Algeria) was sold in Valencia. One of them was 'Muleta, de 30 ãnos, she knows nothing of her husband. She carries a girl of 3 years called Susa and another of two months.' This is very significant, because it illustrates that *muwallada* (which was doubtless given as her 'name') could be translated in Catalan or Castillian as *muleta*, perhaps because the Hispanic scribe was aware of the identity of the two terms or simply because he interpreted the Arabic as such phonetically.[60]

It is interesting that the first definite use of the form *mulato* as applied to humans seems to occur in a proclamation of the king of Portugal dated 1528. In this document the king refers to 'os mulatos moradores na dita ilha' of São Tomé, that is to the island's *mulato* inhabitants. (Previous legislation for São

Tomé dated 1515, 1517 and 1526 had referred only to *escravas* (slaves) and *filhos* (children), or to *negros*, *escravas*, *machos* (males) and their children, or to free *pretos*). In referring to *os mulatos moradores* the king seems to be referring to an entire class of inhabitants without reference to any specific degree of ethnic mixture or without any necessity for offering any legal definition for such persons. We must assume, therefore, that *mulato* in 1528 had a readily understood meaning in both Lisbon and São Tomé. It is conceivable that its meaning was very close to that of *malado* of the 1300s, that is, to refer to persons born and raised in a feudal relationship with local white males and with the Crown. The people in question would have been mixtures of Jewish, African, and Portuguese Christian ancestry, since many Jewish children had been forcibly shipped to São Tomé.[61]

In short, it is not at all clear that the *mulatos moradores* of 1528 were being called *mulatos* because they were hybrids or because they had been freed by the Crown or by their owner-fathers and, thereby, still had a *maladía* type of relationship with their 'patrons'.

It seems clear that we cannot further clarify the origin of *mulato* until we examine other evidence relating to the use of the term in early modern times. As we shall see, there is a possibility that *mulato* went through several fairly significant changes in meaning during the sixteenth century.

MULATO AS A COLOR TERM

Before proceeding to an analysis of such data it is necessary to deal with the possibility that *mulato* in the sixteenth cenury became popular as a color-term, that is, as a word denoting a *mulato* color. Such an interpretation would bring *mulato* in line with most of the competing terms such as *membrillo cocido*, *leonado*, *loro*, *pardo* and *moreno*. There is absolutely no doubt but that *mulato did* become a color term (used for such diverse things as bread, soil, coffee, and human beings). The question is essentially how early this color usage developed and what its inspiration was. 'The most common color of the mule is a brown or bay-brown – bay or bright bay, or piebald being rare; a chestnut tint is sometimes noticed.'[62]

The mule's color falls within the range of *loro* and *membrillo cocido*. Lobo Cabrera remarks that the Fulo (Fulani) people were thought to be 'de color mulato membrillo cocho, as cited by sources from the period' (sixteenth century).[63]

In reviewing early evidence, we find that in the Canary Islands in 1539 a slave girl of 12, Catalina, was classified as a *morisca lora* while in 1558 María, age 35, was classified as a *morisca mulata*. Reference is also made to a *morisca-blanca bozal* (that is, new and non-Spanish-speaking). There is little doubt but that *morisca lora* and *morisca-blanca* refer to color. One cannot be positive but it appears that *morisca-mulata* might also refer to color, *mulata* replacing *lora*. A *morisca* who was known to be half-Spanish would probably not have been given any color designation except, perhaps, *blanca*. The *mulata* could refer to her appearance (color) or to the fact that she was born as a slave in her master's house (*malada* = *mulata*). The latter seems unlikely in this case. Generally, *moriscos* were Muslims who had been forcibly converted to Christianity and their exact parentage was often not known or recorded.

The problem of interpreting such early records will be dealt with below, but here I merely want to cite one or two examples to indicate the *possibility* of a color meaning.

In 1582 a *negro amulatado*, Melchor, age 35, was sold for a big price because he was a technician in a sugar refinery.[64] The use of *amulatado* is significant. It is derived from a verb *amulatar* which literally means 'to be a *mulato*' or 'to be *mulato*-like'. Oudin, in 1625, defines *amulatado* as almost exactly the same as *mulato* (one born of a white and a *more*); however, this noun-like definition seems unsatisfactory. A modern Portuguese dictionary defines *amulatado* as an adjective for 'one having the color of *mulato* and *amulatar* as a verb meaning 'to take the color of *mulato*'. A dictionary of 1889 states that *amulatado* is the past participle of *amulatar-se*: One having the color of *mulato*'.[65]

In any case, a *negro amulatado*, that is, a 'mulatto-ish black' has the 'feel' of referring principally to color or to other physical characteristics. It is equivalent to *negro casi loro* or *loro casi negro*. The only other alternative is to argue that a verb anciently existed for *mulad* (*amuladar*) which had become *amulatar* and meant 'to be a *mulad* or *malado*', that is, born in the master's house, and so on.

The existence of a verbal form, *amulatar*, by the 1580s is quite significant in terms of indicating that the status of being a *mulato* was not simply a permanent passive category imposed by hybrid birth but was an active category affected by perception (as in the case of color) or status (as perhaps in the relationship with one's owner, father, or *patrón*). It should be noted that *negro* could also assume a verbal form in Iberian languages (as in *anegrido* or *anegreado*). This, I would suggest, can only arise where terms such as *mulato* or *negro* do not have the permanent genetic-biological connotations that they now have in English. One can, indeed, say in English: 'he is mulatto-like' or 'she is negro-ish' but such usage can only arise where precise information about ancestry is lacking. It is appearance, or perhaps behavior, which suggests the use of such a phrase. The use of *amulatado* suggests, then, that a person could by 1582 be described as 'like a *mulato*', indicating that appearance or color is being referred to.

Enrico Zaccaria, in his study of *mulatto* in Italian cites early examples wherein Sassetti, travelling with the Portuguese to Cochin and India (1580s) refers to a king as being of good appearance and serious, *di color mulatto*. He also referred to one Zamorino in these terms: 'El color della carne è più chiaro assai che di mulatto.'[66] Clearly, Sassetti (under Portuguese influence, one must assume) was using *mulatto* as a color, not at all as an assertion of genetic character.

In *c.*1601 Rosal wrote: '*loro* they used to call the slave who now we call mulato, *no bien negro*'. Rosal, from Córdoba in Andalucía, was clearly using both *loro* and *mulato* for one who was 'not very black' (*no bien negro*). This would seem to emphasize color as opposed to ancestry.

Francisco Quevedo, in one of his poems (pre-1645) uses the phrase *un pan mulato* which would seem to refer to mulatto-colored bread.[67]

Certainly, in many places where *mulato* is used along with *membrillo cocido* and other color designations one has the feeling that color is being referred to. This is reinforced by the fact that descriptions of slaves, especially runaways, should ordinarily emphasize appearance rather than ancestry.

Nonetheless, the bulk of the above evidence arises somewhat late (1580s, or at least after the 1560s) and we cannot be sure that a color meaning is prior or derivative. Nor can we be sure that the color *mulato* is based upon the color of the mule or the color of the human beings called *mulatos*. The two colors are similar in fact and such a circumstance doubtless would have led to a reinforcement of meaning, no matter which came first. We can be sure, however, that *mulato* was used for a color or a range of colors by the latter part of the sixteenth century. On the other hand, the term appears to have been more complex than denoting *only* a color.

6

Part-Africans and Part-Americans as *Mulatos*

EARLY USE OF *MULATO*

At this point it seems best to leave the subject of the origin of the term *mulato* in order to proceed with explicit definitions and actual usage, prior to 1650. It should be stressed, however, that up to this point we have seen no evidence pointing towards any special reason why *mulato* should have been used for any particular combination of ethnic backgrounds such as for 'black' and 'white' mixed-bloods. How and why the term came to be used for certain mixtures must be discovered in the data still to be examined.

In analyzing early usage the term *mulato* as applied to mules will be noted only in the initial years of documented usage.

The first use of *mulato* in the modern period seems to be in an order issued by the *baylia* (court) of Valencia on February 12, 1498: The court

Commissions Antón Pau, *veguer*, in order that he *lleve a la mulata que* |which, who| is in litigation between Juan Dixer . . . and Caat Moroqua, *moro* . . . , that this one sold to the first at 27 *ducados*, that he has not collected, with damage to him. That both should appear before five days, since if not *la mulata* will be sold, and that which lacks for the price shall be taken of the goods of the *moro*.

Vincenta Cortés interpreted the above litigation as involving a female, human *mulata*. I disagree, however, and believe the dispute was over a female mule. In the documents of the time-period female slaves are usually refered to as *esclavas* or *cautivas*, not merely by a color or caste designation since the latter alone would be legally as well as practically inappropriate. Even a human *mulata* might be free and thus it would be necessary, especially in a legal order, to specify that she was a slave. Moreover, the term *mulato* is not otherwise used for humans until several decades later, while mules were being called *mulatos* in the period in Valencia (as we shall see below).

The price of 27 *ducados* seems high for a human female also, since in 1509 fifty *negros* were sold for 18 *ducados* per head and a ten-year-old *moro* was sold for 15 *ducados*. Nonetheless, it would appear that mules and slaves were sometimes valued at the same price. In Seville in 1518–24, a *negra* of 25 sold for 10,000 *miravedis*, a *negro* of 20 sold for 10,000, and a *negro* of 24 along with a 'mula para su oficio' sold for 20,000. Thus the *mula* was worth about the same price as a male or female slave.

The construction of the document at first might seem to indicate that a human is being described, as in the use of 'a' in 'lleve a la mulata'. However, 'a' is known to be used with animals, occasionally, even today. Most importantly, any slave to be sold had to be registered with the *baylia* and a document such as this one would doubtless refer to the fact, probably noting the date of sale and registration.

In any case, the same *baylia* in 1506 'commissions the veguer Vicente Gascó in order that *lleve a* [he carries to] the court the following *moros . . .* [including] Azmet Jofar, 6 *ducados* that were given to him to buy *mulatas.*'[1] This document has to do with goods in general and it would seem clear that the *mulatas* were either young mules or crutches.

It would seem that 'a' was used with *llevar* (to convey, to carry) in both documents because the form was 'llevar a' rather than because the 'a' denoted a human. Moreover, 'a' was not used before *mulata* later in both documents.

As noted earlier, in 1509 a captive from Oran was one 'Muleta', age 30, who knew nothing of her husband and who carried with her two young children. She was sold with a group of 17 Muslims whose names were normal ones such as Alí, Fátima (a *lora* of 30), Mahamat and Amet.[2]

Before proceeding with Spanish usage let us turn to look at Portuguese data briefly. The available data does not shed much light upon *mulato* in Portuguese prior to the poems and other references to mules cited earlier in this chapter (1520s–1530s).

The earliest reference to a human *mulato* in Portuguese perhaps occurs in the *Commentarios* of Afonso de Albuquerque, first compiled by his son in 1557 and published in 1576. The events, however, relate to a much earlier time-period and the event associated with the phrase *seu mulato* (his mulato), to refer to a servant of Garcia de Sousa, took place in 1513. It is worth reviewing the background to discover, if we can, something about this *mulato.*

Garcia de Sousa arrived in India in 1508 with Albuquerque. He played an active military role in various places in the region, including Malaca, the Red Sea, and Goa. In 1510 he captured a ship bound from Mecca to Calicut, which had two Castillian Jews on board. He also had contact with Cretan (Greek), Russian and Albanian slaves living at Goa.

In 1513 the *mulato* helped Garcia in a battle with Muslims at Aden, a battle in which Albuquerque had 1,700 Portuguese, along with 800 Malabars and Canarese from Goa involved.[3] The *mulato* was doubtless at least 18 years of age and probably born by 1495. But where? He could have been acquired in any of the above-mentioned places (where many captives were taken) and could have been half-Asian, half-Arab, half-European, or half-African, or he could have been a *malado* owing service as discussed earlier.

Whether the term was actually used in 1513 also cannot be known, but it is apparent that the compiler believed that his readers of 1557 would understand something specific by the use of the word. To discover the meaning we must look at other data, specifically from São Tomé island.

The island of São Tomé was colonized from 1471 by the planting there of Europeans, convicts, Jewish children and *negros*. 'All the unmarried men were provided by the Crown with a Negress, avowedly for breeding purposes. . . . the Mulatto children and the slave mothers . . . were subsequently declared to be free by a royal edict of 1515.'⁴ The Jewish children of both sexes were forcefully baptized as Christians and, as they grew up, were married off. An observer of 1506 claimed that: 'few of the women bore children of the white men; very many more bore children of the Negroes while the Negresses bore children of the white men.' In 1515 when the slaves and their *filhos* (children) were freed no use was made of the term *mulato*. This was also true of legislation in 1517 and 1526. In 1528, however, a royal decree extended to the *mulatos moradores* (*mulato* inhabitants) of the island the right to be elected to the council, if they were married men with some property.⁵

It is interesting to note that this 1528 date for the use of *mulato* for humans is at least as old as any of the poems cited using *mulato* for mules (*c*.1526–8). It is also interesting that the king in his decree offered no explanation for his use of the term. Perhaps it is significant that these *mulatos* developed directly as a result of royal policy and were freed directly by the Crown. It is conceivable, therefore, that something of the old concept of *malado* was attached to them (as discussed earlier). Their part-Jewish character might also have contributed to the latter.

In approximately the year 1535 (in an account first published in 1550) a Portuguese pilot described the inhabitants of São Tomé. The Italian text of 1550 states:

vi abitano molti mercatanti portoghese, castigliani, francesi, genovesi; . . . E sono quelli che nascono in detta isola bianchi come noi, ma alle volte accade che detti mercatanti, morendoli le mogli bianche, ne prendono delle negre: nel che non vi fanno tropo difficultà, essendovi arbitatori negri di grande intelletto e ricchi, che allevano le loro figliuole al modo nostro nelli costumi e nel vestire. E quelle che nascono di queste tal negre sono berrettini, e vengono chiamati mulati.

Many Portuguese, Castillian, French and Genoese merchants were living on São Tomé, with white wives, and had children as white as Europeans. But some, when their wives died, lived with a *negre* woman, an accepted practice, since the *negri* inhabitants were both intelligent and rich. Moreover, their *negre* daughters were raised with European customs and clothing. Those who were born of the union of such *negre* women and Europeans were called *mulati* (in the plural) and were *berrettini* in color.⁶

Thus, by 1535, we have a definite statement as to who at least some of the *mulati* (*mulatos*) were: children of the union of European merchants and the daughters of rich Europeanized *negros*. This is quite interesting because it implies a high and positive status for *mulatos*, something utterly at variance with the concept of mule. We can hardly conceive of such people being thought of as 'little mules'. The king's patronage of the *mulatos*, from 1515 onward, also does not suggest a negative attitude.

It is also interesting that *berrettini* was used as the color term for *mulatos* since *berrettini* is the same term used for the Berbers of Mauritania (as their normal color) as well as for Americans on occasion. *Mulato* itself does not seem to have been used as a color term in this 1535 case.

São Tomé was one of the centers for the Portuguese slave trade. We can expect, therefore, that usage might spread rapidly to places including such Spanish colonies as the Canary Islands as well as to Spain and the Caribbean.

The records from the slave market in Las Palmas, Canary Islands, 1514–1600, provide us with an opportunity to analyze the early use of the term *mulato* especially in relation to its gradual replacement of *loro*. The Canary Islands were under Spanish control but contact was maintained with both Portugal and the Portuguese islands. Slaves were obtained also directly from the west coast of North Africa (Muslims of various colors) as well as from the Sierra Leone region and West Africa. Muslims (called *moros* in the early period but usually denominated as *moriscos* during much of the century) were especially numerous in the market from 1520–39 and 1555–79, constituting overall about 12 per cent of those sold. In 1572 Philip II prohibited raids on North Africa but from the 1570s through 1590s there were expeditions to the Agadir region and to other places, although fewer *moriscos* were obtained. Black slaves from West African nations constituted about 70 per cent of the overall totals and were numerous from 1520 through 1539 and 1545 through 1599 and especially so in 1560 through 1599. 'Indian' slaves, so named, were few, but were most numerous between 1546 and 1600.[7]

Slaves classified as *loros*, *mulatos*, *morenos*, or other similar terms will be referred to here as intermediate-colored persons. They were not very numerous, as such, between 1514 aqnd 1557 (only about 14 per cent of the total for the period to 1600 being sold in those years). On the other hand, many Muslims were not categorized by color and it is highly probable that a large percentage of the *moriscos* were of a non-white color (being from regions discussed earlier as inhabited by dark or brown people, from the Iberian standpoint). More than 86 per cent of the intermediate-colored slaves were sold after 1558, when the numbers sold escalated each year. Whether this was due to an increase in island-born mixed-bloods or to the resale of converted, North African-born Muslims or to other causes one cannot say from the data.

As we shall see, the sex ratio of the intermediate slaves sold after 1570 is very unbalanced. In general, the sex ratios resemble *morisco* sex ratios between 1532 and 1569 (*morsicos* were 46 per cent female) but resemble *negro* sex ratios (and those of *indios*) from 1514–1531 and 1570–1600. Overall, the inter-mediate slaves sold were over 70 per cent male and 30 per cent female. (*Negros* were only about 60 per cent male while Indians were 80 per cent male). This unbalanced sex ratio gives the impression of a newly imported slave population, rather than an island-born one. The only other way the imbalance can be explained is to suppose that many island slave-owners were withholding females from the market, either for breeding purposes or for concubinage, or both. Such an explanation is hard to substantiate from the data, especially since *negro* and *indio* sex ratios are quite similar. Moreover, a strong male worker could be deemed as valuable for retention as a female, especially by the agriculturalists who seem to have comprised the majority of sellers of slaves.

More than 250 individual sales involving intermediate categories occurred in the period; however, several slaves were sold more than once. I have attempted to identify the slaves sold several times and to count them only once. The result is a total of 218 to 222 individual persons sold. Table 6.1 reveals the trends in terms of numbers and sex ratios. It is also useful to illustrate the use of intermediate terms by time-periods, as in Table 6.2.

TABLE 6.1   Sales of slaves of intermediate color

		Female	Male	Total	
1514–31	(only *loro* used)	4	10	14	28.5% female
1532–9	(both *loro* and *mulato*)	6	3	9	66.66% female
1540–5		–	–	–	–	–
1546–52	(both *loro* and *mulato*)	3	2	5	60.0% female
1553		–	–	–	–	–
1554	(*mulato* only)	1	1	2	50.0% female
1555–6		–	–	–	–	–
1557–69 increase starts	(*mulato* dominant but *loro* used)	13 or 14	16	29 or 30	46.6% female
1570–86 increase accelerates	(*mulato* very dominant but *loro* used)	18 or 19	44 or 45	62 or 64	29.0% female
1587–1600 greater numbers	(*loro* rare and only for males)	28 or 29	79	107 or 108	26.8% female
Totals		63 or 66	55 or 156	218 or 222	29.8% female

One can see clearly the rapid increase in the use of *mulato* after 1554 and the corresponding decline in *loro*. Moreover, the later use of *loro* is often a modifier for *negro* or is used as a relative color term. Interestingly, the use of both *mulato* and *loro* together for the same person persists (on a minimal scale) throughout the period, from 1532 on.

Do these records, as compiled by Lobo Cabrera, tell us anything about the

TABLE 6.2   The use of intermediate terms by time-periods

Term	1514–31	1532–9	1546–52	1554	1558–69	1570–86	1587–1600
loro	10	2	1	–	–	1	3ᶜ
loro morisco	3	2	–	–	2	–	–
loro, moro	1	–	–	–	–	–	–
loro 'yudo'	–	1	–	–	–	–	–
loro de Berberia	–	1	–	–	–	–	–
negro algo loro	–	–	–	–	1	–	–
negro loro	–	–	–	–	3	1	3
negra casi lora	–	–	–	–	–	1	–
prieta, mas lora que negra	–	–	–	–	–	1	–
loro, mulato	–	1ᵃ	1	–	–	1	1
mulato	–	2	3ᵇ	2	18–19	53–55	99–100
mulato ladino	–	–	–	–	3	2	–
morisco mulato	–	–	–	–	1	–	–
negro amulatado	–	–	–	–	–	1	–
mulato-indio	–	–	–	–	–	1	–
moreno	–	–	–	–	1	–	–
morisco-fulo	–	–	–	–	–	–	1

ᵃresold as *mulato*; ᵇone resold as *negro loro*; ᶜtwo resold as *mulato*.

meaning or nature of the term *mulato*? It is quite clear that *mulato* replaced *loro* and was used in instances where *loro* had been used. For example, in 1523 we find Fátima, age 30, a *blanca berberisca* sold with Matias, 8, *loro* and Bermudo, 12, *loro*. After the 1530s, however, all such cases use *mulato*, as in 1576 when we find Bárbola, 17, *negra* with *su hijo* Juan, age 1, *mulato*. Another example is that of Ignacia, age 30, *negra*, sold in 1584 with Jerónimo, 13, *mulato*. But we also find, in 1549, Juliana, 25, *mulata*, sold with her brother Gaspar, 16, *negro*.

From documents relating to the freeing of slaves one finds: (1) 1562, Juana, *negra*, and *su hija* María, *mulata* were freed by María Martínez, a widow; (2) 1572–4, Juan Garcés named as his heir Melchor, *mulato*, age 2, whom he had had on Barbola, *negra*, *su esclava*; (3) 1557–8, Antón Martin freed *sus hijos* Juanico and Frasquito, *mulatos* and Constanza, *negra*, 'su esclava, madre de los mulatos, de 40 años', and (4) 1585, Juana, *mulata*, is freed thanks to money collected among 'los parientes negros de su madre, Francisca' (among the mother's black relatives).

Thus from 1562 through 1585 cases can be seen where *mulatos* were children of *negras* with the father either being unknown or a Spanish slave owner. Also in 1549 we noted the case of a brother and sister being classified as *negro* and *mulata* respectively.

There are also families sold where the mother was *mulata* and the children were also *mulatos*. In 1573 Beatriz, *mulata*, was sold with Rodrigo, *su hijo*, and a baby, *su hija*, both classed as *mulatos*. In 1579 Catalina, 40, *mulata*, was sold with Francisco, 8, her *mulato* son. In 1582 Antona, 30, *mulata*, was sold with four children, all *mulatos*. In 1591 Bárbola, *mulata*, 40, was sold with her three-month-old *mulato* son. In 1597 Constanza, *mulata*, was sold with her two-year-old *mulatillo* son. Indeed, all of the *mulatas* recorded for sale with children had only *mulato* youngsters.

Thus one finds both *negras* and *mulatas* producing *mulato* children. Unfortunately the fathers' colors are not known in the case of the *mulatas* sold. Since the fathers could easily have been *negros*, *mulatos*, *moriscos* or *indios* (or even native *canarios*), it is not possible to say what this means. It does, however, tend to point towards the use of *mulato* as an appearance term or as a status term, rather than meaning simply 'hybrid'. Certainly some of the fathers could have been 'white' Spaniards, which probably would have resulted in socially or physically white children.

In 1538 a slave owner freed his slave Juana, *de color loro*, because she had had a child, Diego, by his friend Rodrigo de la Barreda. The child was not called *loro* or *mulato*. Similarly, in 1525 liberty was given to Juanico, a boy of two, *de color blanco*, the son of María, *su esclava negra*, by a husband and wife. The child had been born in their house and thus they freed him. In this case, a *negra* produced a white child (but this was seven years before *mulato* began to be used. Nonetheless *loro* could have been utilized.)

Thus there is some evidence that children of *loras* and even *negras* could be white or uncategorized. In this same vein in 1579 Bernardino Palenzuela willed freedom to Juanico, age 2, son of Juana, *mulata*, *mi esclava*. Juanico was referred to only as a *niño*, not as a *mulato*.

We might, therefore, conclude that *mulato* was not an automatic term for hybrids but was reserved for a certain type of appearance or status. But the evidence needs to be further analyzed.

As noted above, the term *loro* continued to be used even after *mulato* had become popular. It is difficult to document any difference in their use other than in a temporal sense. In 1539, for example, freedom was given to a group of slaves including Juan, *loro*. Such usage does not set *loro* apart from *mulato*. In point of fact, there are several cases where *loro* and *mulato* are used interchangeably. First, there were several persons classifed as 'lora, mulata, ladina', 'loro-mulato', and 'mulato loro'. In the usage of the slave registers multiple entries do not ever seem to mean 'half this and half that'. On the contrary, the second term usually modifies or adds to the first.

For example, we find the following: 'blanco-morisco' (white of converted Muslim background), 'negrito, Berbería' (little black, from Barbary), 'negro Fulo' (black of Fulani origin), 'Jalofe, negro-berberisco' (Wolof, black from Barbary), 'negro portugues' (Portuguese black), 'morisca-blanca bozal' (converted Muslim, white, non-assimilated), 'morisco-Fulo' (converted Muslim of Fulani origin), and so on.

In the case of 'lora, mulata, ladina' it is clear that *ladina* (assimilated) modified *lora* and *mulata*. It may be that both of the latter terms were used because the seller or recorder was unsure which to use (because one was replacing the other) and thus used both. On the other hand, it is possible that *mulato* implied something slightly different modified *loro*, or that *loro* modified *mulato*.

I believe, however, that the use of *loro* simply took a while to die out and, in the meantime, some people coupled it with *mulato*. We see, for example, that several *loros* were resold later as *mulatos* and a *mulato* was resold as a *negro loro*. The 'lora, mulata, ladina' mentioned above was resold as a *mulata*.

In 1595 Doña Francisca Ramírez, widow, sold Baltasar, 17, *mulato*. In 1599 she sold Bartolomé, 20, *loro*, to a probable relative. In 1600 that relative sold Bartolomé *mulato*, to Doña Luisa Ramírez, widow. In 1589 Marcos, 14, *loro* was sold by one Hernández to G. Hernández and Chaves, along with Jerónima, 16, *mulata*. In 1593 Marcos, 18, *mulato* was sold by F. Hernández. In 1582 Luis, 11, *mulato* was sold while in 1586, Luis, age 16, *negro loro* was resold. It seems very likely that these examples illustrate the interchangeable use of *mulato* and *loro*, as well as the probability of siblings being denominated by one or the other of the two words.

Note must also be taken of several very important indicators. First, several *mulatos* were referred to as *ladino* or as *morisco*. This proves that a person born in North Africa or elsewhere outside of Spanish control could be called a *mulato*, based, doubtless on appearance alone. A *mulata* slave, Estevanía, 20, was said in 1580 to have run away and that she had been acquired *de buena guerra* (in just war) thus again illustrating that *mulato* could refer to appearance.

We also find reference to Melchor, age 30, in 1580 as a *mulato-indio*, indicating that an Indian could also be called a *mulato* (just as he could be called a *loro*). This is a clear indication that *mulato* could refer to a color. (It would make little sense to interpret *mulato-indio* as meaning 'half-*mulato* and half-Indian'. How could anyone be 'half-*mulato*'?

Nonetheless, we do not find anyone specifically referred to as *de color mulato* in Lobo Cabrera's documents. We find *color negro, color loro, color algo baça*, and so on, but no *color mulato*. I am inclined to believe that *amulatado* is the form of *mulato* used for specific color reference but that otherwise, *mulato* refers to either a generalized appearance or to a specific status, that is, *muwallad* (mestizo) or *malado* (a slave born in the house). The most likely meaning seems to be mixed-blood or having the appearance (color) of a mixed-blood.

Lobo Cabrera believes that the *mulatos* 'were born in the islands or in Barbary, the product of unions between *moro* and black, Canary Islander and black, and white and black. Although many of them were children of whites, they formed part of the slave population, because the child . . . assumed the condition of the mother.' To his list of Muslim and black, canario and black, and white and black we must also add American and black and perhaps white and American, since the term mestizo is not recorded in the Canary Islands in the records.

Lobo Cabrera also believes that prior to about 1550 most of the mixed-bloods were imported from Berbería and were called *loros*. These *mulatos* were then joined after 1550 by mixed-bloods born in the islands. As noted, however, the imbalanced sex-ratios do not confirm this thesis.[8]

The transition from *loro* to *mulato* is a rather sharp one, pinpointed at about 1552. This corresponds extremely well with the first royal decrees relative to *mulatos* in the Caribbean (1530, 1543, 1549) and the last decree relative to *loros* there (1551). This congruence suggests that Spanish officialdom was responsible for the rapid shift in terminology, a shift, however, which is not reflected in Spain itself (at least not in Valencia). This could be explained by the shift being contained in colonial legislation not promulgated in the kingdom of Aragón of which Valencia was a part.

The use of the term *mulato* in relation to the Americas begins by 1530 but before looking at usage in that connection it is best to compare Valencia with the Canary Islands.

In Valencia between 1569 and 1686 *mulato* was not a popular or commonly used term in the records relating to runaway or new slaves. During the period the books of the *baylia* were of three types: those relating to recaptured runaway slaves, those relating to *cautivos* who had fallen into slavery for the first time, and mixed volumes.

By this period *loro* had virtually disappeared from use, being represented by only a few *cautivos* in the 1570s. As previously noted, *membrillo cocido* (365) and *moreno* (59) were both far more common designations than was *mulato* (22). It is significant that *mulato* was used both for runaway slaves (1569–86) and for new slaves (1571–85). In mixed books *mulato* was used from 1594 to 1666 but not in 1666–85. The largest number of *mulatos* for any single book (six) was for new slaves from 1571–8.

It may be that color-descriptive terms were preferred for their aid in identifying a slave. It may also be true that locally born *mulatos* were not recorded unless they ran away. On the other hand, several pieces of evidence point towards *mulato* being a term for appearance including especially its use for new slaves of presumed foreign origin (whose parents could not be known).

It is also significant that in several cases slaves known to have been the mixed-blood children of black (or slave) and white parents were not called *mulatos*. One such was a man picked up as a fugitive in 1564, the son of a slave mother and her owner. He was termed *moreno*. Another I have already referred to earlier as being termed a *negre*. At least one individual was categorized as *llor-mulato*, thus seeming to link the two words.[9]

It may be that *mulato* was simply not popular in Valencia, but in 1637 Philip IV ordered that all male slaves, 'negros, mulatos y berberiscos' be gathered together at Cádiz to serve in the galleys. This usage would seem to support the notion that *mulato* was intended to include all slaves who were neither black nor white (nor Berber), thus basically including all intermediate-colored Christianized slaves. Slaves of *moreno* and *membrillo cocido* color (if not *berberisco*) would be included under *mulato* in that case.[10]

A somewhat similar 'catch-all' usage seems to have developed in Portugal where in *c.*1550, as noted, legislation set aside certain places along the river at

Lisbon for various kinds of slaves. Referred to were *pretos, mulatos, indios* and *mouros*, thus suggesting that *mulato* was a sufficient category to cover all types of slaves who were not *pretos, indios* or *mouros*.[11]

In West Africa one would expect any terms developed for mixed-bloods to refer principally to Portuguese, European or Jewish mixtures with black Africans (although the presence of a certain number of Indians from India and Americans from Brazil is also likely). The term *mulato* continued to be used for mixed-bloods in the area. In 1572 it was noted that the 'whites' of Mina (Ghana)

estaõ amancebados muitos com negras gentias, as ques se tem por averiguado que es perdiçaõ os partos, ou matandoos depois de nacidos, ou fazendoos abortivos, o qual se prova, porque estando amancebados, e crecendo os ventres, naõ há nenhum só mulato em toda a aldea, havendo tantos, donde as negras parem a seu salvo.[12]

Thus many whites had pagan *negras* as mistresses but not a *mulato* was to be seen in the area due to abortions or other means used apparently by the *negras* to prevent the existence of mixed children.

In other areas, such as the Congo, *mulatos* were born. Note has already been made of Lopez and Pigafetta's comment that the children of the Portuguese and *negras* there were called *mulatos* 'by the Spanish'.

An English visitor of the 1590s commented that:

the children in this country are born white, and change their color in two days to a perfect black. As, for example, the Portugals, which dwell in the kingdom of Congo, have sometimes children by the negro woman, and many times the fathers are deceived, thinking when the child is born it is theirs, and within two days it proveth the son or daughter of a negro; which the Portugals do greatly grieve at, for they rejoice when they have a mulato child, though it be a bastard.[13]

This text, first published much later in 1613–25, would seem to indicate either that the native women were practicing birth control or that the children were of half-Portuguese ancestry but only of dark-skin color. If the latter was true (as Duarte Lopez and Pigafetta's evidence would dispute) then the implication is strong that *mulato* was thought of as pointing towards a specific color, at least by the Englishman.

USAGE IN THE AMERICAS

The Spanish Empire in the Americas presented a different situation from Africa, in that there was a multitude of Americans with whom both Africans and Europeans could intermix. The term *mestizo* began to be used in royal proclamations in 1533 but *mulato* appeared irregularly until 1549. Prior to the latter year there were orders given relating to various issues in which *negros* and *mestizos* were mentioned and where, doubtless, the Crown could have intended to include all classes of non-whites. But this is not clear.

As noted earlier, in 1530 the king of Spain sought to prohibit *loros* and *mulatos* from being sent as slaves to the Americas without his special license. This order followed others in 1518–26 which had sought to prohibit heretics, persons condemned before the Inquisition or their relatives, Wolofs, Middle-Easterners (Levantines) or others raised or serving among Muslims (including *negros de Guinea*), New Christians of Jewish or Muslim background, or any *negros ladinos* (who had been in Spain for two years) from going to the Indies without special royal license. The 1530 *cedula* dealt only with slaves. It ordered that: 'slaves shall not pass to the Indies, neither Blancos, Negros, Loros nor Mulatos, without our express license', and if this license was not obtained, the slaves would be confiscated. Moreover, if the slave sent without license was 'Berberisco, de casta de Moros, o Iudios, o Mulato' the head of the fleet had to return the slave to Spain at the cost of the sender. In other words, if the slave was Berber, of the Muslim or Jewish groups, or *mulato*, he or she could not be left in the Indies.

Still more serious was the sending of a *morisco* slave, which would result additionally in a large fine.

Clearly, *moriscos* (conquered and forcibly converted Muslims) were considered the most dangerous (regardless of color). Second most dangerous were other Muslims, Jews, Berbers and *mulatos*. (And presumably the term *loro* used in the first enumeration might also be included under mulato in the second, although *loros* of Muslim or Jewish or Berber background would be covered by reference to those groups specifically). Now why were *mulatos* considered so dangerous by the Crown? Saco comments that

esta ley, sin decir si el mulato pertenecia á secta alguna religiosa, lo equipara al judio en todas las penas que impone; y si en algo lo diferencia del morisco, es en que al introductor de este se le condena además en mil pesos de oro.

Thus, *mulatos* were not mentioned as belonging to a religious sect and yet they were treated the same as Jews.

Negros ladinos had already been prohibited in 1526 and, most likely, *mulatos* and *loros* were now simply being added to the list. Nonetheless, the placing of *mulatos* with Jews, Berbers and Muslims suggests that they were regarded as largely being of suspicious origin. It may well be that many *mulatos* in Spain by 1530 were half-American (or half-*canario*) and were regarded as being especially dangerous because of their potential connections with both rebellious native groups and with Africans.

In 1543 the king ordered that general licenses for the shipment of *negros* to the Americas could not be used for *mulatos* and others 'who are not *negros*', because of 'inconveniences'. In 1549 *mulatos* born in the Americas were referred to in an order to the effect that: 'ningún mulato, ni mestizo, ni hombre que no fuese legítimo, pudiese tener indios, ni oficio real ni público, sin tener para ello especial licencia nuestra.' Thus *mulatos* and *mestizos* were grouped together with all men who were illegitimate and this class was prohibited from having possession of Americans or holding a public office without a special royal licence. In about 1550 mestizos who were not *vecinos* (settlers) or a legitimate son of a *vecino* were prohibited from having Americans in their charge. Also in the same year *encomenderos* of Americans, their relatives and guests, as well as mestizos, *mulatos* and *negros* (free or slave) were prohibited from residing in American villages belonging to the *encomienda*.[14]

In 1563 a general prohibition was issued to prevent anyone living in the villages or missions of Americans who were

> Españoles, Negros, Mulatos, ó Mestizos . . . y los Negros, Mestizos, y Mulatos, demás de tratados mal, se sirven dellos, enseñan sus malas costumbres . . . y en quanto á los Mestizos, y Zambaigos, que son hijos de Indias, nacidos entre ellos, y han de heredar sus casas, y haziendas, porque parece cosa dura separarlos de sus padres, se podrá dispensar.[15]

Thus, all Spaniards, *mestizos*, *mulatos* and *negros* were prohibited because of their abuse of the Americans and their transmission of bad customs, except for *mestizos* and *Zambaígos* who were children of female Americans, and born among them.

The term *zambaígo* will be discussed subsequently. In the above context it can be interpreted as referring to a class of *mulatos* who were half-American and half-African. It is a term used primarily in Peru and adjacent regions.

James Lockhart in his work on Peru covering the years 1532–60 tells us that during that period

> In order to express the classes and categories of mixtures of *negros* with other races, there was only one word of common use: "mulato". Generally the *mulatos* were not seen as a group distinct from the *negros*; a *mulato* was a type of *negro*. The word "zambo" was still not in use, a term which later served to name those born of *negro* and *indígena*. Up to 1560 they were classified as *mulatos*.

(He notes also that specific color terms, such as *membrillo cocido* were also used). Thus the term *mulato*, according to Lockhart, was used for African–American and African–European mixed-bloods. Bowser, another scholar of Peruvian history, states: 'My researches in both Peruvian and Mexican notarial records indicate that zambo was widely used for Afro–Indians in Peru as early as the 16th century, though in Mexico they were still referred to as "mulattoes" as late as 1650.'[16]

Thus both in Mexico and Peru *mulato* was used for American–African mixed-bloods but after 1560 *zambo* (actually *zambaígo*) began to replace *mulato* in the Peru region. This latter subject will be discussed in a separate section later.

It is possible that on certain occasions the term *mestizo* was used so as to embrace all mixed-blood. In 1559, for example, the Spanish Crown extended to *mestizos* the right to come to Spain to study, but *mestizo* was defined as referring to 'hijos de Christianos e Indias' thus implying that the term might otherwise be ambiguous. In any case, *mulato* therefore began to be used more commonly and the ambiguity was perhaps gradually reduced as the two terms were given specialized meanings.

In 1561 *Francisca Mulata* was allowed to travel to Peru from Spain after being requested by her father. By 1562 the 'mestizos y mulatos' were said to be both numerous and dangerous. In 1566 it was ordered that the 'indios y mestizos y mulatos' in Peru not be allowed to carry arms although some had been allowed illegally to do so. In 1568 Philip II ordered that: 'Ningun mulato, ni Zambaígo traiga armas, y los mestizos, que vivieren en lugares de Españoles, y mantuvieren casa, y labrãça, las pueden traer con licencia de el que governare, y no la den á otros.'[17] Thus *mestizos* who lived among and like Spaniards were to be separated out from *mulatos* and *zambaígos*, being allowed under licence to carry arms.

Of great interest are several documents also of 1568. In one the Crown stated:

Nos somos informados que esa tierra [Nueva España] hay mucha cantidad de negros, y que éstos se casan y envuelven con negras e indias, y nacen dellos muchos mulatos, los cuales son mal inclinados, y que ansimismo hay muchos mestizos, hijos de españoles y de indias, y que como no conocen otros deudos sino los de sus madres, se juntan con ellos.

Here we have a clear statement from Spain that *negros* were marrying Americans and that the mixed progeny were called *mulatos*. We also read of the Crown's concern that the *mestizos*, raised by their Native American mothers, were joining with the non-white masses in a threat to Spanish imperialism.

Later in the year the Crown asserted that: 'me ha sido hecha relación que en ella [Nueva España] hay cantidad de los dichos mulatos, hijos de negros e indias y de españoles e negras, que algunos tienen oficios mecánicos y otros sirven a los españoles.'[18] Here we see the term *mulato* used officially and explicitly for both American–African and European–African persons.

As a reflection of the developing colonial caste system in 1571 *negras*, free or slave, and *mulatas* were prohibited from wearing gold, pearls, or silk but an exception was made for those married to Spaniards. The fact that the *mulatas* were assumed to be free indicates that they were children of free American mothers. Many other restrictions on the rights of mixed-bloods and non-whites were also adopted in these years, which do not need to be reviewed here in detail. It is sufficient to point out that the terms *mestizos* and *mulatos* were used in such a way as to usually embrace all classes of mixed-bloods. Occasionally, however, for Peru and adjoining regions the term *zambaígo* was also included.[19]

In 1574 Viceroy Martín Enríquez of Mexico expressed great concern about the rebellions of 'indios, los mestizos y mulatos, y los negros' and also about 'the great increase in numbers of the mulatos, while the mestizos are not so numerous, although there are many among them.' He believed that the *mulatos* were superior in ability and strength to the *mestizos* 'as men are to dolls, since the *mestizos* are sons of Spaniards'. Clearly he was stating that the *mulatos* in question were *not* children of Spaniards. He made this clearer by proposing that the children of 'negros y mulatos con indias sean declarados esclavos y que su santidad prohiba que las indias se casen con negros y mulatos.' Thus he wanted to enslave the children of Americans and *mulatos* or Africans and to outlaw the marriage of the latter with American women.

The situation is made very clear in Juan López de Velasco's *Geografía* (reviewing affairs in the Americas up to 1574): 'Hay, demas de los españoles . . . y de los criollos que de padres y madres españoles han nacido en ellas, muchos mestizos que son hijos de españoles y de indias, o por el contrario, y cada día se van acrecentando más de todas partes.' Thus, in addition to Spaniards and *criollos*, Spaniards born in *las Indias*, there were many *mestizos*, children of Spaniards and Americans and these latter were increasing in all areas. 'Demás de éstos hay muchos mulatos, hijos de negros ye de indias, que se llaman zambaigos, que bienen a ser la gente más peor y vil que en aquellas partes hay; . . . mulatos hijos de españoles y de negras no hay tantos, por las muchas indias que hay ruines de sus personas.' This is, of course, an extremely significant statement, one which must be underscored and referred to again later. In it we find López de Velasco stating that *mulatos* were chilren of Africans and Americans and that they were also called *zambaígos* (in Peru and its vicinity, although he does not specifically say so). He also adds that there were not so many *mulatos* who were children of Spaniards and *negras* because the Spaniards had many American women. This is a very helpful statement in terms of understanding why several definitions for *mulato* in the Americas totally ignore white-Afrian mixed-bloods. The simple fact is that the American–African mixed-bloods far outnumbered the former.

It is also interesting that López states that the *mulatos* or *zambaígos* were coming to be the worst and most vile group in the Americas and that they and the mestizos were putting some regions in danger of separation and rebellion. This must, of course, be considered a compliment to the many *zambo* and native-*zambo* 'republics' which had begun to appear.[20]

In the 1580s Miguel Cabello Balboa wrote a detailed account of the Esmeraldas region of present-day Ecuador including especially coverage of the intermixture of Black Africans with the Americans of the area. Of greatest interest here is his consistent use of the term *mulato* for American–African persons, as in the case of the children of a Nicaraguan mother and an African father who had run away from a Spanish ship: 'Parió allí aquella india de Nicaragua dos hijos, el uno llamado Jhoan y el otro Francisco, de quien trataré más adelante; quiso el negro padre de destos mulatos.' Thus the Nicaraguan American woman gave birth to two *mulatos*, sons of a *negro*. In the region also was a *negro* named Alonso de Illescas, born in Cabo Verde but sent as a young man to Seville and later to South America. Alonso married *una india hermosa*, the daughter of a principal chief, and one of his children is specifically referred to as 'una mulata hija suya', that is, as his *mulata* daughter. These mixed African–American people subsequently created a great deal of difficulty for the Spaniards.

In 1599 several mixed African–American leaders of the Esmeraldas region had their portraits painted together by the Native American artist Adrián Sánchez Galque. This painting has often been reproduced with the leaders referred to as *zambos* but John Leddy Phelan tells us that they are 'incorrectly labelled "mulattoes"' on the painting itself. Clearly this was no mistake, however.

The collaboration of part-African mixed-bloods and *mestizos* with rebel Americans was a danger which spread to the Chichimeca region of north central Mexico. In 1585 a report to the Chichimecos noted that they were going about armed, on horseback, and carried with them 'very skillful *mestizos* and *mulatos* who lead them.'[21]

In 1592 the king stated that:

me ha dicho relación que en ella [Venezuela] hay muchos mulatos hijos de Indias, que pretenden gozar de la libertad que de sus madres les pertenece y salen con ello, de que resultan muchos daños, delitos y excesos que cometen, los cuales cesarían si tuviesen correción y subjeción al servicio de sus encomenderos como sus madres . . . está dada la orden que se ha de tener en esas partes en el tributar los negros y negras, mulatos y mulatas libres que hay.[22]

Thus the king stated that in Venezuela there were many *mulatos*, children of American women, who asserted their freedom and refused to be controlled by the *encomenderos* of their mothers. The king wanted them to pay tribute in accord with an earlier order of 1574.

This is a sufficient review of the usage of the term *mulato* in the Americas, covering 1549–92, to show what *mulato* meant to Spanish royal officialdom. It is very clear that *mulato* primarily referred to American–African mixed-bloods. On the other hand, the term also embraced the rarer Spanish–African mixed-bloods. From this we can easily deduce that *mulato* meant essentially a person who was half-African and half-something-else, a definition very congruent with several of the dictionary definitions to be examined below.

Our explicit evidence falls within the years 1568–92 but we can reasonably infer that usage in 1549–67 would have been the same. As we shall see, usage in the early seventeenth century is essentially the same.

After reviewing this data we can perhaps reinterpret usage in the Canary Islands during the same period, i.e., as *mulato* = half-Black African. But we must be cautious in not too readily embracing such a specifically ancestral definition since there is much evidence that persons could be called *mulatos* whose ancestry was not known. That is, we must allow for something like *mulato* = half-Black African or one having that appearance or, perhaps, one of that color or range of colors. Only in this way can North Africans of brown color fall within the definition.

Now let us return to Portuguese usage. In Brazil I have not found the term *mulato* used during the period 1540s–80s. It may be that *mamaluco* or *mestiço* sufficed to cover any American–African mixed bloods. (There would have been very few Portuguese–African mixed-bloods thanks to the imbalanced sex ratio among African slaves). Of course, there are doubtless sources which I have not seen, but the Jesuit writers do not use *mulato* or such later terms as *caboré*, *cafuso*, *curiboca*, and so on.[23]

By the period of the Dutch invasion, 1630s–50s, *mulato* frequently appears in the sources. There is some indication that it included American–Africans in its meaning. In 1644, for example, the Dutch and Tapuyas raided the quilombo of

Palmares. They took 31 prisoners, among whom were seven 'indios tupís (brasilianos) e alguns mulatinhos', that is Tupís and some young *mulatos*. (These *mulatinhos* were called *mulaetjens* in Dutch.)

Now *mulat* was a new word to the Dutch, not yet incorporated into the ordinary Dutch language. Thus we can assume that its meaning was essentially congruent with Brazilian Portuguese. The clear implication is that the young *mulatos* were half-Tupí and half-African.

Similarly, in 1654 the Dutch and Portuguese entered into a formal treaty which ended their fighting. One passage in the accord states that the Portuguese commander 'gave pardon to all of the rebels especially to Anthony Mendos and all other *Brazilianen*' in the forts and places of Recife, and also to the *'Mulaten/Mamalucquen/* and *Negros'*.

The object of this passage was to guarantee the safety and honorable surrender of all the people who had aided the Dutch including those serving with Antonio Mendes, all of the Brazilians (Tupís) and the *mulaten* (*mulatos*), *mamalucos* and *negros*. No separate term was used for American–African mixed-bloods and we must assume that *mulaten* (and/or *mamalucken*) was used to include them.

It should be noted that Antonio Mendes had captained a company 'de indios tupís, mulatos e negros' for the Dutch.[24]

Since special terms for American–African mixed-bloods did not generally appear until later, we must assume that in this period *mulato* was used for such persons. (It is true that in 1643 George Marcgrave listed the words *curiboca e caboclos'* for African–American mixed-bloods but Dutch documents of the period did not use these terms and perhaps this usage was not yet general. Moreover, *curiboca* is often given the meaning of white and American rather than black and American while *caboclo* has almost universally been treated as being equivalent to *indio*. Marcgrave stated that those 'of Ethiopian mother and European father' were called *mulato*.)[25]

Barlaeus, first published in 1647, mentions *halfzwarten* (half-blacks) as the product of the mixture of whites and *zwarten* in Brazil. He also notes that the mixture of free people (Dutch, Portuguese and Brazilians) with slaves (*negros* and Tapuyas of Maranhão) gave rise to 'Mulaten, Malucken en Mistichos' (*mulatos*, *mamalucos*, and *mestizos*).[26]

A Portuguese law of 1621 prohibited 'negroes, mulattoes, or Indians, although free' from learning the trade of goldsmith. Clearly *mulato* was intended to include African–American mixed-bloods. Somewhat later (pre-1651) a French writer described the Brazilian population as consisting in Negres, Bresiliens, Tapoyos, Molates, Mamelus e Criolles'. Again, 'molates' must have included Red-Black persons, since *mamelus* (*mamalucos*) were usually or always white and American.[27]

Portuguese usage in the Indian Ocean region is reflected in the writings of foreigners who traveled with the Portuguese or who visited their colonies in East Africa and India. In this area it would appear that the Portuguese developed a distinction between *mestiço* and *mulato*, the former being used for mixture with Indians and other Asians, the latter being used for part-Africans. Nonetheless, some confusion may have also existed. As noted earlier, Sassetti referred in 1584–6 to the king of Calicut as being 'di colore di mulatto' and to another individual as being of a similar color. Moreover, it is not always clear that, when a *mulato* is mentioned in early texts, African (as opposed to Indian) ancestry is indicated.[28]

Nonetheless, it does appear that a tendency existed by the 1590s to distinguish between part-African and part-Indian mixed-bloods by the selective use of *mulato* and *mestiço*. Another Italian merchant, Carletti, noted at the Cabo Verde Islands that the Portuguese there were intermixing with *nere* (blacks) and *mulatte*. The latter women were 'born of White and of Black'. On the other hand, in Bengal he used the term *mestrizze* to refer to mixed-bloods. (Sassetti also had noted the use of the latter term in India.)[29]

A French visitor, Pyrard de Laval, spent the years 1601–11 in the region. At the Maldive Islands he mentioned a young servant, age 17: 'he is the son of a *Cafre* [Kaffir] of Ethiopia and of a woman of these islands, that whom they call [a] *Mulastre*'. In India he noted that the Portuguese had many slaves from Africa whom they called *Cafres* and that those descended from Portuguese and *Cafre* or *Negro de Guinea* were called *mulatos* and were held to be the equals of the *mestiços*. Thus *mulato* in its early French form, *mulastre*, was used for both mixed-bloods of African–Maldavian and African–Portuguese background by this traveller.

Pyrard also uses *metisses* and *metifs* (two forms of *mestiço*) to refer to Portuguese soldiers in India.

Approaching the subject of the Portuguese in the Atlantic and Brazil, Pyrard states: 'those who are issues of Portguese and of *Cafres*, they call them *Mulastres*'.[30]

It would appear that in the Indian Ocean area, at least, the Portuguese were developing a system of nomenclature directly analogous to what the Spaniards were doing in the same time period. That is, *mestizo* was being restricted to part-American or part-Indian mixed-bloods while *mulato* was being used for part-African mixed-bloods. But even as in the Americas *mulatos* were also of American–African mixture, so too in Asia it would appear that *mulatos* could be of African–Asian mixture. This same development does not seem to have occurred in Brazil where, as noted earlier, *mestiço* generally retained the very broad meaning of 'mixed'.

EXPLICIT DEFINITIONS OF *MULATO* IN PORTUGUESE

Now let us turn to dictionary definitions and also to the explicit definitions given by other types of writers, through the early seventeenth century primarily. We shall commence with early Portuguese definitions since Cardoso is the first dictionary-maker who seems to have included *mulato* in his work (pre-1569).

Professor Cardoso's dictionary was the first of its type and was reprinted six times through 1694.[31]

Cardoso in his Portuguese–Latin section has: 'mulata, ou mulato = Hybrida, ae' while in the Latin–Lusitanian section he has: 'Hybrida, ae = 0 homem mulato.' *Mestiço* is equated with *Ibria, ae* (1592 printing) and *Hybris, dis. Hybrida, ae* (1643 printing).[32]

Thus *mulato* commences its dictionary life as meaning 'hybrid' (with all of the meanings of *hibrida* discussed earlier) and as essentially the same as *mestiço*. It should be noted that *hibrida* and *mulato* have much the same meaning as *muwallad* in Arabic.

Barbosa, the next dictionary-maker, ignores *mulato* for humans and enters only *mestiço* (1611) with the *hybrida* meaning.[33]

Faria, in his commentary on the *Lusiada* of Camoens (1639) adds some information of interest, as noted earlier. Camoens had referred to the people of the Indian Ocean as *baça* (dark) and Faria states that Camoens was saying that these people were neither white nor black but were like those who in Portugal were called *amulatado* or *pardo* 'because they called *mulatos* the children of black, and white: those of this mixture of parents having a doubtful or neutral color.' This *amulatado* or *pardo* color was seen by Faria as negative. He notes that the children of blacks and whites were called *mulatos*, derived from *mulo*, 'respetando a la calidad de la junta de objetos contrarios.' This 'union of contrary objects' reflects the concept of *hybrida*.

In summary, Faria equates the color of the people of India and the Persian Gulf (*baço*) with *amulatado* or *pardo*. This *mulato-pardo* color is also typical of *mulatos* who are called such because they are hybrids, like the mule. Further, black-white mixed-bloods are called *mulatos* in Portugal but Faria leaves open the possibility that other kinds of mixtures could also be called by the same term.[34]

Pereira (1646) follows Cardoso in that Portuguese *mulato, homem* is equated with Latin *Hybrida*. *Hybris* and *Hybrida* are equated with a series of things including 'o filho de adulterio, porco, ou cão mestiço, etc. o mulato, ou filho de natural, & estrangeiro.' *Hybrida*, in other words, is equivalent to a child of adultery, a mixed dog or pig (or other animal), the mulato, or child of a native and a stranger. Certain of these meanings are taken from ancient Latin authors and it is not clear if 'the mulato' is 'the child of a native and a stranger' or if the latter is simply another meaning. In any case, *mulato* continued to be seen as a word equivalent to 'hybrid'.[35]

A significant change begins to appear as we approach the year 1700. At about that time an Italian, Antonio Zucchelli, visited Portuguese missions in the Congo and then went on to Bahia, Brazil. There, as noted earlier, he remarked on the presence of olive-colored people who he said were 'bastards of the white man, produced by *negre* women'. These people were commonly called 'mulati, overo Pardi'. We cannot be certain that these *olivastro* people did not also have American ancestry since Zucchelli chooses only to emphasize their origin as illegitimate children of sold and prostituted black women. Considering that there were 8,000 to 10,000 of them, he could not possibly have known their actual ancestry.[36]

Nonetheless, the emphasis upon a 'black-white' origin for *mulatos* is typical of the eighteenth century. A 1701 English–Portuguese dictionary has:

mulata = one born of black and white parents
mulato = a man of that mixture between a white and a black.

The meaning of 'black' in this case is not certain but the author has:

Cafra = a she-black-a-moor of Ethiopia
Cafre = the male
Pretinho, preto = negro
Negro ou cafre = a he-black
Negra ou cafre = a she-black.

Thus while *cafre* refers specifically to a black-a-moor of Ethiopia, *negro* refers merely to a black person. The ambiguous English usage of the term 'black' has already been discussed. This is borne out by the translation of 'black' into Portuguese as 'cousa preta, negra, escura ou sombria', covering obscure and dusky (shady) as well as black itself. Moreover, a black-moor is defined as '*mouro, moura*, the natives of Ethiopia' which seems to include *mouros* (Muslims) within the meaning.[37]

A similar situation is presented by a Dutch–Portuguese dictionary of 1718 where we find:

mulata. Een vrows-persoon, welke van witte en swart ouders gebooren is. (A woman born of white and black parents).
mulato homen. Een mans persoon, die van witte en swarte ouders gebooren is. (A male born of white and black parents).

Some light is shed upon the meaning of *swart* by the fact that *negro* or *cafre* is equivalent to *swart, moor, caffer*. We have already noted the Dutch use of *moor* and *swart* for peoples of the East Indies and Brazil, as well as for Africans.[38]

Of greater interest is the work of Bluteau, whose dictionary laid the groundwork for most other Portuguese dictionaries of the eighteenth century. The 1712–20 work has for *mulata, mulato*: 'Filha, & filho de branca, & negra, ou de negro, & de mulher branca. . . . Nata, vel natus ex patre albo, & matre nigra. . . . Tambem poderamos chamar ao mulato *Ibrida*. . . . o que tenho dito sobre *Ibrida* no palavra *Mestiço*.' Thus Bluteau defines the *mulato* as a child of white and *negro* but also notes that one can call the *mulato* '*ibrida*' and directs the reader to his comments regarding *mestiço*. He also quotes Faria (1639) as an illustration.

Under *pardo* Bluteau states:

côr entre branco, & preto . . . (color between white, and black).
Homen pardo. *Vid.* mulato. (Pardo person. See mulato).

For *mestiço*, as already discussed, Bluteau gives the usual meanings for *Hibrida*

including 'nascidos de pays de differentes nacoens. . . . Homen mestiço . . .
Filho de Portuguez, & de India . . . Ibrida.' Thus *mulato*, aside from the black-white meaning, is the same as *pardo* and similar to, or a type of, *ibrida* or *mestiço*.
This leaves considerable latitude for usage, since *mestiço* includes Portuguese and American.

It is also worth noting that Bluteau defines *trigueiro* as a color 'que tira a pardo, que declina a negro' or as the same as *fuscus* and *subniger*. As we shall see, modern Portuguese dictionaries often equate *mulato* with a person of *trigueiro* color, a color similar to *pardo* (except that *pardo* points towards 'dark' while *trigueiro* is a more specific color term from *trigo*, that is, wheat).[39]

An English–Portuguese dictionary of the latter part of the eighteenth century states of *mulata*: 'the daughter of a black and a white; that is of a tawny color'. Tawny as a color has already been discussed.

A French–Portuguese dictionary (1784) continues the black-white definition while also adding under *mulat, mulate, mulâtre*: '*mestiço* . . . mulato; filho de pai, e mai de differente Religiaó, v.g., de hum mouro, e huma Hespanhola' (mixture of different religions as of a Moor and Spanish woman). Under *métif* the dictionary has: 'mistiço, molato, o que he nascido de pai Europeo, e de Mai Indiana, ou de pais de diferentes qualidades, paizes, ou Religiõs . . .' (mixture of different qualities, countries, or religions). I suspect that the definitions emphasizing inter-national and inter-religious mixture reflected a French meaning and were intended for persons who looked up the French word but could read a definition in the Portuguese language. Ten years later a Portuguese–French edition was issued and its definitions, written in both Portuguese and French, do *not* equate *mulato* with *mestiço* and restrict the meaning of the former to the usual black-white mixtures.[40]

In 1789 Antonio de Moraes Silva, born in Brazil, revised Blueau's dictionary. He added to the concept of *mulato* a new ingredient in that a *mulato* was said to be not only the child of a black and a white but also the child 'of *mulato* with white, to a certain degree'. At the same time he also added that a *mestiço* could be the child of a white and a *mulata*. Thus, we find a noticeably more ancestral approach to the concept of *mulato*, with quarter *negro* being so defined. But at the same time such a person could also be a *mestiço*.[41]

No doubt Moraes Silva's definitions reflect the growing racism of his age but also they seem to reflect eitheenth-century classificationist tendencies, as already discussed. It is not clear to what, if any, extent these changes reflect Brazilian usage since Moraes Silva leaves out many Brazilian terms (such as *caboclo* and *curiboca*).

Note has already been taken of S. F. de Mendo Trigoso's translation of Italian *bruni* and *berrettini* as *pardos* and *os amulatados* or *pardos*, respectively. The translator, who died 1821, clearly had no difficulty in regarding the Berbers of Mauritania as a 'mulato-ish' or *pardo* people. This tendency is also reflected in dictionaries of the nineteenth and twentieth centuries which tend to add to the black-white mixture definition a statement about color. Fonseca (1862–3) for example noted that *mulato, mulâtre* were *extrement brun*.

Coelho (1889) states that a *mulato* is one who 'descends' from *branco* and *preta* and, by extension, one who has 'côr escura; trigueiro, moreno'. This emphasis upon appearance is also reflected in the modern revision of Moraes Silva which notes that the term *caboclo* (*Indio*) could be applied to 'Mulato de côr acobreada e cabelos corridos como os brasis', that is, to a copper-colored *mulato* with long hair like an American. At the same time, one can speak of 'indio meio amulatado', that is, 'an Indian half-mulatto-like'.[42]

Following Coelho, most modern dictionaries use expressions for *mulato* such as 'aquele que é escuro; trigueiro' or 'mestiça com sangue negro' or to the color of coffee with milk ('tomar um mulato') or to the color of certain cattle in northern Brazil (orange on the back, the rest black), and so on. Although black-white mixture is mentioned, it seems clear that color and appearance have become hallmarks of a *mulato*, rather than specifically known ancestry. Moreover, the precise nature of that appearance seems highly subjective, since there is evidence that almost any 'sexy', attractive, medium-brown woman might be termed a *mulata* in Brazil, especially if there is a slight hint of African ancestry.[43]

One of the weaknesses of the Portuguese dictionaries over the centuries is their focus on Portuguese rather than Brazilian usage. Another weakness consists in the fascination with 'black and white', a focus understandable given Portuguese colonies in Africa and the widespread use of African slaves in the rest of the empire. Nonetheless, we might also discern in the 'black and white' definitions of *mulato* after 1700 a symbolic usage, replacing the concept of *hibrida* with a concept of the union of opposites (as expressed by Faria in 1639).

Thus we cannot always be sure that *negro* or *preto* meant 'Black African' nor can we be sure that 'white' meant un-mixed Europeans. I have already noted that the Portuguese often referred to Indians and Americans as *negros*. Moreover, the Portuguese in Brazil would, more often than not, be of mixed ancestry. Thus we cannot be satisfied with a literal interpretation of 'black and white = *mulato*'.

A still larger problem emerges when we consider that most of the recent terms used for African–American mixed-bloods in Brazil were not available to the early dictionary-makers. The term *cafuso*, for example, first appears in Pereira (1646) as *carafuz*, 'homo fusca facie'. *Cara fusca*, dusky face, was hardly a concrete designation for American–Africans and there is no indication that Pereira was at all familiar with any Brazilian usages. A 1701 dictionary has '*Carafuz*: one that has a brown, or blackish, or tawny countenance', again, a rather indefinite term, ethnically speaking. Bluteau, who did add some Brazilian terms to his 1727 supplement, has 'Carafuz: termo chulo [new] Homo fusca facie'. We do know, however, that by 1820 *Cafuso* was in use in Brazil to refer to African–American mixed-bloods, but at least two later authors make it refer to African–*mulato* mixtures as well.[44]

Of the two other terms used for African–American mixed persons, *caboré* and *curiboca*, the former seems to be documented only in the nineteenth century. A source of 1876 noted that *cafuso* was used for the American–African mixture in the north of Brazil while *caboré* was used in the south.

In so far as *curiboca* is concerned, we have already discussed Marcgrave's use in the 1640s of this term as being applicable to African–American persons. Simão Marques (1749) also has: *coriboca, filho de negro e india*. On the other hand, most writers seem to agree with Coelho that *cariboca* was used to designate the children of Europeans and Americans. Santamaría states that *cari-boc* meant 'hijo de blanco'. The *diccionario anonymo* of Tupí defines *caryboca* as *mestiço*, while *mulato* is *ceiya*.[45] Thus we cannot be sure that any term was available specifically to refer to African–Americans as distinct from African–Europeans and African–European–Americans, during the early period at least, except for *mulato* (and *pardo*).

Therefore, it is necessary to assume that by using the term 'black and white' the dictionary-makers do not exclude 'black and red' or 'black, white and red'. It perhaps is only that, like so many Europeans, they were utterly transfixed by the black-white nexus either as 'opposites' or as real people.

It seems clear that *mulato* was later used by the Portuguese to include persons who were part-American.[46] For example, in the 1797 census for São Paulo, a place where Tupí had been the vernacular language until just a few decades before, only whites, blacks and mulattoes were identified, according to Russell-Wood. The latter constituted just under 20 per cent of the population. In 1890, when white, black, *caboclo* and *mestiço* categories were used, São Paulo state had 8.24 per cent *caboclos* and 15.72 per cent *mestiços* thus showing that Americans definitely survived in the population. Moreover, the 24 per cent *mestiço–caboclo* total is close to the 20 per cent total for *mulatos* a century earlier.

Many other examples of this type can be cited for Brazil. In general, we can certainly say that *mulato* and *mestiço* tend to be used interchangeably (along with *pardo*) and that African–American–European mixed-bloods would generally fall within the *mulato* category. African–American mixed-bloods (whether called *cafusos* or *cabores*) might often be called *negros* or *pretos*. In either case, however, appearance would largely determine the category used.[47]

Rodrigues specifically states that 'more than 26 percent (26.54%)' of the population of Brazil was 'mixed Negro, Indian, and white' in the 1950 census. What term was used for these African–American–European persons? The census used *mestiço* but Rodrigues' translator calls them mulattoes.[48]

EXPLICIT DEFINITIONS IN SPANISH

Now let us turn to an examination of Spanish definitions, briefly incorporating therein some of the specific statements referred to earlier under usage.

The earliest Spanish dictionaries, those of Nebrija (1495, 1513, et cetera) contain no mention of *mulato* as applied to human beings. This is also the case with Las Casas' Tuscan–Castillian dictionary (1570, 1600). The first documentation occurs instead in reports or legislation relating to the Americas as already discussed. To review that material let us construct a short list:

1568   Royal order defines a *mulato* as a child of *negro* and *india*.
1574   Viceroy Enríquez of México states that *mulatos* are not sons of Spaniards.
1574   López de Velasco states that *mulatos* are children of *negros* and *indias* and, much less commonly, of Spaniards and *negras*.
1583   Cabello Balboa uses *mulato* for American–Africans in Ecuador.
1592   Royal order states that *mulatos* (Venezuela) are *hijos de indias*.
1599   Mixed African–American chieftains from Esmeraldas called *mulatos*.

From the character of these definitions we stated earlier that *mulato* seems to have meant half-Black African and, ordinarily, half-American but with the half-African part being apparently essential. To this must be added, 'or one who looks half-African'.

Interestingly, John Minsheu's English–Spanish dictionary (1599, 1626) states for *mulato, mulata*: 'the son (or daughter) of a blackmoore and one of another nation'. In his 1617 *vocabularium* Minsheu states:

[Latin] Filus maurae & hominis albi coloris vel è contra.
[English] the Sonne of a woman black-moore and a man of another nation, or of a black-more and the woman of another nation.

In his 1617 *Guide* Minsheu has:

mulato, hoc nomine Hispan: vocant genitum ex mauro/patre, & alterius nationis matre, vel è converso.

Thus Minsheu, obviously an excellent student of contemporary Spanish, understood that *mulato* meant half-*mauro* (Latin) or half-Blackmoor (English).[49]

Minsheu's influence was understandably great and many English dictionaries continued his tradition. In 1656, for example, Blount repeated the same definition (half-Blackmore, half-another nation) and added: 'one that is of a mongrel complexion'. Minsheu was followed, in essence, through Kersey's 1708 *Dictionarium*. Most attributed the word directly to Spanish.[50]

In 1602 Garcilaso de la Vega, the half-Inca scholar, after traveling widely (in Europe as well as America) and after interviewing old Spanish soldiers wrote: 'In all of the West Indies, those of us who are born of a Spanish father and an Indian mother are called mestizos, just as in Spain those who are born of a Negro father and an Indian mother or vice versa are called mulatos.'[51]

In 1613, after many decades of research and travel in Peru, Huaman Poma (a Quechua Indian) wrote: 'when mulattoes – a mixture of negro and Indian – produce quadroon children, these children lose all physical trace of their negro origin except for the ear, which still gives them away by its shape and size.'

In 1617 Garcilaso de la Vega's history of Peru was finished. In it he states: 'mulato, hijo de negro e india', that is, that a mulatto is the child of a male

Negro and a female American. He also adds that the word *cholo* was then used for 'the children of mulattoes' but was a Caribbean coastal word used in a derogatory way by the Spaniards. (The term *cholo* later came to apply to various types of mixed-blood Americans in Peru and along the Pacific Coast generally.)[52]

From 1568 through 1617, then, we have seen that American–African persons were called *mulatos* and that they were, in fact, the predominant group so named. Moreover, we have seen both Spanish-based and American-based writers so using the term. Now, however, let us look at several European dictionaries or sources which present a different emphasis. I have already noted that Rosal (*c.*1601) made *mulato* the equivalent of *loro*, using both as names for slaves who were 'no bien negro' (not very black). In 1607 Oudin states of *mulatos*: 'they are half-Moors [*demy Mores*], children who are born of a white man and a *Moresse*, or of a *More* and a white woman'. Oudin also makes Spanish *moro* equivalent to French *more* and *nègre*. His 1625 dictionary adds to the above that *mulatos* 'are of *olivastre* [olive] color. *Mestizo* is defined exactly the same as *mulato*, except that its usage is broader (so as to include 'two races' or two different religions).

The French–Spanish–Dutch version of 1639 remains the same as the 1625 except that a Dutch line is added:

half Mooren gheboren van eenen witten en eene swerte 'tsy man oft vrou/moulack. [Half-Moor, of white and black, a *moulack*.]

Mestizo remains the same as above and is also equivalent to Dutch *moulack*. (The latter may be a corruption of *mamaluco*.)

De la Porte's Spanish–Dutch dictionary (1659) seems to be a copy of Oudin-Rodrigues (1639) and repeats the same definition for *mulato*.[53]

Oudin's work emphasizes a *more*-white mixture but given the ambiguity of *more* (*moor*) in that time period (*more* is equated with Spanish *moro*) and given the use of *moulack* as an equivalent for both *mulato* and *mestizo*, we must regard his definition (half-Moore) as being quite flexible. The use of Dutch *swert* (black) has already been discussed.

Covarrubias (1611) defines *mulato* as 'el que es hijo de negra, y de hõbre blanco' as mentioned earlier. This is a 'black–white' definition which is similar to the Portuguese ones already analyzed. Either Covarrubias was unfamiliar with actual contemporary usage or he was using black and white symbolically.[54]

Now let us turn again to the Americas, looking specifically in the Peruvian direction to see what impact the use of the term *zambaígo* had on the meaning of *mulato*. As noted already, Lockhart states that between 1532 and 1560 only *mulato* was used for African–American mixed persons. Thereafter, *zambaígo* (and later *zambo*) came to be used for such persons, but documents from 1563 onwards often treat the *zambaígo* as a type of *mulato*. But the evidence can be confusing.

In 1615 the viceroy of Peru wrote to his successor that '*mulatos* have resulted' from the mixture of *negros* and *blancos* while *mestizos* derived from white-

American mixture. Nothing was stated about African–Americans. Solórzano, writing from a Peruvian perspective (1620s–40s) states the same thing, in essence, but also notes that

quos Zambahigos, vocant, hoc est ex Aethiopibus, ac foeminis Indis, vel è contrario [Zambaigos, of Ethiopian–American mixture].

In his Spanish translation he notes the growing numbers 'de los Mestizos, Mulatos, y Zambahigos, (que son hijos de Negros, é Indias, ó al contrario).' Solórzano seems to set *Zambahígos* apart from *mulatos* but a law of 1563, repeated in various years through 1646 and even 1681, discussed 'Españoles, Negros, Mulatos, ó Mestizos' and then went on to state that 'los Mestizos, y Zambaigos' who were children of American women, born among the Americans, could be excused from the provisions of the law.[55]

Zambaígo was, in essence, a legal category (in Peru) since persons born of free American mothers were legally distinct from persons born of African or European mothers. Thus we can argue that *Zambaígos* were special kinds of *mulatos* for legal purposes, but usage was bound to vary with the observer of course.

In any case, *mulato* continued to be defined as half-African, half-American in relation to the greater Peruvian region. In 1659 the king wrote to the governor of Tucumán province (now in Argentina) that: 'un esclavo suyo Bentura tiene cinco hijos mulatos de María, su mujer que es india.' Thus the father was a slave (presumably *negro*) and the mother American, while the five children were termed *mulatos*.[56]

The situation in Mexico was quite similar, except that *zambaígo* was seldom used there. I have already quoted Bowser to the effect that 'Afro–Indians' were 'still referred to as "Mulattoes" as late as 1650.' Actually, however, such usage extends much later. In 1682 the king wrote to the viceroy of Mexico that neither 'los españoles (mestizos), ni mulatos, ni otros que no fueren meramente indios de padres y madres' could hold office in American communities. Such persons had to be 'hijos de indio e india legitimos'.

In other words, mixed-bloods of all kinds were excluded from such offices and, moreover, even an American had to be of legitimate descent. The clear implication is that both *mestizos* and *mulatos* could be part-American.[57]

This is certainly borne out by Aguirre Beltrán's study of labels used by the Inquisition in Mexico in the seventeenth century. The author states that: 'these different types of Negros, on mixing with whites and Indians, had descendants which were known by the general term "Mulatto". In order to distinguish between the various types of mulattoes, adjectives denoting color were added.' Aguirre Beltrán then describes various terms for lighter-skinned *mulatos* as well as *mulato prieto*, *mulato pardo* and other names for those who were darker and part-American. 'The "Dark Mulatto" (*mulato pardo*) was the result of the mixture of Negro and Indian. *The dark mulattoes were, without a doubt, the most numerous single group in New Spain.*' (Italics added) He then indicates that local terms, such as *cocho*, *cambujo*, *zambo*, *chino* and *loro* were used for such persons, as well as *color de membrillo, color pardo, color champurrado*, color quebrado, and so on.[58]

I personally am somewhat reluctant to accept Aguirre Beltrán's assumption that light *mulatos* were of white and African ancestry only, or that the terms he discovered offer us a clear statement about ancestry. Certainly some American–African mixed-bloods will resemble Americans and may be easily described by terms giving no hint of African ancestry. In general, a term such as *mulato prieto* should be taken to mean 'dark or black *mulato*' and should not be seen as denominating only persons of three-fourths African and one-fourth American ancestry, as Aguirre Beltrán's chart asserts.

In any case, the evidence seems clear that in the sixteenth and seventeenth centuries the great majority of persons called *mulatos* in the Spanish-controlled Americas were of American and African ancestry. Moreover, many of the less numerous *mulatos claros* (light mulattoes) would have been also part-American since a significant proportion of Spanish-speaking males were, in fact, part-American after the first few generations.

One of the earliest of the various efforts to depict the castes or mixtures of the Americas (dated *c.*1650–1700) and one which probably originated in México states:

de español y negra produce mulato;
de español y india produce mestizo;
de mulato y mestiza produce mulato.
Es torna atras [a "Throwback"].

An African–American mixed-blood was termed a *lobo* (wolf) while a three-quarters American–one-quarter African was termed a *grifo* (griffin). Nonetheless, *mulatos* could be part-American, as indicated.

Later Spanish definitions, such as those of Joseph Gumilla (already discussed) tend towards emphasis upon the black-white origin of *mulatos*. Some interesting variations can be found, however.

In the 1778 and 1790 revisions of Nebrija, for example, *mulato* is defined as *Aethiops hybrida*, that is, as mixed Black African. Such a definition is essentially the same as Minsheu offers us and is sufficient to cover American–African mixtures.

In the twentieth century, Spanish dictionaries, such as that of Pagés, offer a rich variety of meanings for *mulato* (in addition to the mixture of black and white), such as to refer to a person 'de color moreno', or to a person 'que es moreno en su linea' (has some dark-brown ancestry), and also to a type of 'mineral de plata de color obscuro o verde cobrizo' (to types of silver or copper).

Santamaría (1942) adds to the black–white concept:

En Santo Domingo, hijo de mulato y mulata; individuo que forma el tipo de una nueva raza, peculiar de esta isla y que no hay que confundir con el *mulato* propiamente dicho de los otros paises. . . . En el Perú, descendiente de zambo y blanco. . . . – *Mulato torna atras* . . . hijo de mestizo y mulata, o vice versa.

Thus Santamaría feels that using *mulato* to describe the national type of the Dominican Republic should not be confounded with the 'proper' use of *mulato* as found in other countries, but then he goes on to explain that *mulatos* could be mixtures of American–African and white (Peru) and of American–African and white-American (generally). We are, then, left a little confused as to who is the *mulato*, properly so-called.[59]

The problem is, of course, that Santamaría wanted to force the term to conform with prevailing white dictionary definitions when, in fact, he had the knowledge that it did not and told us as much. As we shall see below, more recent Spanish usage in the Americas does *not* conform with normal modern dictionary definitions either.

USAGE AND DEFINITIONS IN OTHER LANGUAGES

It is not necessary to review usage in most other European languages since *mulat* or *mulatte* appears rather late for our purposes and since English will be analyzed separately. Nonetheless, we might find it useful to review a few examples since usage could shed light upon Spanish, Portuguese, and English.

Some examples of early Italian usage have already been given. A modern dictionary defines *mulatto* as

suffuscus . . . (quanto a colore); mixticus (mixtus) . . . (di razza mista). *I mulatti* = mixti.

Thus *mulatto* is seen as denoting a dark, dusky color and people of mixed race.[60]

Usage in French is more significant, perhaps because of the influence of the language. Oudin's dictionary (1607) has already been quoted as defining Spanish *mulato* as a 'demy More' (half-Moore), the child of a white and a *more*. No French word is given as an equivalent, but under *mestizo* the terms *mestif* or *mestis* are given as meaning the same thing. The 1625 and 1639 editions remain the same.

In 1614 Yves d'Evreux states: 'on tient qu'il est Mulâtre François, c'est à dire, nay d'un François et d'Indienne.' Thus *mulâtre* was used for one born from a Frenchman and an Indian.[61]

During the same period (1601–11) Pyrard de Laval traveled to the Indies and, as noted, said that a man born of a 'cafre d'Etiopie & d'une femme' of the Maldive Islands was 'ce qu'on appelle Mulastre'. Later he also stated that the children of Portuguese and *cafres* 'ils les nommêt Mulastres'.

Mulâtre or *mulastre* was slow to appear in French dictionaries. That of d'Arsy (1651) has no such terms, nor does that of Richelet (1707).[62] Nonetheless, the term was being used by the French in the Caribbean region. Du Tertre (1667) noted that the children born of illegitimate relations with *négresses* were 'commonly called *Mulâtres* through all America'. He also relates the term to *mulet* (mule) because the *mulâtres* were born of black and white parents, 'as the

Mulet is produced by two animals of different kind (*espèce*)'. The children were not all white like the French nor all black like *les Negres* but they were a color between the two. Their hair tended to be long like their father's, but also frizzy from their 'black' ancestry.[63]

Clearly the essence of *mulâtre* was identical with that of *métis*, according to Du Tertre, but he chooses to emphasize the African–European mixture only. Elsewhere in the Caribbean region, however, *mulâtre* was being used for French–American mixed-bloods *with no African ancestry*. In the Mobile region (1715) there are references to the children of Frenchmen and Native Americans as 'mulattoes'.[64]

The dictionaries of Marin (1710, 1728, 1743, 1762) are the first I have seen which provide insight into the term:

Mulâtre, Mulate: On appelle ainsi aux Indes & en Espagne, celui qui est né, celle qui est née d'un Indien & d'une Negresse, & aussi de Pere & Mere de differentes Religions, comme l'Enfant d'un More & d'une Espagnole etc.

The Dutch version is:

Mulater: een die uit een Indiaan en een Zwarten, een Moor en een Spaansche vrow geboren is.[65]

Thus, in French, *mulâtre/mulate*, referred to an African–American mixed person or to a child of parents of different religions such as derived from a *More* and a Spaniard. The Dutch does not mention the two different religions.

The Halma dictionaries of 1761 and 1781 contain very similar entries. 'Mulat, mulate ou mulâtre' is defined as being used in the Indies to refer to an *Indien–Nègre* or *Indienne–Nègre* mixture or to a child of parents of different religions.[66]

One might become confused by the above definitions or usages which cover American–African, white-African, white-American, and inter-religious mixtures. But it seems that *mulâtre* was used in just such a broad way. In 1763 an official informed the authorities of Martinique and Guadeloupe that all 'free Negroes' were to be denied permission to leave for France. This had to be clarified by a second letter in which he specified that he meant any 'Negro man or woman, mulatto or mulatress', including people from India and Indians 'who simply constitute another type of colored people'. This would seem to mean that *negre* and/or *mulâtre* could be used for all non-whites.

Richelet's 1765 dictionary repeats the Marin and Halma definitions for *mulat*, *mulate* and *mulâtre*, i.e., *Nègre–Indien* and inter-religious mixtures.[67] Exactly the same is true for Winkelman's 1783 work. The de Sousa-Da Costa e Sá dictionary of 1784 includes basically the same concepts (as already discussed) for French *mulat*, *mulate*, *mulâtre* but states: a child of *negra* and *branco*, a *mestiço*, child of parents of different religions, as of a *mouro* and an *Hespanhola*.[68]

A big change came with the Marin dictionary of 1793 in which a complete shift is made to the *blanc–négresse* definition type. This is also true of the da

Costa e Sá 1794 edition, as well as various nineteenth century dictionaries seen. The only item worthy of note is that Roquette in 1863 equated Portuguese *pardo* with *mulâtre* (in addition to the *blanc–négresse* definition).[69] Between 1783 and 1793, therefore, a decided shift seems to have occurred. It may be that this reflected the loss of Louisiana and Canada and the growing emphasis upon Black African slavery in Haiti and the Caribbean, a change which antedated the 1793–4 dictionaries probably by at least thirty years.

It is also useful to cite a Dutch work of 1824 which, although late, contains a rather interesting summary of the meaning of *Mulatten*: 'Zoo noemt men in de beide Indiën diegenen, welke een blanken of Europeaan tot vader, en een zwarte of ingeborene tot moeder hebben.' Thus in both Indies *mulatten* were children of a European father and a black *or native* mother.

De Spanjaards noemen insgelijks de zoodanige Mulatten, die uit eenen zwarten of Neger en eene Indiaansche vrow geboren zijn, alsmede de kinderen van eenen Moor, of Mohomedaanschen Afrikaan uit Barbarije, en eene Spaansche moeder; en zoo ook in all deze gevallen omgekeered.[70]

Thus the Spaniards name likewise as *mulatten* the children born of black–American and Moor (Muslim African from Barbary)–Spanish mixtures. The compiler, Nieuwenhuis, concludes by stating that all of these cases are reversed or turned around also (i.e., mixtures of the sexes opposite to his examples).

Mulatten, then, were of white-black, white-native, American–African, and Moorish–Spanish mixtures according to Nieuwenhuis, and he provides a much more accurate assessment of reality than one finds in almost any other nineteenth-century work.

Our survey of diverse languages is now concluded except for a brief look at Surinam where in the Sranan Tongo (the creole of the region) *mulato* became *murato*. The use of this term seems quite broad, in that the Carib people living in the western part of Surinam are often called *muratos*, because they 'are visibly mixed with negroids'.[71] This illustrates that *murato* can refer to African–American mixed-bloods, and reflects back especially upon Portuguese usage since many terms in Surinam seem to be borrowed from Brazil.

LATER USAGE IN SPANISH-SPEAKING AMERICA

There are many sources from the Spanish Empire where we come across references to *mulatos* without any immediate indication of ancestry. On the basis of the data compiled herein we must be open to the probability that the majority of such *mulatos*, especially in the sixteenth and seventeenth centuries, were of African and American ancestry. For example, when we read Huaman Poma's *Nueva Crónica y Buen Gobierno* (*c*.1613) and study his drawings of 'criollos, mestizos, y mulatos'; or when we study data from Jamaica and discover that in 1641 a military company was composed of free '*mulatos y negros* and servants of the soldiers' and that another was comprised of 'indios y mulatos horros' (Americans and free *mulatos*) we must be prepared to accept the idea that the *mulatos* were part-American. The same is true when the ousted Jamaica Spaniards complained of pirates and stated that (*c*.1660): 'Also go about some Portuguese . . . and the worst *indios compechanos mulatos* and *negros criollos*, sailors who desire [to live] in the licentious life of the pirate and these are the worst enemies.'[72] Other sources also mention the Maya people of Campeche and the *mulatos* and *negros* who played leading roles among the Dutch and other pirates. We must now be prepared to picture these *mulatos*, as well as those serving in Spanish militia units, as being principally American–African.

It is beyond the scope of this study to trace the precise use of *mulato* after the seventeenth century. On the other hand I would like to present a few examples which illustrate that the term could definitely include a person of American ancestry up to the recent period.

Felix de Azana, who spent the period 1781–1801 along the Paraguayan–Uruguayan–Brazilian border stated that the *pardo* category included the 'mulato (hijo de africano con blanco o indio)'. Thus we have the term *mulato* specifically defined to include African–Americans.[73]

In 1778 in Cuyo (Argentina) there were 9,834 whites, 15,417 *mestizos*, 20,558 *indios*, and 25,548 *negros* and *mulatos*. (Quite clearly these *mulatos* have to be primarily Native–African hybrids).

In 1778 Montevideo had 700 slaves, 594 *libertos*, and 73 Indians, in 1803 it had 899 slaves, 141 *libertos*, and 603 Indians. (It would seem as if many *libertos* became *indios*. *Liberto* had become synonymous with *pardo* and *mulato*).

Censuses of 1785 and 1792 for Indian districts and villages near Córdoba (Argentina) showed large numbers of *negros* and *mulatos* integrated within the American families, according to Rolando Mellafe.

In California in the 1780s and 1790s many cases occurred where part Native Americans were called *mulatos*. For example:

Mestizo José Oliveros married Ana María Carrasca, *mulata* – child is *mulata*;

Mestizo Santiago Pico married Jacinta de la Bastida, *mulata* – children are *mulatos*;

Mulato Francisco Reyes married María Domínguez, *mestiza* – children are *mulatos*.

In 1807 a census of El Salvador included mestizos (white-Native) under the term *mulato*.

In 1809 J. J. Virey stated that the mixture of 'indio y mulata' produces a *mulato prieto* ('black *mulato*').

In 1880 the term *ladino* (used in southern Mexico and Central America) included *mulatos*: 'Those called *ladinos* now were children of Spaniards and Indians, and of *negros* and Indians'.

In 1924 Nicolas León asserted that the mixture of 'indio y mulata' gives *mulata obscuro*.

In 1939 Fernando Romero wrote an article entitled 'José Manuel Valdés,

gran mulato del Peru' (for the *Revista Bimestre Cubana*)
professor and poet, was the son of María del Carmen C
Baltasar Valdés (an Indian musician). Thus we have
American being classified as a *mulato*.[74]

In conclusion, I believe that the Spanish usage of
remarkably consistent in the Americas, for the following 1

Mulato virtually always refers to a person of part-African
The vast majority of persons called *mulatos* were half-Native American in the
sixteenth century; and
A substantial part of those called *mulato* to our own day have been persons of
some degree of Native ancestry.

It would seem that we have established a good case for a reinterpretation of
the early colonial history of the Caribbean, other parts of the Spanish Empire,
and Brazil. If, as we have shown, *mulatos* in the first century of colonization were
principally of American–African descent, then, of course, the formative
character of the slave cultures (plantation and otherwise) and of the early 'free
colored' cultures must be re-examined.

But such a new interpretation requires that we briefly look at evidence which
illustrates the intensity of Black African–American intermixture and establishes
that, indeed, Africans and Native Americans did create a new population of
mulatos.

EVIDENCE OF AFRICAN–AMERICAN MIXTURE

One of the important contributing factors to the widespread mixture of
Americans and Africans was an inbalance of sex ratios among the various
groups (along with population demographics). Virtually all authorities are in
agreement that the Black African sex ratio was highly imbalanced in favor of
males. Franco Silva states that of the *negros* sent to the Americas from Seville in
the early 1500s 'at the least more than 60 per cent approximately' were males.
At Las Palmas in the Canary Islands about 60 per cent of the *negros* were males
and Lobo Cabrera believes that of the slaves sent to the Indies only one-third
were females. In 1524 the Crown decreed that one-third of slave cargoes were
to be females. Of those *bozales* sold in Lima, 1560–1650, 34.5 per cent were
females and, indeed, 40 per cent were females if one includes those born in the
Americas. In 1565 when Menéndez was granted the 'privilege' of importing
500 *negro* slaves into Florida, the Crown saw fit to specify that one-third had to
be women. This requirement (as with the decree of 1524) would indicate that
the tendency had been to import an even greater percentage of males. This
tendency may have continued throughout the colonial period, especially in
newly conquered areas. In 1776, for example, in Minas Gerais (Brazil) there
were 117,171 male *negros* and 49,824 women. In the 1820s the Paraiba Valley
77 per cent of the slaves were males.

speech of 1827 a Brazilian declared that 'only one Negress' was
ted from Africa for every three or four males.' But between 1820–9 the
ssouras coffee region had a ratio of 7 males to 3 females.[76]

Aguirre Beltrán notes that: 'The imbalance of sex and age were important
factors that conditioned African influence on regional cultures: the Negro could
not reconstruct his own family structure in Mexico and turned to interbreeding
with the Indian to balance the disequilibrium of the sexes.' Mörner, after an
extensive study of race mixture in Latin America, states: 'Perhaps there were as
many as three times as many men as there were women among the negroes
brought to the Indies; the ratio may have been even more unequal. . . . Logically
their partners were usually Indian women. In fact, it seems as if many Indian
women preferred them to their own husbands.' Mörner cites a letter from the
viceroy of Mexico to the latter effect, dated 1574. He also indicates that only 10
per cent of the licenses issued by the Crown for passage to the Americas were
for women from 1509–39. Quite a number of these, after 1512, were for
moriscas (women of Islamic background, unmarried, to serve as wives for
Spaniards; but some were slaves).[77]

It would seem very likely that from 65 per cent to 75 per cent of the first
Black African males who established a relationship with a woman would have
done so with a Native woman, not only because of the sex ratio among Africans
but also because of an opposite sex ratio among the Americans. Referring to the
period from the 1560s to 1613 Huaman Poma tells us that the Indian males
died working in the mines of Oropesa (Peru). 'The Indians continued to be
worked to death and only the women remained in the villages.' He also notes
that:

> The city of Lima was full of Indians who had fled from their own villages and were
> living on their wits or acting as servants in Spanish houses. . . . more and more Indians
> were following the example of the fugitives and leaving their villages. Nobody was
> left. . . . I saw also a great number of Indian prostitutes, encumbered with their half-caste
> babies. . . . Even the married ones sold themselves indiscriminately to Spaniards and
> negroes alike. . . . The lowest quarters of the city were full of Indian whores.[78]

We can assume that the same thing was occurring throughout the Empire,
since American women, left with no men and required to pay tribute, would
have perhaps found it necessary to flee their homes.

During the early period (1492–1600) the un-mixed native population of the
West Indies was being vastly reduced from several millions to some few
thousands. Some Black Africans accompanied the earliest Spanish expeditions
but it wasn't until 1501–3 that African slaves were introduced in any numbers.
These persons, who were Christianized slaves from Seville, Spain, soon fled
'and corrupted the Indians' or joined the American rebels so the trade was
halted briefly but renewed after 1504, with one additional suspension. Probably
all were *ladinos* (Spanish-speakers, Christians) until the decade of 1520–30.
Eight thousand or more Black Africans were brought in during the latter
decade and the numbers increased rapidly thereafter.

Slaves soon began to outnumber Spaniards and *mestizos* on the islands and along the Caribbean coasts. By *c.*1565 the ratio was said to be 15,000 to 500 on Borinquen (Puerto Rico), 30,000 to 2,000 on Haiti (or Santo Domingo), with a similar ratio on Cuba. By 1570 it is reported that there were only 25,704 *vecinos* (Spanish and Spanish–American heads of households) in all of the Americas; but Mexico alone had 20,569 Africans, 2,437 *mulatos*, and several million Americans. López de Velasco states that up to the 1570s some '40,000 negros esclavos' were in the American colonies.[79]

Now let us make some rough comparisons. Between the 1490s and the 1570s the Spaniards (including *mestizos* counted as *vecinos*) rose from a few score to 25,000 while the Africans increased from a handful to 40,000. In both cases females would have been outnumbered by at least 2 to 1 (and doubtless there were fewer white females). Thus we may suppose, for purposes of illustration, that in the 1570s there were some 25,000 Spanish and *mestizo* males (*vecinos*) and some 27,000 African males. As possible sexual partners or mates, these males had to choose among 8,000 (or less) Spanish-speaking females, 13,000 (or less) African females and from several millions of American females (the total American population under Spanish control or impact declined from, let us say, 30 to 50 million to probably less than 10 million during the century).

One can easily see that mathematical probability would highly favor both Spaniards and Africans intermarrying with American females, or after several generations of mixture had occurred as in the Caribbean, with *mestizas*, *mulatas* or *indias*. This thesis is certainly borne out by the evidence for the period. (Later, of course, more Spanish-speaking women were introduced with a resultant 'lightening' of the upper levels among the early *mestizos*.)

To the demographics must be added another compelling motive for African–African mixture: freedom. This motive caused great numbers of *negros* to flee to American areas but it also may have caused many males to have children by free American women so that the said children would be free (and also, perhaps, could eventually purchase their father's freedom). As already discussed, many Americans were liberated from formal slavery after 1542 and, thereafter, most American women were technically free persons. A few years passed before this reform was effectively implemented (and it was violated in frontier zones continuously). Nonetheless, the child of a Native woman and a Black African slave was a free person after 1542–50, whereas the child of Spaniard and a Black African slave woman was still a slave. It is this free status of the Red–Black mulatto that Viceroy Enríquez wished to have abolished in 1574 (however, the king failed to enact such a decree).

In point of fact, some Africans may have been able to obtain freedom for themselves directly by marrying a free American woman. The ancient code of Alfonso the Wise allowed for such a means of emancipation until 1526 when the king specifically closed off that avenue. These efforts had to be repeated in 1538 because of reports that Africans were still acquiring freedom by marrying American women in Mexico. Moreover, Enríquez reported in 1574 that 'Indian women would rather marry Negroes than Indians' and that 'Negros prefer to marry Indian women rather than Negresses, so that their children will be born free'.

Is not this American–African mixture precisely the origin of the free mulato (pardo) *population of the Spanish Empire?* Indeed it must be, because the numbers of such free persons greatly accelerated during this period and we find the Spanish directing a great deal of venom towards the *Zambaígos,* as the Red–Black people came to be called in certain regions after 1560, or towards the *mulatos* wherever that term was in use. This free population, freed not by individual Spaniards but by its Native mothers' status, represented a threat especially whenever it existed near hostile Native groups or communities of Red–Black *cimarrones* (runaways).

Note should also be made here that López de Velasco tells us that 'there are not many *mulatos,* children of Spaniards and *negras,* because of the many *indias.*' Solórzano also tells us that, in so far as legitimate marriages were concerned, the Spaniards 'rarely' married American women and it was 'very rare' for them to marry Ethiopians.[80] Thus the creation of the *mulato* was primarily an African–American phenomenon.

Now let us look at a few royal decrees or other sources which clearly make reference to American–African intermixture (not including the definitions already referred to). In 1541 a decree was issued requiring that slaves legally marry because of reports that the *negro* slaves were keeping 'great numbers of Indian women, some of them voluntarily, others against their wishes'. In 1551 a royal *cédula* noted 'that many *negros* have Indian females as *mancebas* (concubines) or treat them badly and oppress them'. The decree was repeated later (1584). In 1572 a decree was issued to the effect that 'los hijos de Negros libres, o esclavos, havidos en Indias por matrimonio, deven pagar tributo como los demás Indios, aunque se pretenda, que no lo son, ni sus padres tributaron.' In short, the children of African males and American females had to pay tribute 'like the rest of the Indians' although 'it is pretended that they are not [Indians].' Earlier in the same year the Crown had imposed the above tribute, even though 'they allege that they are not *indios*', that is, the children of the Africans and Americans were so alleging.[81]

In 1574 the Crown noted that many *negros, negras, mulatos,* and *mulatas* had become free and had acquired some property. Therefore, the payment of tribute was to be imposed on most of them. In 1577 it was noted, however, that it was hard to collect tribute from the above groups because of not having an *asiento* (seat) or *lugar cierto* (certain location). In 1574, as already noted, López de Velasco referred to the large number of *mulatos,* 'hijos de negros y de indias', who were becoming the 'mas peor y vil que en aquellas partes hay'. The *mulatos* (or *zambaígos*) were doubltess difficult to collect tribute from, since many avoided Spanish control or were in active rebellion.

It is significant that in 1674 the Crown was still concerned that the collection of tribute was observed only 'con los indios mulatos y no con los mestizos' in spite of its importance. The implication is that the *indios mulatos* were descendants of female Americans and African or part-African fathers and that the *mestizos* were children of non-tribute paying Spaniards.

In any case, the fact that *mulatos* in general had to pay tribute is a strong indication that, as a class, they were viewed as *not* being children of Spaniards but were instead children of tributaries, that is, of Americans, Africans, or mixed mothers who were *tributarias*. The *mestizo* exemption clearly rested on their biological relationship to the Spaniards.

Doubtless many persons attempted to obtain classification as *mestizos* in order to avoid the head-tax.[82]

In 1595 Philip II decreed that the unmarried 'Españoles, Mestizos, Mulatos, y Zambaigos vagabundos', who were living 'among the *Indios*' be expelled from the latter's villages. Incorrigibles were to be exiled to Chile or to the *islas Filipinas*. We will discuss the Spanish effort to expel non-Americans from Native villages below, but here I wish to cite the above to illustrate that after many years of effort part-Africans were still residing in Native communities.[83]

Specifically as regards the Caribbean, in 1502 'a significant number of negros' were sent to Haiti from Seville. As noted earlier, the next year further shipments were suspended because of the troubles which were produced when the Africans united with the island's American rebels.[84] Thereafter, as discussed earlier, American slaves were being introduced from elsewhere at the same time that African slaves were being brought in. From 1499 through the 1500s the coast of Venezuela was a regular source of slaves for Haiti and other areas. Many slaves were also shipped from Mexico especially via the port of Pánuco, as in 1529–30 when figures of 10,000 to 15,000 are indicated. Such shipments continued through the 1540s, involving thousands. In 1536 the king acknowledged reports of slaves being shipped also from Nicaragua, Peru, and other places and forbade the practice. Americans were also seized regularly in Nuevo León and Florida, the latter from *c.*1513 onward. The Bahamas were virtually emptied of Native People from the 1490s to 1629. It is reported that 40,000 *Lucayos* alone were sent to Haiti and elsewhere.[85] Balboa and his successors also sold slaves from Panama.

Thus it is clear that prior to 1530 (at least) the numbers of American slaves being brought into the West Indies *exceeded* the numbers of Africans, and then remained a significant element of newcomers for several decades, or at least until well after 1542.

In *c.*1530 it was reported that on Haiti 'there are a great many *mestizos* here, sons of Spaniards and Indian women'. This is logical since of the 689 Spaniards on the island in 1514, 107 had Spanish (or *Morisca*) wives and 64 had Native wives. The rest were not legally married but doubtless almost all were living with American *criadas* ('maid-servants') or concubines. Thus it would seem likely that the 2,000–5,000 'Spaniards' living on Haiti in *c.*1560–2 were mostly mixed-bloods, and this would be especially true of the younger men and women and of those who would come into frequent contact with the incoming Black Africans. The mixed children produced by any sexual unions would then be American–Spanish–African rather than simply Black–White.[86]

It should be recalled here that the English also introduced American slaves into the islands, although at a somewhat later date (as did the French, Portuguese and Dutch also). In *c*.1670 Hans Sloane said of the unmixed Americans on Jamaica:

They are not natives of the island, they being all destroyed by the Spaniards, but are usually brought by surprise from the Musquitos [of Nicaragua] or from Florida, or such as were slaves to the Spaniards and taken away from them by the English. They are very good hunters and fishers, but are naught at working in the field or slavish work, and if *chekt* or *drubbed* are good for nothing, therefore are very gently treated and well fed.[87]

In 1682 the Spanish governor of Florida wrote that the English (of South Carolina) were taking Americans to sell as slaves 'como han hecho con muchos, llevandolos a la isla de Barbado; captura aun a los mestizos, nacidos de españoles e indios.' Thus Americans and American–Spanish mixed-bloods from Florida were both being shipped to Barbados as slaves as early as the 1680s and that process continued for years (with other Americans such as those from New England also being sent there, the latter from 1637–77).[88]

As already indicated, in 1592 the Crown made reference to the 'many *mulatos* children of *indias*' in the Venezuela area. Other decrees make it clear that the same thing was true in adjacent coastal areas of Tierra Firme (Colombia and Panama).[89]

As regards the West Indies specifically Ángel Rosenblat suggests that 'in general the great *mestizo* population of the early days had disappeared by being diluted in mixture with the Negro and the Mulatto.'[90] Virtually the reverse has occurred in Mexico and Peru, where the African has been absorbed by the 'Indian' and *mestizo* populations. Let us now look briefly at the latter areas, beginning with Mexico.

In 1553 Viceroy Luis de Velasco of Mexico noted that the *negros* and *mestizos* were much more numerous than the Spaniards. Many Black Africans and mixed-bloods fled to the Americans and, in a report of 1585 already noted, reference is made to *mestizos* and *mulatos* playing leading roles among the Chichimeca rebels of the Zacatecas–Coahuila region. We have also made reference to Viceroy Martín Enríquez' concern that the *mulatos* were becoming very numerous (1574) and that they were tougher than the *mestizos*, the latter being sons of Spaniards. For that reason he proposed that the children of *negros* and *mulatos* with American women be enslaved.[91]

In the New Mexico region in the 1640s the supporters of one faction were said to be 'mestizos y mulatos' while another source states that they were 'a stranger, a Portuguese, and *mestizos* and *sambahigos* sons of female Indians and *negros* or *mulatos*'. In 1680 American rebels in New Mexico were said to include '*mestizos* and mulattoes and people who speak Spanish' or 'coyotes, *mestizos* and mulattoes'. ('Coyotes' may have been three-quarters American, one-quarter European.)[92]

Reference has already been made to two royal orders of 1568 (February 9 and November 4) wherein it was asserted that there were a large number of *mulatos* in New Spain, children of *negros* and *indias*, who were badly inclined, as well as other *mulatos*, children of either *negros* and *indias* or *españoles* and *negras*, who were serving the Spaniards. Also, as noted, Aguirre Beltrán states that the 'dark mulattoes were, without a doubt, the most numerous single group in New Spain' and they were of African–American mixture.'[93]

What transpired with the African–Americans of Mexico in later years? The following figures provide an estimate, with the term *Afromestizo* being used for part-Africans.

1570	20,569 Africans	2,437	*mulatos*
1646	35,089 Africans	116,529	*Afromestizos*
1742	20,131 Africans	226,196	*Afromestizos*
1793	6,100 Africans	369,790	*Afromestizos*
1810	10,000 Africans	624,461	*Afromestizos*

In 1810 Mexico had 3,676,281 *indios* and 1,338,706 'mestizos y mulatos' according to another report.[94]

Garcilaso de la Vega el Inca informs us that in 1553 in Peru there were enough male Africans (*etiopes* or Ethiopians) to enable a rebellious Spaniard, Francisco Hernández, to raise 'una compañía de negros de mas de ciento y cinquenta' and later 'más de treizientos soldados etiopes'. More than 300 African men of fighting age were, therefore, in highland Peru only 21 years after Pizarro's conquest. These rebel soldiers, among other things, robbed the Indians of their property and 'their women and children'.

After Hernández was executed the Spanish viceroy attempted to pacify 'the fugitive *negros* called *cimarrones*' who were living in the mountains. Among these fugitive Africans were some of the above-mentioned rebel soldiers.[95]

No doubt there were some female Africans in Peru but it would seem very unlikely that they could be responsible for the fact that numerous *mulatos* existed there by *c*.1600 (mentioned by Garcilaso as well as by Huaman Poma). In the first place, it is certain that African men greatly outnumbered African women and they had easy access to enslaved or oppressed American women. Secondly, the Spanish men had easy access also to American females. Thirdly, the few African women would doublutess have been largely pre-empted by African men. Finally, very few Spanish women were available before 1590. What conclusion is left?

Lockhart informs us that between 1532 and 1560 *negro* rebel bands sometimes raided Americans and seized women, having many '*mulato* children' by the Native women. By 1562 the 'mestizos y mulatos' in Peru were said to have been both numerous and dangerous.[96]

It would appear that the mixture of Africans and Americans throughout the greater Peruvian region was extremely significant. A group of serologists found in 1962 that of the Americans (Quechua) of Paucarcolla 14.6 per cent were part-African and only 1.1 per cent were part-European. Of course, such studies must be viewed with extreme caution, but other research tends to support extensive mixture. Mario C. Vázquez has noted that 'throughout Peruvian history, Negroes and Indians have engaged in sexual relations. . . . This explains why in 1791 there were more free Negroes and mulattoes (41,398) than Negro slaves (40,337)."[97]

Understandably, the Spanish Crown made gestures from the 1540s (or earlier) onward to prevent the interaction of Black Africans and mixed-bloods with Americans, first in connection with *encomiendas* and later with all American villages and missions (reductions). Such efforts were clearly doomed to failure and, in any case, conflicted with imperial needs for labor in the ports, mines, cities and military posts. Although the Spaniards purported to be concerned about African and mixed-blood exploitation of Americans one can argue that the primary motivation was concern with military rebellion and general dissidence. In 1570 the Spaniards were preoccupied with 'runaway *negros* who mix also with the Indians' in the present Panama region. This mixed African–American population posed a threat to the Peruvian gold and silver shipments and doubtless it provided the non-whites who co-operated with English raiders such as John Oxenham and John Hawkins in the 1560s and 1570s.

By 1599 a group of American–African mixed-bloods, as noted, had established an independent state near Esmeralda, Ecuador. Similarly other American–African 'republics' were established all along the Caribbean. One, called the 'republica Zamba de Nirgua' survived from the sixteenth into the nineteenth century. When Alexander von Humboldt visited the coast of Colombia in the early part of the nineteenth century he found that: 'This mixture of Indians and Negroes is very common in these districts. The women of the copper race feel a great inclination towards that of the African race.' Along the coast of Venezuela and Colombia a great *pardo* population ('población mulata y zamba') continues to exist today. This is also true in Nicaragua, Belize and elsewhere.

In 1625 an Englishman met Luis, a 'mulatto' born in Seville, who had been living with the Caribs of Guadeloupe Island for 12 years. He had fled from Spanish slavery and had an American wife and children. This same traveler, Thomas Gage, noted in *c.*1627 that some two to three hundred 'Blackamoors' were runaways in the eastern Guatemala area and that they were preserving their independence.[98]

The contact between Black Africans, local Native Americans, and new American slaves was both continuous and intimate in the period. There are numerous references to African runaways and rebels joining still-free Americans or fleeing to areas largely populated by the latter. Slave rebellions took place on Borinquen in 1522, on Haiti in 1527, in Panama in 1531, at Amatepeque in Mexico in 1537, and in Peru (as noted earlier). In 1538 slaves and French pirates sacked Havana. From 1533–43 the American cacique Henríquez led a major joint rebellion of Americans and Africans on Haiti.

As already noted, the first African slaves fled to the Natives (1501–3) and that was only a beginning. Individuals or groups fled to the Native Americans in the Carolinas (mid-1520s), on the de Soto expedition (1539–40), on the Coronado expedition (1539–42), on expeditions to Kansas (1541–2, 1549), in

Peru, in Mexico generally, and especially along the coasts of Venezuela, Colombia, Panama, Nicaragua, and Guatemala.

Of course, Africans did not have to run away to be in close proximity to Americans, since both had to work in the Spaniard's mines and plantations, on his ships, at his ports, and so on. In 1565 when Menéndez established St Augustine, Florida, the first thing that he did was to lodge the 'negro slaves' in the 'huts of the Indian village'. He also had at least one *mulato* along on his expedition. The close proximity of Americans and Africans in Florida continued on through the Seminole wars of the 1830s–40s. In 1686, for example, a Spanish military expedition against the English of South Carolina included 'an auxiliary force of Indians and mulattoes'. Virtually every Spanish expedition had many hundreds of such mixed African and Native auxiliary forces or labor groups.'[9]

In conclusion, *it is very clear that Native American–Black African intermixture was very common and that it must have been the major source of the 'free' population of part-African descent everywhere prior to c.1650.* Still further, the continued enslavement of Americans and the undoubted desire of slave owners to retain slaves who were legally free (children of free Native women) must have contributed to American mixture within the slave population as well.

I believe that the probability that Black Africans intermixed more often with Americans than with Europeans in the formative period of colonialism in the Americas has been demonstrated. Also illustrated has been the actual process of American–African mixture in several regions and the development of a very extensive mixed-blood population. Certainly ground has been prepared for the acceptance of the thesis that the term 'mulatto' referred primarily to African–Native-American persons in the Americas.

Moreover, we have seen that the meanings of the term *mulato* must always be discovered in relation to a particular time-period and specific geographical regions. Although, in general, we have seen it evolve from serving as an equivalent of hybrid and *mestizo* to becoming a referent for one who was part-African, we must bear in mind that in French (and, as we shall see, in English) 'mulatto' could be used for an American–European person with no African ancestry during certain periods.

In sum, a re-evaluation of the history of the peopling of the Americas is in order.

7

The Classification of Native Americans as Mulattoes in Anglo-North America

Contemporary scholarly and popular literature in the United States has largely ignored the significance of widespread Native American ancestry among Afroamericans and, also, of African ancestry among many Native groups. The consequences of this neglect are far reaching, and this is especially true in relation to studies of the evolution of music, folk tales, social organization, and other aspects of culture.

In a similar manner, the existence of a large group of 'Red–Black People', part-American and part-African, has been largely overlooked and, in fact, such people have been usually classified as 'Black' by both scholars and North American statutes. Still further, the former existence of comparatively large numbers of Native American slaves has also been ignored generally, with great consequence for both early Native and Afroamerican history.

There are, of course, exceptions to this pattern of overlooking the Red–Black connection. First, there are a large number of biographies and autobiographies, as for example, of musicians or singers such as Adelaide Hall, Willie the Lion Smith, Paul Robeson, Josephine Baker, Bunk Johnson, Lena Horne, Pops Foster, George Lewis, Pearl Bailey, Leadbelly, Tina Turner, and others, all of which have specific reference to Native American ancestry. Secondly, there is Almon W. Lauber's study of *Indian Slavery in Colonial Times* (1913), a work which has been grossly neglected in recent decades. And thirdly, there are several early attempts to document or to note the significance of the Black–American interaction. I wish to cite some of these works so as to illustrate a trend which has not been continued, by and large, since the 1930s.

As early as the late ninteenth century the *Nineteenth Annual Report* of the Bureau of American Ethnology noted that 'a considerable proportion of the blood of the southern Negroes [of the US] is unquestionably Indian.'[1] The 1937 doctoral dissertation of James Hugo Johnston, belatedly published many years later, went further:

there developed, in the colonial period, much intermixture of the Indian and Negro slave. . . . The class commonly called the mulatto is the result, in many instances, of the union of the three racial elements. . . . To the visitor in the south the physical characteristics of many Negro slaves bore witness to their Indian origin. . . . *The mixed race in America today is the result of the union of the Indian, the Negro, and the white man.*[2] (italics added)

Johnston also noted that many Indians were enslaved along the eastern seaboard. 'The end of Indian slavery came with the final absorption of the blood of the Indian by the more numerous Negro slave. But the blood of the Indian did not become extinct in the slave states, for it continued to flow in the veins of the Negro.'[3] In an article published in the *Journal of Negro History* Johnston remarked: 'Where the Negro was brought into contact with the American Indian the blood of the two races intermingled, the Indian has not disappeared from the land, but is now part of the Negro population of the United States.'[4]

The latter statement might offend many Indians today, who still survive, of course, in great numbers as Native Americans, but nonetheless the significance of Johnston's thesis as regards the extent of Native American–African intermixture remains before us. Nor was Johnston alone. Frank H. Russell, in his *The Free Negro in Virginia*, wrote in 1913 that one of the ways in which the 'free colored' population grew was by the mixture of Indians and Negroes. He said also that 'there is no doubt that a considerable element in the free colored population of the nineteenth century was of Indian extraction.'[5]

One can also cite other authorities whose work caused them to consider the intermixture of African and American racial stocks. Helen T. Catterall in her work on slavery in Virginia noted that 'we have shown that the first slaves . . . were Indians, not negroes', and that the enslavement of Americans continued for many, many years.[6] In 1903, a historian of New Jersey noted that 'unions between Indians and Negroes were so commonly frequent, indeed, as to have left permanent impress upon many families of Negroes of the present day.' E. B. Reuter recognized (1927) that African–American mixture had taken place within slavery and said: 'The Indian slaves were gradually absorbed into the black population.'[7]

Also, during the 1920s and 1930s the *Journal of Negro History* frequently featured articles on Black–Native relations in Massachusetts, on Paul Cuffe (an American–African mixed-blood), and on other examples of Red–Black interaction.

Within anthropology a few scholars, such as Ashley Montagu (1944) have recognized the significance of African–American contacts:

With the discovery of the New World, intermixture between the Negroes and the indigenes of the West Indies began almost at once. . . . It must be supposed that these Negroes [from different parts of Africa] were already very thoroughly mixed, among themselves and with the Indians of the islands and of the mainland of Brazil, by the time most of them reached North America. . . . The mingling of Negroes and Indians, of course, occurred first in the West Indies.

It is significant that Montagu recognized that many of the slaves, coming not directly from Africa but from the Caribbean, might have had American ancestry. 'Thus, it may be seen that not only was there much mixture between different varieties of Negroes in the islands, but also complete mixture with the indigenous Indians, and sometimes, with Indians who were not indigenous to these islands.' Montagu also recognized that once the people of African descent had reached North America, inter-mixture with Americans continued: 'The available evidence indicates that ethnic mixture between Indians and Negroes has been of vastly greater proportions than has hitherto been realized. . . . The American Negro population of today is a composite of African, White, and Indian elements.'[8]

Unfortunately, however, the prevailing trend of more recent years has been similar to what happened to Alex Haley's *Roots* when it fell prey to the television script-writers. Haley's book notes that the family absorbed Indian ancestry in the Carolinas but this element was eliminated for television viewing.

There are exceptions to the above trend, however, including J. Leitch Wright, Jr.'s *The Only Land They Know: The Tragic Story of the Americans of the Old South* (1981) and *Creeks and Seminoles* (1986); and Daniel F. Littlefield's studies of *Africans and Seminoles* (1977), *The Cherokee Freedmen* (1978), *Africans and Creeks* (1979), and *The Chickasaw Freedmen* (1980).[9]

Considerable controversy has developed at times among white writers as to how much American ancestry Afroamericans actually possess.[10] This controversy is apparently not found among Afroamericans, many of whom have told this writer of their Indian ancestry. Others related the same thing to Melville Herskovitz, August Meier and other researchers some years ago.[11]

One of the basic problems is to actually go back to the empirical evidence, the historical record, to document the extent of African–American interaction and mixture. To do this, however, one must begin by clarifying the meaning of racial terms as used by early sources.

The primary purpose here is to clarify the use of terms such as 'mulatto' and 'free colored' in the British North American colonies and, incidentally, to shed preliminary light on the relations between Black Africans and Native Americans.

As elsewhere I will use the term 'American' for Indians in the colonial era and 'African' rather than 'negro' for presumably unmixed sub-Saharan Africans.

EXPLICIT DEFINITIONS OF THE TERM 'MULATTO'

English writers began using the term 'mulato', 'mulatow' or 'molato' in the

1590s. The term was borrowed from Spanish and usually referred to persons met with in the Caribbean or South America. Early Spanish definitions of the term make it highly probable, indeed virtually certain, that such persons were usually half-African and half-American. John Minsheu, as already noted, defined 'mulato' in 1599, 1617 and later as a person who was the child of a *mauro* or 'blacke-Moore' and one from 'another nation'.[12] This extremely accurate (and timely) definition reflected Spanish usage very well. Now let us review other early English dictionaries.

John Florio (1611) does not includes 'mulatto' in his dictionary but has 'muletto, a little or young mule' and 'mulo, a horse-mule. Also a bastard or misbegotten.'[13] Henry Cockeram (1623) does not have 'mulatto' but has 'A Black-moore. Ethyope.'[14]

Thomas Blount (1656) continues the Minsheu definition: 'Mulato (Span.) the son of a Blackmore and a man of another Nation, or 'e contra one that is of a mongrel complexion.' A 'muleto' is 'a great mule'.[15]

Edward Phillips (1658) states 'Mulato, (Span.) one whose father is a Blackmore, and his mother of another nation or contrarily.'[16] But in 1702 John Kersey broadens the scope of the concept. 'A Mulatto, the son of a Negro, or Indian woman and of a man of another Nation; or of a Negro man and a woman of another country.'[17] It should be noted that this nicely coincides with Virginia's legal definition of 1705 that a European–American mixed-blood is a mulatto and would seem to reflect some tendency in usage. We may also note that the term 'negro' replaces 'Blackamoor' in the dictionary although the 1708 Kersey usage is somewhat different: 'Mulatto (Sp.) one whose father is a Black-moor, and his mother of another Nation, or whose mother is a Negro, and his father of another country.'[18]

Chamber's *Cyclopedia* (1727–41) states: 'Mulatto, a name given, in the Indies, to those who are begotten by a negro man on an Indian woman; or an Indian man on a negro woman.' This significant definition, so like Kersey's of 1702, undoubtedly reflects Spanish usage as well as practice in South Carolina and other English colonies.[19]

The various dictionaries of N. Bailey (1728–61) define 'Mulatto' as 'one born of parents, of whome one is a Moor, and the other of another Nation'.[20] He also states that a 'Moor' is 'a Native of Mauritania in Africa, a Blackmoor'. This would seem to imply that a mulatto could be the child of a North African and a non-North African, as well as of a Black African and a non-Black African, thus broadening the concept.

A different approach appears in an English–Portuguese dictionary of 1701. The English side does not have the term mulatto while the Portuguese term is defined as 'that mixture between a white and a black'. English 'black' is translated as *escúra* (obscure, dark) and *sombría* (shady, sombre) as well as *negro* and *preto*.

Samuel Johnson, in 1756, is the first English-only dictionary-maker to apparently link mulatto to a black-white mixture. He states 'Mulatto (Spanish) one begot between a white and black'. In 1785 he states 'Mulatto (Spanish;

mulat, French; from *mulus*, Latin). One begot between a white and a black, as a mule between different species of animals.'[21]

Johnson's attitude may well reflect a change in usage and also a growing racism, but we must note that the term 'black' is not defined. James Buchanan (1757) continued the trend: 'Mulatto (S.) one born of parents of whom one is black and the other white'. Buchanan is the first compiler to include a term for other kinds of mixed-bloods: 'Mestizo (S.) the breed of Spaniards with Americans'.[22] The significance of this will be noted later, but it should be stressed here that terms such as half-breed, half-blood, and half-caste never appear (with a racial meaning) in any of the above dictionaries.

Noah Webster in his 1828 dictionary fails to include 'mestizo' but he does have 'Mustee, mestee: A person of mixed breed—West Indies' and 'Mulatto: A person that is the offspring of a negress by a white man, or of a white woman by a negro'.[23]

Thus we can see a rather clear pattern. First, the term 'mulatto' is the *only* term available for referring to persons of mixed race, until 1757. Second, until *c*.1756 'mulatto' usually refers to a person half-African and half-something else but with a half-American, half-another-nation usage in 1702 and American–African in 1727.

After the 1750s the half-'black', half-'white', usage becomes dominant and replaces the half-African, half-another-nation pattern. It should be noted also that from at least 1741 the term 'mulatto' is used to designate a certain type of land or soil, sometimes described as 'a black mould and red earth' (1789) or 'the red or mulatto lands' (1883). This would tend to point in the direction of the term being used as a general marker for some shade of color.

The 1933 edition of *The Oxford English Dictionary* follows that tendency in stating: 'Mulatto [fr. Sp. & Pg. *mulato* young mule, hence one of the mixed race . . .] 1. One who is the offspring of a European and a Negro; also used loosely for any half-breed resembling a mulatto.' This reflects a great deal of early usage, cited by the *OED*, as when a British traveler speaks in 1789 of the 'mulattoes, or as they are called in the East Indies, half-casts [sic]'. Nonetheless, a 1940 dictionary tends to narrow the meaning somewhat: 'Mulatto. A person who is the offspring of a Negro and a white person; a Negro with some white blood. . . . Designating persons of mixed Negro and white blood. . . . Designating soils of a brownish color.'[24] Thus, gradually, the term comes to refer to persons of mixed white European and Black African ancestry, regardless of the exact degree of mixture. This usage is, however, not always the one actually used by legislative bodies and the courts, as will be analyzed below.

It should be noted that *it is very likely that from the beginning the English used the term 'mulatto' to refer to a wide range of brown mixed-bloods, especially since the precise ancestry of most such persons could not be known.* Such usage is reflected in Blount's 1656 definition (above, 'one that is of a mongrel complexion') and also in remarks such as that of Robert Hooke (*c*.1664): 'We find by relations, how much the Negro women do besmeer the offspring of the Spaniard, bringing forth neither white-skinned, nor black, but tawny hided mulattos.'[25]

In fact, virtually all of the early English references to mulattoes (1590s–1600s) are to individuals whose precise ancestry is unknown and whose origin usually has a Spanish connection or at least a West Indian one.

Legal Definitions

Explicit legal (statutory) definitions of the term 'mulatto' are surprisingly few in the colonial period. General usage will be examined below, but first it is necessary to review those explicit references which do exist. We shall begin with Virginia, because that colony is thought to have exercised considerable influence on other areas.[26]

In 1705 Virginia prohibited any 'negro, mulatto, or Indian' from holding any public office. The act further stated:

and for clearing all manner of doubts which hereafter may happen to arise upon the construction of this act, or any other act, who shall be accounted a mulatto: Be it [etc], that the child of an Indian, and the child, grandchild, or great grandchild or a negro shall be deemed, accounted, held, and taken to be a mulatto.[27]

In other words, an American–European mixed-blood was defined as a mulatto, along with all part-Africans to the one-eighth degree. This statute apparently remained unmodified until 1785 when it was enacted that all persons with 'one-fourth or more Negro blood shall . . . be deemed a mulatto'. This remained the legal definition until 1866 when it was modified: 'Every person having one-fourth or more Negro blood shall be deemed a colored person, and every person not a colored person having one-fourth or more Indian blood shall be deemed an Indian.' This use of 'colored person' must be considered in relation to an 1860 statute using 'mulatto' for persons of one-fourth African descent and making 'negro' and 'mulatto' equivalent in all statutes.[28]

It would appear, then, that from 1705 until 1866 the only legal definition applying to mixed Native Americans (excepting those having one-fourth or more African ancestry) was that of 1705. Thus we might at first glance construe that a mixed American–European was legally a mulatto if of one-half or more American blood until that statute of 1866 making such persons 'Indians'. All American–African mixed-bloods remained mulattoes throughout the period, unless having less than one-eighth African ancestry (1705–85) or less than one-quarter African ancestry (1785–1910). After 1910 Virginia reclassified large numbers of persons by extending the 'colored' category to include people with minute amounts of African ancestry.[29]

It should be noted that in actual practice some Virginia officials seem to have assumed, after 1785, that all 'mulattoes' possessed one-quarter or more African ancestry. For example, a white petition asserted in 1843 that the Native Americans of King William County (Pamunkey and Mattaponi reservations): 'all of whome, by the laws of Virginia, would be deemed and taken to be free mulattoes . . . as it is believed they all have one-fourth or more of negro blood.'[30] In 1857 some local whites took away the Pamunkey people's guns.

The Indians complained to the governor and he wrote back that the law in question did not apply to Indians but that 'if any become one fourth mixed with the negro race then they may be treated as free negroes or mulattoes.'[31]

Thus we might conclude that sometime around the War of Independence the term 'mulatto' acquired, in Virginia, the same meaning assigned to it earlier by some English dictionary-makers, that is, that of a part-African person. Still further, it is clear that as late as 1843–57 a person of mixed American–African ancestry was considered to be a 'mulatto'. This differs, of course, from those later dictionary definitions limiting the term to European–African mixed-bloods. (But there are exceptions in usage which will be noted below.)

During the nineteenth century the courts of Virginia seem to have ordinarily limited the use of the term 'mulatto' to persons of one-quarter or more non-white ancestry. For example, in 1847 two brothers of Culpepper County, William and John Ross, were alleged to be 'mulattoes'. The court found that their grandfather David Ross 'was spoken of as a respectable man, though probably a mulatto, was a soldier in the revolution and died in the service.' His wife was probably white, and his son's wife 'certainly' was. The Supreme Court held that the Ross brothers were legally 'white'.[32]

South Carolina was another early leader in developing racial classification terms, somewhat independent of Virginia. Spanish practice seems to have greatly influenced this colony, especially in the use of the term 'mustee' or 'mustizo' (*mestizo*) for a certain type of part–American mixed-blood. The government of colonial South Carolina would appear to have almost never directly defined racial terms but one instance is of great value to us.

In 1719 South Carolina decided who should be an 'Indian' for tax purposes, since American slaves were taxed at a lesser rate than African slaves. The act stated: 'And for preventing all doubts and scruples that may arise what ought to be rated on mustees, mulattoes, etc., all such slaves as are not entirely Indian shall be accounted as negroe.'[33]

This is an extremely significant passage because it clearly asserts that 'mustees' and 'mulattoes' were persons of part-American ancestry. My own judgement (to be discussed later) is that a mustee was primarily part-African and American and that a mulatto was usually part-European and American. The act is also significant because it asserts that part–Americans with or without African ancestry could be counted as negroes, thus having an implication for all later slave censuses.

As will be indicated below, South Carolina colonial legislation makes frequent reference to negroes, mulattoes, mustees and Indians, both as slaves and as free persons. This usage continued into the nineteenth century but new meanings were gradually assigned to the terms. An important factor was doubtless the complete assimilation of American slaves into the general slave population, and, to some extent, a similar absorption of Americans within the free 'colored' group.

In any case, there are many court cases from 1829 onward involving a discussion of the term 'mulatto'. In that year the Supreme Court stated that when the words negro, mulatto, etc. are used in statutes 'for the purpose of designating a class, they are to be interpreted by their common acceptation' which in the case of mulatto meant 'offspring of a black and a white'.[34]

There is no legal definition of the term [mulatto] . . . in the first of the cases . . . [a judge said] that a mulatto was the offspring of parents, one . . . white, and the other black; and that he was disposed to think that where the white blood predominated, this disqualification [of mulatto status] ought not to attach. . . . It is certainly true that every admixture of African blood with the European, or white, is not to be referred to the degraded class. It would be dangerous and cruel to subject to this disqualification, persons bearing all the features of a white, on account of some remote admixture of negro blood; nor has the term mulatto, or person of colour, I believe, been popularly attributed to such a person. . . . *where there is a distinct and visible admixture of negro blood, the person is to be denominated a mulatto, or person of colour* . . . [it is] a question very proper for a jury.[35] (italics added)

South Carolina judges, in other words, gradually extended the term to be virtually an equivalent to 'colored person' and to include persons visibly part-African, regardless of actual degree of blood. In 1846 this was stated even more explicitly:

The constant tendency of this class [mulattoes] to assimilate to the white, and the desire for elevation, present frequent cases of embarrassment and difficulty. . . . It would be difficult, if not impolitic, to define by . . . inflexible rules the lines of separation. . . . the question of the reception of colored persons into the class of citizens must partake more of a political than a legal character, and, in a great degree, be decided by public opinion, expressed in the verdict of a jury.[36]

Regardless of the appearance of 'liberality' the court consistently drew the line at somewhere between one-eighth and one-sixteenth African ancestry, a line formalized in many other states at that date. Still further, the father of the litigant, one Elijah Bass, although showing some unspecified non-European features, had apparently been treated as a white man and his children had married white people. Thus the court was in some ways more conservative than the local white community. (And it is possible that Bass had American ancestry, since Bass people often have Indian affiliation in the South.)

It is clear from a decision of 1850 that persons of American descent, in order to escape from the status of mulatto or colored person had to prove that they were 'of free Indian descent, unmixed with African blood'. The case is as follows: Amelia Marchant was challenged as a witness on the grounds that she was a person of color. It was argued on her behalf that her grandparents were free Indians and also that her father, James Mitchell, was a Portuguese. Opponents said that Mitchell had associated with colored persons and was so considered. The verdict was in Marchant's favor, that is, that she was of free Indian ancestry and that she had no African blood. The Supreme Court reviewed the case and reversed the verdict, in spite of the fact that the Mitchells had paid no capitation tax (charged to free colored people) and that James Mitchell had apparently married a white woman. The grounds for reversal were, in part, that many Indians had been enslaved and that the Mitchells came under the status of colored persons, apparently because they could not prove descent from 'free' Indians 'in amity' with South Carolina.[37]

If nothing else, this 1850 case illustrates that persons of American blood could still be considered to be mulattoes or colored persons in South Carolina, especially if a suspicion of African ancestry existed.

In Georgia (which usually followed the lead of South Carolina) a wealthy Spanish–Floridian of alleged mixed African and American ancestry was held to be a mulatto by a lower court. The higher court in 1856 reversed this decision and held him to be a white man.[38]

The other English colonies in North America seemingly failed to develop legal definitions for the various racial terms used in their statutes. Court cases occasionally shed light on meanings, as in Delaware where a woman was freed from slavery because she was descended in the female line from a 'native of Asia' (her grandmother). Slavery, it was said, extended only to 'negroes and mulattoes' descended from a 'female Negro'. Her father was a 'negro' and she apparently was classified as a mulatto.[39]

Many states adopted legal definitions after 1800. They are typified by the following examples.

Indiana (1817): Every person other than a negro, of whose grandfathers or grandmothers any one is or shall have been a negro, though his other progenitors may have been a white, shall be deemed a mulatto, and so every person who shall have one-fourth part or more of negro blood.

(Indiana also asserted that 'no negro, mulatto, or Indian' could be witness in cases involving white persons.)[40]

California (1850): persons having one-eighth or more of negro blood shall be deemed mulattoes, and persons having one-half of Indian blood, shall be deemed Indians. . . . no black or mulatto person, or Indian . . .

shall give evidence in a case involving a white person.[41]

In general, the statutes defining the term 'mulatto' always do so in such a way as to include virtually any American–African hybrid, provided that the African ancestry is one-quarter or more, one-eighth or more, and so on, depending on the time period. Alabama, however, tended to classify all part-Americans and part-Africans in the same 'colored' group:

All negroes, mulattoes, Indians and all persons of mixed blood descended from negro or Indian ancestors, to the third generation inclusive, though one ancestor of each generation only have been a white person, whether bond or free, shall be taken, and deemed incapable in law, to be witnesses . . . except for or against each other.[42]

In 1859 an Alabama court classified mixed persons of apparently part-American, part-African, and part-European descent as mulattoes.[43]

Census and Other Extra-Legal Definitions

Colonial tax-rolls seldom give racial characteristics but there are exceptions which will be reviewed when pertinent. In Virginia many early tax rolls are missing; however, one can use fairly continuous records from *c.*1783 onward. There seems to be a common trend in these documents, as reflected by the rolls of Charles City County. From 1783 to the early 1800s no race is given for free persons – all are classified (for tax purposes) as 'white-tithable'. From 1809 to 1812 'free negro' is placed after the names of some free persons but mixed-bloods are still treated as white. Beginning in 1813, however, the word 'mulatto' appears beside mixed-people's names, along with 'free negro' for others. Persons who can be identified as Chickahominy Indians or as ancestors of the present-day Chickahominy are uniformly classified as mulattoes.

A similar trend occurs in King William, King and Queen, Caroline, and Essex Counties, except that Indians living on the two small reservations in King William (Pamunkey and Mattaponi) generally do not appear on the tax rolls (since their land was not taxable). On the other hand, relatives of the reservation Indians having taxable property or living off-reservation normally are classified as 'mulatto' or 'free colored'. In the other counties Indians are classified as above but also in several cases as 'F.N.' (free negro). It is very rare to see a person classified as 'Indian' in pre-Civil War Virginia records and *never* in the above counties (where the bulk of Indians were then concentrated).[44]

A similar situation exists in relation to early United States records. The first census (1790) forced the local enumerator to place all free persons in two categories: 'white' or 'all other free persons except Indians not taxed'. Most families known to be of Indian extraction in Maryland, North Carolina, South Carolina, and elsewhere (Virginia is missing) were placed in the 'all other free persons' category. Occasionally, however, the enumerator also wrote in their specific racial status. Thus we find in South Carolina, Jordan Chavers of Cheraw classified as 'mulatoe' and Hannah Shavis of Edgefield classified as 'mulatto'. The Chavers–Chavis name is widely associated with Indian communities in both North and South Carolina.[45]

The 1800, 1810, 1820 and 1830 censuses use the 'free person of color' category for most non-whites, including Indians. Thus the Native families of Robeson County, North Carolina, and all Virginia counties are always classified as 'colored' persons. Carter Woodson's *The Free Negro Heads of Families in the United States in 1830*, being and indexing of the 'free colored' population, includes many thousands of Indians. For example, the entire Cherokee Indian population of Carroll County, Georgia was included as colored persons, with names such as Rattlesnake, Ekoah, Watta, Tah-ne-cul-le-hee, Wasotta, Keecha, Widow Swimmer, Pumpkinpile, Charles Vann, and so on. One also finds people like Stephen Jumper in Rockingham County, North Carolina, Charles Moose in the same county, and 'Indian Bill' of Westchester County, New York, classified as people of color, along with the general Indian population in county after county.[46]

In 1834 a special census was taken of the Choctaw Indian people. In it we find the following revealing entries:

Jacob O'Rare, a mulatto, half Indian and half negro.
James Blue, a Negro–Indian man, has an Indian wife.
William Lightfoot, a mulatto, half Indian and half Negro.
Jim Tom, half-breed Negro, has an Indian wife.
Jacob Daniel, has a half Indian and half Negro for a wife.[47]

In the 1840 US census the 'free colored' category continues to be used for most non-whites.

In 1850 US census enumerators were instructed 'in enumerating colored persons to write "B" or "M" in the space on the schedule.' The 'B' presumably stood for 'Black' and the 'M' for 'Mulatto' (although 'mixed' seems to be the more correct modern rendering). In both 1850 and 1860 these racial terms were not defined by the census officials.

In Virginia one finds that all of the Indians of the central tidewater counties were classified as 'M', including the residents of the Pamunkey and Mattaponi reservations, with a few exceptions in King William County where one or two were classified as 'B'. (The 'B' should be placed in context, since early Virginia tax-rolls (such as those of the 1780s) divided all tithable persons between 'white souls' and 'black souls'. The term 'black' or 'B' is, therefore, open to various interpretations.)

The same pattern appears in Norfolk County, Virginia where many members of the Nansemond Indian group living near Portsmouth were classifed as 'M'. This is especially significant since the Nansemonds were categorized as 'I' (for Indian) on an 1860 local tax roll. At various dates, certificates were apparently issued to Nansemond Indian people, such as the following: 'William Bass, the bearer, tall, swarthy, dark eyes . . . is of English and Indian descent with no admixture of negro blood, numbered as a Nansemun by his own choosing.' This was in 1742. But in the following century many Nansemonds were harassed as 'mulattoes' and listed in the 1850 census with 'M' after their names. Nonetheless, a local county court ruled in 1833 that they were 'not free negroes or mulattoes, but are of Indian descent'.

Here we have a clear indication that *some* whites were still using the term 'mulatto' for people with no African ancestry, even in the nineteenth century, while the judiciary was holding to the letter of Virginia's 1785 law (requiring African ancestry).[48]

All in all, some 37 per cent of the free people of color in 1850 were classified as 'M' while only about one-twelfth of the slaves were so categorized.[49] It seems clear that a good many of the free people classed as 'M' were, in fact, Indians or of Indian descent.

It is helpful, at this point, to review a few specific cases so as to shed light on actual practice. An interesting one is that of the Dungee family. The name appears to originate in King William County, Virginia, as it is found nowhere else in the 1790 US census or in the Virginia tax-rolls of 1782–5 examined by this writer. In 1782 a Joseph and John Dungee are recorded as 'white' tithables in King William. In 1783 John 'Dungary' is age 21 plus, has four 'white souls' in his household and no 'negroes' (slaves). In 1810 John Dungey is still listed as a 'white' tithable. By that date Dungees had also appeared in other Virginia counties. All are listed in the census as 'free colored' (except for one woman in Middlesex, classed as 'white'), and the situation is similar in 1820. On the tax-rolls of King William County after 1813 the Dungees are all listed as mulattoes. John Dungy specifically appears as a mulatto on the King and Queen County tax rolls for 1813.[50]

In 1825 an interesting document was submitted to the General Assembly of Virginia: 'Your petitioners John Dungie and Lucy Ann, his wife who are free persons of colour residing in King William County ask permission respectfully to represent to the Senate and House of Delegates of Virginia that your Petitioner John (who is descended from the aborigines of this Dominion), was born free.'[51] Lucy Ann (Littlepage) his wife, was an emancipated slave, half-African and half-white (the daughter of a wealthy planter). They, therefore, had to petition to remain in Virginia since she was required by law to leave the state.

Respected white planters endorsed the petition by stating that: 'Capt. Dungee is a Free born native of Virginia, was raised in the calling of a sailor and has for many years been the Commander of a vessel, constantly employed in the navigation of the Chesapeake Bay and the Rivers of Virginia.'[52]

By 1830 Dungees had spread to Tennessee, South Carolina, Ohio, New York and various parts of Virginia. Those in Virginia and Tennessee were all classified as free persons of color. In 1840 the same is true. In 1850 all of the Dungees in King William County, Virginia were classified as either 'M' or 'B' even though all were living on or near the Mattaponi or Pamunkey Indian reservations.[53]

A similar situation exists in relation to other prominent Indian families. The Sampson family contributed a great many students to the Indian college at William and Mary (Thomas 1754; John 1764; George 1769, 1775; Reubin 1775; Edmund 1776). An 1812 petition of the Pamunkey Tribe lists John, William and Henry Sampson as among the 'Headmen and Chiefs'.[54] It would appear that during that period many Sampsons left to settle elsewhere where they were in 1810 and later classified as 'free people of color'. The 1850 census for King William County classifies all of the Sampsons (all on the Pamunkey Reservation) as mulattoes ('M') including Thomas. In 1865 Thomas Sampson was re-elected a headman at Pamunkey.[55]

The same thing is true for the Langston family at Pamunkey, a family which contributed students to the Indian school at William and Mary College before the Revolutionary War. In 1830 and 1840 their descendants are classified as 'free colored' and in the 1850 as 'mulattoes' without exception. The same is true for all of the prominent Pamunkey and Mattaponi families, even including those of Rhoda Arnold and Molly Holt, two ladies from whom a visitor acquired some Indian words in 1844.[56]

Many photographs of Indian people in central tidewater Virginia were taken by anthropologists in the 1890s–1920s. These photographs illustrate rather clearly that the people being described in the records as mulattoes are of complex racial origin, with Native American features predominating.[57]

Another interesting case is afforded by the Nottoway Tribe, a reservation group in Southampton County, Virginia. In 1808 a partial census of the tribe identified, for example, Littleton Scholar (age 51) as an Indian (full-blood) with a white wife. In the 1830 US census, however, Littleton's sons Billy and Ned are listed as free people of color. (And all of the surviving full-blood Nottoways are listed in the same manner.) In 1844 an 'enumeration of free negroes and mulattoes' in Southampton County listed 'certain mulatto children' including Alex, Bob, Samuel and Gideon Scholar, all children of a white mother.[58]

The Scholars do not appear to have had any African ancestry but are regarded nonetheless as mulattoes. Most of the other Nottoways, with some African ancestry, are classified as mulattoes or as free negroes.

Another case involves the Scott family of Indians in Richmond, Virginia. William Scott was listed as an Indian in the tax-rolls of the 1780s. By 1810 'Billy Scott' was called a free person of color, with nine in his household. By 1850 the oldest 'William Scott' in the area, age 49, was classified as an 'M' in the census, as was his probable son. (All other William Scotts were classed as either 'B' or 'M' in Henrico County.) In 1853 the Grand Jury charged 'William Scott', senior, a free negro for 'retailing ardent spirits to be drunk at the place where sold' without a license. The defendant 'moved the court to permit him to withdraw his pleas of "not guilty" and to plead that he was not a free negro . . . but an Indian'. The court held that to be immaterial since the charge was the same for whites, Indians, or free negroes.[59]

The William Scott claiming to be an Indian in 1853 was doubtless the same person as the Scott, age 49, classed as an 'M' in the 1850 census, since the latter had property worth $3,000 and could read. Doubtless he owned a store or shop of some kind.

Many other examples could be cited, including that of the widespread Going (Goen, Gowin) family descended probably from 'Gowin, an Indian servant to Mr Thomas Bushrod' who was to be free in 1676. This Gowin, in turn, may be the child of one 'Mihill Gowen negro late servant' who was discharged from service in 1657 in York County and who had a son named William born to a woman belonging to a white lady. The latter gave up all claims on the child but it is possible that he was later indentured. (This is not the only example of the interchangeable use of 'Negro' and 'Indian' in Virginia.)

By 1754 many of the Gowens had moved to Granville, North Carolina, where Thomas, Michael, and Edward Gowen were all listed as 'mulatto' members of a militia company. Going/Gowen descendents are classified as free people of color (rarely as white) in the censuses through 1840 in Virginia, Tennessee and North Carolina. In 1850 they are usually classified as 'M' throughout the south.[60]

In 1870 the term 'mulatto' was defined by US Census officials 'to include quadroons, octoroons, and all persons having any respectable trace of African blood' thus taking the definition far beyond the legal statutes of any states at that date.[61] Quite clearly, large numbers of people of Native American ancestry would be included under such a definition.

In 1880 and 1900 there were no published instructions, but in 1890 a 'black' was defined as a person with 'three-fourths or more "black blood"', other persons with any proportion of 'black' blood being classified as 'mulattoes', 'quadroons', or 'octoroons'. In 1910 'black' included all 'full-blooded Negroes' while 'mulatto' included 'all other persons having some proportion or perceptible trace of Negro blood.'[62] All of these definitions, of course, allowed broad scope to local white census-takers and went beyond the statutory definitions of 'mulatto' in most states.

Later censuses also tended to increase the size of the 'negro' group by including most persons of mixed Indian and African ancestry. For example, the 1930 census-takers were instructed to count as Indians those of mixed white and Indian ancestry 'except where the percentage of Indian blood is very small' or when the person 'is regarded as a white person . . . where he lives'. But this same reasoning was not applied to the African–American hybrids. Such people 'shall be returned as a Negro unless the Indian blood *predominates* and the status as an Indian is generally accepted in the community'. The 1940 census instructions required that an American–African hybrid be counted as a Negro unless the Native ancestry '*very definitely predominates* and he is *universally* accepted in the community as an Indian'. (italics added)[63]

Thus, although the term 'mulatto' ceases to be used in US censuses, the general tendency is to use the term negro to include all Indian–Black persons who earlier would have been categorized under the former term. In short, 'mulatto' had become subsumed completely under 'negro'. We can be reasonably certain, I would suggest, that in many parts of the country white census-takers would have counted as negro virtually all Indians showing African ancestry except in counties where the Indians openly resisted such a classification.[64]

It is interesting to note that in the most recent US census (1980) persons of part-Indian ancestry had to be very alert if they wished to be counted as an Indian. Census rules forbade a person being counted in more than one racial category and no 'mixed' status was allowed. Thus a person who checked more than one box was to be counted only with the first category marked and 'white' came first, 'black' second, and 'Indian' third. In short, any person who checked both 'black' and 'Indian' would be counted as 'black' only.[65]

Aside from census records, there are a few other extra-statutory definitions of the term 'mulatto' which are of interest. Examples will be cited in more or less chronological order.

In *c.*1648 an Englishman (Thomas Gage) who had lived in Mexico and Guatemala wrote a book which made frequent use of the terms 'mulatto' and 'mestizo'. The latter was defined as a Spanish–American mixture while 'mulatto' is used very frequently but only clarified in this passage:

Nay, a blackamoor or tawny young maid and slave will make hard shift, but she will be in fashion. . . . The attire of this baser sort of people of blackamoors and mulattoes (which are of a mixed nature, of Spaniards and blackamoors) is so light, and their carriage so enticing, that many Spaniards . . . disdain their wives for them . . . their bare, black, and tawny breasts are covered with bobs hanging from their chains of pearls.[66]

Gage, an ex-Catholic priest, was describing his memory of Mexico City after the passage of twenty years and we may suspect that his definition of 'mulatto' is not intended to be precise as to the exact genetic make-up of the part-African people he was describing. Subsequently, he frequently refers to Indians, mestizos, mulattoes, and blackamoors in Guatemala, Nicaragua, Panama, and elsewhere, but he never introduces any term for African–American hybrids as such. Are we to believe that in such a heavily American region there were no American–African mixed-bloods embraced within his 'mulatto' category?

In 1673 an Englishman from Virginia visited the Tomahitan (Euchee) people living to the west in the Appalachian Mountains. They took him on an expedition to Spanish Florida, to a 'negro town' where they killed a negro man. Later it was reported: 'The Tomahitans have amongst them many brass pots and kettles from three gallons to thirty. They have two mullato women all ye white and black people they take they put to death since their twenty men were barbarously handled [by the Spaniards or "hairey people"][67]. It seems quite clear that these 'mullato' women were neither white nor black but were of mixed race, including American ancestry, since it would make no sense to kill whites and blacks but keep people who were mixed white and black. A 'Spanish Indian boy' was also spared by the Tomahitans and was brought to Virginia by them.

In the 1684–99 period Ann Wall, a white woman, was convicted in Virginia of having 'two mulattoe bastards by a negro'. This illustrates a tendency found in some records and indicates that the term 'mulatto' could have been applied to children of some other type of father as well.[68] This is borne out by a statement of Helen T. Caterall, summarizing records of the seventeenth century. She states that the servant (but non-slave) class included: 'mulatto servants (whose servitude was the penalty for having a white mother and an Indian, negro, or mulatto father [a law reenacted in 1705] or, after 1723, for being descended in the maternal line from such a combination of ancestors).'[69]

in 1704 a British writer refers directly to an Indian as a mulatto. He writes: 'I shall observe your Caution, says my Moletto Comrade [the Indian].'

In 1706 a girl described as a 'molatta or mustee' became pregnant in Accomack County, Virginia. She would have been punished with servitude but an Indian, Edward Bagwell, stepped forward to assume all costs. This clearly implies that she was half-American and that either of the two terms – mulatto or mustee – was a referent to such people.

In 1715 a South Carolina English missionary baptized a 'mulatto' girl whose mother he reported as an Indian and whose father he said was a white trader.[70]

During the period 1717–21 an Englishman named Hugh Jones lived in Virginia. In 1724 he published a book in which he stated: 'The [slave] children belong to the master of the woman that bears them; and such as are born of a Negroe and a European are called Molattoes; but such as are born of an Indian and Negroe are called Mustees.'[71] Some doubt is cast on Jones' accuracy or reliability in that the term 'mustee' seldom appears in any records of Virginia that I have examined. Instead one finds the following: 'A reward is offered [in 1782] for a runaway slave who, according to the description, was the offspring of an Indian and a negress; but he is called a mulatto.'[72]

Another example occurred in 1818 when Virginia judges considered a case where a free person was sold as a slave to defraud a buyer; 'the free man sold, was not proved to be either a negro or mulatto, but by one witness, who said he had heard that he was the offspring of a white woman by an Indian.'[73]

This would indicate that as late as 1818 the term 'mulatto' could be applied to a white–Indian mixed-blood by Virginia jurists (in spite of the evidence cited in the previous section).

From 1803 to the Civil War all free people of color in Virginia were required to register. The register for Essex County has survived and in it we find many Indian people listed but none are called Indians. Classifications given include black, dark brown, tawney, very dark mulatto, dark mulatto, shade lighter than a dark mulatto, bright mulatto, very bright mulatto, and very bright mulatto almost white. One man, the son of a non-white father (of Indian extraction judging from his family name) and a white mother was described in 1844 as 'color bright mulatto . . . with hair somewhat like a white persons'. His brother, a son of the same white man, was described as a bright mulatto with 'long hair'.[74] No doubt the hair was being worn long because of Indian identity since this was common for Native Americans in Virginia through the 1890s at least.

It should be noted that all of the persons with Indian family names registered in Essex, with the exception of one woman and her children, were 'born free'.

In Delaware in the 1850s several legal cases developed when laws designed to control 'free negroes and mulattoes' were applied to Indian communities in that state. One set of cases was designed to prevent certain Indians of Sussex County from buying or selling arms and ammunition. The Indians were found to be mixed with some vague degree of African ancestry and, therefore, legally mulatto.[75] Similarly, a relative of one of the above Indians, Peter B. Socum, was arrested for having entered the state, since the Revised Code prohibited entry by 'free negroes and free mulattoes'. He was fined and jailed but the judgement was reversed in 1856 because he had been a resident at the time the act had been passed.[76]

One more example will be given to show that the term 'mulatto' was regularly used to include persons of part-Indian ancestry. In North Carolina in the 1870s a white woman wrote a book about the people now known as the Lumbee Indians of Robeson County. The author traces the ancestry of many Lumbees and takes note of white and Indian as well as African ancestors. Nonetheless, all are referred to as 'bright' mulattoes, light mulattoes, or simply as mulattoes. She notes that the area of their settlement was called: 'Scuffletown, from the act of the mulattoes inhabiting that region congregating in Lowrie's grocery and after imbibing pretty freely of whiskey, in engaging in the broad shuffle, and also from the fact that it was generally a scuffle with the mulattoes to live.' She describes a Lumbee resistance leader, Henry Berry Lowrie, as follows: '[His color was] of a mixed white and yellow, partaking of an admixture, resembling copper, the Indian color however, still predominating, although the white and black remain apparent. . . . He wore a dark goatee, his hair was straight and black like an Indian's.'[77] Nonetheless, he was a mulatto to white North Carolinians of 1875, even as his people were recorded as mulattoes in the US census.

In the same year there is testimony from the Robeson County attorney before a Congressional committee in which he says that 'the Mulattoes' of Robeson, as he termed the Lumbees, 'were a mixture of Cherokee and Portuguese'.[78] The use of the term 'Portuguese' may have been a euphemism for 'African', but nonetheless it seems clear that the term 'mulatto' was still being used in a very broad way.

The situation historically in North Carolina tax records and other document is summarized by Robert K. Thomas as follows (for the Lumbee people):

Most individuals are listed most commonly as Mulattoes. In that time in North Carolina the legal category Mulatto meant having one white parent and one non-white parent. The non-white parent could be either Indian or Negro. Some individuals in these families are listed as white, a few are listed as black, and occasionally an individual is listed as an Indian. . . . this meant full-blood Indian. . . . by definition, a mixed-blood Indian would be a Mulatto.[79]

A similar situation existed in Tennessee where the so-called Melungeon people (probably Saponi–Powhatan) of Hawkins, Grainger and nearby counties were often classed as 'free colored' and mulatto, but occasionally also as white.[80] A white writer of *c.*1890 asserted of these people: 'A great many declare them mulattoes, and base their belief upon the ground that at the close of the civil war negroes and Malungeons stood upon precisely the same social footing, "free man of color" all.' One official said that the Malungeon 'isn't a nigger and he isn't an Indian, and he isn't a white man'. The author adds: 'In appearance they bear a striking resemblance to the Cherokees, and they are believed by the people around about to be a kind of half-breed Indian. Their complexion is reddish brown, totally unlike the mulatto.'[81] Here, of course, we sense that the writer of 1890 has a feeling that the term 'mulatto' ought *not* to be applied to persons whose shade of brownness (and probably other features) do not resemble those of an African–white hybrid.

This same confusion over the use of the term 'mulatto' is exemplified by the status of a similar group of mixed Indian people in South Carolina, called variously 'Brass Ankles', 'Redbones', 'Yellow People', and so on, until recently. Although frequently classified as mulattoes in earlier census records, these people in the 1940s were being variously called mulattoes, yellow people, 'half-niggers', and 'half-Indians' by the local whites. Some were being accepted as whites also, albeit with reluctance. (The term mustee or mestizo had reportedly disappeared from local usage.)[82]

Runaway Slave Advertisements

Advertisements for runaway slaves occasionally contain information which sheds light on racial terms. The term 'mulatto' is sometimes used for persons whose background cannot be documented, but very often American ancestry is specifically indicated. In the following examples from Virginia, North Carolina and South Carolina, references to Americans held as slaves will also be included, along with those specifically using the term 'mulatto'.

We shall begin with Virginia:

1737 (1738): Amos, a 'Mulatto Man Slave . . . he is about 6 Feet high, with broad face and Shoulders, has bushy Hair and is a Native of this Country, altho he has the Countenance of a Madegascar.'

1752 Ran away from Somerset County, Maryland, 'a tall Slim Mulatto Man Slave, . . . looks much like unto an Indian and will endeavour to pass for such; had with him a strip'd Indian Match-coat.'

1772 Ran away 'a dark Mulatto Man Slave named Manuel, about five Feet nine Inches high, thirty years of age . . . and has bushy Hair; he has been used to go by Water, has much the appearance of a Sailor, and is a tolerably good Shoemaker; he was born in the Spanish West Indies, speaks Spanish fluently.'

1772 Ran away from Cumberland a 'Mulatto Man named Jim, who is a Slave, but pretends to have a Right to his Freedom. His father was an Indian, of the name of Cheshire, and very likely will call himself James Cheshire, or Chink.' He has 'long black hair resembling an Indian's.'

1773 Ran away with 'a Negro Fellow named Fortune . . . a Wench named Aminta . . . has much the Look of an Indian, and is so, her Mother having been brought from the Spanish Main to Rhode Island, has long black hair.' They were brought from Rhode Island.

1773 Ran away from Amelia County 'a Negro man of the name of Tom . . . of a yellowish complexion, much the appearance of an Indian. . . . His hair is of a different kind from that of a Negro's, rather more of the Indian's, but partaking of both, which though short, he frequently ties behind.'

1775 Ran away from Cumberland 'a Mulatto man slave named Sancho. . . . Absconded with him a white servant woman. . . . I expect they will change their names and endeavour to pass for husband and wife, as free people.'

1775 Ran away from Bute County, North Carolina, 'a Slave named Charles, of the Indian breed'.

1776 Ran away from Amherst County a 'Negro Fellow named Ben.' He used the name John Savage on a previous flight 'and has an Indian Woman for his wife who some Time ago lived in Goochland.'

1777   Ran away from Blandfield, in Essex County, 'a Negro Man named John
       Twopence . . . 40 years of age, of a yellowish complexion, a good
       countenance.' Twopence people were later regarded as Indians in
       neighboring King William County.
1777   Ran away from Amelia County 'a large young Mulatto Fellow named
       Sam, of the Indian breed. I expect he is in James City county, as he has a
       Mother who lives there.'
1785   Ran away from Dinwiddie County one Joe. 'He is a dark Mulatto . . .
       has a bushy head of hair, and is of the Indian breed; is an excellent
       sawyer . . . plays on the violin.' (Changed his name to Peter Tony.)
1790   Ran away from Southampton 'a lad about 18 or 19 years of age called
       Ben Whitehead, he is of the Indian breed and almost white, has coarse
       straight hair of a dark brown colour and black eyes . . . is a carpenter . . .
       and he can read.'[83]

The above evidence shows not only that Americans were still being held as
slaves in Virginia as late as 1790 but that in 1772, 1777 and 1785 the term
'mulatto' was explicitly used for persons of American ancestry. In one of the
cases the mulatto was also part-African but in the other two instances no
African ancestry is specifically indicated.

In 1764 a 'Mulatto or Mustee slave, called Tony' ran away from New Bern,
North Carolina. He had 'long stiff black hair, and greatly the looks and colour
of an Indian.' In 1775 a 'Slave of the Indian Blood named Charles, of a very
light Complexion' ran away from Bute County. He had been branded with a 'R'
on the right cheek and a 'T' on the left. He had 'long straight black hair'.[84]

South Carolina newspapers feature numerous advertisements for 'mustee'
slaves (usually of American–African mixture). The term 'mulatto' seems to have
been used less commonly. Nonetheless a few examples can be found, along
with evidence for continued American–African interaction up to the Revolutionary War period.

1738   Ran away, 'an Indian Man, named Peter.'
1740   Deserted from the sloop May-flower 'a tall rough Spanish Indian
       Fellow . . . also a well set Spanish Negro Fellow.'
1746   Ran away 'a tall lusty young Wench, can speak good English,
       Chickesaw, and perhaps French, the Chickesaws having taken her from
       the French settlements on Mississippi.' She fled with her negro
       husband.
1748   Ran away from Cohansey in New Jersey 'a very lusty Negro Man named
       Sampson, aged about 58 years, and has some mixture of Indian Blood in
       him. . . . He has taken with him a boy named Sam, who was born of an
       Indian woman, and looks much like an Indian only his Hair. . . . They
       both talk Indian very well, and it is likely have dress'd themselves in an
       Indian dress, and gone towards Carolina.'
1749   Ran away 'a slave between a mulato and a mustee, named Peter. . . . and
       can read currently well. . . . And was to have gone off with Mr Maxwell's

mustee fellow named Abraham. . . . 'tis supposed . . . he will harbour about Santee (where he hath a wife,) Pedee (where he hath many acquaintance,) Four-Holes, Seludy, or New-Windsor.'

1753 Ran away 'a mullatto girl (of the Indian breed) named Nancy, about 18 or 19 years old, has . . . long black hair.'

1761 Ran away 'a mulatto wench named Betty. . . .She is short and square made, has short Indian hair, is well known in Charles-Town.'

1762 Ran away 'a stout black Negro man . . . named Crack.' With him went 'a free Indian wench, wife to the fellow Crack, who had a child with her about two years of age: A white man was also seen in the canow with them'.

1770 A pilot boat taken by Jack 'a Negro Man' brought up in England and Tony, 'a brown Indian Man, speaks good English and Spanish'.

1771 Ran away 'a young mulatto or mustee wench, named Mary.' Well known at Ashley-River 'where she formerly lived, and was enticed away by her mother, an Indian wench, named Sarah, who lives at . . . Stono Plantation.'

1773 Ran away a 'Negro man, named Nero' and 'a Mulatto or half-Indian Man, named Frank, well made, about nineteen or twenty years old.'[85]

Aside from illustrating American–African contacts, the advertisements specifically ascribe American ancestry to mulattoes in 1753, 1771 and 1773 and, by inference, in 1761. The girl described as mustee or mulatto in 1771 was specifically stated to be the daughter of an American mother, thus implying that if her father was white she was a mulatto, while if black she was a mustee.

It would appear that in South Carolina mulatto was used for European–American (lighter) mixed persons while in Virginia mulatto was used for both European–American and African–American persons. In any event, it would seem clear from the foregoing that the term 'mulatto' has been used frequently so as to include persons of American ancestry, whether mixed with African or not. Before drawing any conclusions, however, it is necessary to examine a mass of data of a more indirect nature.

DEFINITIONS BY INFERENCE

As noted earlier in several places, there is a strong tendency for the English to use the term 'mulatto' in a general sort of sense, as to refer to any mixed-blood, to any brown person, or to some type of mixed origin. This usage is reflected in 1613 when Purchas asks: 'why then are the Portugalls children and Generations White, or Mulatos at most' and in 1657 when Ligon refers to 'A great fat man . . . his face not so black as to be counted a Molotto' or, as in Defoe's *Robinson Crusoe* (1719) 'My face, the color of it was really not so Moletta like, as one might expect.' Still more interesting is a reference in 1664 to 'Purgatory, which is a device to make men be mulatas, as the Spaniard calls half Christians'.[86] Thus, a half-'heathen' might be called a mulatto, a usage very much in keeping with colonial attitudes towards both Americans and Africans.

As stated before, the earliest English usage of the term 'mulatto' seems to relate to individuals whose precise ancestry was not known, or who were associated with the Spanish. For example, in 1590 at Puerto Rico 'a mulatto named Pedro, who knew everything about our condition, deserted to the Spaniards' and in 1595 one of Sir Francis Drake's pilots was a 'mulato' who sailed from Plymouth but who was probably a Canary Islander in origin. Drake was also aided by a 'Mulatow and an Indian' on the coast of Jamaica.[87]

During the same general period Richard Hawkins sailed along the coast of western South America and put in at San Mathew (San Mato) Bay in the Ecuador area. In this area, Hawkins states, the Spaniards from Guayaquil had established a post but the Americans 'being a people of stomacke and presumption, they suffered themselves to bee persuaded and led by a Molato. This leader many years before had fled unto them from the Spaniards.' With the 'molato's' help the Americans forced the Spaniards to retreat to Quito, the nearest Spanish settlement.

No doubt most of the early mulattoes mentioned by the English were African–American mixed-bloods. This, however, is not the case with Andrew Battell's use of the term for Portuguese–African children born in the Congo (mentioned in a work published in the 1613–25 period).[88]

In 1632 the London Company wrote Captain Daniel Elfrye 'condemning his indiscretion in too freely entertaining a Mullato, as you call him, in the island [Providence Island], and in taking a Spanish frigate'. And in 1666 the Virginia House of Burgesses recorded that 'a Mulato named Manuel' was freed the previous year after being judged 'no slave and sent to serve as other Christians servants do.' In 1658 a London merchant went to 'Chelsea College' to see if any prisoners there 'had lived as slaves and servants in the Indies' and would be willing to go to Virginia. 'Two mulattoes offered to go rather than remain eternally in prison.' And in 1678 a 'Spanish Mullatto, by name Anthonio' was sold by a Bostonian for ten years' service in Virginia.[89]

This rather general, imprecise use of the term continued. Two more specific examples will suffice: In 1724 the *Boston Gazette* reported that the crew of a Spanish 'pirate' ship off Virgina 'consists of about 60 Spaniards, including the Negros and Molattos, 14 English, and 18 French.' In 1728 an English party surveying the Virginia–North Carolina border reported: 'we came upon a family of mulattoes that called themselves free, though by the shyness of the master of the house . . . their freedom seemed a little doubtful. It is certain many slaves shelter in this obscure part of the world.'[90] An even more explicit example of the usage is also from Virginia. In 1670 a law was adopted which confirmed the practice that all slaves converted to Christianity before coming to Virginia served for only a fixed term as servants. In 1682 this act was changed because 'many negroes, Moors, mulattoes, and others' born in a heathen country and of heathen parents but converted to Christianity elsewhere had been avoiding full slave status. Quite clearly, the 'mulattoes' now to be made life-slaves were persons born in a non-Christian land to non-Christian parents, that is, Native Americans, Africans, Asians, and so on. Thus their precise ancestry could not be known.[91]

Another body of data which needs to be cited consists in reviewing lists of racial groups, usually in statutes, which serve to show that the term 'mulatto' embraced people of American ancestry. The first colonies to be sampled will be those where the term 'mustee' is never used in the statutes, beginning with Virginia:

1657–8	negroes and Indians.
1670	negro or Indian.
1672	negro, molatto, Indian slave, or servant for life [apprehension of runaways].
1680	negro or other slave; all negro and molatto children tithable at age 16 [Indian women age 16 up added in 1682].
1682	negros, Moors, mollatoes or Indians [except 'Turkes' and Moors in amity]; negroes, Moores, mollatoes, and others; negroe, moor, or molatto.
1691	negroes, mulattoes, and other slave or slaves; negroes, mulattoes, and Indians; negro, mulatto, or Indian; negro or mulatto; negro or mulatto (cannot be set free unless transported).
1705	Popish recusants, convict negroes, mulattoes, and Indian servants and others, not being Christians; no negroes, mulattoes or Indians, although Christians, Jews, or Moors, Mahometans, or other infidels; negro, mulatto, or Indian, Jew, Moor, Mahometan, or other infidel; negro or mulatto; negro, mulatto or Indian; [also definition of a mulatto given, includes child of an Indian].
1723	Free negro, mulatto, or Indian slaves.
1732	Free negroes, mulattos, or Indians; negros, mulattos, and Indians; that no negro, mulatto, or Indian slaves shall be set free; mulatto or Indian women; that no free negro, mulatto, or Indian, whatsover, shall here after have any vote.
1732	negroes, mulattos, and Indians; negroes, mulattos and Indians [cannot be witness except in capital slave trials].
1744	any free negro, mulatto, or Indian [can be a witness in non-white cases].
1748	for the better government of negroes, mulattoes, and Indians, bond or free [re-enacted 1753].

1769   free negros, mulattos and Indian women or the wives of free
             negroes, mulattos and Indians, except slaves.
1777   negroes and mulattoes.
1779   negro or mulatto servant or slave.
1792–1812   free negroes and mulattoes; no Indians listed as such.[92]

One can see that from 1682 through 1769 the usual pattern was to mention
three groups: negroes, mulattoes, and Indians. In most cases, we are dealing
with limitations being placed on the civil and property rights of such people and,
therefore, we must assume that it was always the intention of the government of
Virginia to subject African–American mixed-bloods (and probably European–
American mixed-bloods if of one-half Native blood) to the same proscriptions
as were imposed on European–African hybrids. The term 'mulatto' is clearly a
'catch-all' to cover all mixed people of whatever variety. Fortunately, in the case
of Virginia, this interpretation is confirmed by the statute of 1705.
    Maryland sources have the following:

1692   negroes or other slaves [marriage outlawed with whites].
1715   any negroes . . . or mulatto slave [cannot marry whites].
1717   No negro or mulatto slave, free negro, or mulatto born of a white
             woman . . . or any Indian slave or free Indian . . . [can testify where
             any Christian white is involved]; negroes or mulattoes . . . except
             mulattoes born in white women.
1728   free mulatto women . . . , negroes and other slaves, and free negro
             women.
1846–7   Repeats terms in statute of 1717 including negro, mulatto, Indian
             slave, free Indian, et cetera [otherwise 1803–60, free negro and
             negro used almost exclusively].[93]

(It should be noted that a number of Indian or part-Indian communities
survived in Maryland. Many are called mulattoes in the 1790 census.)
    In Delaware there are these references:

1721   negro or mulatto slaves;
             mulatto children [by white mothers];
             negro or mulatto women [no fornication with, by white men].
1739   free negroes [children to be bound out].
1760   children of white woman by negro or mulatto fathers . . . and
             [free] negroes [to be protected from enslavement].
1767   free negroes and mulattoes [are bad example to slaves].
1776   negro, Indian, or mulatto slave.
1787–1852   negro and mulatto used exclusively except for 'colored persons'
             in 1826.
1866   free negroes and free mulattoes [to be punished the same as
             white persons].[94]

(Several Indian communities survived in Delaware. They seem to be called mulattoes or colored people.)

Massachusetts sources offer the following quotations:

1652	all Scotchmen, negroes, and Indians.
1656	negroes or Indians.
1669–1776	Slave statutes refer to 'all slaves' or 'negro or other slaves'.
1692	Negro, Indian or mulatto [cannot marry whites].
1694	negroes, mulattoes and Indian servants.
1695	Negroes, Mulattoes and Indian servants.
1698	Indian, molato, or negro servant or slave.
1703	molatto or negro slaves;
	Indians, mulattoes, and negroes.
1705	Negro and mulatto;
	negro or mulatto;
	negro or mulatto.
1786	negro, Indian, or Mulatto [cannot marry whites].[95]

Maine continued the style of Massachusetts:

1821   negro, Indian or mulatto [cannot marry whites].[96]

Connecticut uses these terms:

1650	Indians and negroes.
1660	Indian or negros.
1677	runaway Indians.
1708	negro and mulatto servants and slaves.
1711	negro, mulatto, and Spanish Indians . . . servants.
1715	Indians and other slaves.
1723	negro and Indian servants and slaves.
1730	negro, Indian, and mulatto slaves.
1769	Indian, negro, or mulatto slave.
1774	Indian, negro, or mulatto slave.
1784	free negroes;
	Indian, negro or mulatto slave;
	negro or mulatto child.
1788	free negro, Indian, or mulatto;
	such negroes or mulattoes.
1797	negro or mulatto child.
1848	any Indian, negro or mulatto slave.[97]

Rhodes Island usage is:

1712	negroes or Indian slaves.
1715	Indian slaves.
1728	mulatto or negro slaves.
1750	Indian, negro or mulatto servants or slaves.

1766   Indian slaves [reprint of 1715].
1770   free negroes and mulattoes.
1784   negroes, mulattoes, and others [freed].[98]

In New Hampshire:

1714   Indian, negro, or molatto servant or slave;
        Indian slaves.
1718   Indian or negro servant.[99]

Pennsylvania records list:

1700   servants or negroes, etc., Indian slaves [not to be imported after 1706].
1711   Indians and negroes [prohibitory duty on].
1721   Indian and negro slaves or servants.
1725   Free negroes [idle people]; no free negro or mulatto to entertain any negro, Indian or mulatto slave.
1738   [Philadelphia]: negroes, mulattoes and Indian servants and slaves.
1780   negroes and mulattoes [and] others; negro and mulatto; thereafter only negro and mulatto appear.

Finally, there are a couple of references from Kentucky:

1798   negro, or mulatto, or Indian, bond or free [cannot strike a white].
1799   negroes, mulattoes, and Indians [cannot serve in militia].

and Indiana:

1817   No negro, mulatto, or Indian [can be a witness in white cases.][100]

The above examples are duplicated by ones from others states, and together they should illustrate the thesis that the term 'mulatto' can only be interpreted as referring to mixed persons with Native American ancestry being a potential part of the mixture, especially during the periods when Indians are identified as being servants or slaves alongside of Africans. It is apparent that no other terms, such as 'half-breed' or 'mustee', are utilized. 'Mulatto' is, therefore, the only legal referent to racially mixed persons of whatever background.

At this point, it would be well to note other evidence showing that the mixed African–American people in Massachusetts (a rather numerous group) were consistently referred to as 'mulattoes' (or as people of color). Paul Cuffe, the noted half-Indian, half-Black mariner and merchant, referred to himself and his relations in petitions as: of 'our Colour', 'Indian men', 'Indian men', and 'all free Negroes and molattoes'.

Similarly, Crispus Attucks who died in the Boston Massacre was of Native American extraction but called a mulatto. 'He is usually described as a mulatto, but it seems probably that he was a Natick Indian from Framingham who was also of Negro blood.'[101]

An 1847 report stated that most of the Indians in Massachusetts 'are of mixed blood; mostly Indian and African'. Throughout the eighteenth and nineteenth centuries Massachusetts reports make reference to three classes of people in Indian communities: Indians, mulattoes, and Negroes (or later, Indians and people of color). A 1767 report stated that at Mashpee there were various 'wigwams' and 'shingled houses' belonging to and inhabited by 'Indians and mulattoes'. It would seem that the term 'mulatto' was used for white–Indian mixed-bloods as well as for African–Indian hybrids. An 1802 report notes that 'the inhabitants of Marshpee are denominated Indians, but very few of the pure race are left. There are negroes, mulattoes, and Germans.' The 1808 census counted 357 'Indians, negroes and mulattoes' there.[102]

Now we should look at the colonies using the term 'mustee' in official statutes, since they present a slightly more complex problem. In essence, four racial terms (Indian, Negro, Mulatto, Mustee) are used in situations where six groups existed (Africans, Americans, American–Africans, American–Europeans, European–Africans, European–African–Americans). The problem, then, is to decide which of the four mixed groups are represented under which of the two terms available for mixed people. As noted earlier, the meaning of the term 'mustee' will be analyzed separately but my interpretation is, in essence, that mulatto means primarily African–European or European–American and mustee primarily African–American. (But by the 1790s mustee also refers to an African–European–American hybrid of a 'yellowish' or light character.)

South Carolina uses the following terms:

1690 negro or Indian slaves.

1703 [duties on] negro slaves imported and Indian slaves exported.

1712 An Act for the better ordering . . . of negroes and slaves refers first to negroes and other slaves and then repeatedly to 'negroes, mulattoes, mestizoes, and Indians' [all of whom have been sold are slaves]; any negro or Indian slave, or any other slave [can be baptized but is not free].

1716 [Only white men and no other can vote].

1718 [will] all my slaves, whether Negroes, Indians, mustees, or Molattoes.

1719 [For tax purposes] all mustees and mulattoes [slaves who are not pure Indian] are to be counted as negroes.

1720 such negroes, mulattoes, mustees, and Indian slaves [for militia service].

1722 any negro, mulatto, mustee or Indian slave (repeat of 1712);
Spanish Indians, mustees, negroes and mulattoes.

1735 said negro or Indian, mulatto or mestizo;
any negro, mulatto, mustee or Indians.

1740 All negros, Indians [free Indians in amity . . . , and negroes, mulattoes or mestizoes who are now free, excepted], mulattoes, or mestizoes . . . and all their issue . . . are . . . absolute slaves, and shall follow the condition of the mother; every negro, Indian, mulatto, and mestizo is a slave unless the contrary can be made to appear . . . (but) Indians in amity . . . expected.

1741   [Spanish force includes 800 men, whites, mustees and negroes, and 200 Indians; refers to 1706 event].

1751   [Treaty with Cherokee Nation] If any Negro or Mulatto shall desert . . . the Indians shall . . . apprehend him . . . and no Trader shall carry into the Indian Country any Negro or other slave.

1768   [Battle fought in SC with] a numerous collection of outcast mulattoes, mustees, and free negroes.

1784   [Charleston swarms with] blacks, mulattoes and mestizos. . . . there are here many free negroes and mulattoes.

1789   [Tax imposed on all] negroes, mustizos, and mulattoes.

1792   slaves or negroes, mulattoes, Indians, Moors, or mestizoes bound for a term of years [entry prohibited].

1800   [Unlawful for any] free negro, mulatto, or mestizo [to enter]; [also applies to] other persons of color.

1922   [Unlawful for whites to marry] an Indian, Negro, Mulatto, Mestizo, or half-breed.[103]

It is quite clear that the 'mestizo' class remained legally significant in South Carolina for a considerable period, while the pure Indian group is treated somewhat separately after about 1750 when the colonial authorities began to see the Creeks, Cherokees, and so on, as important pawns in the political-economic struggle with Virginia, the French, and the 'Northern' (pro-French) tribes. Likewise, most 'settlement Indians' were by then viewed as useful allies and/or as having become mestizos or mulattoes.

North Carolina records have the following:

1669   [Taxable are] every white male, aged 16; and every slave, negro, mulatto or Indian . . . age 12.

1705   Negro Indyan and Mallotta slaves [sold in Chowan County].

1715   [fine for a white person marrying] negroes, mulattoes, or Indians.

1723   [Act for added tax on all] free negroes, mulattos, mustees, and such persons . . . as now or hereafter shall be intermarried with any such persons.

1741   [Fine for a white person marrying] an Indian, Negro, Mustee, or Mulatto . . . or any person of mixed Blood to the Third Generation, bond or free.
        negro, mulatto or Indian slaves [cannot be freed];
        negroes, mulattoes, bond and free to the third generation, and Indian servants and slaves [cannot testify in white cases].

1750   Every negro, mulatto or mustee, and every other person of mixed blood to the fourth generation, 12 years of age [is tithable]; [earlier act referred to every slave, negro, mulatto, or Indian, male or female, age 12].[104]

1777   'Indians, negroes, etc.' [cannot be witnesses in white cases].

1826   All free mulattoes descended from negro ancestors to the fourth generation inclusive . . . shall be deemed free persons, and persons of mixed blood.

1835 [At State Constitutional Convention one delegate proposed]: that no free negro, mulatto, or person of mixed blood [can vote if convicted of a serious crime or unless he has $500 worth of property; defeated 64–65, thus leaving vote only to free white males].

1838 a free negro, or free person of color to the third generation [cannot marry a white].

In New York:

1684 Indians and Negros [as slaves];
Negros and Indians (as slaves).

1688 Negros and Indians.

1702 [tax on] every Negro or Indian slave [imported];
Negro or Indian slave [suppression of evidence];
Indian and negroes;
negroes and Indians.

1706 [to encourage baptism of] negroe, Indian and mulatto slaves;
All and every negro, Indian, mulatto and mestee bastard child . . . who . . . shall be born of any negro, Indian, mulatto, or mestee, shall follow ye state and Condition of the Mother and be esteemed . . . a slave.

1708 Negro, Indian and other slaves.

1712 No negro, Indian or mulatto hereafter made free shall enjoy . . . any houses, lands, tenements . . . within the colony.

1717 Negroe, Indian, or Malatto slave (several times).

1741 Spanish Negroes, Negro and other slaves (in slave insurrection).

1768 No squaw Mustee or mulatto female shall . . . have any house or cellar, or wigwam (in Smithtown, NY).

1788 Every negro, mulatto, or mestee . . . who . . . is a slave . . . shall continue as such . . . (but) the children of every negro, mulatto, or mestee woman, being a slave, shall follow the . . . condition of the mother.

1806 'people of color' means mulattoes, mustees, costees, etc., all colors from black to white.

1811 [Certificate of freedom needed by] blacks or mulattoes [seeking to vote].

1814 men of color; free blacks.

1817 Every negro, mulatto, or mustee [shall be free by 1827 if born before 1799].

1824 No negro or mulatto [shall vote in the councils of the Stockbridge Indians].

1827 [an act against kidnapping persons] other than negroes, mulattoes, or mustees.[105]

And finally in New Jersey:

1694 negroes and other slaves; negroes and Indians.

1702 [Baptism gives no freedom to] any negro, Indian or mulatto slave.

1713 Indian, negro or mulatto slaves.

1739 [Duty proposed on] Indian, Negroe and Mollatto slaves imported.

1751   servants, negroes and mulatto slaves.
1769   [Duty levied on] all negro, Indian or mulatto slaves [except from other colonies].
1798   that every negro, Indian, mulatto or mustee [is still a slave if had been one];

  free negroes;

  negro, mulatto, mestee, or Indian.[106]

(The term 'mustee' seems to have been introduced very late into New Jersey in spite of much evidence of Indian slavery in the colony.)

Finally, we may note that the federal act of 1807 prohibiting the general importation of slaves refers repeatedly to 'any negro, mulatto, or person of color'. Are we to believe that slaves of Native American ancestry could still be legally imported from Spanish Florida or Texas perhaps? In any case, African–American persons must have been covered by the act.[107]

There are also many descriptions of 'mulattoes' found in court cases and runaway slave advertisements which attest to Indian-looking persons being regarded as mulattoes or to Indian features being within the range of characteristics ascribed to mulattoes. A few examples should suffice: First, a man named Robbins was denied the right to vote in North Carolina. In the 1856 court case it was noted that 'his father was a dark colored man with straight hair, and that his grandfather was a dark red-faced mulatto, with dark straight hair'. In a Kentucky case in 1848 it was alleged that a girl's mother was Jin, 'a mulatto woman and a slave'. Others said Jin was a free Indian woman. The girl, Rose Landerdale, was very white looking and 'has more or less Indian blood in her'. There was strong evidence that she was 'a bound or indented Indian girl, to be free at the age of 18 or 21'.

In the case of *Gobu v. Gobu* (North Carolina) a person secured his freedom because of possible Indian ancestry. As an infant he had been found in a barn. He was later described as being 'of an olive color, between black and yellow, had long hair, and a prominent nose. . . . such persons may have descended from Indians in both lines; or at least in the maternal; they may have descended from a white person in the maternal line or from mulatto parents originally free.' In 1768 in New Jersey an advertisement was placed for 'a molatto man, named Samuel Wright' born near Hampton, Virginia. He had 'bushy' hair and was 'rather red'. Finally, in 1890, Bret Harte summed up things well when he said that Boone Culpepper's wife was 'variosly believed to be a gypsy, a Mexican, a bright mulatto, a Digger Indian'.[108]

Many other examples could be cited of a similar nature.

IMPLICATIONS OF THE MEANING OF 'MULATTO'

In 1793 a prominent Cherokee leader, Little Turkey, declared that the Spaniards were not 'real white people, and what few I have seen of them looked like mulattoes, and I would never have anything to say to them'.[109] This statement, designed to please Anglo–Saxon ears, is perplexing only if we conceive of the term 'mulatto' as referring to a narrow mixture of Black African and European Caucasian. The 'Spaniards' of Florida and Louisiana were, of course, largely mixed with Arawak–Carib and North American native ancestry, as well as with Black African and North African.

What conclusions can we arrive at, after reviewing the various types of evidence discussed?

First, we have found that no term was available to the English to refer to people of mixed race or intermediate ('mongrel') appearance from the sixteenth century until the eighteenth century except for mulatto. The term 'half-breed' seems to appear by 1751 in South Carolina (but is used primarily for European–American hybrids living in Native-controlled areas).[110] The term 'people of color' appears by 1777 in North Carolina and by 1800 in South Carolina. It is, however, primarily popularized by Federal use in the census of 1800 and adopted gradually in the statutes of most states in the next two or three decades.[111]

'Mustee' is used by 1712 in South Carolina but its use tends to be restricted to a few colonies only on the mainland, although it was also adopted in Jamaica and Trinidad. As noted, dictionaries do not cite 'mestizo' until 1757.

In the formative period of interracial contact, from the 1590s through *c.*1700–50, the term 'mulatto' must generally refer to any type of mixed-blood, as is corroborated by the Virginia legislation of 1705. Still further, 'mulatto' remains the only term commonly used for mixed-bloods in Virginia, Maryland, Delaware and all of the New England colonies. Not enough evidence is available for Pennsylvania, while in New Jersey 'mulatto' is always the primary term used, 'mustee' being rare.

Although many early dictionaries specify that 'mulatto' refers to a half-African person, enough evidence has been assembled to show that the word was used also for mixed-bloods (or even Native Americans) who had no African ancestry.

In general, the term seems to be best translated as 'mixed', although at times 'a brown-colored person' might be a more apt rendering.

We can be certain, I believe, that most American–African hybrids were called mulattoes (until being called 'colored' or even 'negro' at a later date.) We can also, I think, be certain that European–American and European–American–African hybrids were also called 'mulattoes', except (and as above also) where the term 'mustee' was in common use.

It would seem that those many students of North American history and society who have been fascinated solely with the Black–White nexus or who have conceived of Black and Native American history as being two largely separate streams are going to have to re-examine their assumptions. This will have great implications for the study of the diffusion of central traits in areas as diverse as folk-tales, music, social structure, folk language and religion. Especially important will be the construction of the basic 'plantation' and 'free non-white' cultures, both in North America and around the Caribbean, into which all later slaves and free people became subsequently immersed.

We must also re-examine the myth of the 'lusty' white men who produced an entire race of 'mulattoes', the image so exuberantly portrayed by several writers. It must be kept in mind that the early documented cases of white parentage run into the dozens, or hundreds at the most, in any given colony, while the numbers of Indians forcibly merged into the slave population in South Carolina alone seems to exceed the total of white parentage cases for *all* of the colonies. Admittedly there is a great deal of hearsay, sometimes inflammatory, evidence relating to the sexually active white planter and overseer, but hearsay evidence must, in the end, give way before concrete empirical data.

The 'free colored' population before the Revolutionary War developed largely by the natural growth of a people descended from parents and especially mothers who were born free and not from manumissions.[112] These free mothers were ordinarily, therefore, of European, Native American, or mixed ancestry.

It would seem clear that the entire conception of the origin of non-African ancestry within the United States' Afroamerican population requires rigorous re-examination. In 1712 John Norris provided advice to prospective planters: he told them to buy fifteen Negro men and eighteen Indian women, or, if they were starting out small, 'a good Negro man' and 'a good Indian woman'.[113] The implications of such evidence must now, at last, be taken to heart.

Finally, a new look needs to be taken at the many surviving Native American communities, primarily along the east coast, who have been denied recognition because of being classified in the past as mulattoes or people of color. Needless to state, the presence of African ancestry should be no bar to state and federal recognition as Indians but, in addition, the use of the terms analyzed herein provides no evidence, in and of itself, of specific African descent. That racial mixture has occurred is obvious but its significance for ethnic and cultural self-definition is a quite separate matter.

8
Mustees, Half-Breeds and Zambos

I have earlier introduced evidence relating to the terms 'mestizo', 'mustee', and 'zambo', but it is still necessary to explore these concepts in greater depth, since all have direct relevance to the classification of people of American and African ethnic backgrounds in Anglo-North America and the Caribbean.

THE TERM 'MUSTEE'

The forms 'mustee', 'mestizo', and 'mestee' were used commonly in the South Carolina region, in New York, and also in such British Caribbean colonies as Jamaica and Trinidad and in India. They clearly are derived from Spanish *mestizo* and Old French *mestis* (now *métis*).[1] The term means 'mixed' but came, in Spanish America, to refer most commonly to persons of European and American ancestry, as opposed to part-Africans.

Historians of North America have not been in agreement as to the meaning of the term in the English colonies. Peter H. Wood (in *Black Majority*) states that 'the term . . . came to be used in South Carolina to distinguish those who were part Indian, and the remainder of their ancestry was often African.' Winthrop D. Jordan, in an article about mulattoes, said: 'the term mustee . . . was used to describe a mixture which was in part Indian, usually Indian–Negro but occasionally Indian–white. The term was in common use only in the Carolinas, Georgia and to some extent New York.' The meaning is narrowed to a very precise one by Joel Williamson (1980) who states: 'there was also miscegenation between American Indians and Negroes. Offspring of such unions were usually called "mustees".'[2]

From the 1560s onward, and especially after the 1620s, the English came into frequent contact with Spanish-speaking mixed-bloods, many of whom were associated with the crews of ships raiding Spanish fleets and who were later captured and enslaved. In securing slaves the English seem to have been quite willing to abduct Spanish-speaking, Christianized persons, whether of

American, African, or part-European ancestry. In 1682, for example, the governor of Spanish Florida wrote that the English of South Carolina were capturing Native Americans to sell as slaves 'as they have done with many, carrying them to the island of Barbado; they also capture the mestizos, born of Spaniards and Indians.'[3]

We must assume, because of the enslavement of mestizos who were Spanish-speaking and because of the extensive contact of the English of the Caribbean and Carolina with Spanish culture, that the term was, initially at least, taken over into English with its ordinary Spanish meaning. The problem is that early Spanish (and European Spanish generally) used the term *mestizo* in a very general way. This is reflected in Minsheu's English–Spanish dictionary of 1599 where *mestizo* is defined as referring to a mixed-blood or a 'mungrill'. The one example given by Minsheu was of the mixture of 'a blacke-Moore and a Christian'. This approach was repeated in 1617 and 1623.

Nonetheless, in the Americas after the middle of the sixteenth century *mestizo* was usually used in Spanish for an American–European mixed-blood. This usage is reflected in the first appearance of 'mestizo' in a monolingual English dictionary, that of James Buchanan in 1757. He states that it was derived from Spanish and meant 'the breed of Spaniards with Americans'.[4]

Other eighteenth-century dictionaries do not include either mestizo or mustee, among them editions of Samuel Johnson's work through 1785. The 1828 edition of Noah Webster's dictionary has no entry for mestizo but 'mustee, mestee' does appear and is defined as 'A person of mixed breed' as used in the West Indies. A sharp change occurs between that date and 1848 when John Russell Bartlett has 'Mestee: In the West Indies, the child of a white person and a quadroon.' For 'Mustee ' he directs the reader to proceed to 'mulatto' and gives the origin as French *Métis* and Spanish *Mestizo*. Under 'mulatto' we find *mustafina*, child of a white and a mustee and under 'Negro' we find *Metif* as a mixture of white and 'quarteron' with a Louisiana derivation.[5]

John Ogilvie's dictionary (1885 edition) has 'Mestee, see Mestizo. The offspring of a white and a quadroon (West Indies).' The term 'Mustee' is treated as the same. Under 'Mestizo, Mestino' we find 'the offspring of a Spaniard or Creole and an American Indian'. John Farmer (1889) tells us under 'Mustee' to see 'Mulatto'. There we find that 'Metis or metif' is the child of a white and quarteron, in a list clearly derived from Bartlett or some Louisiana source. The *Oxford English Dictionary* (1933) has: 'Mustee, mestee, corrupt, Mestizo' and 'the offspring of a white and a quadroon; also, loosely, a half-caste'.[6]

From other evidence, which I will cite later, it seems clear that the terms under review went through several changes of meaning which the above dictionary definitions do not completely clarify. Therefore, I will proceed to non-dictionary definitions to round out the picture.

A 1712 English traveler defines 'the Mustees, begot by Spaniards on Indian women'.[7]

In 1715 North Carolina adopted a law on marriage, re-enacted in 1741. This act fined any white person who should marry 'an Indian, Negro, Mustee or Mulatto . . . or any person of mixed bood to the Third Generation, bond or free'. In 1852 the North Carolina Supreme Court dealt with a case where one Melton, 'of Indian descent' (to an unknown degree) had been charged with illegally marrying a white woman. This charge was made under acts of 1836 and 1838 which essentially re-enacted the prohibitions of 1715 and 1741. The court held:

> . . . it cannot be supposed it was the intention of the Legislature to forbid marriages between white persons and persons of Indian blood, howsoever far removed. . . . they must have meant that the offense . . . should be a marriage within the degrees specified in the Act of 1836. [This was "any person of mixed-blood to the third generation".][8]

It seems possible that the term 'mustee' as used in the original acts could be interpreted as referring to American–European hybrids.

In 1717 South Carolinians purchased a 'Mustee Boy' at the Cherokee Factory and brought him down 'from thence among the Indian slaves in June last'. He was to serve for a term of nineteen years and 'that the said boy shall not be exported or carried off or shipped from this province, during that term'. He was also to become a Christian and learn a trade. The group in question, of 'Indian slaves and Charikee Burdens', came down from 'Savano Town'. Thus it seems quite probable that this youth was of European–American descent, both because of place of origin and because he was being treated as a servant for a term. An American–African hybrid would probably have been treated as a simple slave.[9]

In 1719 South Carolina imposed a lesser tax on Indian slaves than on others. The act also stated: 'And for preventing all doubts and scruples that may arise what ought to be rated on mustees, mulattoes, etc., all such slaves as are not entirely Indian shall be accounted as negroe.'[10] From this we know that both mustees and mulattoes were part-American (or could be). It is necessary to stress that 'mulatto' was sometimes used for American–European hybrids, as discussed earlier with examples from Virginia and South Carolina. It was sometimes necessary to use the phrase 'mulatto or mustee' in areas (such as Virginia and Massachusetts) where the latter term was perhaps little understood. For example: in 1706 a girl in Accomack County, Virginia was called a 'molatta or mustee' but because an Indian came to her financial assistance it seems clear that she was half-Indian.[11] Similarly, the *Boston Evening Post* in 1763 carried an advertisement for a runaway who was 'a Molatta or Mustee Servant, of about 24 years of age . . . and was a soldier last summer'.[12] In 1715 an English missionary baptized a 'mulatto' girl in South Carolina whose parents he reported as being Indian and white.[13]

In 1722 South Carolina passed an act which noted that 'the importation of Spanish Indians, mustees, negroes and mulattoes may be of dangerous consequence.' Given the fact that this has specific reference to Spanish Florida or other Spanish areas, the term 'mustee' could be interpreted as being the same as Spanish *mestizo*.[14]

From 1717 through 1721 Hugh Jones resided in Virginia. After returning to England he wrote a book (published 1724) which states: 'such as are born of a Negroe and a European are called Molattoes; but such as are born of an Indian and Negroe are called Mustees'.[15] This would seem to contradict actual practice in Virginia where all half-Americans (whether of half-European or half-African mixture) were legally classed as mulattoes by 1705. Still further, the term 'mustee' is almost never used in Virginia records.[16]

In 1750 North Carolina decided that all white males, age 16 or more, and 'every negro, mulatto, or mustee, and every other person of mixed blood to the fourth generation, 12 years of age' should pay tithes. This replaced a 1669 act which had made white males tithable if age 16 and upwards, and every slave, 'negro, mulatto, or Indian, male or female, age 22'.[17]

It would seem quite clear that the term 'mulatto' as used in 1669 covered African–American mixed-bloods since it would have been absurd to have exempted them from tax. From this one can reason that the addition of 'mustee' and 'of mixed blood' in the 1750 act was designed to specifically encompass American–European hybrids. It is also likely that only 'Indians' living in Native-controlled areas or on reservations were exempted in 1750 and that non-reservation Indians were considered to be 'mustees' and tithable. (It may be, however, that between 1669 and 1750 many African–American mixed-bloods had been born and that these are the people called mustees).

In 1751–3 the governor of South Carolina reported that 'under cover of the Name of Senecas, Nittewegas, frequently come into our Settlements . . . carrying off some of our Settlement Indians, People born among us, and who are not at War with any Nation whatever, and such of our slaves as had the least tincture of Indian blood in them.' In a separate letter he notes that six Savannahs (Shawnees) had been captured. He thinks that: 'they have carried off some of our friendly Indians . . . and [I] have sent two of the six prisoners to you to be sent, or detained by you as you may judge it most likely to obtain the good end of having our friendly Indians or Mustee slaves sent back.'[18] Perhaps one should not make too much of this, but it could be argued that the term 'mustee' was beginning to be used for any part-American person by the 1750s.

In 1777 De Menonville utilized the term *métis* to refer to the 'mixed-breeds' of the Spanish Empire from Panama to Mexico (but he uses 'mulatto' when referring to Cuba).[19] In this case French *métis* stands for Spanish *mestizo*.

More significantly, in 1777 the very careful observer William Bartram uses 'mustee' to refer to a young Creek man of three-quarters Indian and one-quarter European ancestry. Bartram, who had spent many years in North Carolina and along the St John's River, journeyed throughout the southern region in 1773–7. From Mobile he was guided by the young man, 'a Mustee Creek, his mother being a Chactaw slave [among the Creeks], and his father a halfbreed, betwixt a Creek and a white man'. This young man, called 'the Indian' as well as 'the young Mustee' had 'Chactaw blood in his veins from his mother . . . and by his father had been instructed in reading, writing and arithmetic, and could speak English very well.' The young man had traveled to the Choctaws pretending to be a white trader but his hosts discovered that his father was a Creek and tried to kill him. He, however, had escaped to Mobile.[20]

Clearly, then, a very well-informed person was using 'mustee' to refer to European–American mixed-bloods as late as the Revolutionary War period. There is no indication that the Choctaw mother possessed any African ancestry.

In 1781–96 there are three references to the colors of 'mustees' which tend strongly to support the above usage. First, there is a reference (from India) to 'a slave boy, pretty white or colour of Musty'. Second, a reference to Sumatrans being lighter than 'the Mustees or halfbreed, of the rest of India'. Thirdly, from Surinam, 'the Samboe dark, and the Mulatto brown, the Maesti fair'.[21]

It may be, however, that usage in the Caribbean and East Indies, where 'mustee' pointed towards a very light color, was not especially typical of the South Carolina area. The term 'mustee' appears frequently in advertisements for runaway slaves in that province from at least 1733 through the 1790s while 'mestizo' or 'mustizo' appears from 1760 through 1784 although with less frequency. I cannot discover any difference in usage between the two forms, although such a difference is possible.

As has been noted, the terms 'mulatto' and 'mustee' could both be used in South Carolina for half-American persons. In 1771, for example, reference was made to 'a young mulatto or mustee wench, named Mary . . . enticed away by her mother, an Indian wench, named Sarah'. We also read in 1753 of 'a mullatto girl (of the Indian breed) named Nancy [with] . . . long black hair'. In 1773 reference was made to 'a Mulatto or half Indian man, named Frank' and in 1780 an advertisement was placed for 'A likely mustee woman named Isabella [age 26]. . . . She was with her two children, the eldest a mulatto boy named Jack, about 6 years old, the other a girl about three months. She [Isabella] wears her hair very long. . . . She may endeavor to pass for a free woman.' From the above we may infer that 'mulatto' was definitely used for half-American persons and, looking at the evidence as a whole, we can suggest that such persons were either of European–American ancestry or that they tended to show little if any African features. Thus the child of a mustee could be a mulatto, as above.

Isabella, with long hair, seems to have leaned in the American direction. This is also the case with other persons classed as mustees or mestizos in South Carolina advertisements. I will list some examples:

1733 'a Mustee Wench, that may be taken for an Indian. . . . and may be taken to be a French Wench.'
1734 'a Mustee Woman, named Sue, with long black hair'.
1743 'two Mustee Fellows, one called Tom . . . about six Feet nine Inches high; the other call'd Billey . . . and more of an Indian Colour than the former. . . . speaks tolerable good English.' [Their mother was American.]
1744 'a Mustee Fellow named Johny . . . with a Roman nose'.

1747 'a . . . slim Mustee Fellow, named Mingo'. [*Mingo* may be the Choctaw word for headman.]
1759 'a Mustee Fellow named Toney, has much the appearance of an Indian both in his hair and complexion'.
1764 'a Mulatto or Mustee Slave, called Tony, . . . with long stiff black hair, and greatly the Looks and Colour of an Indian'.
1769 a 'Mustizo (or rather Indian breed)'.

But not all of the mustees were persons of American appearance. Many clearly possessed African ancestry or were children of one known African parent.

1743 'A Mustee Fellow named Nedd . . . short curl'd Hair, but not woolly, thick lip'd, small eyes'.
1756 'Peter, a Mustee . . . with black curl'd hair' [listed among 'the following negroes'].
1759 'a Negro woman named HAGAR, with her child Fanny, a Mustee'.
1767 'a black mustee fellow, named CUPID . . . has a very thick head of hair'.
1768 'A MUSTEE FELLOW called Jacob . . . has a bushy head and round visage'.
1772 a 'slim Negro Wench, named CATHARINA . . . and carried away with her a Mustee Child (her Daughter) about Six Years old'.
1774 Frank, 'of a yellowish or mustee complexion, . . . would feign dress, the wool of his head in the maccaroni taste, the which being that of a mustee, he has teazed into side locks, and a queue, but when too lazy to comb, ties his head with a handkerchief.'
1775 'Jemmy, a Mustee Fellow . . . sharp visaged, not flat nosed, which shews the Indian blood more than the negro'.

In addition to the above, there are several mustees listed as negroes but who are otherwise undescribed. There are also three mustee men with African names (two named Cudjoe and one named Cuffee), suggesting an African parent or, at least, close association with Africans.

From the above we can assert that mustees could be half-African and that they could range in color from 'yellowish' to 'black'. We might conclude, therefore, that mustees as a group were variable in appearance, having in common some acknowledged degree of American ancestry. In 1738 we read of a 'Mustee Wench, named Diana, and a little Negro boy, named March', from which we might conclude that the child of a mustee and an African would be classed as negro.

In certain cases the advertiser was unsure of the exact background of the runaway slave. In 1749 we read of a 'slave between a mulatto and a mustee, named Peter. . . . 'tis supposed he will attempt to pass for a free man.'

It may well be that 'appearance' rather than precise ancestry was often pointed towards. In 1759 reference was made to 'March a mustee fellow . . . and Daphne his wife, a yellow wench'. In 1783 we read of 'a mustee man slave, born in Caracoa [Curaçao?]' who had been employed as a sailor in the West

Indies and who spoke 'all the languages used there'. In this case, he must have looked like a mustee since his exact parentage could hardly have been known in South Carolina.

In a similar vein are some slave advertisements of the 1790s from South Carolina: 'a Mustee Fellow named James . . . of a Yellow Complexion, bushy hair' and 'Bob, a carpenter Fellow, of a yellowish complexion, mustee, has bushy hair . . . and speaks rather more proper than Negroes in general. Dorcas, his wife, also has a Yellowish complexion, and bushy hair.' They also had two children, a girl Willoughby and an infant.

There is also one advertisement from Virginia which refers to a mustee of part-African background. In 1777 from Middlesex County there escaped 'a mustee complexioned man slave, named SAM. . . . Nature has furnished him with a covering for his head, which when grown out is thick and bushy. . . . He is, it is supposed, lurking about . . . in King & Queen County.' There were quite a few American people in the King and Queen County area, adjoining the Essex and Carolina boundaries, and it is possible that Sam was trying to join them.[22]

Taken together, we can say that 'mustee' was a term used for part-American persons (usually slaves) who were mixed with either European or African or both. In South Carolina, where the term was most common, 'mustee' seems to have come to refer to a person of yellow-brown or darker color who exhibited either American or part-African features, while 'mulatto' seems to have been used for lighter, part-European-looking mixed-bloods of American background.

By the 1770s–1790s, however, mustees seem to be usually described as being of a yellowish hue.

The term 'yellow person' needs also to be discussed briefly, because there was a tendency for Indian-derived groups in several areas to be so denominated (in a manner similar to Brazil, where *caboclo* reportedly means copper-colored, as well as among modern Chicanos, who on occasion use the phrase *raza de bronce* to refer to themselves). In Delaware, for example, the Nanticoke people were called 'yellow people' and the mixed-Indians of South Carolina have also been called thus in modern times.[23]

There are many advertisements and court records referring to 'Yellow people', as in New Jersey in 1769 when 'an indented servant man, who calls himself William Kelly' ran away. He was 'a yellow fellow, part Indian, and part Negroe'. Also, Ben 'a yellowish Negro . . . bushy hair' and Jack 'also yellowish' – both spoke Dutch and English. Also, Ben a Negro of Newark, of 'a yellow cast' and, in 1768, Samuel Wright 'a molatto man . . . bushy hair . . . and rather red'. None of these persons are called mustees (perhaps because the term was rarely used in New Jersey).

Many runaway slaves in South Carolina were described as of yellow color. It would seem that yellow-brown as well as lighter shades could be so denominated, since in 1771 we read of a 'well made fellow, of the Guinea country, yellow complexion.'[24]

In 1820 an exploring expedition met a group of Cherokees at Rocky Bayou who were led by 'a Metiff chief known as Tom Graves, and his wife of aboriginal race'. They had 'several slaves of African descent'. 'Metiff' is a variation of _métis_.[25]

In any case, it would appear that the term 'mustee' began to go through a gradual change in meaning during the eighteenth century, doubtless due to the fact that slaves of European–American ancestry were intermarrying extensively with slaves of African ancestry (in whole or part). Also, as slaves, these mustees began to be considered to be 'negroes' since 'negro' was becoming practically synonymous with 'slave'. In 1759 one Saunders, a runaway, was described as 'a Carolina born Negro man . . . of the Mustee breed' and in 1775: 'You are hereby ordered . . . to apprehend . . . John Swan, a reputed free negro or mestizo man.'[26]

In South Carolina there are various late eighteenth-century references to 'mustees' or 'mestizos': in 1768 a battle was fought with a group of 'outcast mulattoes, mustees, and free negroes'; in 1784 Charleston 'Swarms with blacks, mulattoes and mestizos', in 1789 South Carolina imposed a tax per head on all 'negroes, mustizos, and mulattoes'; and in 1792 the same state moved to prohibit 'bringing in slaves or negroes, mulattoes, Indians, Moors, or mestizoes bound for a term of years'[27]

During the nineteenth century the South Carolina courts had to clarify the meaning of 'mustee' in a series of cases involving persons of Native American ancestry. In essence, cases began to arise where such persons sought relief from burdens placed on all non-whites (such as being tried by special courts without a jury and being subject to a special capitation tax) or from slavery itself. The basic law remained the Act of 1740 which stated that 'every negro, Indian, mulatto, and mestizo is a slave unless the contrary can be made to appear' but 'Indians in amity with his government' were excepted, in which case 'the burden of proof shall lie on the defendant' charged with seeking to hold such a person in slavery. The act had recognized the existence of 'free Indians in amity . . . and negroes, mulattoes, or mestizoes who are now free', but, clearly, it was quite easy to enslave such persons. In the case of Indians or mustees, for example, many tribes had been at war when their members were enslaved but were at peace in 1740. What was their status under the act?[28]

Even more difficulty can be envisioned for persons of Indian descent whose tribal origins had been in a remote period or whose tribe no longer existed. Those tens of thousands who had been shipped to Barbados and other colonies were, of course, utterly helpless unless by chance they were returned to South Carolina.

In any case, a certain liberality reached the South Carolina Supreme Court in the early part of the nineteenth century and the 'Indians in amity' clause was interpreted favorably in several cases, such as _Adam Garden v. Justices_ (1814). The plaintiff sought to be removed from the magistrates court's jurisdiction on the grounds that he was not a slave but descended from 'a free Indian woman in amity'. It was argued that 'Adam was born a slave . . . of an Indian woman' who was also 'owned'. He had brothers and sisters in slavery. In 1795 he was sold and Adam and his mother agreed to refund the purchase price to secure freedom. This was done but in 1799 the sheriff sought to collect the capitation tax and Adam had to pay, although he had petitioned to be exempt.

One witness said: 'Indians were permitted to remain on plantations, and were considered free. . . . an old woman . . . made an affadavit . . . that . . . she knew Adam, the son of Flora . . . , daughter of Rachel, a free born Indian woman . . . brought into this State by – Superintendent of Indian Affairs, who . . . bought her from an Indian nation.' The justices found Adam 'to be of free Indian descent, and declined to take cognizance of his offence'.[29]

There is no mention of any African ancestry in this case. It should also be noted that no solid proof was given that Rachel was derived from a nation in amity with South Carolina.

In an 1817 case a family sought exemption from the capitation tax on the grounds that they were from Santo Domingo (Haiti) and were of East Indian and white ancestry. The tax ordinance stated 'that . . . every other free . . . person of colour, whether a descendent of an Indian or otherwise' should have to pay. The court held that:

the word Indian means unquestionably slave Indians, for it is a fact . . . well known, that the Indians of the Country were formerly made slaves, it cannot, then, be extended to the descendents of an East Indian and a white man, nor indeed to the descendents of any other free Indian not impregnated with the blood of the negro.[30]

Thus we see that the class of Indians mixed only with whites or of pure Indian descent was by 1817 to be differentiated from persons of mixed Native and African ancestry. This was, of course, a radical departure from the Act of 1740 and from many other early statutes, but was perhaps made politically necessary by successful white people having some degree of American ancestry.

In any case, the above trend was carried further in 1836–8 when Charlotte Miller 'the descendent of an Indian woman living in Charlotte [?] about fifty years ago' was to be tried by the non-white court under the Act of 1740. The court decided unanimously that the words 'free Indians in amity . . . mean Indians domiciled in this State, although disconnected with any tribe.' Charlotte Miller, therefore, could not be tried under the Act of 1740.

In 1838 in a related case it was said that Charlotte Miller's 'grandmother was an Indian woman, living in Charleston at least fifty years before trial – her mother was the child of a white man by that same Indian woman, and that she herself was the child of a white man.' The court held that 'the term "mustizo" used in the Act of 1740, signified the issue of a negro and an Indian.'[31]

Here we see that in order to maintain the notion that the Act of 1740 did not apply to American–European hybrids it was necessary to define 'mustizo' so as to have the latter refer to part-African persons.

A more conservative and anti-Indian trend appeared in the court by 1850 when a case arose because the testimony of Amelia Marchant was objected to on the grounds that she was a free colored person. It was testified that her grandparents were 'free Indians' but her father, James Mitchell 'was said to be Portuguese. . . . none of the family had ever paid a capitation tax'. Opposing testimony asserted that 'Mitchell . . . was considered a colored person. He served as a Pioneer in the Artillery, and associated with colored persons.' Another witness recalled that if Mitchell had 'been a mulatto, they would not have permitted Nancy [a white] to marry him'. A jury said that Amelia Marchant was a 'free person of color'.

On appeal it was argued that:

free Indians have been invariably tried by a judge and jury . . . "Indians in amity excepted" [Act of 1740] means all Indians not in hostility. But with many exceptions, as those of Indian slaves – Indians from time to time in hostility – or declared slaves, as the Yamasees were. . . . The whole State policy in making slaves of Indians, was temporary. . . . ought we . . . to hold in the category of slaves . . . the spare remnants of the red man?

Another judge disagreed, stating perhaps more accurately that: 'The colonists . . . seized and enslaved as many as they could take of the hostile tribes . . . The number . . . was very great; so that after supplying the wants of the colony, many were shipped to the West Indies.' He argued that 'Indians in amity' only applied to independent nations or tribes and not to other Americans. Still further, an earlier verdict that the defendants were 'of free Indian descent, unmixed with African blood' was reversed.[32]

The above case would seem to mean that 'mestizos' could be held to be covered by the various acts against other non-whites unless they could prove both freedom from African ancestry and descent from independent tribes in amity.

It is worth noting in passing that the above evidence tends strongly to show that South Carolina developed a racial caste system of the Caribbean (and Latin American) type, with many subtle gradations. This contradicts those scholars who have tried to argue that Anglo-North America tended everywhere to have only two free castes: white and black. If the latter did develop, it developed at a later date.

The term 'mestee' was used in New York colonial and state statutes in 1706 and 1788, while 'mustee' appeared in 1817 and 1827. No definitions have been found. Similarly in 1798 a New Jersey statute used 'mustee' without a definition.

Nonetheless, in 1768 a local ordinance was adopted as follows: 'No Squaw Mustee or Mulatto female shall . . . have any house or cellar, or wigwam, standing in the bounds of said Smithtown.' This would seem to imply that 'mustee' referred to an American–European mixed-blood since it would make no sense to exempt 'half-breeds' from such an ordinance (but, of course, 'mulatto' could have been intended to cover American–European mixed-bloods). Similarly, in 1832, it was reported in the US Congress that 'the people in the neighborhood of the Menomonee village [Wisconsin] . . . he denominated mustee French and pronounced incapable of self-government.'[33] Thus the term continued to refer to European–American hybrids, apparently, in the north.

A similar situation was presented by evidence from Iere (Trinidad) in the Caribbean where it was noted in 1838 that the Indians of that island were

fast merging on extinction – from no fault of the local government, nor from any disease: the births amongst the Indian woman exceed the deaths in the usual ratio; the fact is, that the Indian men . . . choose mates of other races, and the women do the same, hence out of every seven children born of an Indian mother during the last thirty years, there are scarcely two of pure blood . . . ; this will decrease their population; for those of the mixed race, whether they be Samboes (between Negroes and Indians), or Mustees (between European and Indians), or the countless castes that the admixture between the African, European, and Indian tribes produce, they are not the real aboriginal race, and leave the inactive community of Indians as soon as they reach the years of discretion.[34]

Thus the term 'mustee' retained the meaning of American–European in Iere.

Elsewhere in the Caribbean area the term under study seems to have diverged considerably in meaning from that of Trinidad and South Carolina, although further detailed research in parish registers may eventually clarify usage. In the latter part of the seventeenth century Wafer noted that 'where an European lies with an Indian woman, the child is always a *Mostese*, or Tawney, as is well known to all who have been in the West Indies, where there are *Mostesa's.*' This is quite different from what one finds in later definitions originating from the island of Jamaica where modern sources tend to equate 'mustee' with a person of one-eighth American and seven-eighths European ancestry (as noted earlier), in other words, a very light-skinned person who, doubtless, looked 'white'.

Before looking at the evidence, it should be noted that persons of American race, unmixed and mixed with Spanish or African, survived the British occupation of Jamaica in 1656. They formed a large part of the original free people of color on the island, since the British were forced to recognize their free status after a period of armed resistance. Subsequently, the British brought in large numbers of additional Americans as slaves and servants, the greater part from Central America (but probably many also from South Carolina, Virginia and New England). For example, in the decade after 1712 the British purchased more than 2,000 Catholic Indian and *mestizo* slaves from the Miskito Indians of Nicaragua and others were purchased from Indians in Darién (Panama). In the period 1674–1701 fifty-one out of 600 estates in Jamaica included Indian servants or slaves. American slaves were also taken from Jamaica to New York and Virginia in the eighteenth century.

Charles H. Wesley in a 1932 article noted that: 'A Parish Register of Kingston referred to the persons baptized as blacks or Negro, Sambo, quadroon, mustee, brown, persons of color, and Indian'.[35] In 1774 Edward Long reported that 'the inhabitants of [Jamaica] . . . may be distinguished under the following classes: Creoles, or natives; whites, Blacks, Indians, and their varieties.' Thus, it is clear that through the end of the eighteenth century there were enough people of American descent in Jamaica to doubtless require the use of special terms (mustee, sambo, etc.) for part-American mixed-bloods.

Long gives us the following relevant definitions: the child of a 'negro' and a 'mulatta' is a 'sambo de mulatta'; the child of an Indian and a 'mulatta' is a 'Mestize'; the child of an Indian and a 'negro' is a 'Sambo de Indian'; the child of a 'Sambo de Indian' and a 'Sambo de Mulatta' is a 'Givero' (probably 'Jíbaro'), supposedly the worst type of mixed-blood. But then he goes on to state that 'these distinctions do not prevail in Jamaica' but are used by the Spaniards elsewhere. (It seems possible that Long simply borrowed all or part of these definitions from a book on Peru in English, published in 1748, in which it is also said that the 'Giveros' are the offspring of Sambo de Mulattos and Sambo de Indians.)[36]

Nonetheless, the concept of a 'mestize' being one-half American, one-fourth European, and one-fourth African was probably not borrowed from Spanish usage. It may reflect the fact that Americans in Jamaica were overwhelmingly mixing with people of African descent as opposed to Europeans.

Bryan Edwards, writing in 1787–92, offers a rather confusing picture. He states: 'I proceed now to persons of mixed blood (usually termed People of Colour). . . . all the different classes . . . are not easily discriminated. In the British West Indies they are commonly known by the names of Samboes, Mulattoes, Quadroons and Mestizos; but the Spaniards . . . have many other and nicer distinctions.' He then proceeds to give some Spanish terms of the same type as presented by Long and also by Bartlett and Farmer for Louisiana, probably derived from Cuba. He also quotes a Spaniard as saying: 'between the Mulatto and the Negro, there is an intermediate race, which they call Sambos, owing their origin to a mixture between one of those with an Indian, or among themselves.' Edwards also states: 'All . . . whether called in common parlance Mestizes, Quadroons, or Mulattoes, are deemed by law Mulattoes' in Jamaica.

Confusion enters because a footnote was added presumably by Edwards to the following effect:

A *Sambo* is the offspring of a Black woman by a Mulatto man or *vice versa*; *Mulatto*, of a Black woman by a white man. *Mestize* on Mustee of a Quadroon woman by a white man. The offspring of a Mestize by a white man are white by law. A Mestize therefore in our islands is, I suppose, the Quinteron of the Spaniards.[37]

My tentative explanation of the above is that the presence of the American race was unknown to Edwards and that he was, and perhaps other white people were, attempting to explain the meaning of terms such as 'mestizo' and 'zambo' solely on the basis of African–European mixtures. Two other pertinent factors need to be borne in mind: First, white people often do not actually know the correct ancestry of non-whites but simply make guesses (which doubtless are often very inaccurate); and, second, it may be that a person of one-eighth African ancestry, and seven-eighths European, was thought to resemble a 'mestizo' of American–European descent so closely that the two castes were confounded. Similarly, a three-fourths African, one-fourth European was called a 'Sambo' because he or she resembled a half-American, half-African (to whom the designation more traditionally applied). More likely, however, many of the 'mustees' and 'sambos' of *c.*1800 actually had some degree of American ancestry and it was simply too difficult to separate it out with appropriate terms.

Later in the nineteenth century Charles H. Eden noted that the 'people of colour' of Jamaica were placed into various subdivisions based upon the degree of European ancestry. After a brief listing of terms he states: 'it is not requisite to dwell upon this subject, although it is one of great importance in the eyes of the coloured population.'[38] Thus the non-African and non-European mixed population had internalized the racial-caste grading system and, according to Eden, regarded the various categories as being important. It may well be, however, that the system had become essentially an appearance-based color-ranking system and not a statement of precise ancestry. Thus a 'mustee' would *not* be a person of one-eighth African and seven-eighths European ancestry but rather 'the highest rank' among non-whites, that is, one who was known to have some non-white ancestry but who was, nonetheless, lighter-skinned or more European-looking than a 'quadroon' or a 'mulato', and so on.

I believe that this latter interpretation is the most likely, considering the 300 years of mixture between the 1500s and the 1800s. For our purposes, though, one thing remains apparently clear: 'mustee' or 'mestizo' seems always to have referred to a light-colored mixed-blood and never to an African–American hybrid without European ancestry.

In summary, the terms 'mustee' and 'mestizo' as used in the British Caribbean colonies would seem to always refer to American–European hybrids until perhaps the 1770s–1790s when mixed-bloods of a light color were also included, at least in some parts of the Caribbean. Thereafter usage becomes somewhat less certain, but it seems clear that the term continues to refer to a light-colored, part-American person or to one who resembles such an individual. The term may also be used in the East Indies to refer to a mixed-blood of European and Indian (or other non-European) ancestry.

We have seen no empirical evidence that 'mustee' was ever used simply to refer to any type of mixed-blood without regard to ancestry. The term 'mulatto' seems to have fulfilled that function for English-speakers until such descriptions as 'half-breed' and 'half-caste' came into vogue. These latter terms do not appear early enough to be of any significance for the formative period of race mixture in the Americas, but a brief review is in order to better clarify the use of 'mustee' and also 'mulatto'.

HALF-BREEDS, HALF-BLOODS AND HALF-CASTES

'Half-breed' (or 'half-bred') originally had nothing to do with race mixture. In 1701 one author used the phrase 'Half-bred and of the Mongrel Strain of mischief' but such a concept is not actually applied in North America until much later. No early dictionaries, including that of Noah Webster (1828), use it in a racial context. On the frontiers of South Carolina it begins to appear by 1751 as in a reference to Andrew White, a 'half-breed fellow' at Keawohee in the Cherokee nation. White had killed a European and helped six negroes to run away.[39]

In 1752 one Vann, in the Cherokee nation, had 'no less than three Negroes, one Mulatto, and a half-bred Indian now living with him. . . . the Mulatto is one of Scott's sons who escaped out of prison.' From 1754 to 1757 there are numerous references to 'halfbreeds', all living in the Cherokee, Catawba, Creek, Pedee, or Chicasaw nations. But one cannot be sure that all such persons were of American–European mixture. Bartram in 1777 has to specify: 'a halfbreed, betwixt a Creek and a white man'.[40]

In the early eighteenth century a man who had lived many years among the Creeks stated that if a person was to travel among the latter he would 'see the number of half-breeds of whites, negroes, and all others that have mixed'. A South Carolina court case of 1835–57 had reference to a half-African, half-European person as a 'half-breed'. (And in Britain, in 1860, half-English, half-Irish persons are referred to as 'half-breeds.')[41]

The term 'half-breed', therefore, was used in a general way and could refer to more than one type of racial mixture. The same is true of 'half-blood', a term originally used for half-sisters or half-brothers. In 1844 there is a reference in Tennessee to Margaret Morgan a 'half-blood Cherokee' but a Virginia petition of 1833 refers to a half-African, half-European woman as a 'half-blood' and the *Southern Literary Messenger* of 1840 asked the question 'are there any descendents of this tribe of the African intermarriage, in the degree of half-bloods?'[42]

'Half-breed' and 'half-blood' in North America, therefore, were used to refer to American–African, American–European and European–African persons, a usage totally different from 'mustee' or 'mestizo' and more akin to 'mulatto'.

'Half-caste' never seems to have become popular in North America, appearing in India by the 1789–93 period and spreading to Africa and, later, the West Indies. It is used as in a 1789 reference: 'Mulattoes, or as they are called in the East Indies, half-casts'. But American-derived mixed-bloods could also be called thus in Trinidad, as when a very old Native American lady is called in 1838 'a half-cast Indian' (Señora Trinidada).[43]

The term 'quadroon' or 'quarteron' might also be mentioned. It is generally supposed by later dictionaries that this designation refers to a person of one-quarter African ancestry but in 1857 Thomas S. Woodward speaks of a Creek leader (three-fourths European) as 'Billy Weatherford, the Quadroon'.[44]

ZAMBOS, SAMBOS AND *ZAMBAÍGOS*

The Spaniards came to use several terms for American–African hybrids, including *mulato* (which came to apply also to European–African hybrids), *zambaígo* or *zambo*, *lobo* (wolf), *chino* and *grifo*. The use of these terms was often local, as with *lobo*, but *zambo* or *sambo* spread to English-speaking colonies.

The origin of the term *Zambaígo* is obscure but it is interesting to note that in

1501 Rodrigo de Bastidas reached the *puerto de Zamba* along the Caribbean coast of Colombia. Zamba was also called *los Coronados* because all of the Americans there wore *grandes coronas* (crowns). It was near Caramari (Cartagena), and in the early 1530s was still a prominent village. (A Zamba woman who had been taken to Haiti was brought back in 1533 to serve as an interpreter.) A coastal Colombian leader's name is also given as 'Tamalaísa Zambo' in the same period.

Zamba is also an African name, common among the Wolof people, and usually used for males. In the records of Valencia one finds many slaves with such a name, as 'un negro de 14 años, de Jalof, llamado Zamba'. Females were also recorded, as in the same year (1491): 'una negra de Jalof de 8 años, llamada Zamba'. Other forms were *Zambia* and *Zambico*. Most were from Jalof (Wolof) but a few were listed as being of 'Mandinga' or 'Seni'. In Seville one *Zamba*, a girl of 7 years, was sold in 1499.

The term *zambo* also appears in Spanish and other languages as a word referring to bow-legs ('Zambo de piernas a lo águila imperial', bow-legged as the imperial eagle).[45]

Lockhart indicates that *zambo* had not appeared in Peruvian usage prior to 1560, *mulato* being used for American–African mixed-bloods. In 1563 the Spanish Crown prohibited 'negros, mulatos ó mestizos' from living in American communities but 'en quanto á los Mestizos, y Zambaigos, que son hijos de Indias, nacidos entre ellos, y han de heredar sus casas, y haziendas, porque parece cosa dura separarlos de sus padres, se podrá dispensar.' Thus *zambaígos* and *mestizos* who were sons of American mothers, born among Americans, and entitled to inherit property, were exempted from the prohibition.

A decade later López de Velasco wrote that there were in the Indies 'muchos mulatos, hijos de negros y de indias, que se llaman zambaigos, que bienen a ser la gente más peor y vil que en aquellas partes hay.' Thus, *zambaígos* were *mulatos*, children of Africans and American women, and were coming to be the worst people (from the Spanish perspective).

Thereafter Spanish royal decrees occasionally made reference to *zambaígos* in connection usually with *Tierra Firme* (Colombia–Panama) or Peru. In the 1620s Solórzano also refers to *Zambahigos* as children of Ethiopians and Americans, while in 1680 certain *zambaígos* were referred to in a royal decree relating to the Provincia de las Charcas (Rio de la Plata–Paraguay area).

In general, the term *zambaígo* seems to have appeared first in the Peru region (where López de Velasco and Solórzano both served) or in the Colombia–Panama area. Nonetheless, it is actually used by the Crown in Spain prior to general adoption by Spanish writers in the Americas (Cabello Balboa, for example, uses *mulato* and not *zambaígo* in Ecuador in the 1580s). The term spread both to the north and to the south but its introduction into Mexico is comparatively late.

The shortened form *zambo* is used by Solórzano in 1647 ('los *Zambos*, o' *Zambahigos*, que son hijos de Negro, é India, ó al contrario', children of Africans and Americans).[46]

Since there was a great amount of mixture between Americans and Africans in the Cartagena area of Colombia it is very possible that the place-name Zamba was the origin of the term. On the other hand, *Zambaígo* is rather close to the Wolof name *Zambico* (which could, however, be an Iberian diminutive of *Zamba*, the more common Wolof name). It seems certain, however, that *Zambaígo* is completely distinct from the word meaning bow-legged (unless that proves to be a borrowing from an African or American language).

In 1643 in New Mexico a 'Sambahigo' was described as a child of an Indian woman and a 'negro' or a 'mulato'. In other words, a 'Sambahigo' would be half-American and half-African or three-quarters American and one-quarter African. In Peru it appears that by the 1700s a *mulato* was seen as a lighter-colored hybrid than a *zambo*. One Peruvian definition of this period characterizes a *zambo* as being the child of a *negro y mulato* but *mulato* probably refers to a part-American person.

In the 1740s the mixture of a 'negro y sus mezclas con indio' (an African or part-African with an American) was said to produce a *zambo de negro* or a *zambo de mulato* and so on. The term *zambo* appears to point towards the American component, modified by the kind of person involved in the mixture. By the late 1700s and early 1800s most Spanish writers defined *Zambaígo* (or *Zambo* and *Sambuyo*) as being a mixture of one-half American with some combination of African and American, usually with some European ancestry as well. One partial exception is in Peru where *negro* and *mulata* and *negro* and *india* both yielded *zambo* or *sambo de indio* children. Again, however, *mulato* in Peru implied American ancestry. One also finds such variations as 'dark Zambos' being children of 'Zambos' and Africans, and so on.[47]

In the British West Indies the term began to be used quite early. A free non-white named William Sambo was baptized in the 1690s in Barbados (where many Americans from Surinam and North America had been enslaved) and it is said that 'already in the seventeenth century the most favourite name was Sambo' among slaves.[48] In 1774 Edward Long asserted that the mixture of 'Negro' and American produced 'Sambo de Indian' while a 'Negro' and a 'Mulatta' produced 'Sambo de Mulatta'. This usage seems, however, to have been borrowed from a 1748 English book about Peru which, in turn, was based on the Peruvian usage cited above. Long tells us that 'these distinctions . . . do not prevail in Jamaica'. Nonetheless, they are partially repeated by Edwards in 1787–92 and by James M. Phillippo in 1843.[49]

Edwards mentions 'Sambo' as one of the racial names used in the British West Indies. He states that a '*Sambo* is the offspring of a Black woman by a Mulatto man or *vice versa*' but he goes on to note a Spanish source to the effect that 'Samboes' owe their origin to a mixture between an American and either a 'negro' or a 'mulatto', or 'among themselves'. In Jamaica all of the castes were legally considered to be 'mulattoes'.[50]

In 1811 the New York *Evening Post* carried an advertisement for a runaway slave described as 'a black boy, named Joab, aged 14 . . . and has likely features, of a yellowish complexion (being a sambo)'.[51] Sambo was also a common name among slaves in the North American British colonies. In the early nineteenth century James Swaby, a 'Sambo', rose to some prominence in Jamaica.[52]

During the nineteenth century the idea began to be popularized that a 'sambo' was a mixture of African and 'mulatto'. An 1833 novel, *Peter Simple*, by Captain Frederick Marryat states: 'A quadroon looks down on a mulatto, while a mulatto looks down on a sambo, that is, half mulatto half negro'. On the other hand, a much more reliable source, E. L. Joseph, a resident of Trinidad for thirty years, states (1838) that 'Samboes' were a mixture 'between Negroes and Indians'.[53]

Other sources continue the same notion. Reid's *Rifle Rangers* (1851) notes that in Mexico 'you meet with a strange race – the cross of the negro with the ancient inhabitants of the country – the "Zamboes"'. Similarly, in 1896 an English visitor to Venezuela refers to 'the Zambos, the offspring of the imported negro and the native Indian stock'.[54]

Farmer in his dictionary of 'Americanisms' (1889) states under 'Sambo': 'a name applied to all colored persons, but originally used to designate the offspring of a black person and a mulatto; also sometimes the child of an Indian and a negro. Spelt also *Zambo*.' The *Encyclopedia Britannica* of the same period noted that 'Zambo' could refer to any half-breed (sic), 'but mostly the issue of Negro and Indian parents' except in the United States, the West Indies and Peru where 'Negro' and 'Mulatto' were involved.[55]

As regards the West Indies, by the nineteenth century it is more than likely that few pure Americans remained in Jamaica while, at the same time, the genes of many thousands of Americans had been absorbed into the population, primarily among people classified as 'colored' or 'black'. The nineteenth century use of terms such as 'sambo', 'mulatto' and 'mustee' must be analyzed within that context. It is simply not possible to accept the standard definitions of the late period because, with one or two exceptions, they ignore the fact that the people who are being called 'sambos', and so on, are very likely part-American as well as part-African. It should also be noted that Jamaica maintained close relations with the Miskito Coast of Nicaragua where the term *zambo* for American–African mixtures was in common use.

A similar situation doubtless prevailed in Louisiana where American slaves were still being absorbed for many years after 1803 but where the greatest numbers had already merged into the 'colored' or 'black' groups.[56]

In such regions most white figures were, of course, not concerned with the precise ancestry of non-whites. Instead, as the century wore on and as emancipation, social unrest, arnd abolitionism became paramount issues, the white ruling classes became more and more fearful of the 'black' masses still held in slavery and of the possible collusion of the mixed groups with the slaves. They began to see a white–black division, or white–brown–black, and whether a black or a brown was part-Indian was rather irrelevant in that context.

My conclusion is that the term 'zambo' ordinarily referred to an American–African hybrid but perhaps to one who had some degree of European ancestry also. Based on the total evidence, I believe that 'zambos' tended to have marked

Indian features, along with clear evidence of African mixture. With this in mind, we can say that 'zambos' would tend to stand somewhat between light brown 'mulattoes' and pure Africans and, therefore, the term might have come in certain colonies to embrace similar 'dark' but not pure African persons.

Nonetheless, we must stress again that most white observers would have no idea whatsoever of the actual ancestry of a person called a 'zambo' (after two or three centuries of complex intermixture). The presence of American as well as African ancestry should be considered likely, especially whenever being a 'sambo' is a self-affirmation of a non-white communal designation.

The term *Grifo* or *Griffe* occupies a somewhat similar position. In the 1650–1700 period it is said to have designated a person of three-quarters American and one-quarter African ancestry (in Mexico).[57]

It seems very likely that the term *grifo* went through some changes of meaning as it spread to French-speaking areas (such as Louisiana), but since it does not seem to have been adopted in the English colonies, it is sufficient merely to note its existence as another term referring to a type of American–African mixed-blood.

Jíbaro ('Givero' in Long) is another term referring to American or part-American persons in the Spanish-speaking West Indies and Ecuador–Peru. We do not need to trace its history here since it did not pass into English usage until the modern period when it is used to refer to the Indian-like people of interior Borinquen (Puerto Rico). It seems to denote non-white people (or tribes, as in Ecuador) who are thought to be 'bronco' or 'wild'.

Another term used was *chino* (borrowed perhaps from *china*, a female, in Quechua). A 1672 report makes reference to *los indios chinos* in various parts of Mexico. It isn't clear exactly what is meant but it would seem *not* to refer to imported *indios chinos* from the East Indies. Later the term, as in *la china poblana*, came to refer to a certain type of mixed Red–Black person who resembled (in all probability) a Filipino or Eastern Indonesian.[58] It should be noted that many Malayo–Polynesian peoples, such as the South Moluccans, resembled Red–Black hybrids.

In conclusion, the terms under review here are significant in understanding the early history of African–American intermixture in North America even though their use must be seen in relation to the much more common (and general) use of 'mulatto'. The latter term, along with 'people of color', always remained the ordinary way of referring to American–African or American–African–European mixed-bloods. The use of 'mustee' and 'zambo' was always localized. 'Half-breed', 'half-caste', and so on, are clearly very general terms (in the period under review) and cannot be used except with the meaning of 'mixed'.

9

Native Americans as Pardos and People of Color

PEOPLE OF COLOR AND PARDOS:
LATIN AMERICA AND THE CARIBBEAN

I have shown that in many areas of the British colonies persons of American ancestry were frequently classified as mulattoes, with or without mixture with Africans. I have also analyzed the evolution of other racial terms used to refer to part-American persons, such as 'mustee', 'zambo', 'half-breed' and 'half-blood'. One result of the above studies has been to show that the word 'mulatto' was the only term used for 'mixed-blood' in the English language until about 1700 and that it remained the dominant term in the Atlantic seaboard colonies from Virginia northwards until perhaps 1790–1810 when 'colored' began to be occasionally used.

Many examples of the use of 'people of color' to refer to Americans have been cited in the above studies but it is necessary, nonetheless, to deal specifically with this topic. It has commonly been assumed by many writers that the so-called 'free' people of color living in the United States prior to the Civil War were always of African ancestry and that the words 'Negro', 'Black', and 'African' or 'Afro-American' can be freely substituted for 'colored'. My research questions this assumption and also the assumption that such persons were 'free'. In fact, they were 'restricted' subjects of the British Crown and, later, of the United States. Their social character also requires empirical study rather than *a priori* assignment to a single racial or social category.

All of the European empires in the Americas possessed a need for labor, a need which was commonly met by the enslavement of any non-white or non-Christian person who could be captured or purchased. Americans, Black Africans, Muslim North Africans, South Asians, and Asians were all subject to seizure and sale and all found their way, in varying proportions, to the slave plantations or mines of the Americas. In addition, Americans were often reduced to a near-slave status (peonage etc.) or to the status of low-wage laborers. Needless to state, race mixture rapidly occurred. This process was doubtless accelerated by the sexual imbalances found among African slaves (with relatively few women being transported) and by the common tendency to enslave more American women and children than men or by high death-rates among American males.[1] Thus a growing African–American hybrid population developed, along with perhaps smaller European–African and European–American–African groups.

Many of the mixed-bloods remained in slavery because their mothers were slaves (generally slavery was inherited in the female line). In colonies such as South Carolina, New Jersey and Brazil, to name but three, it was possible during all or most of the colonial period to maintain an American woman as a slave and thus slavery was transmitted in the female line even if it was non-African in origin.

Nonetheless, a sizeable non-white 'free' population began to develop. In most areas it evolved from free American mothers, because everywhere there were such women. In a few areas, free white mothers contributed mixed children and, of course, white fathers extended freedom to some mixed children. Manumissions, on the whole, cannot be considered as playing a major role, though, in the *initial* formation of the non-slave mixed population.

In any case, this growing population occupied an intermediate position between the Europeans and the enslaved. In some cases its lighter members were accepted as 'white' and rose to prominence in the colonial social systems.[2] On the whole, however, the restricted non-slaves were reduced to, or maintained in, an inferior status.

In many parts of the colonial empires such persons were primarily of American racial ancestry and maintained an identity as 'Indians', speaking the native language, and so on. But in many areas, such as parts of Argentina, coastal Brazil, in the entire Caribbean region, and along the Atlantic seaboard of North America the mixture of races and languages gradually produced a class of people who were denationalized and who were speaking dialects of Guaraní-Tupí, Portuguese, Spanish, French, English, Dutch or so-called 'Creole' languages.

It is my intention here to concentrate upon the 'colored' population in British North America. Nonetheless, it is useful to make reference to developments in Brazil and other regions in order to illustrate the widespread existence of this intermediate group and the common presence of Americans or part-Americans within its composition.

I have already discussed the evolution of the terms *pardo*, *moreno* and *mulato* in the Portuguese and Spanish areas of the Americas, illustrating that these terms were often applied to persons of American ancestry. Of these terms, *pardo* is the most directly analogous to English 'colored'. Since *pardo* is a very significant term it is well to briefly review its early usage, emphasizing that in the late fifteenth and early sixteenth centuries it was applied by the Portuguese to 'dusky' or brown-colored peoples such as the Idzāgen (Berbers) of northwest Africa and the unmixed Americans of Brazil.[3] The Portuguese who first reached Brazil in 1500 stated specifically that the Americans were *pardos*, that is, 'de aspecto esta gente são homems pardos'. *Pardo* color was said to be intermediate between *branco* and *preto* (between white and black).[4]

A modern-day Brazilian dictionary (Nascentes) defines *pardo* as:

de côr intermediaria entre o preto e o branco, quasi escuro. . . . Pessoa mestiça, de côr parda, filho de mulatos. [Of color intermediate between black and white, almost dark. . . . A mixed person, of *pardo* color, a child of *mulatos*].[5]

Thus the basic meaning of *pardo* as a brown color intermediate between white and black remains, but in addition reference is made to persons of mixed racial background. C. R. Boxer, a historian of the Portuguese Empire, defines a *pardo* as a 'Coloured man; mixed blood, often with the connotation of negro blood'. In another book he says: 'colored; often synonymous with mulatto'.

Many Portuguese dictionaries since that of Bluteau (eighteenth century) tend to equate *pardo* with *mulato*. This is, however, a very misleading definition because the term *mulato* is highly ambiguous and also because *pardo* in actual use continues to refer to people who (in English at least) would not today be called mulattoes. Constancio (1836) for example, notes that *pardo* referred to a 'côr . . . escura como a dos mulatos'. He states that 'Homens pardos' were 'baços de pele'. In short, *pardos* were dark-skinned, of an obscure color like *mulatos*. Moraes Silva states: 'De côr entre branco e preto. . . . Diz-se daquele que tem pele escura ou trigueira; muito moreno.'

Agreeing with the definition of Nascentes, Moraes Silva states that *pardos* are of a color between black and white, of obscure or wheat color, very brown.[6]

Pardo, then, is not the equivalent of modern English mulatto since it refers to a range of intermediate colors and *not* to a specific type of ancestry. To understand this better we must briefly examine modern Brazilian usage in order to somewhat clarify the confusion which exists with terms such as *pardo*, *mestiço*, and *mulato*.

Modern Brazilian writers often equate *pardo* with *mestiço* (mixed) and *mulato* (mixed) in Portuguese. In fact Octavio Ianni in his *As Metamorfoses do Escravo* (1962) specifically equates *pardo*, *mestiço* and *mulato* in his text. He also lumps *pardos*, *mestiços* and *caboclos* (Americans) together to form a total of *mulatos* for the 1872 and 1890 censuses.[7]

Pardo (and Spanish *loro*) commenced as a term for essentially brown people such as Berbers and Native Brazilians. Later, mixed-bloods who possessed a similar color were naturally and logically encompassed by the same term. But it is quite clear that *pardo* continued in its essential meaning of intermediate color and could have included unmixed (and especially assimilated) Americans as well as all types of brown mixed-bloods. This is made very clear in census reports for various provinces or states of Brazil where large numbers of Americans and part-American mixed-bloods were present but where only the terms *branco* (white), *pardo* (dusky brown), *preto* (black), *negro*, or *mulato* are used in the census.

For example, historians seem to agree that the São Paulo region was one of extremely heavy American ancestry and mixture, with, in fact, relatively few pure Europeans or Africans through the mid-eighteenth century. A. J. R. Russell-Wood notes:

Even in São Paulo, where until the middle of the eighteenth century Tupí rather than Portuguese was the common language, the 1797 population of 158,450 was made up of 89,323 white, 38,650 blacks, and 30,487 mulattoes. In 1800 this population had increased to 94,349 whites, 34,311 blacks, and 39,884 mulattos.

Russell-Wood's statement was based, in part, upon Rodrigues who, however, uses 'mestizo' or 'mixed' instead of 'mulato' for the 1797 census (in English translation). Judging from other censuses of the time, it seems likely that either *mestiço* or *pardo* was used in the original, but whichever term was used makes little difference since we are faced with the task of explaining where the *mamalucos* and *caboclos* (Americans) are in a census using only the categories of white, black, and *mulato–mestiço–pardo*.[8]

The 1815 census for São Paulo reproduced by the Bavarian scholars Spix and Martius uses the terms white, black, and *Braune* (brown) in the original German edition (translated as white, black, and 'mulattoes' in an English edition). This suggests that *pardo* was the original Portuguese category although Rodrigues' English translator uses 'mestizo'. In any case, almost 26 per cent of the population were in the *Braune* category.

The 1890 census for São Paulo, which uses the category of *caboclo* (in addition to *mestiço*), has 8.24 per cent of the population in that category. The term *caboclo* is defined variously by current authorities but it is interpreted as meaning *indígena* or *índio* by the author of the text of the *Diccionario Histórico, Geográphico e Ethnográphico do Brasil* (1922). Forty years later Ianni interprets *caboclo* as referring to 'os hibridos de aborigines e brancos', that is as mixed white and American. This interpretation is apparently disputed by Salles who uses *índio* as distinct from *mestiço do índio* ('O mestiço do índio, e o caboclo') and who specifically defines the *caboclo* as one born of 'Indio x Indio' (two American parents). Moreover, the terms *indio* and *caboclo* are used interchangeably when speaking of the same category in the 1872 and 1890 censuses and, more significantly, the *mestiço* category (i.e., mixed) was clearly set apart from *caboclo* by the designers of the censuses.

In any event, we can be certain that more than 8 per cent of the São Paulo population in 1890 were American-looking, even if not of biologically 'pure' ancestry. Quite clearly, then, Americans and part-Americans were residing in São Paulo province in earlier (and later) years when only categories such as *mestiço*, *pardo* (or *mulato*) were used for 'brown' people. It would seem obvious that they are mentioned in most of the censuses only as *brancos* (probably the lighter-skinned), *pardos* and *mestiços* (the brown-skinned), *pretos* and *negros* (the ones mixed with African or those serving as slaves who were also dark brown).

The same situation clearly exists in the Brazilian area of Parana (Paranaguá–Curitiba) which was developed primarily by persons of American race (many as slaves) or part-American mixed-bloods. Ianni, in his study of the region, makes this abundantly clear, and a census of 1776 shows that about 20 per cent of the slaves were *administrados* (*indios*) and these alone comprised almost 5 per cent of the total population. Free Americans and part-Americans are, however, lost in the *branco*, *pardo*, *negro* and *mulato* categories used in various censuses through 1854. For 1767 Ianni states that 'a presença do negro, aborigine e mestiços na comunidade é geral' (the presence of the negro, American and mixed-bloods in the community – of Curitiba – is general). And yet the count for that year has only *brancos* and *escravos*.

In 1854 specifically American *aldeias* (settlements) existed in Parana, but the census of that year includes only the categories of *branco*, *mulato* (*pardo*), and *negro*. The 1872 census utilizes the category of *caboclos* who constituted about 7 per cent while the *pardos* constituted about 25 per cent. Ianni states 'em 1872 os *pardos* reuniam 34.59% dos habitantes', thus totaling the *caboclos* and *pardos* together as *pardos* – but he also refers to both the totals of *pardos* and *caboclos* in 1872 and of *mestiços* and *caboclos* in 1890 as 'mulatos'. In any case, it is rather clear that Americans in Parana were called *brancos*, *pardos*, and so on, during the years between 1776 and 1872.[9]

The same phenomenon can be observed in Pará province where a census of 1793 used *brancos*, *pretos*, *indios* and *mestiços*, while one of 1856 used only *pardos* and *pretos* for non-whites. Clearly the term *pardo* was used to include all non-whites who were not considered to be black (the population was 20 per cent *caboclo* in 1890).

In Bahia the census of 1775 uses the terms *brancos*, *pardos* and *pretos*. Thales de Acevedo notes that 64 per cent of the population consisted in 'pretos e mestiços de vários tipos, *mulatos*, *mamelucos*, *cabôclos*, cafusos e outros.' Thus the term *pardo* is interpreted as including *mamelucos*, *caboclos* and *cafusos*, all part-American groups. A count of 1807 utilizes the same categories while one of 1824 (reported by Spix and Martius) separates out whites, blacks (*neger*), Americans (*Indianer*), and *farbige* (colored, probably *pardo*). The 1890 census identifies 7.83 per cent of the population as *caboclo* while 46.19 per cent is termed *mestiço*. Acevedo states: 'agora a mestiçagem fazia preponderar francamente os *pardos* sôbre os tipos extremos.' Thus in stating that the *pardos* are clearly predominating due to race mixture, Acevedo is equating *pardo* with *mestiço* and probably *caboclo*.[10]

The 1940 and 1950 Brazilian censuses utilized the categories of *branco*, *pardo* and *preto*. In the latter year the *pardo* category included 26.54 per cent of the population, of whom Rodrigues states: 'more than 26 per cent (26.54%) [is] Negro, Indian, and white', thus equating the *pardo* group with part-American as well as part-African people. Rodrigues' English translators replace *pardo* with 'mestizo' at one point and with 'mulatto' at another, thus adding a measure of confusion for English-speaking readers. Rodrigues goes on to say that the division of the census into three groups

is extremely imprecise. . . . it permits classification by sight, according to features, hair, and color of skin. Many light mulattoes . . . must appear to be white. Mestizos appearing to be white are included as white. . . . In the white group, then, one finds not only true whites but also white phenotypes, that is, Afro-white and Indian-white mestizos reverting to white type. In the Negro group there are Negroes and Negro phenotypes, mulattoes and *cafuzos* [Indian–Negro] reverting to the Negro type. Finally, the mestizo [pardo] classification shows the greatest lack of precision, for mulattoes . . . are not distinguished from *caboclos*.

Thus American ancestry can be found, according to Rodrigues, in all three categories – *branco*, *pardo*, and *preto*.

Salles also notes, as regards the same census classifications, that:

Na nomenclatura oficial do IBGE [Census Bureau], os mestiços são designados *pardos*, palavra ambígua, mas de uso generalizado, que engloba indifferentemente as diversas categorias de mestiços de cruzamento branco ameríndio, mas também do negro ameríndio e demais mestiçamentos oriundo da miscigenação.

Thus the system used causes all *mestiços* to be placed under the 'ambiguous' word *pardo*, which indiscriminately covers all types of mixed-bloods such as white and American and black and American.

The IBGE itself, as quoted by Marvin Harris, in 1961 noted that 'the label "white" is bestowed with a liberality that would be inconceivable in Washington. . . . However, it would be extremely difficult to clearly separate *brancos morenos* from *pardos de matiz claro* and *pardos de matiz escuro* from *pretos*.' That is, it would be hard to separate 'brown' whites from *pardos* of light color and *pardos* of dark color from blacks. The IBGE notes that in many areas *pretos* were called *pardos* and *pardos* were called *pretos*.

Of course, the use of such terms is of no value whatsoever in a country where there is an absolute continuum of shadings with no breaks. But that is also true in the United States (and the rest of the Americas) where so-called racial terms bear no relationship to reality. The Brazilian problem seems to be compounded for outside observers by North American scholars who so often insist upon translating *mestiço* and *pardo* as 'mulatto' which, in modern English, results in a grave distortion of the tri-racial character of the *pardo-mestiço* group. Also serious is the tendency of some to lump all *pardos*, *mestiços* and *pretos* together as 'colored' people (or as negroes), meaning by 'colored' *not* non-white but only negro and part-negro.[11]

I have already noted that in *c.*1769–70 a military company of *pardo* men was authorized in Pará along with one for *pretos*. Salles suggests that these *pardos* might have been Americans, perhaps because the latter group was so numerous in that province (still constituting almost 20 per cent in 1890).

Further support for the viewpoint that the *pardo* category included persons of American ancestry is to be found in the term *pardavasco*. This is defined as an: 'individuo *pardo*, no geral mestiço de negro e índio; índio meio amulatado, acaboclado, pardusco. [a *pardo* individual, in general a mixed-blood of African and American; an American who is mulatto-ized and *caboclo*-ized, clear grayish color].' Salles specifically defines a *pardo* as a 'descendent of secondary crossings' such as between 'mulato x mameluco', that is, as a person of white, African and American ancestry.

Euclides da Cunha in his classic work *Os Sertões* states:

Teoricamente, ele (o tipo brasileiro) seria o pardo, para que convergem os cruzamentos sucessivos do mulato, do cariboca e do cafuz. [Theoretically the Brazilian type would be the *pardo*, because of the blending together of the successive mixture of the *mulato*, the *cariboca* (American–European) and the *cafuz* (American–African)].[12]

From this perspective, then, a *pardo* would be seen as a product of the blending of the American, African and European racial strains.

I have gone into this analysis of the Portuguese–Brazilian concept at some length because the evolution of the term *pardo* is rather analogous to what takes place with 'colored' in English usage. The exact correspondence or degree of divergence will become clear only after other data is examined, but at the very least we can see that Portuguese *pardo* suffers from the same tendency as 'colored', that is, to be distorted by those modern writers who choose to emphasize only African and European components and who tend to disregard the American element in mixed populations.

In the Spanish Empire the terms *pardo* and *moreno* also begin to be applied to a broad range of mixed-bloods of free status, although in certain regions *cholo*, *ladino* and *gente de razón* were used for persons not living as traditional 'Indians' or as slaves. *De razón* (rational) was often used for persons not living in a traditional American way in northern Mexico and California. In 1774 a royal official noted that the different castes were called *de razón* which resulted from the mixture, in varying proportions, of whites, Indians, and negroes. This mixture resulted in 'great familial confusion.' But in California *de razón* was used as a rough synonym for 'civilized' and was thus a much broader term than *pardo*.

Santamaría defines the *Cholo* as a 'casta que resulta del cruzamiento de la raza blanca con la indígena y en general, mestizo, Criollo, etc., o por extensión, gente baja. . . . En Mejico por lo general indio medio civilizado. . . . En Costa Rica . . . cualquier persona muy morena.' Thus *cholo*, although primarily applying to American–European mixed-bloods could be used for a wide range of brown people of generally low social status. In many respects, *de razón*, *ladino* and *cholo* correspond to one of the current meanings of *caboclo* in Brazil, that is, to refer to 'detribalized' persons of American or part-American ancestry living a way of life intermediate between the bulk of coastal Brazilians, on the one hand, and traditional Americans, on the other.

I have already cited examples from the Spanish Empire to show that the term *pardo* was utilized for persons of American ancestry. For example, in the latter part of the eighteenth century Felix de Azana stated that the *pardos* included American–Europeans, African–Europeans, and African–Americans in the Río de la Plata–Paraguay region. Santamaría states that the term *pardo* is applied to *mulatos* in Argentina and the Caribbean, to American–*mulato* mixed-bloods in Brazil, and to the children of Europeans and either Americans or Africans in other countries 'y más generalmente a toda la gente de color, incluso el negro del país, como en Cuba y Puerto Rico' (that is, to refer to all people of color even including blacks in Cuba and Puerto Rico). Santamaría also notes that in Tabasco *pardo* was used in a manner similar to that cited for *cholo*, namely, to refer to a lower-class person.

There is general agreement among most authors that *pardo* is now used for all mixed-bloods or people of color (along with the term *casta*). Rosenblat also notes that military companies of 'pardos y morenos' in Buenos Aires included Americans, while Mellafe, referring perhaps to a slightly earlier period, identifies *pardos* as mixtures of African and American (the same as *zambos*).

In California one can find examples of how *pardo* was used, and these bearing out Mellafe to a degree. In the 1780s and 1790s *pardo* was *not* used as a general term for all mixed-bloods (*casta* being used instead, along with the more ambiguous *de razón*). In the 1790 census for San José we find:

1 Antonio Acevez, 50, *mulato*, from San Bartolomé (Durango), married to Feliciana Cortes, 50, *mestiza*; two children.
2 Manuel Gonzalez, 70, *indio*, from Valle de San Bantolo (Durango), married to Gertrudis Acevez, 20, *parda*; two sons by a previous marriage.
3 Antonio Romero, 40, *pardo*, from Guadalajara, married to Petra Acevez, *parda*; one son.

This would seem to indicate that *pardo* was used in California for the child of a *mulato* and a *mestizo*. On the other hand, it should be noted that several probable sons of Antonio Acevez were classified as *mulatos* at San Francisco in 1790. But as I have shown elsewhere *mulato* was also used for the progeny of *mulatos* and *mestizos* in California. Both terms, therefore, could refer to an American–African–European mixed-blood.

In any case, it is certain that *pardos* could be part-American in the Spanish Empire in all periods.

The Spanish and Portuguese Empires certainly saw the development of a large non-European population which was, at the same time, not living in a traditional American way and was legally non-slave. After a few generations, it was not possible to determine the precise ancestry of individuals in this large group nor was it of any major significance, since phenotype and life-style (rather than genotype) determined caste position. In Spanish California, for example, I have shown that racial status frequently changed (in a white or light direction) as economic or social position improved.[13]

This is not to say that European officials did not attempt to record the racial character of individuals, but I would argue that appearance (phenotype) and/ or social status determined the category used rather than any accurate assessment of actual ancestry (genotype), which could hardly be known for most persons who were not recent slaves.

The development in the Iberian colonies of the group to which are applied the various adjectives, *pardo*, *moreno*, *cholo*, *ladino*, *caboclo*, *mulato* and *mestizo* corresponds to a similar phenomenon in the British colonies. In the latter case, fewer specific racial terms were used in official records but locally a great many correspondences with Latin America appear. A few examples will be given.

The Portuguese, for instance, used terms such as *Indios mansos* (tame Indians), *mamalucos* (Portuguese–American mixed-bloods), and *caboclos* (literally copper-colored people) to refer to Christianized, detribalized, or semi-incorporated Americans. In the British colonies terms such as 'tributary Indians', 'settlement Indians' and 'praying Indians' were used for the same class of persons. Later their descendants were often called mulattoes and coloreds or, in certain areas, *métis* and half-breeds.

Locally also, the British settlers evolved many terms to refer to various mixed types, such as tawny, dark mulatto, bright mulatto, yellow people, etc. Occasionally such terms almost approached the designation of a class or group (especially bright mulatto, yellow people and mustee in South Carolina) but generally they were used only as descriptive terms for individuals or particular families. This usage may not, however, be very different from Spanish Portuguese practice since the use of terms such as *cafuso* (African–American), *mamaluco*, *mestizo*, etc., may well refer simply to individual appearance or family reputation and not to any precise knowledge of ancestry.

In this connection, it should be noted again that the late-eighteenth- and early nineteenth–century efforts by European writers to develop catalogues of precise racial terms for areas such as the Spanish Empire, Louisiana, the Caribbean, etc., are the product of *post-hoc* scientific rationalism and not of actual usage. That is, systematically inclined writers, influenced by the general classification tendency in natural history, sought to make *belated* sense out of a myriad of racial terms. But I am inclined to believe that such 'systems' were never actually used in any precise way, since in fact the ancestry of individuals could usually not be known.

Mörner, following Aguirre Beltrán, points out that the eighteenth century paintings of various mixed racial types with appropriate terminology 'should not be taken too seriously because they express erudite imagination and genealogical concern rather than social reality. The complex terminologies do highlight the increasing absurdity of a genealogical criterion for social classification in a multiracial environment.'[14]

In any case, broad all-encompassing categories became necessary in all of the colonies. Thus, in Mexico, the term *mestizo* has gradually come to refer to almost everyone who is not a traditional *indio* or a *blanco*. *Mestizo* has come to encompass all Spanish-speaking brown or light-brown persons even if they are American in appearance or have some degree of African ancestry. Thus *mestizo* has lost any precise racial meaning and has become a social designation, although one pointing towards the possession of a degree of indigenous Mexican (American) ancestry.

Similarly, terms such as *cholo* and *caboclo* have tended to become social class terms in South America while *ladino* occupies a similar position in Central America. *Gens de couleur* in Louisiana and *kleurling* in the Dutch colonies (along with *Kreool* in Surinam) evolved also in this direction.

In the British colonies of North America a similar process seems to have occurred because the complex intermixture of Americans, Africans, and

Europeans gave rise to a class of people who, like the *mestizos* of Mexico or the *pardos* of Brazil, were so highly mixed that previously popular terms no longer seemed broad enough to encompass the group. In North America, the term 'mulatto', widely used for mixed-bloods of any type, was becoming legally more specialized (that is, to refer to any part-African of more than one-sixteenth, one-eighth or one-quarter African ancestry). Yet many of the non-whites looked like Americans or Europeans rather than Africans and thus the term 'mulatto' (perhaps) needed replacement by a more general term. Moreover, some 'free' people were African in appearance.

As we shall see, however, the terms 'free mulatto' and 'free negro' continued to be used for a long time after the term 'free colored' was introduced. Still further, it was never certain whether 'colored' should be used for people of African appearance or only for people of a mixed or brown (intermediate) color.

In the English-speaking Caribbean a strong tendency existed (and still exists) for the term 'colored' to be used only for 'brown' as opposed to 'black' people. Harry Hoetink, in his study of Curaçao society, repeatedly cites sources distinguishing between *kleurlingen* (coloreds) and *negers* although some modern Dutch definitions are of such a nature as to encompass all non-whites under *kleurlingen*.[15] In South Africa, of course, the 'coloreds' are clearly distinguished from members of native nationalities still speaking African languages.

A modern Dutch dictionary defines *kleurling* as:

Iemand met kleur . . . met een gekleurde huid. . . . Naam voor nakomelingen uit vermengingen van blanken (Europeanen) met niet-blanken. . . . Als een meer algemene naam, . . . voor: iemand, behorende tot de niet-blanke mensen-rassen [someone of color, with a colored skin. . . . The name for mixed persons resulting from mixing of whites (Europeans) with non-whites. . . . As a more general name for someone from a non-white race.]

But the dictionary adds, for *Kleurlingen*:

Hieronder verstaat men in de Nederlands W. I.-koloniën . . . de gehele niet-blanke bevolking maar alleen de personen ontstaan uit kruising van blanken met negers of indianen of met andere kleurlingen. [Those in the Dutch West Indian colonies . . . understand by this not the entire non-white people, but only the people resulting from the crossing of whites with negroes or Indians or with other colored persons.][16]

A major Dutch encyclopedia reiterates the above, that is, that *kleurlingen* refers either to all non-white (non-European) peoples or to 'half-bloods'. It states that 'nowadays' *kleurling* is preferred to 'half-bloed' as a descriptive term for all types of mixed-bloods.

It is clear that the term *kleurlingen* was used for Americans as well as part-Americans. The *Encyclopedie* of Dutch West India speaks of the population of Bonaire as including 'kleurlingen, afstammende van Indianen en Negers, met een geprononceerd Indianen-type, zoals op Aruba.' Thus, colored people of mixed American and African background existed showing pronounced American features, along with a more numerous group showing African features. A census of the population of Bonaire in 1833 has only *blanken* (whites), *gekleurden* (coloreds), and *zwarten* (blacks), thus showing that all non-whites except 'blacks' were classified as *kleurlingen* (apparently the Americans of Bonaire were all of mixed blood by 1816).

Similarly in 1833 Aruba had only whites, coloreds, and blacks in spite of the agreement of most authorities that significant numbers of Americans were living (and still live) on that island. Menkman notes that while a few Americans still survived on Curaçao in 1795, the most numerous group of *genuine Indianen* were living on Aruba where they, along with the "*mestiezen en Zambos*" (mestizos and zambos) were able to form a militia company under a lieutenant of their own blood. He states also that in 1816 Aruba had 564 genuine (unmixed) *Indianen* and 336 slaves. The 1833 census has 1,817 free *gekleurden*, 71 free *zwarten*, and 393 slaves.[17]

Thus the term 'colored', in Dutch, could certainly embrace Americans as well as persons of mixed American–European or American–African ancestry.

As regards French usage, Léo Elisabeth notes that:

The French islands [Guadeloupe, Martinique, et cetera] were a singular and lasting refuge for the Carib Indians, and the Caribs were generally considered to have been free always. While the Indians were in certain cases ascriptively and legally distinguished from the free colored of African and slave descent, they were in other instances lumped together with the emancipated people of color.

Elisabeth then cites a source from the 1760s wherein it is asserted that 'people from India and Indians' constitute 'another type of colored people' and should be grouped together with people of African descent. Between 1687 and 1694 Caribs were entered separately in the census returns for the French Caribbean colonies but from 1696 onwards only the term 'free colored' was used, at least on Martinique.[18]

In the area of the United States a tendency developed by the late nineteenth century to equate 'colored' with 'negro' and to use both terms interchangeably.

The National Association for the Advancement of Colored People (and predecessor groups) used the term in this way.

Nonetheless, the story of the evolution of the concept is complex and requires a review of usage.

THE TERM 'COLORED' IN NORTH AMERICA

John Russell Bartlett in his *Dictionary of Americanisms* (*c.*1860) defined 'Colored' as 'a term applied to persons who have negro blood in their veins'. This definition is not, however, in accord with earlier usage. In 1807, for example, the United States adopted an act to prohibit the importation of slaves. The act repeatedly refers only to 'any negro, mulatto, or person of color'. Either we have to interpret 'person of color' as referring to *all* non-whites or we have to accept the notion that American, American–European, Asiatic, and Northern

African persons could still be imported as slaves after 1807. This latter is not an impossibility either, as Americans were still being enslaved in New Mexico, Arizona–Sonora, and along the 'wild coast' of Venezuela–Colombia and the Guianas during the first half of the nineteenth century.[19]

In any case, the most general use of the term 'colored' (or its predecessor 'all other free persons') occurs in relation to the United States census from 1790 onward. Until 1850 the United States chose not to list non-whites and whites together in the same manner. Non-whites were treated separately, in the sense that they were enumerated in separate columns which provided less information. In 1790 non-whites were referred to as 'all other free persons'. Subsequently this group was listed as 'free people of color'.

Generally speaking, it was left to the local census-taker to distinguish between colored and uncolored. Quite clearly, however, *all* persons considered to be non-white were to be enumerated as colored persons except for Indians who were not taxed, that is, Indians living on non-taxable lands who paid no property or poll taxes. In the 1830 census we can find numerous examples of Indians who were enumerated as free persons of color, including all of the Cherokee Indians in Carroll County, Georgia. Because most of these Cherokees have native names we can safely assume that they were of unmixed American race.

In the 1850 census enumerators were told: 'in enumerating colored persons to write "B" or "M" in the space on the schedule'. The 'B' apparently stood for 'black' or 'dark' while the 'M' stood for mulatto, mixed or brown. The same method was used in 1860.

The vast majority of American Indian people in Virginia and North Carolina were classified as colored people in 1850, with an 'M' being placed after their names. A few were classed as 'B'.

Some 37 per cent of the free people in the United States classified as non-white in 1850 were categorized as 'M' while only about one-twelfth of the slaves were so classed. It is clear that a significant proportion of the 'M' group, and certainly some of the 'B' group as well, were of American or part-American descent. This was, of course, also true in 1830, 1840 and other census years.

In my study of the term 'mulatto' in North America I have reviewed detailed evidence showing specifically how individual Indians were classified as 'persons of color' in Virginia and elsewhere in the census records. It is not necessary to review that data here except to say that it is quite certain that Native Americans were often classified in that manner in the slave states.[20]

It seems likely that the United States from 1790 through 1860 did not intend taxpaying Indians to be counted as white people. The only category left would then be the 'all other free people' or the 'free colored' category. That North Carolina, Virginia, Georgia and other states chose to enumerate most or all Indians as colored persons must be seen as being in accord with the intentions of the United States government.

The South Carolina Area

It is now necessary to proceed to an examination of specific colonies or states, because usage is usually best illustrated by local sources.

South Carolina usage, in general, resembles that of the Caribbean in that 'free colored' were often distinguished from 'free negro' or 'free black' people. In 1823 the Supreme Court stated that 'in this country . . . the universal understanding (is) that when a servant is spoken of, a person of color is meant'.[21] In 1852 the court added. 'It is not according to the use of language in this region to speak of one altogether black as a person or color. The phrase is almost exclusively applied to one of mixed blood and color.'[22] In 1895 George Tillman, speaking at the South Carolina Constitutional Convention asserted that 'there was not a full blooded Caucasian on the floor of the convention. Every member had in him a certain mixture of Mongolian, Arab, Indian, or *other colored blood.*'[23] (italics added)

In these quotations we see an apparent change, from using 'colored' to refer to mixed-bloods to a later usage in which Indian blood is categorized, *per se*, as 'colored'. But the same tendency can be found in an Act (1823) which sought to imprison free colored seamen so as to be sure that they did not settle permanently in South Carolina. However, this act did not apply to 'free American Indians, free Moors, or Lascars, or other colored subjects of countries beyond the Cape of Good Hope'.[24] In other words, American Indians, Moors, and Lascars (south Asians) were 'colored' people although not Africans. (This act was also adopted by Georgia in 1829.)

In the nineteenth century, then, we can see that for South Carolina and Georgia the term 'colored' was applicable to a broad range of people but essentially can be translated as 'non-white' though not including unmixed West Africans. Let us proceed, however, to clarify usage still further.

The non-slave, colored population of South Carolina was composed of people who were not always treated identically. A number of sub-groups existed, including Native Americans, mixed-bloods in general, and mulattoes born of white mothers. In general, lighter shades of color or possession of a white mother resulted in differential treatment, but the degree of close association with uncolored persons and acceptance of the latter's cultural values was also a factor. There is much evidence for a tolerant attitude towards brown or light brown persons who associated with whites and behaved like them. Such persons could marry white people and produce children or grandchildren acceptable as whites (provided that no 'relapse' into the colored or black worlds occurred).

In 1807 the Court held that David Burden, 'a man of color' could testify because he was born of a white woman, since 'it was determined in this court, by all the judges, that any person of color, if the issue of a free white woman, is entitled to give evidence . . . in our courts.'[25] The race of the father seems to have been irrelevant in such an instance.

In 1789 a 'capitation tax' was imposed upon all 'negroes, mustizos, and mulattoes' in South Carolina. In 1817 the courts considered the case of certain descendants of an East Indian woman who had married a white man in Haiti. The judges quoted the ordinance as stating 'that . . . every other . . . person of color, whether a descendent of an Indian or otherwise' shall have to pay the poll tax. The court held that the Indians in question were 'slave Indians' and that the descendants of free Indians and Asian Indians were not included. Indeed, the court held that a descendant of a free Indian must have some African ancestry to be so taxed.[26]

Here, then, we have the court introducing a lenient interpretation in so far as lighter persons with no African ancestry were concerned. The original legislation clearly had intended to include Indians as people of color liable to taxation, but by 1817 the judges were inclined to exempt those who were not part-African. In any case, those persons of mixed American and African ancestry were still to be regarded as taxable colored persons.

By 1850 the South Carolina court had adopted a more conservative attitude. One judge stated that 'the colonists . . . seized and enslaved as many (Indians) as they could take of the hostile tribes. . . . The number . . . was very great; so that after supplying the wants of the colony, many were shipped to the West Indies.' Thus a special status for Indians (exempting some from laws affecting people of color generally) was to be available only to those Indians who were specifically descended from independent nations or tribes 'in amity' with South Carolina.[27]

In reality, however, the 1817 and 1850 decisions are not in conflict since both are based upon the notion that certain kinds of Native Americans were exempt not because of race but because of alliances and because of the language of the original governing legislation. This legislation (1712–40) had stated that:

all negroes, Indians (free Indians in amity with this government, and negroes, mulattoes, or mestizoes who are new free, excepted), mulattoes, or mestizoes, who are now or who shall here after be in this province, and all their issue and offspring born, or to be born, shall be, and they are hereby declared to be and remain forever hereafter, absolute slaves, and shall follow the condition of the mother.

Also:

every negro, Indian, mulatto, and mestizo is a slave unless the contrary can be made to appear (but) Indians in amity with this government excepted, in which case the burden of proof shall lie with the defendant.

Any 'negro, mulatto, mustee or Indian slave' could apply for freedom under the above rules.[28] Thus 'Indians in amity' was a key phrase in determining later court decisions, not Indian blood *per se*. Nonetheless, there was some judicial sympathy for Indians in general who were not part-African, as noted, although this was often not applied evenly.

In 1825, for example, one Gray was charged with insolence against a white man. He was tried by a court for colored people and appealed on the grounds that he was descended from 'a free Indian woman in amity'. His appeal was rejected by a Circuit Court judge and he was punished. The Supreme Court ruled that the Circuit Court judge had erred in rejecting Gray's application but refused to take any action since he had been whipped already.[29] In a different case, in 1814, the Supreme Court ruled in a more liberal manner as regards one Adam Garden, the descendant of an Indian woman.[30]

The South Carolina Supreme Court considered, in a number of cases, the dividing line between white and colored. In general, the line was to be determined by appearance and culture but principally by acceptance as 'white' by local white juries.[31] The ambiguity of South Carolina statutes made it possible for non-whites to be rewarded or punished in a capricious manner and the effect was undoubtedly to better control all classes of mixed or brown persons who might aspire to favorable treatment.

In 1831 the South Carolina Court stated:

There is no legal definition of the term (mulatto). It . . . would be dangerous and cruel to subject to this disqualification, persons bearing all the features of a white, on account of some remote admixture of negro blood; nor has the term mulatto, or person of colour, I believe, been popularly attributed to such a person. . . . where there is a distinct and visible admixture of negro blood, the person is to be denominated a mulatto, or person of colour.

The Supreme Court denied the argument of an earlier judge, to the effect that a person could be white if the white blood predominated (as in a person of one-quarter African ancestry) but referred approvingly to a Louisiana statute allowing one-eighth Africans to be white. The matter was 'a question very proper for a jury', but the Court left little leeway: 'the witness was a quadroon, and such an one is clearly . . . a mulatto, or person of color.'[32]

We may be sure that all American–African mixed-bloods would be considered to be colored person but very brown American–European mixed-bloods might also be so regarded. In an 1835 case the Supreme court stated:

We cannot say what admixture . . . will make a colored person. . . . The condition . . . is not to be determined solely by . . . visible mixture . . . but by reputation . . . and it may be . . . proper that a man of worth . . . should have the rank of a white man, while a vagabond of the same degree of blood should be confined to the inferior caste. . . . It is hardly necessary to say that a slave cannot be a white man.[33]

In several instances the Supreme Court does not seem to have specified (or known) what kind of non-white ancestry was involved. In 1840, for instance, one Bass was described as 'a free man of colour' even though the Bass name is a common one among Indian descendants. In an 1843 case a group of people were charged with being 'free mulattoes' who were required to pay the *per capita* tax levied on 'free persons of color'. They were descended from a white woman who had married 'Tan', described simply as 'a colored man'. A daughter, Lydia Tan, had married a Dutchman and their daughter, Sally, had married a white man. Two sons of Sally were judged to be white by a jury. In any case, 'Tan' was never described racially, except as a man of color.[34]

An 1846 case emphasized that:

It would be difficult, if not impolitic, to define by . . . inflexible rules the line of separation. . . . the question of the reception of colored persons into the class of citizens must partake more of a political than a legal character, and, in a great degree, be decided by public opinion, expressed in the verdict of a jury.

In this particular case a revolutionary soldier named 'Bass' had married a woman described as a 'much respected mulatto woman', daughter apparently of a white woman. The son of the above, one Elijah Bass, showed 'plainly the corrupt blood' but was never subjected to the *per capita* tax on colored persons. The Court stated that Elijah Bass

is not a clear-blooded white man; but has always been treated by his neighbors as a free white man. He visits and is visited by them as a free White man, eats with them at their tables, and they with him at his, and is honest and industrious.

He was married to a white woman and owned land and slaves. His children, who looked white, were intermarried with whites and 'if any people tinged with African blood are worthy to be rated as white', it should be them. Nonetheless, one jury held the children to be 'free mulattoes'. The Supreme Court allowed the 'free mulatto' verdict to stand in a 3–2 decision but the grandchildren of Elijah Bass were judged to be whites.[35]

Thus one can see how 'political' indeed was the line between colored and white. It seems quite clear that many persons of American ancestry were regarded in South Carolina as colored persons (or as mulattoes), especially when poor or when living in association with part-Africans. Census records for the mixed Indian people of northeastern South Carolina (variously called 'Brass Ankles', 'Redbones', 'Yellow People', etc., until recently) usually classify them as 'colored' or 'mulattoes'.[36]

Many persons who were classified as 'colored' retained a specific knowledge of their American ancestry. Some attempted to challenge the application of the capitation tax to colored people of American racial background. In 1858, for example, Frederick Chavis, Lewis Chavis, Durany Chavis, James Jones, Bartley Jones, Mary Jones, Jonathan Williams, and Polly Dunn petitioned the South Carolina legislature to the effect that:

the first six petitioners above named, to wit, the Chavis & Jones families, are free persons of color being descendants of Indian ancestors. The other two, to wit, Jonathan Williams & Polly Dunn are free colored persons alleged to be descended from, or mixed with the blood of the negro race. . . .

Your petitioners of the Indian blood, that is to say, Frederick, Lewis & Durany Chavis, James, Bartley & Mary Jones, pray your Honorable body to say whether by free persons of color, they mean to include descendants of Indians, or only those who are mixed with negro blood, in order that your petitioners may know whether they are liable for this tax or not.

Wesley D. White found that in the 1860 census for Edgefield County, James A. Jones and Fred Chevers were both married to 'white' women and that all of their children were then classified as 'white'.

It is not known what result was obtained from the above petition. In any case, the status of these families illustrates the complex, tri-racial character of the 'colored' people of South Carolina and also helps to dispel the notion that only a two-caste system for free people (white and 'negro') existed in the British North American slave colonies (as has been argued by some writers).[37]

In those regions greatly influenced by South Carolina we find evidence also that persons of American ancestry could be classified as people of color. Reference has already been made to Georgia's classification of numerous Cherokee people (unmixed in all probability) as persons of color in the 1830 census. In 1835 Georgia passed an act regulating 'free persons of color' and requiring registration. The act, however, did not apply to 'any American Indian, free Moor, or Lascar, but the burden of proof, in all cases of arrest of any person of color, shall be on such person of color, to show himself or herself exempt from the operations of this act.'[38]

In Florida we find that an 'Appalachacola' Indian man named Tom Factor had married a 'negro' woman who, along with their children, was carried off by Georgia white men and held as a slave. A daughter, Sarah Factor, was called 'a coloured woman' in 1838.[39]

In Alabama the state code seems to have placed all persons of American ancestry, to one-eighth blood, in the same category with part-Africans:

all negroes, mulattoes, Indians and all persons of mixed blood, descended from negro or Indian ancestors, to the third generation inclusive, though one ancestor of each generation may have been a white person, whether bond or free; shall be taken, and deemed incapable in law, to be witnesses . . . except for or against each other.[40]

In 1851–2 certain 'free persons of color' were declared to be 'citizens' of Alabama 'as fully as they would be if they were not of Indian descent'.[41]

In 1859 there was a case against 'Maria Louisa (Woman of Color)' in Alabama, involving a white man who sought to hold her as a slave. Her mother 'was a woman of yellowish complexion' who always had acted free and had died in 1839 in New Orleans. 'Her mother seemed to be of Indian or Mexican descent, and had the charactistic features of an Indian Mexican, or Mexican Indian.' The presumption must be, according to the Court, that she was free since the presumption of slavery 'applies only to Africans, or persons having negro blood'.[42]

Certain it is, then, that in both Georgia and Alabama persons of American race, with no African ancestry, were called 'colored'; while in Florida a mixed African–American woman was called 'colored'.

North Carolina

North Carolina was also quite influential as regards its legal definitions of caste position and prohibitions of interracial marriage. In general, Americans and Africans and their descendants were placed in the same category until *c.*1826, and there was no legal tendency to treat part-American persons in a favored manner with one exception: In the nineteenth century the presumption of a slave status applied only to persons of unmixed African ancestry and not to persons colored by American blood. (Doubtless even this difference could not have been applicable in the early period when American slaves were common.) In a court case of 1802 the decision stated:

> I acquiesce in the rules . . . with respect to the presumption of every black person being a slave. . . . But I am not aware that the doctrine of presuming against liberty, has been urged in relation to persons of mixed blood, or to those of any color between the two extremes of black and white; and I do not think it reasonable that such a doctrine should receive the least countenance. Such persons may have descended from Indians in both lines, or at least in the maternal. . . . The plaintiff, attempting to obtain freedom was of an olive color, between black and yellow; had long hair and a prominent nose.

He had been found in a barn as an infant, born of unknown parents. The court recognized his freedom.[43]

In another case in 1853 a man named Alfred Nichols obtained his freedom, because any shade of color lighter than black led to a presumption of liberty. Nichols 'was of a brown color, between that of an African and a mulatto' and was known as a free man. He was judged to be 'a man of color' and free.[44]

One key difference, then, between 'people of color' and 'free negroes' was that colored persons had the presumption of freedom in their favor, while free Africans had to prove their freedom by means of documents or testimony. The burden of proof, in other words, fell on the free Africans.

Another difference, however, was that free colored persons were often of American ancestry, as opposed to African. Several scholars have noted that the Indians of North Carolina were often classified as 'people of color'.[45] Court cases make this quite clear also. In 1821 one John Locklier was called 'a coloured man' while the name Locklier is confined to the Indians of Robeson County and surrounding areas. In 1841–3 one William P. Waters claimed that he was not a 'man of color' because 'he was descended from Portuguese, and not from Negro or Indian ancestors.' In 1853 a Locklear was judged to be a free person of color incapable of carrying arms. In 1857 a William Chavers (also a Lumbee or Robeson County Indian name) was charged 'as a free person of color' with carrying a shotgun. Chavers was able to win his case eventually 'because he is charged as "a free person of color" whereas . . . the act . . . makes it penal for any 'free negro' to carry arms. . . . Free persons of color may be . . . persons colored by Indian blood. . . . The indictment cannot be sustained.[46] The Supreme Court held specifically that 'free negro' and 'free person of color' were not legally identical terms.

It is quite clear, then, that Americans could be colored persons in North Carolina (and that 'free negroes' were not the only 'persons of color' before the Civil War). This concept is reinforced by the application of marriage laws in North Carolina. An act of 1715, re-enacted in 1741 and remaining in effect until 1836, specified that a white person could not marry: 'an Indian, Negro, Mustee, or Mulatto . . . or any person of Mixed Blood to the Third Generation.'

This prohibition was re-enacted in 1838 and in 1866. Under it, in 1852, a man was charged with illegally being married to a white woman.

Melton is of Indian descent [but in what degree the Jury could not say] and . . . Byrd is a white woman; and they allege that they were legally married. [It is held that] it cannot be supposed it was the intention of the legislature to forbid marriages between white persons and persons of Indian blood, however far removed. . . . when in 1838 they extend the penalty in the Fifth Section of the 71st chapter of the Act of 1836, they must have meant that the offence . . . should be a marriage within the degrees specified in the Act of 1836 (any person of mixed-blood to the third generation).[47]

The Marriage Act of January 8, 1839 (enacted 1838) is quoted in a court decision as stating that all marriages 'between a white person and a free negro, or a free person of color to the third generation, shall be void.'[48] Thus the terms 'mixed-blood' and 'person of color' could be used interchangeably in North Carolina and definitely included persons of part-American ancestry.

Virginia

Some years ago Frank H. Russell, in his work on *The Free Negro in Virginia*, recognized that one of the ways in which the free colored population grew was by the mixture of Africans and Americans: 'there is no doubt that a considerable element in the free colored population of the nineteenth century was of Indian extraction.'[49] Russell also noted that prior to the War of Independence manumissions were rare.[50] Free persons of color, then, had to be descended largely from free women, that is, American or European women.

We can be sure that all persons of mixed African and American ancestry were classified as colored persons (or as 'negroes') prior to the Civil War. In addition, there is a large body of evidence showing that virtually all Indians residing in Virginia, whether part-African or not, were also classified as 'people of color'. Under the laws of Virginia from 1705 until at least 1785 the 'child of an Indian' was legally categorized as a 'mulatto', along with persons of one-eighth or more African ancestry. In 1785 the term 'mulatto' was applied to persons of only one-quarter or more African ancestry, thus allowing some persons to become white (or Indian) who had legally been 'mulatto' previously. It is not clear if the 1705 definition was replaced, as regards American ancestry, and court decisions and other evidence are contradictory on this point. Nonetheless, in practice, the term continued to be applied to virtually all reservation and off-reservation Indians in tax records, census enumerations, and in the 'free negro' registration book of at least one county.[51] In 1866, after the Civil War, the following language was adopted: 'Every person having one-fourth or more Negro blood shall be deemed a colored person, and every person not a colored person having one-fourth or more Indian blood shall be deemed an Indian.'[52] Here we see an apparent change, in that the 'colored persons' category was made to include unmixed Black Africans as well as mixed persons and, of course, persons of three-quarters American ancestry if the other quarter was

African. This change was anticipated in 1860 when Virginia had made the terms 'negro' and 'mulatto' equivalent in all statutes. By 1866 both terms were to be subsumed under the category of 'colored'.

It should be noted that most local records prior to 1860 differentiate between 'free mulattoes' and 'free negroes' but there are instances where the distinction is not maintained.

The Native American communities were, of course, vitally affected by these changes. Such communities might now be divided into at least two categories of people: 'Indians' (with less than one-quarter African ancestry) and 'colored' (with one-quarter or more African ancestry). What ensued was a one-hundred-year struggle to resist the 'colored' category, a struggle fought with uneven success and one which served to poison African–American Indian relations as well as to split communities, churches, and even families. It is beyond the scope of this study to go into that story but one remark should be made and that is that the Native American communal resistance to the term 'colored' after the Civil War seems to have been based on the fact that 'colored', in the white mind, had become equivalent to 'negro' and that its acceptance by Indians would have amounted to a voluntary change in ethnic identity.

In the twentieth century Virginia broadened the term 'colored' to include all Indians with any trace of African ancestry, if living off reservation, and with more than one-thirty-second African ancestry, if living on a reservation. For all governmental purposes Indians were treated as 'colored' persons until recently, but in at least one or two counties the lighter families were treated, in practice, in a different manner from their relations elsewhere.[53]

The local tax-rolls of Virginia seem to show a common trend from *c.*1783 onward. Until about 1812 people who can be identified as Indians or as being of mixed blood are listed under the 'white-tithable' column while only a few free Africans are labeled as 'free negroes'. From *c.*1813 onward, however, the word 'mulatto' is used beside the names of Indians and mixed-bloods, with 'free negro' used for people of presumably dark complexion.

In these local records few of the Indians of Virginia are designated as 'Indians', the overwhelming majority being called 'mulattoes' or 'free colored'. In certain counties an 'F.N.' ('Free Negro') was placed after the names of a few families who may have been Indian.[54]

From 1803 until the Civil War all free people of color in Virginia were required to register. The register of Essex County has survived and in it many Rappahannock Indian families were registered, usually as 'mulattoes'. The book was entitled 'Register of Free Negroes' but a high percentage of the people were, in fact, of Indian extraction.[55]

One of the few persons listed as 'Indian' in the early Virginia tax records was William Scott of Richmond. By 1810, however, 'Billy Scott' was called a free person of color in the census, and his descendants were apparently all classified as 'M' in the census records. Nonetheless, a William Scott, senior, was still claiming to be an Indian in 1853.[56]

Many other examples can be cited to show that Indians were called 'people of color'. In 1825 John Dungie (Dungee), 'who is descended from the aborigines of this Dominion' was called specifically a free person of color in a petition submitted to the Virginia legislature.[57]

As already noted, the census records of Virginia through 1830 uniformly place all Indians in the 'free colored' category, while those of 1840 and 1850 categorize virtually all as 'M'. These persons include the members of reservation tribal councils, chiefs, and some persons identified in other sources as having no African ancestry. For example an 1808 partial census of the Nottoway tribe identified Littleton Scholar as a full-blood Indian with a white wife. In the 1830 census, however, his sons Ned and Billy were listed as free people of color.[58]

It is abundantly clear, then, that persons of Amerian and American–European ancestry, along with persons of American–African ancestry, were commonly categorized as people of color in Virginia prior to the Civil War.

Other Eastern States

As noted previously, many persons of American background are classified as 'persons of color' in the census records of Maryland, Delaware, and other eastern states. But in some of the states the terms 'negro' and 'mulatto' continued to be used in local records and statutes, up to the Civil War. Maryland, for example, often seems to use 'free negro' to refer to all free non-whites although 'mulatto' and 'Indian' also occasionally appear in statutes. In 1717 the legislature decided that: 'no negro or mulatto slave, free negro, or mulatto born of a white woman, during his time of servitude by law, or any Indian slave or free Indian, natives of this or the neighboring provinces, be admitted [to testify where any] Christian white person is concerned.' This act was repeated in 1846–7 except that the white person did not have to be a Christian to be immune from non-white testimony.

Quite clearly the acts of 1717 and 1846–7 were designed to preclude all non-white testimony and yet certain categories of non-whites are not specifically identified (i.e., American–Africans, mulattos who are free but not born of a white woman, etc.). We must assume, I believe, that Maryland intended the term 'free negro' to embrace all such persons.

The concept 'people of color' is used in an 1831–2 statute but otherwise 'free negro', 'negro', and 'mulatto' are the common terms.[59] It seems quite clear that the Indians who remained in Maryland were usually placed under one of these categories, especially since all of the Piscataway Indian families located in the 1790 census have 'mulatto' written after their names.[60]

Delaware follows a similar pattern. The Nanticoke Indians in the 1830 census, for example, are all listed under the 'free people of color' column but 'F.N.' has been inserted beside virtually all of their names. An Act of 1826 refers to 'colored persons' but generally 'free negro' and 'mulatto' are used in statutes. After a long struggle the Nanticoke Indians succeeded in having a separate school system established (1881) but they were referred to in the enabling act as 'a certain class of colored persons'. Their schools were called 'The Indian River School Districts for a certain class of colored persons'. The legislature also stated: 'Provided that no one shall be a member of this corporation who does not belong to the class of colored persons to which those mentioned in Section One belong.' Clearly, the legislature insisted upon referring to the Indian River Nanticokes as 'colored people' but agreed to differentiate them from other 'colored people' because of their Indian background, and to allow them to exclude non-Indians from membership.[61]

There were significant numbers of African–American mixed-bloods in both New Jersey and New York, and some also in Pennsylvania. They seem to have often been referred to as 'negroes' or, as in the case of 'Indian Bill' of Westchester County, New York (1830) classed as 'persons of color'. New York referred to 'men of color' in 1814, and in 1817 under 'persons of color' were listed 'every negro, mulatto, or mustee', thus encompassing all slaves of whatever mixture. In 1806 the expression 'people of color' was defined as 'mulattoes, mustees, costees, etc., all colors from black to white'. In 1817 the *New York Spectator* referred to Paul Cuffe (half-Indian, half-African) as an example whereby 'the free people of color . . . may see the manner in which they may require [acquire] competency and reputation'.[62]

In New England it appears that many persons of American blood were classified as 'people of color', at least for census purposes. On the other hand, Massachusetts seem to have used 'people of color' primarily to refer to American–African or American–African–European mixed-bloods. Throughout the nineteenth century, references are made to 'Indian, mulatto and negro people' living in Indian communities in that state, along with 'Indians and people of color'.

In 1861, however, the Fall River Indians were referred to as 'colored people' in a report. Also in 1861, the Indians of Yarmouth were said to be almost white. They were 'so little colored, that it would hardly be noticed by one not acquainted with the fact.' The Middleborough Indians were said to have integrated into the general community 'as the other colored population of the state'. Nonetheless, a legislative act of 1861 allowed many Indian tribal members – referred to as 'Indian or person of color' – to acquire full Massachusetts citizenship. If they did so they could not later return to an Indian legal status. The act dealt with 'All Indians and descendants of Indians' and made reference to 'any Indian or person of color, belonging to either of the tribes'.[63]

Thus we have clear evidence that in Massachusetts the term 'colored' was used for tribal members and, on occasion at least, for entire Indian groups. Nonetheless, it is likely that 'colored' was usually reserved for mixed-bloods. An 1849 report states: 'the whole number of Indians and people of colour connected with them, not including Natick, is 847. There are about six or eight Indians, of pure blood, in the state, . . . all the rest are of mixed blood; mostly Indian and African.[64]

In 1857 New Hampshire adopted a statute stating that 'any person of color or of African descent' cannot be deprived of the right to vote.[65] This would seem to imply that 'persons of color' could be of American Indian or other non-white descent.

States West of the Appalachians

Kentucky appears to have followed Virginia usage, in general, and we find that 'negroes, mulattoes, and Indians' are together placed in the same inferior category by law. An Act of 1798 stated: 'that if any negro, or mulatto, or Indian bond or free, shall at any time lift his or her hand in opposition to any person not being a negro, mulatto or Indian, (it is) declared punishable . . . with thirty lashes.' A court decision of 1820 invalidated the above because the act subjected 'the free persons of color' to punishment merely upon a white person's oath.[66]

Tennessee followed the pattern of North Carolina, in general, although the precise treatment of unmixed Indians is not clear from my data. From 1794 'Negroes and persons of mixed-blood to the third generation' were prohibited from testifying in white cases and in 1822 punishment was provided for any white person who 'shall presume to live with any negro, mustee, or mulatto . . . as man and wife.' The above groups were apparently regarded as 'colored'.

In 1834 the franchise was limited to 'free white men' except that colored persons of less than one-eighth non-white ancestry could vote. Apparently the 'Malungeon' (Saponi–Powhatan) mixed people of northeastern Tennessee were categorized as 'free persons of color' by the same constitutional convention.[67]

The newer states seem not to have clearly categorized unmixed Indians as colored persons but it is certain that African–American mixed bloods were so designated. Ohio legislation refers repeatedly to 'black and mulatto persons' or to 'negro and mulatto persons' but these terms seem not to have been defined until 1849 when separate schools for colored children were authorized. At that date it was decided that 'the term colored, as used in this act, shall be construed as being of the same signification as the term "black or mulatto", as used in former acts.' In general, it would appear that a person of one-half or more African descent was understood to come under the above definition.[68]

Indiana in 1817 adopted language as follows:

Every person other than a negro, of whose grandfathers or grandmothers any one is or shall have been a negro, though his other progenitors may have been a white, shall be deemed a mulatto, and so every person who shall have one-fourth part or more of negro blood.

In 1843 Arkansas adopted a similar act, entitling it as being for 'free persons of color': 'every person not a full negro, who shall be one fourth or more negro, shall be deemed a mulatto.'[69] Thus the tendency to separate 'negro' from 'colored' or 'mulatto' was preserved and all African–American mixed-bloods would be included under the latter categories.

Indiana also discriminated against 'negroes, mulattoes and Indians' as did

Illinois in 1818 and 1829. In the latter year a mulatto was defined by Illinois to be a person of one-quarter or more Negro blood while 'every person who shall have one-half Indian blood shall be deemed an Indian'. At the same time an act stated that a 'person of color, negro, or mulatto' cannot marry a white person. 'Persons of color' would seem to embrace Indians or at least persons of American–African mixture.[70]

Most other western states tended to place Indians, some part-Indians, Africans and some part-Africans (along with Asians and Hawaiians) in the same inferior category of non-citizens. But the term 'colored' is, it would appear, seldom used as a general designation for non-whites. On the other hand, California authorized segregated schools in 1870 for children 'of African or Indian descent' and in San Francisco at least these schools were known to be 'for colored children'.[71]

POST-CIVIL WAR USAGE

The latter half of the nineteenth and the first half of the twentieth centuries saw many persons equating 'colored' with 'negro' and 'negro' with 'colored', at least in the United States. Such usage arose not only from white racist efforts to place all non-whites (or at least persons of African ancestry) in a single catch-all category but also from Afroamerican efforts to secure internal unity. Some Afroamerican groups emphasized 'colored' as their unifying term, a category which undoubtedly was more palatable to some mixed-bloods than was 'negro'. Some groups did, however, find 'negro' preferable and promoted its usage in a variety of ways.

In any case, the close association of 'negro' and 'colored' after *c.*1860 had the effect, no doubt, of making the latter term so closely associated with having African ancestry that it could no longer be used to encompass all non-whites except in the ex-slave states (where, as already noted, many Indians continued to be categorized as colored persons but with the often unsubstantiated assumption of their having some degree of African ancestry).

More recently some non-white poets and writers have begun to revive the concept of 'people of color' as being applicable to all non-whites (or all 'Third World People'). This usage has been made possible, no doubt, by the fact that the Afroamerican population in the United States has largely abandoned the use of 'colored' as a self-designation.

PEOPLE OF COLOR:
A UNIQUE AND COMPLEX CATEGORY

In our analysis of the historical meaning of racial terms we must avoid the mistake of reading back into the past contemporary definitions. From this perspective it has been very dangerous and counterproductive to substitute 'free negro', 'free black', African or Afroamerican for 'free colored' as used before the Civil War.

In so doing scholars have not only misled us as to ethnic make-up of the free non-white population, but they have also helped to obscure the distinctive character of Atlantic Seaboard society before and after the Civil War. What I mean by this is that it seems highly likely that pre-Civil War society was much more ethnically diverse and culturally pluralistic, at least in so far as non-whites were concerned. After the Civil War and Reconstruction periods 'Jim Crow' racism advanced far beyond what had existed before and a much more polarized social situation ensued.

'Free Negro' implies, I think, a much more culturally and ethnically unified group of people, and also one thoroughly circumscribed by the black-white conflict.

But the 'free people of color' included all kinds of persons and all kinds of communities, from Indian reservations, to Indian rural communities, to mixed Indian–African–white populations, to European–African mixed-bloods, to free Africans, etc. It included not only a vast range of colors but a range of cultures and living situations, both urban and rural. And what is more, it was an extremely assimilative sector of society, mixing and blending three races (and sometimes Asians as well).

I have discussed this aspect of the 'free colored' world separately and thus it is not necessary to proceed further here. I do want to summarize, however, the conclusions I have reached about the meaning of the term 'colored' in the United States prior to the Civil War.[72]

I believe that the evidence indicates that the 'free people of color' generally consisted in all non-European persons of whatever racial ancestry except: (1) unmixed Indians living on a federal reservation or when living as independent nations; (2) unmixed Indians living in recognized Indian towns in a few states such as Massachusetts (but this is only a partial exception); and (3) free persons of unmixed African ancestry according to the usage common in many southern states.

We can be quite certain, however, that there was no solid line between 'free colored persons' and 'free negroes', unmixed Indians, or even whites before the Civil War. The 1850 census for Charles City County, Virginia (a heavily slave county) shows white women living in the same household with non-white men, and vice versa, as well as many 'M' (mixed people) being married to 'B' (black or dark) people.[73]

Thus we cannot suppose that the 'free colored' population was a 'fixed' entity. It was dynamic and constantly changing.

But above all, we cannot make the mistake of translating 'colored' as 'negro', black, or African. It must, before the Civil War, be generally translated as 'people who are colored with some shade intermediate between the extremes of white and black', that is, with much the same meaning as Portuguese *pardo*.

Finally, I believe that it will be quite important for scholars to study the evolution of 'colored', mixed groups in the Americas on a comparative basis without becoming locked into paradigms formed essentially by North American white racism and fascination with only the black–white nexus.

For, after all, the mixture of American, African and European (with Asian also) has produced tens of millions of 'cosmic' persons who have become the dominant population in many regions of the Americas. And, moreover, many of the descendants of the 'free colored' before the Civil War still live, even today, as mixed people or as American Indians in spite of the pressures of racism and the categories imposed by outsiders.

The 'tunnel vision' of seeing pre-Civil War 'free persons of color' as simply a stage in the evolution of modern-day Afroamericans must be revised in favor of a more complex analysis which recognizes the tri-racial origins of the population and which also sees their relationship to both contemporary Afroamericans and Native Americans and their relevance to comparative research with similar populations elsewhere in the Americas.

10
African–American Contacts and the Modern Re-Peopling of the Americas

AFRICAN AND AMERICAN CONTACTS IN PRE-COLUMBIAN
TIMES

The evidence seems rather convincing that Americans reached the British Isles and the coast of Europe long before 1492 and perhaps as early as *c*. 50 BC. The navigational capabilities of Americans, as well as favorable ocean currents, also suggest the possibility of contacts with the Azores, and perhaps the Canary Islands and the coast of Africa.

I have not examined critically the claims made by others for possible ancient African contacts with America but the evidence presented herein is suggestive of interaction shortly prior to 1492. The reports of 'black' traders in the Caribbean and of 'black' people living in Panama (by 1513) cannot be ignored.

Much work remains to be done. The archaeology, ethnology, art, oral literature and documentary records must all be examined from Iceland and Ireland to southern Africa with a view to the discovery of evidence relating to American influences. The task has hardly commenced, since heretofore few scholars have been looking for the effects of American arrivals in either Europe or Africa.

Similarly, much work remains in terms of the evidence of African contacts with America. Someone must, for example, trace carefully the history of the 'black' village near Cuarecua, Panama, after 1513, to shed further light on its origin. Those who also advocate an African presence in ancient America must go beyond pointing out a particular image as having so-called African features and must proceed to the placing of the image in a complete cultural–historical process. If, for example, the giant heads of the Olmec culture were of African inspiration, then we must be shown where in the Africa of 800–300 BC such heads were also being carved.

I have established the high probability also that Americans kidnapped by the Norse reached northern Europe in the 1000s and early 1400s, and the possibility that Americans from Newfoundland and elsewhere may have been taken to Portugal or other parts of Europe in the 1490s or even earlier. Nonetheless, the slave trade initiated by Columbus in the Caribbean and by the Portuguese in Brazil constituted a decisive stage in the escalation of African–American contacts of an intensive nature.

AMERICAN–AFRICAN CONTACTS IN AFRICA AND EUROPE

The presence of Native Americans in Europe and Africa in significant numbers from the 1490s onward has been overlooked by the scholarly world in general. Nonetheless, the subject is of very great significance indeed because of the tremendous Native American cultural impact upon both continents, especially in the horticultural realm. Now, however, we can demonstrate enough intensity of contact to allow for the diffusion of American techniques (e.g., pipe-making or cassava production), crops, ideas (individual freedom, utopian socialism), folklore, music, art, medicine, and so on, not by some indirect means but through direct American contact within Europe and Africa.

Evidence has been presented in the preceding pages to show that Columbus planned to sell American slaves to the African islands controlled by Spain and Portugal as early as the mid–1490s and that it is extremely likely that the Portuguese began to use native Brazilians in Africa as early as the first decade of the sixteenth century. Native American contacts with Africa intensified as Angola and West Africa became ever more entwined with Brazil and, especially, with the direct Dutch use of Native American auxiliary troops in the conquest of Angola, Elmina (Ghana) and the Portuguese islands of the Gulf of Guinea (1639–1640s).

We have been able to outline the possible extent of Native American presence in places such as Angola, Ghana, Spain, Portugal, the Netherlands, and so on, but we have not exhausted the subject. Quite the contrary; it will be necessary for other scholars to conduct detailed, in-depth studies in all of the countries mentioned.

We can be sure, however, that a new chapter in the social and cultural history of Africa and Europe will be opened, once the American presence is acknowledged and further investigated.

THE CLARIFICATION OF THE MEANINGS OF
COLOR AND 'RACIAL' TERMS

The greater part of this study has been taken up with the extremely crucial task of showing that the modern European and North American tendency to be obsessed with 'black-white' relations (to the near exclusion of multi-ethnic and time-depth, comparative perspectives) has led to significant distortions in the use of color and 'racial' terms, such as 'colored', black, negro, mulatto, mustee, *pardo*, *loro*, and several others.

I have been able to clarify the evolution of many of these terms, in so far as they bear upon American–African relations. In general, I am able to show that all of these terms have historically been applicable to persons of American ancestry and that one cannot read back into previous centuries the current dictionary definitions of such words without serious error.

Of considerable significance has been the documentation that Americans were often called *negros*, blacks, negroes, and *mooren* in various languages (along with other non-white peoples) and that it is very dangerous to assume that each and every person referred to as *negro* or 'black' was African. This is especially pertinent to analyses relating to the character of slaves being shipped from or within the Americas.

Also of great significance has been our showing that 'mulatto' in several languages included persons of half- or part-American ancestry and that in the Spanish colonies in the Americas most *mulatos* in the sixteenth and seventeenth centuries were of American–African background, *not* European–African. Generally speaking, it would seem that *mulato* referred to a person who was part-African and part-not African, but, in French and North American colonial English, *mulâtre* and 'mulatto' could refer to a European–American mixed-blood. This was also true of *mulat* in Dutch.

The evidence also shows that Native Americans were commonly referred to as 'people of color' or its equivalent in various languages (*kleurlingen*, *pardos*, *loros*, colored people). This is of great significance for the social history of the United States, Brazil, Argentina, and the Americas in general since it has often been assumed (by English-speaking scholars especially) that 'people of color' in the United States or *pardos* in Brazil should be regarded as 'negroes' or people of 'black' identity.

It has been shown that it is historically unsound to ignore the possible American ancestry of people referred to in sources as colored, *pardos*, and so on. This is also true of people called *mulatos*, as discussed above.

The collective significance of these findings consists principally in their creating an absolute obligation for the radical revision of our views relative to the nature of the modern (post-1500) re-peopling of the Americas. In addition, however, these findings require that a new critical look be taken at some of the most common notions current regarding the history of race relations, slavery, the evolution of plantation societies, and the development of 'free colored' populations in the Americas.

THE EVOLUTION OF RACISM AND CASTE TERMINOLOGY

As the reader will recall, some Europeans from the 1200s through the early 1500s utilized terms such as *negro*, *loro*, *pardo*, *olivastre* and *berretino* to refer to persons of intermediate and dark color-shades. These terms were then supplemented by a proliferation of others such as *leonado*, *membrillo cocido*, *moreno*, and *trigueño*. The significant thing about these terms is that it would appear that they were not used as 'race' or caste names, they were not used in a genealogical sense, nor did they point towards anything more than appearance, generally speaking.

In 1552 the *Historia* of Francisco López de Gómara appeared and within it the author included an interesting statement about human physical variation. In it he remarked upon the marvellous variety of colors created by God for human beings and how, although whites and blacks seem to be of totally opposite colors, there is really a progression of colors, almost by grades (*casi por grados*). There are whites of many shades of white, *bermejos* (reddish people) of many degrees of redness, and blacks of many kinds of blackness. Moreover, from white to *bermejo* one moves through *descolorido* (uncolored pale whites) and *rubio* (blonde, golden) and from black one moves through *cenizoso* (ash-colored), *moreno* (dark brown), *loro* (intermediate brown) and *leonado* (lionish). The Native Americans are *leonado* or, in general, *membrillos cochos* (stewed quince color), *tiriciados* (yellowish) or *castaños* (chestnut), according to López.[1]

The perspective of López, in seeing a great variety of colors not associated with any concept of separate 'races', is significant and, I believe, typical of most observers prior to modern times. Especially in the Mediterranean world we have noted the use of a great variety of color terms and an awareness of many gradations in human physical types. In sum, I think that we can say that the general view was that human types changed gradually and blended into one another.

Moreover, I believe that we can assert that it was more important (for the Iberians at least) that a person was a Muslim and an Arab or Berber than that he was black, brown, or white in color or that his hair was *crespo* (kinky), curly or straight.

In Europe itself most of the non-whites who arrived prior to the current century were gradually absorbed into the general population and thus a racial caste system failed to evolve locally. But in the European colonies, as has been pointed out, a fundamental shift occurred coincident with the adoption of terms such as *mestizo* and *mulato* and with the conquest or control of large masses of Americans, Africans, and Asians.

As noted in this study, the evolution of the term *mestizo* (or hybrid) seems to reflect a very significant shift in European thinking, a shift in direction of racism. 'Hybrid' formerly referred to almost any type of mixture including that between 'wild' and 'tame' or between 'citizen' and 'stranger'. *Mestizo* commenced its history as an equivalent of 'hybrid' and originally was applicable to animals as well as humans, and to mixture that was religious, ethnic or cultural as well as 'racial'.

But gradually European colonialists began to place greater and greater emphasis upon a narrowed concept of *mestizaje* which began to upset the balance between cultural and biological factors. The Spanish and Portuguese varieties of colonialism never abandoned cultural factors completely (for example, differentiating between *mestizos* of 'legitimate' birth or who were raised among Spaniards and *mestizos* raised among Americans). British North American colonialists followed, at first, the same path (differentiating, in some colonies, between mulattoes born of a white mother and those born of American or African mothers, for example). But in the nineteenth century, and especially after the US Civil War, greater and greater emphasis was placed upon wholly biological or 'racial' categorization and differentiation in North America.

Generally speaking, a study of colonial legislation reveals that terms such as *preto*, *mestizo*, *mulato*, *zambahígo*, mustee, and so on, were utilized largely *to exclude*. From the early 1500s onward we can trace a whole series of laws in the various empires in which the rights extended to Spaniards, Portuguese, Britons and other white persons were *denied* to persons categorized as negroes, mulattoes, blacks, mustees, mestizos, and so forth. The primary use of such terms in legislation was *to exclude* persons so categorized from the ordinary rights and privileges enjoyed by white subjects of the respective colonial powers.

Of course, it is true that the terms themselves did not originally cause this exclusion. Exclusion resulted from the social reality of colonial exploitation. The Spaniards, instead of denying to *mulatas* the right to wear expensive jewelry and silk clothes, could have simply said that any woman of African and Spanish or African and American (Indian) ancestry could not wear such items. Terms such as *mulata* were simply shorthand, efficient ways for referring to certain kinds of people without describing them in detail.

On the other hand, it is also true that once developed, terms such as *negro*, *mulato*, 'Indian', and 'half-breed' came to possess a power of their own, facilitating the stereotyping of people. Moreover, as racism developed as a cancer in European colonial settings, this stereotyping came to have a greater and greater 'racial' as opposed to 'cultural' content, especially in North America.

THE RE-PEOPLING OF THE AMERICAS

'Racial' stereotyping as well as the use of caste categories fostered by colonialism have had the effect of distorting our understanding of the re-peopling of the Americas. I have provided a critical and theoretical basis upon which a new approach to this subject can be erected, a basis informed by the empirical examination of the evidence relating to the meaning of ethnic terms in given spatial or temporal realms as opposed to simply making deductive assumptions based upon myths of the recent past or of the present.

One of our major tasks now is to clarify the nature of the re-peopling of the Americas, that is, the population recovery which followed the declines of the sixteenth century (or subsequent centuries, depending on the area).

The centuries which followed Columbus' incursion into the Caribbean saw a radical decline in the population of the Americas, as has been pointed out earlier. Subsequently the population began to recover, but with an important difference. That is, in many areas the subsequent population has seemed to be African or mixed (or European) in appearance, rather than Native American.

Many scholars have assumed that the repopulation process, particularly in the circum-Caribbean region, was one of the *replacement* of Americans by Africans and African–European mixed-bloods. This is the common picture provided for the re-peopling of the Caribbean islands, the southern United States, and parts of coastal mainland South America.

My research establishes, beyond any doubt, that the above picture is erroneous. There has essentially been no *replacement* of Native Americans (considered on a broad scale). What has in fact happened is that *American survivors and African survivors* (because huge numbers of Africans also died in the process) *have merged together to create the basic modern populations of much of the Greater Caribbean and adjacent mainland regions.*

Of course, as the years have passed the process of merger has proven to be uneven. Some areas (such as Mexico and Peru) have become phenotypically 'Indian' while other areas (such as many of the islands) have become phenotypically 'African'. In general, of course, one finds a wide range of sub-groups since merger has been uneven and European and Asian genes have also been absorbed.

In simplistic terms, nonetheless, we can suggest the broad significance of American–African intermixture by referring to the Eastern Neo–American mixed population and the Western Neo–American mixed population. Both groups have arisen (or are arising) from the mixture of African, American, European and some Asian elements, with the African element being relatively stronger in Eastern Neo–American and the Native American element being relatively stronger in Western Neo–American, as discussed at the close of chapter 2.

In short, persons may 'look' African but have Native American ancestry, or 'look' indigenous American but have African ancestry, and not only may individuals lean in one direction or the other, but the population of entire regions may seem to fall into one category or another.

By the nineteenth century it seems quite certain that Afroamericans, whether living in Latin America, the Caribbean or in North America, had absorbed considerable amounts of Native American ancestry. Similarly, many North American and circum-Caribbean native groups had absorbed varying amounts of African ancestry, from New England to the entire rim of Central and South America. But in many cases we are dealing with 300 to 400 years (twenty generations) of intermixture of a very complex sort. Very seldom would we be looking at, for example, a half-American, half-African person in the later nineteenth century, but rather at a person both of whose parents might have varying amounts of African and American ancestry derived at different intervals and from extremely diverse sources – as from American nations as different as the Narragansett or Pequot and the Carib or Arawak, or from African nations as diverse as the Mandinka, Yoruba, and Malagasy.

The ancestry of modern-day Americans, whether of 'black' or 'Indian' appearance, is often (or usually) quite complex indeed. It is sad that many such persons have been forced by racism into arbitrary categories which tend to render their ethnic heritage simple rather than complex. It is now one of the principal tasks of scholarship to replace the shallow one-dimensional images of non-whites with more accurate multi-dimensional portraits.[2]

Notes

INTRODUCTION

1 Broadsheet, Mimeographed, 'Fight Racism: Drop All Charges against Black Youth', October 1981.
2 Richard Ligon, *A True and Exact History of the Island of Barbadoes* (London:Cass, 1970), pp. 15–17.
3 Beverly Fleet, *Virginia Colonial Abstracts*, vol. 15, Sixth Collection, pp. 2ff; and William Nelson, ed., *Documents Relating to the Colonial History of New Jersey* (Patterson: The Call, 1904), vol. 26, p. 267.
4 James Hugo Johnston, *Race Relations in Virginia and Miscegenation in the South, 1776–1860* (Amherst: University of Massachusetts Press, 1970), pp. 196–7.

CHAPTER 1 AFRICANS AND AMERICANS: INTER-CONTINENTAL CONTACTS ACROSS THE ATLANTIC, TO 1500

1 The word 'American' will be used for American Indians, Amerindians and Native Americans in the colonial period, and 'African' or 'Black African' will be used for sub-Saharan Africans in order to avoid premature use of the ambiguous 'Indian' and 'Negro'. The word 'Indian' was used for Pacific Islanders, Indonesians, Filipinos, etc. by the Spanish and English. See, for example, the reference to an Indian cacique from Manila and the *indios chinos* and *japoneses* cited by Magnus Mörner, *Race Mixture and the History of Latin America* (Boston: Little, Brown, 1967), p. 66 and n; and the reference to Filipinos as *los Indios* by the king of Spain in 1574, quoted in Silvio Zavala, *Los Esclavos Indios en Nueva España* (Mexico City: Colegio Nacional, 1967), p. 201. See ibid., p. 236, for the liberation of 'indios chinos o indios filipinenses' in Mexico in 1572.
2 Jan Carew, 'Children of the Sun' in Andrew Salkey, ed. *Caribbean Folk Tales and Legends* (London: Bogle-L'Ouverture, 1980), pp. 88, 94–5, 98.
3 The movie *Black Orpheus* depicts a macumba ceremony in Rio de Janeiro where American, African and European elements are mixed. See also Melville J. Herskovitz and Frances J. Herskovitz, 'Afro-Bahian Religious Songs', Album L-13, *Folk Music of Brazil* (Washington, DC: Library of Congress, 1947) pp. 2, 6–9;

Russell G. Hamilton, Jr, 'The Present State of African Cults in Bahia', *Journal of Social History*, vol. 3 (1970), pp. 364n, 370.

4 *Het Huwelijk Contract*, painting by Jan Steen, exhibited in the Boymans-van Beuningen Museum, Rotterdam, Netherlands, on loan from the Hermitage, Leningrad, July 1985.

5 See, for example, Leo Wiener, *Africa and the Discovery of America* (1920) and *Mayan and Mexican Origins* (1926); Ivan Van Sertima, ed., *African Presence in Early America* (1987) and *They Came Before Columbus* (1976); and Michael Bradley, *The Black Discovery of America* (1981).

6 Ian Whitaker, 'The Scottish Kayaks and the "Finn-men" ', *Antiquity*, vol. XXVIII (1954), p. 101; Thor Heyerdahl, 'Comment', in *Current Anthropology*, vol. 4 (1963), p. 73; Lindsey Scott, 'Drift Timber in the West', *Antiquity*, no. 99, pp. 151–3 as cited in Whitaker, 'Scottish Kayaks'; Carroll L. Riley, J. Charles Kelley, Campbell W. Pennington and Robert L. Rands, eds, *Man across the Sea: Problems of Precolumbian Contacts* (Austin: University of Texas Press, 1971), p. 17; Gert Noorter, *Old Kayaks in the Netherlands* (Leiden: Brill, 1971), pp. 6, 64, 69; M. Smallegange, *Nieuwe Cronijk van Zeeland* (Middelburg, 1696), vol. I, book IV, p. 489; Jean Merrien, *Christopher Columbus: the Mariner and the Man*, trans. Maurice Michael (London: Odhams, 1958) pp. 64–5; Jean Merrien, *Lonely Voyagers*, trans: J. H. Watkins (London: Hutchinson, 1954) pp. 37–8, 264.

7 Merrien, *Lonely Voyagers*, p. 35; Merrien, *Christopher Columbus*, p. 60; E. F. Greenman, 'The Upper Paleolithic and the New World', *Current Anthropology*, vol. 4 (1963), p. 61. Robert Heizer, in his study of whaling, noted that there were similarities between certain aspects of Inuit culture and that of prehistoric Finnmark (Samiland). He states that 'we may suspect a genetic connection between these American and Scandinavian cave arts. . . . Connection between Eskimo and Scandinavian cultures is a generally accepted fact'. This would refer to a period of at least 2,000 to 3,000 years ago. See Robert Fleming Heizer, 'Aboriginal Whaling in the Old and New Worlds', Doctor of Philosophy dissertation, University of California, Berkeley, 1941, pp. 34, 93–6, 108, 142. Only in the Finnmark region and in North America had archaeology revealed prehistoric evidence of whale-hunting (p. 40).

8 Bartolomé de las Casas, *Historia de las Indias*, edición de Augustín Millares Carlo (Mexico City: Fondo de Cultura Economica, 1951), vol. I, p. 67.

9 Ibid., vol. I, p. 138.

10 Luis de Cadamosto, *Viagens*, trans. Sebastião Francisco de Mendo Trigoso (Lisbon: Portugalia, no date), pp. 38–41; 'Le Navigazioni de Alvise de Ca'da Mosto e Pietro di Sintra' in Giovanni Battista Ramusio, *Navigazioni e Viaggi* (Turin: Einaudi, 1979), vol. I, pp. 480–5; also see lists of Canario names in Vicenta Cortés, *La Esclavitud en Valencia durante el Reinado de los Reyes Católicos, 1479–1516* (Valencia: Archivo Municipal y Ayuntamiento, 1964), and Alfonso Franco Silva, *Regesto Documental sobre la Esclavitud Sevillana, 1453–1513* (Seville: Universidad de Sevilla, 1979).

11 Las Casas, *Historia*, vol. I, p. 206. One authority argues that small vessels were safer than large ones (of over 30 feet length) and that coastal water is more dangerous than the open sea. See Thor Heyerdahl, *Early Man and the Ocean* (London: Allen & Unwin, 1978), pp. 44–5. Also see Riley et al., *Man across the Sea*, p. 9.

12   Andrés Bernaldez, *Memorias del Reinado de los Reyes Católicos* (Madrid: Real Academia de la Historia, 1962), pp. 275ff; Cecil Jane, *The Voyages of Christopher Columbus* (London: Argonaut, 1930), pp. 313, 318; W. H. Brett, *The Indian Tribes of Guiana; Their Condition and Habits* (London: Bell and Daldy, 1868), p. 488n.

13   Jane, *Voyages*, pp. 150, 163–4, 188–9, 201, 206, 229.

14   Ibid., p. 287; Las Casas, *Historia*, vol. I. p. 325.

15   Bernal Díaz del Castillo, *The Discovery and Conquest of Mexico*, trans. A. P. Maudslay, ed. Irving A. Leonard (New York: Grove, 1956), pp. 6–18, 21, 27; Clinton R. Edwards, 'Possibilities of Pre-Columbian Maritime Contacts among New World Civilizations', *Mesoamerican Studies*, vol. 4 (1969), pp. 3–10; Riley et al., *Man across the Sea*, pp. 11–12, 85, 259, 262; José Antonio Saco, *Historia de la Esclavitud de los Indios en el Nuevo Mundo* Havana: Cultural, 1932), vol. I, pp. 169–70. Saco also cites examples of Carib captives at Haiti escaping homeward in canoas (p. 168), and of the maritime capabilities of the Americans of the Gulf of Coquibacoa (Venezuela) where the people lived in houses erected over the water. By 1499–1500 they had already become hostile towards Spaniards, doubtless due to news from the Antilles or Haiti (pp. 119–22).

16   John Lawson, *History of North Carolina* (Richmond: Garrett and Massie, 1952), p. 7.

17   Bernard G. Hoffman, *Cabot to Cartier: Sources for a Historical Ethnography of Northeastern North America, 1497–1550* (Toronto: University of Toronto, 1961), pp. 108, 110.

18   Peter Lindeström, *Geographica Americae*, ed Amandus Johnson (Philadelphia: Swedish Colonial Society, 1925), pp. 237–8.

19   Antonio Pigafetta, *Primer Viaje en Torno del Globo*, trans. Carlos Amoretti (Buenos Aires: Espasa–Calpe, 1954), p. 41; Juan (Hans) Staden, *Vera Historia y Descripción de un País de las Salvages . . . en el Nuevo Mundo América*, trans. and ed. Edmundo Wernicke (Buenos Aires: Coni, 1944), p. 132.

20   Serafim Leite, ed., *Monumenta Brasiliae* (Rome: Societatis Iesu, 1960), vol. IV, pp. 131–2, 244.

21   See Thor Heyerdahl, *American Indians in the Pacific* (London: Allen & Unwin, 1952); Heyerdahl, *Early Man and the Ocean*, pp. 233, 353.

22   Pliny, *Natural History*, trans. H. Rackham (London: Heinemann, 1938), vol. I, book II, pp. 303–5.

23   Alexander S. Taylor, 'Indianology', Third Series, 1862, in the *California Farmer*, p. 82, Bancroft Library, University of California, Berkeley; Las Casas, *Historia*, vol. I, p. 71. The same data is in Joseph de Acosta, *The Natural and Moral History of the Indies*, trans. Edward Grimston (London: Hakluyt, 1880), vol. I, p. 55. See also Jan de Laet, *Notae ad Dissertationem Hugonis Grotii* (Amsterdam: Elzivirium, 1643), p. 79.

24   E. E. Evans and C. F. C. Hawkes, 'An Eskimo Harpoon-head', *Ulster Journal of Archaeology*, vol. III (1940).

25   Whitaker, 'Scottish Kayaks', p. 102n; *Proceedings of the Society of Antiquaries of Scotland*, vol XI (1876), p. 407, as cited in Whitaker.

26   H. Osterman, ed., *Knud Rasmussen's Posthumous Notes on the Life and Doings of the East Greenlanders in Olden Times* (Copenhagen: Retzels, 1938), p. 53. Such Inuit accidental voyages might help to explain the development of whaling in Norwegian–Sami areas from c.400 AD onward as well as the diffusion of the skin-covered boat in the British Isles and Scandinavia. See Heizer, *Aboriginal Whaling*,

pp. 14, 24, 28ff, 92–3 and passim for a discussion of the appearance of whaling in Europe.

27 Las Casas, *Historia*, vol. I, p. 67; Hernando Colón, *Vida del Almirante, Don Cristóbal Colón*, ed. Ramón Iglesia (Mexico City: Fondo de Cultura Economica, 1947), p. 51; Merrien, *Christopher Columbus*, p. 244.

28 Las Casas, *Historia*, vol. I, p. 500; Jane, *Voyages*, p. 270

29 Las Casas, *Historia*, vol. II, pp. 17–18.

30 Ibid., vol. I, p. 304; vol. II, pp. 18–19. It may be noted that in 1501 Spaniards captured certain Americans *de color moreno* in the Gulf of Urabá (Darién, now Panama). The term *moreno* is ambiguous but suggests a dark brown color. Saco, *Esclavitud de los Indios*, vol. I, p. 134.

31 Ca 'da Mosto, 'Navigazioni' in Ramusio, *Navigazioni*, pp. 498–9; Cadamosto, *Viagens*, pp. 74–5.

32 Ibid., pp. 127, 160; Ramusio, *Navigazioni*, pp. 524, 541. But see also Stewart C. Malloy, 'Traditional African Watercraft: A New Look' in Ivan van Sertima, ed., *Blacks in Science: Ancient and Modern* (New Brunswick: Transaction Books, 1983).

33 Pedro Mártir de Anglería, *Décadas del Nuevo Mundo* (Buenos Aires: Bajel, 1944), pp. 198–201; Francisco López de Gómara, *Historia General de las Indias* (Madrid: Calpe, 1922), vol. I, pp. 144, 162; vol. II, p. 241–2. See also Samuel Purchas, *Purchas his Pilgrimage, or Relations of the World and the Religions Observed in All Ages* (London: Stansby, 1613), p. 610.

34 Liete, *Monumenta Brasiliae*, vol. II, pp. 99, 117; vol. III, p. 95; vol. IV, p. 411n.

35 Heyerdahl, 'Comment', p. 73; Andrés Bernaldez, in Jane, *Voyages*, p. 313.

36 José Honório Rodrigues, *Brazil and Africa*, trans. Richard A. Mazzara and Sam Hileman (Berkeley: University of California Press, 1965), p. 103.

37 'Navigazione da Lisboa all' Isola di San Tomé, . . . per un Piloto Portoghese' and 'Descrizione del' Africa di Leone Africano', both in Ramusio, *Navigazioni*, vol. I, pp. 391, 584.

38 'Informação da Mina', Sept. 29, 1572, in António Brasio, ed., *Monumenta Missionaria Africana* (Lisbon: Agencia Geral do Ultramar, 1953), vol. III, p. 102.

39 Leite, *Monumenta Brasiliae*, vol. III, pp. 406, 463.

40 Ibid., vol. IV, p. 33.

41 Gabriel Soares de Sousa, *Tratado Descriptivo do Brasil em 1587*, ed. Francisco Adolpho de Varnhagem (São Paulo: Editoria Nacional, 1938), pp. 207–9.

42 Jorge Marcgrave, *Historia Natural do Brasil*, trans. José Procopio de Magalhães (São Paulo: Impresa Oficial del Estado, 1942), pp. 137, 141, 274.

43   Richard Ligon, *A True and Exact History of the Island of Barbadoes* (London:Cass, 1970); Lionel Wafer in William Dampier, *A Collection of Voyages* (London: Knapton, 1729), pp. 9–10; and see also Acosta, *History*, pp. 242–3; Pero de Magalhães de Gândavo, *Tratado da Província do Brasil* (Rio de Janeiro: Instituto Nacional do Livro, 1965), p. 169; François Pyrard de Laval, *Voyage Contenant sa Navigation aux Indes* (Paris : Thiboust, 1619), p. 128 (part I), p. 387 (part II). Juan de Castellanos, in writing of the 1530s, lists *plátanos* (bananas) as one of the fruits of the Cartagena region of Colombia, prior to Spanish settlement. Juan de Castellanos, *Elegías de Varones Ilustres, de Indias* (Madrid : Rivadeneyra, 1857), pp. 366–7.

44 Columbus thought he saw *iñames* (yams) in the Caribbean; however, he may have confused the yam with mandioca-cassavi or with the *patata* (sweet potato). Jane,

Voyages, pp. 198, 202, 209; Las Casas, *Historia*, vol. I, p. 396; see also Van Sertima, *Blacks in Science*, pp. 20–1; Heyerdahl, *Early Man and the Ocean*, p. 68ff, 80–5, 219–36; Karl H. Schwerin, 'Winds across the Atlantic', *Mesoamerican Studies*, vol. 6 (1970), pp. 2, 3–6, 9, 11–17, 18–20, 23–5; Riley et al., *Man across the Sea*, pp. xiiff, 23–9, 36–7, 266–92, 309ff.

45 Isaac de la Peyrere, *Relation du Groenland* (Paris: Courbe, 1647), pp. 10ff and de la Peyrere, *Histoire du Groenland* in *A Collection of Documents on Spitzbergen and Greenland* (London: Hakluyt, 1855), p. 188; de la Peyrere, *Relation de l'Islande* (Paris: Billaine, 1663), pp. 85, 94, 102; Julius E. Olson and Edward Gaylord Bourne, eds, *The Northmen, Columbus and Cabot 985–1503* (New York: Scribner's, 1906) pp. 10–11; Kaj Birket-Smith, *Ethnography of the Egedesminde District* (Copenhagen: Bianco Lunos, 1924), p. 7; Gwyn Jones, *The Norse Atlantic Sage* (London: Oxford, 1964), p. 157; Finn Gad, *The History of Greenland* (London: Hurst, 1970), vol. I, p. 88; Samuel Eliot Morrison, *The European Discovery of America, The Northern Voyages A.D. 500–1600* (New York: Oxford University Press, 1971), p. 56.

46 'Eirik the Red's Saga' in Jones, *The Norse Atlantic Saga*, p. 186.

47 Ibid., pp. 161, 187; and Gad, *History*, p. 49.

48 Morrison, *European Discovery*, p. 59; Gad, *History*, pp. 52, 55, 60, 88; Jones, *The Norse Atlantic Saga*, pp. 96–7

49 Whitaker, 'Scottish Kayaks', p. 101.

50 Gad, *History*, p. 173; Birket-Smith, *Ethnography*, p. 8.

51 Birket-Smith, *Ethnography*, p. 7.

52 Ibid., p. 8.

53 Peyrere, 'Histoire du Groenland', p. 207; Riley et al, *Man across the Sea*, p. 279.

54 Morrison, *European Discovery*, pp. 60–1.

55 Ibid., p. 60; Gad. *History*, p. 161.

56 J. T. Jenkins, *A History of the Whale Fisheries* (Port Washington, New York: Kennikat, 1971), p. 64; Ivan T. Sanderson, *Follow the Whale* (Boston: Little Brown, 1956), p. 141; Charles de la Roncière, *Histoire de la Marine Française* (Paris: Plon-Nourrit, 1914), vol. II, pp. 398–400; Louwrens Hacquebord and René de Bok, *Spitsbergen 79° N. B.* (Amsterdam: Elsevier, 1981), pp. 14–15, 20; Philippe Veyrin, *Les Basques* (Bayonne: Musée Basque, 1947), pp. 45–6; Martín Fernández de Navarrete, *Colección de los Viages y Descubrimientos* (Madrid: Imprenta Real, 1829), vol. III, pp. 177–8; Heizer, *Aboriginal Whaling*, p. 32; Merrien, *Christopher Columbus*, p. 64.

57 Morrison, *European Discovery*, pp. 95–6, 163, 166, 203, 205, 208; Henry Harrisse, *The Discovery of North America* (Amsterdam: Israel, 1961), pp. 4ff; J. Corominas, *Diccionario Crítico Etimológico de la Lengua Castellana* (Berne: Franche, 1954), p. 445; Hoffman, *Cabot to Cartier*, pp. 19, 202; Adolfo Lafarga Lozano, *Los Vascos en el Descubrimiento y Colonización de América* (Bilbao: Gran Enciclopedia Vasca, 1973), p. 26; Birket-Smith, *Ethnography*, p. 8; Gad, *History*, p. 181.

58 António Brasio, *Os Pretos em Portugal* (Lisbon: Agencia Geral das Colonias, 1944), pp. 10–11.

59 Cortés, *La Esclavitud*, pp. 318–35.

60 Henry Harrisse, *Découverte et Évolution Cartographique de Terre-Neuve et des Pays Circonvoisins* (Paris: Welter, 1900), pp. 45–6; David Beers Quinn, *England and the Discovery of America, 1481–1620* (New York: Knopf, 1974), pp. 117–18; J. A. Pires de Lima, *Mouros, Judeus e Negros na História de Portugal* (Oporto: Livraria

Civilização, 1940), p. 60; Morrisson, *European Discovery*, pp. 180, 215–16; Hoffman, *Cabot to Cartier*, pp. 26–9

61 Las Casas, *Historia*, vol. I, pp. 71, 352.

62 Jane, *Voyages*, pp. 151, 174, 186, 203, 261, 264; Tzvetan Todorov, *The Conquest of America: The Question of the Other*, trans. Richard Howard (New York: Harper & Row, 1984), p. 46.

63 Silvio Zavala, *Estudios Indianos* (Mexico City: Colegio Nacional, 1948), pp. 56, 98–100, Las Casas, *Historia*, vol. I, p. 448; vol II, pp. 88–9; Navarrete, *Colección*, vol I, p. 173, 232–3.

64 Las Casas, *Historia*, vol. I, pp. 446–7; Saco, *Esclavitud de los Indios*, vol. I, pp. xvi–xvii, 90–110, 123.

65 Ibid., vol. II, pp. 71–2; Todorov, *Conquest*, p. 47.

66 Details about the shipment of the 3,000 plus slaves can be found in Las Casas, *Historia*, vol. I, pp. 366, 397–8, 405, 408–10, 421–3, 439, 465, 467; vol. II, pp. 74, 87, 93; Zavala, *Estudios Indianos*, pp. 100n, 101n, 104; Carolyn Thomas Foreman, *Indians Abroad 1493–1938* (Norman: University of Oklahoma Press, 1943), pp. 3–7; Jane, *Voyages*, pp. 104–8; Saco, *Esclavitud de los Indios*, vol. I, pp. 99–111, 123. Isabel's anger only achieved the freeing of a very small number of Americans, since all those previously sent to Spain remained as slaves and new expeditions of 1499–1500 specifically authorized the taking of more slaves. See Saco, *Esclavitud de los Indios*, vol. I, p. 126 and Antonio Muro Orejón, 'La Primera Capitulación con Vicente Yáñez Pinzon para Descubrir en Las Indias, 6 Junio 1499', *Anuário de Estudios Americanos*, vol. IV (1947), pp. 746–7.

67 Las Casas, *Historia*, vol. I, pp. 324–6.

68 Jane, *Voyages*, pp. 256–8; Bernaldez, *Memorias*, pp. 278ff; Las Casas, *Historia*, vol. I, p. 355.

69 Todorov, *Conquest*, pp. 47–9.

70 Ibid., pp. 5, 133.

CHAPTER 2 THE INTENSIFICATION OF CONTACTS: TRANS-ATLANTIC SLAVERY AND INTERACTION, AFTER 1500

1 Yçe de Chebir, 'Suma de los Principales Mandamientos y Devedamientos de la Ley y Çunna' and 'Leyes de Moros' in *Memorial Histórico Español* (Madrid: Real Academia de la Historia, 1853), vol. V, pp. 63, 334, 368.

2 Joaquín Miret y Sans, 'La Esclavitud en Cataluña en los Ultimos Tiempos de la Edad Media', *Revue Hispanique*, vol. XLI (1917), pp. 11–14, 17–18, 23, 34, 36, 38–9, 41–3, 49, 56–7, 68, 80, 89n; Charles Verlinden, *L'Esclavage dans l'Europe Médiévale* (Bruges: De Tempel, 1955), vol. I, pp. 279–83.

3 Domenico Gioffrè, *Il Mercato degli Schiavi a Genova nel Secolo XV* (Genoa: Bozzi, 1971), p. 31 and n; Verlinden, *L'Esclavage*, Vol. I, pp. 285–6; the Indian Ocean was referred to as the *oceano Indico*. Cortés, *La Esclavitud*, p. 60. See also *Indico* in Richard Konetzke, ed., *Colección de Documentos para la Historia de la Formación Social de Hispanoamérica, 1493–1810* (Madrid: Consejo Superior de Investigaciones Científicas, 1953), p. xxv.

4 Manuel Heleno, *Os Escravos em Portugal* (Lisbon: Empresa do Anuário Comercial, 1933), pp. 135, 145, 170; A. H. de Oliveira Marques, *History of Portugal* (New York: Columbia University Press, 1972), pp. 55, 61, 80.

5 Heleno, *Os Escravos*, pp. 111–12.

6   Ibid., p. 138; Alfonso Franco Silva, *La Esclavitud en Sevilla y su Tierra a Fines de la Edad Media* (Seville: Diputación Provincial, 1979), p. 40.

7   Franco Silva, *La Esclavitud*, pp. 42, 66–7, 71. See John Ure, *Prince Henry the Navigator* (London: Constable, 1977) for general discussion of Portuguese activity.

8   Ibid., pp. 135–7; Antonio Pigafetta, 'Viaggio' in Ramusio, *Navigazioni*, vol. I, p. 889n; Todorov, *Conquest*, p. 40; Antonio Domínguez Ortiz, *The Golden Age of Spain 1516–1659*, trans. James Casey (London: Weidenfeld and Nicolson, 1971), pp. 163–4; *Reppertorio das Ordenaçoēs e Leys do Reyno de Portugal* (Lisbon: S. Vicente Fora, 1749), pp. 221–2; Jacques Heers, *Esclaves et Domestiques au Moyen–Age dans le Monde Méditerranéen* (Paris: Fayard, 1981), pp. 223f; Antonio Domínguez Ortiz, 'La Esclavitud en Castilla durante la Edad Moderna', *Estudios de Historia Social de España* (Madrid: Instituto Balmes, 1952), pp. 380–1; José Antonio Saco, *Historia de la Esclavitud desde los Tiempos mas Remotos hasta Nuestros Días* (Barcelona: Jepús, 1877), vol. III, pp. 184–6, 202, 283, 285.

9   Ure, *Prince Henry*, p. 167.

10   Diego Ortiz de Zúñiga, *Ánales Eclesiasticos y Seculares . . . de Sevilla* (Madrid: Imprenta Real, 1677, p. 374; Verlinden, *L'Esclavage*, vol. I, pp. 566–7n.

11   Many scholars have studied the question of slavery and its legitimacy, espcially in relation to *canarios* and Americans. Such studies need, however, always to be supplemented by examinations of the lists of slaves actually being sold and their disposition. See Zavala, *Estudios Indianos*, for a general discussion of the enslavement of *canarios* and Americans. See also Silvio Zavala, 'Relaciones Históricas entre Indios y Negros en Iberoamérica', *Revista de las Indias*, Bogotá, vol. XXVIII (1946), pp. 53–65, for the relationship of African slavery to the above. See also Cortés, *La Esclavitud en Valencia* and Franco Silva, *La Esclavitud en Sevilla* for detailed records of actual slavery practices in Spain. See especially Saco, *Esclavitud de los Indios*, vol. I, pp. 110–11, 119–23, 125–6, 128, 130, 132, 135, 143–5, 156–7, 167, 242–3, 259, 264–5, 294, for evidence relating to the reality of slavery in contrast to questions of legality.

12   Hoffman, *Cabot to Cartier*, p. 29; Harrisse, *Découverte et Évolution Cartographique*, pp. 45–6; Pires de Lima, *Mouros*, p. 60.

13   Morrison, *European Discovery*, pp. 180, 211–16, 225; Hoffman, *Cabot to Cartier*, pp. 26–8; Quinn, *England and the Discovery*, pp. 117–18.

14   Cortés, *La Esclavitud*, pp. 318, 335, 356, 455, 471.

15   Franco Silva, *Regesto Documental*, years 1510–13; Franco Silva, *La Esclavitud*, pp. 312n, 314n.

16   Hoffman, *Cabot to Carier*, pp. 114, 116.

17   James Lockhart, *El Mundo Hispanoperuano 1532–1560* (Mexico City: Fondo de Cultura Económica, 1982), pp. 220–1; Frederick P. Bowser, *The African Slave in Colonial Peru 1524–1650* (Stanford: Stanford University Press, 1974), pp. 40–3, 346.

18   Franco Silva, *La Esclavitud en Sevilla*, p. 69; Cortés, *La Esclavitud*, p. 58.

19   Brasio, *Monumenta Missionaria Africana*, vols I and III.

20   Manuel Lobo Cabrera, *La Esclavitud en las Canarias Orientales en el Siglo XVI* (Tenerife: Cabildo Insular, 1982), p. 364.

21   Hoffman, *Cabot to Cartier*, p. 125; 'Navigazión del Capitano Pedro Alvares [Cabral] Scritta per un Piloto Portoghese' in Ramusio, *Navigazioni*, vol. I, p. 652; Harrisse, *The Discovery of North America*, pp. 69, 175, 184 and n, 188n, 299, 450,

574, 577; José Antonio Gonsalves de Mello, *Tempo dos Flamengos* (São Paulo: Olympio, 1947), pp. 144–5, 145n.

22 Hoffman, *Cabot to Cartier*, pp. 32, 65, 68–9, 128, 185–6; Harrisse, *The Discovery of North America*, pp. 299, 452, 574; Navarette, *Colección*, vol. III, pp. 176ff; Harrisse, *Découverte et Évolution Cartographique*, pp. 34, 54. Also see Corominas, *Diccionario Crítico, Bacalao*.

23 See the sources cited in n. 22 above, and also Veyrin, *Les Basques*, p. 46.

24 Hoffman, *Cabot to Cartier*, pp. 34–5.

25 Ibid., pp. 31, 169–70; Harrisse, *Découverte et Évolution Cartographique*, p. 162.

26 See, for example, Gonzalo Fernández de Oviedo, *Historia General y Natural de las Indias* (Madrid: Biblioteca de Autores Españoles, 1959), book 16, p. 107; book 24, p. 418, for description of Americans as *loros*.

27 Robert Southey, *History of Brazil* (London: Longman, 1822), pp. 1, 5, 26; John Hemming, *Red Gold: the Conquest of the Brazilian Indians* (London: Macmillan, 1978), pp. 183, 158n, 569n; Foreman, *Indians Abroad*, pp. 7–8; Franco Silva, *Regesto Documental*, year 1500; Muro Orejón, 'La Primera Capitulación', pp. 746–7; Saco, *Esclavitud de los Indios*, vol. I, pp. 119–26, 128–32, 135, 143–5, 156.

28 Harrisse, *The Discovery of North America*, p. 574; Antonio Pigafetta, 'Viaggio', in Ramusio, *Navigazioni*,. vol. II, pp. 879ff; Henry Harrisse, *John Cabot, the Discoverer of North America and Sebastian his Son* (New York: Argosy-Antiquarian, 1968), pp. 223–5, 422; Foreman, *Indians Abroad*, pp. 1–11; Saco, *Esclavitud de los Indios*, vol. I, pp. 154–6, 158ff, 164ff, 173–5, 179ff, 241.

29 See especially Silvio Zavala, *Los Esclavos Indios en Nueva España* (Mexico City: Colegio Nacional, 1967), pp. 20, 21, 51, 94; Zavala, *Estudios Indianos*, pp. 100ff; Saco, *Esclavitud de los Indios*,, vol I, pp. 259, 264–5, 294.

30 Zavala, *Estudios Indianos*, pp. 102, 118–19; Saco, *Esclavitud de los Indios*, vol. I, pp. 157–8, 242–3.

31 Navarrete, *Colección*, vol. II, pp. 246–7; Zavala, *Estudios Indianos*, pp. 102–4; Saco, *Esclavitud de los Indios*, vol. I, pp. 259, 264–5, 294.

32 Zavala, *Estudios Indianos*, discusses all of these categories except for neophytes in the missions. The latter's status is discussed in Jack D. Forbes, *Native Americans of California and Nevada* (Happy Camp, California: Naturegraph, 1982); Jack D. Forbes, *Warriors of the Colorado* (Norman: University of Oklahoma Press, 1965).

33 Girolamo Benzoni, *History of the New World* (London: Hakluyt, 1857), pp. 11, 78.

34 Foreman, *Indians Abroad*, p. 12; Todorov, *Conquest*, p. 129; Vittorio Lanternani, *Religions of the Oppressed* (New York: New American Library, 1965), pp. 151–2.

35 Southey, *Brazil*, p. 23.

36 Hemming, *Red Gold*, pp. 10ff, 39, 531; Alexander Marchant, *From Barter to Slavery: The Economic Relations of the Portuguese and Indians in the Settlement of Brazil, 1500–1580* (Baltimore: Johns Hopkins, 1942), pp. 29, 34, 37, 72n; Saco, *Esclavitud de los Indios*, vol. I, p. 134.

37 Marchant, *From Barter to Slavery*, p. 71; Zavala, *Estudios Indianosx*, pp. 119–20.

38 Maurilio de Gouveia, *História da Escravidão* (Rio de Janeiro: Tupy, 1955), p. 52.

39 Joseph de Anchieta, *Cartas, Informações, Fragmentos Históricos e Sermoes, 1554–1594* (Rio de Janeiro: Civilização Brasileira, 1933), p. 315; Leite, *Monumenta Brasilae*, passim.

40 Staden, *Vera Historia*, pp. 19 and n, 59, 76. See also Hans Staden, *Naaukeurige Versameling der . . . Zee en Landreysen* (Leiden: Van der Aa, 1707), p. 5.

41   Ulrich Schmidel, 'Voyage of Ulrich Schmidt' in *The Conquest of the River Plate (1535–1555)* (London: Hakluyt, 1891), pp. 85–8.

42   Anchieta, 'Informação do Brasil' in Anchieta, *Cartas*, pp. 318–23.

43   Jaime Cortesão, ed., *Jesuitas e Bandeirantes no Tape, 1615–1641* (Rio de Janeiro: Biblioteca Nacional, 1969), pp. 299, 305, 318; Hemming, *Red Gold*, p. 274.

44   Gouveia, *História da Escravidão*, pp. 53ff; see also Vicente Salles, *O Negro na Pará* (Pará: Universidade, 1971).

45   C. R. Boxer, *The Golden Age of Brazil 1695–1750* (Berkeley: University of California Press, 1962), p. 243.

46   Ettore Marcucci, ed., *Lettere Edite e Inedite di Filippo Sassetti* (Florence: Felice le Monnier, 1855), p. 123; Hemming, *Red Gold*, pp. 264–5.

47   John Vogt, *Portuguese Rule on the Gold Coast 1469–1682* (Athens, Georgia: University of Georgia Press, 1979), pp. 38, 57, 73; Rodrigues, *Brazil and Africa*, pp. xiv, 107.

48   Ibid., p. 24.

49   C. R. Boxer, *Fidalgos in the Far East, 1550–1770* (Hong Kong: Oxford University Press, 1968), p. 12; and Japanese drawings seen by this writer at the Rijksmuseum voor Volkenkunde, Leiden, Netherlands, 1984.

50   Pigafetta, *Primer Viaje*, pp. 41 and n, 98, 140; Boxer, *Fidalgos in the Far East*, pp. 197ff; see also Donald Chipman, 'Isabel Moctezuma: Pioneer of Mestizaje' in David G. Sweet and Gary B. Nash, eds, *Struggle and Survival in Colonial America* (Berkeley: University of California Press, 1981), pp. 214ff for similar data on the Spanish Empire.

51   C. R. Boxer, *The Dutch in Brazil, 1624–1654* (Oxford: Clarendon Press, 1957), p. 198; José Antonio Gonsalves de Mello, *Henrique Dias: Governador dos Pretos, Criollos e Mulatos do Brasil* (Recife: Universidade, 1954), pp. 26–8, 63n; Rodrigues, *Brazil and Africa*, pp. 21–3.

52   Boxer, *The Golden Age*, pp. 260, 301; C. R. Boxer, 'The Colour Question in the Portuguese Empire, 1415–1825', *Proceedings of the British Academy*, vol. XLVII (1961), p. 132n; Rodrigues, *Brazil and Africa*, pp. 23–4.

53   Southey, *Brazil*, p. 417 and n.

54   Pires de Lima, *Mouros*, p. 61; Cortés, *Esclavitud*, p. 59n.

55   Manuel de Silveira Cardozo, 'Antonio de Gouveia: Adventurer and Priest' in Sweet and Nash, *Struggle and Survival*, p. 144; Brasio, *Os Pretos em Portugal*, pp. 12, 14; Verlinden, *L'Esclavage*, vol. I, p. 837; A. C. de C. M. Saunders, *A Social History of the Black Slaves and Freedmen in Portugal, 1441–1555* (Cambridge: Cambridge University Press, 1982), p. 211n.

56   Verlinden, *L'Esclavage*, vol. I, p. 837.

57   Brasio, *Os Pretos em Portugal*, p. 111n.

58   Ibid., pp. 75–9, 82, 88, 89.

59   Lobo Cabrera, *La Esclavitud, venta de indios* in appendices.

60   Franco Silva, *Regesto Documental*, years 1472–1513.

61   Fernández de Oviedo, *Historia General*, book 16, p. 107; see also Julio Cejador y Franca, *Tesoro de la Lengua Castellana* (Madrid: Perlado, Paez, 1910), pp. 99–100.

62   Franco Silva, *La Esclavitud*, p. 138 and n.

63   Franco Silva, *Regesto Documental*, years 1508, 1513.

64   Ibid., years 1500–13; Franco Silva, *La Esclavitud*, pp. 141–2, 149.

65   Franco Silva, *La Esclavitud*, pp. 60 and n, 61n, 112, 141–2, 148–9, 149n, 164n, 234–8, 247, 249, 325.

66 Antonio Domínguez Ortiz, *Orto y Ocaso de Sevilla* (Seville: Universidad, 1974), p. 102 and n; Domínguez Ortiz, 'La Esclavitud', pp. 375, 392.
67 Domínguez Ortiz, *Orto y Ocaso*, pp. 102–3.
68 Domínguez Ortiz, 'La Esclavitud', pp. 380–1.
69 Vicente Graullera Sanz, *La Esclavitud en Valencia en los Siglos XVI y XVII* (Valencia: Instituto Valenciano de Estudios Históricos, 1978), p. 210.
70 Domínguez Ortiz, 'La Esclavitud', p. 380.
71 See, for example, Hans Staden, *Vera Historia*, pp. 4n, 13.
72 Cortés, *La Esclavitud*, pp. 218, 221, 230, 243, 298–9, 333, 350, 367, 401, 407, 414, 416, 427, 442, 444–5, 451, 452, 453, 461, 467, 471, for cases illustrating the analysis made; see pp. 60, 471 for data on the Brazilian natives.
73 Cortés, *La Esclavitud*, pp. 60, 196, 275, 372, 387, 428, 444, 451, 452, 465, 471.
74 Sanz, *La Esclavitud*, pp. 126–7, 129, 134.
75 *Recopilación de las Leyes destos Reynos* (Madrid: Barrio y Angulo, 1640), libro 8, titulo II, p. 295.
76 Zavala, *Estudios Indianos*, p. 119 and n.
77 Domínguez Ortiz, *The Golden Age*, p. 165.
78 Zavala, *Estudios Indianos*, p. 103–4.
79 Lobo Cabrera, *La Esclavitud*, pp. 146–51, 155, 158.
80 Ibid., pp. 141, 155–6; also *Ventas de Indios*, *Ventas de Mulatos* and *Ventas de Negros* in appendices.
81 Cortés, *La Esclavitud*, pp. 279, 308.
82 Hans Staden, *The True History of his Captivity*, trans. and ed. Malcolm Letts (London: Routledge, 1928), pp. 120, 176n, 183n.
83 J. A. Goris, 'Slavernij te Antwerpen in de XVIde eeuw', in *Bijdragen tot de Geschiedenis*, vol. 15 (1923), pp. 541–4; Saunders, *A Social History*, p. 188 n.
84 Hessel Gerritsz, 'Journaux et Nouvelles', *Anais da Biblioteca Nacional*; J. de Laet, *L'Histoire du Nouveau Monde*, 1640; both as cited in Gonsalves de Mello, *Tempo dos Flamengos*, pp. 231–2; Brett, *Indian Tribes*, p.70.
85 Helen T. Catterall, *Judicial Cases Concerning American Slavery and the Negro* (Washington, DC: Carnegie, 1929) vol. I, pp. 55–6, 60 and n, 76–7; Allen W. Trelease, *Indian Affairs in Colonial New York* (Ithaca: Cornell University Press, 1960) pp. 81, 158–9; Elizabeth Donnan, *Documents Illustrative of the Slave Trade to America* (Washington, DC: Carnegie, 1932), vol. III, p. 405.
86 John Codman Hurd, *The Law of Freedom and Bondage in the United States* (New York: Negro Universities Press, 1968), vol. I, p. 277n; Trelease, *Indian Affairs*, p. 81; Foreman, *Indians Abroad*, pp. 29–30.
87 C. M. Schulten, *Nederlandse Expansie in Latijns Amerika: Brazilië, 1624–1654* (Bussum: Fibula-van Dishoeck, 1968), pp. 14ff; Johann Gregor Aldenburgk, 'Relação da Conquista e Perda da Cidade do Salvador pelos Holandeses em 1624–1625', trans. Edgard de Cerqueira Falcão, *Brasiliensia Documenta*, vol. I (1961), pp. 173 ff.
88 Gonsalves de Mello, *Tempo dos Flamengos*, pp. 233, 263, 265; Boxer, *The Dutch in Brazil*, pp. 58, 135–6, 157, 185, 267–8; Hemming, *Red Gold*, p. 288.
89 Gonsalves de Mello, *Tempo dos Flamengos*, pp. 166–9, 219–20, 223, 247–8.
90 Gonsalves de Mello, *Tempo dos Flamengos*, pp. 229 and n, 242–3, 255 and n, 270; Schulten, *Nederlandse Expansie*, p. 74; Johan Nieuhof, *Gedenkweerdige Brasilianese Zee en Lant Reize* (Amsterdam: van Meurs, 1682), p. 215.
91 Boxer, *The Dutch in Brazil*, pp. 84, 107; Gonsalves de Mello, *Tempo dos Flamengos*,

pp. 246n, 260n; Rodrigues, *Brazil and Africa*, pp. 19–21; Nieuhof, *Zee en Lant Reize*, pp. 7–8.

92   Personal correspondence from Albert van Dantzig, 13 May 1984; Aad van den Heuvel, *William Bosman in Goud en Slaven* (Amsterdam: Meulenhoff, 1981), p. 23; E. van den Boogart, 'Infernal Allies: the Dutch West India Co. and the Tarairiu 1631–1654' in E. van den Boogart, ed., *Johan Maurits van Nassau–Siegen 1604–1679* (The Hague: Maurits Stichting, 1979), p. 528; M. Hemmersam, *West-Indianische Reisz Beschreibung* (Nürnberg: Fürst, 1663), p. 113.

93   Boxer, *The Dutch in Brazil*, p. 245. Additional information on the *Tapoeijers* is provided in Caspar Barlaeus, *Nederlandsch Brazilie onder het Bewind van Johan Maurits–Grave van Nassau, 1637–1644* (The Hague: Nijhoff, 1923), pp. 53, 76, 156, 240, 396, 415; Arnoldus Montanus, *De Nieuwe en Onbekende Weereld of Beschryving van America* (Amsterdam: Meurs, 1671), pp. 371, 373.

94   Gonsalves de Mello, *Tempo dos Flamengos*, p. 227; J. A. Rogers, *Sex and Race: Negro–Caucasian Mixing in all Ages and all Lands* (New York: Rogers, 1967), vol. I, p. 124.

95   Jean Baptiste DuTertre, *HIstoire Générale des Antilles* (Paris: Jolly, 1667–71), vol. I, pp. 460, 462, 476, 500–1; vol. II, p. 493. See also Gwendolyn Midlo Hall, 'Saint Dominique' and Leo Elisabeth, 'The French Antilles' in David W. Cohen and Jack P. Greene, *Neither Slave nor Free: The Freedmen of African Descent in the Slave Societies of the New World* (Baltimore: Johns Hopkins, 1972), pp. 135, 178.

96   Hemming, *Red Gold*, pp. 441–2; Brett, *Indian Tribes*, pp. 49 and n, 50, 70, 315–18, 478–81, 493; Boxer, *The Dutch in Brazil*, p. 137; David I. Sweet, 'Francisca: Indian Slave', in Sweet and Nash, *Struggle and Survival*, pp. 276–8; Almon W. Lauber, *Indian Slavery in Colonial Times within the Present Limits of the United States* (New York: Privately printed, 1913), p. 318; Richard S. Dunn, *Sugar and Slaves: The Rise of the Planter Class in the English West Indies, 1624–1713* (London: Cape, 1973), pp. 61, 71, 74, 227; Frans L. Wojchiechowski, 'De Indianen van de Westindische Eilanden', *Nieuw West-Indische Gids* (1980), pp. 132–3; John Gabriel Stedman, *Narrative of a Five Years' Expedition* (Barre, Mass.; Imprint Society, 1971), vol. II, p. 325.

97   J. H. J. Hamelberg, *De Nederlanders op de West-Indische Eilanden* (Amsterdam: Emmering, 1979), pp. 208–10; Paul Robert, *Dictionnaire . . . de Langue Française* (Paris: Société du Nouveau Littre, 1959), *Macaron, Macaronique*; A. Kluyver et al., *Woordenboek der Nederlandse Taal* (The Hague and Leiden: Nijhoff, Sijthoff, 1913), *Makron, Makaron*; E. Zerolo, M. de Toro y Gómez, E. Isaza, *Diccionario de Lengua Castellana* (Paris: Garnier, 1911), *Macarron, Macarronea*; Francisco J. Santamaria, *Diccionario General de Americanismos* (Mexico City: Editorial Robredo, 1942), *Macamacrans*; Lathan A. Windley, *Runaway Slave Advertisements* (Westport, Connecticut: Greenwood, 1983), vol. III, p. 696.

98   G. P. Jansen, *Nederlandsch Papiaments Handwoordenboek* (Scherpenheuvel: St Vincentiusgesticht, 1947), *Macaron*; H. D. Benjamins and J. F. Snelleman, eds, *Encyclopedia Nederlandsche West-Indie* (The Hague: Nijhoff, 1914), p. 458; W. R. Menkman, *De Nederlanders in het Caraibische Zeegebied* (Amsterdam: Kampen, 1942), p. 68; Kluyver, *Woordenboek der Nederlandse Taal, Makron, Makaron*.

99   Stedman, *Narrative*, vol. II, p. 324.

100 Staden, *The True Story*, pp. 175n, 177, 178n; John Hemming, *Het Rode Goud* (Utrecht: Spectrum, 1980), p. 23; Southey, *Brazil*, p. xxxvii, 39, 414, 422;

Schulten, *Nederlandse Expansie*, pp. 14–16; Serafim Leite, ed., *Novas Cartas Jesuíticas* (São Paulo: Editora Nacional, 1940), p. 109; Soares de Sousa, *Tratado Descriptivo*, pp. 404–5.

101 Miret y Sans, 'La Esclavitud', p. 89n.

102 Foreman, *Indians Abroad*, pp. 8–9; Harrisse, *Découvertes et Évolution Carto-graphique*, p. 162.

103 Foreman, *Indians Abroad*, pp. 12–14, 32; Hoffman, *Cabot to Cartier*, pp. 108–12.

104 William Renwick Riddell, 'The Slave in Canada', *Journal of Negro History*, vol. V (1920), pp. 266–7; Lauber, *Indian Slavery*, pp. 86f, 93, 98.

105 Marcel Giraud, *History of French Louisiana*, trans. Joseph C. Lambert (Baton Rouge: Louisiana State University Press, 1974), vol. I, pp. 180–1, 203–5, 326; Du Tertre, *Histoire Générale*, vol. II, p. 493; Lauber, *Indian Slavery*, pp. 83ff, 90–1, 95, 98.

106 Zavala, *Estudios Indianos*, p. 120n.

107 R. W. Chambers, *Thomas More* (London: Cape, 1962), pp. 139–40; Hoffman, *Cabot to Cartier*, p. 17; Quinn, *England and the Discovery*, p. 118; Morrison, *European Discovery*, pp. 219–20; Foreman, *Indians Abroad*, p. 8; Hemming, *Het Rode Goud*, p. 23; Sydney Lee, 'The Call of the West', *Scribner's Magazine*, vol. XLII (1907), pp. 316–17.

108 Ibid., p. 318; Foreman, *Indians Abroad*, pp. 14–15.

109 Quinn, *England and the Discovery*, pp. 390, 403, 419–22, 428, 430; Foreman, *Indians Abroad*, pp. 16–19; Lee, 'The Call of the West', pp. 321–2; W. D. Cooley, ed., *Sir Francis Drake, His Voyage, 1595* (London: Hakluyt Society, 1849), vol. 4, pp. 36, 54.

110 Neal Salisbury, 'Squanto: Last of the Patuxets', in Sweet and Nash, *Struggle and Survival*, pp. 233–5; Foreman, *Indians Abroad*, p. 20.

111 Folarin Shyllon, *Black People in Britain 1555–1833* (London: Institute of Race Relations, 1977), p. 6; Peter Fryer, *Staying Power: the History of Black People in Britain* (London: Pluto, 1984), pp. 110–12; Foreman, *Indians Abroad*, pp. 23–4.

112 J. W. Schulte Nordholt, *The People that Walk in Darkness*, trans. M. B. van Wijngaarden (New York: Ballantine, 1970), p. 12; Leach, *Flintlock and Tomahawk*, pp. 225–6; Donnan, *Documents*, vol. III, p. 4n; Hurd, *Law of Freedom and Bondage*, vol. I, p. 269n; Lauber, *Indian Slavery*, pp. 127, 311.

113 A. Judd Northrop, 'Slavery in New York', *State Library Bulletin*, History (New York), (1908), p. 309.

114 Foreman, *Indians Abroad*, pp. 30–1; Hurd, *Law of Freedom and Bondage*, vol. I, pp. 230, 241; Lauber, *Indian Slavery*, pp. 106, 118, 119, 133, 185, 198; Giraud, *History*, vol. I, pp. 181, 203–5, 326; Verner W. Crane, *The Southern Colonial Frontier 1678–1732* (Ann Arbor: University of Michigan, 1959), pp. 113–14; Zavala, *Los Esclavos Indios*, p. 236.

115 Shyllon, *Black People in Britain*, pp. 11, 122; Fryer, *Staying Power*, pp. 27 and n, 28–31; 'Scotch Indians in Scotland', *Quarterly Journal of the Society of American Indians*, vol. 3 (1915), p. 231.

116 Gert Noorter, *Old Kayaks in the Netherlands* (Leiden: Brill, 1971), pp. 5ff, 73; Bente Dam–Mikkelsen and Torben Lundbaek, *Etnografiske Genstende Danske Kunstkammer 1650–1800* (Copenhagen: National Museet, 1980), pp. 3–14; Whitaker, 'Scottish Kayaks', pp. 99ff; Ian Whitaker, 'The Scottish Kayaks Reconsidered', *Antiquity*, vol LI (1977), pp. 41ff.

117 Lauber, *Indian Slavery*, p. 293; Foreman, *Indians Abroad*, pp. 181–4.

118 'An Account of the Moskito Indians' in Dampier, *A Collection*, pp. 8–11.
119 Hurd, *Law of Freedom and Bondage*, vol. II, pp. 97, 105.
120 H. N. Sherwood, 'Paule Cuffe', *Journal of Negro History*, vol. 8 (1923), pp. 153, 157–73.
121 Boxer, *The Golden Age*, pp. 10, 14, 21, 23, 242–4, 269, 301, 322; A. J. R. Russell-Wood, *The Black Man in Slavery and Freedom in Colonial Brazil* (London: Macmillan, 1982), p. 29.
122 Rodrigues, *Brazil and Africa*, pp. 126, 138.
123 Hemming, *Red Gold*, pp. 441–3; Salles, *O Negro no Pará*, pp. 92, 104, 321, 324–5, 328; Rodrigues, *Brazil and Africa*, pp. 150–1; Brett, *Indian Tribes*, pp. 318, 478.
124 Mary Karasche, 'Damiana da Cunha: Castechist and Sertanista' in Sweet and Nash, *Struggle and Survival*, p. 118n; Boxer, *Golden Age*, pp. 267, 277–80, 284–5, 289–301; Octavio Ianni, *As Metamorfoses do Escravo* (São Paulo: Européia do Livro, 1962), pp. 41–2, 45, 60n, 77, 87.
125 Jack D. Forbes, *Apache, Navaho and Spaniard* (Norman: University of Oklahoma Press, 1960), pp. 179, 271–2 and index; Forbes, *Warriors of the Colorado*, index; Forbes, *Native Americans of California and Nevada*, pp. 34, 37, 43, 49–50, 56, 67, 72–4, 78, 85; L. R. Bailey, *Indian Slave Trade in the Southwest* (Los Angeles: Westernlore, 1966); Jack D. Forbes, 'Historical Survey of the Indians of Sonora, 1821 to 1910' in *Ethnohistory*, vol. 4 (1957), pp. 347, 355–6; Jack D. Forbes, *The Indian in America's Past* (Englewood Cliffs: Prentice-Hall, 1964), pp. 89–97; Ronald Wright, *Cut Stones and Crossroads: A Journey in the Two Worlds of Peru* (Harmondsworth: Penguin, 1986), p. 132.
126 Franco Silva, *La Esclavitud*, pp. 96n, 103 and n.
127 Ibid., p. 45.
128 Rodrigues, *Brazil and Africa*, pp. XIV, XV; see also Gonzalo Aguirre Beltrán, 'African Influences in the Development of Regional Cultures in the New World', in *Plantation Systems of the New World* (Washington, DC: Pan American Union, 1959), especially p. 70.
129 Ibid., pp. 103–6.
130 See, for example, Spanish legislation in the *Recopilación de Leyes de los Reynos de Indias*, libro VI, titulo X, ley 19, fo. 237; titulo IX, ley 15, fo. 231; titulo IX, ley 14, fo. 231; titulo XII, ley 16, fo. 243, as well as others; Todorov, *Conquest*, p. 136; Lockhart, *El Mundo Hispanoperuano*, pp. 219, 242; Gonsalves de Mello, *Tempo dos Flamengos*, pp. 207n, 215; Stedman, *Narratives*, vol. II, p. 325; William S. Willis, 'Divide and Rule: Red, White and Black in the Southeast', *Journal of Negro History*, vol. 48 (1963); José Antonio Saco, *Historia de la Esclavitud de la Raza Africana en el Nuevo Mundo* (Barcelona: Jepús, 1879), vol. I, p. 154; Hubert Howe Bancroft, *History of the North Mexican States and Texas* (San Francisco: The History Co., 1890), vol. I, pp. 454, 457, 460; David M. Davidson, 'Negro Slave Control and Resistance in Colonial Mexico, 1519–1650', *Hispanic-American Historical Review*, vol. XLVI (1966), pp. 239–40, 243–4, 247, 251–2; Edgar F. Love, 'Legal Restrictions on Afro–Indian Relations in Colonial Mexico', *Journal of Negro History*, vol. LV (1970), 131ff; Stuart B. Schwartz, 'The Mocambo: Slave Resistance in Colonial Bahia', *Journal of Social History*, vol. 3 (1970), pp. 322–4, 332.
131 Franco Silva, *La Esclavitud*, p. 103; Rodrigues, *Brazil and Africa*, p. 159 and n; Bowser, *The African Slave*, p. 254; Lobo Cabrera, *La Esclavitud*, pp. 146–8; Russell-Wood, *The Black Man*, p. 112; Donnan, *Documents*, vol. III, pp. 19–40; Peter H. Wood, *Black Majority: Negroes in Colonial South Carolina* (New York: Knopf, 1974), pp. 154–5; Jack D. Forbes, 'The Evolution of the Term Mulatto: A

Chapter in Black–Native American Relations', *Journal of Ethnic Studies*, vol 10 (1982), pp. 45ff; Jack D. Forbes, 'Mulattoes and People of Color in Anglo-North America: Implications for Black–Indian Relations', *Journal of Ethnic Studies*, vol. 12 (1984), pp. 17ff; Schwartz, 'The Mocambo', pp. 325–6.

132 See, for example, Laurence Foster, *Negro–Indian Relationships in the South-East* (Philadelphia: Privately printed, 1935); Kenneth W. Porter, 'Relations Between Negroes and Indians within the Present Limits of the U.S.', *Journal of Negro History*, vol. XVII (1932); Kenneth W. Porter, 'Florida Slaves and Free Negroes in the Seminole War, 1835–1842', *Journal of Negro History*, vol. XXVIII (1943); C. R. Boxer, *Golden Age*, p. 260; Leite, *Monumenta Brasiliae*, vol. III, p. 95; vol. IV, p. 411n; Kenneth W. Porter, 'Negroes and Indians on the Texas Frontier, 1831–1876', *Journal of Negro History*, vol. XLI (1956), pp. 193ff; Schwartz, 'The Mocambo', pp. 320–1, 324–6.

133 Davidson, 'Negro Slave Control', pp. 243–52; Gonsalves de Mello, *Tempo dos Flamengos*, pp. 216–17; Stedman, *Narrative*, vol. II, pp. 314–15; Brett, *Indian Tribes*, p. 59.

134 Rodrigues, *Brazil and Africa*, p. 45. See also Aguirre Beltrán, 'African Influences', pp. 64–5.

CHAPTER 3   NEGRO, BLACK AND MOOR: THE EVOLUTION OF THESE TERMS AS APPLIED TO NATIVE AMERICANS AND OTHERS

1 The People v. Hall, Oct. 1, 1854, in Robert Heizer and Alan J. Almquist, eds, *The Other Californians* (Berkeley: University of California Press, 1971), pp. 232–3.

2 I shall use the term 'American' to refer to the native American people during the colonial period especially, so as to avoid confusion with other peole called 'Indians'. Likewise, whites will generally be called 'Europeans' and Black Africans will be 'Africans'.

3 See chs 5, 6 and 8.

4 Brasio, *Os Pretos em Portugal*, p. 10; Gioffrè, *Il Mercato degli Schiavi*, p. 31; Miret y Sans, 'L'Esclavage'.

5 Franco Silva, *La Esclavitud*, pp. 96n, 103n; Lobo Cabrera, *La Esclavitud*, pp. 360–1, 364, 367, 369; *Recopilación de leyes . . . de Indias*, ley 21, titulo 26, libro 9, tomo 4, fo. 5.

6 Goris, 'Slavernij te Antwerpen', pp. 541–2; Todorov, *Conquest*, pp. 130–1; Max Steck, *Dürer and his World*, trans. J. Maxwell Brownjohn (London: Thames & Hudson, 1964), pp. 66, 108, 114; Bernadette Bucher, *Icon and Conquest*, trans. Basia Miller Gulati (Chicago: University of Chicago Press, 1981), p. 32; Walter Koschatzky and Alice Strobl, *Die Dürer Zeichnungen der Albertina* (Salzburg: Residenz Verlag, 1971), p. 324; Elizabeth G. Holt, *A Documentary History of Art* (New York: Doubleday, 1957), vol. I, pp. 324–5. Interestingly the Japanese language reportedly utilized only 'white' and 'black' to refer to skin color. See Hiroshi Wagatsuma, 'The Social Perception of Skin Color in Japan' in *Daedalus*, vol. 96 (1967), p. 411.

7 *Le Dictionnaire des Six Langages* (Rouen: Le Villain, 1625), *niger*.

8 Cesar Oudin, *Tesoro de las dos Lenguas Francesa y Española* (Paris: Marc Orry, 1607), *negro*.

9 Francisco Javier Simonet, *Glosario de Voces Ibericas y Latinas Usadas entre los Mozárabes* (Madrid: Real Academia de la Historia, 1888), pp. 353–4; the term

mauros reportedly stems from Greek μαυρος (*mairos*), a word meaning ' black' today along with μελας (*melas*). In contemporary Greek μαυριζω (*mairizo*) means 'to blacken', μαυριλα (*mairila*) means 'blackness', and so on. Originally the term seems to have been borrowed from the name for the people of the present region of Morocco and Algeria, the Mauri, but it is possible that it did not come into Latin from Greek. New Testament and classical Greek seem to use μελας (*melas*) or derivations thereof for 'black' and not μαυρος (*mairos*). The latter must be a late borrowing in Greek. In classical Greek a blackamoor is μελαμβροτος (melambrotos) while a negro or blackamoor is Αιθιοψ (*Aithiops*). See George Ricker Berry, *The Classic Greek Dictionary* (Chicago: Follett, 1962), 'negro', 'blackamoor', 'black'; George C. Divry, *Modern English–Greek and Greek–English Desk Dictionary* (New York: Divry, 1971), 'black'; Gerhard Kittel, *Theological Dictionary of the New Testament*, trans. and ed. Geoffrey W. Bromiley (Grand Rapids: Erdmans, 1964–76), vol. IV, pp. 549ff.

10   Simonet, *Glosario*, p.353; Francisco Carletti, *Ragionamenti sopra le Cose da Lui Vedute ne' Suoi Viaggi* (Florence: Manni, 1701), p. 3.

11   Oudin, *Tesoro* (1607), *moreno*.

12   Brasio, *Os Pretos em Portugal*, p. 10.

13   Dubhaltach Mac Firbisigh, *Annals of Ireland: Three Fragments*, ed. John O'Donovan (Dublin: Irish Archaeological and Celtic Society, 1868), pp. 159–63.

14   J. Verdam, *Middlenederlandsch Woordenboek* (The Hague: Nijhoff, 1912), 'zwart'; Saco, *Historia de la Esclavitud*, vol. III, pp. 125, 141n.

15   Fryer, *Staying Power*, pp. 2–4.

16   Pigafetta, 'Viaggio' and 'Navigazione del Mar Rosso fino alle Indie secondo Arriano', in Ramusio, *Navigazioni e Viaggi*, vol. II, pp. 505, 874; Pigafetta, *Primer Viaje*, p. 41; Bernaldez, *Memorias*, p. 276; Hoffman, *Cabot to Cartier*, p. 108; Joseph Gumilla, *El Orinoco* (Madrid: Fernandez, 1745), p. 81.

17   Leite, *Monumenta Brasiliae*, vol. I, pp. 108–10, 110n.

18   Ibid., vol. I, pp. 119–22.

19   Ibid., vol. I, pp. 244, 258, 270, 325 and n.

20   Ibid., vol. I, pp. 376n, 381–2; Leite, *Novas Cartas Jesuiticas*, pp. 24–5, 67, 83, 146–52.

21   Leite, *Monumenta Brasiliae*, vol. I, p. 404; vol. II, pp. 58–9, 58n.

22   Ibid., vol. II. 'Dialogo Sobre a Conversão do Gentio', pp. 319 and n, 320, 334, 340.

23   Ibid., vol. II, pp. 372, 387, 433–4, 438; vol. III, pp. 20–2, 37, 39, 43, 47.

24   Ibid., vol. III, pp. 66, 95, 101, 438, 502; vol. IV, p. 204 and n.

25   Ibid., vol. II, pp. 84, 115, 441–2; Anchieta, *Cartas*, pp. 258, 315, 318, 322.

26   Soares de Sousa, *Tratado Descriptivo*, pp. 143, 209, 405.

27   Southey, *Brazil*, p. 417 and n; Gonsalves de Mello, *Tempo dos Flamengos*, p. 204; Schwartz, 'The Mocambo', p. 325.

28   Leite, *Novas Cartas Jesuiticas*, p. 310.

29   Raphael Bluteau, *Vocabulario Portuguez e Latino* (Coimbra: Companhia de Jesus, 1712), *Mameluco*; Marcgrave, *Historia Natural*, p. 268; Georgi (Marcgrave) Margravi de Liebstad and Guilielmi Pisonis, *Historia Naturalis Brasiliae* (Amsterdam: Elzevirium, 1648), p. 268.

30   Georg Friederici, *Amerikanistisches Wörterbuch* (Hamburg: De Gruyter, 1947), pp. 446–7; 'Directorio que se deve observar nas Povoacoens dos Indios do Pará, Maranhão' as cited by Russell-Wood, *The Black Man*, pp. 42–3.

31 Rodrigues, *Brazil and Africa*, pp. 73–5.
32 C. R. Boxer, *Race Relations in the Portuguese Colonial Empire 1415–1825* (Oxford: Clarendon Press, 1963), pp. 64–5, 65n, 66–7, 74. The famous Portuguese poet Camoens in the *Lusiadas* refers on several occasions to Indians as *negros*. See vol. VIII, p. 93 and vol. IX, p. 12; cited in Leite, *Monumenta Brasiliae*, vol. II, pp. 319–20.
33 Hieronymus Cardoso, *Dictionarium Latino Lusitanicum* (Olissapone, Lisbon: Lopezii, 1592), *preto, negro*; Agostinho Barbosa, *Dictionarium Lusitanicolatinum* (Bracharae, Portugal: Basto, 1611), *Baça, Negra, Preta*.
34 A. J. [Alexander Justice?], *A Compleat Account of the Portuguese Language* (London: Janenay, 1701), 'Blackness', 'Black', 'Black-moor'.
35 Bluteau, *Vocabulario, negro, preto, pretinho*.
36 Emmanuel de Sousa and Joachim Joseph da Costa e Sa, *Nouveau Dictionanaire François-Portugais* (Lisbon: Borel and Borel, 1784), *negre*; Francisco Solano Constancio, *Nova Diccionario Critico e Etymologico da Lingua Portuguesa* (Paris: Casimir, 1836), *negro, preto*.
37 José Ignacio Roquette, *Nouveau Dictionnaire Portugais–Français* (Paris: Ailland, Guillard, 1863), *negra, negro*.
39 Brasio, *Os Pretos em Portugal*, p. 18.
39 Eduardo Pinheiro, *Dicionário da Lingua Portuguesa* (Oporto: Figueirinhas, *c*.1945), under *Negra* and *Negro*.
40 Boxer, 'The Colour Question', pp. 129–30, 132. See also Saunders, *A Social History*, p. xii.
41 Marcucci, *Lettere Edite e Inedite di Filippo Sassetti*, p. 312.
42 Saunders, *A Social History*, p. xiii.
43 Cortés, *La Esclavitud*, pp. 217–408; Franco Silva, *La Esclavitud*, p. 138; Lobo Cabrera, *La Esclavitud*, pp. 360–1, 364, 367, 369.
44 Ibid., *Ventas de Negros* 1514–1600; p. 179.
45 Domínguez Ortiz, 'La Esclavitud, p. 410.
46 Cortés, *La Esclavitud*, pp. 333, 350, 367, 445, 451–3.
47 Ibid., pp. 318, 335, 356, 455, 471; Franco Silva, *La Esclavitud*, pp. 312n, 314n; Franco Silva, *Regesto Documental*, years 1510–13. It is interesting to note that the Spanish Crown allowed the enslavement of 'negros o loros o otros' to be found in the Americas, in instructions issued in 1499 and 1500. This may, however, represent uncertainty as to whether *negros* or *loros* would be found in South America. See Muro Orejón, 'La Primera Capitulación', pp. 746–7; Saco, *Esclavitud de los Indios*, vol. I, p. 126.
48 Cortés, *La Esclavitud*, pp. 275, 372, 387, 428, 444, 451, 452, 465, 471.
49 Sebastián de Covarrubias Orozco, *Tesoro de la Lengua Castellana o' Española* (Madrid: Sanchez, 1611), *negro*.
50 Graullera Sanz, *La Esclavitud*, pp. 106–11, 213.
51 Ibid., p. 210.
52 Domínguez Ortiz, 'La Esclavitud', p. 392.
53 See, for example, *Recopilación de Leyes de los Reynos de Indias*, tomo II, ley 14, libro VI, titulo IX, fo. 231; Woodbury Lowery, *The Spanish Settlements in the United States* (New York: Knickerbocker, 1911), pp. 14–15; H. Hoetink, *Slavery and Race Relations in the Americas* (New York: Harper & Row, 1973), p. 164.
54 Cesar Oudin and Juan Francisco Rodriguez (reputed authors), *Den Grooten Dictionaris en Schat van Drij Talen* (Antwerp: Trognesius, 1639), entry for *negro*;

Arnoldus de la Porte, *Den Nieuwen Dictionaris ofti Schadt der Duytse ende Spaensche Talen* (Antwerp: Verdussen, 1659); F. Claes, ed., *De Thesaurus Van Plantijn* (The Hague: Mouton, 1972), *Moor;* Goris, 'Slavernij te Antwerpen', pp. 541–4; Frederic Verachter, ed., *Albrecht Dürer en de Nederlanden* (Antwerp: De la Croix, 1840), p. 72.

55 Staden, *Vera Historia*, pp. 13 and n, 19n, 26; Staden, *True History*, p. 16; Staden, *Naaukeurige Versameling*, pp. 5, 9; Schmidel, *Derrotero*, p. 39n.

56 Duarte López and Filippo Pigafetta, *Relação do Reino de Congo*, trans. Rosa Carpeans (Lisbon: Agencia Geral do Ultramar, 1951), p. 29; Filippo Pigafetta and Duarte López, *De Beschrijvinghe*, trans. Martijn Everart (Amsterdam: Claesz, 1956), Capittel II, III; Duarte López and Filippo Pigafetta, *Description du Royaume de Congo*, trans. Willy Bal (Louvain: Nauwelaerts, 1963), p. 23.

57 Michael Hemmersam, *Reise nach Guinea und Brasilien* (The Hague: Nijhoff, 1930), pp. 39, 87; Hemmersam, *West-Indianische Reise*, pp. 36, 113.

58 Wouter Schoutens, *Oost-Indische Voyagie* (Amsterdam: Meurs and van Someren, 1676), pp. 12, 20, 28, 40, 72, 77, 179.

59 A. O. Exquemelin, *Historie de Boecaniers, of Vrybuyters van America* (Amsterdam: Ten Hoorn, 1700), p. 11; A. O. Exquemelin, *De Americaensche Zee-rovers* (Amsterdam: De Spieghel, 1931), vol. I, p. 21.

60 Martin Wintergerst, *Reisen auf dem Mittelländischen Meere* (The Hague: Nijhoff, 1932; pp. 26, 29–31, 78, 80.

61 Nicolaus de Graaff, *Reysen . . . na de Vier Gedeeltens des Werelds . . . Oost-Indise Spiegel* (Hoorn, Netherlands: Rijp, 1704), pp. 9, 11, 207.

62 *Les Epithetes de M. de la Porte, Parisien* (Paris: Buon, 1571), *Mores, Aethiopiens;* Theophilo Golio, *Onomasticon Latinogermanicum* (Straatsburg, Netherlands, no publisher, 1579), *Massagetae, Mauritani, Aethiopia;* Junius, *Nomenclator Omnium Rerum Propria Nomina variis Linguis* (Antwerp: Plantin, 1583), *Aethiopia;* Anthoni Smyters, *Epitheta dat Zijn Bynamen ofti Toenamen* (Rotterdam: Waesberghe, 1620), *mooren;* Cornelii Kiliaan, *Dictionarium Teutonico-Latinum* (Antwerp: Plantin, 1588), *Moor, Moorman;* Mathias Sasbout, *Dictionaire Fleming – Francoys* (Antwerp: Waesberge, 1576), *Moor;* Cornelii Kiliaan, *Etymologicum Teutonicae Linguae sive Dictionarium* (The Hague: Mouton, 1972), *Moor;* Elae Edouard Leon Mellema, *Dictionaire ou Promptu-aire Francois–Flameng* (Rotterdam: Waesbergue, 1602), *More;* Ian Louys d'Arsy, *Le Grand Dictionaire Francois–Flamen* (Rotterdam: Waesbergue, 1651); Pieter Marin, *Nieuw Nederduits en Frans Woordenboek* (Amsterdam: de Groot, 1701).

63 William Sewels, *Neder-Duytsch en Engelsch Woordenboek* (Amsterdam: Swart, 1691); D. van Hoogstratten, *Nieuw Woordenboek der Nederlantsche en Latijnsche Tale* (Amsterdam: Boom, 1704), *moor.*

64 A. Alewyn and Jan Collé, *Vocabulario das Duas Linguas Portugueza e Flamenga* (Amsterdam: Vandenderge, 1718), *pardo, negro, cafre;* M. Noel Chomel, *Algemeen . . . Woordenboek* (Leiden: LeMair, 1771), pp. 2044, 2046, 2057.

65 O. R. F. W. Winkelman, *Dictionnaire François-Hollandois* (Utrecht: Wild, 1783).

66 J. L. Terwen, *Etymologisch Handwoordenboek der Nederduitsche Taal* (Gouda: van Goor, 1844), *Moor;* P. G. Witsen Geysbeek, *Woordenboek der Zamenleving* (Amsterdam: Diederichs, *c.*1845), *Moor;* A. Kluyver et al., *Woordenboek der Nederlandsche Taal* (The Hague and Leiden: Nijhoff, Sijthoff, 1913), *Moor, Neger, Negerkoelie;* A. Beets et al., *Woordenboek der Nederlandsche Taal* (The Hague: Nijhoff and Sijthoff, 1912), *Zwart.* The modern use of *Zwart* is based on personal

observations and interviews. For *nègre* etc. being equal to 'slave' see Abraham Blussé, *Dictionnaire Portatief François et Hollandois* (Dordrecht: Blussé, 1815), *nègre*; John Holtrop, *A New English and Dutch Dictionary* (Dordrecht–Amsterdam: Blussé and Holtrop, 1789), 'negro'; Winkelman, *Dictionnaire François–Hollandois*, *nègre, maure*. For 'Indian' being translated as *zwart* see Pieter Marin, *Dictionnaire Complet François et Hollandois* (Amsterdam: Uytwerf, 1728), *mestif ou métif* and *metif ou métis*. For *negerkoelies* see Frederick van Eeden, *Studies* (Amsterdam: Versluys, 1904), p. 185.

67   See examples in Lauber, *Indian Slavery*, pp. 289, 311; John S. Bassett, ed., *The Writings of Colonel William Byrd* (New York: Doubleday, 1901), pp. 8–9; Hurd, *The Law of Freedom and Bondage*, vol. 2, p. 95; *The Oxford English Dictionary* (Oxford: Clarendon Press, 1933), 'Negro'; Fryer, *Staying Power*, pp. 27–8; John Minsheu, *The Guide into Tongues* (London: Browne, 1617), pp. 314–15; Henry Cockeram, *The English Dictionarie* (Menston: Scolar Press, 1968), 'Black-moore'; Minsheu and Percivale, *A Dictionarie* (1599), *Mora* to *Morisco, Negra* to *Negro, Prieto* and 'Moore', 'Blackemoore.' See also Minsheu and Percivale, *A Dictionary* (1623), which is the same for these terms.

68   Donnan, *Documents*, vol. IV, p. 68; James Hugo Johnston, *Race Relations in Virginia and Miscegenation in the South, 1776–1860* (Amherst: University of Massachusetts Press, 1970), p. 194; Ex parte Leland, cited in Catterall, *Judicial Cases*, vol. II, p. 311.

69   Folarin Shyllon, *Black People in Britain 1555–1833* (London: Institute of Race Relations, 1977), p. 6.

70   Ibid., p 11.

71   Ibid., p. 122.

72   Fryer, *Staying Power*, p. 27n; Foreman, *Indians Abroad*, p. 86; William B. Weeden, *Economic and Social History of New England, 1620–1789* (New York: Hillary House, 1963), vol. II, p. 454.

73   Wylie Sypher, *Guinea's Captive Kings: British Anti-Slavery Literature of the XVIIIth Century* (Chapel Hill: University of North Carolina Press, 1942), p. 106.

74   William Young, *An Account of the Black Charaibs* (London: Cass, 1971), pp. 8–9, 13–14, 18, 23, 27, 30, 42.

75   See, for example, Nancy L. Solien, 'West Indian Characteristics of the Black Carib' in Michael M. Horowitz, ed., *Peoples and Cultures of the Caribbean* (New York: National History Press, 1971), pp. 133ff; also see David Lowenthal, *West Indian Societies* (London: Oxford University Press, 1972), pp. 178–86.

76   Catterall, *Judicial Cases*, vol. I, pp. 55, 56, 60.

77   Ibid., vol. 1, pp. 58, 78.

78   Hurd, *Law of Freedom*, vol. 1, p. 233; Catterall, *Judicial Cases*, vol. 1, p. 63; Wesley Frank Craven, *White, Red and Black: The Seventeenth Century Virginian* (Charlottesville: University of Virginia Press, 1971), p. 98.

79   Mattie Emma Edwards Parker, ed., *North Carolina Higher Court Records, 1697–1701* (Raleigh: Department of Archives and History, 1971), p. 528.

80   Donnan, *Documents*, vol. 3, pp. 463, 466, 470, 477, 499, 500; vol. 4, pp. 175–9.

81   'Vestry Book of King William Parish', *Virginia Magazine of History and Biography*, vol. XII, pp. 23, 26.

82   J. Leitch Wright, *The Only Land They Knew: The Tragic Story of the Indians of the Old South* (New York: Free Press, 1981), p. 252; 'Eighteenth-Century Slave Advertisements', *Journal of Negro History*, vol. I (1915), p. 176.

83   Wilbert E. Moore, 'Slave Law and the Social Structure', *Journal of Negro History*, vol. XXVI (1941), pp. 182–3.

84   Peter H. Wood, *Black Majority: Negroes in Colonial South Carolina* (New York: Knopf, 1974), p. 99.

85   Johnston, *Race Relations in Virginia*, pp. 275–6.

86   Anna Bustill Smith, 'The Bustill Family', *Journal of Negro History*, vol. X (1925), pp. 638–44.

87   Northrup, *Slavery in New York*, p. 306.

88   Lathan A. Windley, *Runaway Slave Advertisements*, vol. I, pp. 181, 323, 327.

89   Wright, *The Only Land They Knew*, p. 256; this work, ch. 7; William A. Craigie and James R. Hulbert, *A Dictionary of American English* (Chicago: University of Chicago Press, 1940), vol. 3, p. 1512; Windley, *Runaway Slave Advertisements*, vol. III, pp. 32, 81, 150, 182, 191, 196.

90   Windley, *Runaway Slave Advertisements*, vol. I, p. 234.

91   Johnston, *Race Relations in Virginia*, p. 280; Helen C. Roundtree, 'The Indians of Virginia: A Third Race in a Biracial State', MS, 1976, in Virginia State Library, Indian file.

92   Roundtree, 'The Indians of Virginia', pp. 8, 10.

93   'Eighteenth-Century Slave Advertisements', p. 172.

94   Sherwood, 'Paul Cuffe', pp. 158, 163, 164, 165, 172.

95   Luther P. Jackson, 'Free Negroes of Petersburg, Virginia', *Journal of Negro History*, vol. XII (1927), pp. 368, 380, 381.

96   See discussions of such records in chs 6 and 8.

97   Johnston, *Race Relations in Virginia*, p. 285.

98   Kenneth W. Porter, 'Florida Slaves and Free Negroes in the Seminole War, 1835–1842', *Journal of Negro History*, vol. XXVIII (1943), p. 393, 397; Johnston, *Race Relations in Virginia*, p. 230.

99   Gunter Wagner, *Yuchi Tales* (Publications of the American Ethnological Society, 1931).

100   Catterall, *Judicial Cases*, vol. II, pp. 79, 209, 381; State v. Oxendine, *North Carolina Reports*, vol. 19, p. 435 (2 Devereux and Battle).

101   Roundtree, 'The Indians of Virginia', p. 13.

102   Hurd, *Law of Freedom*, vol. 2, p. 165.

103   Wright, *The Only Land They Knew*, p. 259.

104   George Chamberlain, 'African and American', *Science*, vol. XVII (1891), p. 87.

105   C. A. Weslager, *Delaware's Forgotten Folk* (Philadelphia: University of Pennsylvania Press, 1943), p. 38.

106   Catterall, *Judicial Cases*, vol. II, p. 431.

107   Ibid., vol. I, p. 231; vol. II, pp. 132, 176; Hurd, *Law of Freedom*, vol. II, pp. 17, 18, 19, 128; Edward Byron Reuter, *Race Mixture* (New York: McGraw–Hill, 1931), pp. 96–7.

108   See chs 6, 7 and 8 of this work. See also William Bartram, *Travels through North and South Carolina, Georgia, East and West Florida* (Savannah: Beehive Press, 1973), pp. 481–3.

109   *Negro Population in the United States, 1790–1915* (Washington, DC: Bureau of the Census, 1917), p. 207; Felix Cohen, *Handbook of Federal Indian Law* (Washington, DC: Government Printing Office, 1942), p. 2 and n; Arthur C. Parker, 'The Status and Progress of Indians as Shown by the Thirteenth Census', *The Quarterly Journal of the Society of American Indians*, vol. III (1915), pp. 188–90; James

Mooney, 'The Powhattan Confederacy: Past and Present', *The American Anthropologist*, n.s., vol. 9 (1907), p. 148.
110 Elmer Rusco, *Good Time Coming? Black Nevadans in the 19th Century* (Westport, Connecticut: Greenwood, 1975), pp. 217–18; Weslager, *Delaware's Forgotten Folk*, p. 18.
111 US Census instructions in my possession; along with verbal statements from Bureau of Census officials.

CHAPTER 4 *LOROS, PARDOS* AND *MESTIZOS*: CLASSIFYING BROWN PEOPLES

1 Pauli de La Garde, ed., *Petri Hispani de Lingua Arabici Libri Duo* (Gottingae: Hoyer, 1883), pp. 295, 321–2; Hans Wehr, *A Dictionary of Modern Written Arabic*, ed. J. Milton Cowan (Wiesbaden: Harrassowitz, 1979), pp. 236, 239, 302, 719; Elias A. and Ed. E. Elias, *Modern Dictionary, English–Arabic* (Cairo: Elias, 1968), 'brown', 'Red Indian', 'mulatto', 'negro', 'black'; Munir Ba'albaki, *Al-Mawrid: A Modern English–Arabic Dictionary* (Dar el-ilm: Lil-Malayen, 1973), 'brown', 'black'; Hasan S. Karmi, *Al Manar: An English–Arabic Dictionary* (New York: St. Martin's, 1971), 'mulatto'; and interviews with Arabic-speaking informants.
2 Ludwig Wittgenstein, *Remarks on Colour*, ed. G. E. M. Anscombe (Berkeley: University of California Press, 1977), pp. 25e, 26e, 28e, 29e, 33e, 37e, 48e; Josef Albers, *Interaction of Color* (New Haven: Yale University Press, 1975), pp. 1, 3, 12; Ralph Hattersley, *Photographic Lighting: Learning to See* (Englewood Cliffs: Prentice-Hall, 1979), pp. 4, 22, 27, 74–5, 93–4.
3 *The Oxford English Dictionary*, 'hybrid'; Charlton T. Lewis, *A Latin Dictionary* (Oxford: Clarendon Press, 1879), *hybrida*.
4 Antonio de Nebrija, *Diccionario Latino–Español* (Barcelona: Puvill-Editor, 1979), *hybrida, hybris*; Cardoso, *Dictionarium* (1592), *mulato, hybrida*; Hieronymo Cardoso, *Dictionarium Latino Lusitanicum* (Lisbon: Anueres, 1643), *mestiço*.
5 Antonio de Nebrija, *Dictionarium ael. Antonii Nebrissensis* (1554 dedication; 1561 date), *hybridas*; Bento Pereira, *Prosodia in Vocabularium Bilingue Latinum et Lusitanum* (Ebora, Portugal): Academiae, 1750), *hybrida, mestizo, mulato*; Barbosa, *Dictionarium* (1611), *mestiço*.
6 Emmanuel Pina Cabral, *Magnum Lexicon, Latinum et Lusitanum* (Lisbon: Regiae Officinae, 1780), *Ibrida*; also the 1802 edition (Lisbon: Ferreira), *Ibrida*; Antonio de Nebrija, *Dictionarium Emendatum* (Matriti: de Urrutia, 1790), *mulato, mestizo, hybris*; de Nebrija and Lopez de Rubiños, *Dictionarium Redivivum* (Matriti: Michaelem, 1778), *mulato, mestizo*.
7 See, for example, Miret y Sans, 'La Esclavitud', p. 12; Franco Silva, *La Esclavitud*, pp. 138–9; Verlinden, *L'Esclavage*, vol. I, pp. 280, 366; J. Segura, *Aplech de documents*, p. 165, as cited in Verlinden, vol. I, p. 366; Heers, *Esclaves et Domestiques*, p. 223; Lobo Cabrera, *La Esclavitud*, pp. 141, 153–4; Cortés, *La Esclavitud*, p. 62.
8 Heleno, *Os Escravos*, pp. 111–12; Saunders, *A Social History*, p. xiii.
9 Franco Silva, *La Esclavitud*, p. 153; Lobo Cabrera, *La Esclavitud*, pp. 141, 154, 173; Domínguez Ortiz, 'La Esclavitud', pp. 395–6.
10 Dwight M. Hoover, *The Red and the Black* (Chicago: Rand McNally, 1976), pp. 67–9.
11 Gumilla, *El Orinoco*, pp. 81–5, 90. See also charts and plates reproduced in Angel

Rosenblat, *El Mestizaje y las Castas Coloniales* (Buenos Aires: Editorial Nova, 1954), pp. 163–79.

12 See, for example, Magnus Mörner, 'The History of Race Relations in Latin America: Some Comments on the State of Research', *Latin American Research Review*, vol. I (1966), pp. 20–1; Gonzalo Aguirre Beltrán, 'Races in 17th Century Mexico', *Phylon*, vol 6 (1945), p. 213.

13 Marvin D. Harris, 'Racial Identity in Brazil', *Luso-Brazilian Review*, vol. I (1964), pp. 22–4, 26–7.

14 Mörner, 'The History of Race Relations', pp. 26–7; Minsheu, *A Dictionarie, raça*.

15 Miret y Sans, 'La Esclavitud', pp. 11–14; Verlinden, *L'Esclavage*, vol. I, pp. 279–83, 366; Simonet, *Glosario*, p. 316; Corominas, *Diccionario, loro* II.

16 Miret y Sans, 'La Esclavitud', pp. 34n, 42.

17 Gioffrè, *Il Mercato*, p. 31 and n.

18 Jaume Roig, *Spill o Libre de les Dones* (Valencia, 1461) as cited by Corominas, *Diccionario, loro* II and Cortés, *La Esclavitud*, p. 61.

19 Yçe de Chebir, 'Suma' in *Memorial Histórico Español*, vol. V, p. 334.

20 Franco Silva, *La Esclavitud*, pp. 40, 103n, 138 and n, 153, 249, 266n, 268n, 270n, 292n, 298, 312n, 318n, 319n, 320n; Franco Silva, *Regesto Documental*, years 1472–1513.

21 Verlinden, *L'Esclavage*, vol. I, pp. 566–7; Ortíz de Zúñiga, *Anales*, p. 374.

22 Franco Silva, *La Esclavitud*, pp. 266n, 270n.

23 Cortés, *La Esclavitud*, pp. 220, 229, 231, 237, 239, 242, 244, 274, 281, 283, 285, 289, 292, 298–9, 305, 308, 310–12, 321–2, 323, 324, 329, 332, 339–42, 344, 347, 349, 355, 358, 361, 364, 375, 385, 393–4, 398, 406, 410, 417, 419, 424, 433, 435, 438, 445, 451, 453, 455, 459, 460, 464–5, 471.

24 Lobo Cabrera, *La Esclavitud, ventas de mulatos, ventas de moriscos, ventas de negros.*

25 Ibid., p. 361; Franco Silva, *La Esclavitud*, p. 138.

26 Las Casas, *Historia*, vol. I, pp. 138, 204–5; Cortés, *La Esclavitud*, p. 36; Bernaldez, *Memorias*, p. 276; letter of Jaime Ferrer to Columbus, Aug. 5, 1495 in Fernández de Navarrete, *Colección*, vol. II, p. 128; Muro Orejón, *'La Primera Capitulación'*, pp. 746–7; Saco, *Esclavitud de los Indios*, vol. I, p. 126.

27 Fernández de Oviedo, *Historia General*, book 16, pp. 7, 107; book 24, p. 418.

28 Francisco de Quevedo, *Obra Poética*, ed. José Manuel Blecua (Madrid: Castalia, 1969), vol.III, p. 415.

29 Antonio de Nebrija, *Vocabulario Español–Latino* (Madrid: Real Academia Española, 1951), *loro*; John Minsheu and Richard Percivale, *A Dictionarie in Spanish and English* (London: Bollifant, 1599), *loro*; Oudin, *Tesoro* (1607), *loro*; Oudin, *Tesoro*(1625), *loro*; Oudin and Rodrigues, *Le Grande Dictionaire, loro*; John Minsheu, *Vocabularium Hispanico–Latinum et Anglicum* (London: Browne, 1617), *loro*; Saco, *Historia de la Esclavitud*, vol. III, pp. 125, 141n.

30 Julio Cejador y Franca, *Vocabulario Medieval Castellano* (New York: Las Americas, 1968), *loro*; Cejador y Franca, *Tesoro de la Lengua Castellana*, vol. L, pp. 99–100; Antonio de Nebrija and López de Rubiños, *Dictionarium Redivivum, laurus, loro*; Antonio de Nebrija, *Dictionarium Emendatum*, loro; Aniceto de Pagés, *Gran Diccionario de la Lengua Castellana* (Barcelona, Fomento Comercial del Libro, 1901), *loro*; Giuseppe Pasini, *Vocabulario Italiano e Latino* (Venice: Molinari, 1823, *lauro*.

31 Graullera Sanz, *La Esclavitud*, pp. 119, 125–7, 127n, 133–4, 190, 194, 213, 221, 222–4, 227.

32 Domínguez Ortiz, 'La Esclavitud', p. 410. A little girl from Orán of 'nación Africana' was described as *morena de rostro*, 1607, Madrid. Ibid., p. 424.
33 Lobo Cabrera, *La Esclavitud*, p. 140.
34 Aguirre Beltrán, 'Races in 17th Century Mexico', pp. 214, 216; Lockhart, *El Mundo Hispanoperuano*, p. 224.
35 *Recopilación de Leyes de los Reynos de Indias*, libro VII, titulo V, ley 15, fo. 287; tomo IV, libro IX, titulo XXVI, ley 17, fo. 4 and ley 18 fo. 4 and leyes 11, 15, 19, fo. 4; Saco, *La Esclavitud de la Raza Africana*, vol. I, pp. 152–3.
36 Rosenblat, *El Mestizaje*, p. 179.
37 Corominas, *Diccionario, loro*; Cejeador y Franca, *Tesoro*, vol. L, p. 99.
38 Soares de Sousa, *Tratado Descriptivo*, p. 405.
39 Pereira, *Prosodia, louro*.
40 Brasio, *Monumenta Missionaria*, vol. I, p. 441 and n; Brasio, *Os Pretos em Portugal*, pp. 20, 25; Gonsalves de Mello, *Temp dos Flamengos*, pp. 170, 223, 247.
41 *Le Dictionnaire des Six Langages* (1625), *griseus*; Domínguez Ortíz, 'La Esclavitud', p. 383n; Graullera Sanz, *La Esclavitud*, p. 123.
42 Corominas, *Diccionario, pardo*; Nebrija, *Vocabulario* (*c.*1495), *pardo*; Joaquím de Santa Rosa de Viterbo, *Elucidario das Palavras, Termos, e Frases Que em Portugal Antiguamente se Usárão* (Lisbon: Ferreira, 1798), *pardo*.
43 Kelvin M. Parker, 'Vocabulario de la Crónica Troyana', *Acta Salamanticensia*, Filosofia y Letras, vol. XII (Universidad de Salamanca, 1958–9), pp. 262–5.
44 Saunders, *A Social History*, pp. xiii, 180n.
45 Diary of Pedro Álvares Cabral and Letter of Pero Vaz de Caminha in José Manuel García, ed., *Viagens dos Descobrimentos* (Lisbon: Presença, no date), pp. 247, 270, 271. See also diary of Vasco da Gama in same source.
46 'Navigazión del Capitano Pedro Álvares Scritta per un Piloto Portoghese', in Ramusio, *Navigazioni*, vol. I, p. 624.
47 'Navigazioni di Alvise da Ca'da Mosto' in Ramusio, *Navigazioni*, vol. I, pp. 486–7, 494–5.
48 Cadamosto, *Viagens*, pp. 49, 52, 65, 67.
49 Staden, *Vera Historia*, p. 117; Staden, *The True History*, p. 136.
50 Leite, *Monumenta Brasiliae*, passim; Magalhaes de Gandavo, *Tratado*; Soares de Sousa, *Tratado*, pp. 361, 405.
51 López and Pigafetta, *Relação*, pp. 25, 29; Pigafetta and López, *Description*, p. 23.
52 Luis de Camoens, *Lusiadas* with commentary by Manuel de Faria e Sousa (Madrid: Coello, 1639), p. 503.
53 Boxer, 'The Colour Question', pp. 119, 133.
54 Antonio Zucchelli, *Relazione del Viaggio e Missione di Congo* (Venice: Giavarina, 1712), p. 69, VII and VIII; Soares de Sousa, *Tratado*, p. 143.
55 Salles, *O Negro na Pará*, p. 62.
56 Cardoso, *Dictionarium* (1592), *pardo, baca*; Cardoso, *Dictionarium* (1643), *pardo, baca*; Barbosa, *Dictionarium, baca*; Pereira, *Prosodia, parda, carafuz*.
57 Bluteau, *Vocabulario* (1712–20), *negro, pardo, trigueiro*.
58 Alewyn and Collë, *Vocabulario, pardo*; Antonio Vieyra Transtagano, *Dictionary of the Portuguese and English Languages* (London: Camper, 1783), *cabra, pardo*; Rafael Bluteau with Antonio Moraes Silva, *Diccionaris da Lingua Portugueza* (Lisbon: Ferreira, 1789), *pardo*; Joaquím José da Costa e Sá, *Diccionario Portuguez–Francez e Latino* (Lisbon: Ferreira, 1794), *cabra, pardo*.

59 Constancio, *Novo Diccionario, pardo*; H. Michaelis, *Novo Diccionario da Lingua Portugueza e Allemã* (Leipzig: Brockhaus, 1891), *pardo*.

60 Antonio de Nebrija, *Dictionarium Aelii Antonii Nebrissensis Hispaniariom in Latinum* (Brocario: Guillelmi, 1520), *pardo*; *Quinque Linguarum, Latinae, Teuthonica, Gallicae, Hispanicae, Italicae* (Antwerp: Steels, 1534), *pardillo*; Oudin, *Tesoro* (1611), *pardo*.

61 Minsheu, *Vocabularium, baco, pardo*; Minsheu, *The Guide*, 'Browne'; Minsheu, *A Dictionarie* (1599), *pardo, pardisco*.

62 *Le Dictionnaire des Six Langages* (1625), *griseus*; De la Porte, *Den Nieuwen Dictionaris* (1659), *pardo*; Nebrija, *Dictionarium Redivivum, pardo*; Nebrija, *Dictionarium Emendatum, pardo color*; Pagés, *Gran Diccionario, pardo*; Francisco J. Santamaría, *Diccionario General de Americanismos* (Mexico City: Robredo, 1942), *pardo*.

63 Aguirre Beltrán, 'Races in 17th Century Mexico', chart and pp. 215–16, 218.

64 Juan de Solórzano Pereira, *Política Indiana*, ed. Francisco Ramíro de Valenzuela (Madrid: Ibero-Americana, 1972), p. 448; *Recopilación de Leyes de los Reynos de Indias*, libro VII, titulo V, fo. 286.

65 Aguirre Beltrán, 'Races in 17th Century Mexico', pp. 215–16; Saco, *Esclavitud de los Indios*, vol. I. p. 134; Gumilla, *El Orinoco*, pp. 81–2.

66 Oudin, *Tesoro* (1607), *moreno*; Minsheu, *Vocabularium, moreno color*; Minsheu, *A Dictionarie, moreno color, hombre moreno*, 'Browne coloured'; also John Minsheu and Richard Percivale, *A Dictionary* (1623).

67 *Recopilación de Leyes de los Reynos de Indias*, libro VII, titulo V, fo. 287; Konetzke, *Colección*, vol. II, p. 565.

68 Antenor Nascentes, *Dicionário da Lingua Portuguesa* (Brazil: Imprensa Nacional, 1943–66), *moreno*.

69 Mörner, *Race Mixture*, p. 56.

70 Konetzke, *Colección*, vol. II, p. 722.

71 Gumilla, *El Orinoco*, pp. 81–2.

72 Verlinden, *L'Esclavage*, vol. I, pp. 285–6; Gioffrè, *Il Mercato*, p. 31; Ramusio, *Navigazioni*, vol. I, p. 624; vol. II, pp. 505, 874, 885, 889; López and Pigafetta, *Description*, p. 23; Carlo Battisti and Giovanni Alessio, *Dizionario Etimologico Italiano* (Florence: Barbèra, 1950), *berrettino, bruno*.

73 Fryer, *Staying Power*, pp. 28, 29, 31; and *Oxford English Dictionary*, 'tawny'.

74 Thomas Gage, *Travels in the New World*, ed. J. Eric Thompson (Norman: University of Oklahoma Press, 1958), pp. 68–9.

75 Minsheu, *The Guide*, 'browne'; Minsheu, *Vocabularium, moreno*; Minsheu, *Dictionarie, loro*; *Oxford English Dictionary*, 'dun', 'brown', 'tawny'.

76 Cejador y Franca, *Vocabulario Medieval, mozárabe*.

77 Nebrija, *Vocabulario* (*c*.1495), *mestizo*; Nebrija, *Dictionarium* (1520), *mestizo*; Santa Rosa de Viterbo, *Elucidario, mestiço, mistiço*; Cardoso, *Dictionarium* (1592), *mestizo*; Cardoso, *Dictionarium* (1643), *mestiço*.

78 Minsheu, *A Dictionarie*, 'mestizo'; Minsheu, *Vocabularium, mestizo*; Minsheu, *The Guide*, 'mongrill'.

79 Oudin, *Tesoro* (1607), *mestizo, métis, mestif, podenco*; Oudin, *Tesoro* (1625), the same terms; Oudin and Rodrigues, *Den Grooten Dictionaris* (1639–40), the same terms.

80 Covarrubias, *Tesoro* (1611), *mestizo*; Barbosa, *Dictionarium, mestiço*; Pereira, *Prosodia, mestiço, hybris*; De la Porte, *Den Nieuwen Dictionaris, mestizo*; Francisco

Sobrino, *Dicionario Nuevo de las Lenguas Española y Francesa* (Brussels: Foppens, 1721), *mestizo*.

81 Nebrija and Rubiños, *Dictionarium Redivivum*, *mestizo*; Nebrija, *Dictionarium Emendatum*, *mestizo*, *hybris*; Santamaría, *Diccionario*, *mestizo*.

82 Justice, *Vocabularium*, *mestiço*; Bluteau, *Vocabularium* (1712), *mestiço*; Bluteau and Moraes Silva, *Diccionaris*, *mestiço*; Alewyn and Collë, *Vocabulario*, *mestiço*; de Sousa and da Costa e Sá, *Nouveau Dictionnaire*, *mulâtre*, *metif*; da Costa e Sá, *Diccionario Portuguez–Francez e Latino*, *mestiço*.

83 Vieyra, *Dictionary*, *mestiço*; Constancio, *Nova Diccionario*, *mestiço*; J-I. Roquette, *Nouveau Dictionnaire Portugais–Français* (Paris: Aillaud, *c.*1900), *mestiço*; Nascentes, *Dicionário*, *mulato*; Pinheiro, *Dicionário*, *pardo*, *mestiço*; Ersílio Cardoso and Jean Rousé, *Grande Dicionario Portugùes–Francês de Domingo de Azevedo* (Lisbon: Bertrand, 1953), *mestiço*; Francisco Fernandes, *Dicionário Brasileiro Contemperâneo* (Porto Alegre: Globo, 1967), *mulato*; Antonio de Moraes Silva, *Grande Dicionário da Lingua Portugueza* (Lisbon: Confluencia, 1954), eds Augusto Moreno Cardoso Jr and José Pedro Machado, *mameluco*, *caboré*.

84 Boxer, 'Race Relations', pp. 62ff, 78; Carletti, *Ragionamenti*, p. 255; Pyrard de Laval, *Voyage*, pp. 66, 128, 131; Sebastião Rodolfo Dalgado, *Glosario Luso–Asiatico* (Coimbra: Imprensa da Universidade, 1921), *mestiço*, *topaz*; Marcucci, *Lettere Edite*,. p. 280.

85 Leite, *Monumenta Brasiliae*, vol. I, pp. 258, 361; Plinio Ayrosa, *Termos Tupís no Português do Brasil* (São Paulo: Departemento de Cultura, 1937), *mamaluco*.

86 Mörner, *Race Mixture*, pp. 70–1.

87 Konetzke, *Colección*, vol. I, pp. 147, 168, 256, 427; *Recopilación de Leyes de los Reynos de Indias*, libro VII, titulo IV, ley 4, fo. 285 and titulo VII, ley 4, fo. 296; libro VI, titulo IX, ley 14, fo. 231, etc.

88 Solórzano, *Politica Indiana*, p. 445; Juan de Solórzano, *De Indianum Iure* (Lyons: Anisson, 1671), p. 208.

89 Aguirre Beltrán, 'Races in 17th Century Mexico', pp. 217–18.

90 Domínguez Ortiz, 'La Esclavitud', p. 395; Cortés, *La Esclavitud*, p. 62.

91 Rosenblat, *Mestizaje*, pp. 77, 158n, 166, 179; Carlos M. Rama, 'The Passing of the Afro–Uruguayans from Caste Society into Class Society', in Magnus Mörner, ed., *Race and Class in Latin America* (New York: Columbia University Press, 1970), p. 35; C. R. Boxer, *The Portuguese Seaborne Empire, 1415–1825* (London: Hutchinson, 1969), pp. 389–90; Bowser, *The African Slave*, p. 249; Santamaría, *Diccionario*, *cholo*.

CHAPTER 5   THE *MULATO* CONCEPT: ORIGIN AND INITIAL USE

1 Corominas, *Diccionario*, *mulo*; Pagés, *Gran Diccionario*, p. 860.

2 Covarrubias, *Tesoro* (1611), *mulato*, *muleto*, *mulo*.

3 Solórzano, *Indianum Iure*, p. 208.

4 Solórzano, *Política Indiana*, p. 445.

5 Faria e Souza, *Lusiada*, *Comentadas*, Canto 10, Oitava 100, p. 503.

6 Bluteau, *Vocabulario*, *mulato*.

7 É. Lévi-Provençal, *Histoire de l'Espagne Musulmane* (Paris: Maisonneuve, 1953), III, pp. 178, 186.

8 Coriminas, *Diccionario*, *mulo*; Wilhelm Meyer-Lübke, *Grammatik der Romanischen*

Sprachen (Leipzig: Reisland, 1902), pp. 547–8; Saco, *Historia de la Esclavitud*, III, pp. 125, 140–1; Simonet, *Glosario*, p. 387.

9   Nebrija, *Diccionario Latino–Español* (1492), *mulus*, *burdo*, *hinnus*, *hinnulus*, *ginny*; Nebrija, *Vocabulario Español-Latino* (1945), *muleto*; Nebrija, *Vocabulario de Romance en Latin*, ed. Gerald J. MacDonald (Madrid: Castalia, 1973), *muleto*. See also P. G. W. Clarke, *Oxford Latin Dictionary* (Oxford: Clarendon Press, 1983), for *ginnus*, *hinnus*, *hinnulus*; and Pliny, *Natural History*, vol. 3, book VIII, pp. 120–3.

10 Nebrija and López de Rubiños, *Dictionarium Redivivum*, *mulo*, *muleta*; Nebrija, *Dictionarium Emendatum*, *mulo*, *muleta*.

11 Cardoso, *Dictionarium* (1592) and (1643), mulato, *muleta*, *mulo*.

12 Cristóbal de las Casas, *Vocabulario de las Dos Lenguas Toscana y Castellana* (Venice: Alberti, 1600), *mulo*, *muleta*.

13 Oudin, *Tesoro* (1607 and 1625), *mulet*, *muleta*, *mulato*.

14 Oudin and Rodrigues, *Le Grand Dictionaire* (1639), *mulet*; Nebrija, *Vocabulario de Romance*, *mohino*; George C. Divry, *Modern English–Greek and Greek–English Desk Dictionary* (New York: Divry, 1971), 'mule'.

15 Covarrubias, *Tesoro*, *muleto*.

16 Barbosa, *Dictionarium*, *mulo*, *mulato*, *muleto*; John Florio, *Queen Anna's New World of Words or Dictionarie of the Italian and English Tongues* (Menston: Scolar Press, 1968), *muleto*, *mulo*.

17 Minsheu, *Vocabularium*, *mulato*, *muleta*, *mulo*; Minsheu, *Guide*, 'mongrill', *burdo*. In Minsheu, *A Dictionarie* (1599) is:

Muléta roma, a shee colt of an asse and a horse.
Mulétada, a herd of mules.
Mulétas, crutches or stilts to go on.
Muléto rómo, a he colt of an horse and an asse.

18 Pereira, *Prosodia*, *mulato*, *muleto*.

19 De la Porte, *Den Nieuwen Dictionaris*, *mula*, *muleto*; Justice, *A Complete Account*, *mulato*; Alewyn and Collë, *Vocabulario*, *mulato*.

20 Bluteau, *Vocabulario*, *mulato*.

21 Corominas, *Diccionario*, *macho*; Santa Rosa de Viterbo, *Elucidario*, *mulato*; Minsheu, *A Dictionarie* (1599) has for *macho*: 'the male kinde of any creature, the man, a smiths sledge, or great hammer. Also a hee goat.'

22 Sobrino, *Diccionario*,, *muleto*; Pagés, *Gran Diccionario*, *mulato*, *muleto*, *muleta*; Zerolo, Toro y Gómez, and Isaza, *Diccionario*, same terms.

23 Nascentes, *Dicionário*, *mulato*, *muleta*; Antenor Nascentes, *Dicionário da Lingua Portuguesa* (Brazil: Imprensa Nacional, 1966), same terms; Jorge Amado, *Tereza Batista, Cansada de Guerra* (Lisbon: Europa–America, 1978), p. 19.

24 Pasini, *Vocabulario*, *mulo*, *muletto*; Oreste Badellino, *Dizionario Italiano–Latino* (Turin: Rosenberg & Sellier, 1970), *muletto*; Wilhelm Meyer-Lübke, *Romanisches Etymologisches Wörterbuch* (Heidelberg: Winter, 1930), p. 473.

25 Marin, *Dictionnaire* (1710), *mulet*; Francois Halma, *Le Grand Dictionaire Francois et Flamend* (Amsterdam: Rudolph & Wetstein, 1717), *mulet*.

26 George Fleming, 'Mule', *Werner Encyclopaedia* (Akron: Werner, 1909), vol. XVII, pp. 19–20.

27 Encyclopaedia Judaica (Jerusalem: Keter, 1971), 'mule'.

28 Gil Vicente, *Obras Completas*, ed. Marques Braza (Lisbon: Sá da Costa, 1942), vol. II, p. 242 and n; vol. VI, p. 8.

29 Dalgado, *Glossário, mulato.*
30 Santa Rosa de Viterbo, *Elucidario, mulato;* Fleming, 'Mule', p. 20.
31 Pagés, *Gran Diccionario, mulato;* Cortés, *La Esclavitud,* pp. 294, 343.
32 Corominas, *Diccionario, macho.*
33 Francisco del Rosal, *La Razon de Algunos Refranes,* ed. B. Bussell Thompson (London: Tamesis, 1975), p. 71. Minsheu, *A Dictionarie* (1599) has for *mulas:* 'high-heeled shoes, or pantofles. Also mules.' The former meaning reminds one of the use of *muletas* for stilts or crutches.
34 Cortés, *La Esclavitud,* p. 465.
35 Corominas, *Diccionario, mulo.*
36 Wehr, *A Dictionary,* pp. 296, 1196, 1286; Elias, *Modern Dictionary,* 'date-palm, date tree', 'half-breed', 'half-caste', 'hybrid', 'mestizo', 'mulatto', 'mule'; John Wortabet and Harvey Porter, *English–Arabic and Arabic–English Dictionary* (New York: Ungar, 1954), 'mulatto', 'mule'; N. S. Doniach, ed., *The Oxford English–Arabic Dictionary of Current Usage* (Oxford: Clarendon Press, 1972), 'half-breed', 'half-caste', 'hybrid', 'mix', 'mulatto', 'mule'; Ba'albaki, *Al-Mawrid,* 'mulatto', 'mule'; Karmi, *Al Manar,* 'mulatto', 'mule'; de la Garde, ed., *Petri Hispani,* p. 317.
37 Corominas, *Diccionario, mulo;* Wehr, *A Dictionary,* p. 283; discussions with Arabic-speaking informants.
38 Corominas, *Diccionario, mulo.*
39 Oliveira Marques, *History of Portugal,* vol. I, pp. 32, 69, 71.
40 *Grande Enciclopédia Portuguesa e Brasileira* (Lisbon: Editorial Enciclopedia, post–1945), *muladi.*
41 Ángel González Palencia, *Historia de la España Musulmana* (Barcelona: Editorial Labor, 1925), p. 123.
42 Simonet, *Glosario,* pp. xxxv, cxxix; Simonet, *Historia de los Mozárabes,* pp. xiv–xvi as cited in Lévi–Provençal, *Histoire,* vol. III, p. 180n.
43 William C. Atkinson, *A History of Spain and Portugal* (Harmondsworth: Penguin, 1960), pp. 47, 50; Lévi–Provençal, *Histoire,* vol. III, pp. 180–1, 217.
44 Santa Rosa de Viterbo, *Elucidario, malado.*
45 Ibid., *malada, maladía;* Saco, *Historia de la Esclavitud,* vol. III, pp. 106–7, 153n, 154; Lévi–Provençal, *Histoire,* vol. III, pp. 210–13. Lévi–Provençal states that *maullatus* was used to designate 'recommendees' derived from Mozarabic emigration from Muslim areas to areas falling newly under Christian control (tenth century).
46 W. H. Engelmann, *Glossaire des Mots Espagnols et Portugais Dérivés de l'Arabe* (Leiden: Brill, 1861), pp. 87, 320.
47 Corominas, *Diccionario, muladi, mulo.*
48 R. Dozy and W. H. Englemann, *Glosaire des Mots Espagnols et Portugais Dérivés de l'Arabe,* 2nd edition (Leiden: Brill, 1869), p. 384.
49 Leopoldo Eguilaz y Yanguas, *Glosario Etimológico de las Palabras Españolas de Origen Oriental* (Granada: La Lealtad, 1886), *mulato.* See also P. J. Veth, *Uit Oost en West: Verklaring van Eenige Uitheemsche Woorden* (Arnhem: Gouda Quint., 1889), pp. 93–7, for supporting data on *muwallad.*
50 Pagés, *Gran Diccionario, muladi;* Zerolo, Toro y Gomez, and Isaza, *Diccionario, muladi.*
51 Pinheiro, *Dicionario, malado, maladía, maladio.*
52 José Pedro Machado, *Dicionário Etimológico da Lingua Portuguosa* (Lisbon: Confluencia, 1952, 1967), *muladi.*

53 *Diccionario de la Lengua Española* (Madrid: Real Academia Española, 1984), *muladi*.

54 Wehr, *A Dictionary*, pp. 1285–6.

55 Informant.

56 Leon Carl Brown, 'Color in Northern Africa' in John Hope Franklin, ed., *Color and Race* (Boston: Beacon, 1968), p. 192.

57 Doniach, *English–Arabic Dictionary*, 'half-caste', 'half-breed', 'hybrid', 'mulatto'; Karmi, *Al-Manar*, 'mulatto'; Elias, *Modern Dictionary*, 'half-caste', 'hybrid', 'mestizo', 'mulatto', 'mulattress'; 'mulattress'; Ba'albaki, *Al-Mawrid*, 'mulatto'.

58 Lévi–Provençal, *Histoire*, vol. III, pp. 182–7.

59 Rodrigues, *Brazil and Africa*, pp. 32, 45.

60 Cortés, *La Esclavitud*, p. 381.

61 Brasio, *Monumenta Missionaria Africana*, vol. I, pp. 331, 376, 391–2, 472, 500–1; Ramusio, *Navigazioni*, vol. I, p. 578; Boxer, 'Race Relations', p. 15.

62 Fleming, 'Mule', p. 20.

63 Lobo Cabrera, *La Esclavitud*, p. 140.

64 Ibid., *ventas de moriscos, ventas de negros*.

65 Oudin, *Tesoro* (1625), *amulatado*; Artur Bivar, *Dicionário General e Analógico da Lingua Portuguesa* (Oporto: Ouro, 1952), vol. II p. 381; F. Adolpho Coelho, *Diccionario Manual Etymologico da lingua Portuguesa* (Lisbon: Plantier, 1889), *amulatado*.

66 Enrico Zaccaria, *L'Elemento Iberico nella Lingua Italiana* (Bologna: Cappelli, 1927), p. 282; Marcucci, ed., *Lettere . . . de Sasseti*, pp. 224, 302.

67 Corominas, *Diccionario, loro*; Zerolo, Toro y Gómez, & Isasza, *Diccionario, mulato*.

CHAPTER 6 PART-AFRICANS AND PART-AMERICANS AS *MULATOS*

1 Cortés, *La Esclavitud*, pp. 62, 294, 343, 369, 387; Franco Silva, *La Esclavitud*, p. 321. In 1513 a *lor* slave, Sebastián, 17, of Seville was traded for 'un macho de silla' (a riding mule?) and 'el dinero que faltaba'. Cortés, *La Esclavitud*, p. 438.

2 Ibid., p. 381.

3 Afonso de Albuquerque, *The Commentaries of the Great Afonso Dalboquerque*, trans. Walter de Gray Birch (London: Hakluyt Society, 1875), vol. I, pp. 1, 20–1, 38, 45, 81, 89, 140, 142, lxxxix, xxxv.

4 Boxer, 'The Colour Question', p. 116.

5 Boxer, 'Race Relations', pp. 15–16; Brasio, *Monumenta Missionaria Africana*, vol. I, pp. 331, 376, 391–2, 472, 500–1.

6 'Navigazione da Lisboa all'Isola di San Tomé. . . . per un Piloto Portoghese', in Ramusio, *Navigazioni*, vol. I, p. 578; and Boxer, 'Race Relations', p. 15. It is interesting that the words *tiburoni* (sharks) and *batatas* (sweet potatoes) had already spread from the Caribbean to West African waters by 1535. See Ramusio, *Navigazioni*, vol. I, pp. 570, 582.

7 Lobo Cabrera, *La Esclavitud*, pp. 31, 125, 146–8, 151–2 and appendices.

8 Ibid., pp. 141, 154–5, 173, 242, 266, 271, 360–1, 364, 367, 370, 374, 379, 382–3, and appendices ('ventas de negros, de mulatos, de moriscos, de indios').

9 Graullera Sanz, *La Esclavitud*, pp. 125, 126–7, 127n, 194.

10 Domínguez Ortiz, 'La Esclavitud', pp. 400–1.

11 Brasio, *Os Pretos em Portugal*, p. 111n.

12 'Informação de Mina' in Brasio, *Monumenta Missionaria Africana*, vol. III, p. 90.

13 Andrew Battell, *The Strange Adventures of Andrew Battell*, ed. E. G. Ravenstein (London: Hakluyt Society, 1901), p. 49.

14 Konetzke, *Colección*, vol. I, p. 256; *Recopilación de Leyes . . . de Indias*, tomo II, libro VI, titulo XII, ley 13, fo. 243 and ley 14, fo. 231; tomo IV, libro IX, titulo XXVI, ley 17, ley 21, ley 11, ley 15, ley 19, fos 1–5; Saco, *Esclavitud de la Raza Africana*, vol. I, pp. 152–3.

15 *Recopilación de Leyes . . . de Indias*, libro VI, titulo III, ley 21, fo. 200.

16 Lockhart, *El Mundo Hispanoperuano*, p. 224; Bowser, *The African Slave*, p. 384n.

17 *Recopilación de Leyes . . . de Indias*, libro IV, titulo XXVI, ley 23, fo. 4; libro VI, titulo III, ley 17, fo. 200; libro VII, titulo V, ley 14, fo. 287; Konetzke, *Colección*, vol. I, p. 420; Bowser, *The African Slave*, p. 273; Rosenblat, *Mestizaje*, p. 89.

18 Konetzke, *Colección*, vol. I, pp. 427, 435.

19 *Recopilación de Leyes . . . de Indias*, libro V, titulo 8, ley 40, fo. 167; libro VI, titulo VI, ley 7, fo. 218; libro VII, titulo IV, fo. 284–7; libro VII, titulo V, fo. 290–1; Konetzke, *Colección*, vol. I, pp. 479, 489; Rosenblat, *Mestizaje*, pp. 151–3.

20 Rosenblat, *Mestizaje*, pp. 64–5; Juan López de Velasco, *Geografía y Descripción Universal de las Indias* (Madrid: Atlas, 1971), p. 22.

21 Zavala, *Los Esclavos Indios*, pp. 192–3; Miguel Cabello Balboa, 'Verdadera Descripción y Relación Larga de la Provincia y Tierra de las Esmeraldas . . .', *Obras* (Quito: Ecuatoriana, 1945), vol. I, pp. 21, 25–6; John Leddy Phelan, *The Kingdom of Quito in the Seventeenth Century* (Madison: University of Wisconsin Press, 1967), p. 8.

22 Konetzke, *Colección*, vol. I, pp. 623–4.

23 Brasio, *Monumenta Brasilae*, passim; Anchieta, *Cartas*; Magalhaes de Gandavo, *Tratado*; Soares de Sousa, *Tratado*.

24 Gonsalves de Mello, *Tempo dos Flemengos*, pp. 216–17, 229; *Accord van Brasilien, Mede van 't Recif, Maurits-Stadt, Ende de Omleggende Forten van Brasil* (Amsterdam: Claes Lambrechtsz. van der Wolf, 1654), p. 7.

25 Marcgravi (Marcgrave) and Pisonis, *Historia Naturalis*, p. 268; Marcgrave, *Historia Natural*, p. 268; Friederici, *Americanistisches Wörterbuch*, p. 437.

26 Barlaeus, *Nederlandsch Brazilië*, pp. 76, 156.

27 Rodrigues, *Brazil and Africa*, p. 58; Gonsalves de Mello, *Tempo dos Flamengos*, p. 147. Schwartz, 'The Mocambo', pp. 325–6, provides evidence of marriages between Africans and Americans in colonial Bahia.

28 Zaccaria, *L'Elemento Iberico*, p. 282; Dalgado, *Glossário, mulato*.

29 Carletti, *Ragionamenti*, pp. 5–6, 255; Marcucci, *Lettere Edite*, p. 280.

30 Pyrard de Laval, *Voyage*, pt I, p. 328; pt II, pp. 32, 65–6, 128, 131, 236; Dalgado, *Glossário, mulato*.

31 Innocencio Francisco da Silva, *Diccionario Bibliografico Portuguez* (Lisbon: Imprensa Nacional, 1859), vol. III, p. 259.

32 Cardoso, *Dictionarium* (1592), *mulato, hybrida, mestiço*; (1643), same terms.

33 Barbosa, *Dictionarium, mulato, mestiço*.

34 Faria, *Lusiadas, Comentadas*, p. 503.

35 Pereira, *Prosodia, mulato, Hybris, Hybrida*.

36 Zucchelli, *Relazioni*, p. 69.

37 Justice, *A Compleat Account, cafra, mulata, Pretinho, Negro*.

38 Alewyn and Collë, *Vocabulario, mulato, negro*.

39 Bluteau, *Vocabulario, mulato, mestiço, pardo, Trigueiro*.

40 Vieyra Transtagano, *Dictionary, mulato, mulata*; de Sousa and da Costa e Sá,

Nouveau Dictionnaire, mulat, métif; da Costa e Sá, *Diccionario, mulato, mestiço.*
41 Bluteau and Moraes Silva, *Diccionaris, mulato, mestiço, pardo.*
42 Cadamosto, *Viagens,* pp. 49, 52, 65, 67; Fonseca, *Novo Diccionario, mulato;* Roquette, *Nouveau Dictionnaire, mulato, pardo;* Moraes Silva, *Grande Dicionário, caboclo, pardavasco.*
43 Bivar, *Dicionário,* vol. II, pp. 382, *mulato;* Nascentes, *Dicionário, mulato; Grande Enciclopédia Portguguesa, mulato;* Pinheiro, *Dicionário, mulato;* Fernandes, *Dicionário, mulato.* Some persons would equate modern Brazilian *mulata* with 'dancer'. However, I have before me an illustrated article in the Portuguese (Lisbon) newspaper *Exito,* Dec. 24, 1986, entitled 'Mulatas do Brasil pro nosso fim de ano' in which the seven *mulatas* are all brown-skinned beauties with a mixture of Native American, African and European features.
44 Pereira, *Prosodia, carafuz;* Justice, *A Compleat Account, carafuz;* Raphael Bluteau, *Supplemento ao Vocabulario Portuguez e Latino* (Lisbon: da Sylva, 1727), *carafuz;* Constancio, *Novo Diccionario, caboclo;* Cardoso and Rousé, *Grande Dicionário, cafuz;* Johann Baptist von Spix and Carl F. P. von Martius, *Travels in Brazil, in the Years 1817–1820* (London: Longman, 1824), vol. I, pp. 323–4; Pinheiro, *Dicionário, cafuso.*
45 Coelho, *Diccionário, cariboca;* Santamaría, *Diccionario, cariboca;* Julio Platzmann, ed., *O Diccionario Anonymo da Lingua Geral do Brasil* (Leipzig: Teubner, 1896), *mestiço, mulato;* Friederici, *Amerikanistisches Wörtenbuch, caburé, cafuzo;* Moraes Silva, *Grande Dicionario, cariboca, caboré,* Simão Marques, *Brasilia Pontifica,* pp. 140–1 as cited in Leite, *Monumenta Brasiliae,* vol. IV, p. 431n.
46 Boxer, *Fidalgos in the Far East,* p. 199; Salles, *O Negro na Para,* p. 104.
47 Russell-Wood, *The Black Man,* p. 49; *Diccionario Histórico, Geográphico e Ethnográphico do Brasil* (Rio de Janeiro: Imprensa Nacional, 1922), p. 278; Rodrigues, *Brazil and Africa,* p. 75.
48 Rodrigues, *Brazil and Africa,* pp. 73–6.
49 Konetzke, *Colección,* vol. I, pp. 427, 435, 623–4; López de Velasco, *Geografía,* p. 22; Rosenblat, *Mestizaje,* pp. 64–5; and see discussion of Spanish usage earlier in this chapter; Minsheu, *A Dictionarie* (1599) 'mulato'; Minsheu, *Vocabularium,* 'mulato'; Minsheu, *Guide,* p. 314, 'mongrill'; Walter W. Skeat, *An Etymological Dictionary of the English Language* (Oxford: Clarendon, 1924), 'mulatto'.
50 Thomas Blount, *Glossographia* (Menston: Scolar Press, 1969), 'mulato'; Edward Phillips, *The New World of English Words* (Menston: Scolar Press, 1969), 'mulato'; John Kersey, *Dictionarium Anglo–Britannicum or a New English Dictionary* (Menston: Scolar Press, 1969), 'mulatto'.
51 Garcilaso de la Vega (el Inca), *The Florida of the Inca,* trans. & ed. John Grier Varner and Jeanette Johnson Varner (Austin: University of Texas Press, 1951), pp. 105–6.
52 Huaman Poma (Felipe de Ayala), *Letter to a King,* ed. Christopher Dilke (New York: Dutton, 1978), p. 162; Garcilaso de la Vega, *Comentários Reales* as quoted in Rosenblat, *Mestizaje,* p. 173.
53 Oudin, *Tesoro* (1607), *mulato, moro, mestizo;* Oudin. *Tesoro* (1652), *mulato, mestizo;* Oudin and Rodrigues (1639) *Den Grooten Dictionaris, mulato, mestizo, more;* Corominas, *Diccionario, loro;* De la Porte, *Den Nieuwen Dictionaris, mulato.*
54 Covarrubias, *Tesoro* (1611), *mulato.*
55 Lockhart, *El Mundo Hispanoperuano,* p. 224; Relación del Marqués de Montesclaros in Luis Torres de Mendoza, ed., *Colección de Documentos Inéditos* (Vaduz:

Kraus, 1964), vol. VI, p. 224; Solórzano, *De Indianum Iu.*
Solórzano, *Política Indiana*, pp. 442, 447, 449; *Recopilación de L.*
libro VI, título III, ley 21, fo. 200; Konetzke, *Colección*, vol II, p

56 Ibid., vol. II, p. 480.
57 Bowser, *The African Slave*, p. 384n; Konetzke, *Colección*, vol. II, ¡
58 Aguirre Beltrán, 'Races in 17th Century Mexico', pp. 214–16 an
59 Rosenblat, *Mestizaje*, p. 172; Gumilla, *El Orinoco*, pp. 81, 83, 85, 8\ _.ᴜ, ɪNebrija
   and López de Rubiños, *Dictionarium Redivivum*, *mulato*; Nebrija, *Dictionarum
   Emendatum*, *mulato*; Pagés, *Gran Diccionario*, *mulato*; Santamaría, *Diccionario*,
   mulato.
60 Badellino, *Dizionario*, *mulatto*.
61 Oudin, *Tesoro* (1607), *mulato*, *mestizo*; Oudin, *Tesoro* (1625), *mulato*; Oudin and
   Rodrigues, *Den Grooten Dictionaris*, *mulato*; Friederici, *Amerikanistisches Wörterbuch*, p. 437.
62 Pyrard de Laval, *Voyage*, pt. I, p. 328; pt II, p. 236; d'Arsy, *Le Grand Dictionaire*;
   Pierre Richelet, *Le Grand et Nouveau Dictionaire Francois et Flamand* (Brussels:
   Grieck, 1707).
63 Du Tertre, *Histoire*, p. 512.
64 Giraud, *A History*, p. 280.
65 Marin, *Dictionnaire Complet* (1710, 1728, 1743, 1762), *mulâtre*.
66 Halma, *Le Grand Dictionnaire* (1761), 1781), *mulat*.
67 Leo Elizabeth, 'The French Antilles' in Cohen and Greene, *Neither Slave Nor
   Free*, p. 135; Pierre Richelet, *Le Grand Dictionnaire Francois et Flamand* (Brussels:
   Fricx, 1765), *mulat*.
68 Winkelman, *Dictionnaire*, *mulat*; de Sousa and da Costa e Sá, *Nouveau
   Dictionnaire*, *mulat*.
69 Pieter (Pierre) Marin, *Dictionnaire François et Hollandois* (Amsterdam: Changuion,
   1793), *mulat*; da Costa e Sá, *Diccionario* (1794), *mulato*; Roquette, *Nouveau
   Dictionnaire* (1863), *pardo*.
70 G. Nieuwenhuis, *Algemeen Woordenboek van Kunsten en Wetenschappen* (Zutphen:
   Thieme, 1824), *mulatten*.
71 Peter Kloos, 'Amerindians of Surinam', in *De Indianen in Suriname*, p. 3, a hand-
   out of the author. Also published in *The Situation of the Indian in South America*.
72 Francisco Morales Padrón, *Jamaica Española* (Seville: Escuela de Estudios
   Hispano–Americanos, 1952), pp. 273–4, 430.
73 Rosenblat, *Mestizaje*, pp. 157–8, Mörner, *Race Mixture*, p. 56.
74 Rama, 'The Passing of the Afro–Uruguayans' in Morner, *Race and Class*, pp. 31,
   35; Mörner, *Race Mixture*, pp. 70n, 110; Rosenblat, *Mestizaje*, pp. 70, 131, 164 and
   n, 175–6, 178–9; Jack D. Forbes, 'Black Pioneers: The Spanish-Speaking Afro–
   Americans of the Southwest', *Phylon*, vol. 27 (1966), pp. 235, 237–8; Rolando
   Mellafe, *Negro Slavery in Latin America*, trans. J. W. S. Judge (Berkeley: University
   of California Press, 1975), p. 103.
75 Franco Silva, *La Esclavitud*, p. 103; Lobo Cabrera, *La Esclavitud*, pp. 146, 148;
   Bowser, *The African Slave*, p. 254; Lowery, *The Spanish Settlements*, p. 143;
   Mörner, *Race Mixture*, p. 121 and n.
76 Rodrigues, *Brazil and Africa*, pp. 159 and n.
77 Mörner, *Race Mixture*, p. 16, 30; Zavala, *Los Esclavos Indios*, p. 105; Rosenblat,
   Mestizaje, p. 56; Aguirre Beltrán, 'African Influences', in *Plantation Systems of the
   New World*, p. 70.

    Huaman Poma, *Letter to a King*, pp. 221, 241.
79   C. H. Haring, *The Spanish Empire in America* (New York: Oxford University Press, 1947), pp. 219, 221; López de Velasco, Geografía, p. xxiv.
80   López de Velasco, *Geografía*, p. 22; Solórzano, *De Indianum Iure*, p. 208; Davidson, 'Negro Slave Control', pp. 239–40; Love, 'Legal Restrictions', pp. 135–6.
81   Mörner, *Race Mixture*, p. 38; Rosenblat, *Mestizaje*, pp. 64–5, 156; *Recopilación de Leyes . . . de Indias*, libro VII, titulo V, ley 7, fo. 286; libro VI, titulo V, ley 8, fo. 209; libro VII, titulo V, ley 2, fo. 285.
82   *Recopilación de Leyes . . . de Indias*, libro VII, titulo V, ley 3, fo. 285; López de Velasco, *Geografía*, p. 22; Konetzke, *Colección*, vol. II, p. 610; Aguirre Beltrán, 'Races in 17th Century Mexico', p. 218.
83   *Recopilación de Leyes . . . de Indias*, libro VII, titulo IV, ley II, fo. 284.
84   Franco Silva, *La Esclavitud*, p. 95.
85   Rosenblat, *Mestizaje*, p. 75; Zavala, *Los Esclavos Indios*, pp. 20, 21, 51, 94; Frederick A. Ober, 'Aborigines of the West Indies', *Proceedings of the American Antiquarian Society*, vol. 9 (1893), p. 273; Saco, *Esclavitud de los Indios*, vol. I, pp. 164ff, 241.
86   Mörner, *Race Mixture*, pp. 25–6; Hoetink, *Slavery and Race Relations*, p. 164.
87   Quoted in Ober, 'Aborigines', p. 282. American slaves were still in Jamaica as late as 1747 when one was sold to Virginia.
88   Zavala, *Los Esclavos Indios*, p. 236; see Crane, *Southern Colonial Frontier*, for many southern examples; also see Lauber, *Indian Slavery*, pp. 119–33, 180, 185, 272, 314. See also Jerome S. Handler, 'The Amerindian Slave Population of Barbados in the Seventeenth and Early Eighteenth Centuries', *Caribbean Studies*, vol. 8 (1968), pp. 38–64.
89   Konetzke, *Colección*, vol. I, pp. 489, 623–4.
90   Rosenblat, *Mestizaje*, p. 54.
91   Ibid., p. 64–5, 156; Zavala, *Los Esclavos Indios*, pp. 192–3; also see Zavala's index for references to *negros* in the mines with Americans; Mörner, *Race Mixture*, p. 38. See also Davidson, 'Negro Slave Control', pp. 243ff, 247; and Love, 'Legal Restrictions', pp. 131ff, for excellent discussions of African–American interaction in Mexico. Davidson presents data on a *palenque* in Mexico with American women (p. 247).
92   Petition of Alonso Vaca, *c.*1643, in Patronato 244, Ramo VII, Archivo General de Indias, Seville; Forbes, *Apache, Navaho and Spaniard*, pp. 135, 138–9, 148, 189 and n; Charles W. Hackett, *The Revolt of the Pueblo Indians* (Albuquerque: University of New Mexico Press, 1942), vol. II, pp. 322–55.
93   Konetzke, *Collección*, vol. I, pp. 427, 435; Aguirre Beltrán, 'Races in 17th Century Mexico', p. 216.
94   Rosenblat, *Mestizaje*, pp. 30, 65n, 66.
95   Garcilaso de la Vega (el Inca), *Historia General del Peru*, ed Ángel Rosenblat (Buenos Aires: Emce, n.d.), vol. III, pp. 131–2, 191.
96   Lockhart, *El Mundo Hispanoperuano*, p. 242; Rosenblat, *Mestizaje*, p. 89.
97   Mario C. Vázquez, 'Immigration and Mestizaje in Nineteenth-Century Peru', in Mörner, *Race and Class*, pp. 91–3.
98   Gage, *Travels*, pp. 22, 96, 195–6; Rosenblat, *Mestizaje*, pp. 69, 73–4, 77, 167; Mörner, *Race Mixture*, p. 20.
99   Haring, *Spanish Empire*, pp. 219, 221; Huaman Poma, *A Letter to a King*, pp. 113,

191; de la Vega, *The Florida of the Inca*, pp. 333, 346–7; Bancroft, *History of the North Mexican States and Texas*, vol. I, pp. 454, 457, 460; Forbes, *Apache, Navaho and Spaniard*, pp. 8, 22, 42, 76; see also Jack D. Forbes, *Afro–Americans in the Far West* (Washington, DC: Government Printing Office, 1969); Crane, *Southern Colonial Frontier*, p. 31; Lowery, *Spanish Settlements*, pp. 160, 194.

CHAPTER 7   THE CLASSIFICATION OF NATIVE AMERICANS AS
MULATTOES IN ANGLO-NORTH AMERICA

1 James Mooney, 'Myths of the Cherokee', in *Nineteenth Annual Report*, Bureau of American Ethnology, 1897–8, pt 1, p. 233.
2 Johnston, *Race Relations in Virginia*, pp. 171–2, 281, 292.
3 Ibid., pp. 272–3, and also p. 269.
4 James Hugo Johnston, 'Documentary Evidence of the Relations of Negroes and Indians', *Journal of Negro History*, vol. XIV (1929), p. 43.
5 John H. Russell, *The Free Negro in Virginia 1619–1865* (Baltimore: Johns Hopkins, 1913), pp. 41. 130.
6 Catterall, *Judicial Cases,*. vol. I, p. 63.
7 Robert B. Lee, *New Jersey as a Colony and as a State* (Trenton: 1903), vol. I, pp. 65–6 as cited in Johnston, *Race Relations*, p. 274; Edward Byron Reuter, *The American Race Problem, A Study of the Negro* (New York: Crowell, 1927), pp. 122–3. See also Reuter, *Race Mixture*, pp. 47–9.
8 M. F. Ashley Montagu, 'Origins of the American Negro', *Psychiatry: Journal of the Biology and Pathology of Interpersonal Relations*, vol. 7 (1944) pp. 169–72.
9 See, for example, Wright, *The Only Land They Knew*, pp. 128–50, 248–78.
10 See, for example, articles by D. F. Roberts and Bentley Glass in the *American Journal of Human Genetics*, 7 (1955), pp. 361–85.
11 Melville J. Herskovitz, *The American Negro* (New York: Knopf, 1928), pp. 8–10; August Meier, 'A Study of the Racial Ancestry of the Mississippi College Negro', *American Journal of Physical Anthropology*, n.s., vol. 7 (1947), pp. 227–39. See also John H. Spurgeon and Howard V. Meredith, 'Skin Color Comparisons among Ethnic Groups of College Men', *American Journal of Physical Anthropology*, vol. 64 (1984), pp. 413–18. Of the 197 South Carolina students of African background studied, over half (40 per cent to 57 per cent) had American ancestry. Meier's data from somewhat further west contained a slightly higher percentage of American background.
12 Minsheu, *A Dictionarie*, *mulata, mulato*; Minsheu, *Vocabularium*, *mulato*; Minsheu, *Guide*, 'mongrill'; Skeat, *An Etymological Dictionary*, 'mulatto'.
13 Florio, *Queen Anna's New World of Words*.
14 Cockeram, *The English Dictionarie*.
15 Blount, *Glossographia*.
16 Phillips, *The New World of English Words*.
17 Kersey, attrib., *A New English Dictionary*.
18 Kersey, *Dictionarium Anglo–Britanicum*.
19 *The Oxford English Dictionary* (Oxford: Clarendon Press, 1933), 'mulatto'.
20 N. Bailey, *The Universal Etymological English Dictionary*, editions as follows (London: Darby, 1728), (London: Ware: 1749), (London: Osborne, 1961) and others.
21 Justice, *Vocabularium*, 'mulato', 'black'; Samuel Johnson, *A Dictionary of the English*

Language (London: Knapton, 1756), vol. II and (London: Rivington, 1785) vol. 2.

22   James Buchanan, *Linguae Britannicae* (Menston: Scolar Press, 1967).

23   Noah Webster, *An American Dictionary of the English Language* (New York: Johnson, 1970). This definition is contained also in dictionaries such as John Russell Bartlett, *Dictionary of Americanisms* (Boston: Little Brown, 1860 [1859]) and John S. Farmer, *Americanisms – Old and New* (London: Poulter, 1889).

24   *The Oxford English Dictionary*, 'mulatto'; Mitford M. Mathews, *A Dictionary of Americanisms* (Chicago: University of Chicago Press, 1951), 'mulatto'; Craigie and Hulbert, *A Dictionary*, vol 3, pp. 1565f.

25   Robert Hooke, *Micrographia* (London: Marotyn, *c.*1667), pp. 206–7.

26   Hurd, *The Law of Freedom and Bondage*, vol. I, p. 228.

27   Ibid., vol. I, p. 238; also Lauber, *Indian Slavery*, p. 254. In 1733 Jamaica defined 'mulatto' so as to include all persons with African ancestry to the third degree. See Winthrop D. Jordan, 'American Chiaroscuro: the Status and Definition of Mulattoes in the British Colonies', *William and Mary Quarterly*, vol. 19 (1962), p. 198. In 1644 Antigua passed an ordinance against copulation between Christians and 'heathens', the latter being Negroes and Indians. Any mulatto children were to be enslaved to age 18 or 21 according to Dunn, *Sugar and Slaves*, p. 228 and n. In fact, however, the law and a revision of 1672 never utilized the term mulatto. Colonial Office 154/1, pp. 41, 49–51, (Leeward Islands Mss. Laws, 1644–1673). Public Records Office.

28   Jane Purcell Guild, *Black Laws of Virginia* (Richmond: Whittet and Shepperson, 1936), pp. 25, 29, 30 and n, 33.

29   Ibid., p. 35.

30   Archives of Virginia, Petition 13733, King William County, 1843.

31   Helen Roundtree, 'The Indians of Virginia', ms. in Archives of Virginia, Indian File, p. 13.

32   Dean v. Commonwealth, 4 Grattan 541, June 1847.

33   Wood, *Black Majority*, p. 99n.

34   State v. Richard Scott, 1 Bailey 270, June 1829; see also Catterall, *Judicial Cases*, vol. 2, p. 339.

35   State v. Davis, State v. Hanna, 2 Bailey 558, Dec. 1831; also Catterall, *Judicial Cases*, vol. 2, p. 346.

36   Catterall, *Judicial Cases*, vol. 2, p. 401.

37   Catterall, *Judicial Cases*, vol. 2, pp. 415–16.

38   Johnston, *Race Relations*, pp. 202–3.

39   Phillis v. Lewis, 1 Delaware Cas. 417, in Daniel J. Boorstin (ed.), *Delaware Cases 1792–1830* (St. Paul: West, 1943), pp. 503–5.

40   Hurd, *Law of Freedom and Bondage*, vol. II, p. 128.

41   Heizer and Almquist, *The Other Californians*, p. 236.

42   Ivey v. Hardy, 2 Port. 548, 1852; *Revised Alabama Code* 1852, Sect. 2276.

43   Johnston, *Race Relations*, p. 204. This interpretation is based, though, on the assumption that a 'griffe' was part-American and part-African. Such an interpretation would be in accord with French usage of the term *mulatto*. A French writer (1614) used *mulatto* to refer to a mixture of French and Indian, while in 1715 the children of Frenchmen and American women in the Mobile region were called 'mulattoes'. Corominas, *Diccionario*, vol. 3, p. 475; Giraud, *A History of French Louisiana*, p. 280.

44 Tax rolls of Charles City, New Kent, King William, Essex, King and Queen, and Caroline counties, Archives of Virginia, Richmond.

45 *First Census of the United States*, South Carolina, 1790, pp. 46–62.

46 Carter G. Woodson, *The Free Negro Heads of Families in the United States in 1830* (Washington, DC: Association for Study of Negro Life and History, 1925) pp. 21, 121–2, 184.

47 *American State Papers, Public Lands* (Washington, DC, 1834–5), vol. VII, p. 39, as cited in Johnston, *Race Relations*, p. 290 and Johnston, 'Documentary Evidence', p. 41.

48 See *The Lower Norfolk County Virginia Antiquary*, vol. 3 (1899), pp. 12–18; U.S. Census 1850, various counties. In the case of John Bass of Norfolk the 'm' has been erased. See p. 255, 1850 Census, Norfolk County, Va., and Albert D. Bell, *Bass Families of the South* (Rocky Mount, N.C., 1941) pp. 5–16.

49 *Negro Population in the United States, 1790–1915* (Washington, DC: Bureau of the Census, 1918), p. 67.

50 Tax rolls of King William County, 1782–1815, Virginia Archives; Tax rolls of King and Queen County, 1813, Virginia Archives; US Census, Virginia, 1810, 1820.

51 Petition of John and Lucy Ann Dungie, 1825, King William petitions, Virginia Archives.

52 Endorsements to the above, Virginia Archives.

53 Woodson, *Free Negro Heads of Families* (index); US Census, King William County, Virginia, 1830, 1840, 1850.

54 Communication, 'List of Indian Students Enrolled', from Librarian, William and Mary College; Petition of Headmen and Chiefs of Pamunkey Tribe, King William petitions, 1812, Virginia Archives.

55 US Census, King William County, 1830, 1840, 1850; also other counties in Virginia; Frank G. Speck, 'Chapters on the Ethnology of the Powhatan Tribes of Virginia', *Indian Notes and Monographs*, vol. 1 (1928), p. 303; Pamunkey Petition, Dec. 4, 1812, Virginia Archives.

56 US Census, King William County, 1830, 1840, 1850; also Rev. Dalrymple, in *The Historical Magazine* (New York), vol. 5 (1858), p. 182.

57 See photographs in the National Anthropological Archives, Smithsonian Institution, under Chickahominy, Pamunkey, Rappahannock, Mattaponi tribes. Many also published in works of Frank G. Speck and in *Attan-Akamik* (Powhatan) newspaper.

58 'Nottoway Tribe of Indians, Advice Relative Thereto', No. 1, July 18, 1808, Southampton County, Virginia Archives; US Census, Southampton County, 1830, 1850; Auditor report, No. 161. 1844, Southampton County, Virginia Archives.

59 Augusta B. Fothergill and John Mark Naugle, *Early Virginia Taxpayers, 1782–87* (n.p., n.p., 1940); US Census, Henrico county, 1810, 1850; Commonwealth v. Scott, cited in Catterall, *Judicial Cases,*, vol. I, p. 220.

60 Catterall, *Judicial Cases*, vol. I, pp. 58, 78; Edward Thomas Price, Jr, 'Mixed-Blood Populations of Eastern United States' (Ph.D. dissertation, Geography, University of California, Berkely, 1950), pp. 171–3; US Census, 1850, Grainger County, Tennessee and Lawrence County, Alabama; Woodson, *Free Negro Heads of Families* (see index), various Virginia and North Carolina censuses (see indexes

for 1790–1850); Worth S. Ray, *Colonial Granville County and its People* (Baltimore: Southern Book Co., 1956), p. 292; Russell, *The Free Negro*, pp. 47–8.

61 Ibid., p. 185n. See also Roundtree, 'The Indians of Virginia', p. 20.

62 *Negro Population in the U.S., 1790–1915*, pp. 185n, 207.

63 Cohen, *Handbook of Federal Indian Law*, p. 2 and n.

64 Major battles developed in certain Virginia counties over whether Indians could record themselves under that designation.

65 US Census instructions, 1980, printed sheets received from the Bureau of the Census.

66 Gage, *Travels in the New World*, pp. 68–9. See also pp. xvii, xliii, 25, 67, 95, 190–4, 198–9, 200, 202, 204, 215, 269, 315–17, 322, 327.

67 Letter of Aug. 22, 1674 of Abraham Wood, in Clarence Walworth Alvord and Lee Bidgood, *The First Expeditions of the Trans-Allegheny Region by the Virginians 1650–1674* (Cleveland: Arthur H. Clark, 1912) pp. 213–14, 216, 219.

68 Johnston, *Race Relations*, p. 175.

69 Catterall, *Judicial Cases*, vol. I, p. 53.

70 T. Brown, *Walk Round Land*, vol. III, pp. iii, 9, as quoted in *The Oxford English Dictionary*, (1933), 'mulatto'; Wright, *The Only Land They Knew*, pp. 98, 256.

71 Hugh Jones, *The Present State of Virginia*, ed. Richard L. Morton (Chapel Hill: University of North Carolina Press, 1956), p. 76.

72 Russell, *The Free Negro*, p. 130n.

73 Mercer v. Commonwealth, 2 VA., *c.*144, in Catterall, *Judicial Cases*, Vol. I, p. 130.

74 *Register of Free Negroes*, Essex County Court House, Tappahannock, Virginia, vols I and II.

75 Weslager, *Delaware's Forgotten Folk*, p. 31.

76 Peter B. Socum als. Delaware, *Houston's Delaware Reports*, vol. I, (new 6) p. 204.

77 Mary C. Norment, *The Lowrie History* (Wilmington: Daily Journal, 1875), pp. 5–20.

78 Robert K. Thomas, 'A Report on Research of Lumbee Origins', ms., undated (*c.*1976–9), p. 5.

79 Ibid., pp. 37–8. See also Brewton Berry, *Almost White* (New York: Macmillan, 1963), p. 50 and Douglas Rights, *The American Indian in North Carolina* (Winston-Salem: Blair, 1957), p. 148.

80 Price, 'Mixed-Blood Populations', pp. 171–3; US Census, Hawkins County, Tennessee, 1830.

81 William Allen Dromgoole, 'The Malungeons', *The Arena*, No. XVI (1891), pp. 470–3. See also US Census, Grainger County, Tennessee 1850.

82 Brewton Berry, 'The Mestizos of South Carolina', *American Journal of Sociology*, vol. 51 (1945), pp. 34–41. See also Berry, *Almost White*, pp. 46–8.

83 Windley, *Runaway Slave Advertisements*, vol. I, pp. 5, 27, 124, 125, 131, 174, 177–8, 181, 186, 230–1, 323, 325, 411.

84 New Bern, *North Carolina Magazine, or Universal Intelligencer*, 1764; *North Carolina Gazette*, April 7, 1775, p. 3; April 14, 1775; Dec. 22, 1775; as copied by Wesley D. White, Jr. and provided to the author.

85 Windley, *Runaway Slave Advertisements*, vol. 3, pp. 32, 41, 71, 81, 94, 122, 192, 212, 322, 434, 670.

86 See *The Oxford Dictionary of the English Language* (1933) and Samuel Johnson, *A Dictionary of the English Language*, ed. H. J. Todd (London: Longman, 1827).

87 John White's Report in Stephen Lorant, ed., *The New World* (New York: Dull,

Sloan & Pearce, 1965), p. 170; Thomas Maynarde, 'Sir Francis Drake, his Voyage, 1595', and 'Relación de lo Sucedido en San Juan de Puerto Rico de las Indias' in W. D. Cooley, ed., *Sir Francis Drake, his Voyage, 1595* (London: Hakluyt Society, 1849), vol. 4, pp. 22, 36, 54.

88 C. R. D. Bethune, ed., *The Observations of Sir Richard Hawkins in his Voyage to the South Sea, 1593* (London: Hakluyt Society, 1847), pp. 181–2; Battell, *Strange Adventures*, p. 49.

89 Russell, *The Free Negro in Virginia*, p. 31; Catterall, *Judicial Cases*, vol. I, pp. 58, 60; Alex Brown, *The Genesis of the United States* (Boston, 1897), pp. 885–6; Edward D. Neill, *Virginia Carolorum* (Albany: Munsell, 1886), p. 365.

90 Donnan, *Documents*, vol. IV, p. 119; Bassett, ed., *The Writings of Colonel William Byrd*, p. 75.

91 Russell, *The Free Negro in Virginia*, p. 39.

92 Hurd, *The Law of Freedom and Bondage*, vol. I, pp. 230–45; vol. II, pp. 2–3, 5, 7–10, 12; Russell, *Free Negro in Virginia*, pp. 39, 51, 95; Lauber, *Indian Slavery*, pp. 229, 254–5, 278; 3 Hening 86–8, 250, in Catterall, *Judicial Cases*, vol. I, p. 68n; Craven, *White, Red and Black*, p. 102.

93 Lauber, *Indian Slavery*, pp. 253, 255; Hurd, *The Law of Freedom and Bondage*, vol. I, pp. 252–3; vol. II, pp. 20–4. See also Joel Williamson, *New People: Miscegenation and Mulattoes in the United States* (New York: Free Press, 1980), pp. 11, 13. He cites a Maryland census of 1755 which identifies only whites, blacks and mulattoes.

94 *Laws of the State of Delaware, 1866* (Dover, Delaware: Kirk, 1966), pp. 160–1; Hurd, *Law of Freedom and Bondage*, vol. II, pp. 74, 76–81; vol. I, pp. 291–3.

95 Ibid., vol. I, pp. 261–3; vol. II, p. 29; Lauber, *Indian Slavery*, pp. 230–1, 253, 290.

96 Hurd, *Law of Freedom and Bondage*, vol. II, p. 34.

97 Lauber, *Indian Slavery*, p. 290; Hurd, *Law of Freedom and Bondage*, vol. I, pp. 268, 270–2; vol. II, pp. 42–3, 47.

98 Donnan, *Documents*, vol. 3, p. 111; Hurd, *Law of Freedom and Bondage*, vol. I, p. 276; vol. II, pp. 48, 50.

99 Ibid., vol. I, pp. 266–7.

100 Lauber, *Indian Slavery*, p. 290; Hurd, *Law of Freedom and Bondage*, vol. II, pp. 14–15, 68–72, 128, 177, 217; vol. I, pp. 288–91.

101 Sherwood, 'Paul Cuffe', pp. 153, 162–5; Chamberlain, 'African and American', p. 86; Porter, 'Relations', p. 318.

102 Carter G. Woodson, 'The Relations of Negroes and Indians in Massachusetts', *Journal of Negro History*, vol. 5 (1920), pp. 48ff; Johnson, 'Documentary Evidence', p. 26; Porter, 'Relations', p. 311; Chamberlain, 'Africans and Americans', p. 86.

103 Craigie and Hulbert, *A Dictionary*, vol. 3, p. 1512; Wood, *Black Majority*, pp. 99 and n, 154–5; Lauber, *Indian Slavery*, pp. 277–8, 290, 315; Hurd, *Law of Freedom and Bondage*, vol. I, pp. 297–311; vol. II, pp. 95–6; William L. McDowell, *Documents Relating to Indian Affairs, 1750–1754* (Columbia: South Carolina Archives, 1958), p. 190; Herbert Aptheker, 'Maroons within the Present Limits of the United States', *Journal of Negro History*, vol. 24 (1939), p. 169; Johann D. Schoeph, 'Travels in the Confederation', *Journal of Negro History*, vol. 1 (1915), p. 406; Thomas Cooper, ed., *The Statutes at Large of South Carolina* (Columbia: Johnston, 1839), vol. 5, p. 135; Reuter, *Race Mixture*, p. 94. Georgia's basic law was a 1770 copy of South Carolina's 1740 statute. See Hurd, *Law of Freedom and Bondage*, vol. I, p. 311.

104   William S. Price, Jr., ed., *North Carolina Higher Court Records 1702–1708* (Raleigh: Department of Archives and History, 1974), p. 204; Lauber, *Indian Slavery*, pp. 227, 253, 254, 278; Guion Griffis Johnson, *Ante-Bellum North Carolina: A Social History* (Chapel Hill: University of North Carolina Press, 1937), pp. 499, 591.

105   Hurd, *Law of Freedom and Bondage*, vol. I, pp. 280 and n, 281; vol. II, pp. 52–8; Lauber, *Indian Slavery*, p. 272; Northrup, 'Slavery in New York', pp. 256–7, 260, 264–5, 272–3, 278, 305; Craigie and Hulbert, *A Dictionary*, vol. 3, p. 1512.

106   Donnan, *Documents*, vol. 3, p. 450; Lauber, *Indian Slavery*, pp. 237, 271; Hurd, *Law of Freedom and Bondage*, pp. 280n, 282–5.

107   Donnan, *Documents*, vol. IV, p. 666.

108   Catterall, *Judicial Cases*, vol. 1, pp. 388–9; vol. 2, pp. 18–19, 198, 488–9; Nelson, *Documents*, vol. 26, p. 227; See also pp. 444, 454, 458. Bret Harte, *Heritage of Didlow Marsh*, p. 14, cited in Craigie and Hulbert, *A Dictionary*, vol 3, p. 1565. See also Edwin Bryant, *What I Saw in California* (Santa Ana: Fine Arts, 1936), p. 322. Bryant, in describing native Hawaiians, says: 'Their complexion resembles that of a bright mulatto.'

109   Willis, 'Divide and Rule', p. 157.

110   McDowell, *Documents Relating to Indian Affairs, 1750–1754*, pp. 68, 83.

111   Hurd, *Law of Freedom and Bondage*, vol. 2, pp. 82, 95.

112   See *Proceedings and Debates of the Convention of North Carolina, . . . 1835* (Raleigh: Gales, 1836), pp. 351–2; also Russell, *The Free Negro*, pp. 51ff.

113   Crane, *Southern Colonial Frontier*, p. 113 and n.

CHAPTER 8   MUSTEES, HALF-BREEDS AND ZAMBOS

1   John Ogilvie, *The Imperial Dictionary*, revised Charles Annandale (London: Blackie, 1885), 'Mestizo'.

2   Wood, *Black Majority*, p. 99; Jordan, 'American Chiaroscuro', pp. 185–6; Williamson, *New People*, pp. xii, 39.

3   Zavala, *Los Esclavos Indios*, p. 236.

4   Buchanan, *Linguae Britannicae*, 'Mestizo'; Minsheu, *A Dictionarie*, 'mestizo'; Minsheu, *Vocabularium*, 'mestizo'; Minsheu, *The Guide*, 'mongrill'.

5   Johnson, *A Dictionary of English* (1785); Webster, *An American Dictionary*; Bartlett, *Dictionary of Americanisms*.

6   Ogilvie, *The Imperial Dictionary*; Farmer, *Americanisms*; *The Oxford English Dictionary*.

7   Rogers, *Voyage* as cited in *The Oxford English Dictionary* (1933) under 'mustee'.

8   Johnson, *Ante-Bellum North Carolina*, pp. 590–1; Lauber, *Indian Slavery*, p. 253; State v. Melton and Byrd, Burke 49, Dec. 1852, p. 253, in Catterall, *Judicial Cases*, vol. 2, p. 171.

9   William L. McDowell, ed., *Journals of the Commissioners of the Indian Trade 1710–1718* (Columbia: South Carolina Archives, 1955), pp. 198–9.

10   S. C. Statutes, III, 77 as cited in Wood, *Black Majority*, p. 99n.

11   Wright, *The Only Land They Knew*, pp. 98, 256.

12   'Eighteenth Century Slave Advertisements', p. 200.

13   Wright, *The Only Land They Knew*, p. 256.

14   Lauber, *Indian Slavery*, p. 290.

15 Jones, *The Present State of Virginia*, p. 76.
16 See previous chapter.
17 Lauber, *Indian Slavery*, p. 227; Hurd, *The Law of Freedom and Bondage*, vol. I, p. 294n.
18 McDowell, *Documents, 1750–1754*, p. 463.
19 'De Menonville's Travels to Guaxaca' in John Pinkerton, ed., *Voyages and Travels* (London: Longman, 1812), vol. 13, p. 850.
20 Bartram, *Travels*, pp. 438, 441, 442, 444, 504.
21 *The Oxford English Dictionary* (1933), under 'mustee'. 'The Maesti fair' is quoted by Stedman from an unnamed source. A footnote identifies the 'Maesti' as being the offspring of a European and a 'Quaderon', that is, as one-eighth African. He spells it 'Mestico' elsewhere. See Stedman, *Narrative*, vol. I, p. 161; vol. II, plate 54.
22 'Eighteenth Century Slave Advertisements', pp. 171–3; Windley, *Runaway Slave Advertisements*, vol. I, p. 259; vol. III, pp. 6, 9, 32, 54–5, 57–8, 64, 76, 81, 94, 122, 150, 152, 171–3, 182, 191, 196, 261, 274, 276, 315, 322, 473, 571–2, 670, 696, 719; The New Bern *North Carolina Magazine or Universal Intelligencer*, June 29, 1764, p. 40, as copied by Wesley White and furnished to the author.
23 Weslager, *Delaware's Forgotten Folk*, pp. 11ff; Berry, 'The Mestizos of South Carolina', p. 34.
24 Nelson, *Documents*, pp. 227, 444, 454, 458; Windley, *Runaway Slave Advertisements*, vol. III, p. 670.
25 Cited by Chamberlain, 'African and American', p. 88.
26 Wright, *The Only Land They Knew*, p. 256; Craigie and Hulbert, *A Dictionary*, vol. 3, p. 1512.
27 Aptheker, 'Maroons', p. 169; Schoepf, 'Travels in the Confederation', p. 406; Cooper, *The Statutes at Large of South Carolina*, p. 135; Hurd, *The Law of Freedom and Bondage*, vol. 2, p. 95.
28 Lauber, *Indian Slavery*, p. 315.
29 Adam Garden v. Justices, 4 Strobhart 459, 1814, in Catterall, *Judicial Cases*, vol. 2, p. 299.
30 Ex parte Ferrett, 1 Mill 194, 1817, in Catterall, *Judicial Cases,*, vol. 2, p. 302.
31 Charlotte Miller v. Justices, 4 Strobhart 450, 1836 and Miller v. Dawson, Dudley 174, 1838, in Catterall, *Judicial Cases*, vol. 2, p. 362–6.
32 State v. Belmont, 4 Strobhart 445, 1850, in Catterall, *Judicial Cases*, vol. 2, pp. 415–16.
33 Craigie and Hulbert, *A Dictionary*, vol. 3, p. 1512; Hurd, *Law of Freedom and Bondage*, vol. 2, pp. 52, 55, 57, 62–3; vol. 1, p. 281; Northrup, *Slavery in New York*, pp. 265, 305.
34 E. L. Joseph, *History of Trinidad*, (Trinidad: Mills, 1938), pp. 102–3.
35 Wright, *The Only Land They Knew*, p. 145; Dunn, *Sugar and Slaves*, pp. 74, 269. Lauber, *Indian Slavery*, p. 318; Donnan, *Documents*, vol. 3, p. 475; Friederici, *Amerikanistiches Wörterbuch*, p. 408; Charles H. Wesley, 'The Negro in the West Indies, Slavery and Freedom', *Journal of Negro History*, vol. XVII (1932), p. 52.
36 Edward Long, *The History of Jamaica* (London: Pass, 1970), pp. 260–1; *The Oxford English Dictionary (1933)*, see 'Sambo'.
37 Bryan Edwards, *The History, Civilisation and Commerce of the British Colonies in the West Indies* (New York: Arno, 1972), Part II, pp. 16–17, 95. In 1813 it was proposed to grant white status to 'Mestizoes'. See Gad J. Heuman, 'Between

Black and White: Brown Men in Jamaican Society and Politics, 1823–1865',
doctoral dissertation, Yale University, 1975, p. 32.

38 Charles H. Eden, *The West Indies* (London: Low, 1880), p. 60.

39 *The Oxford English Dictionary* (1933), 'Half-Bred'; Webster, *An American
Dictionary*, 'half-bred'; McDowell, *Documents . . .* , 1750–1754, pp. 68–83.

40 McDowell, *Documents . . .* , *1750–1754*, p. 251; William L. McDowell, Jr, ed.,
Documents Relating to Indian Affairs, 1754–1765, (Columbia: University of South
Carolina Press, 1970), pp. 20, 86, 107, 111, 191, 299, 368, 495; Bartram, *Travels*,
p. 438.

41 Thomas S. Woodard, *Reminiscenses* (Monterey: Barrett and Wimbisu, 1859), p.
33; State v. Cantey, 2 Hill, S.C. Rep., 278 (1857) in Catterall, *Judicial Cases*, vol.
2, p. 358; *The Oxford English Dictionary* (1933), 'Half-breed'.

42 Catterall, *Judicial Cases*, vol. 2, p. 522; Johnston, *Race Relations*, p. 235; Craigie
arnd Hulbert, *A Dictionary*, vol. 2, p. 1207.

43 *The Oxford English Dictionary* (1933), 'Half-caste'; Joseph, History of Trinidad, p.
19.

44 Woodward, *Reminiscenses*, p. 6.

45 Saco, *La Esclavitud de los Indios*, vol. I, p.133; Castellanos, *Elegías de Varones*, pp.
316, 368, 374, 376; Franco Silva, *Regesto Documental*, year 1499; Cortés, *La
Esclavitud*, pp. 239, 248, 291, 305, 310, 314–16, 318, 321, 323, 361, 396, 402,
406; Corominas, *Diccionario*, 'zambo'.

46 Bowser, *The African Slave*, pp. 116, 384n; Lockhart, *El Mundo Hispanoperuano*, p.
224; *Recopilación de Leyes . . . de Indias*, libro VI, titulo III, ley 21, fo. 200; López de
Velasco, *Geografía*, p. 22; Konetzke, *Colección*, vol. I, pp. 489, 598, 623–4; vol. II,
pp. 718, 728–9; Solórzano Pereira, *De Indiarum Iure*, vol. II, p. 209; Solórzano
Pereira, *Politica Indiana*, pp. 447, 449.

47 See Forbes, 'The Evolution of the Term Mulatto', pp. 15, 18, 22–5; Rosenblat,
Mestizaje, pp. 167–4; Corominas, *Diccionario*, 'Zambo'.

48 Dunn, *Sugar and Slaves*, pp. 252, 255.

49 Long, *History of Jamaica*, p. 261; *The Oxford English Dictionary*, (1933), 'Sambo';
James J. Phillippo, *Jamaica: Its Past and Present State* (Westport, Connecticut:
Greenwood, 1970), pp. 143–4.

50 Edwards, *History*, vol. II, pp. 17–95. Stedman, having served in Surinam, defines
a 'Samboe' as a mixture being 'between a mulatto and a black, being of a deep
copper-coloured complexion, with dark hair, that curls in large ringlets'. Stedman,
Narrative, vol. I, p. 326; vol. II, p. 275.

51 Farmer, *Americanisms*, 'Sambo'.

52 Gad J. Heuman, 'White over Brown over Black: the Free Coloureds in Jamaican
Society during Slavery and after Emancipation', *The Journal of Caribbean History*,
vol. 14 (1981), p. 57.

53 *The Oxford English Dictionary* (1933), 'Sambo'; Joseph, *History of Trinidad*, pp.
102–3.

54 *The Oxford English Dictionary* (1933), 'Sambo'.

55 Ibid., and Farmer, *Americanisms*, 'Sambo'.

56 Alice Dunbar Nelson, 'People of Color in Louisiana', *Journal of Negro History*, vol.
I (1915), p. 367.

57 Rosenblat, *El Mestizaje*, p. 172. Also see *The Oxford English Dictionary* (1933),
'Griff'; Bartlett, *Dictionary*, 'Griffe'; Farmer, *Americanisms*, 'Griffe'; Dupree v. the
State, 33 *Alabama Decisions*, in Catterall, *Judicial Cases*, pp. 380–5; John H. Burma,

Spanish-Speaking Groups in the United States (Durham: Duke University Press, 1954), p. 175.
58 Corominas, *Diccionario*, 'China'; Zavala, *Los Indios Esclavos*, p. 228. See also pp. 215, 236–8; and Gonzalo Aguirre Beltrán, 'The Integration of the Negro into the National Society of Mexico', in Mörner, *Race and Class*, p. 24.

CHAPTER 9 NATIVE AMERICANS AS PARDOS AND PEOPLE OF COLOR

1 Wright, *The Only Land They Knew*, p. 149; Russell-Wood, *The Black Man*, pp. 112, 115.
2 Many mixed-bloods played prominent roles in the conquest of Peru, Chile, New Mexico and Brazil. For example, see Boxer, *The Golden Age*, p. 17; Boxer, *Fidalgos in the Far East*, p. 199.
3 Saunders, *A Social History*, pp. xiii, 180n.
4 Diary of Pedro Alvares Cabral and Carta de Pero Vaz de Caminha in Garcia, ed., *Viagems dos Descobrimentos*, pp. 247, 270, 271.
5 Nascentes, *Dicionário*,(1966), *pardo*.
6 Boxer, *The Portuguese Seaborne Empire*, p. 390; Boxer, *The Golden Age*, p. 372; Da Costa e Sá, *Diccionario, pardo*; Constancio, *Novo Diccionario, pardo*; Roquette, *Nouveau Dictionnaire, pardo*; Candido de Figueiredo, *Pequeno Diccionario da Língua Portugueza* (Lisbon: Portugal–Brasil, 1924), *pardo*; Pinheiro, *Dicionario, pardo*; Moraes Silva, *Grande Dicionário, pardo*; Bivar, *Diccionario*, vol. II, *pardo*.
7 Ianni, *As Metamorfoses*, pp. 45, 91, 92, 94, 103, 118, 119, 126.
8 Russell-Wood, *The Black Man*, p. 49; Ianni, *As Metamorfoses*, pp. 36–41, 45, 47; Boxer, *The Golden Age*, pp. 10, 14, 21, 23, 242–4, 322; Rodrigues, *Brazil and Africa*, p. 54; A. J. R. Russell-Wood, 'Colonial Brazil', in Cohen and Greene, *Neither Slave nor Free*, p. 98.
9 Ianni, *As Metamorfoses*, pp. 45, 60n, 70 and n, 87, 90, 94, 95, 100, 103 and n, 118, 119, 126, 127; *Diccionário Histórico, Geográphico e Ethnográphico do Brasil*, pp. 278, 280, 281, 284; Salles, *O Negro na Pará*, pp. 80, 94; Spix and Martius, *Travels*, vol. II, p. 32; Johann Baptist von Spix and Carl Friedrich Phil. von Martius, *Reise in Brasilien* (Munich: Lindauer, 1823), book III, p. 239.
10 Salles, *O Negro na Pará*, pp. 70–1, 74; Spix and Martius, *Reise*, vol. II, p. 659; Thales de Azevedo, 'Índios, Brancos e Pretos no Brasil Colonial', *América Indígena*, vol. XIII (1953), pp. 123–4.
11 Rodrigues, *Brazil and Africa*, pp. 40, 73–6; Salles, *O Negro na Pará*, p. 78; Harris, 'Racial Identity', pp. 21–2; Herbert S. Klein, 'The Colored Freedman in Brazilian Slave Society', *Journal of Social History*, vol. 3 (1969), pp. 36, 41, 43, 50.
12 Moraes Silva, *Grande Dicionário* (1954), vol. VII, pp. 815, 817; Euclides da Cunha, *Os Sertões* (Rio de Janeiro: Azevedo, 1954), p. 68; Salles, *O Negro na Pará*, pp. 62, 94.
13 Forbes, 'Black Pioneers', pp. 233–46; Sr Fiscal Areche, 'Reflexiones sobre el Reyno de Nueva España', in Virreinato de Mexico, II, bound manuscript 568, Biblioteca del Museo Naval, Madrid; Santamaría, *Dioccionario, cholo, pardo*; Mellafe, *Negro Slavery*, pp. 114–15; Rosenblat, *El Mestizaje*, pp. 77, 158n, 166, 179; Mörner, *Race Mixture*, pp. 70–1; Bowser, *The African Slave*, p. 249; Rama, 'The Passing of the Afro–Uruguayans', in Mörner, *Race and Class*, p. 35.
14 See, for example, the elaborate systems discussed in Rosenblat, *El Mestizaje*. See also Mörner, 'The History of Race Relations', pp. 26–7.

15   Harry Hoetink, *Het Patroon van de Oude Curaçaose Samenleving* (Aruba: De Wit, 1971), pp. 77, 79–82, 85, 87, 92, 109, 111, 124, 130, 162–3. Also M. D. Teenstra, *De Nederlandsch West-Indische Eilanden* (Amsterdam, Emmerling, 1977), vol. II, pp. 189, 196.

16   J. Herisius et al., *Woordenboek der Nederlandse Taal* (The Hague: Nijhoff, 1941), *kleurling.*

17   *Grote Winkler Prins Encyclopedie* (Amsterdam: Elsevier, 1977), *kleurlingen, Half-bloed*; Benjamins and Snelleman, *Encyclopedie, Bonaire*, p. 144; Teenstra, *De Niederlandsch West-Indische Eilanden*, vol. II, pp. 190, 196; Menkman, *De Nederlanders in het Caraibische Zeegebied*, pp. 162, 203.

18   Elisabeth, 'The French Antilles' in Cohen and Greene, *Neither Slave nor Free*, pp. 134–5, 147–8, 337.

19   Bartlett, *Dictionary*, p. 92; Wojchiechowski, 'De Indianen van de Westindische Eilanden', pp. 132–3; Donnan, *Documents*, vol. IV, p. 666.

20   See ch. 6.

21   State v. Calder as cited in Catterall, *Judicial Cases*, vol. 2, p. 321.

22   Thorne v. Fordham, in Ibid., vol. 2, p. 431.

23   Johnston, *Race Relations*, p. 161n.

24   Hurd, *The Law of Freedom and Bondage*, vol. 2, pp. 97, 105.

25   Catterall, *Judicial Cases*, vol. 2, p. 289.

26   Ibid., vol. 2, p. 302; and Cooper, ed., *The Statutes at Large of South Carolina*, vol. 5, p. 135.

27   State v. Belmont (1850) as cited in Catterall, *Judicial Cases*, vol. 2, pp. 411, 415.

28   Lauber, *Indian Slavery*, pp. 277, 278, 315.

29   Catterall, *Judicial Cases*, vol. 2, p. 330.

30   Ibid., vol. 2, p. 299.

31   Ibid., vol. 2, pp. 334, 339, 346, 358, 377, 385–6, 401.

32   State v. Davis, State v. Hanna, in Ibid., vol. 2, p. 346.

33   State v. Cantey, in Ibid., vol. 2, p. 358.

34   Ibid., vol. 2, pp. 377, 385–6.

35   Ibid., p. 401.

36   US Census records for Marlboro County, South Carolina, 1830–1850; and Berry, 'The Mestizos of South Carolina', pp. 34–41. See also Berry, *Almost White*, p. 50.

37   General Assembly Petitions, 1859, #12, South Carolina Archives and United States Census for Edgefield County, South Carolina, 1860, both as copied and examined by Wesley D. White, Jr, and furnished to the author. See Laura Foner, 'The Free People of Color in Louisiana and St Dominique', *Journal of Social History*, vol. 3 (1970), pp. 406–7 for an exposition of the 'two-caste' perspective for the United States.

38   Hurd, *Law of Freedom and Bondage*, vol. 2, pp. 106–7.

39   Johnston, *Race Relations*, pp. 228–9; Johnston, 'Documentary Evidence', vol. XIV (1929), p. 39.

40   Ivey v Hardy, 2 Port. 548 (*Alabama Decisions*), 1835; *Revised Alabama Code*, 1852, Section II, 2276.

41   Hurd, *Law of Freedom and Bondage*, vol. 2, p. 152.

42   Fanelly v. Maria Louisa (Woman of Color), 34 Alabama 284, 1859.

43 Gobu v. E. Gobu, in Catterall, *Judicial Cases*, vol. 2, pp. 18–19.
44 Nichols v. Bell, in Ibid., vol. 2, p.176.
45 Rights, *The American Indian*, p. 148; and Robert Thomas, 'A Report on Research of Lumbee Origins', ms, p. 15.
46 Catterall, *Judicial Cases*, vol. 2, pp. 102, 173–4 209, 317.
47 State v. Melton and Byrd, Ibid., vol. 2, p. .171; Johnson, *Ante-Bellum North Carolina*, pp. 590–1; Lauber, *Indian Slavery*, p.253.
48 State v. Hairston, 1868, 63 *North Carolina Reports* (Phillips), p. 452.
49 Russell, *The Free Negro in Virginia*, pp. 41, 129–30.
50 Ibid., pp. 51–2.
51 See ch. 6.
52 Guild, *Black Laws*, pp. 25, 29–30, 33.
53 For example, in King and Queen County certain Indians were allowed to attend white schools. This was not true, however, in neighboring Caroline County where even white-looking children were required to attend 'colored' schools. Some Indians tried to maintain 'Indian' schools to avoid going to 'colored' schools.
54 Tax rolls of Charles City, New Kent, King William, Essex, King and Queen, and Caroline Counties, Archives of Virginia, Richmond, Virginia.
55 *Register of Free Negroes*, Essex County Court House, Tappahannock, Virginia, vols I and II.
56 See ch. 6.
57 See ch 6; and Petition of John and Lucy Dungie, 1825, King William petitions, Virginia Archives, Richmond, Virginia.
58 See ch. 6; 'Nottoway Tribe of Indians, Advice Relative Thereto', no. 1, July 18, 1808, Southampton County, Virginia Archives, Richmond, Virginia.
59 Hurd, *Law of Freedom and Bondage*, vol. I., pp. 252–3; vol. II, pp. 20–4.
60 US Census, Maryland, 1790, Charles County.
61 Hurd, *Law of Freedom and Bondage*, vol. II, pp. 74, 76, 77, 78, 79 80, 81; *Laws of the State of Delaware*, 1881, pp. 378–9; US Census, Delaware, 1830, Kent, Sussex and other counties. See also Woodson, *The Free Negro Heads of Families in the United States in 1830*, Delaware section.
62 Hurd, *Law of Freedom and Bondage*, vol. II, pp. 54–5, 58; *Balance* (1806) as cited in Craigie and Hulbert, *A Dictionary of American English*, vol. 3, p. 1512; Sherwood, 'Paul Cuffe', p. 225; Woodson, *Free Negro Heads of Families*, p. 110.
63 For example, persons bearing the names of the Indian relatives of Paul Cuffe in 1830 are 'free colored'. Woodson, *Free Negro Heads of Families*, pp. 65, 67, 68, 69. See also Woodson, 'The Relations of Negroes and Indians in Massachusetts', pp. 48ff, 50–3, 58.
64 Johnson, 'Documentary Evidence', p. 26.
65 Hurd, *Law of Freedom and Bondage*, vol. II, p. 36.
66 Ibid., vol. II, pp. 14 and n, 15.
67 Ibid., vol. II, pp. 89–90, 92, 93; Catterall, *Judicial Cases*, vol. II, p. 537; Dromgoole, 'The Malungeons', p. 470.
68 Hurd, *Law of Freedom and Bondage*, vol. II, pp. 116–19, 121–2.
69 Ibid., vol. II, pp. 128, 173.
70 Ibid., vol. II, pp. 132, 135.
71 Heizer and Almquist, *The Other Californians*, pp. 239–40.
72 See Jack D. Forbes, 'Envelopment, Proletarianization and Inferiorization: Some

Aspects of Colonialism's Impact upon Native Americans and other People of Color in Eastern North America', ms.

73 United States Census, 1850, Charles City County, Virginia.

CHAPTER 10 AFRICAN–AMERICAN CONTACTS AND THE MODERN RE-PEOPLING OF THE AMERICAS

1 López de Gómara, *Historia General*, vol. I, pp. 241–2.

2 Jack D. Forbes, "The Manipulation of Race, Caste, and Identity: Classifying Afroamericans, Native Americans, and Red-Black People," *Journal of Ethnic Studies* 17(4), Winter 1990, 1–51; and "Envelopment, Proletarianization and Inferiorization . . . ," *Journal of Ethnic Studies*, 18(4), Winter 1991, 95–122.

Bibliography

MANUSCRIPT AND UNPUBLISHED MATERIALS

Archivo General de Indias, Seville, Spain: Petition of Alonso Vaca, 1643, Patronato 244, Ramo VII.

Biblioteca del Museo Naval, Madrid, Spain: Sr. Fiscal Areche, 'Reflexiones sobre el Reyno de Nueva España', Virreinato de Méjico, II, bound manuscript, 568.

British Public Record Office, Kew, Richmond: Leeward Island Mss. Laws, 1644–73, Colonial Office 154/1.

Essex County Court House, Tappahanock, Virginia: Register of Free Negroes, volumes I and II, bound manuscript.

National Archives and Records Service, Washington, D.C. United States Census records as follows:

1790 for South Carolina, Virginia, North Carolina, Maryland.
1800 for Virginia (various counties).
1810 for Virginia (various counties).
1820 for Virginia (various counties).
1830 for Virginia (various counties).
1830 for South Carolina (Marlboro County).
1830 for Delaware (various counties).
1830 for Tennessee (Hawkins County).
1840 for Virginia (various counties).
1850 for Virginia (various counties).
1850 for Tennessee (Grainger County).
1850 for Alabama (Lawrence County).
1850 for North Carolina (Robeson County).
1850 for South Carolina (several counties).

National Anthropological Archives, Smithsonian Institution, Washington D.C. Photographic collections: Chickahominy, Mattaponi, Pamunkey, Rappahannock tribes.

Virginia Archives, Richmond, Virginia:

'Nottoway Tribe of Indians, Advice Relative Thereto', No. 1, July 18, 1808, Southampton County.

Southampton County, Auditor Report, no. 161, 1844.

Petition 13733, King William County, 1843.
Petition of John and Lucy Ann Dungie, 1825, King William Petitions.
Helen Roundtree, 'The Indians of Virginia', manuscript, Indian File.
Petition of Headmen and Chiefs of the Pamunkey Tribe, 1812, King William Petitions.
Pamunkey Petition, Dec. 4, 1812, King William Petitions.
Tax Rolls of Charles City, New Kent, King William, Essex, King and Queen, and Caroline Counties, c.1782–1815, microfilm.

Manuscripts in the Author's Possession

'Fight Racism: Drop All Charges Against Black Youth', Oct. 1981, mimeographed broadsheet, Bradford, England.
'List of Indian Students Enrolled' at William and Mary College, communication from the Librarian.
Robert K. Thomas, 'A Report on Research of Lumbee Origins', typed ms., c.1976–9.

NEWSPAPERS

Attan-Akamik
Tsen-Akamak

LEGAL CITATIONS

The citation of legal cases follows law review practice. Sources cited may be found in law libraries under:

Alabama Decisions
Delaware, *Laws of the State of Delaware*
Delaware Reports; *North Carolina Reports* (Phillips)
Revised Alabama Code
South Carolina Reports
Virginia Reports
Virginia Statutes at Large (Hening)

BOOKS AND ARTICLES

Accord van Brasilien, med van't Recif, Maurits-stadt, ende de omleggende Forten van Brasil. Amsterdam: Claes Lambrechtsz. Van der Wolf, 1654.
Acosta, Joseph de. *The Natural and Moral History of the Indies*, trans. Edward Grimston. London: Hakluyt Society, 1880.
Agassiz, Louis. *A Journey in Brazil.* London: Trübner, 1868.
Aguirre Beltrán, Gonzalo. 'African Influences in the Development of Regional Cultures in the New World', *Plantation Systems of the New World.* Washington, D.C.: Pan American Union, 1959.
——. 'Races in Seventeenth Century Mexico', *Phylon* 6 (1945).
Albers, Josef. *Interaction of Color.* New Haven: Yale University Press, 1975.
Aldenburgk, Johann Gregor. 'Relação da Conquista e Perda da Cidade do Salvador pelos Holandeses em 1624–1625,' trans. Edgard de Cerqueira Falcão, in *Brasiliensia Documenta*, vol. I (1961).

Albuquerque, Afonso de. *The Commentaries of the Great Afonso Dalboquerque*, trans. by Walter de Gray Birch. London: Hakluyt Society, 1875.

Alewyn, A., and Jan Collë. *Vocabulario das duas Linguas Portugueza e Flamenga*. Amsterdam: Vandenderge, 1718.

Alvord, Clarence Walworth and Lee Bidgood. *The First Expeditions of the Trans–Allegheny Region by the Virginians, 1650–1674*. Cleveland: Arthur H. Clark, 1912.

Amado, Jorge. *Tereza Batista, Cansada de Guerra*. Lisbon: Europa–America, 1978.

Anchieta, Joseph de. *Cartas, Informações, Fragmentos Históricos e Sermoes, 1554–1594*. Rio de Janeiro: Civilização Brasileira, 1933.

Aptheker, Herbert. 'Maroons Within the Present Limits of the United States'. *Journal of Negro History*, vol. 24, 1939.

Atkinson, William C. *A History of Spain and Portugal*. Harmondsworth: Penguin, 1960.

Ayrosa, Plinio. *Termos Tupis no Português do Brasil*. São Paulo: Departemento de Cultura, 1937.

Azevedo, Thales de. 'Índios, Brancos e Pretos no Brasil Colonial'. *América Indígena* vol. 13 (1953).

Ba'albaki, Munir. *Al-Mawrid: A Modern English–Arabic Dictionary*. Darel-ilm: Lil-Malayen, 1973.

Badellino, Oreste. *Dizionario Italiano–Latino*. Turin: Rosenberg and Sellier, 1970.

Bailey, L. R. *Indian Slave Trade in the Southwest*. Los Angeles: Westernlore, 1966.

Bailey, N. *The Universal Etymological English Dictionary*. London: Darby, 1728.

——. *The Universal Etymological English Dictionary*. London: Ware, 1749.

——. *The Universal Etymological English Dictionary*. London: Osborne, 1961.

Bancroft, Hubert Howe. *History of the North Mexican States and Texas*. San Francisco: The History Co., 1890.

Barbosa, Agostinho. *Dictionarium Lusitanicolatinum*. Bracharae: Laurentii de Basto, 1611.

Barlaeus, Caspar. *Nederlandsch Brazilie onder het Bewind van Johan Maurits–Grave van Nassau, 1637–1644*. The Hague: Nijhoff, 1923.

Barlement, Noel van, attrib. *Dictionariolum et Colloquia Octo Linguarum*. Antwerp: Aertsens, 1622.

Barrantes, Ramiro, Peter E. Smouse, James V. Neal, Harvey W. Mohrenweiser, and Henry Gershowitz. Migration and Genetic Infrastructure of the Central American Guyami and their Affinities with Other Tribal Groups. *American Journal of Physical Anthropology*, 58(1982), 201–214.

Bartlett, John Russell. *Dictionary of Americanisms*. Boston: Little, Brown, 1860 (1859).

Bartram, William. *Travels Through North and South Carolina, Georgia, East and West Florida*. Savannah: Beehive Press, 1973.

Bassett, John S., ed. *The Writings of Colonel William Byrd*. New York: Doubleday, 1901.

Bates, Henry Walter. *The Naturalist on the River Amazon*. London: Murray, 1892.

Battell, Andrew. *The Strange Adventures of Andrew Battell*, ed. E. G. Ravenstein. London: Hakluyt Society, 1901.

Battisti, Carlo and Giovanni Alessio. *Dizionario Etimologico Italiano*. Firenze: Barbèra, 1950.

Beets, A., et al. *Woordenboek der Nederlandsche Taal*. The Hague: Nijhoff and Sijthoff, 1912.

Bell, Albert D. *Bass Families of the South*. Rocky Mount, N.C., 1941.

Benjamins, H. D. and J. F. Snelleman, eds. *Encyclopedie van Nederlandsche West-Indië*. The Hague: Nijhoff, 1914.

Benzoni, Girolamo. *History of the New World*. London: Hakluyt Society, 1857.

Bernaldez, Andrés. *Memorias del Reinado de los Reyes Católicos*. Madrid: Real Academia de la Historia, 1962.

Berry, Brewton. *Almost White*. New York: Macmillan, 1963.

——. 'The Mestizos of South Carolina'. *American Journal of Sociology*, vol. 51 (1945).

Berry, George Ricker. *The Classic Greek Dictionary*. Chicago: Follett, 1962.

Bethune, C. R. D. ed., *The Observations of Sir Richard Hawkins in His Voyage to the South Sea, 1593*. London: Hakluyt Society, 1847.

Biard, F. *Deux Années au Brésil*. Paris: Hachette, 1862.

Birket-Smith, Kaj. *Ethnography of the Egedesminde District*. Copenhagen: Bianco Lunos, 1924.

Bivar, Artur. *Dicionário General e Analógico da Lingua Portuguesa*. Porto: Ouro, 1952.

Blount, Thomas. *Glossographia*. Menston: Scolar Press, 1969.

Blussé, Abraham. *Dictionnaire Portatief François et Hollandois* Dordrecht: Blussé, 1815.

Bluteau, Raphael. *Supplemento ao Vocabulario Portuguez e Latino*. Lisbon: da Sylva, 1727.

——. *Vocabulario Portuguez e Latino*. Coimbra: Companhia de Jesus, 1712.

——. *Vocabulario Portuguez e Latino*. Lisbon: Pascoal da Sylva, 1720.

Bluteau, Rafael and António de Moraes Silva. *Diccionaris da Lingua Portugueza*. Lisbon: Ferreira, 1789.

Boogart, E. van den. 'Infernal Allies: the Dutch West India Co. and the Tarairiu, 1631–1654' in E. van den Boogart, ed. *Johan Maurits van Nassau–Siegen 1604–1679*. The Hague: Maurits Stichting, 1979.

Boorstin, Daniel J., ed. *Delaware Cases, 1792–1830*. St. Paul: West, 1943.

Bowser, Frederick P. *The African Slave in Colonial Peru, 1524–1650*. Stanford: Stanford University Press, 1974.

Boxer, C. R. 'The Colour Question in the Portuguese Empire, 1415–1825'. *Proceedings of the British Academy*, vol. XLVII (1961).

——. *The Dutch in Brazil, 1624–1654*. Oxford: Clarendon Press, 1957.

——. *Fidalgos in the Far East, 1550–1770*. Hong Kong: Oxford University Press, 1968.

——. *The Golden Age of Brazil 1695–1750*. Berkeley: University of California Press, 1962.

——. *The Portuguese Seaborne Empire 1415–1825*. London: Hutchinson, 1969.

——. *Race Relations in the Portuguese Colonial Empire 1415–1825*. Oxford: Clarendon Press, 1963.

Brasio, António, ed. *Monumenta Missionaria Africana*. Lisbon: Agencia Geral do Ultramar, 1953.

——. *Os Pretos em Portugal*. Lisbon: Agencia Geral das Colonias, 1944.

Brett, W. H. *The Indian Tribes of Guiana; Their Condition and Habits*. London: Bell and Daldy, 1868.

Brown, Alex. *The Genesis of the United States*. Boston, 1897.

Bryant, Edwin. *What I Saw in California*. Santa Ana: Fine Arts, 1936.

Buarque de Holanda, Sérgio. *Raízes do Brasil*. Rio de Janeiro: Olympio, 1956.

Buchanan, James. *Linguae Britannicae*. Menston: Scolar Press, 1967.

Bucher, Bernadette. *Icon and Conquest*, trans. Basia Miller Gulati. Chicago: University of Chicago Press, 1981.

Burma, John H. *Spanish-Speaking Groups in the United States*. Durham: Duke University Press, 1954.

Buve, R. Th. J. 'Traffic of American Indians and Negroes to Holland During the 17th and 18th Centuries – Its Social Implications', *XXVII Congreso Internacional de Americanistas*, separada del vol. 4. Seville, 1966.

Byard, P. J. and F. C. Lees. 'Skin Colorimetry in Belize. II. Inter- and Intra-Population Variation'. *American Journal of Physical Anthropology*, vol. 58 (1982).

Cabello Balboa, Miguel. 'Verdadera descripción y relación larga de la Provincia y Tierra de las Esmeraldas. . . . ', *Obras*, Quito: Ecuatoriana, 1945, I.

Ca'da Mosto, Lúis de. *Viagens*, trans. from Italian by Sebastião Francisco de Mendo Trigoso, notes by Augusto Reis Machado, Lisbon: Portugália, no date.

Camoens, Luis de. *Lusiadas*, with commentary by Manuel de Faria e Sousa, Madrid: Coello, 1639.

Cardoso, Ersílio and Jean Rousé. *Grande Dicionario Português–Francês de Domingo de Azevedo*, Lisbon: Bertrand, 1953.

Cardoso, Hieronymus. *Dictionarium Latino Lusitanicum*. Lisbon: Lopezii, 1592.

——. *Dictionarium Latino Lusitanicum*. Lisbon: Anueres, 1643.

Carletti, Francisco. *Ragionamenti sopra le Cose da Lui Vedute ne' Suoi Viaggi*. Florence: Manni, 1701.

Casas, Cristobal de las. *Vocabulario de las Dos Lenguas Toscana y Castellana*. Venice: Alberti, 1600.

Castellanos, Juan de. *Elegías de Varones Ilustres de Indias*. Madrid: Rivadeneyra, 1857.

Catterall, Helen T. *Judicial Cases Concerning American Slavery and the Negro*. Washington, D.C.: Carnegie, 1929.

Cauvet, G. *Les Berbères en Amérique*. Algiers: Bringau, 1930.

Cejeador y Franca, Julio. *Tesoro de la Lengua Castellana*. Madrid: Perlado, Paez, 1910.

——. *Vocabulario Medieval Castellano*. New York: Las Americas, 1968.

Chamberlain, George. 'African and American', *Science*, vol. XVII (1891).

Chambers, R. W. *Thomas More*. London: Cape, 1962.

Chebir, Yçe de. 'Suma de los Principales Mandamientos y Devedamientos de la Ley y Çunna', *Memorial Histórico Español*, vol. V. Madrid: Real Academia de la Historia, 1853.

Chomel, M. Noel. *Algemeen . . . Woordenboek*. Leiden: LeMair, 1771.

Claes, F., ed. *De Thesaurus Van Plantijn*. The Hague: Muton, 1972.

Clarke, P. G. W. *Oxford Latin Dictionary*. Oxford: Clarendon Press, 1983.

Cockeram, Henry. *The English Dictionarie*. Menston: Scolar Press, 1968.

Coelho, F. Adolfo. *Diccionario Manual Etymologico da Lingua Portuguesa*. Lisbon: Plantier, 1889.

Cohen, David W. and Jack P. Greene, eds. *Neither Slave nor Free: The Freedman of African Descent in the Slave Societies of the New World*. Baltimore: Johns Hopkins, 1972.

Cohen, Felix. *Handbook of Federal Indian Law*. Washington, D.C.: Government Printing Office, 1942.

Colloquia et Dictionariolum Octolinguarium. Amsterdam: Lavrentii, 1622.

Colón, Hernando. *Vida del Almirante, Don Cristóbal Colón*, ed. Ramón Iglesia. Mexico City: Fondo de Cultura Economica, 1947.

Constancio, Francisco Solano. *Novo Diccionario Critico e Etymologico da Lingua Portugesa*. Paris: Casimir, 1836.

Cooley, W. D., ed. *Sir Francis Drake, His Voyage, 1595*. London: Hakluyt Society, 1849.

Cooper, Thomas, ed. *The Statutes at Large of North Carolina*. Columbia: Johnston, 1839.

Corominas, J. *Diccionario Crítico Etimológico de la Lengua Castellana*. Berne: Franche, 1954.

Cortés, Vicenta. *La Esclavitud en Valencia durante el Reinado de los Reyes Catolicos (1479–1516)*. Valencia: Archivo Municipal y Ayuntamiento, 1964.

Cortesão, Jaime, ed. *Jesuitas e Bandeirantes no Tape, 1615–1641*. Rio de Janeiro: Biblioteca Nacional, 1969.

Costa e Sá, Joaquím José da. *Diccionario Portuguez–Francez e Latino*. Lisbon: Ferreira, 1794.

Covarrubias Orozco, Sebastian de. *Tesoro de la Lengua Castellana, o' Española*. Madrid: Sanchez, 1611.

——. *Tesoro de la Lengua Castellano, o' Española*. Madrid: Noydens, 1647.

Craigie, William A. and James R. Hulbert. *A Dictionary of American English*. Chicago: University of Chicago Press, 1940.

Crane, Verner W. *The Southern Colonial Frontier, 1678–1732*. Ann Arbor: University of Michigan Press, 1959.

Craven, Wesley Frank. *White, Red and Black: The Seventeenth Century Virginian*. Charlottesville: University of Virginia Press, 1971.

Cunha, Euclides da. *Os Sertões*. Rio de Janeiro: Azevedo, 1954.

Dalgado, Sebastião Rodolfo. *Glosario Luso–Asiatico*. Coimbra: Imprensa da Universidade, 1921.

Dalrymple, Rev. note, in *The Historical Magazine* (New York), vol. 5 (1858).

Dam-Mikkelsen, Bente and Torben Lundbaek. *Etnografiske Genstende Danske Kunstkammer 1650–1800*. Copenhagen: National Museet, 1980.

Dampier, William. *A Collection of Voyages*. London: Knapton, 1729.

d'Arsy, Ian Louys. *Le Grand Dictionaire François–Flamen*. Rotterdam: Waesbergue, 1651.

Davidson, David M. 'Negro Slave Control and Resistance in Colonial Mexico, 1519–1650', *Hispanic–American Historical Review*, vol. XLVI (1966).

D'Azevedo, J. Lucio. *Historia dos Cristiaños novos Portugueses*. Lisbon: Teixeira, 1921.

Díaz del Castillo, Bernal. *The Discovery and Conquest of Mexico*, trans. A. P. Maudslay, ed. Irving A. Leonard. New York: Grove, 1956.

Le Dictionnaire des Six Langages. Rouen: Le Villain, 1625.

Diccionario de la Lengua Española. Madrid: Real Academia Española, 1984.

Diccionario Histórico, Geográphico e Ethnográphico do Brasil. Rio de Janeiro: Instituto Historico, Imprensa Nacional, 1922.

Dictionaire et Colloques en Quatre Langues . . . Woorden-Boeck ende T' Samen–Spraken, in vier Talen. Bruxelles, Mommart, 1647.

Divry, George C., ed. *Modern English–Greek and Greek–English Desk Dictionary*. New York: Divry, 1971.

Domínguez Ortiz, Antonio. 'La Esclavitud en Castilla durante la Edad Moderna', *Estudios de Historia Social de España*. Madrid: Instituto 'Balmes' de Sociologia, (1952).

——. *The Golden Age of Spain 1516–1659*, trans. James Casey. London: Weidenfeld and Nicolson, 1971.

——. *Orto y Ocaso de Sevilla*. Seville: Universidad, 1974.

Doniach, N. S., ed. *The Oxford English–Arabic Dictionary of Current Usage*. Oxford: Clarendon Press, 1972.

Donnan, Elizabeth, ed. *Documents Illustrative of the Slave Trade to America*. Washington, D. C.: Carnegie, 1932.

Dozy, R. and W. H. Engelmann. *Glossaire des Mots Espagnols et Portugais Dérivés de l'Arabe*. Leiden: Brill, 1869 and Paris: Maisonneuve, 1869.

Dromgoole, William Allen. 'The Malungeons', *The Arena*, No. XVI (1891).

Dunn, Richard S. *Sugar and Slaves: The Rise of the Planter Class in the English West Indies, 1624–1713.* London: Cape, 1973.

Du Tertre, Jean Baptiste. *Histoire Générale des Antilles.* Paris: Jolly, 1667–1671.

Eden, Charles H. *The West Indies.* London: Low et al., 1880.

Edwards, Bryan. *The History, Civilisation and Commerce of the British Colonies in the West Indies.* New York: Arno, 1972.

Edwards, Clinton R. 'Possibilities of Pre-Columbian Maritime Contacts among New World Civilizations', *Mesoamerican Studies*, vol. 4 (1969).

Eeden, Frederick van. *Studies.* Amsterdam: Versluys, 1904.

Eguilaz y Yanguas, Leopoldo. *Glosario Etimológico de las Palabras Españoles de Origen Oriental.* Granada: La Lealtad, 1886.

'Eighteenth-Century Slave Advertisements', *Journal of Negro History*, vol. I (1915).

Elias, A. and Ed E. Elias. *Modern Dictionary, English–Arabic.* Cairo: Elias, 1968.

Encyclopaedia Judaica. Jerusalem: Keto, 1971.

Engelmann, W. H. *Glossaire des Mots Espagnols et Portugais Dérivés de L'Arabe.* Leiden: Brill, 1861.

Evans, E. E. and Hawkes, C. F. C. 'An Eskimo Harpoon-head from Tara Co. Down (?)' in *Ulster Journal of Archaeology*, vol. III (1940).

Exquemelin, A. O. *De Americaensche Zee-Rovers.* Antwerpen and Amsterdam: De Sikkel and De Spieghel, 1931.

——. *Historie der Boecaniers, of Vrybuyters van America.* Amsterdam: Ted Hoorn, 1700.

Farmer, John S. *Americanisms – Old and New.* London: Poulter, 1889.

Fernandes, Francisco. *Dicionário Brasileiro Contemperneo.* Porto Alegre: Globo, 1967.

Fernández de Navarrete, Martín. *Colección de los Viages y Descubrimientos.* Madrid: Imprenta Real, 1825. I.

——. *Colección de los Viages y Descubrimientos.* Buenos Aires: Editorial Guarania, 1945. II.

——. *Colección de los Viages y Descubrimientos.* Madrid: Imprenta Real, 1829. III.

Fernández de Oviedo, Gonzalo. *Historia General y Natural de las Indias.* Madrid: Biblioteca de Autores Españoles, 1959.

Figueiredo, Candido de. *Pequeno Diccionario da Língua Portugueza.* Lisbon: Portugal–Brasil, 1924.

Fleet, Beverly. *Virginia Colonial Abstracts*, vol. 15, Sixth Collection.

Fleming, George. 'Mule', *Werner Encyclopaedia.* Akron: Werner, 1909. V. XVII, pp. 19–20.

Florio, John. *Queen Anna's New World of Words or Dictionarie of the Italian and English Tongues.* Menston: Scolar Press, 1968.

Foner, Laura. 'The Free People of Color in Louisiana and St Dominique', *Journal of Social History*, vol. 3 (1970).

Fonseca, Jose da. *Novo Diccionario Francez–Portuguez.* Paris: Aillaud, Moulon, 1862.

Forbes, Jack D. *Afro-Americans in the Far West.* Washington, D.C.: Government Printing Office, 1969.

——. *Apache, Navaho and Spaniard.* Norman: University of Oklahoma Press, 1960.

——. 'Black Pioneers: The Spanish-Speaking Afro-Americans of the Southwest', *Phylon*, vol. 27. (1966).

——. 'The Evolution of the Term Mulatto: A Chapter in Black–Native American Relations', *Journal of Ethnic Studies*, vol. 10 (1982).

——. 'Historical Survey of the Indians of Sonora, 1821 to 1910', *Ethnohistory*, vol. 4 (1957).

——. *The Indian in America's Past.* Englewood Cliffs: Prentice-Hall, 1964.

——. 'Mulattoes and People of Color in Anglo-North America: Implications for Black–Indian Relations'. *Journal of Ethnic Studies*, vol. 12 (1984).

——. *Native Americans of California and Nevada*. Happy Camp, California: Naturegraph, 1982.

——. *Warriors of the Colorado*. Norman: University of Oklahoma Press, 1965.

Foreman, Carolyn Thomas. *Indians Abroad 1493–1938*. Norman: University of Oklahoma Press, 1943.

Foster, Laurence. *Negro–Indian Relationships in the South-East*. Philadelphia: Privately printed, 1935.

Fothergill, Augusta B., and John Mark Naugle. *Early Virginia Taxpayers, 1782–87*. No place, no publisher, 1940.

Franco, M. Helena L. P., Tania A. Weaver, and F. M. Salzano. 'Blood Polymorphisms and Racial Admixture in Two Brazilian Populations', *American Journal of Physical Anthropology*, vol. 58 (1982).

Franco Silva, Alfonso. *La Esclavitud en Sevilla y su Tierra A Fines de la Edad Media*. Seville: Diputación Provincial, 1979.

——. *Los Esclavos de Sevilla*. Seville: Diputación de Sevilla, 1980.

——. *Regesto Documental sobre la Esclavitud Sevillana, 1453–1513*. Seville: Universidad de Sevilla, 1979.

Franklin, John Hope, ed. *Color and Race*, Boston: Beacon, 1968.

Friederici, Georg. *Amerikanistisches Wörterbuch*. Hamburg: De Gruyter, 1947.

Fryer, Peter. *Staying Power: The History of Black People in Britain*. London: Pluto, 1984.

Gad, Finn. *The History of Greenland*. London: Hurst, 1970.

Gage, Thomas. *Travels in the New World*, ed. J. Eric Thompson. Norman: University of Oklahoma Press, 1958.

García, José Manuel. *Viagens dos Descobrimentos*. Lisbon: Presença, no date.

Geysbeek, P. G. Witsen. *Woordenboek der Zamenleving*. Amsterdam: Diederichs, *c.*1845.

Gioffré, Domenico. *Il Mercato degli Schiavi á Genova nel Secolo XV*. Genova: Bozzi, 1971.

Giraud, Marcel. History of French Louisiana, trans. Joseph C. Lambert. Baton Rouge: Louisiana State University Press, 1974.

Glass, Bentley. 'On the Unlikelihood of Significant Admixture of Genes from the North American Indian in the Present Composition of the Negroes of the United States', *American Journal of Human Genetics*, vol. 7 (1955).

Golio, Theophilo. *Onomasticon Latinogermanicum*. Straatsburg: no publisher, 1579.

Gonsalves de Mello, José Antonio. *Henrique Dias: Governador dos Pretos, Criollos e Mulatos do Brasil*. Recife: Universidade, 1954.

——. *Tempo dos Flamengos*. São Paulo: Olympio, 1947.

González Palencia, Ángel. *Historia de la España Musulmana*. Barcelona: Editorial Labor, 1925.

Goris, J. 'Slavernij te Antwerpen in de XVIde eeuw', *Bijdragen tot de Geschiedenis*, vol. 15 (1923).

Gouveia, Maurilio de. *História da Escravidão*. Rio de Janeiro: Tupy, 1955.

Graaff, Nicolaus de *Reysen . . . na de Vier Gedeeltens des Werelds also . . . . Africa, America en Europa. Oost-Indise Spiegel*. Hoorn: Feyken Rijp, 1704.

Grande Enciclopédia Portuguesa e Brasileira. Lisbon, Rio de Janeiro: Editorial Enciclopedia, after 1945.

Graullera Sanz, Vicente. *La Esclavitud en Valencia en los Siglos XVI y XVII*. Valencia: Instituto Valenciano de Estudios Históricos, 1978.

Greenman, E. F. 'The Upper Paleolithic and the New World', *Current Anthropology*, vol. 4 (1963).

Grote Winkler Prins Encyclopedie. Amsterdam: Elsevier, 1977.

Guild, Jane Purcell. *Black Laws of Virginia.* Richmond: Whittet and Shepperson, 1936.

Gumilla, Joseph. *El Orinoco: Ilustrado y Defendido, Historia Natural y Geographica.* Madrid: Fernandez, 1745.

Hackett, Charles W. *The Revolt of the Pueblo Indians.* Albuquerque: University of New Mexico Press, 1942.

Hacquebord, Lowrens and René de Bok. *Spitsbergen 79° N.B.* Amsterdam: Elsevier, 1981.

Halma, Francois. *Le Grand Dictionaire Francois et Flamend.* Amsterdam: Rudolph & Wetstein, 1717.

Hamelberg, J. H. J. *De Nederlanders op de West-Indische Eilanden.* Amsterdam: Emmering, 1979.

Hamilton Jr, Russell G. 'The Present State of African Cults in Bahia', *Journal of Social History*, vol. 3 (1970).

Handler, Jerome S. 'The Amerindian Slave Population of Barbados in the Seventeenth and Early Eighteenth Centuries', *Caribbean Studies*, vol. 8 (1968).

Haring C. H. *The Spanish Empire in America.* New York: Oxford University Press, 1947.

Harris, Marvin D. 'Racial Identity in Brazil', *Luso–Brazilian Review*, vol. 1 (1964).

Harrisse, Henry. *Découverte et Évolution Cartographique de Terre–Neuve et des Pays Circonvoisins.* Paris: Welter, 1900.

——. *The Discovery of North America.* Amsterdam: Israel, 1961.

——. *John Cabot, the Discoverer of North America and Sebastian his Son.* New York: Argosy–Antiquarian, 1968.

Hattersley, Ralph. *Photographic Lighting: Learning to See.* Engelwood Cliffs: Prentice-Hall, 1979.

Heers, Jacques. *Esclaves et Domestiques au Moyen–Age dans le Monde Méditerranéen.* Paris: Fayard, 1981.

Heizer, Robert F. and Alan J. Almquist, eds. *The Other Californians.* Berkeley: University of California Press, 1971.

Heleno, Manuel. *Os Escravos em Portugal.* Lisbon: Empresa do Anuário Comercial, 1933.

Hemmersam, Michael. *West-Indianische Reiszbeschreibung.* Nürnberg: Paulus Fürst, 1663.

——. *Reise nach Guinea und Brasilien 1639–1645.* The Hague: Nijhoff, 1930.

Hemming, John. *Het Rode Goud.* Utrecht: Spectrum, 1980.

——. *Red Gold: The Conquest of the Brazilian Indians.* London: Macmillan, 1978.

Herisius, J., et al. *Woordenboek der Nederlandse Taal.* The Hague: Nijhoff, 1941.

Herskovitz, Melville J. *The American Negro.* New York: Knopf, 1928.

Herskovitz, Melville J. and Frances J. Herskovitz. 'Afro–Bahian Religious Songs', Album L-13, *Folk Music of Brazil.* Washington D.C.: Library of Congress Archive of Folk Song (1947, 1971).

Heuman, Gad J. 'White over Brown over Black: The Free Coloureds in Jamaican Society during Slavery and after Emancipation', *The Journal of Caribbean History.* vol. 14 (1981).

Heuvel, Aad van den. *William Bosman in Goud en Slaven.* Amsterdam: Meulenhoff, 1981.

Heyerdahl, Thor. *American Indians in the Pacific.* London: Allen & Unwin, 1952.

——. 'Comment', in *Current Anthropology*, vol. 4 (1963).

——. *Early Man and the Ocean*. London: Allen & Unwin, 1978.

Hoetink, H. *Het Patroon van de Oude Curaçaose Samenleving*. Aruba: DeWit, 1971.

——. *Slavery and Race Relations in the Americas: Comparative Notes on their Nature and Nexus*. New York: Harper & Row, 1973.

——. *The Two Variants in Caribbean Race Relations: A Contribution to the Sociology of Segmented Societies*, trans. Eva M. Hooykaas. London: Oxford University Press, 1967.

Hoffman, Bernard G. *Cabot to Cartier: Sources for a Historical Ethnography of Northeastern North America, 1497–1550*. Toronto: University of Toronto, 1961.

Holt, Elizabeth G. *A Documentary History of Art*. New York: Doubleday, 1957.

Holtrop, John. *A New English and Dutch Dictionary*. Dordrecht/Amsterdam: Blusse and Holtrop, 1789.

Hoogstratten, D. van. *Nieuw Woordenboek der Nederlantsche en Latijnsche Tale*. Amsterdam: Boom, 1704.

Hooke, Robert. *Micrographia*. London: Marotyn, *c.*1667.

Hoover, Dwight W. *The Red and The Black*. Chicago: Rand McNally, 1976.

Horowitz, Michael M., ed. *Peoples and Cultures of the Caribbean*. New York: National History Press, 1971.

Hurd, John Codman. *The Law of Freedom and Bondage in the United States*. New York: Negro Universities Press, 1968.

Ianni, Octavio. *As Metamorfoses do Escravo*. São Paulo: Européia do Livro, 1962.

Jackson, Luther P. 'Free Negroes of Petersburg, Virginia', *Journal of Negro History*, vol. XII (1927).

Jane, Cecil. *The Voyages of Christopher Columbus*. London: Argonaut, 1930.

Jansen, G. P. *Nederlandsch Papiaments Handwoordenboek*. Scherpenheuval: St Vicentius-gesticht, 1947.

Jenkins, J. T. *A History of the Whale Fisheries*. Port Washington, New York: Kennikat, 1971.

Johnson, Guion Griffis. *Ante–Bellum North Carolina: A Social History*. Chapel Hill: University of North Carolina Press, 1937.

Johnson, Samuel. *A Dictionary of the English Language*. London: Knapton, 1756.

——. *A Dictionary of the English Language*. London: Rivington, 1785.

——. *A Dictionary of the English Language*. Ed. H. J. Todd. London: Longman, 1827.

Johnston, James Hugo. 'Documentary Evidence of the Relations of Negroes and Indians', *Journal of Negro History*, vol. XIV (1929).

——. *Race Relations in Virginia and Miscegenation in the South, 1776–1860*. Amherst: University of Massachusetts Press, 1970.

Jones, Gwyn. *The Norse Atlantic Saga*. London: Oxford, 1964.

Jones, Hugh. *The Present State of Virginia*, ed. Richard L. Morton. Chapel Hill: University of North Carolina Press, 1956.

Jordan, Winthrop D. 'American Chiaroscuro: the Status and Definition of Mulattoes in the British Colonies', *William and Mary Quarterly*, vol. 19 (1962).

Joseph, E. L. *History of Trinidad*. Trinidad: Mills, 1938.

Junius. *Nomenclator Omnium Rerum Propria Nomina Variis Linguis*. Antwerp: Plantin, 1583.

[?Justice, Alexander] (A. J.). *A Compleat Account of the Portuguese Language Being a Copious Dictionary*. London: Janenay, 1701.

Karmi, Hasan S. *Al Manar: An English–Arabic Dictionary*. New York: St. Martin's, 1971.

Kersey, John. *Dictionarium Anglo–Britannicum or a New English Dictionary.* Menston: Scolar Press, 1969.

Kiliaan, Cornelii. *Dictionarium Teutonico–Latinum.* Antwerp: Plantin, 1588.

———. *Etymologicum Teutonicae Linguae Sive Dictionarium.* The Hague: Mouton, 1972.

Kittel, Gerhard. *Theological Dictionary of the New Testament,* trans. and ed. Geoffrey W. Bromiley. Grand Rapids: Erdmans, 1964–76.

Klein, Herbert S. 'The Colored Freedmen in Brazilian Slave Society', *Journal of Social History,* vol. 3 (1969).

Kloos, Peter. 'De Indianen in Suriname' reprint of 'Amerindians of Surinam', *The Situation of the Indian in South America.* Geneva: World Council of Churches, 1972.

Kluyver, A., et al. *Woordenboek der Nederlandsche Taal.* The Hague, Leiden: Nijhoff, Sijthoff, 1913.

Konetzke, Richard, ed. *Colección de Documentos para la Historia de la Formación Social de Hispanoamérica, 1493–1810.* Madrid: Consejo Superior de Investigaciones Cientíiicas, 1953.

Koschatzky, Walter and Alice Strobl. *Die Dürer Zeichnungen der Albertina.* Salzburg: Residenz Verlag, 1971.

Kramers, J. *Nouveau Dictionnaire Néerlandais–Français.* Gouda: van Goor, 1883.

Lacavalleria, V. E. *Dictionario Castellano, Dictionario Françòis, Dictionario Catala.* Barcelona: Pere Lacavalleria, 1642.

Laet, Jan de. *Notae ad Dissertationem Hugonis Grotii de Origine Gentium Americanarum et Observationes.* Amsterdam: Elzivirium, 1643.

La Garde, Pauli de. *Petri Hispani de Lingua Arabica Libri Duo.* Gottingae: Hoyer, 1883.

Lanternani, Vittorio. *Religions of the Oppressed.* New York: New American Library, 1965.

Las Casas, Bartolomé de. *Historia de las Indias.* Edition of Augustin Millares Carlo. Mexico: Fondo de Cultura Economica, 1951.

Lauber, Almon W. *Indian Slavery in Colonial Times within the Present Limits of the United States.* New York: Privately printed, 1913.

Lawson, John. *History of North Carolina.* Richmond: Garrett and Massie, 1952.

Layrisse, M., Z. Layrisse, and J. Wilbert. 'The Blood Group Antigens in Guajiro Indians', *American Journal of Physical Anthropology,* n.s. vol. 19 (1961).

Leach, Douglas Edward. *Flintlock and Tomahawk.* New York: Norton, 1966.

Lee, Sydney. 'The Call of the West', *Scribner's Magazine,* vol. XLII (1907).

Leite, Serafim, ed. *Novas Cartas Jesuíticas.* São Paulo: Editora Nacional, 1940.

———. *História da Companhia de Jesus no Brasil.* Rio de Janeiro: Instituto de Livro, 1949.

———. *Monumenta Brasiliae.* Rome: Societatis Iesu, 1956–60.

Lévi-Provençal, É. *Histoire de l'Espagne Musulmane.* Paris: Maisonneuve, 1953.

Lewis, Charlton T. *A Latin Dictionary.* Oxford: Clarendon Press, 1879.

Ligon, Richard. *A True and Exact History of the Island of Barbadoes.* London: Cass, 1970.

Lindeström, Peter. *Geographia Americae,* ed. Amandus Johnson. Philadelphia: Swedish Colonial Society, 1925.

Lobo Cabrera, Manuel. *La Esclavitud en las Canarias Orientales en el Siglo XVI.* Tenerife: Cabildo Insular de Gran Canaria, 1982.

Lockhart, James. *El Mundo Hispanoperuano 1532–1560.* Mexico City: Fondo de Cultura Economica, 1982.

Long, Edward. *The History of Jamaica.* London: Pass, 1970.

Lopez, Duarte and Pigafetta, Filippo. *Description du Royaume de Congo et des Contrées Environnantes,* trans. Willy Bal. Louvain: Nauwelaerts, 1963.

——. *Relaçao do Reino de Congo e das Terras Circunvizinhas*, trans. Rosa Carpeans. Lisbon: Agencia Geral do Ultramar, 1951.

López de Gómara, Francisco. *Historia General de las Indias*. Madrid: Calpe, 1922.

López de Velasco, Juan. *Geografía y Descripción Universal de las Indias*. Madrid: Atlas, 1971.

Lorant, Stephen, ed. *The New World*. New York: Dull, Sloan & Pearce, 1965.

Love, Edgar F. 'Legal Restrictions on Afro-Indian Relations in Colonial Mexico', *Journal of Negro History*, vol. LV(2) (1970).

Lowenthal, David. *West Indian Societies*. London: Oxford University Press, 1972.

The Lower Norfolk County Virginia Antiquary, vol. 3, 1899.

Lowery, Woodbury. *The Spanish Settlements in the United States*. New York: Knickerbocker, 1911.

Lozano, Adolfo Lafarga. *Los Vascos en el Descubrimiento y Colonización de América*. Bilbao: Gran Enciclopedia Vasca, 1973.

MacFirbisigh, Dubhaltach. *Annals of Ireland: Three Fragments*, ed. John O'Donovan. Dublin: Irish Archaeological and Celtic Society, 1868.

Machado, Jose Pedro. *Dicionário Etimológico da Lingua Portuguesa*. Lisbon: Confluencia, 1952, 1967.

Magalhães de Gândavo, Pero de. *Tratado da Província do Brasil*. Rio de Janeiro: Instituto Nacional do Livro, 1965.

Mally, Stewart C. 'Traditional African Watercraft: A New Look,' in Ivan Van Sertima, ed., *Blacks in Science: Ancient and Modern*. New Brunswick: Transaction Books, 1983.

Marcgrave, George (Jorge). *Historia Natural do Brasil*, trans. José Procopio de Magalhães. São Paulo: Imprensa Oficial del Estado, 1942.

Marcgrave (Marcgravi), Georgi and Guilielmi Pisonis. *Historia Naturalis Brasiliae*. Amsterdam: Elzevirium, 1648.

Marchant, Alexander. *From Barter to Slavery: The Economic Relations of the Portuguese and Indians in the Settlement of Brazil, 1500–1580*. Baltimore: Johns Hopkins, 1942.

Marcucci, Ettore, ed. *Lettere Edite e Inedite di Filippo Sassetti*. Florence: Felice le Monnier, 1855.

Marin, Pieter (Pierre). *Dictionnaire Complet François et Hollandois*. Amsterdam: Uytwerf, 1728.

——. *Dictionnaire François et Hollandois*. Amsterdam: Changuion, 1793.

——. *Nieuw Nederduits en Frans Woordenboek*. Amsterdam: de Groot, 1701.

Markham, Clements R., ed. *The Letters of Amerigo Vespucci*. London: Hakluyt Society, 1894.

Mártir de Anglería, Pedro. *Décadas del Nuevo Mundo*. Buenos Aires: Bajel, 1944.

Mathews, Mitford M. *A Dictionary of Americanisms*. Chicago: University of Chicago Press, 1951.

McDowell, William L., ed. *Documents Relating to Indian Affairs, 1750–1754*. Columbia: South Carolina Archives, 1958.

——. *Documents Relating to Indian Affairs, 1754–1765*. Columbia: University of South Carolina Press, 1970.

——. *Journals of the Commissioners of the Indian Trade 1710–1718*. Columbia: South Carolina Archives, 1955.

Meier, August. 'A Study of the Racial Ancestry of the Mississippi College Negro', *American Journal of Physical Anthropology*, vol. 7 (1949).

Mellafe, Rolando. *Negro Slavery in Latin America*, trans. J. W. S. Judge. Berkeley: University of California Press, 1975.

Mellema, Elae Edouard Leon. *Dictionaire ou Promptu-aire Francois–Flameng*. Rotterdam: Waesbergue, 1602.

Menkman, W. R. *De Nederlanders in het Caraibische Zeegebied*. Amsterdam: Kampen, 1942.

Merrien, Jean. *Christopher Columbus: the Mariner and the Man*, trans. Maurice Michael. London: Odhams, 1958.

——. *Lonely Voyagers*, trans. J. H. Watkins. London: Hutchinson, 1954.

Meyer-Lübke, Wilhelm. *Grammatik der Romanischen Sprachen*. Leipzig: Reisland, 1902.

——. *Romanisches Etymologisches Wörterbuch*. Heidelberg: Winter, 1930.

Michaelis, H. *Novo Diccionario da Lingua Portugueza e Allemã*. Leipzig: Brockhaus, 1891.

Minsheu, John. *The Guide Into the Tongues or a Dictionary of Eleven Languages*. London: Browne, 1617.

——. *Vocabularium Hispanico–Latinum et Anglicum (A Most Copious Spanish Dictionarie, with Latine and English)*. London: Browne, 1617.

Minsheu, John and Richard Percivale. *A Dictionarie in Spanish and English*. London: Bollifant, 1599.

——. *A Dictionary in Spanish and English*. London: John Haviland, 1623.

Miret y Sans, Joaquín. 'La Esclavitud en Cataluña en los Ultimos Tiempos de la Edad Media'. *Revue Hispanique*. vol. XLI, 1917.

Montagu, M. F. Ashley. 'Origins of the American Negro', *Psychiatry: Journal of the Biology and Pathology of Interpersonal Relations*, vol. 7 (1944).

Montanus, Arnoldus. *De Nieuwe en Onbekende Weereld of Beschryving van America*. Amsterdam: Meurs, 1671.

Mooney, James. 'Myths of the Cherokee', in *Nineteenth Annual Report*, Bureau of American Ethnology, 1897–8, part 1.

——. 'The Powhattan Confederacy: Past and Present', *American Anthropologist*, n.s., vol. 9 (1907).

Moore, Wilbert E. 'Slave Laws and the Social Structure', *Journal of Negro History*, vol. 26, 1941.

Moraes Silva, António de. *Grande Dicionário da Lingua Portugueza*, eds Augusto Moreno Cardoso Jr. and José Pedro Machado. Lisbon: Confluencia, 1954.

Morales Padrón, Francisco. *Jamaica Española*. Seville: Escuela de Estudios Hispano–Americanos, 1952.

Mörner, Magnus. 'The History of Race Relations in Latin America: Some Comments on the State of Research', *Latin American Research Review*, vol. 1 (1966).

——, ed. *Race and Class in Latin America*. New York: Columbia University Press, 1970.

——. *Race Mixture in the History of Latin America*. Boston: Little, Brown, 1967.

Morrison, Samuel Eliot. *The European Discovery of America, The Northern Voyages A.D. 500–1600*. New York: Oxford University Press, 1971.

Muro Orejón, Antonio. 'La Primera Capitulación con Vicente Yáñez Pinzon para Descubrir en las Indias (6 Junio 1499)', *Anuário de Estudios Americanos*, vol. IV (1947).

Nascentes, Antenor. *Dicionário da Lingua Portuguesa*. Brazil: Imprensa Nacional, 1943–66.

——. *Dicionário da Lingua Portuguesa*. Brazil: Dept. de Imprensa Nacional, 1966.

Nebrija, Antonio de. *Dictionarium Aelii Antonii Nebrissensis Hispaniariom in Latinum*. Brocario: Guillelmi, 1520.

——. *Dictionarium ael. Antonii Nebrissensis*. No publisher, ded. 1554; 1561 on back.

——. *Dictionarium Emendatum*. Matriti: de Urrutia, 1790.

——. *Diccionario Latino–Español (1492)*. Barcelona: Puvill-Editor, 1979.

——. *Vocabulario Español–Latino (c.1495)*. Madrid: Real Academia Española, 1951.
——. *Vocabulario de Romance en Latin*, ed. Gerald J. MacDonald. Madrid: Castalia, 1973.
——. *Vocabularius Nebrissensis*. 1511; copy British Library, no publisher, no place.
Nebrija, Antonio de and Lopez de Rubiños. *Dictionarium Redivivum*. Matriti: Michaelem, 1778.
Negro Population in the United States, 1790–1915. Washington, D.C.: Bureau of the Census, 1918.
Neill, Edward D. *Virginia Carolorum*. Albany: Munsell, 1886.
Nelson, Alice Dunbar. 'People of Color in Louisiana', *Journal of Negro History*. vol. 1 (1915).
Nelson, William, ed. *Documents Relating to the Colonial History of New Jersey*. Patterson: The Call, 1904.
Nieuhof, Johan. *Gedenkweerdige Brasiliaense Zee an Lant Reize, 1640–1649*. Amsterdam: van Meurs, 1682.
Nieuwenhuis, G. *Algemeen Woordenboek van Kunsten en Wetenschappen*. Zutphen: Thieme, 1824.
Noorter, Gert. *Old Kayaks in the Netherlands*. Leiden: Brill, 1971.
Norment, Mary C. *The Lowrie History*. Wilmington: Daily Journal, 1875.
Northrop, A. Judd. 'Slavery in New York', *State Library Bulletin*, History (New York) (1908).
Ober, Frederick A. 'Aborigines of the West Indies', *Proceedings of the American Antiquarian Society*, vol. 9 (1893).
Ogilvie, John. *The Imperial Dictionary*, revised by Charles Annandale. London: Blackie, 1885.
Oliveira Marques, A. H. de. *History of Portugal*. New York: Columbia University Press, 1972.
Olson, Julius E. and Edward Gaylord Bourne, eds. *The Northmen, Columbus and Cabot 985–1503*. New York: Scribner's, 1906.
Ortiz de Zúñiga, Diego. *Ánales Eclesiasticos y Seculares . . . de Sevilla*. Madrid: Imprenta Real, 1677.
Osterman, H., ed. *Knud Rasmussen's Posthumous Notes on the Life and Doings of the East Greenlanders in Olden Times*. Copenhagen: Retzels, 1938.
Oudin, César (and Juan Francisco Rodriguez?). *Den Grooten Dictionaris en Schat van Drij Talen; Le Grand Dictionaire et Trésor de Trois Langues; el Grande Dictionario Thesoro de las Tres Lenguas*. Antwerp: Trognesius, 1639–40.
Oudin, César. *Tesoro de las dos Lenguas Española y Francesa*. Brussels: Hubert Antoine, 1625.
——. *Tesoro de las dos Lenguas Francesa y Española*. Paris, 1621.
——. *Tesoro de las dos Lenguas Francesa y Española*. Paris: Marc Orry, 1607.
The Oxford English Dictionary. Oxford: Clarendon Press, 1933.
Pagés, Aniceto de. *Gran Diccionario de la Lengua Castellana*. Barcelona: Fomento Comercial del Libro, 1901.
Parker, Arthur C. 'The Status and Progress of Indians as Shown by the Thirteenth Census', *The Quarterly Journal of the Society of American Indians*, vol. III (1915).
Parker, Kelvin M. 'Vocabulario de la Crónica Troyana', *Acta Salamanticensia*, Filosofía y Letras, vol. XII. Salamanca: Universidad de Salamanca, 1958–9.
Parker, Mattie Emma Edwards, ed. *North Carolina Higher Court Records, 1697–1701*. Raleigh: Dept. of Archives and History, 1971.

Pasini, Giuseppe. *Vocabulario Italiano e Latino.* Venice: Molinari, 1823.

Pereira, Bento. *Prosodia in Vocabularium Bilingue Latinum, et Lusitanum (1646).* Eborao, Portugal: Academiae, 1750.

Peyrere, Isaac de la. *Relation du Groenland.* Paris: Courbe, 1647.

——. 'Histoire du Groenland' (1647) in *A Collection of Documents on Spitzbergen and Greenland.* London: Hakluyt Society, 1855.

——. *Relation de l'Islande.* Paris: Billaine, 1663.

Phelan, John Leddy. *The Kingdom on Quito in the Seventeenth Century.* Madison: University of Wisconsin Press, 1967.

Phillippo, James J. *Jamaica: Its Past and Present State.* Westport: Greenwood, 1970.

Phillips, Edward. *The New World of English Words.* Menston: Scolar Press, 1969.

Pigafetta, Antonio. *Primer Viaje en Torno del Globo,* trans. Carlos Amoretti. Buenos Aires: Espasa–Calpe, 1954.

Pigafetta, Philips (Filippo) and Edoat (Duarte) Lopez. *De Beschrijvinghe vant Groot Ende Vermaert Coninckrijck van Congo,* trans. Martijn Everart. Amsterdam: Claesz, 1596.

Pina Cabral, Emmanuel. *Magnum Lexicon, Latinum et Lusitanum.* Lisbon: Regiae Officinae, 1780.

——. *Magnum Lexicon, Latinum et Lusitanum.* Lisbon: Ferreira, 1802.

Pinheiro, Eduardo. *Dicionário da Lingua Portuguesa.* Oporto, Figueirinhas, *c.*1945.

Pinkerton, John, ed. *Voyages and Travels.* London: Longman, 1812.

Pires de Lima, J. A. *Mouros, Judeus e Negros na História de Portugal.* Oporto: Livraria Civilização, 1940.

Platzmann, Julio, ed. *O Diccionario Anonymo da Lingua Geral do Brasil.* Leipzig: Teubner, 1896.

Pliny. *Natural History,* trans. H. Rackham. London: Heinemann, 1938.

Poma, Huaman (Felipe de Ayala). *Letter to a King,* ed. Christopher Dilke. New York: Dutton, 1978.

Porte, M. de la. *Les Epithètes de M. de la Porte, Parisien.* Paris: Buon, 1571.

Porte, Arnoldus de la. *Den Nieuwen Dictionaris oft Schadt der Duytse ende Spaensche Talen.* Antwerp, Verdussen, 1659.

Porter, Kenneth W. 'Florida Slaves and Free Negroes in the Seminole War, 1835–1842', *Journal of Negro History,* vol. XXVIII (1943).

——. 'Negroes and Indians on the Texas Frontier, 1831–1876', *Journal of Negro History,* vol. XLI (1956).

——. 'Relations between Negroes and Indians within the Present Limits of the United States', *Journal of Negro History,* vol. XVII (1932).

Price, William S., Jr., ed. *North Carolina Higher Court Records 1702–1708.* Raleigh: Department of Archives and History, 1974.

Proceedings and Debates of the Convention of North Carolina . . . 1835. Raleigh: Gales, 1836.

Purchas, Samuel. *Purchas his Pilgrimage, or Relations of the World and the Religions Observed in all Ages.* London: Stansby, 1613.

Pyrard de Laval, François. *Voyage Contenant sa Navigation aux Indes.* Paris: Thiboust, 1619.

Quevedo, Francisco de. *Obra Poetica,* ed. José Manuel Blecua. Madrid: Castalia, 1969.

Quinn, David Beers. *England and the Discovery of America 1481–1620.* New York: Knopf, 1974.

Quinque Linguarum, Latinae, Teuthonicae, Gallicae, Hispanicae, Italicae. Antwerp: Steels, 1534.

Ramusio, Giovanni Battista, ed. *Navigazioni e Viaggi.* Turin: Einaudi, 1979.

Ray, Worth S. *Colonial Granville County and its People*. Baltimore: Southern Book Co., 1956.

Recopilación de las Leyes destos Reynos. Madrid: Barrio y Angulo, 1640.

Recopilación de Leyes de los Reynos de Indias. Madrid: 1681.

Reppertorio das Ordenações e Leys do Reyno de Portugal. Lisbon: S. Vicente Fora, 1749.

Reuter, Edward B. *The American Race Problem, A Study of the Negro*. New York: Crowell, 1927.

——. *Race Mixture: Studies in Intermarriage and Miscegenation*. New York: McGraw-Hill, 1931.

Richelet, Pierre. *Le Grand et Nouveau Dictionnaire Francois et Flamand*. Brussels: Grieck, 1707.

——. *Le Grand Dictionnaire Francois et Flamand*. Brussels: Friex, 1765.

Riddell, William Renwick. 'The Slave in Canada', *Journal of Negro History*, vol. V (1920).

Rights, Douglas. *The American Indian in North Carolina*. Winston-Salem: Blair, 1957.

Riley, Carroll, L., J. Charles Kelley, Campbell W. Pennington and Robert L. Rands, eds. *Man across the Sea: Problems of Precolumbian Contacts*. Austin: University of Texas Press, 1971.

Robert, Paul. *Dictionnaire . . . de Langue Française*. Paris: Société du Nouveau Littré, 1959.

Roberts, D. F. 'The Dynamics of Racial Intermixture in the American Negro: Some Anthropological Considerations', *American Journal of Human Genetics*, vol. 7 (1955).

Rodrigues, José Honório. *Brazil and Africa*, trans. Richard A. Mazzara and Sam Hileman. Berkeley: University of California Press, 1965.

Rogers, J. A. (Joel Augustus). *Sex and Race: Negro–Caucasian Mixing in all Ages and all Lands*. New York: J. A. Rogers, 1942–72.

Roncière, Charles de la. *Histoire de la Marine Française*. Paris: Plon-Nourrit, 1914.

Roquette, José Ignacio. *Nouveau Dictionnaire Portugais–Français*. Paris: Aillaud, Guillard, 1863.

——. *Nouveau Dictionnaire Portugais–Français*. Paris: Aillaud, c.1900.

Rosal, Francisco del. *La Razon de Algunos Refranes*, ed. B. Bussell Thompson. London: Tamesis, 1975.

Rose, Peter I. *The Subject is Race: Traditional Ideologies and the Teaching of Race Relations*. New York: Oxford University Press, 1968.

Rosenblat, Angel. *El Mestizaje y las Castas Coloniales*. Buenos Aires: Editorial Nova, 1954.

Rusco, Elmer. *Good Time Coming? Black Nevadans in the 19th Century*. Westport, Connecticut: Greenwood, 1975.

Russell, John H. *The Free Negro in Virginia, 1619–1865*. Baltimore: Johns Hopkins, 1913.

Russell-Wood, A. J. R. *The Black Man in Slavery and Freedom in Colonial Brazil*. London: Macmillan, 1982.

Saco, José Antonio. *Historia de la Esclavitud de la Raza Africana en el Nuevo Mundo*. vol. I, Barcelona: Jepús, 1879; vol. II, Havana: Alvarez, 1893.

——. *Historia de la Esclavitud de los Indios en el Nuevo Mundo*. Havana: Cultural, 1932.

——. *Historia de la Esclavitud desde los Tiempos mas Remotos hasta Nuestros Días*. vol. I, Paris: La Hure, 1875; vol. II, Paris : Kugelmann, 1875; vol. III, Barcelona: Jepús, 1877.

Salkey, Andrew, ed. *Caribbean Folk Tales and Legends*. London: Bogle-L'Ouverture, 1980.

Salles, Vicente. *O Negro no Pará*. Pará: Universidade Federal do Pará, 1971.
Sanderson, Ivan T. *Follow the Whale*. Boston: Little, Brown, 1956.
Santamaría, Francisco J. *Diccionario General de Americanismos*. Mexico City: Editorial Robredo, 1942.
Santa Rosa de Viterbo, Joaquim de. *Elucidario das Palavras, Termos, e Frases que em Portugal Antiguamente se Usáraõ*. Lisbon: Ferreira, 1798.
Sasbout, Mathias. *Dictionaire Fleming–Francoys*. Antwerp: Waesberge, 1576.
Saunders, A. C. de C. M. *A Social History of Black Slaves and Freedmen in Portugal, 1441–1555*. Cambridge: Cambridge University Press, 1982.
Schmidel, Ulrich. *Derrotero y Viaje a España y las Indias*, trans. Edmundo Wernicke. Santa Fe, Argentina: Univ. Nacional del Litoral, 1938.
———. 'Voyage of Ulrich Schmidt' in *The Conquest of the River Plate (1535–1555)*. London: Hakluyt, 1891.
Schoeph, Johann D. 'Travels in the Confederation', *Journal of Negro History*, vol. 1 (1915).
Schoutens, Wouter. *Oost-Indische Voyagie*. Amsterdam: Meurs and van Someren, 1676.
Schulte Nordholt, J. W. *The People that Walk in Darkness*, trans. M. B. van Wijngaarden. New York: Ballantine, 1970.
Schulten, C. M. *Nederlandse Expansie in Latijns Amerika: Brazilië, 1624–1654*. Bussum: Fibula-van Dishoeck, 1968.
Schwartz, Stuart B. 'The Mocambo: Slave Resistance in Colonial Bahia', *Journal of Social History*, vol. 3 (1970).
Schwerin, Karl H. 'Winds Across the Atlantic', *Mesoamerican Studies*, vol. 6 (1970).
'Scotch Indians in Scotland', *Quarterly Journal of Society of American Indians*, vol. 3 (1915).
Sewel, William. *Neder–Duytsch en Engelsch Woordenboek*. Amsterdam: Swart, 1691.
———. *A Complete Dictionary English and Dutch*. Amsterdam: de Veer, 1766.
Sherwood, H. N. 'Paul Cuffe', *Journal of Negro History*, vol. 8 (1923).
Shyllon, Folarin. *Black People in Britain 1555–1833*. London: Institute of Race Relations, 1977.
Silva, Innocencio Francisco da. *Diccionario Bibliografico Portuguez*. Lisbon: Imprensa Nacional, 1859.
Simonet, Francisco Javier. *Glosario de Voces Ibericas y Latinas Usadas entre los Mozárabes*. Madrid: Real Academia de la Historia, 1888.
Skeat, Walter W. *An Etymological Dictionary of the English Language*. Oxford: Clarendon Press, 1924.
Smallegange, M. *Nieuwe Cronijk van Zeeland*. Middelburg: 1696.
Smith, Anna Bustill. 'The Bustill Family', *Journal of Negro History*, vol. X (1925).
Smyters, Anthoni. *Epitheta dat Zijn Bynamen oft Toenamen*. Rotterdam: Waesberghe, 1620.
Soares de Sousa, Gabriel. *Tratado Descriptivo do Brasil em 1587*, ed. Francisco Adolpho de Varnhagem. São Paulo : Editoria Nacional, 1938.
Sobrino, Francisco. *Dicionario Nuevo de las Lenguas Española y Francesa*. Brussels: Foppens, 1721.
Solórzano Pereira, Juan de. *De Indiarum Iure*. Lyons: Lavrentii Anisson, 1671.
———. *Politica Indiana*, ed. Francisco Ramiro de Valenzuela. Madrid: Ibero–Americana, 1972.
Sousa, Emmanuel de and Joachim Joseph da Costa e Sa. *Nouveau Dictionnaire François–Portugais*. Lisbon: Borel and Borel, 1784.

Southey, Robert. *History of Brazil.* London: Longman, 1822.

Speck, Frank G. 'Chapters on the Ethnology of the Powhatan Tribes of Virginia', *Indian Notes and Monographs*, vol. I (1928).

Spix, Johann Baptist von and Carl F. P. von Martius. *Reise in Brasilien.* Munich: Lindauer, 1823.

———. *Travels in Brazil, in the Years 1817–1820.* London: Longman, 1824.

Spurgeon, John H. and Howard V. Meredith. 'Skin Color Comparisons among Ethnic Groups of College Men', *American Journal of Physical Anthropology*, vol. 64 (1984).

Staden, Hans. *Naaukeurige Versameling der . . . Zee en Landreysen.* Leiden: Van der Aa, 1707.

———. *The True History of his Captivity*, trans. and ed. Malcolm Letts. London: Routledge, 1928.

Staden, Juan (Hans). *Vera Historia y Descripción de un País de las Salvages . . . en el Nuevo Mundo America*, trans. and ed. Edmundo Wernicke. Buenos Aires: Coni, 1944.

Steck, Max. *Dürer and his World*, trans. J. Maxwell Brownjohn. London: Thames & Hudson, 1964.

Stedman, John Gabriel. *Narrative of a Five Years' Expedition.* Barre, Mass.: Imprint Society, 1971.

Sweet, David G. and Gary B. Nash. *Struggle and Survival in Colonial America.* Berkeley : University of California Press, 1981.

Sypher, Wylie. *Guinea's Captive Kings: British Anti-Slavery Literature of the XVIIIth Century.* Chapel Hill: University of North Carolina Press, 1942.

Taylor, Alexander S. 'Indianology', Third Series, 1862, in the *California Farmer*, Bancroft Library, University of California, Berkeley.

Teenstra, M. D. *De Nederlandsch West-Indische Eilanden.* Amsterdam: Emmerling, 1977.

Terwen, J. L. *Etymologisch Handwoordenboek der Nederduitsche Taal.* Gouda: van Goor, 1844.

Todorov, Tzvetan. *The Conquest of America: The Question of the Other*, trans. Richard Howard. New York: Harper & Row, 1984.

Torres de Mendoza, Luis, ed. *Colección de Documentos Inéditos.* Vaduz: Kraus, 1964.

Trelease, Allen W. *Indian Affairs in Colonial New York.* Ithaca: Cornell University Press, 1960.

Tricentenario de Vinda dos Primeiros Portuguezes ao Ceará 1603–1903. Ceará: Minerva, 1903.

Ure, John. *Prince Henry the Navigator.* London: Constable, 1977.

Van Sertima, Ivan, ed. *Blacks in Science: Ancient and Modern.* New Brunswick: Transaction Books, 1983.

———. *They Came before Columbus: The African Presence in Ancient America.* New York: Random House, 1977.

Vega, Garcilaso de la (el Inca). *The Florida of the Inca*, trans. and ed. John G. and Jeanette J. Varner. Austin: University of Texas Press, 1951.

———. *Historia General del Peru*, ed. Ángel Rosenblat. Buenos Aires: Emce, no date.

Verachter, Frederic, ed. *Albrecht Dürer en de Nederlanden.* Antwerpen: De la Croix, 1840.

Verdam, J. *Middlenederlandsch Woordenboek.* The Hague: Nijhoff, 1912.

Verlinden, Charles. *L'Esclavage dans l'Europe Médiévale.* Bruges: De Tempel, 1955.

'Vestry Book of King William Parish', *Virginia Magazine of History and Biography*, vol. XII.

Veth, P. J. *Uit Oost en West: Verklaring van eenige Uitheemsche Woorden.* Arnhem: Gouda Quint., 1889.

Veyrin, Philippe. *Les Basques.* Bayonne: Musée Basque, 1947.
Vicente, Gil. *Obras Completas,* ed. Marques Braga. Lisbon: Sá da Costa, 1942.
Vieyra Transtagano, Antonio. *Dictionary of the Portuguese and English Languages in two parts.* London: Camper, 1783.
Vogt, John. *Portuguese Rule on the Gold Coast, 1469–1682.* Athens, Georgia: University of Georgia Press, 1979.
Wagatsuma, Hiroshi. 'The Social Perception of Skin Color in Japan', *Daedalus,* vol. 96 (1967).
Wagner, Gunter. *Yuchi Tales.* Publications of the American Ethnological Society, 1931.
Webster, Noah. *An American Dictionary of the English Language.* New York: Johnson, 1970.
Weeden, William B. *Economic and Social History of New England, 1620–1789.* New York: Hillary House, 1963.
Wehr, Hans. *A Dictionary of Modern Written Arabic (Arabic–English),* ed. J. Milton Cowan. Weisbaden: Harrassowitz, 1979.
Weslager, C. A. *Delaware's Forgotten Folk.* Philadelphia: University of Pennsylvania Press, 1943.
Wesley, Charles H. 'The Negro in the West Indies, Slavery and Freedom', *Journal of Negro History,* vol. XVII (1932).
Whitaker, Ian. 'The Scottish Kayaks and the "Finnmen"', *Antiquity,* vol. XXVIII (1954).
———. 'The Scottish Kayaks Reconsidered', *Antiquity,* vol. LI (1977).
Williamson, Joel. *New People: Miscegenation and Mulattoes in the United States.* New York: Free Press, 1980.
Willis, William S. 'Divide and Rule: Red, White and Black in the Southeast', *Journal of Negro History,* vol. 48 (1963).
Windley, Lathan A. *Runaway Slave Advertisements.* Westport, Connecticut: Greenwood, 1983.
Winkleman, O. R. F. W. *Dictionaire François–Hollandois.* Utrecht: Wild, 1783.
Wintergerst, Martin. *Reisen auf dem Mittelländischen Meere.* The Hague: Nijhoff, 1932.
Wittgenstein, Ludwig. *Remarks on Colour,* ed. G. E. M. Anscombe, trans. Linda L. McAlister and Margarete Schattle. Berkeley: University of California Press, 1977.
Wojchiechowski, Frans L. 'De Indianen van de Westindische Eilanden', *Nieuw West-Indische Gids* (1980).
Wood, Peter H. *Black Majority: Negroes in Colonial South Carolina.* New York: Knopf, 1974.
Woodard, Thomas S. *Reminiscenses.* Monterey: Barrett and Wimbisu, 1859.
Woodson, Carter G. *The Free Negro Heads of Families in the United States in 1830.* Washington, D.C.: Association for the Study of Negro Life and History, 1925.
———. 'The Relations of Negroes and Indians in Massachusetts', *Journal of Negro History,* vol. 5 (1920).
Wortabet, John and Harvey Porter. *English–Arabic and Arabic–English Dictionary.* New York: Ungar, 1954.
Wright, J. Leitch. *The Only Land They Knew: The Tragic Story of the Indians of the Old South.* New York: Free Press, 1981.
Wright, Ronald. *Cut Stones and Crossroad: A Journey in the Two Worlds of Peru.* Harmondsworth: Penguin, 1986.
Young, William. *An Account of the Black Charaibs.* London: Cass, 1971.
Zaccaria, Enrico. *L'Elemento Iberico nella Lingua Italiana.* Bologna: Cappelli, 1927.
Zavala, Silvio. *Estudios Indianos.* Mexico City: Colegio Nacional, 1948.

——. *Los Esclavos Indios en Nueva España*. Mexico City: Colegio Nacional, 1967.
——. 'Relaciones Históricas entre Indios y Negros en Iberoamérica', *Revista de las Indias*, Bogotá, vol. XXVIII (1946).
Zerolo, E., M. de Toro y Gómez, E. Isaza. *Diccionario de la Lengua Castellana*. Paris: Garnier, 1911[?] or 1926.
Zucchelli, Antonio. *Relazione del Viaggio e Missione di Congo*. Venezia: Giavarina, 1712.

UNPUBLISHED DISSERTATIONS

Heizer, Robert Fleming. 'Aboriginal Whaling in the Old and New Worlds', Anthropology, University of California, Berkeley, 1941.
Heuman, Gad J. 'Between Black and White: Brown Men in Jamaican Society and Politics, 1823–1865', Yale University, 1975.
Price Jr., Edward Thomas. 'Mixed-Blood Populations of the Eastern United States as to Origins, Locations, and Persistence'. Geography, University of California, Berkeley, 1950.

Index

Index by Isobel McClean and the author

Jack D. Forbes, who is of Native American ancestry, is director of Native American Studies at the University of California, Davis. He is the author of several books, including *Apache, Navaho, and Spaniard* and *Essays in Red, Black, and White.*